FREQUENTLY USED SYMBOLS AND ABBREVIATIONS (CONTINUED)

k_s	Required Return on Common Stock
m	Number of times per year interest is compounded
M	Bond's Par Value
M/B	Market/Book Ratio
MACRS	Modified Accelerated Cost Recovery System
MNC	Multinational Company
MP	Market Price per Share
MRP	Materials Requirement Planning
n	• Number of Outcomes Considered • Number of Periods—Typically, Years • Years to Maturity
N	Number of Days Payment Can Be Delayed by Giving up the Cash Discount
N_d	Net Proceeds from the Sale of Debt (Bond)
N_n	Net Proceeds from the Sale of New Common Stock
N_p	Net Proceeds from the Sale of the Preferred Stock
NCAI	Net Current Asset Investment
NFAI	Net Fixed Asset Investment
NPV	Net Present Value
O	Order Cost Per Order
OC	Operating Cycle
OCF	Operating Cash Flow
P	Price (value) of asset
P_0	Value of Common Stock
$PBDT_t$	Profits Before Depreciation and Taxes in year t
PD	Preferred Stock Dividend
P/E	Price/Earnings Ratio
PMT	Amount of Payment
Pr	Probability
PV	Present Value
PVA_n	Present Value of an n-Year Annuity
$PVIF_{i,n}$	Present Value Interest Factor for a Single Amount Discounted at i Percent for n Periods
$PVIFA_{i,n}$	Present Value Interest Factor for an Annuity When Interest is Discounted Annually at i Percent for n Periods
Q	• Order Quantity in Units • Sales Quantity in Units
R_F	Risk-Free Rate of Interest
RADR	Risk-Adjusted Discount Rate
ROA	Return on Total Assets
ROE	Return on Common Equity
S	Usage in Units per Period
SML	Security Market Line
t	Time
T	Firm's Marginal Tax Rate
V	• Value of an Asset or Firm • Venture Capital
V_C	Value of Entire Company
V_D	Value of All Debt
V_P	Value of Preferred Stock
V_S	Value of Common Stock
VC	Variable Operating Cost per Unit
w_j	• Proportion of the Portfolio's Total Dollar Value Represented by Asset j • Proportion of a Specific Source of Financing j in the Firm's Capital Structure
WACC	Weighted Average Cost of Capital
WMCC	Weighted Marginal Cost of Captial
YTM	Yield to Maturity
ZBA	Zero Balance Account
σ	Standard Deviation
Σ	Summation Sign

PRINCIPLES OF

MANAGERIAL FINANCE BRIEF

The Addison-Wesley Series in Finance

Chambers/Lacey
Modern Corporate Finance: Theory and Practice

Copeland/Weston
Financial Theory and Corporate Policy

Dufey/Giddy
Cases in International Finance

Eakins
Finance: Investments, Institutions, and Management

Eiteman/Stonehill/Moffett
Multinational Business Finance

Gitman
Principles of Managerial Finance

Gitman
Principles of Managerial Finance —Brief Edition

Gitman/Joehnk
Fundamentals of Investing

Gitman/Madura
Introduction to Finance

Hughes/MacDonald
International Banking: Text and Cases

Madura
Personal Finance

McDonald
Derivatives Markets

Megginson
Corporate Finance Theory

Melvin
International Money and Finance

Mishkin/Eakins
Financial Markets and Institutions

Moffett
Cases in International Finance

Moffett/Stonehill/Eiteman
Fundamentals of Multinational Finance

Rejda
Principles of Risk Management and Insurance

Solnik
International Investments

Addison Wesley

Boston San Francisco New York
London Toronto Sydney Tokyo Singapore Madrid
Mexico City Munich Paris Cape Town Hong Kong Montreal

Lawrence J. Gitman

Principles of Managerial Finance

Brief

Third Edition

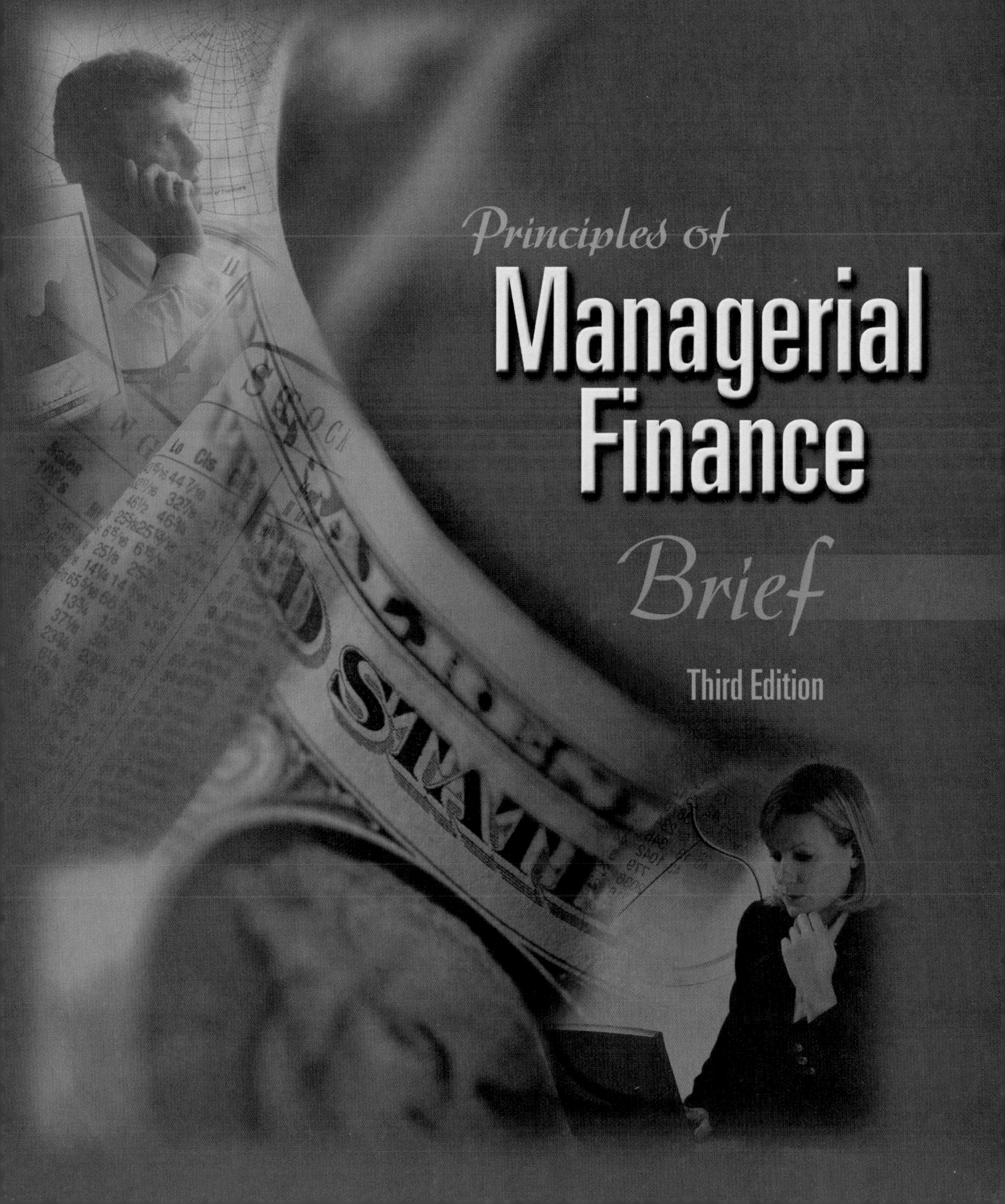

Editor-in-Chief: Denise Clinton
Acquisitions Editor: Donna Battista
Senior Project Manager: Mary Clare McEwing
Development Editor: Ann Torbert
Managing Editor: Jim Rigney
Production Supervisor: Nancy Fenton
Marketing Manager: Adrienne D'Ambrosio
Media Producer: Jennifer Pelland
Supplements Editor: Andrea Basso
Assistant Editor: Amy Gembala
Project Coordination, Text Design, Art Studio,
and Electronic Page Makeup: Thompson Steele, Inc.
Design Manager: Regina Hagen Kolenda
Cover Designer: Regina Hagen Kolenda
Cover Photographs: © Lee Atherton/SuperStock;
© Don Carstens/Brand X Pictures;
© Didier Boutet/Brand X Pictures/PictureQuest
Senior Manufacturing Buyer: Hugh Crawford

Library of Congress Cataloging-in-Publication Data

Gitman, Lawrence J.
Principles of managerial finance : brief.-- 3rd ed.
p. cm.
Includes index.
ISBN 0-201-78480-7 (alk. paper)
1. Corporations--Finance. 2. Business enterprises--Finance. I. Title.
HG4011.G52 2002
658.15--dc21

2002018473

ISBN 0-201-78480-7

1 2 3 4 5 6 7 8 9 10—RNT—06 05 04 03 02

Dedicated to the memory
of my mother, Dr. Edith Gitman,
who instilled in me the importance
of education and hard work

Brief Contents

Contents

Part 4 Long-Term Financial Decisions 387

Part 5 Short-Term Financial Decisions 491

Preface

The desire to write *Principles of Managerial Finance* came out of my experience teaching the introductory managerial finance course early in my academic career. When I began teaching full time, I was not very far removed from my own undergraduate studies and therefore could appreciate the difficulties some of my students were having with the textbook we used. They wanted a book that spoke to them in plain English. They wanted a book that tied concepts to reality. And they wanted not just description, but demonstration of concepts, tools, and techniques. Recognizing that, I decided that I would write an introductory finance text that would effectively resolve these concerns.

Three years later, in 1976, the first edition of *Principles of Managerial Finance* was published. Its initial market success was driven by its conversational tone, wide use of examples set off in the text, and coverage of short-term finance. We've continued to build on these strengths over the past 27 years, numerous translations, and more than 500,000 U.S. users. The Brief Edition evolved from these years of work. Based on significant market feedback from adopters, non-adopters, and finance practitioners, it incorporates the learning system from *Principles of Managerial Finance* with a more focused and streamlined table of contents.

As before, my goal in the third Brief Edition of *Principles* is to satisfy the needs of professors and students. Like the first edition, the third uses plain English, ties concepts to reality, and demonstrates concepts, tools, and techniques. It incorporates a proven learning system, which integrates pedagogy with concepts and practical applications. It concentrates on the concepts, tools, techniques, and practices that are needed to make keen financial decisions in an increasingly competitive business environment. The strong pedagogy and generous use of examples make the text an easily accessible resource for long-distance learning and self-study programs.

The third Brief Edition has been specifically designed to fit the one-term financial management course. It is intended for those professors who want to provide students with a thorough introduction to corporate finance that focuses on the fundamental concepts, tools, techniques, and practices of financial management. I've "right-sized" the book for the one-term course by eliminating from my longer *Principles* book topics that will be covered in subsequent courses. Specifically, I've eliminated the chapter on corporate mergers and the separate chapter on international managerial finance, although discussions and examples of international finance appear in appropriate chapter discussions throughout. In addition, the chapter from the longer book that contains discussion of hybrid and derivative securities is not included in the Brief Edition. Also, coverage of capital budgeting in the Brief Edition is presented in two chapters, compared to three chapters in the longer book. Finally presentation of many topics has been streamlined throughout. The resulting presentation thoroughly covers all basic topics, yet is four chapters and about 235 pages shorter than *Principles of Managerial Finance,* Tenth Edition, upon which it is based.

The text's organization, described in detail in the following pages, conceptually links the firm's actions and its value as determined in the securities market. Each major decision area is presented in terms of both risk and return factors and their potential impact on the owners' wealth. A new "Focus on Value" element at the end of each chapter helps reinforce the student's understanding of the link between the financial manager's actions and share value.

Although the text is sequential, instructors can assign almost any chapter as a self-contained unit. This flexibility enables instructors to customize the text to various teaching strategies and course lengths.

We live in a world in which both international and ethical considerations cannot be divorced from the study of business in general and finance in particular. As in prior editions, discussions of international dimensions of chapter topics are integrated throughout the book. For example, Chapter 5 discusses the risks and returns associated with international diversification. In each chapter in which international coverage is included, the international material is integrated into learning goals and end-of-chapter materials. In terms of ethics, four new *In Practice* boxes address some of the most significant ethical issues that financial managers have faced as they attempt to sail the sometimes-rough waters of the business world.

In organizing each chapter, I have adhered to a managerial decision-making perspective, relating decisions to the firm's overall goal of wealth maximization. Once a particular concept has been developed, its application is illustrated by an example. These examples demonstrate, and solidify in the student's thought, financial decision-making considerations and their consequences.

From classroom to boardroom, the third Brief Edition of *Principles of Managerial Finance* can help users get to where they want to be. I hope that your review of the third edition confirms my belief that it is better than ever—more relevant, more accurate, and more effective than its prior edition. I hope that you agree that this *Principles of Managerial Finance, Brief,* Third Edition, meets your needs for the one-term managerial finance course.

New Structure and Revised Content

As we made plans to publish the third *Brief* Edition, market feedback indicated to us that a revised chapter structure would better meet the needs of professors teaching the course. Besides improving the text's focus on creating shareholder value and the effectiveness of the conceptual presentation, the new structure has enabled us to shorten the book a bit, in line with market trends. After carefully testing ideas for the new structure with both adopters and non-adopters, we decided to reduce the number of chapters from 17 to 14. The major changes and their benefits are shown in the following table.

Revisions Made to *Principles of Managerial Finance, Brief,* Third Edition

	Revisions	Benefits
PART 1: Introduction to Managerial Finance	Chapters restructured to improve focus and reduce number from 4 to 3.	Provides a broad understanding of the role and scope of managerial finance, financial statements and ratio analysis, the firm's cash flows, and cash and profit plans.
Chapter 1: The Role and Environment of Managerial Finance	Material on the institutions and tax environment (from Chapter 2 in the second edition) folded into Chapter 1.	Provides integrated coverage of the environmental aspects of managerial finance.
Chapter 2: Financial Statements and Analysis	Financial statement review material (from Chapter 4 in the second edition) integrated with financial statement analysis material (from Chapter 5 in the second edition). Now includes a market ratio category.	The review of financial statements is now logically followed by the analysis of those statements.
Chapter 3: Cash Flow and Financial Planning	Material on cash flow (Chapter 4 of the second edition) with added coverage of operating and free cash flow is integrated with coverage of financial planning (from Chapter 14 in the second edition).	The concept of cash flow serves as a logical introduction to the procedures used to prepare cash and profit plans.
PART 2: Important Financial Concepts	Bond and stock valuation coverage (in Chapter 8 of the second edition) split into separate chapters that include more descriptive material. The number of chapters in this part increases from 3 to 4.	Separately focuses attention on all aspects of bonds, including valuation, and then on all aspects of stocks, including valuation.
Chapter 4: Time Value of Money (Chapter 6 in the second edition)	Significantly restructured and expanded. Now covers future value and then present value of single sums, ordinary annuities, and mixed streams; then covers compounding interest more frequently than annually; and finally, several applications of time value that now includes finding an unknown number of periods. Sample spreadsheets have been added throughout the chapter.	Provides a more logical parallel development of future and present values and then covers refinements (which can be more readily skipped).
Chapter 5: Risk and Return (Chapter 7 in the second edition)	Table of popular sources of risk and discussions of historic return data added, including standard deviations and risk premiums, to updated risk and return coverage.	Increases reader understanding and interest in a naturally conceptual discussion.
Chapter 6: Interest Rates and Bond Valuation	Integrates material on interest rates and the description of bonds (in Chapter 3 in the second edition) with the basic valuation model and the bond valuation material (in Chapter 8 in the second edition).	Focuses discussion on all aspects of bonds—interest rates, characteristics, and valuations—thereby adding clarity.

(*continued*)

Revisions Made to *Principles of Managerial Finance, Brief,* Third Edition (continued)

	Revisions	Benefits
Chapter 7: Stock Valuation	Integrates the material describing the characteristics of common and preferred stock (in Chapter 3 in the second edition) with the common stock valuation material (in Chapter 8 of the second edition). Now includes a new discussion of issuing common stock and covers venture capital and the free cash flow valuation model.	Improves understanding of all of the important aspects of common and preferred stock—characteristics, issuance, and valuation.
PART 3: Long-Term Investment Decisions	Thorough updating and tightening, with minor adjustments made in response to user and reviewer suggestions.	Improves accuracy and focus in all chapters.
Chapter 8: Capital Budgeting Cash Flows	Introductory discussion streamlined, motive for recognizing changes in net working capital in the initial investment clarified, and cash flow development discussions improved.	Imparts better focus and improves understanding of the rationale and procedures for developing relevant cash flows.
Chapter 9: Capital Budgeting Techniques: Certainty and Risk	All discussions improved and tightened and time lines for NPV and IRR calculations added. The detailed trial-and-error approach for calculating IRR now moved to the Web site. Computation demonstrations added, discussion of certainty equivalents eliminated, time lines for risk-adjusted discount rate calculations included, and a new discussion of the rationale for and demonstration of the application of real options in capital budgeting added.	Provides clear understanding of the importance, rationale, and key differences among the most popular capital budgeting techniques and provides a lucid discussion of the application of capital budgeting techniques.
PART 4: Long-Term Financial Decisions	All discussions updated and tightened; minor adjustments made in response to user and reviewer feedback.	Improves accuracy and focus in all chapters.
Chapter 10: The Cost of Capital (Chapter 11 in second edition)	Trial-and-error approach for finding the cost of debt eliminated. All other discussions updated and refined.	Improves readability and focus in all discussions.
Chapter 11: Leverage and Capital Structure (Chapter 12 in second edition)	All data updated; discussions of all topics tightened and refined.	Improves readability and focus in all discussions.
Chapter 12: Dividend Policy (Chapter 13 in second edition)	Streamlined discussion of dividend reinvestment plans; all other discussions updated and refined.	Improves readability and focus in all discussions.

(*continued*)

Revisions Made to *Principles of Managerial Finance, Brief,* Third Edition (continued)

	Revisions	Benefits
PART 5: Short-Term Financial Decisions	Completely restructured to reduce number of chapters from 4 to 2, by moving the material in Chapter 14 of the second edition to become part of Chapter 3 in this edition and then combining Chapters 15, 16, and 17 from the second edition to become two chapters—13 and 14.	Discussions focus solely on the management of current accounts—current assets and current liabilities—thereby improving understanding.
Chapter 13: Working Capital and Current Assets Management	A brief overview of working capital management (in Chapter 15 in the second edition) provided. Develops the cash conversion cycle (in Chapter 16 in the second edition) that is used to anchor the discussions in the two chapters in this part, and discusses current assets management—inventory, accounts receivable (both in Chapter 17 in the second edition), and cash receipts and disbursements (in Chapter 16 in the second edition).	Greatly improves understanding of the procedures for managing current assets and how they relate to the firm's goal of minimizing cash requirements.
Chapter 14: Current Liabilities Management	Updated and tightened discussion of the characteristics of the firm's key sources of short-term financing—spontaneous, unsecured, and secured; explains their role in terms of cost and with regard to the firm's cash conversion cycle.	Focuses solely on short-term financing; uses the cash conversion cycle to link it to the cash minimization goal.

Gitman's Proven Teaching/Learning System

Users of *Principles of Managerial Finance, Brief* have praised the effectiveness of the book's teaching/learning system, which has been hailed as one of its hallmarks. The system, driven by a set of carefully developed learning goals, has been retained and polished in the Third Edition. Key elements of the teaching/learning system are illustrated and described below.

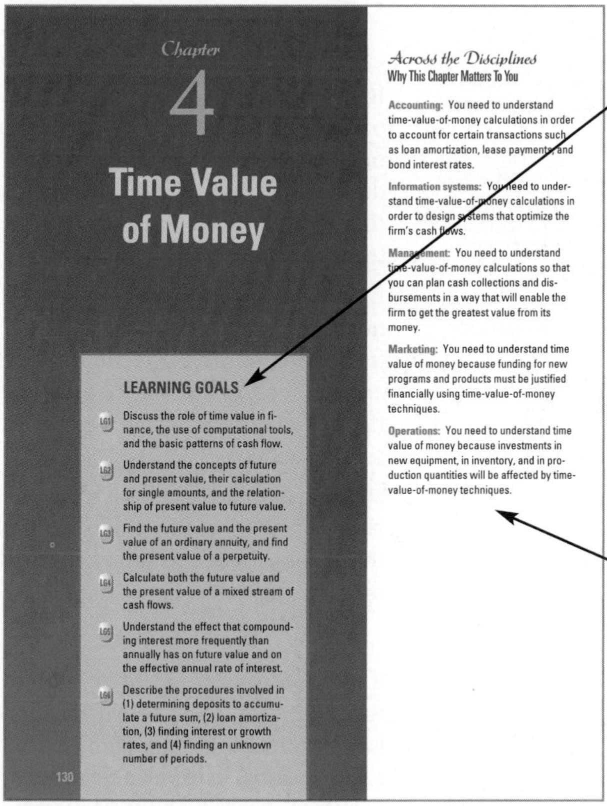
Chapter

4

Time Value of Money

LEARNING GOALS

LG1 Discuss the role of time value in finance, the use of computational tools, and the basic patterns of cash flow.

LG2 Understand the concepts of future and present value, their calculation for single amounts, and the relationship of present value to future value.

LG3 Find the future value and the present value of an ordinary annuity, and find the present value of a perpetuity.

LG4 Calculate both the future value and the present value of a mixed stream of cash flows.

LG5 Understand the effect that compounding interest more frequently than annually has on future value and on the effective annual rate of interest.

LG6 Describe the procedures involved in (1) determining deposits to accumulate a future sum, (2) loan amortization, (3) finding interest or growth rates, and (4) finding an unknown number of periods.

130

Across the Disciplines
Why This Chapter Matters To You

Accounting: You need to understand time-value-of-money calculations in order to account for certain transactions such as loan amortization, lease payments, and bond interest rates.

Information systems: You need to understand time-value-of-money calculations in order to design systems that optimize the firm's cash flows.

Management: You need to understand time-value-of-money calculations so that you can plan cash collections and disbursements in a way that will enable the firm to get the greatest value from its money.

Marketing: You need to understand time value of money because funding for new programs and products must be justified financially using time-value-of-money techniques.

Operations: You need to understand time value of money because investments in new equipment, in inventory, and in production quantities will be affected by time-value-of-money techniques.

Six **Learning Goals** at the start of the chapter anchor the most important concepts and techniques to be learned in the chapter. The learning goal icons reappear next to related text sections and again in the chapter-end summary, end-of-chapter homework materials, and supplements such as the Study Guide and Test Bank.

New! Every chapter opens with a feature that discusses the intersection of the finance topics covered in the chapter with the concerns of other major business disciplines. **Across the Disciplines** shows students majoring in accounting, information systems, management, marketing, and operations why the chapter matters to them, and it encourages them to appreciate the numerous cross-disciplinary interactions that routinely occur in business.

LG2 **Single Amounts**

The most basic future value and present value concepts and computations concern single amounts, either present or future amounts. We begin by considering the future value of present amounts. Then we will use the underlying concepts to learn how to determine the present value of future amounts. You will see that although future value is more intuitively appealing, present value is more useful in financial decision making.

Learning goal and PMF "Toolbox" icons appear next to first-level text headings. The learning goal icon ties chapter content to learning goals. The "toolbox" is a system of icons that signals resources such as software tutorials, problem-solving routines, and spreadsheet templates, where these apply to the topic at hand.

PMF Toolbox Icons

The PMF Tutor software, packaged with the book, extends self-testing opportunities beyond those on the printed page. Through user-friendly menus, students can access over 40 problem types, constructed by random-number generation for a nearly inexhaustible supply of new problems. The Tutor icon flags all the Tutor applications in the text.

The PMF Problem-Solver software, packaged with the book, contains 27 short menu-driven programs. Once students have learned the concept needed to solve a particular problem, they can use the Problem-Solver to do the mathematical computations using data they input.

The PMF Excel Spreadsheet Templates software, packaged with the book, provide preprogrammed spreadsheet templates that correspond to marked end-of-chapter problems.

EXAMPLE As noted, Pam Valenti wishes to find the present value of \$1,700 to be received 8 years from now, assuming an 8% opportunity cost.

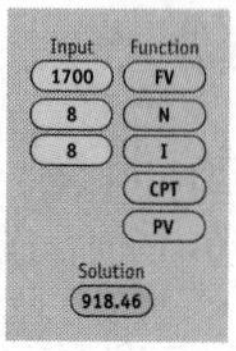

Table Use The present value interest factor for 8% and 8 years, $PVIF_{8\%, 8 \text{ yrs}}$, found in Table A–2, is 0.540. Using Equation 4.12, \$1,700 × 0.540 = \$918. The present value of the \$1,700 Pam expects to receive in 8 years is \$918.

Calculator Use Using the calculator's financial functions and the inputs shown at the left, you should find the present value to be \$918.46. The value obtained with the calculator is more accurate than the values found using the equation or the table, although for the purposes of this text, these differences are insignificant.

Spreadsheet Use The present value of the single future amount also can be calculated as shown on the following Excel spreadsheet.

	A	B
1	PRESENT VALUE OF A SINGLE FUTURE AMOUNT	
2	Future value	\$1,700
3	Interest rate, pct per year compounded annually	8%
4	Number of years	8
5	Present value	\$918.46

Entry in Cell B5 is =–PV(B3,B4,0,B2).
The minus sign appears before PV to change the present value to a positive amount.

Examples are an important component of the book's learning system. Clearly set off from the text, they provide an immediate and concrete demonstration of how to apply financial concepts, tools, and techniques.

Examples in certain chapters, most notably in Chapter 4, demonstrate the time value of money techniques. Those examples show the use of time lines, factor tables, financial calculators, and spreadsheets.

New! Spreadsheet Solutions accompany most calculator solutions and show the inputs, solutions, and cell formulas of the spreadsheets.

$$\text{Present value interest factor} = PVIF_{i,n} = \frac{1}{(1+i)^n} \qquad (4.11)$$

Appendix Table A–2 presents present value interest factors for \$1. By letting $PVIF_{i,n}$ represent the appropriate factor, we can rewrite the general equation for present value (Equation 4.9) as follows:

$$PV = FV_n \times (PVIF_{i,n}) \qquad (4.12)$$

This expression indicates that to find the present value of an amount to be received in a future period, n, we have merely to multiply the future amount, FV_n, by the appropriate present value interest factor.

Key Equations are printed in blue throughout the text to help readers identify the most important mathematical relationships. The variables used in these equations are for convenience printed on the front endpapers of the book.

ordinary annuity
An annuity for which the cash flow occurs at the *end* of each period.

annuity due
An annuity for which the cash flow occurs at the *beginning* of each period.

invested at the end of each of the next 5 years).

Types of Annuities

There are two basic types of annuities. For an **ordinary annuity,** the cash flow occurs at the *end* of each period. For an **annuity due,** the cash flow occurs at the *beginning* of each period.

For help in study and review, Key Terms and their definitions appear in the margin when they are first introduced. These terms are also boldfaced in the index and appear in the Glossary.

Review Questions

4–8 What is the difference between an *ordinary annuity* and an *annuity due?* Which always has greater future value and present value for identical annuities and interest rates? Why?

4–9 What are the most efficient ways to calculate the present value of an ordinary annuity? What is the relationship between the *PVIF* and *PVIFA* interest factors given in Tables A–2 and A–4, respectively?

4–10 What is a *perpetuity?* How can the present value interest factor for such a stream of cash flows be determined?

Review Questions, which appear at the end of each major section of the chapter, challenge students to stop and test their understanding of key concepts, tools, techniques, and practices before they move on to the next section.

In Practice

FOCUS ON **ETHICS** "Doing Well by Doing Good"

Hewlett-Packard (H-P) was founded in 1939 by Bill Hewlett and Dave Packard on the basis of principles of fair dealing and respect—long before anyone coined the expression "corporate social responsibility." H-P credits its ongoing commitment to "doing well by doing good" as a major reason why employees, suppliers, customers, and shareholders seek it out. H-P is clear on its obligation to increase the market value of its common stock, yet it strives to maintain the integrity of each employee in every country in which it does business. Its "Standards of Business Conduct" include a provision that triggers immediate dismissal of any employee who is found to have told a lie. Its internal auditors are expected to adhere to all of these standards, which set forth the "highest principles of business ethics and conduct," according to H-P's 2000 annual report.

Maximizing shareholder wealth is what some call a "moral imperative," in that stockholders are owners with property rights, and in that managers as stewards are obliged to look out for owners' interests. Many times, doing what is right is consistent with maximizing the stock price, but what if integrity causes a company to lose a contract or causes analysts to reduce the rating of the stock from "buy" to "sell"? The objective to maximize shareholder wealth holds, but company officers must do so within ethical constraints. Those constraints occasionally limit the alternative actions from which managers may choose. Some critics have mistakenly assumed that the objective of maximizing shareholder wealth is somehow the cause of unethical behavior, ignoring the fact that *any* business goal might be cited as a factor pressuring individuals to be unethical.

U.S. business professionals have tended to operate from within a strong moral framework based on early-childhood moral development that takes place in families and religious institutions. This does not prevent all ethical lapses, obviously. But it is not surprising that chief financial officers declare that the number-1 personal attribute that finance grads need is ethics—which they rank above interpersonal skills, communication skills, decision-making ability, and computer skills. H-P is aware of this need and has institutionalized it in the company's culture and policies.

In Practice boxes offer insight into important topics in finance, through the experiences of real companies, both large and small. There are three different categories of boxes.

New! Focus on Ethics boxes help students appreciate important ethical issues in finance.

New! Focus on e-Finance boxes describe how companies are using new technologies in their application of finance principles.

Focus on Practice boxes take a corporate focus that relates a business event to a specific financial concept or technique.

All three types of boxes provide readers with a solid grounding in the practice of finance in the real world.

SUMMARY

FOCUS ON VALUE

Time value of money is an important tool that financial managers and other market participants use to assess the impact of proposed actions. Because firms have long lives and their important decisions affect their long-term cash flows, the effective application of time-value-of-money techniques is extremely important. Time value techniques enable financial managers to evaluate cash flows occurring at different times in order to combine, compare, and evaluate them and link them to the firm's **overall goal of share price maximization.** It will become clear in Chapters 6 and 7 that the application of time value techniques is a key part of the value determination process. Using them, we can measure the firm's value and evaluate the impact that various events and decisions might have on it. Clearly, an understanding of time-value-of-money techniques and an ability to apply them are needed in order to make intelligent value-creating decisions.

New! The Summary now begins with a Focus on Value feature, which explains how the chapter's content relates to the firm's goal of maximizing owner wealth. This feature helps reinforce understanding of the link between the financial manager's actions and share value.

REVIEW OF LEARNING GOALS

LG1 **Discuss the role of time value in finance, the use of computational tools, and the basic patterns of cash flow.** Financial managers and investors use time-value-of-money techniques when assessing the value of the expected cash flow streams associated with investment alternatives. Alternatives can be assessed by either compounding to find future value or discounting to find present value. Because they are at time zero when making decisions, financial managers and investors rely primarily on present value techniques. Financial tables, financial calculators, and computers and spreadsheets can streamline the application of time value techniques. The cash flow of a firm can be described by its pattern—single amount, annuity, or mixed stream.

LG2 **Understand the concepts of future and present value, their calculation for single amounts, and the relationship of present value to future value.** Future value relies on compound interest to mea-

The **Review of Learning Goals** restates each learning goal and summarizes the key material that was presented to support mastery of that goal.

SELF-TEST PROBLEMS (Solutions in Appendix B)

LG2 LG5 ST 4–1 **Future values for various compounding frequencies** Delia Martin has $10,000 that she can deposit in any of three savings accounts for a 3-year period. Bank A compounds interest on an annual basis, bank B compounds interest twice each year, and bank C compounds interest each quarter. All three banks have a stated annual interest rate of 4%.

Self-Test Problems, keyed to the learning goals and tools in the PMF Toolbox, give students an opportunity to strengthen their understanding of topics by doing a sample problem before they begin homework materials. Solutions are provided in Appendix B at the back of the book, easily located by the green stripe on the edge of the pages.

LG2 4–5 **Future value** You have $1,500 to invest today at 7% interest compounded annually.

a. Find how much you will have accumulated in the account at the end of (1) 3 years, (2) 6 years, and (3) 9 years.
b. Use your findings in part a to calculate the amount of interest earned in (1) the first 3 years (years 1 to 3), (2) the second 3 years (years 4 to 6), and (3) the third 3 years (years 7 to 9).
c. Compare and contrast your findings in part b. Explain why the amount of interest earned increases in each succeeding 3-year period.

LG2 4–6 **Inflation and future value** As part of your financial planning, you wish to purchase a new car exactly 5 years from today. The car you wish to purchase costs $14,000 today, and your research indicates that its price will increase by 2% to 4% per year over the next 5 years.

a. Estimate the price of the car at the end of 5 years if inflation is (1) 2% per year, and (2) 4% per year.
b. How much more expensive will the car be if the rate of inflation is 4% rather than 2%?

A comprehensive set of **Problems,** containing more than one problem for each concept, tool, or technique, provides a wide range of assignable materials. A short descriptor at the beginning of the problem identifies the concept or technique that the problem has been designed to test. Problems labeled as "Integrative" tie together related topics. All problems are keyed to the learning goals and, where appropriate, to the tools in the PMF Toolbox. Guideline answers to selected end-of-chapter problems appear in Appendix C.

CHAPTER 4 CASE **Finding Jill Moran's Retirement Annuity**

Sunrise Industries wishes to accumulate funds to provide a retirement annuity for its vice president of research, Jill Moran. Ms. Moran by contract will retire at the end of exactly 12 years. Upon retirement, she is entitled to receive an annual end-of-year payment of $42,000 for exactly 20 years. If she dies prior to the end of the 20-year period, the annual payments will pass to her heirs. During the 12-year "accumulation period" Sunrise wishes to fund the annuity by making equal annual end-of-year deposits into an account earning 9% interest. Once the 20-year "distribution period" begins, Sunrise plans to move the accumulated monies into an account earning a guaranteed 12% per year. At the end of the distribution period, the account balance will equal zero. Note that the first deposit will be made at the end of year 1 and that the first distribution payment will be received at the end of year 13.

Chapter Cases call for application of concepts and techniques to a more complex realistic situation than in the regular problems. These cases help strengthen practical application of financial tools and techniques.

WEB EXERCISE

Go to Web site *www.arachnoid.com/lutusp/finance_old.html*. Page down to the portion of this screen that contains the financial calculator.

1. To determine the FV of a fixed amount, enter the following:

   Into PV, enter −1000; into **np**, enter 1; into **pmt**, enter 0; and, into **ir**, enter 8.

A **Web Exercise** at the end of the chapter links the chapter topic to a related site on the Internet and asks students to use information there to answer questions. These exercises capture student interest while teaching about financial-related sites.

Supplements to the Third Edition

The *PMF* Teaching/Learning System includes a variety of useful supplements for teachers and for students.

Teaching Tools for Instructors

The key teaching tools available to instructors are the *Instructor's Manual,* testing materials, and *PowerPoint Lecture Presentations.*

Instructor's Manual *Compiled by Frederick P. Schadler, East Carolina University.* This comprehensive resource pulls together the teaching tools so that instructors can use the textbook easily and effectively in the classroom. Each chapter provides an overview of key topics and detailed answers and solutions to all review questions, end-of-chapter problems, and chapter cases. At the end of the manual are practice quizzes and solutions.

Testing Material *Created by Hadi Salavitabar, SUNY–New Paltz.* Thoroughly revised to accommodate changes in the text, the Test Bank consists of a mix of true/false, multiple choice, and essay questions. For quick test selection and construction, each chapter features a handy chart for identifying type of question, skill tested by learning goal, and level of difficulty. The Test Bank is available in both printed and electronic formats, including Windows or Macintosh *TestGen-EQ* files and Microsoft Word files.

Instructors can download the *TestGen-EQ* version of the Test Bank into *QuizMaster-EQ,* an online testing program for Windows and Macintosh that enables users to conduct timed or untimed exams at computer workstations. After completing tests, students can see their scores and view or print a diagnostic report of those topics or objectives requiring more attention. When installed on a local-area network, *QuizMaster-EQ* allows instructors to save the scores on disk, print study diagnoses, and monitor progress of students individually or by class section and by all sections of the course.

PowerPoint Lecture Presentations *Created by Daniel J. Borgia, Florida Gulf Coast University.* Available for Windows or Macintosh on the Instructor's Resource CD-ROM, this presentation combines lecture notes with art from the textbook.

Instructor's Resource CD-ROM Electronic files of the *Instructor's Manual, Test Bank,* and *PowerPoint Lecture Presentations* are available on one convenient CD-ROM, compatible with both Windows and Macintosh computers. The electronic versions allow instructors to customize the support materials to their individual classroom needs.

Learning Tools for Students

Beyond the book itself, students have access to several resources for success in this course: the *PMF* CD-ROM, *Study Guide,* and the *Principles of Managerial Finance, Brief,* Third Edition Web site.

PMF CD-ROM Software Packaged with new copies of the text at no additional cost, the *PMF* CD-ROM Software, created by KMT Software, contains three state-of-the-art software tools: the *PMF Tutor,* the *PMF Problem-Solver,* and the *PMF Excel Spreadsheet Templates.* Documentation and practical advice for using the *PMF* CD-ROM appear in Appendix D of the textbook.

PMF Tutor The *PMF Tutor* extends self-testing opportunities beyond those of the printed page. The Tutor helps students to identify and solve various types of managerial finance problems. Part of the *PMF* Toolbox, the Tutor icon flags all the Tutor applications in the text. Through user-friendly menus, students can access over 40 different problem types, constructed by random-number generation for a nearly inexhaustible supply of problems with little chance of repetition. Routines include financial ratios, time value of money, valuation, capital budgeting, and cost of capital.

PMF Problem-Solver The *PMF Problem-Solver* contains 27 short menu-driven programs to accelerate learning by providing an efficient way to perform financial computations. The Problem-Solver icon points out all the related applications throughout the text of this popular provision of the *PMF* Toolbox. Referenced to specific chapters and sections for quick review of techniques, the routines include financial ratios, cash budgets, time value of money, bond and stock valuation, capital budgeting techniques, and cost of capital.

PMF Excel Spreadsheet Templates The *PMF Excel Spreadsheet Templates* provide users with preprogrammed spreadsheet templates for inputting data and solving problems using perhaps the most popular and widely accepted practical software application. The template files correspond to selected end-of-chapter problems.

Study Guide *Prepared by Stanley G. Eakins, East Carolina University.* The *Study Guide* is an integral component of the *PMF* Learning System. It offers many tools for studying finance. Each chapter contains the following features: chapter summary enumerated by learning goals; topical chapter outline, also broken down by learning goals for quick review; sample problem solutions; study tips; a full sample exam with the answers at the end of the chapter; and thumbnail printouts of the *PowerPoint Lecture Presentations* to facilitate classroom note taking.

Principles of Managerial Finance, Brief Third Edition Web Site The Web site to accompany this textbook, located at *www.aw.com/gitman,* contains valuable links, self-assessment quizzes, and much more. The quizzes, created by Christopher Riley of the State University of New York, New Paltz, consist of ten multiple-choice questions per chapter.

In addition to the Companion Web site, the course content is available in CourseCompass™ and Blackboard versions. CourseCompass™ is a nationally hosted, dynamic, interactive online course management system powered by Blackboard, leaders in the development of Internet-based learning tools. This easy-to-use and customizable program enables professors to tailor content and functionality to meet individual course needs. To see a demo, visit *www.coursecompass.com*. Please contact your local sales representative for more information on obtaining course content in these various formats.

Acknowledgments

To My Colleagues, Friends, and Family

No textbook can consistently meet market needs without continual feedback from colleagues, students, practitioners, and members of the publishing team. Once again, I invite colleagues to relate their classroom experiences using this book and its package to me at San Diego State University, or in care of the Acquisitions Editor in Finance, Addison-Wesley Publishing Company, 75 Arlington Street, Suite 300, Boston, Massachusetts 02116. Your constructive criticism will help me to continue to improve the textbook and its Teaching/Learning System still further.

Addison-Wesley and former publisher HarperCollins sought the advice of a great many excellent reviewers, all of whom strongly influenced various aspects of this book. My special thanks go to the following individuals who analyzed the manuscript in previous editions:

Saul W. Adelman
M. Fall Ainina
Gary A. Anderson
Ronald F. Anderson
Gene L. Andrusco
Antonio Apap
David A. Arbeit
Allen Arkins
Saul H. Auslander
Peter W. Bacon
Richard E. Ball
Alexander Barges
Charles Barngrover
Michael Becker
Scott Besley
Douglas S. Bible
Charles W. Blackwell
Russell L. Block
Calvin M. Boardman
Paul Bolster
Robert J. Bondi
Jeffrey A. Born
Jerry D. Boswell
Denis O. Boudreaux
Kenneth J. Boudreaux
Wayne Boyet
Ron Braswell
Christopher Brown
William Brunsen
Samuel B. Bulmash
Francis E. Canda
Omer Carey
Patrick A. Casabona
Robert Chatfield
K. C. Chen
Roger G. Clarke
Terrence M. Clauretie
Mark Cockalingam
Thomas Cook
Maurice P. Corrigan
Mike Cudd
Donnie L. Daniel
Prabir Datta
Joel J. Dauten
Lee E. Davis
Richard F. DeMong
Peter A. DeVito
James P. D'Mello
R. Gordon Dippel
Thomas W. Donohue
Vincent R. Driscoll
Betty A. Driver
Lorna Dotts
David R. Durst
Dwayne O. Eberhardt
Ronald L. Ehresman
Ted Ellis
F. Barney English
Greg Filbeck
Ross A. Flaherty
Rich Fortin
Timothy J. Gallagher
George W. Gallinger
Gerald D. Gay
R. H. Gilmer
Anthony J. Giovino
Philip W. Glasgo
Jeffrey W. Glazer
Joel Gold

Ron B. Goldfarb
Dennis W. Goodwin
David A. Gordon
J. Charles Granicz
C. Ramon Griffin
Reynolds Griffith
Lewell F. Gunter
Melvin W. Harju
Phil Harrington
George F. Harris
George T. Harris
John D. Harris
R. Stevenson Hawkey
Roger G. Hehman
Harvey Heinowitz
Glenn Henderson
Russell H. Hereth
Kathleen T. Hevert
J. Lawrence Hexter
Douglas A. Hibbert
Roger P. Hill
Linda C. Hittle
James Hoban
Hugh A. Hobson
Keith Howe
Kenneth M. Huggins
Jerry G. Hunt
Mahmood Islam
James F. Jackson
Stanley Jacobs
Dale W. Janowsky
Jeannette R. Jesinger
Nalina Jeypalan
Timothy E. Johnson
Roger Juchau
Ashok K. Kapoor
Daniel J. Kaufman, Jr.
Joseph K. Kiely
Terrance E. Kingston
Thomas M. Krueger
Lawrence Kryzanowski
Harry R. Kuniansky
Richard E. La Near
William R. Lane
James Larsen
Rick LeCompte
B. E. Lee
Scott Lee
Michael A. Lenarcic
A. Joseph Lerro
Thomas J. Liesz
Timothy Hoyt McCaughey
Christopher K. Ma
James C. Ma
Dilip B. Madan
Judy Maese
Brian Maris
Daniel S. Marrone
William H. Marsh
John F. Marshall
Linda J. Martin
Stanley A. Martin
Charles E. Maxwell
Jay Meiselman
Vincent A. Mercurio
Joseph Messina
John B. Mitchell
Gene P. Morris
Edward A. Moses
Tarun K. Mukherjee
William T. Murphy
Randy Myers
Lance Nail
Donald A. Nast
G. Newbould
Gary Noreiko
Dennis T. Officer
Kathleen J. Oldfather
Kathleen F. Oppenheimer
Richard M. Osborne
Jerome S. Osteryoung
Prasad Padmanabahn
Roger R. Palmer
Don B. Panton
John Park
Ronda S. Paul
Bruce C. Payne
Gerald W. Perritt
Gladys E. Perry
Stanley Piascik
Mary L. Piotrowski
D. Anthony Plath
Jerry B. Poe
Gerald A. Pogue
Ronald S. Pretekin
Fran Quinn
Walter J. Reinhart
Jack H. Reubens
William B. Riley, Jr.
Ron Rizzuto
Gayle A. Russell
Patricia A. Ryan
Murray Sabrin
Kanwal S. Sachedeva
R. Daniel Sadlier
Hadi Salavitabar
Gary Sanger
William L. Sartoris
Carl J. Schwendiman
Carl Schweser
Jim Scott
John W. Settle
Richard A. Shick
A. M. Sibley
Surendra S. Singhvi
Stacy Sirmans
Barry D. Smith
Gerald Smolen
Ira Smolowitz
Jean Snavely
Joseph V. Stanford
John A. Stocker
Lester B. Strickler
Elizabeth Strock
Philip R. Swensen
John C. Talbott
Gary Tallman
Harry Tamule
Richard W. Taylor
Rolf K. Tedefalk
Richard Teweles
Kenneth J. Thygerson
Robert D. Tollen
Emery A. Trahan
Pieter A. Vandenberg
Nikhil P. Varaiya
Oscar Varela
Kenneth J. Venuto
James A. Verbrugge
Ronald P. Volpe
John M. Wachowicz, Jr.
William H. Weber III
Herbert Weinraub
Jonathan B. Welch
Grant J. Wells

Larry R. White
Peter Wichert
C. Don Wiggins
Howard A. Williams
Richard E. Williams
Glenn A. Wilt, Jr.
Bernard J. Winger
Tony R. Wingler
I. R. Woods
John C. Woods
Robert J. Wright
Richard H. Yanow
Seung J. Yoon
Charles W. Young
Philip J. Young
Joe W. Zeman
J. Kenton Zumwalt
John T. Zeitlow
Tom Zwirlein

The following individuals provided extremely useful comments for the preparation of the third edition:

Alaak Alshawa, *Concordia College*
John Ewert, *College of Santa Fe*
Frank R. Falegin, *Robert Morris College*
James D. Keys, *Florida International University*
Winford Naylor, *Santa Barbara City College*
Susanne Polley, *SUNY at Cortland*
Jan M. Serrano, *Stephen F. Austin State University*
Lowell E. Stockstill, *Wittenberg University*
Richard W. Taylor, *Arkansas State University*
Douglas Waggle, *Berry College*
John Zeitlow, *Mount Vernon Nazarene College*

My special thanks go to all members of my book team whose vision, creativity, and ongoing support helped me to engineer all elements of the Teaching/Learning System: to Marlene Bellamy of Writeline Associates for preparing the chapter opening vignettes, e-finance and corporate focus In Practice boxes, and Web exercises; to Bernard W. Weinrich of St. Louis Community College, Forest Park Campus, for preparing the marginal annotations; to John Zeitlow, Mount Vernon Nazarene College, for preparing the ethics In Practice boxes; to Hadi Salavitabar of the State University of New York—New Paltz for revising the Test Banks; to Fred Schadler of East Carolina University for updating the *Instructor's Manual;* to Stan Eakins of East Carolina University for revising the *Study Guide;* to Daniel J. Borgia of Florida Gulf Coast University for preparing the *PowerPoint Lecture Presentations;* to Chris Riley of the State University of New York—New Paltz for generating the online quizzes; to Bill Megginson of the University of Oklahoma for revising the chapter on international managerial finance, which was originally prepared by Mehdi Salhizadeh of San Diego State University; and to KMT software for developing the *PMF Brief* CD-ROM software.

I'm pleased by and proud of all their efforts, and I'm confident that those who use the book—both instructors and students—will appreciate everything they've done to add new features of interest and to ensure accuracy, consistency, and accessibility throughout the package.

A standing ovation and hearty round of applause also go to the publishing team assembled by Addison-Wesley—including Donna Battista, Amy Gembala, Adrienne D'Ambrosio, Mary Clare McEwing, Gina Kolenda, Nancy Fenton, Jennifer Pelland, and others who worked on the book—for the inspiration and the perspiration that define teamwork. Nancy Freihofer and all the people at Thompson Steele, Inc., deserve an equally resounding ovation. Applause is also due Ann Torbert, whose development skills, creativity, expertise, and hard work have contributed to the book's standard of excellence. Also, special thanks to the formidable Addison-Wesley sales force in finance, whose ongoing efforts keep the business fun!

Finally, and most important, many thanks to my wife, Robin, and to our children, Zachary and Jessica, for patiently providing support, understanding, and good humor throughout the revision process. To them, I will be forever grateful.

—Lawrence J. Gitman

To the Student

Because you have a good many options for getting your assigned reading materials, I appreciate your choosing this textbook as the best means for learning. You shouldn't be disappointed. To meet your needs and time constraints, my product team and I have put together in this textbook an effective learning system. It integrates a variety of learning tools with the concepts, tools, techniques, and practical applications you'll need to learn about managerial finance. We have carefully listened to the compliments and complaints of students and of professors who have used earlier editions of this textbook in their coursework, and we have worked hard to present the most important concepts and practices of managerial finance in a clear and interesting way.

This book is loaded with features designed to motivate your study of finance and to help you learn the course material. For an overview and explanation of those features, go back to page xxvii ("Gitman's Proven Teaching/Learning System"). The page views and descriptions there will walk you through the features included in the book.

Some words of advice about a few specific features: First, pay attention to the learning goals, which will help you focus attention on what material you need to learn, where you can find it in the chapter, and whether you've mastered it by the end of the chapter.

Second, at the end of each major text section are Review Questions. It may be tempting to rush past those questions, but try to resist doing so. Pausing briefly to test your understanding of the key concepts, tools, techniques, and practices in the section you've just read will help you cement your understanding of that material. Give yourself an honest assessment of whether you've understood what you've read. If you haven't, go back (even briefly) and review anything that seemed unclear.

Third, look for (or make) opportunities to talk with classmates or friends about what you're reading and learning in the course. Being able to talk about the concepts and techniques of finance demonstrates how much you've learned, uncovers things you haven't yet understood fully, and gives you valuable practice for class and (eventually) the business world. While you're talking, don't neglect to discuss the issues raised in the Focus on Ethics boxes in the book, which look at some of the types of opportunities to do right (or not) that people in business sometimes face.

Packaged with new copies of this book is a CD that contains three useful pieces of software. Opportunities to apply these tools in conjunction with certain parts of the text are indicated by the use of an icon in the margin of the book. The laptop PC icon refers to the *PMF Brief Tutor*, which will use random number generation to create additional problems for you to solve. The CD icon refers to the *PMF Brief Problem-Solver*, which will do the routine mathematical computations of certain problems when you input the correct data. (Of course, you need to understand the concept in order to know what numbers to put in, but it's nice to have a "number-cruncher" right at hand.) The icon that looks like a spreadsheet refers to the *PMF Excel Spreadsheet Templates*. It indicates selected problems that can be solved using Excel spreadsheet templates. For more on these tools and other additional study resources, see page xxxii ("Learning Tools for Students").

Given today's rapidly changing technology, who knows what might be available next? We are striving to keep pace with your needs and interests, and want to hear your ideas for improving the teaching and learning of finance. Please feel free to share your ideas with us by e-mailing *finance@aw.com*.

I wish you all the best in this course, and in your academic and professional careers.

—Lawrence J. Gitman
San Diego State University

Part 1

Introduction to Managerial Finance

Chapter

1

The Role and Environment of Managerial Finance

LEARNING GOALS

LG1 Define *finance,* the major areas of finance and the opportunities available in this field, and the legal forms of business organization.

LG2 Describe the managerial finance function and its relationship to economics and accounting.

LG3 Identify the primary activities of the financial manager within the firm.

LG4 Explain why wealth maximization, rather than profit maximization, is the firm's goal and how the agency issue is related to it.

LG5 Understand the relationship between financial institutions and markets, and the role and operations of the money and capital markets.

LG6 Discuss the fundamentals of business taxation of ordinary income and capital gains.

Across the Disciplines

Why This Chapter Matters To You

Accounting: You need to understand the relationships between the firm's accounting and finance functions; how the financial statements you prepare will be used for making investment and financing decisions; ethical behavior by those responsible for a firm's funds; what agency costs are and why the firm must bear them; and how to calculate the tax effects of proposed transactions.

Information systems: You need to understand the organization of the firm; why finance personnel require both historical and projected data to support investment and financing decisions; and what data are necessary for determining the firm's tax liability.

Management: You need to understand the legal forms of business organization; the tasks that will be performed by finance personnel; the goal of the firm; the issue of management compensation; the role of ethics in the firm; the agency problem; and the firm's relationship to various financial institutions and markets.

Marketing: You need to understand how the activities you pursue will be affected by the finance function, such as the firm's cash and credit management policies; the role of ethics in promoting a sound corporate image; and the role the financial markets play in the firm's ability to raise capital for new projects.

Operations: You need to understand the organization of the firm and of the finance function in particular; why maximizing profit is not the main goal of the firm; the role of financial institutions and markets in providing funds for the firm's production capacity; and the agency problem and the role of ethics.

The field of finance directly affects the lives of every person and every organization. Many areas for study and a large number of career opportunities are available in finance. The purpose of this chapter is to acquaint you with the study of finance, the managerial finance function, and the goal of the firm. The chapter also describes financial institutions and markets, and business taxation. Finance will affect your working life in whatever area of study you choose to concentrate.

LG1

Finance and Business

The field of finance is broad and dynamic. It directly affects the lives of every person and every organization. There are many areas and career opportunities in the field of finance. Basic principles of finance, such as those you will learn in this textbook, can be universally applied in business organizations of different types.

What Is Finance?

finance
The art and science of managing money.

Finance can be defined as the art and science of managing money. Virtually all individuals and organizations earn or raise money and spend or invest money. Finance is concerned with the process, institutions, markets, and instruments involved in the transfer of money among individuals, businesses, and governments.

Major Areas and Opportunities in Finance

The major areas of finance can be summarized by reviewing the career opportunities in finance. These opportunities can, for convenience, be divided into two broad parts: financial services and managerial finance.

Financial Services

financial services
The part of finance concerned with the design and delivery of advice and financial products to individuals, business, and government.

WWW

Financial services is the area of finance concerned with the design and delivery of advice and financial products to individuals, business, and government. It involves a variety of interesting career opportunities within the areas of banking and related institutions, personal financial planning, investments, real estate, and insurance. Career opportunities available in each of these areas are described at this textbook's Web site at *www.aw.com/gitman.*

Managerial Finance

managerial finance
Concerns the duties of the financial manager in the business firm.

financial manager
Actively manages the financial affairs of any type of business, whether financial or nonfinancial, private or public, large or small, profit-seeking or not-for-profit.

Managerial finance is concerned with the duties of the financial manager in the business firm. **Financial managers** actively manage the financial affairs of any type of businesses—financial and nonfinancial, private and public, large and small, profit-seeking and not-for-profit. They perform such varied financial tasks as planning, extending credit to customers, evaluating proposed large expenditures, and raising money to fund the firm's operations. In recent years, the changing economic and regulatory environments have increased the importance and complexity of the financial manager's duties. As a result, many top executives have come from the finance area.

Another important recent trend has been the globalization of business activity. U.S. corporations have dramatically increased their sales, purchases, investments, and fund raising in other countries, and foreign corporations have likewise increased these activities in the United States. These changes have created a need for financial managers who can help a firm to manage cash flows in different currencies and protect against the risks that naturally arise from international transactions. Although these changes make the managerial finance function more complex, they can also lead to a more rewarding and fulfilling career.

Legal Forms of Business Organization

The three most common legal forms of business organization are the *sole proprietorship*, the *partnership*, and the *corporation*. Other specialized forms of business organization also exist. Sole proprietorships are the most numerous. However, corporations are overwhelmingly dominant with respect to receipts and net profits. Corporations are given primary emphasis in this textbook.

Sole Proprietorships

sole proprietorship
A business owned by one person and operated for his or her own profit.

A **sole proprietorship** is a business owned by one person who operates it for his or her own profit. About 75 percent of all business firms are sole proprietorships. The typical sole proprietorship is a small business, such as a bike shop, personal trainer, or plumber. The majority of sole proprietorships are found in the wholesale, retail, service, and construction industries.

unlimited liability
The condition of a sole proprietorship (or general partnership) allowing the owner's total wealth to be taken to satisfy creditors.

Typically, the proprietor, along with a few employees, operates the proprietorship. He or she normally raises capital from personal resources or by borrowing and is responsible for all business decisions. The sole proprietor has **unlimited liability;** his or her total wealth, not merely the amount originally invested, can be taken to satisfy creditors. The key strengths and weaknesses of sole proprietorships are summarized in Table 1.1.

Partnerships

partnership
A business owned by two or more people and operated for profit.

A **partnership** consists of two or more owners doing business together for profit. Partnerships account for about 10 percent of all businesses, and they are typically larger than sole proprietorships. Finance, insurance, and real estate firms are the most common types of partnership. Public accounting and stock brokerage partnerships often have large numbers of partners.

articles of partnership
The written contract used to formally establish a business partnership.

Most partnerships are established by a written contract known as **articles of partnership.** In a *general* (or *regular*) *partnership,* all partners have unlimited liability, and each partner is legally liable for all of the debts of the partnership. Strengths and weaknesses of partnerships are summarized in Table 1.1.

Corporations

corporation
An artificial being created by law (often called a "legal entity").

A **corporation** is an artificial being created by law. Often called a "legal entity," a corporation has the powers of an individual in that it can sue and be sued, make and be party to contracts, and acquire property in its own name. Although only about 15 percent of all businesses are incorporated, the corporation is the domi-

TABLE 1.1 Strengths and Weaknesses of the Common Legal Forms of Business Organization

	Sole proprietorship	Partnership	Corporation
Strengths	• Owner receives all profits (and sustains all losses) • Low organizational costs • Income included and taxed on proprietor's personal tax return • Independence • Secrecy • Ease of dissolution	• Can raise more funds than sole proprietorships • Borrowing power enhanced by more owners • More available brain power and managerial skill • Income included and taxed on partner's tax return	• Owners have *limited liability,* which guarantees that they cannot lose more than they invested • Can achieve large size via sale of stock • Ownership (stock) is readily transferable • Long life of firm • Can hire professional managers • Has better access to financing • Receives certain tax advantages
Weaknesses	• Owner has *unlimited liability*—total wealth can be taken to satisfy debts • Limited fund-raising power tends to inhibit growth • Proprietor must be jack-of-all-trades • Difficult to give employees long-run career opportunities • Lacks continuity when proprietor dies	• Owners have *unlimited liability* and may have to cover debts of other partners • Partnership is dissolved when a partner dies • Difficult to liquidate or transfer partnership	• Taxes generally higher, because corporate income is taxed, and dividends paid to owners are also taxed • More expensive to organize than other business forms • Subject to greater government regulation • Lacks secrecy, because stockholders must receive financial reports

nant form of business organization in terms of receipts and profits. It accounts for nearly 90 percent of business receipts and 80 percent of net profits. Although corporations are involved in all types of businesses, manufacturing corporations account for the largest portion of corporate business receipts and net profits. The key strengths and weaknesses of large corporations are summarized in Table 1.1.

stockholders
The owners of a corporation, whose ownership, or *equity,* is evidenced by either common stock or preferred stock.

common stock
The purest and most basic form of corporate ownership.

dividends
Periodic distributions of earnings to the stockholders of a firm.

board of directors
Group elected by the firm's stockholders and having ultimate authority to guide corporate affairs and make general policy.

The owners of a corporation are its **stockholders,** whose ownership, or *equity,* is evidenced by either common stock or preferred stock.[1] These forms of ownership are defined and discussed in Chapter 7; at this point suffice it to say that **common stock** is the purest and most basic form of corporate ownership. Stockholders expect to earn a return by receiving **dividends**—periodic distributions of earnings—or by realizing gains through increases in share price.

As noted in the upper portion of Figure 1.1, the stockholders vote periodically to elect the members of the board of directors and to amend the firm's corporate charter. The **board of directors** has the ultimate authority in guiding corporate affairs and in making general policy. The directors include key corporate personnel as well as outside individuals who typically are successful businesspeople and executives of other major organizations. Outside directors for major corporations

1. Some corporations do not have stockholders but rather have "members" who often have rights similar to those of stockholders—that is, they are entitled to vote and receive dividends. Examples include mutual savings banks, credit unions, mutual insurance companies, and a whole host of charitable organizations.

FIGURE 1.1 Corporate Organization
The general organization of a corporation and the finance function (which is shown in yellow)

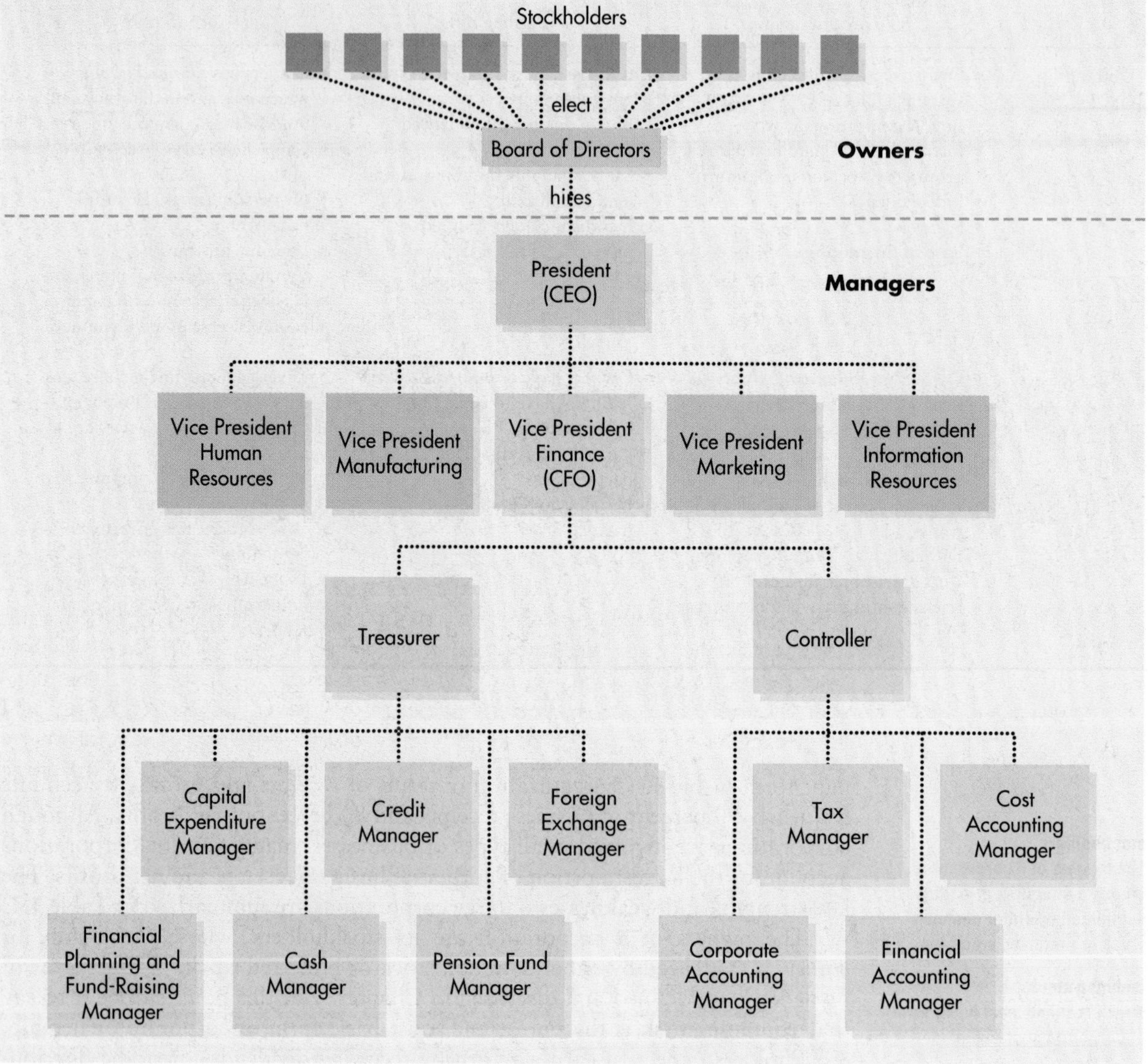

are generally paid an annual fee of $10,000 to $20,000 or more. Also, they are frequently granted options to buy a specified number of shares of the firm's stock at a stated—and often attractive—price.

president or chief executive officer (CEO)
Corporate official responsible for managing the firm's day-to-day operations and carrying out the policies established by the board of directors.

The **president** or **chief executive officer (CEO)** is responsible for managing day-to-day operations and carrying out the policies established by the board. The CEO is required to report periodically to the firm's directors.

It is important to note the division between owners and managers in a large corporation, as shown by the dashed horizontal line in Figure 1.1. This separation and some of the issues surrounding it will be addressed in the discussion of *the agency issue* later in this chapter.

Other Limited Liability Organizations

A number of other organizational forms provide owners with limited liability. The most popular are *limited partnerships (LPs), S corporations (S corps), limited liability corporations (LLCs),* and *limited liability partnerships (LLPs)*. Each represents a specialized form or blending of the characteristics of the organizational forms described before. What they have in common is that their owners enjoy limited liability, and they typically have fewer than 100 owners. Each of these limited liability organizations is described at the book's Web site at *www.aw.com/gitman*.

The Study of Managerial Finance

An understanding of the concepts, techniques, and practices presented throughout this text will fully acquaint you with the financial manager's activities and decisions. Because most business decisions are measured in financial terms, the financial manager plays a key role in the operation of the firm. People in all areas of responsibility—accounting, information systems, management, marketing, operations, and so forth—need a basic understanding of the managerial finance function.

All managers in the firm, regardless of their job descriptions, work with financial personnel to justify laborpower requirements, negotiate operating budgets, deal with financial performance appraisals, and sell proposals at least partly on the basis of their financial merits. Clearly, those managers who understand the financial decision-making process will be better able to address financial concerns and will therefore more often get the resources they need to attain their own goals. The "Across the Disciplines" element that appears on each chapter-opening page should help you understand some of the many interactions between managerial finance and other business careers.

As you study this text, you will learn about the career opportunities in managerial finance, which are briefly described in Table 1.2. Although this text focuses

TABLE 1.2 Career Opportunities in Managerial Finance

Position	Description
Financial analyst	Primarily prepares the firm's financial plans and budgets. Other duties include financial forecasting, performing financial comparisons, and working closely with accounting.
Capital expenditures manager	Evaluates and recommends proposed asset investments. May be involved in the financial aspects of implementing approved investments.
Project finance manager	In large firms, arranges financing for approved asset investments. Coordinates consultants, investment bankers, and legal counsel.
Cash manager	Maintains and controls the firm's daily cash balances. Frequently manages the firm's cash collection and disbursement activities and short-term investments; coordinates short-term borrowing and banking relationships.
Credit analyst/manager	Administers the firm's credit policy by evaluating credit applications, extending credit, and monitoring and collecting accounts receivable.
Pension fund manager	In large companies, oversees or manages the assets and liabilities of the employees' pension fund.
Foreign exchange manager	Manages specific foreign operations and the firm's exposure to fluctuations in exchange rates.

on publicly held profit-seeking firms, the principles presented here are equally applicable to private and not-for-profit organizations. The decision-making principles developed in this text can also be applied to personal financial decisions. I hope that this first exposure to the exciting field of finance will provide the foundation and initiative for further study and possibly even a future career.

Review Questions

1–1 What is *finance?* Explain how this field affects the lives of everyone and every organization.
1–2 What is the *financial services* area of finance? Describe the field of *managerial finance.*
1–3 Which legal form of business organization is most common? Which form is dominant in terms of business receipts and net profits?
1–4 Describe the roles and the basic relationship among the major parties in a corporation—stockholders, board of directors, and president. How are corporate owners compensated?
1–5 Briefly name and describe some organizational forms other than corporations that provide owners with limited liability.
1–6 Why is the study of managerial finance important regardless of the specific area of responsibility one has within the business firm?

LG2 LG3

The Managerial Finance Function

People in all areas of responsibility within the firm must interact with finance personnel and procedures to get their jobs done. For financial personnel to make useful forecasts and decisions, they must be willing and able to talk to individuals in other areas of the firm. The managerial finance function can be broadly described by considering its role within the organization, its relationship to economics and accounting, and the primary activities of the financial manager.

Organization of the Finance Function

treasurer
The firm's chief financial manager, who is responsible for the firm's financial activities, such as financial planning and fund raising, making capital expenditure decisions, and managing cash, credit, the pension fund, and foreign exchange.

controller
The firm's chief accountant, who is responsible for the firm's accounting activities, such as corporate accounting, tax management, financial accounting, and cost accounting.

The size and importance of the managerial finance function depend on the size of the firm. In small firms, the finance function is generally performed by the accounting department. As a firm grows, the finance function typically evolves into a separate department linked directly to the company president or CEO through the chief financial officer (CFO). The lower portion of the organizational chart in Figure 1.1 (on page 6) shows the structure of the finance function in a typical medium-to-large-size firm.

Reporting to the CFO are the treasurer and the controller. The **treasurer** (the chief financial manager) is commonly responsible for handling financial activities, such as financial planning and fund raising, making capital expenditure decisions, managing cash, managing credit activities, managing the pension fund, and managing foreign exchange. The **controller** (the chief accountant) typically handles the accounting activities, such as corporate accounting, tax management, financial accounting, and cost accounting. The treasurer's focus tends to be more external, the controller's focus more internal. *The activities of the treasurer, or financial manager, are the primary concern of this text.*

If international sales or purchases are important to a firm, it may well employ one or more finance professionals whose job is to monitor and manage the firm's exposure to loss from currency fluctuations. A trained financial manager can "hedge," or protect against such a loss, at reasonable cost by using a variety of financial instruments. These **foreign exchange managers** typically report to the firm's treasurer.

foreign exchange manager
The manager responsible for monitoring and managing the firm's exposure to loss from currency fluctuations.

Relationship to Economics

The field of finance is closely related to economics. Financial managers must understand the economic framework and be alert to the consequences of varying levels of economic activity and changes in economic policy. They must also be able to use economic theories as guidelines for efficient business operation. Examples include supply-and-demand analysis, profit-maximizing strategies, and price theory. The primary economic principle used in managerial finance is **marginal analysis,** the principle that financial decisions should be made and actions taken only when the added benefits exceed the added costs. Nearly all financial decisions ultimately come down to an assessment of their marginal benefits and marginal costs.

marginal analysis
Economic principle that states that financial decisions should be made and actions taken only when the added benefits exceed the added costs.

EXAMPLE

Amy Chen is a financial manager for Strom Department Stores, a large chain of upscale department stores operating primarily in the western United States. She is currently trying to decide whether to replace one of the firm's online computers with a new, more sophisticated one that would both speed processing and handle a larger volume of transactions. The new computer would require a cash outlay of $80,000, and the old computer could be sold to net $28,000. The total benefits from the new computer (measured in today's dollars) would be $100,000. The benefits over a similar time period from the old computer (measured in today's dollars) would be $35,000. Applying marginal analysis, Amy organizes the data as follows:

Benefits with new computer	$100,000	
Less: Benefits with old computer	35,000	
(1) Marginal (added) benefits		$65,000
Cost of new computer	$ 80,000	
Less: Proceeds from sale of old computer	28,000	
(2) Marginal (added) costs		52,000
Net benefit [(1) – (2)]		$13,000

Because the marginal (added) benefits of $65,000 exceed the marginal (added) costs of $52,000, Amy recommends that the firm purchase the new computer to replace the old one. The firm will experience a net benefit of $13,000 as a result of this action.

Relationship to Accounting

The firm's finance (treasurer) and accounting (controller) activities are closely related and generally overlap. Indeed, managerial finance and accounting are not often easily distinguishable. In small firms the controller often carries out the finance function, and in large firms many accountants are closely involved in various finance activities. However, there are two basic differences between finance and accounting; one is related to the emphasis on cash flows and the other to decision making.

Emphasis on Cash Flows

accrual basis
In preparation of financial statements, recognizes revenue at the time of sale and recognizes expenses when they are incurred.

cash basis
Recognizes revenues and expenses only with respect to actual inflows and outflows of cash.

The accountant's primary function is to develop and report data for measuring the performance of the firm, assessing its financial position, and paying taxes. Using certain standardized and generally accepted principles, the accountant prepares financial statements that recognize revenue at the time of sale (whether payment has been received or not) and recognize expenses when they are incurred. This approach is referred to as the **accrual basis.**

The financial manager, on the other hand, places primary emphasis on *cash flows,* the intake and outgo of cash. He or she maintains the firm's solvency by planning the cash flows necessary to satisfy its obligations and to acquire assets needed to achieve the firm's goals. The financial manager uses this **cash basis** to recognize the revenues and expenses only with respect to actual inflows and outflows of cash. Regardless of its profit or loss, a firm must have a sufficient flow of cash to meet its obligations as they come due.

EXAMPLE

Thomas Yachts, a small yacht dealer, sold one yacht for $100,000 in the calendar year just ended. The yacht was purchased during the year at a total cost of $80,000. Although the firm paid in full for the yacht during the year, at year-end it has yet to collect the $100,000 from the customer. The accounting view and the financial view of the firm's performance during the year are given by the following income and cash flow statements, respectively.

Accounting View (accrual basis)		Financial View (cash basis)	
Thomas Yachts Income Statement for the Year Ended 12/31		Thomas Yachts Cash Flow Statement for the Year Ended 12/31	
Sales revenue	$100,000	Cash inflow	$ 0
Less: Costs	80,000	Less: Cash outflow	80,000
Net profit	$ 20,000	Net cash flow	($80,000)

In an accounting sense Thomas Yachts is profitable, but in terms of actual cash flow it is a financial failure. Its lack of cash flow resulted from the uncollected account receivable of $100,000. Without adequate cash inflows to meet its obligations, the firm will not survive, regardless of its level of profits.

As the example shows, accrual accounting data do not fully describe the circumstances of a firm. Thus the financial manager must look beyond financial statements to obtain insight into existing or developing problems. Of course, accountants are well aware of the importance of cash flows, and financial managers use and understand accrual-based financial statements. Nevertheless, the financial manager, by concentrating on cash flows, should be able to avoid insolvency and achieve the firm's financial goals.

Decision Making

The second major difference between finance and accounting has to do with decision making. Accountants devote most of their attention to the *collection and presentation of financial data.* Financial managers evaluate the accounting statements, develop additional data, and *make decisions* on the basis of their assessment of the associated returns and risks. Of course, this does not mean that accountants never make decisions or that financial managers never gather data. Rather, the primary focuses of accounting and finance are distinctly different.

Primary Activities of the Financial Manager

In addition to ongoing involvement in financial analysis and planning, the financial manager's primary activities are making investment decisions and making financing decisions. Investment decisions determine both the mix and the type of assets held by the firm. Financing decisions determine both the mix and the type of financing used by the firm. These sorts of decisions can be conveniently viewed in terms of the firm's balance sheet, as shown in Figure 1.2. However, the decisions are actually made on the basis of their cash flow effects on the overall value of the firm.

Review Questions

1–7 What financial activities is the treasurer, or financial manager, responsible for handling in the mature firm?
1–8 What is the primary economic principle used in managerial finance?
1–9 What are the major differences between accounting and finance with respect to emphasis on cash flows and decision making?

FIGURE 1.2

Financial Activities
Primary activities of the financial manager

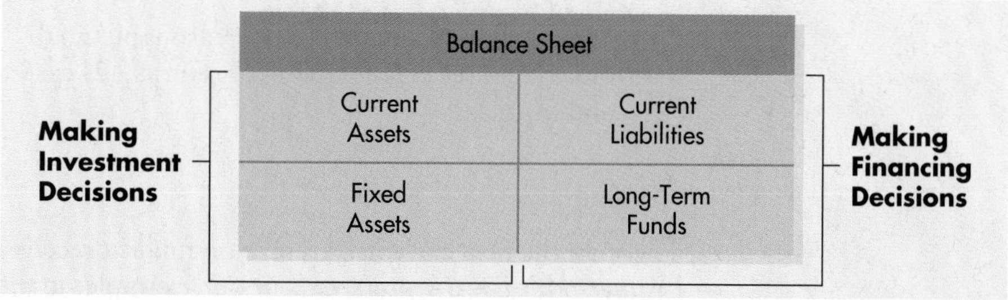

1–10 What are the two primary activities of the financial manager that are related to the firm's balance sheet?

LG4

Goal of the Firm

As noted earlier, the owners of a corporation are normally distinct from its managers. Actions of the financial manager should be taken to achieve the objectives of the firm's owners, its stockholders. In most cases, if financial managers are successful in this endeavor, they will also achieve their own financial and professional objectives. Thus financial managers need to know what the objectives of the firm's owners are.

Maximize Profit?

Some people believe that the firm's objective is always to maximize profit. To achieve this goal, the financial manager would take only those actions that were expected to make a major contribution to the firm's overall profits. For each alternative being considered, the financial manager would select the one that is expected to result in the highest monetary return.

earnings per share (EPS)
The amount earned during the period on behalf of each outstanding share of common stock, calculated by dividing the period's total earnings available for the firm's common stockholders by the number of shares of common stock outstanding.

Corporations commonly measure profits in terms of **earnings per share (EPS)**, which represent the amount earned during the period on behalf of each outstanding share of common stock. EPS are calculated by dividing the period's total earnings available for the firm's common stockholders by the number of shares of common stock outstanding.

EXAMPLE

Nick Bono, the financial manager of Harpers, Inc., a manufacturer of fishing gear, is choosing between two investments, Rotor and Valve. The following table shows the EPS that each investment is expected to have over its 3-year life.

	Earnings per share (EPS)			
Investment	Year 1	Year 2	Year 3	Total for years 1, 2, and 3
Rotor	$1.40	$1.00	$0.40	$2.80
Valve	0.60	1.00	1.40	3.00

In terms of the profit maximization goal, Valve would be preferred over Rotor, because it results in higher total earnings per share over the 3-year period ($3.00 EPS compared with $2.80 EPS).

But is profit maximization a reasonable goal? No. It fails for a number of reasons: It ignores (1) the timing of returns, (2) cash flows available to stockholders, and (3) risk.

Timing

Because the firm can earn a return on funds it receives, *the receipt of funds sooner rather than later is preferred.* In our example, in spite of the fact that the total earnings from Rotor are smaller than those from Valve, Rotor provides much greater earnings per share in the first year. The larger returns in year 1 could be reinvested to provide greater future earnings.

Cash Flows

Profits do *not* necessarily result in cash flows available to the stockholders. Owners receive cash flow in the form of either cash dividends paid them or the proceeds from selling their shares for a higher price than initially paid. Greater EPS do not necessarily mean that a firm's board of directors will vote to increase dividend payments.

Furthermore, higher EPS do not necessarily translate into a higher stock price. Firms sometimes experience earnings increases without any correspondingly favorable change in stock price. Only when earnings increases are accompanied by increased future cash flows would a higher stock price be expected.

Risk

risk
The chance that actual outcomes may differ from those expected.

Profit maximization also disregards **risk**—the chance that actual outcomes may differ from those expected. A basic premise in managerial finance is that a tradeoff exists between return (cash flow) and risk. *Return and risk are in fact the key determinants of share price, which represents the wealth of the owners in the firm.*

risk-averse
Seeking to avoid risk.

Cash flow and risk affect share price differently: Higher cash flow is generally associated with a higher share price. Higher risk tends to result in a lower share price because the stockholder must be compensated for the greater risk. In general, stockholders are **risk-averse**—that is, they want to avoid risk. When risk is involved, stockholders expect to earn higher rates of return on investments of higher risk and lower rates on lower-risk investments. The key point, which will be fully developed in Chapter 5, is that differences in risk can significantly affect the value of an investment.

Because profit maximization does not achieve the objectives of the firm's owners, it should *not* be the goal of the financial manager.

Maximize Shareholder Wealth

The goal of the firm, and therefore of all managers and employees, is *to maximize the wealth of the owners for whom it is being operated.* The wealth of corporate owners is measured by the share price of the stock, which in turn is based on the timing of returns (cash flows), their magnitude, and their risk. When considering each financial decision alternative or possible action in terms of its impact on the share price of the firm's stock, *financial managers should accept only those actions that are expected to increase share price.* Figure 1.3 depicts this process. Because share price represents the owners' wealth in the firm, maximizing share price will maximize owner wealth. Note that *return (cash flows) and risk are the key decision variables in maximizing owner wealth.* It is important to recognize that earnings per share (EPS), because they are viewed as an indicator of the firm's future returns (cash flows), often appear to affect share price. Two important issues related to maximizing share price are economic value added (EVA®) and the focus on stakeholders.

FIGURE 1.3

Share Price Maximization

Financial decisions and share price

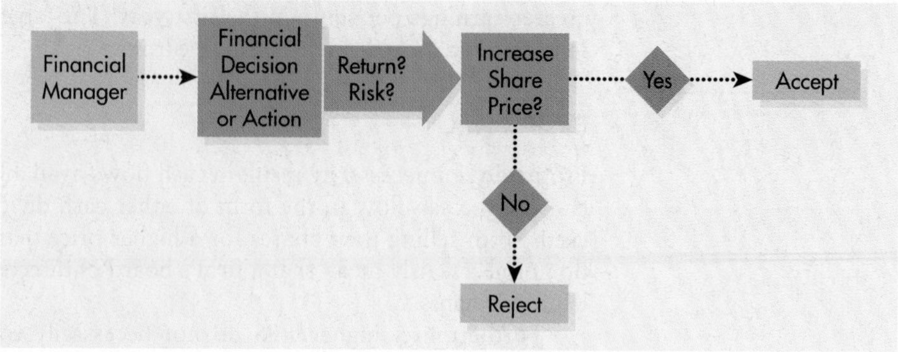

Economic Value Added (EVA®)

economic value added (EVA®) A popular measure used by many firms to determine whether an investment contributes positively to the owners' wealth; calculated by subtracting the cost of funds used to finance an investment from its after-tax operating profits.

Economic value added (EVA®) is a popular measure used by many firms to determine whether an investment—proposed or existing—contributes positively to the owners' wealth. EVA® is calculated by subtracting the cost of funds used to finance an investment from its after-tax operating profits. Investments with positive EVA®s increase shareholder value and those with negative EVA®s reduce shareholder value. Clearly, only those investments with positive EVA®s are desirable. For example, the EVA® of an investment with after-tax operating profits of $410,000 and associated financing costs of $375,000 would be $35,000 (i.e., $410,000 – $375,000). Because this EVA® is positive, the investment is expected to increase owner wealth and is therefore acceptable. (EVA®-type models are discussed in greater detail as part of the coverage of stock valuation in Chapter 7.)

What About Stakeholders?

stakeholders Groups such as employees, customers, suppliers, creditors, owners, and others who have a direct economic link to the firm.

Although maximization of shareholder wealth is the primary goal, many firms broaden their focus to include the interests of *stakeholders* as well as shareholders. **Stakeholders** are groups such as employees, customers, suppliers, creditors, owners, and others who have a direct economic link to the firm. A firm with a *stakeholder focus* consciously avoids actions that would prove detrimental to stakeholders. The goal is not to maximize stakeholder well-being but to preserve it.

The stakeholder view does not alter the goal of maximizing shareholder wealth. Such a view is often considered part of the firm's "social responsibility." It is expected to provide long-run benefit to shareholders by maintaining positive stakeholder relationships. Such relationships should minimize stakeholder turnover, conflicts, and litigation. Clearly, the firm can better achieve its goal of shareholder wealth maximization by fostering cooperation with its other stakeholders, rather than conflict with them.

The Role of Ethics

In recent years, the ethics of actions taken by certain businesses have received major media attention. Examples include an agreement by American Express Co. in early 2002 to pay $31 million to settle a sex- and age-discrimination lawsuit filed on behalf of more than 4,000 women who said they were denied equal pay and promotions; Enron Corp.'s key executives indicating to employee-shareholders in mid-2001 that the firm's then-depressed stock price would soon recover while, at the same time, selling their own shares and, not long after, taking the firm into bankruptcy; and Liggett & Meyers' early 1999 agreement to fund the payment of more than $1 billion in smoking-related health claims.

ethics
Standards of conduct or moral judgment.

Clearly, these and similar actions have raised the question of **ethics**—standards of conduct or moral judgment. Today, the business community in general and the financial community in particular are developing and enforcing ethical standards. The goal of these ethical standards is to motivate business and market participants to adhere to both the letter and the spirit of laws and regulations concerned with business and professional practice. Most business leaders believe businesses actually strengthen their competitive positions by maintaining high ethical standards.

Considering Ethics

Robert A. Cooke, a noted ethicist, suggests that the following questions be used to assess the ethical viability of a proposed action.[2]

1. Is the action arbitrary or capricious? Does it unfairly single out an individual or group?
2. Does the action violate the moral or legal rights of any individual or group?
3. Does the action conform to accepted moral standards?
4. Are there alternative courses of action that are less likely to cause actual or potential harm?

Clearly, considering such questions before taking an action can help to ensure its ethical viability.

Today, more and more firms are directly addressing the issue of ethics by establishing corporate ethics policies and requiring employee compliance with them. Frequently, employees are required to sign a formal pledge to uphold the firm's ethics policies. Such policies typically apply to employee actions in dealing with all corporate stakeholders, including the public. Many companies also require employees to participate in ethics seminars and training programs. To provide further insight into the ethical dilemmas and issues sometimes facing the financial manager, a number of the *In Practice* boxes appearing throughout this book are labeled to note their focus on ethics.

Ethics and Share Price

An effective ethics program is believed to enhance corporate value. An ethics program can produce a number of positive benefits. It can reduce potential litigation and judgment costs; maintain a positive corporate image; build shareholder confidence; and gain the loyalty, commitment, and respect of the firm's stakeholders. Such actions, by maintaining and enhancing cash flow and reducing perceived

2. Robert A. Cooke, "Business Ethics: A Perspective," in *Arthur Andersen Cases on Business Ethics* (Chicago: Arthur Andersen, September 1991), pp. 2 and 5.

In Practice

FOCUS ON ETHICS "Doing Well by Doing Good"

Hewlett-Packard (H-P) was founded in 1939 by Bill Hewlett and Dave Packard on the basis of principles of fair dealing and respect—long before anyone coined the expression "corporate social responsibility." H-P credits its ongoing commitment to "doing well by doing good" as a major reason why employees, suppliers, customers, and shareholders seek it out. H-P is clear on its obligation to increase the market value of its common stock, yet it strives to maintain the integrity of each employee in every country in which it does business. Its "Standards of Business Conduct" include a provision that triggers immediate dismissal of any employee who is found to have told a lie. Its internal auditors are expected to adhere to all of these standards, which set forth the "highest principles of business ethics and conduct," according to H-P's 2000 annual report.

Maximizing shareholder wealth is what some call a "moral imperative," in that stockholders are owners with property rights, and in that managers as stewards are obliged to look out for owners' interests. Many times, doing what is right is consistent with maximizing the stock price, but what if integrity causes a company to lose a contract or causes analysts to reduce the rating of the stock from "buy" to "sell"? The objective to maximize shareholder wealth holds, but company officers must do so within ethical constraints. Those constraints occasionally limit the alternative actions from which managers may choose. Some critics have mistakenly assumed that the objective of maximizing shareholder wealth is somehow the cause of unethical behavior, ignoring the fact that *any* business goal might be cited as a factor pressuring individuals to be unethical.

U.S. business professionals have tended to operate from within a strong moral framework based on early-childhood moral development that takes place in families and religious institutions. This does not prevent all ethical lapses, obviously. But it is not surprising that chief financial officers declare that the number-1 personal attribute that finance grads need is ethics—which they rank above interpersonal skills, communication skills, decision-making ability, and computer skills. H-P is aware of this need and has institutionalized it in the company's culture and policies.

risk, can positively affect the firm's share price. *Ethical behavior is therefore viewed as necessary for achieving the firm's goal of owner wealth maximization.*[3]

The Agency Issue

We have seen that the goal of the financial manager should be to maximize the wealth of the firm's owners. Thus managers can be viewed as *agents* of the owners who have hired them and given them decision-making authority to manage the firm. Technically, any manager who owns less than 100 percent of the firm is to some degree an agent of the other owners. This separation of owners and managers is shown by the dashed horizontal line in Figure 1.1 on page 6.

In theory, most financial managers would agree with the goal of owner wealth maximization. In practice, however, managers are also concerned with their personal wealth, job security, and fringe benefits. Such concerns may make managers reluctant or unwilling to take more than moderate risk if they perceive that taking too much risk might jeopardize their jobs or reduce their personal

3. For an excellent discussion of this and related issues by a number of finance academics and practitioners who have given a lot of thought to financial ethics, see James S. Ang, "On Financial Ethics," *Financial Management* (Autumn 1993), pp. 32–59.

wealth. The result is a less-than-maximum return and a potential loss of wealth for the owners.

The Agency Problem

From this conflict of owner and personal goals arises what has been called the **agency problem,** the likelihood that managers may place personal goals ahead of corporate goals. Two factors—market forces and *agency costs*—serve to prevent or minimize agency problems.

agency problem
The likelihood that managers may place personal goals ahead of corporate goals.

Market Forces One market force is *major shareholders,* particularly large institutional investors such as mutual funds, life insurance companies, and pension funds. These holders of large blocks of a firm's stock exert pressure on management to perform. When necessary, they exercise their voting rights as stockholders to replace underperforming management.

Another market force is the *threat of takeover* by another firm that believes it can enhance the target firm's value to restructuring its management, operations, and financing. The constant threat of a takeover tends to motivate management to act in the best interests of the firm's owners.

Agency Costs To minimize agency problems and contribute to the maximization of owners' wealth, stockholders incur **agency costs.** These are the costs of monitoring management behavior, ensuring against dishonest acts of management, and giving managers the financial incentive to maximize share price.

The most popular, powerful, and expensive approach is to *structure management compensation* to correspond with share price maximization. The objective is to give managers incentives to act in the best interests of the owners. In addition, the resulting compensation packages allow firms to compete for and hire the best managers available.

The two key types of compensation plans are incentive plans and performance plans. **Incentive plans** tend to tie management compensation to share price. The most popular incentive plan is the granting of **stock options** to management. These options allow managers to purchase stock at the market price set at the time of the grant. If the market price rises, managers will be rewarded by being able to resell the shares at the higher market price.

Many firms also offer **performance plans,** which tie management compensation to measures such as earnings per share (EPS), growth in EPS, and other ratios of return. **Performance shares,** shares of stock given to management as a result of meeting the stated performance goals, are often used in these plans. Another form of performance-based compensation is **cash bonuses,** cash payments tied to the achievement of certain performance goals.

agency costs
The costs borne by stockholders to minimize agency problems.

incentive plans
Management compensation plans that tend to tie management compensation to share price; most popular incentive plan involves the grant of *stock options.*

stock options
An incentive allowing managers to purchase stock at the market price set at the time of the grant.

performance plans
Plans that tie management compensation to measures such as EPS, growth in EPS, and other ratios of return. *Performance shares* and/or *cash bonuses* are used as compensation under these plans.

performance shares
Shares of stock given to management for meeting stated performance goals.

cash bonuses
Cash paid to management for achieving certain performance goals.

The Current View of Management Compensation

The execution of many compensation plans has been closely scrutinized in recent years. Both individuals and institutional stockholders, as well as the Securities and Exchange Commission (SEC), have publicly questioned the appropriateness of the multimillion-dollar compensation packages that many corporate executives receive. For example, the three highest-paid CEOs in 2001 were (1) Lawrence Ellison, of Oracle, who earned $706.1 million; (2) Jozef Straus, of JDS Uniphase, who earned $150.8 million; and (3) Howard Solomon, of Forest Laboratories, who earned $148.5 million. Tenth on the same list was Timothy Koogle, of Yahoo!, who earned $64.6 million. During 2001, the compensation of the average CEO of a major U.S. corporation declined by about 16 percent from 2000. CEOs of 365 of the largest U.S. companies surveyed by *Business Week,* using data from Standard & Poor's EXECUCOMP, earned an average of $11 million in total compensation; the average for the 20 highest paid CEOs was $112.5 million.

Recent studies have failed to find a strong relationship between CEO compensation and share price. Publicity surrounding these large compensation packages (without corresponding share price performance) is expected to drive down executive compensation in the future. Contributing to this publicity is the SEC requirement that publicly traded companies disclose to shareholders and others both the amount of compensation to their highest paid executives and the method used to determine it. At the same time, new compensation plans that better link managers' performance with regard to shareholder wealth to their compensation are expected to be developed and implemented.

Unconstrained, managers may have other goals in addition to share price maximization, but much of the evidence suggests that share price maximization—the focus of this book—is the primary goal of most firms.

Review Questions

1–11 For what three basic reasons is profit maximization inconsistent with wealth maximization?

1–12 What is *risk?* Why must risk as well as return be considered by the financial manager who is evaluating a decision alternative or action?

1–13 What is the goal of the firm and therefore of all managers and employees? Discuss how one measures achievement of this goal.

1–14 What is *economic value added (EVA®)?* How is it used?

1–15 Describe the role of corporate ethics policies and guidelines, and discuss the relationship that is believed to exist between ethics and share price.

1–16 How do market forces, both shareholder activism and the threat of takeover, act to prevent or minimize the *agency problem?*

1–17 Define *agency costs,* and explain why firms incur them. How can management *structure management compensation* to minimize agency problems? What is the current view with regard to the execution of many compensation plans?

LG5

Financial Institutions and Markets

Most successful firms have ongoing needs for funds. They can obtain funds from external sources in three ways. One is through a *financial institution* that accepts savings and transfers them to those that need funds. Another is through *financial markets,* organized forums in which the suppliers and demanders of various types of funds can make transactions. A third is through *private placement.* Because of the unstructured nature of private placements, here we focus primarily on financial institutions and financial markets.

Financial Institutions

financial institution
An intermediary that channels the savings of individuals, businesses, and governments into loans or investments.

Financial institutions serve as intermediaries by channeling the savings of individuals, businesses, and governments into loans or investments. Many financial institutions directly or indirectly pay savers interest on deposited funds; others provide services for a fee (for example, checking accounts for which customers pay service charges). Some financial institutions accept customers' savings deposits and lend this money to other customers or to firms; others invest customers' savings in earning assets such as real estate or stocks and bonds; and some do both. Financial institutions are required by the government to operate within established regulatory guidelines.

Key Customers of Financial Institutions

The key suppliers of funds to financial institutions and the key demanders of funds from financial institutions are individuals, businesses, and governments. The savings that individual consumers place in financial institutions provide these institutions with a large portion of their funds. Individuals not only supply funds to financial institutions but also demand funds from them in the form of loans. However, individuals as a group are the *net suppliers* for financial institutions: They save more money than they borrow.

Business firms also deposit some of their funds in financial institutions, primarily in checking accounts with various commercial banks. Like individuals, firms also borrow funds from these institutions, but firms are *net demanders* of funds. They borrow more money than they save.

Governments maintain deposits of temporarily idle funds, certain tax payments, and Social Security payments in commercial banks. They do not borrow funds *directly* from financial institutions, although by selling their debt securities to various institutions, governments indirectly borrow from them. The government, like business firms, is typically a *net demander* of funds. It typically borrows more than it saves. We've all heard about the federal budget deficit.

Major Financial Institutions

The major financial institutions in the U.S. economy are commercial banks, savings and loans, credit unions, savings banks, insurance companies, pension funds, and mutual funds. These institutions attract funds from individuals, businesses, and governments, combine them, and make loans available to individuals and businesses. Descriptions of the major financial institutions are found at the textbook's Web site at *www.aw.com/gitman*.

Financial Markets

financial markets
Forums in which suppliers of funds and demanders of funds can transact business directly.

Financial markets are forums in which suppliers of funds and demanders of funds can transact business directly. Whereas the loans and investments of institutions are made without the direct knowledge of the suppliers of funds (savers), suppliers in the financial markets know where their funds are being lent or invested. The two key financial markets are the money market and the capital market. Transactions in short-term debt instruments, or marketable securities, take place in the *money market*. Long-term securities—bonds and stocks—are traded in the *capital market*.

private placement
The sale of a new security issue, typically bonds or preferred stock, directly to an investor or group of investors.

public offering
The nonexclusive sale of either bonds or stocks to the general public.

primary market
Financial market in which securities are initially issued; the only market in which the issuer is directly involved in the transaction.

secondary market
Financial market in which preowned securities (those that are not new issues) are traded.

To raise money, firms can use either private placements or public offerings. **Private placement** involves the sale of a new security issue, typically bonds or preferred stock, directly to an investor or group of investors, such as an insurance company or pension fund. Most firms, however, raise money through a **public offering** of securities, which is the nonexclusive sale of either bonds or stocks to the general public.

All securities are initially issued in the **primary market.** This is the only market in which the corporate or government issuer is directly involved in the transaction and receives direct benefit from the issue. That is, the company actually receives the proceeds from the sale of securities. Once the securities begin to trade between savers and investors, they become part of the **secondary market.** The primary market is the one in which "new" securities are sold. The secondary market can be viewed as a "preowned" securities market.

The Relationship Between Institutions and Markets

Financial institutions actively participate in the financial markets as both suppliers and demanders of funds. Figure 1.4 depicts the general flow of funds through and between financial institutions and financial markets; private placement transactions are also shown. The individuals, businesses, and governments that supply and demand funds may be domestic or foreign. We next briefly discuss the money market, including its international equivalent—the *Eurocurrency market.* We then end this section with a discussion of the capital market, which is of key importance to the firm.

The Money Market

money market
A financial relationship created between suppliers and demanders of *short-term funds.*

The **money market** is created by a financial relationship between suppliers and demanders of *short-term funds* (funds with maturities of one year or less). The money market exists because some individuals, businesses, governments, and

FIGURE 1.4

Flow of Funds

Flow of funds for financial institutions and markets

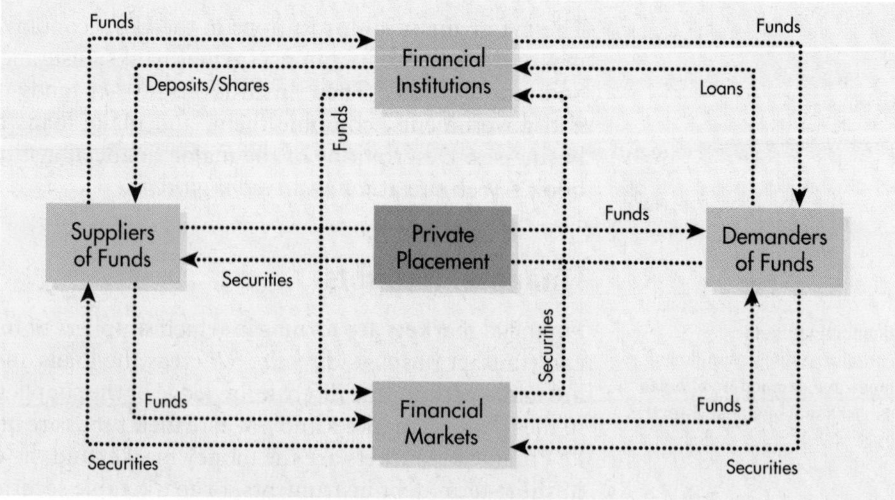

financial institutions have temporarily idle funds that they wish to put to some interest-earning use. At the same time, other individuals, businesses, governments, and financial institutions find themselves in need of seasonal or temporary financing. The money market brings together these suppliers and demanders of short-term funds.

marketable securities
Short-term debt instruments, such as U.S. Treasury bills, commercial paper, and negotiable certificates of deposit issued by government, business, and financial institutions, respectively.

Most money market transactions are made in **marketable securities**—short-term debt instruments, such as U.S. Treasury bills, commercial paper, and negotiable certificates of deposit issued by government, business, and financial institutions, respectively. (Marketable securities are described in Chapter 13.)

The Operation of the Money Market

The money market is not an actual organization housed in some central location. How, then, are suppliers and demanders of short-term funds brought together? Typically, they are matched through the facilities of large New York banks and through government securities dealers. A number of stock brokerage firms purchase money market instruments for resale to customers. Also, financial institutions purchase money market instruments for their portfolios in order to provide attractive returns on their customers' deposits and share purchases. Additionally, the Federal Reserve banks become involved in loans from one commercial bank to another; these loans are referred to as transactions in **federal funds.**

federal funds
Loan transactions between commercial banks in which the Federal Reserve banks become involved.

In the money market, businesses and governments demand short-term funds (borrow) by *issuing* a money market instrument. Parties who supply short-term funds (invest) *purchase* the money market instruments. To issue or purchase a money market instrument, one party must go directly to another party or use an intermediary, such as a bank or brokerage firm, to make the transaction. The secondary (resale) market for marketable securities is no different from the primary (initial issue) market with respect to the basic transactions that are made. Individuals also participate in the money market as purchasers and sellers of money market instruments. Although individuals do not issue marketable securities, they may sell them in the money market to liquidate them prior to maturity.

The Eurocurrency Market

The international equivalent of the domestic money market is called the **Eurocurrency market.** This is a market for short-term bank deposits denominated in U.S. dollars or other easily convertible currencies. Historically, the Eurocurrency market has been centered in London, but it has evolved into a truly global market.

Eurocurrency market
International equivalent of the domestic money market.

Eurocurrency deposits arise when a corporation or individual makes a bank deposit in a currency other than the local currency of the country where the bank is located. If, for example, a multinational corporation were to deposit U.S. dollars in a London bank, this would create a Eurodollar deposit (a dollar deposit at a bank in Europe). Nearly all Eurodollar deposits are *time deposits.* This means that the bank would promise to repay the deposit, with interest, at a fixed date in the future—say, in 6 months. During the interim, the bank is free to lend this dollar deposit to creditworthy corporate or government borrowers. If the bank cannot find a borrower on its own, it may lend the deposit to another international bank. The rate charged on these "interbank loans" is called the **London**

London Interbank Offered Rate (LIBOR)
The base rate that is used to price all Eurocurrency loans.

Interbank Offered Rate (LIBOR), and this is the base rate that is used to price all Eurocurrency loans.

The Eurocurrency market has grown rapidly, primarily because it is an unregulated, wholesale, and global market that fills the needs of both borrowers and lenders. Investors with excess cash to lend are able to make large, short-term, and safe deposits at attractive interest rates. Likewise, borrowers are able to arrange large loans, quickly and confidentially, also at attractive interest rates.

The Capital Market

capital market
A market that enables suppliers and demanders of *long-term funds* to make transactions.

The **capital market** is a market that enables suppliers and demanders of *long-term funds* to make transactions. Included are securities issues of business and government. The backbone of the capital market is formed by the various *securities exchanges* that provide a forum for bond and stock transactions.

Key Securities Traded: Bonds and Stocks

bond
Long-term debt instrument used by business and government to raise large sums of money, generally from a diverse group of lenders.

The key capital market securities are bonds (long-term debt) and both common and preferred stock (equity, or ownership). **Bonds** are long-term debt instruments used by business and government to raise large sums of money, generally from a diverse group of lenders. *Corporate bonds* typically pay interest *semiannually* (every 6 months) at a stated *coupon interest rate*. They have an initial *maturity* of from 10 to 30 years, and a *par*, or *face*, *value* of $1,000 that must be repaid at maturity. Bonds are described in detail in Chapter 6.

EXAMPLE

Lakeview Industries, a major microprocessor manufacturer, has issued a 9 percent coupon interest rate, 20-year bond with a $1,000 par value that pays interest semiannually. Investors who buy this bond receive the contractual right to $90 annual interest (9% coupon interest rate × $1,000 par value) distributed as $45 at the end of each 6 months (1/2 × $90) for 20 years, plus the $1,000 par value at the end of year 20.

preferred stock
A special form of ownership having a fixed periodic dividend that must be paid prior to payment of any common stock dividends.

As noted earlier, shares of *common stock* are units of ownership, or equity, in a corporation. Common stockholders earn a return by receiving dividends—periodic distributions of earnings—or by realizing increases in share price. **Preferred stock** is a special form of ownership that has features of both a bond and common stock. Preferred stockholders are promised a fixed periodic dividend that must be paid prior to payment of any dividends to common stockholders. In other words, preferred stock has "preference" over common stock. Preferred and common stock are described in detail in Chapter 7.

Major Securities Exchanges

securities exchanges
Organizations that provide the marketplace in which firms can raise funds through the sale of new securities and purchasers can resell securities.

Securities exchanges provide the marketplace in which firms can raise funds through the sale of new securities and purchasers of securities can easily resell them when necessary. Many people call securities exchanges "stock markets," but this label is misleading because bonds, common stock, preferred stock, and a variety of other investment vehicles are all traded on these exchanges. The two key types of securities exchanges are the organized exchange and the over-the-counter exchange. In addition, important markets exist outside the United States.

organized securities exchanges
Tangible organizations that act as *secondary markets* where outstanding securities are resold.

Organized Securities Exchanges **Organized securities exchanges** are tangible organizations that act as *secondary markets* where outstanding securities are resold. Organized exchanges account for about 46 percent of the *total dollar volume* of domestic shares traded. The best-known organized exchanges are the New York Stock Exchange (NYSE) and the American Stock Exchange (AMEX), both headquartered in New York City. There are also regional exchanges, such as the Chicago Stock Exchange and the Pacific Stock Exchange.

Most exchanges are modeled after the New York Stock Exchange, which accounts for about 93 percent of the total annual dollar volume of shares traded on *organized* U.S. exchanges. In order for a firm's securities to be listed for trading on an organized exchange, a firm must file an application for listing and meet a number of requirements. For example, to be eligible for listing on the NYSE, a firm must have at least 2,000 stockholders owning 100 or more shares; a minimum of 1.1 million shares of publicly held stock; pretax earnings of at least $6.5 million over the previous 3 years, with no loss in the previous 2 years; and a minimum of $100 million in stockholders' equity. Clearly, only large, widely held firms are candidates for NYSE listing.

To make transactions on the "floor" of the New York Stock Exchange, an individual or firm must own a "seat" on the exchange. There are a total of 1,366 seats on the NYSE, most of which are owned by brokerage firms. Trading is carried out on the floor of the exchange through an *auction process*. The goal of trading is to fill *buy orders* at the lowest price and to fill *sell orders* at the highest price, thereby giving both purchasers and sellers the best possible deal.

Once placed, an order to buy or sell can be executed in minutes, thanks to sophisticated telecommunication devices. New Internet-based brokerage systems enable investors to place their buy and sell orders electronically. Information on publicly traded securities is reported in various media, both print, such as the *Wall Street Journal,* and electronic, such as MSN Money Central Investor (*www.moneycentral.msn.com*).

over-the-counter (OTC) exchange
An intangible market for the purchase and sale of securities not listed by the organized exchanges.

The Over-the-Counter Exchange The **over-the-counter (OTC) exchange** is an intangible market for the purchase and sale of securities not listed by the organized exchanges. OTC traders, known as *dealers,* are linked with the purchasers and sellers of securities through the *National Association of Securities Dealers Automated Quotation (Nasdaq) system.*

This sophisticated telecommunications network provides current bid and ask prices on thousands of actively traded OTC securities. The *bid price* is the highest price offered by a dealer to purchase a given security, and the *ask price* is the lowest price at which the dealer is willing to sell the security. The dealer in effect adds securities to his or her inventory by purchasing them at the bid price and sells securities from the inventory at the ask price. The dealer expects to profit from the *spread* between the bid and ask prices. Unlike the auction process on the organized securities exchanges, the prices at which securities are traded in the OTC market result from both competitive bids and negotiation.

Unlike the organized exchanges, the OTC handles *both* outstanding securities and new public issues, making it both a *secondary* and a *primary market.* The OTC accounts for about 54 percent of the *total dollar volume* of domestic shares traded.

Eurobond market
The market in which corporations and governments typically issue bonds denominated in dollars and sell them to investors located outside the United States.

foreign bond
Bond that is issued by a foreign corporation or government and is denominated in the investor's home currency and sold in the investor's home market.

international equity market
A market that allows corporations to sell blocks of shares to investors in a number of different countries simultaneously.

International Capital Markets Although U.S. capital markets are by far the world's largest, there are important debt and equity markets outside the United States. In the **Eurobond market,** corporations and governments typically issue bonds denominated in dollars and sell them to investors located outside the United States. A U.S. corporation might, for example, issue dollar-denominated bonds that would be purchased by investors in Belgium, Germany, or Switzerland. Through the Eurobond market, issuing firms and governments can tap a much larger pool of investors than would be generally available in the local market.

The foreign bond market is another international market for long-term debt securities. A **foreign bond** is a bond issued by a foreign corporation or government that is denominated in the investor's home currency and sold in the investor's home market. A bond issued by a U.S. company that is denominated in Swiss francs and sold in Switzerland is an example of a foreign bond. Although the foreign bond market is much smaller than the Eurobond market, many issuers have found this to be an attractive way of tapping debt markets in Germany, Japan, Switzerland, and the United States.

Finally, the **international equity market** allows corporations to sell blocks of shares to investors in a number of different countries simultaneously. This market enables corporations to raise far larger amounts of capital than they could raise in any single national market. International equity sales have also proven to be indispensable to governments that have sold state-owned companies to private investors during recent years.

The Role of Securities Exchanges

efficient market
A market that allocates funds to their most productive uses as a result of competition among wealth-maximizing investors that determines and publicizes prices that are believed to be close to their true value.

Securities exchanges create continuous liquid markets in which firms can obtain needed financing. They also create **efficient markets** that allocate funds to their most productive uses. This is especially true for securities that are actively traded on major exchanges, where the competition among wealth-maximizing investors determines and publicizes prices that are believed to be close to their true value. The price of an individual security is determined by the demand for and supply of the security. The competitive market created by the major securities exchanges provides a forum in which share price is continuously adjusted to changing demand and supply.

Review Questions

1–18 Who are the key participants in the transactions of financial institutions? Who are net suppliers and who are net demanders?

1–19 What role do *financial markets* play in our economy? What are *primary* and *secondary* markets? What relationship exists between financial institutions and financial markets?

1–20 What is the *money market?* How does it work?

1–21 What is the *Eurocurrency market?* What is the *London Interbank Offered Rate (LIBOR)* and how is it used in this market?

1–22 What is the *capital market?* What are the primary securities traded in it?

1–23 What role do securities exchanges play in the capital market? How does the *over-the-counter exchange* operate? How does it differ from the *organized securities exchanges?*

1–24 Briefly describe the international capital markets, particularly the *Eurobond market* and the *international equity market.*

1–25 What are *efficient markets?* What determines the price of an individual security in such a market?

LG6

Business Taxes

Taxes are a fact of life, and businesses, like individuals, must pay taxes on income. The income of sole proprietorships and partnerships is taxed as the income of the individual owners; corporate income is subject to corporate taxes. Regardless of their legal form, all businesses can earn two types of income: ordinary and capital gains. Under current law, these two types of income are treated differently in the taxation of individuals; they are not treated differently for entities subject to corporate taxes. Frequent amendments in the tax code, such as the *Economic Growth and Tax Relief Reconciliation Act of 2001* (reflected in the following discussions), make it likely that these rates will change before the next edition of this text is published. Emphasis here is given to *corporate taxation.*

Ordinary Income

ordinary income
Income earned through the sale of a firm's goods or services.

The **ordinary income** of a corporation is income earned through the sale of goods or services. Ordinary income is currently taxed subject to the rates depicted in the corporate tax rate schedule in Table 1.3.

TABLE 1.3 Corporate Tax Rate Schedule

	Tax calculation		
Range of taxable income	Base tax	+	(Marginal rate × amount over base bracket)
\$ 0 to \$ 50,000	\$ 0	+	(15% × amount over \$ 0)
50,000 to 75,000	7,500	+	(25 × amount over 50,000)
75,000 to 100,000	13,750	+	(34 × amount over 75,000)
100,000 to 335,000[a]	22,250	+	(39 × amount over 100,000)
335,000 to 10,000,000	113,900	+	(34 × amount over 335,000)
Over \$10,000,000	3,400,000	+	(35 × amount over 10,000,000)

[a]Because corporations with taxable income in excess of \$100,000 must increase their tax by the lesser of \$11,750 or 5% of the taxable income in excess of \$100,000, they will end up paying a 39% tax on taxable income between \$100,000 and \$335,000. The 5% surtax that raises the tax rate from 34% to 39% causes all corporations with taxable income between \$335,000 and \$10,000,000 to have an *average tax rate* of 34%.

EXAMPLE

Western Manufacturing, Inc., a small manufacturer of kitchen knives, has before-tax earnings of $250,000. The tax on these earnings can be found by using the tax rate schedule in Table 1.3:

$$\begin{aligned}\text{Total taxes due} &= \$22{,}250 + [0.39 \times (\$250{,}000 - \$100{,}000)] \\ &= \$22{,}250 + (0.39 \times \$150{,}000) \\ &= \$22{,}250 + \$58{,}500 = \underline{\underline{\$80{,}750}}\end{aligned}$$

From a financial point of view, it is important to understand the difference between average and marginal tax rates, the treatment of interest and dividend income, and the effects of tax deductibility.

Average Versus Marginal Tax Rates

average tax rate
A firm's taxes divided by its taxable income.

The **average tax rate** paid on the firm's ordinary income can be calculated by dividing its taxes by its taxable income. For firms with taxable income of $10,000,000 or less, the average tax rate ranges from 15 to 34 percent, reaching 34 percent when taxable income equals or exceeds $335,000. For firms with taxable income in excess of $10,000,000, the average tax rate ranges between 34 and 35 percent. The average tax rate paid by Western Manufacturing, Inc., in the preceding example was 32.3 percent ($80,750 ÷ $250,000). As a corporation's taxable income increases, its average tax rate approaches and finally reaches 34 percent. It remains at that level up to $10,000,000 of taxable income, beyond which it rises toward but never reaches 35 percent.

marginal tax rate
The rate at which *additional income* is taxed.

The **marginal tax rate** represents the rate at which *additional income* is taxed. In the current corporate tax structure, the marginal tax rate on income up to $50,000 is 15 percent; from $50,000 to $75,000 it is 25 percent; and so on, as shown in Table 1.3. Western Manufacturing's marginal tax rate is currently 39 percent because its next dollar of taxable income (bringing its before-tax earnings to $250,001) would be taxed at that rate. To simplify calculations in the text, *a fixed 40 percent tax rate is assumed to be applicable to ordinary corporate income.*

EXAMPLE

If Western Manufacturing's earnings go up to $300,000, the marginal tax rate on the additional $50,000 of income will be 39 percent. the company will therefore have to pay additional taxes of $19,500 (.39 × $50,000). Total taxes on the $300,000, then, will be $100,250 ($80,750 + $19,500). To check this figure using the tax rate schedule in Table 1.3, we would get a total tax liability of $22,500 + [.39 × ($300,000 − $100,000)] = $22,250 + $78,000 = $100,250—the same value obtained by applying the marginal tax rate to the added income and adjusting the known tax liability.

The *average tax rate* tends to be most useful in evaluating taxes historically, and the *marginal tax rate* is more frequently used in financial decision making. Given our focus on financial decision making, *the tax rates used throughout this text are assumed to represent marginal tax rates.*

double taxation
Occurs when the already once-taxed earnings of a corporation are distributed as cash dividends to stockholders, who must pay taxes on them.

Interest and Dividend Income

In the process of determining taxable income, any *interest received* by the corporation is included as ordinary income. Dividends, on the other hand, are treated differently. This different treatment moderates the effect of **double taxation,** which occurs when the already once-taxed earnings of a corporation are distributed as cash dividends to stockholders, who must pay taxes on them. Therefore, dividends that the firm receives on common and preferred stock held in other corporations, and representing less than 20 percent ownership in them, are subject to a 70 percent exclusion for tax purposes.[4]

intercorporate dividends Dividends received by one corporation on common and preferred stock held in other corporations.

Because of the dividend exclusion, only 30 percent of these **intercorporate dividends** are included as ordinary income. The tax law provides this exclusion to avoid *triple taxation*. Triple taxation would occur if the first and second corporations were taxed on income before the second corporation paid dividends to its shareholders, who must then include the dividends in their taxable incomes. The dividend exclusion in effect eliminates most of the potential tax liability from the dividends received by the second and any subsequent corporations.

EXAMPLE

Checker Industries, a major manufacturer of molds for the plastics industry, during the year just ended received \$100,000 in interest on bonds it held and \$100,000 in dividends on common stock it owned in other corporations. The firm is subject to a 40% marginal tax rate and is eligible for a 70% exclusion on its intercorporate dividend receipts. The after-tax income realized by Checker from each of these sources of investment income is found as follows:

	Interest income		Dividend income
(1) Before-tax amount	\$100,000		\$100,000
Less: Applicable exclusion	0	(0.70 × \$100,000) =	70,000
Taxable amount	\$100,000		\$ 30,000
(2) Tax (40%)	40,000		12,000
After-tax amount [(1) − (2)]	\$ 60,000		\$ 88,000

As a result of the 70% dividend exclusion, the after-tax amount is greater for the dividend income than for the interest income. Clearly, the dividend exclusion enhances the attractiveness of stock investments relative to bond investments made by one corporation in another.

Tax-Deductible Expenses

In calculating their taxes, corporations are allowed to deduct operating expenses, as well as interest expense. The tax deductibility of these expenses reduces their after-tax cost. The following example illustrates the benefit of tax deductibility.

EXAMPLE

Two companies, Debt Co. and No Debt Co., both expect in the coming year to have earnings before interest and taxes of \$200,000. Debt Co. during the year

4. The exclusion is 80% if the corporation owns between 20 and 80% of the stock in the corporation paying it dividends; 100% of the dividends received are excluded if it owns more than 80% of the corporation paying it dividends. For convenience, we are assuming here that the ownership interest in the dividend-paying corporation is less than 20%.

will have to pay $30,000 in interest. No Debt Co. has no debt and therefore will have no interest expense. Calculation of the earnings after taxes for these two firms is as follows:

	Debt Co.	No Debt Co.
Earnings before interest and taxes	$200,000	$200,000
Less: Interest expense	30,000	0
Earnings before taxes	$170,000	$200,000
Less: Taxes (40%)	68,000	80,000
Earnings after taxes	$102,000	$120,000
Difference in earnings after taxes	$18,000	

Whereas Debt Co. had $30,000 more interest expense than No Debt Co., Debt Co.'s earnings after taxes are only $18,000 less than those of No Debt Co. ($102,000 for Debt Co. versus $120,000 for No Debt Co.). This difference is attributable to the fact that Debt Co.'s $30,000 interest expense deduction provided a tax savings of $12,000 ($68,000 for Debt Co. versus $80,000 for No Debt Co.). This amount can be calculated directly by multiplying the tax rate by the amount of interest expense $(0.40 \times \$30,000 = \$12,000)$. Similarly, the $18,000 *after-tax cost* of the interest expense can be calculated directly by multiplying one minus the tax rate by the amount of interest expense $[(1 - 0.40) \times \$30,000 = \$18,000]$.

The tax deductibility of certain expenses reduces their actual (after-tax) cost to the profitable firm. Note that both for accounting and tax purposes *interest is a tax-deductible expense, whereas dividends are not.* Because dividends are not tax deductible, their after-tax cost is equal to the amount of the dividend. Thus a $30,000 cash dividend has an after-tax cost of $30,000.

Capital Gains

capital gain
The amount by which the sale price of an asset exceeds the asset's initial purchase price.

If a firm sells a capital asset (such as stock held as an investment) for more than its initial purchase price, the difference between the sale price and the purchase price is called a **capital gain.** For corporations, capital gains are added to ordinary corporate income and taxed at the regular corporate rates, with a maximum marginal tax rate of 39 percent.[5] To simplify the computations presented in the text, as for ordinary income, *a fixed 40 percent tax rate is assumed to be applicable to corporate capital gains.*

EXAMPLE ▼ Loos Company, a manufacturer of pharmaceuticals, has pretax operating earnings of $500,000 and has just sold for $40,000 an asset that was purchased 2 years ago for $36,000. Because the asset was sold for more than its initial pur-

[5]. The *Omnibus Budget Reconciliation Act of 1993* included a provision that allows the capital gains tax to be halved on gains resulting from investments made after January 1, 1993, in startup firms with a value of less than $50 million that have been held for at least 5 years. This special provision, which is intended to help startup firms, is ignored throughout this text.

chase price, there is a capital gain of $4,000 ($40,000 sale price – $36,000 initial purchase price). The corporation's taxable income will total $504,000 ($500,000 ordinary income plus $4,000 capital gain). Because this total is above $335,000, the capital gain will be taxed at the 34% rate (see Table 1.3), resulting in a tax of $1,360 (0.34 × $4,000).

Review Questions

1–26 Describe the tax treatment of *ordinary income* and that of *capital gains.* What is the difference between the *average tax rate* and the *marginal tax rate?*

1–27 Why might the *intercorporate dividend* exclusion make corporate stock investments by one corporation in another more attractive than bond investments?

1–28 What benefit results from the tax deductibility of certain corporate expenses?

Using This Text

The organization of this textbook links the firm's activities to its value, as determined in the securities markets. The activities of the financial manager are described in the five parts of the book. Each major decision area is presented in terms of both return and risk factors and their potential impact on owners' wealth. Coverage of international events and topics is integrated into the chapter discussions.

The text has been developed around a group of learning goals—six per chapter. Mastery of these goals results in a broad understanding of managerial finance. These goals have been carefully integrated into a learning system. Each chapter begins with a numbered list of learning goals. Next to each major text heading is a "toolbox," which notes by number the specific learning goal(s) addressed in that section. At the end of each section of the chapter (positioned before the next major heading) are review questions that test your understanding of the material in that section. At the end of each chapter, the chapter summaries, self-test problems, and problems are also keyed by number to each chapter's learning goals. By linking all elements to the learning goals, the integrated learning system facilitates your mastery of the goals.

Also keyed to various parts of the text is the *PMF Brief CD-ROM Software,* a disk for use with IBM PCs and compatible microcomputers. The disk contains three different sets of routines:

1. The *PMF Brief Tutor* is a user-friendly program that extends self-testing opportunities in the more quantitative chapters beyond those included in the end-of-chapter materials. It gives immediate feedback with detailed solutions and provides tutorial assistance (including text references). Text discussions and end-of-chapter problems with which the *PMF Brief Tutor* can be used are marked with a .

2. The *PMF Brief Problem-Solver* can be used as an aid in performing many of the routine financial calculations presented in the book. A disk symbol, , identifies those text discussions and end-of-chapter problems that can be solved with the *PMF Brief Problem-Solver.*
3. The *PMF Brief Excel Spreadsheet Templates* can be used with Microsoft Excel to input data and carry out "what-if" types of analyses in selected chapters. These problems are marked by the symbol .

A detailed discussion of how to use the *PMF Brief CD-ROM Software*—the *Tutor,* the *Problem-Solver,* and the *Excel Spreadsheet Templates*—is included in Appendix D at the back of this book.

Each chapter ends with a case that integrates the chapter materials. Where applicable, the symbols for the *PMF Brief Problem-Solver* and/or the *PMF Brief Tutor* identify case questions that can be solved with the aid of these programs. The chapter-end cases can be used to synthesize and apply related concepts and techniques.

SUMMARY

FOCUS ON VALUE

Chapter 1 established the primary goal of the firm—**to maximize the wealth of the owners for whom the firm is being operated.** For public companies, which are the focus of this text, value at any time is reflected in the stock price. Therefore, management should act only on those alternatives or opportunities that are expected to create value for owners by increasing the stock price. Doing this requires management to consider the returns (magnitude and timing of cash flows) and the risk of each proposed action and their combined impact on value.

REVIEW OF LEARNING GOALS

LG1 **Define *finance,* the major areas of finance and the opportunities available in this field, and the legal forms of business organization.** Finance, the art and science of managing money, affects the lives of every person and every organization. Major opportunities in financial services exist within banking and related institutions, personal financial planning, investments, real estate, and insurance. Managerial finance is concerned with the duties of the financial manager in the business firm. It offers numerous career opportunities, as shown in Table 1.2. The recent trend toward globalization of business activity has created new demands and opportunities in managerial finance.

The legal forms of business organization are the sole proprietorship, the partnership, and the corporation. The corporation is dominant in terms of business receipts and profits, and its owners are its common and preferred stockholders. Stockholders expect to earn a return by receiving dividends or by realizing gains through increases in share price. The key strengths and weaknesses of the common legal forms of business organization are summarized in Table 1.1.

LG2 **Describe the managerial finance function and its relationship to economics and accounting.** All areas of responsibility within a firm interact with finance personnel and procedures. In large firms, the managerial finance function might be handled by a separate department headed by the vice president of finance (CFO), to whom the treasurer and controller report. The financial manager must understand the economic environment and relies heavily on the economic principle of marginal analysis to make financial decisions. Financial managers use accounting but concentrate on cash flows and decision making.

LG3 **Identify the primary activities of the financial manager within the firm.** The primary activities of the financial manager, in addition to ongoing involvement in financial analysis and planning, are making investment decisions and making financing decisions.

LG4 **Explain why wealth maximization, rather than profit maximization, is the firm's goal and how the agency issue is related to it.** The goal of the financial manager is to maximize the owners' wealth, as evidenced by stock price. Profit maximization ignores the timing of returns, does not directly consider cash flows, and ignores risk, so it is an inappropriate goal. Both return and risk must be assessed by the financial manager who is evaluating decision alternatives. The wealth-maximizing actions of financial managers should also reflect the interests of stakeholders, groups who have a direct economic link to the firm. Positive ethical practices help the firm and its managers to achieve the firm's goal of owner wealth maximization.

An agency problem results when managers, as agents for owners, place personal goals ahead of corporate goals. Market forces, in the firm of shareholder activism and the threat of takeover, tend to prevent or minimize agency problems. Firms incur agency costs to monitor managers' actions and provide incentives for them to act in the best interests of owners. Stock options and performance plans are examples of such agency costs.

LG5 **Understand the relationship between financial institutions and markets, and the role and operations of the money and capital markets.** Financial institutions serve as intermediaries by channeling into loans or investments the savings of individuals, businesses, and governments. The financial markets are forums in which suppliers and demanders of funds can transact business directly. Financial institutions actively participate in the financial markets as both suppliers and demanders of funds.

In the money market, marketable securities (short-term debt instruments) are traded, typically through large New York banks and government securities dealers. The Eurocurrency market is the international equivalent of the domestic money market.

In the capital market, transactions in long-term debt (bonds) and equity (common and preferred stock) are made. The organized securities exchanges provide secondary markets for securities. The over-the-counter exchange, a telecommunications network, offers a secondary market for securities and is a primary market in which new public issues are sold. Important debt and equity markets—the Eurobond market and the international equity market—exist outside of the United States. The securities exchanges create continuous liquid markets for needed financing and allocate funds to their most productive uses.

LG6 **Discuss the fundamentals of business taxation of ordinary income and capital gains.** Corporate income is subject to corporate taxes. Corporate tax rates are applicable to both ordinary income (after deduction of allowable expenses) and capital gains. The average tax rate paid by a corporation ranges from 15 to nearly 35 percent. (For convenience, we assume a 40 percent marginal tax rate in this book.) Corporate taxpayers can reduce their taxes through certain provisions in the tax code such as intercorporate dividend exclusions and tax-deductible expenses.

SELF-TEST PROBLEM (Solution in Appendix B)

LG6 **ST 1–1** **Corporate taxes** Montgomery Enterprises, Inc., had operating earnings of $280,000 for the year just ended. During the year the firm sold stock that it held in another company for $180,000, which was $30,000 above its original purchase price of $150,000, paid 1 year earlier.

a. What is the amount, if any, of capital gains realized during the year?
b. How much total taxable income did the firm earn during the year?
c. Use the corporate tax rate schedule given in Table 1.3 to calculate the firm's total taxes due.
d. Calculate both the *average tax rate* and the *marginal tax rate* on the basis of your findings.

PROBLEMS

LG1 **1–1** **Liability comparisons** Merideth Harper has invested $25,000 in Southwest Development Company. The firm has recently declared bankruptcy and has $60,000 in unpaid debts. Explain the nature of payments, if any, by Ms. Harper in each of the following situations.

a. Southwest Development Company is a sole proprietorship owned by Ms. Harper.
b. Southwest Development Company is a 50–50 partnership of Ms. Harper and Christopher Black.
c. Southwest Development Company is a corporation.

LG2 **1–2** **Accrual income versus cash flow for a period** Thomas Book Sales, Inc., supplies textbooks to college and university bookstores. The books are shipped with a proviso that they must be paid for within 30 days but can be returned for a full refund credit within 90 days. In 2003, Thomas shipped and billed book titles totaling $760,000. Collections, net of return credits, during the year totaled $690,000. The company spent $300,000 acquiring the books that it shipped.

a. Using accrual accounting and the preceding values, show the firm's net profit for the past year.
b. Using cash accounting and the preceding values, show the firm's net cash flow for the past year.
c. Which of these statements is more useful to the financial manager? Why?

LG4 **1–3** **Identifying agency problems, costs, and resolutions** Explain why each of the following situations is an agency problem and what costs to the firm might result from it. Suggest how the problem might be dealt with short of firing the individual(s) involved.

a. The front desk receptionist routinely takes an extra 20 minutes of lunch to run personal errands.
b. Division managers are padding cost estimates in order to show short-term efficiency gains when the costs come in lower than the estimates.
c. The firm's chief executive officer has secret talks with a competitor about the possibility of a merger in which (s)he would become the CEO of the combined firms.

d. A branch manager lays off experienced full-time employees and staffs customer service positions with part-time or temporary workers to lower employment costs and raise this year's branch profit. The manager's bonus is based on profitability.

LG6 1–4 **Corporate taxes** Tantor Supply, Inc., is a small corporation acting as the exclusive distributor of a major line of sporting goods. During 2003 the firm earned \$92,500 before taxes.

a. Calculate the firm's tax liability using the corporate tax rate schedule given in Table 1.3.
b. How much are Tantor Supply's 2003 after-tax earnings?
c. What was the firm's *average tax rate,* based on your findings in part **a**?
d. What is the firm's *marginal tax rate,* based on your findings in part **a**?

LG6 1–5 **Average corporate tax rates** Using the corporate tax rate schedule given in Table 1.3, perform the following:

a. Calculate the tax liability, after-tax earnings, and average tax rates for the following levels of corporate earnings before taxes: \$10,000; \$80,000; \$300,000; \$500,000; \$1.5 million; \$10 million; and \$15 million.
b. Plot the average tax rates (measured on the *y* axis) against the pretax income levels (measured on the *x* axis). What generalization can be made concerning the relationship between these variables?

LG6 1–6 **Marginal corporate tax rates** Using the corporate tax rate schedule given in Table 1.3, perform the following:

a. Find the marginal tax rate for the following levels of corporate earnings before taxes: \$15,000; \$60,000; \$90,000; \$200,000; \$400,000; \$1 million; and \$20 million.
b. Plot the marginal tax rates (measured on the *y* axis) against the pretax income levels (measured on the *x* axis). Explain the relationship between these variables.

LG6 1–7 **Interest versus dividend income** During the year just ended, Shering Distributors, Inc., had pretax earnings from operations of \$490,000. In addition, during the year it received \$20,000 in income from interest on bonds it held in Zig Manufacturing and received \$20,000 in income from dividends on its 5% common stock holding in Tank Industries, Inc. Shering is in the 40% tax bracket and is eligible for a 70% dividend exclusion on its Tank Industries stock.

a. Calculate the firm's tax on its operating earnings only.
b. Find the tax and the after-tax amount attributable to the interest income from Zig Manufacturing bonds.
c. Find the tax and the after-tax amount attributable to the dividend income from the Tank Industries, Inc., common stock.
d. Compare, contrast, and discuss the after-tax amounts resulting from the interest income and dividend income calculated in parts **b** and **c**.
e. What is the firm's total tax liability for the year?

LG6 1–8 **Interest versus dividend expense** Michaels Corporation expects earnings before interest and taxes to be \$40,000 for this period. Assuming an ordinary tax rate of 40%, compute the firm's earnings after taxes and earnings available for common stockholders (earnings after taxes and preferred stock dividends, if any) under the following conditions:

a. The firm pays $10,000 in interest.
b. The firm pays $10,000 in preferred stock dividends.

LG6 **1–9 Capital gains taxes** Perkins Manufacturing is considering the sale of two nondepreciable assets, X and Y. Asset X was purchased for $2,000 and will be sold today for $2,250. Asset Y was purchased for $30,000 and will be sold today for $35,000. The firm is subject to a 40% tax rate on capital gains.

a. Calculate the amount of capital gain, if any, realized on each of the assets.
b. Calculate the tax on the sale of each asset.

LG6 **1–10 Capital gains taxes** The following table contains purchase and sale prices for the nondepreciable capital assets of a major corporation. The firm paid taxes of 40% on capital gains.

Asset	Purchase price	Sale price
A	$ 3,000	$ 3,400
B	12,000	12,000
C	62,000	80,000
D	41,000	45,000
E	16,500	18,000

a. Determine the amount of capital gain realized on each of the five assets.
b. Calculate the amount of tax paid on each of the assets.

CHAPTER 1 CASE Assessing the Goal of Sports Products, Inc.

Loren Seguara and Dale Johnson both work for Sports Products, Inc., a major producer of boating equipment and accessories. Loren works as a clerical assistant in the Accounting Department, and Dale works as a packager in the Shipping Department. During their lunch break one day, they began talking about the company. Dale complained that he had always worked hard trying not to waste packing materials and efficiently and cost-effectively performing his job. In spite of his efforts and those of his co-workers in the department, the firm's stock price had declined nearly $2 per share over the past 9 months. Loren indicated that she shared Dale's frustration, particularly because the firm's profits had been rising. Neither could understand why the firm's stock price was falling as profits rose.

Loren indicated that she had seen documents describing the firm's profit-sharing plan under which all managers were partially compensated on the basis of the firm's profits. She suggested that maybe it was profit that was important to management, because it directly affected their pay. Dale said, "That doesn't make sense, because the stockholders own the firm. Shouldn't management do what's best for stockholders? Something's wrong!" Loren responded, "Well, maybe that explains why the company hasn't concerned itself with the stock price. Look, the only profits that stockholders receive are in the form of cash dividends, and this firm has never paid dividends during its 20-year history. We as stockholders therefore don't directly benefit from profits. The only way we benefit is for the stock price to rise." Dale chimed in, "That probably explains why the firm is being sued by state and federal environmental officials for dumping pollutants in the adjacent stream. Why spend money for pollution control? It increases costs, lowers profits, and therefore lowers management's earnings!"

Loren and Dale realized that the lunch break had ended and they must quickly return to work. Before leaving, they decided to meet the next day to continue their discussion.

Required

a. What should the management of Sports Products, Inc., pursue as its overriding goal? Why?
b. Does the firm appear to have an *agency problem?* Explain.
c. Evaluate the firm's approach to pollution control. Does it seem to be *ethical?* Why might incurring the expense to control pollution be in the best interests of the firm's owners in spite of its negative impact on profits?
d. On the basis of the information provided, what specific recommendations would you offer the firm?

WEB EXERCISE

At the Careers in Finance Web site, *www.careers-in-finance.com*, you will find information on career opportunities in seven different areas of finance. First click on **Corporate Finance** in the **Areas to Explore** section and use the various subsections to answer the following questions:

1. What are the primary responsibilities of the financial manager?
2. Summarize the types of skills a financial manager needs.
3. Describe the key job areas in corporate finance.
4. What are the salary ranges for the following positions in corporate finance: rookie financial analyst, credit manager, chief financial officer? How do these compare to salaries at General Motors or PepsiCo?

Now return to the home page and click on either **Commercial Banking** or **Investment Banking.**

5. How do careers in the area you chose (commercial banking or investment banking) compare to careers in corporate finance in terms of skills required, responsibilities, and salaries?

Remember to check the book's Web site at

www.aw.com/gitman

for additional resources, including additional Web exercises.

Chapter

2

Financial Statements and Analysis

LEARNING GOALS

- LG1 Review the contents of the stockholders' report and the procedures for consolidating international financial statements.
- LG2 Understand who uses financial ratios, and how.
- LG3 Use ratios to analyze a firm's liquidity and activity.
- LG4 Discuss the relationship between debt and financial leverage and the ratios used to analyze a firm's debt.
- LG5 Use ratios to analyze a firm's profitability and its market value.
- LG6 Use a summary of financial ratios and the DuPont system of analysis to perform a complete ratio analysis.

Across the Disciplines

Why This Chapter Matters To You

Accounting: You need to understand the stockholders' report and preparation of the four key financial statements; how firms consolidate international financial statements; and how to calculate and interpret financial ratios for decision making.

Information systems: You need to understand what data are included in the firm's financial statements in order to design systems that will supply such data to those who prepare the statements and to those in the firm who use the data for ratio calculations.

Management: You need to understand what parties are interested in the annual report and why; how the financial statements will be analyzed by those both inside and outside the firm to assess various aspects of performance; the caution that should be exercised in using financial ratio analysis; and how the financial statements affect the value of the firm.

Marketing: You need to understand the effects your decisions will have on the financial statements, particularly the income statement and the statement of cash flows, and how analysis of ratios, especially those involving sales figures, will affect the firm's decisions about levels of inventory, credit policies, and pricing decisions.

Operations: You need to understand how the costs of operations are reflected in the firm's financial statements and how analysis of ratios, particularly those involving assets, cost of goods sold, or inventory, may affect requests for new equipment or facilities.

All companies gather financial data about their operations and report this information in financial statements for interested parties. These statements are widely standardized, and so we can use the data in them to make comparisons between firms and over time. Analysis of certain items of financial data can identify areas where the firm excels and, also, areas of opportunity for improvement. This chapter reviews the content of financial statements and explains categories of financial ratios and their use.

LG1

The Stockholders' Report

generally accepted accounting principles (GAAP)
The practice and procedure guidelines used to prepare and maintain financial records and reports; authorized by the *Financial Accounting Standards Board (FASB).*

Financial Accounting Standards Board (FASB)
The accounting profession's rule-setting body, which authorizes *generally accepted accounting principles (GAAP).*

Securities and Exchange Commission (SEC)
The federal regulatory body that governs the sale and listing of securities.

stockholders' report
Annual report that publicly owned corporations must provide to stockholders; it summarizes and documents the firm's financial activities during the past year.

letter to stockholders
Typically, the first element of the annual stockholders' report and the primary communication from management.

Every corporation has many and varied uses for the standardized records and reports of its financial activities. Periodically, reports must be prepared for regulators, creditors (lenders), owners, and management. The guidelines used to prepare and maintain financial records and reports are known as **generally accepted accounting principles (GAAP).** These accounting practices and procedures are authorized by the accounting profession's rule-setting body, the **Financial Accounting Standards Board (FASB).**

Publicly owned corporations with more than $5 million in assets and 500 or more stockholders[1] are required by the **Securities and Exchange Commission (SEC)**—the federal regulatory body that governs the sale and listing of securities—to provide their stockholders with an annual **stockholders' report.** The annual report summarizes and documents the firm's financial activities during the past year. It begins with a letter to the stockholders from the firm's president and/or chairman of the board.

The Letter to Stockholders

The **letter to stockholders** is the primary communication from management. It describes the events that are considered to have had the greatest impact on the firm during the year. It also generally discusses management philosophy, strategies, and actions, as well as plans for the coming year. Links at this book's Web site (*www.aw.com/gitman*) will take you to some representative letters to stockholders.

WWW

The Four Key Financial Statements

The four key financial statements required by the SEC for reporting to shareholders are (1) the income statement, (2) the balance sheet, (3) the statement of retained earnings, and (4) the statement of cash flows.[2] The financial statements

1. Although the Securities and Exchange Commission (SEC) does not have an official definition of *publicly owned,* these financial measures mark the cutoff point it uses to require informational reporting, regardless of whether the firm publicly sells its securities. Firms that do not meet these requirements are commonly called "closely owned" firms.

2. Whereas these statement titles are consistently used throughout this text, it is important to recognize that in practice, companies frequently use different titles. For example, General Electric uses "Statement of Earnings" rather than "Income Statement" and "Statement of Financial Position" rather than "Balance Sheet." Bristol Myers Squibb uses "Statement of Earnings and Retained Earnings" rather than "Income Statement." Pfizer uses "Statement of Shareholders' Equity" rather than "Statement of Retained Earnings."

from the 2003 stockholders' report of Bartlett Company, a manufacturer of metal fasteners, are presented and briefly discussed.

Income Statement

income statement
Provides a financial summary of the firm's operating results during a specified period.

The **income statement** provides a financial summary of the firm's operating results during a specified period. Most common are income statements covering a 1-year period ending at a specified date, ordinarily December 31 of the calendar year. Many large firms, however, operate on a 12-month financial cycle, or *fiscal year,* that ends at a time other than December 31. In addition, monthly income statements are typically prepared for use by management, and quarterly statements must be made available to the stockholders of publicly owned corporations.

Table 2.1 presents Bartlett Company's income statements for the years ended December 31, 2003 and 2002. The 2003 statement begins with *sales revenue*—the total dollar amount of sales during the period—from which the *cost of goods sold* is deducted. The resulting *gross profits* of $986,000 represent the amount remaining to satisfy operating, financial, and tax costs. Next, *operating expenses,* which include selling expense, general and administrative expense, lease expense, and depreciation expense, are deducted from gross profits.[3] The resulting *operating profits* of $418,000 represent the profits earned from producing and selling products; this amount does not consider financial and tax costs. (Operating profit is often called *earnings before interest and taxes,* or *EBIT.*) Next, the financial cost—*interest expense*—is subtracted from operating profits to find *net profits* (or *earnings*) *before taxes.* After subtracting $93,000 in 2003 interest, Bartlett Company had $325,000 of net profits before taxes.

Next, taxes are calculated at the appropriate tax rates and deducted to determine *net profits* (or *earnings*) *after taxes.* Bartlett Company's net profits after taxes for 2003 were $231,000. Any preferred stock dividends must be subtracted from net profits after taxes to arrive at *earnings available for common stockholders.* This is the amount earned by the firm on behalf of the common stockholders during the period.

dividend per share (DPS)
The dollar amount of cash distributed during the period on behalf of each outstanding share of common stock.

Dividing earnings available for common stockholders by the number of shares of common stock outstanding results in *earnings per share (EPS).* EPS represents the number of dollars earned during the period on behalf of each outstanding share of common stock. In 2003, Bartlett Company earned $221,000 for its common stockholders, which represents $2.90 for each outstanding share. The actual cash **dividend per share (DPS),** which is the dollar amount of cash distributed during the period on behalf of each outstanding share of common stock, paid in 2003 was $1.29.

Balance Sheet

balance sheet
Summary statement of the firm's financial position at a given point in time.

The **balance sheet** presents a summary statement of the firm's financial position at a given point in time. The statement balances the firm's *assets* (what it owns) against its financing, which can be either *debt* (what it owes) or *equity* (what was

3. Depreciation expense can be, and frequently is, included in manufacturing costs—cost of goods sold—to calculate gross profits. Depreciation is shown as an expense in this text to isolate its impact on cash flows.

TABLE 2.1 Bartlett Company Income Statements ($000)

	For the years ended December 31	
	2003	2002
Sales revenue	$3,074	$2,567
Less: Cost of goods sold	2,088	1,711
Gross profits	$ 986	$ 856
Less: Operating expenses		
Selling expense	$ 100	$ 108
General and administrative expenses	194	187
Lease expense[a]	35	35
Depreciation expense	239	223
Total operating expense	$ 568	$ 553
Operating profits	$ 418	$ 303
Less: Interest expense	93	91
Net profits before taxes	$ 325	$ 212
Less: Taxes (rate = 29%)[b]	94	64
Net profits after taxes	$ 231	$ 148
Less: Preferred stock dividends	10	10
Earnings available for common stockholders	$ 221	$ 138
Earnings per share (EPS)[c]	$ 2.90	$ 1.81
Dividend per share (DPS)[d]	$ 1.29	$ 0.75

[a]Lease expense is shown here as a separate item rather than being included as part of interest expense, as specified by the FASB for financial-reporting purposes. The approach used here is consistent with tax-reporting rather than financial-reporting procedures.

[b]The 29% tax rate for 2003 results because the firm has certain special tax write-offs that do not show up directly on its income statement.

[c]Calculated by dividing the earnings available for common stockholders by the number of shares of common stock outstanding—76,262 in 2003 and 76,244 in 2002. Earnings per share in 2003: $221,000 ÷ 76,262 = $2.90; in 2002: $138,000 ÷ 76,244 = $1.81.

[d]Calculated by dividing the dollar amount of dividends paid to common stockholders by the number of shares of common stock outstanding. Dividends per share in 2003: $98,000 ÷ 76,262 = $1.29; in 2002: $57,183 ÷ 76,244 = $0.75.

provided by owners). Bartlett Company's balance sheets as of December 31 of 2003 and 2002 are presented in Table 2.2. They show a variety of asset, liability (debt), and equity accounts.

current assets
Short-term assets, expected to be converted into cash within 1 year or less.

current liabilities
Short-term liabilities, expected to be paid within 1 year or less.

An important distinction is made between short-term and long-term assets and liabilities. The **current assets** and **current liabilities** are *short-term* assets and liabilities. This means that they are expected to be converted into cash (current assets) or paid (current liabilities) within 1 year or less. All other assets and liabilities, along with stockholders' equity, which is assumed to have an infinite life, are considered *long-term,* or *fixed,* because they are expected to remain on the firm's books for more than 1 year.

TABLE 2.2 Bartlett Company Balance Sheets ($000)

	December 31	
Assets	**2003**	**2002**
Current assets		
Cash	$ 363	$ 288
Marketable securities	68	51
Accounts receivable	503	365
Inventories	289	300
Total current assets	$1,223	$1,004
Gross fixed assets (at cost)[a]		
Land and buildings	$2,072	$1,903
Machinery and equipment	1,866	1,693
Furniture and fixtures	358	316
Vehicles	275	314
Other (includes financial leases)	98	96
Total gross fixed assets (at cost)	$4,669	$4,322
Less: Accumulated depreciation	2,295	2,056
Net fixed assets	$2,374	$2,266
Total assets	$3,597	$3,270
Liabilities and Stockholders' Equity		
Current liabilities		
Accounts payable	$ 382	$ 270
Notes payable	79	99
Accruals	159	114
Total current liabilities	$ 620	$ 483
Long-term debt (includes financial leases)[b]	$1,023	$ 967
Total liabilities	$1,643	$1,450
Stockholders' equity		
Preferred stock—cumulative 5%, $100 par, 2,000 shares authorized and issued[c]	$ 200	$ 200
Common stock—$2.50 par, 100,000 shares authorized, shares issued and outstanding in 2003: 76,262; in 2002: 76,244	191	190
Paid-in capital in excess of par on common stock	428	418
Retained earnings	1,135	1,012
Total stockholders' equity	$1,954	$1,820
Total liabilities and stockholders' equity	$3,597	$3,270

[a]In 2003, the firm has a 6-year financial lease requiring annual beginning-of-year payments of $35,000. Four years of the lease have yet to run.

[b]Annual principal repayments on a portion of the firm's total outstanding debt amount to $71,000.

[c]The annual preferred stock dividend would be $5 per share (5% × $100 par), or a total of $10,000 annually ($5 per share × 2,000 shares).

In Practice

FOCUS ON PRACTICE Extraordinary? Not to the FASB!

To most of us, the events of September 11, 2001, would certainly qualify as extraordinary. The plane crashes that took thousands of lives, destroyed the World Trade Center Towers, and damaged part of the Pentagon were circumstances well outside what we consider "ordinary." Yet, several weeks after the tragedy the Financial Accounting Standards Board (FASB) announced that the terrorist attack did not constitute an extraordinary event—at least not in accounting terms.

As a result, companies will not be able to separate costs and expenses related to the disaster as extraordinary on their financial statements. Those expenses will show up as normal operating costs in the continuing operations section of the income statement.

Explained Tim Lucas, chair of the FASB Emerging Issues Task Force, "The task force understood that this was an extraordinary event in the English-language sense of the word. But in the final analysis, we decided it wasn't going to improve the financial reporting system to show it [separately]."

The FASB task force had prepared a draft document with guidelines on accounting for disaster-related costs as extraordinary. As they considered how to apply these recommendations, they realized that the impact of the attack was so far-ranging that it was almost impossible to divide direct financial and economic effects from the weakening economic conditions prior to September 11. Nor was it possible to develop one set of guidelines appropriate for all industries. FASB members were concerned that companies would blame negative financial performance on the attacks when in fact the costs were unrelated. As one member pointed out, almost every company was affected in some way. Because the whole business climate changed, "it almost made it ordinary."

Companies will, however, be able to separate costs they believe to be attributable to September 11 in the footnotes to financial statements and in management's discussion of financial results.

Sources: Jennifer Davies, "Will Attacks Cover Up Weak Earnings?" *San Diego Union-Tribune* (October 14, 2001), pp. H1, H6; Steve Liesman, "Accountants, in a Reversal, Say Costs from the Attack Aren't 'Extraordinary,'" *Wall Street Journal* (October 1, 2001), pp. C1-2; Keith Naughton, "Out of the Ordinary," *Newsweek* (October 15, 2001), p. 9.

As is customary, the assets are listed from the most liquid—*cash*—down to the least liquid. *Marketable securities* are very liquid short-term investments, such as U.S. Treasury bills or certificates of deposit, held by the firm. Because they are highly liquid, marketable securities are viewed as a form of cash ("near cash"). *Accounts receivable* represent the total monies owed the firm by its customers on credit sales made to them. *Inventories* include raw materials, work in process (partially finished goods), and finished goods held by the firm. The entry for *gross fixed assets* is the original cost of all fixed (long-term) assets owned by the firm.[4] *Net fixed assets* represent the difference between gross fixed assets and *accumulated depreciation*—the total expense recorded for the depreciation of fixed assets. (The net value of fixed assets is called their *book value.*)

Like assets, the liabilities and equity accounts are listed from short-term to long-term. Current liabilities include *accounts payable,* amounts owed for credit purchases by the firm; *notes payable,* outstanding short-term loans, typically from commercial banks; and *accruals,* amounts owed for services for which a bill may not or will not be received. (Examples of accruals include taxes due the government and wages due employees.) **Long-term debt** represents debt for which

long-term debt
Debts for which payment is not due in the current year.

4. For convenience the term *fixed assets* is used throughout this text to refer to what, in a strict accounting sense, is captioned "property, plant, and equipment." This simplification of terminology permits certain financial concepts to be more easily developed.

payment is not due in the current year. *Stockholders' equity* represents the owners' claims on the firm. The *preferred stock* entry shows the historical proceeds from the sale of preferred stock ($200,000 for Bartlett Company).

Next, the amount paid by the original purchasers of common stock is shown by two entries: common stock and paid-in capital in excess of par on common stock. The *common stock* entry is the *par value* of common stock. **Paid-in capital in excess of par** represents the amount of proceeds in excess of the par value received from the original sale of common stock. The sum of the common stock and paid-in capital accounts divided by the number of shares outstanding represents the original price per share received by the firm on a single issue of common stock. Bartlett Company therefore received about $8.12 per share [($191,000 par + $428,000 paid-in capital in excess of par) ÷ 76,262 shares] from the sale of its common stock.

paid-in capital in excess of par
The amount of proceeds in excess of the par value received from the original sale of common stock.

Finally, **retained earnings** represent the cumulative total of all earnings, net of dividends, that have been retained and reinvested in the firm since its inception. It is important to recognize that retained earnings *are not cash* but rather have been utilized to finance the firm's assets.

retained earnings
The cumulative total of all earnings, net of dividends, that have been retained and reinvested in the firm since its inception.

Bartlett Company's balance sheets in Table 2.2 show that the firm's total assets increased from $3,270,000 in 2002 to $3,597,000 in 2003. The $327,000 increase was due primarily to the $219,000 increase in current assets. The asset increase in turn appears to have been financed primarily by an increase of $193,000 in total liabilities. Better insight into these changes can be derived from the statement of cash flows, which we will discuss shortly.

Statement of Retained Earnings

The **statement of retained earnings** reconciles the net income earned during a given year, and any cash dividends paid, with the change in retained earnings between the start and the end of that year. Table 2.3 presents this statement for Bartlett Company for the year ended December 31, 2003. The statement shows that the company began the year with $1,012,000 in retained earnings and had net profits after taxes of $231,000, from which it paid a total of $108,000 in dividends, resulting in year-end retained earnings of $1,135,000. Thus the net increase for Bartlett Company was $123,000 ($231,000 net profits after taxes minus $108,000 in dividends) during 2003.

statement of retained earnings
Reconciles the net income earned during a given year, and any cash dividends paid, with the change in retained earnings between the start and the end of that year.

TABLE 2.3 Bartlett Company Statement of Retained Earnings ($000) for the Year Ended December 31, 2003

Retained earnings balance (January 1, 2003)		$1,012
Plus: Net profits after taxes (for 2003)		231
Less: Cash dividends (paid during 2003)		
Preferred stock	($10)	
Common stock	(98)	
Total dividends paid		(108)
Retained earnings balance (December 31, 2003)		$1,135

TABLE 2.4 Bartlett Company Statement of Cash Flows ($000) for the Year Ended December 31, 2003

Cash Flow from Operating Activities		
Net profits after taxes	$231	
Depreciation	239	
Increase in accounts receivable	(138)[a]	
Decrease in inventories	11	
Increase in accounts payable	112	
Increase in accruals	45	
Cash provided by operating activities		$500
Cash Flow from Investment Activities		
Increase in gross fixed assets	($347)	
Change in business interests	0	
Cash provided by investment activities		(347)
Cash Flow from Financing Activities		
Decrease in notes payable	($ 20)	
Increase in long-term debts	56	
Changes in stockholders' equity[b]	11	
Dividends paid	(108)	
Cash provided by financing activities		(61)
Net increase in cash and marketable securities		$ 92

[a]As is customary, parentheses are used to denote a negative number, which in this case is a cash outflow.

[b]Retained earnings are excluded here, because their change is actually reflected in the combination of the "net profits after taxes" and "dividends paid" entries.

Statement of Cash Flows

statement of cash flows
Provides a summary of the firm's operating, investment, and financing cash flows and reconciles them with changes in its cash and marketable securities during the period.

The **statement of cash flows** is a summary of the cash flows over the period of concern. The statement provides insight into the firm's operating, investment, and financing cash flows and reconciles them with changes in its cash and marketable securities during the period. Bartlett Company's statement of cash flows for the year ended December 31, 2003, is presented in Table 2.4. Further insight into this statement is included in the discussion of cash flow of in Chapter 3.

Notes to the Financial Statements

notes to the financial statements
Footnotes detailing information on the accounting policies, procedures, calculations, and transactions underlying entries in the financial statements.

Included with published financial statements are explanatory notes keyed to the relevant accounts in the statements. These **notes to the financial statements** provide detailed information on the accounting policies, procedures, calculations, and transactions underlying entries in the financial statements. Common issues addressed by these notes include revenue recognition, income taxes, breakdowns of fixed asset accounts, debt and lease terms, and contingencies. Professional securities analysts use the data in the statements and notes to develop estimates of the value of securities that the firm issues, and these estimates influence the actions of investors and therefore the firm's share value.

Consolidating International Financial Statements

Financial Accounting Standards Board (FASB) Standard No. 52
Mandates that U.S.-based companies translate their foreign-currency-denominated assets and liabilities into dollars, for consolidation with the parent company's financial statements.

So far, we've discussed financial statements involving only one currency, the U.S. dollar. The issue of how to consolidate a company's foreign and domestic financial statements has bedeviled the accounting profession for many years. The current policy is described in **Financial Accounting Standards Board (FASB) Standard No. 52,** which mandates that U.S.-based companies translate their foreign-currency-denominated assets and liabilities into dollars, for consolidation with the parent company's financial statements. This is done by converting all of a U.S. parent company's foreign-currency-denominated assets and liabilities into dollar values using the exchange rate prevailing at the fiscal year ending date (the current rate). Income statement items are treated similarly. Equity accounts, on the other hand, are translated into dollars by using the exchange rate that prevailed when the parent's equity investment was made (the historical rate). Further details on this procedure can be found at the book's Web site at *www.aw.com/gitman* or in an intermediate accounting text.

Review Questions

2–1 Describe the purpose of each of the four major financial statements.
2–2 Why are the notes to the financial statements important to professional securities analysts?

LG2

Using Financial Ratios

ratio analysis
Involves methods of calculating and interpreting financial ratios to analyze and monitor the firm's performance.

The information contained in the four basic financial statements is of major significance to various interested parties who regularly need to have relative measures of the company's operating efficiency. *Relative* is the key word here, because the analysis of financial statements is based on the use of *ratios* or *relative values.* **Ratio analysis** involves methods of calculating and interpreting financial ratios to analyze and monitor the firm's performance. The basic inputs to ratio analysis are the firm's income statement and balance sheet.

Interested Parties

Ratio analysis of a firm's financial statements is of interest to shareholders, creditors, and the firm's own management. Both present and prospective shareholders are interested in the firm's current and future level of risk and return, which directly affect share price. The firm's creditors are interested primarily in the short-term liquidity of the company and its ability to make interest and principal payments. A secondary concern of creditors is the firm's profitability; they want assurance that the business is healthy. Management, like stockholders, is concerned with all aspects of the firm's financial situation, and it attempts to produce financial ratios that will be considered favorable by both owners and creditors. In addition, management uses ratios to monitor the firm's performance from period to period.

Types of Ratio Comparisons

Ratio analysis is not merely the calculation of a given ratio. More important is the *interpretation* of the ratio value. A meaningful basis for comparison is needed to answer such questions as "Is it too high or too low?" and "Is it good or bad?" Two types of ratio comparisons can be made: cross-sectional and time-series.

Cross-Sectional Analysis

cross-sectional analysis
Comparison of different firms' financial ratios at the same point in time; involves comparing the firm's ratios to those of other firms in its industry or to industry averages.

benchmarking
A type of *cross-sectional analysis* in which the firm's ratio values are compared to those of a key competitor or group of competitors that it wishes to emulate.

Cross-sectional analysis involves the comparison of different firms' financial ratios at the same point in time. Analysts are often interested in how well a firm has performed in relation to other firms in its industry. Frequently, a firm will compare its ratio values to those of a key competitor or group of competitors that it wishes to emulate. This type of cross-sectional analysis, called **benchmarking,** has become very popular.

Comparison to industry averages is also popular. These figures can be found in the *Almanac of Business and Industrial Financial Ratios, Dun & Bradstreet's Industry Norms and Key Business Ratios, Business Month, FTC Quarterly Reports, Robert Morris Associates Statement Studies, Value Line,* and industry sources.[5] A sample from one available source of industry averages is given in Table 2.5.

Many people mistakenly believe that as long as the firm being analyzed has a value "better than" the industry average, it can be viewed favorably. However, this "better than average" viewpoint can be misleading. Quite often a ratio value that is far better than the norm can indicate problems that, on more careful analysis, may be more severe than had the ratio been worse than the industry average. It is therefore important to investigate significant deviations *to either side* of the industry standard.

EXAMPLE In early 2004, Mary Boyle, the chief financial analyst at Caldwell Manufacturing, a producer of heat exchangers, gathered data on the firm's financial performance during 2003, the year just ended. She calculated a variety of ratios and obtained industry averages. She was especially interested in inventory turnover, which reflects the speed with which the firm moves its inventory from raw materials through production into finished goods and to the customer as a completed sale. Generally, higher values of this ratio are preferred, because they indicate a

5. Cross-sectional comparisons of firms operating in several lines of business are difficult to perform. The use of weighted-average industry average ratios based on the firm's product-line mix or, if data are available, analysis of the firm on a product-line basis can be performed to evaluate a multiproduct firm.

TABLE 2.5 Industry Average Ratios (2001) for Selected Lines of Business[a]

Line of business (number of concerns reporting)[b]	Current ratio (X)	Quick ratio (X)	Sales to inventory (X)	Collection period (days)	Total assets to sales (%)	Total liabilities to net worth (%)	Return on sales (%)	Return on total assets (%)	Return on net worth (%)
Department	6.2	1.9	6.0	2.9	34.3	19.7	4.0	8.5	14.6
stores	3.0	0.8	4.7	8.0	50.9	62.0	1.8	3.3	6.5
(167)	1.9	0.3	3.3	34.7	68.2	164.9	0.6	0.9	2.0
Electronic	3.6	1.8	19.0	34.7	36.4	121.4	7.1	11.7	23.9
computers	1.8	1.0	9.1	55.9	59.7	230.4	1.8	3.5	9.8
(91)	1.3	0.6	5.3	85.4	102.3	428.4	(0.8)	(3.1)	2.0
Grocery	2.5	0.9	31.0	1.1	14.4	46.2	2.2	9.9	24.3
stores	1.5	0.4	19.7	2.9	20.3	128.4	0.8	3.9	11.1
(541)	1.0	0.2	14.0	5.8	31.3	294.2	0.3	1.0	3.8
Motor	2.0	1.0	11.2	18.5	27.9	95.9	3.7	9.7	24.1
vehicles	1.5	0.7	8.7	26.7	39.0	174.3	1.9	3.7	15.6
(38)	1.2	0.3	5.8	47.5	59.2	393.9	0.6	1.4	3.4

[a]These values are given for each ratio for each line of business. The center value is the median, and the values immediately above and below it are the upper and lower quartiles, respectively.

[b]Standard Industrial Classification (SIC) codes for the lines of business shown are, respectively: SIC #5311, SIC #3571, SIC #5411, SIC #3711.

Source: "Industry Norms and Key Business Ratios," Copyright © 2001 Dun & Bradstreet, Inc. Reprinted with permission.

quicker turnover of inventory. Caldwell Manufacturing's calculated inventory turnover for 2003 and the industry average inventory turnover were as follows:

	Inventory turnover, 2003
Caldwell Manufacturing	14.8
Industry average	9.7

Mary's initial reaction to these data was that the firm had managed its inventory significantly *better than* the average firm in the industry. The turnover was nearly 53% faster than the industry average. Upon reflection, however, she realized that a very high inventory turnover could also mean very low levels of inventory. The consequence of low inventory could be excessive stockouts (insufficient inventory). Discussions with people in the manufacturing and marketing departments did in fact uncover such a problem: Inventories during the year were extremely low, the result of numerous production delays that hindered the firm's ability to meet demand and resulted in lost sales. What had initially appeared to reflect extremely efficient inventory management was actually the symptom of a major problem.

Time-Series Analysis

time-series analysis
Evaluation of the firm's financial performance over time using financial ratio analysis.

Time-series analysis evaluates performance over time. Comparison of current to past performance, using ratios, enables analysts to assess the firm's progress. Developing trends can be seen by using multiyear comparisons. As in cross-sectional analysis, any significant year-to-year changes may be symptomatic of a major problem.

Combined Analysis

The most informative approach to ratio analysis combines cross-sectional and time-series analyses. A combined view makes it possible to assess the trend in the behavior of the ratio in relation to the trend for the industry. Figure 2.1 depicts this type of approach using the average collection period ratio of Bartlett Company, over the years 2000–2003. This ratio reflects the average amount of time it takes the firm to collect bills, and lower values of this ratio generally are preferred. The figure quickly discloses that (1) Bartlett's effectiveness in collecting its receivables is poor in comparison to the industry, and (2) Bartlett's trend is toward longer collection periods. Clearly, Bartlett needs to shorten its collection period.

Cautions About Using Ratio Analysis

Before discussing specific ratios, we should consider the following cautions about their use:

1. Ratios with large deviations from the norm only indicate *symptoms* of a problem. Additional analysis is typically needed to isolate the *causes* of the problem. The fundamental point is this: Ratio analysis merely directs attention to potential areas of concern; it does not provide conclusive evidence as to the existence of a problem.
2. A single ratio does not generally provide sufficient information from which to judge the *overall* performance of the firm. Only when a group of ratios is

FIGURE 2.1

Combined Analysis
Combined cross-sectional and time-series view of Bartlett Company's average collection period, 2000–2003

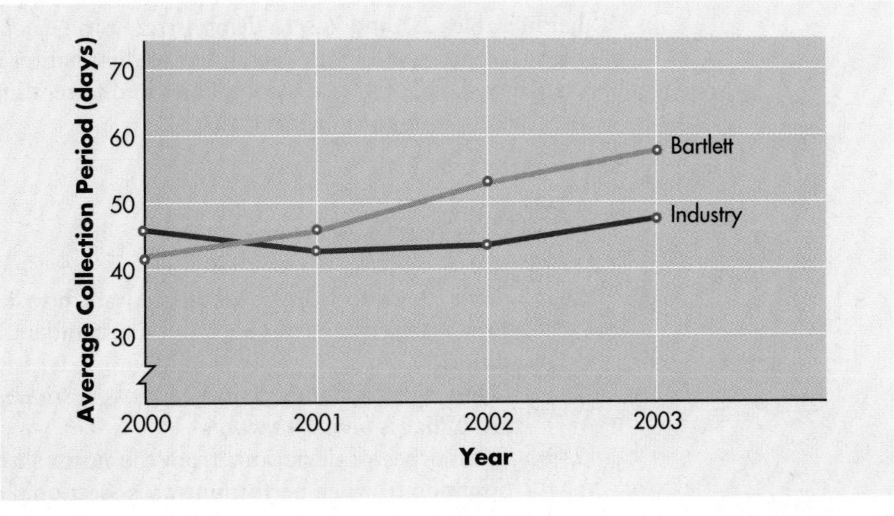

used can reasonable judgments be made. However, if an analysis is concerned only with certain *specific* aspects of a firm's financial position, one or two ratios may be sufficient.

3. The ratios being compared should be calculated using financial statements dated at the same point in time during the year. If they are not, the effects of *seasonality* may produce erroneous conclusions and decisions. For example, comparison of the inventory turnover of a toy manufacturer at the end of June with its end-of-December value can be misleading. Clearly, the seasonal impact of the December holiday selling season would skew any comparison of the firm's inventory management.
4. It is preferable to use *audited financial statements* for ratio analysis. If the statements have not been audited, the data contained in them may not reflect the firm's true financial condition.
5. The financial data being compared should have been developed in the same way. The use of differing accounting treatments—especially relative to inventory and depreciation—can distort the results of ratio analysis, regardless of whether cross-sectional or time-series analysis is used.
6. Results can be distorted by *inflation,* which can cause the book values of inventory and depreciable assets to differ greatly from their true (replacement) values. Additionally, inventory costs and depreciation write-offs can differ from their true values, thereby distorting profits. Without adjustment, inflation tends to cause older firms (older assets) to appear more efficient and profitable than newer firms (newer assets). Clearly, in using ratios, care must be taken to compare older to newer firms or a firm to itself over a long period of time.

Categories of Financial Ratios

Financial ratios can be divided for convenience into five basic categories: liquidity, activity, debt, profitability, and market ratios. Liquidity, activity, and debt ratios primarily measure risk. Profitability ratios measure return. Market ratios capture both risk and return.

As a rule, the inputs necessary to an effective financial analysis include, at a minimum, the income statement and the balance sheet. We will use the 2003 and 2002 income statements and balance sheets for Bartlett Company, presented earlier in Tables 2.1 and 2.2, to demonstrate ratio calculations. Note, however, that the ratios presented in the remainder of this chapter can be applied to almost any company. Of course, many companies in different industries use ratios that focus on aspects peculiar to their industry.

Review Questions

2–3 With regard to financial ratio analysis, how do the viewpoints held by the firm's present and prospective shareholders, creditors, and management differ?

2–4 What is the difference between *cross-sectional* and *time-series* ratio analysis? What is *benchmarking?*

2–5 What types of deviations from the norm should the analyst pay primary attention to when performing cross-sectional ratio analysis? Why?

2–6 Why is it preferable to compare ratios calculated using financial statements that are dated at the same point in time during the year?

LG3

Liquidity Ratios

liquidity
A firm's ability to satisfy its short-term obligations *as they come due.*

The **liquidity** of a firm is measured by its ability to satisfy its short-term obligations *as they come due*. Liquidity refers to the solvency of the firm's *overall* financial position—the ease with which it can pay its bills. Because a common precursor to financial distress and bankruptcy is low or declining liquidity, these ratios are viewed as good leading indicators of cash flow problems. The two basic measures of liquidity are the current ratio and the quick (acid-test) ratio.

Current Ratio

current ratio
A measure of liquidity calculated by dividing the firm's current assets by its current liabilities.

The **current ratio,** one of the most commonly cited financial ratios, measures the firm's ability to meet its short-term obligations. It is expressed as follows:

$$\text{Current ratio} = \frac{\text{Current assets}}{\text{Current liabilities}}$$

The current ratio for Bartlett Company in 2003 is

$$\frac{\$1,223,000}{\$620,000} = 1.97$$

Generally, the higher the current ratio, the more liquid the firm is considered to be. A current ratio of 2.0 is occasionally cited as acceptable, but a value's acceptability depends on the industry in which the firm operates. For example, a current ratio of 1.0 would be considered acceptable for a public utility but might be unacceptable for a manufacturing firm. The more predictable a firm's cash flows, the lower the acceptable current ratio. Because Bartlett Company is in a business with a relatively predictable annual cash flow, its current ratio of 1.97 should be quite acceptable.

Quick (Acid-Test) Ratio

quick (acid-test) ratio
A measure of liquidity calculated by dividing the firm's current assets minus inventory by its current liabilities.

The **quick (acid-test) ratio** is similar to the current ratio except that it excludes inventory, which is generally the least liquid current asset. The generally low liquidity of inventory results from two primary factors: (1) many types of inventory cannot be easily sold because they are partially completed items, special-purpose items, and the like; and (2) inventory is typically sold on credit, which means that it becomes an account receivable before being converted into cash. The quick ratio is calculated as follows:[6]

$$\text{Quick ratio} = \frac{\text{Current assets} - \text{Inventory}}{\text{Current liabilities}}$$

6. Sometimes the quick ratio is defined as (cash + marketable securities + accounts receivable) ÷ current liabilities. If a firm were to show as current assets items other than cash, marketable securities, accounts receivable, and inventories, its quick ratio might vary, depending on the method of calculation.

The quick ratio for Bartlett Company in 2003 is

$$\frac{\$1{,}223{,}000 - \$289{,}000}{\$620{,}000} = \frac{\$934{,}000}{\$620{,}000} = 1.51$$

A quick ratio of 1.0 or greater is occasionally recommended, but as with the current ratio, what value is acceptable depends largely on the industry. The quick ratio provides a better measure of overall liquidity only when a firm's inventory cannot be easily converted into cash. If inventory is liquid, the current ratio is a preferred measure of overall liquidity.

Review Question

2–7 Under what circumstances would the current ratio be the preferred measure of overall firm liquidity? Under what circumstances would the quick ratio be preferred?

LG3

Activity Ratios

activity ratios
Measure the speed with which various accounts are converted into sales or cash—inflows or outflows.

Activity ratios measure the speed with which various accounts are converted into sales or cash—inflows or outflows. With regard to current accounts, measures of liquidity are generally inadequate because differences in the *composition* of a firm's current assets and current liabilities can significantly affect its "true" liquidity. It is therefore important to look beyond measures of overall liquidity and to assess the activity (liquidity) of specific current accounts. A number of ratios are available for measuring the activity of the most important current accounts, which include inventory, accounts receivable, and accounts payable.[7] The efficiency with which total assets are used can also be assessed.

Inventory Turnover

inventory turnover
Measures the activity, or liquidity, of a firm's inventory.

Inventory turnover commonly measures the activity, or liquidity, of a firm's inventory. It is calculated as follows:

$$\text{Inventory turnover} = \frac{\text{Cost of goods sold}}{\text{Inventory}}$$

7. For convenience, the activity ratios involving these current accounts assume that their end-of-period values are good approximations of the average account balance during the period—typically 1 year. Technically, when the month-end balances of inventory, accounts receivable, or accounts payable vary during the year, the average balance, calculated by summing the 12 month-end account balances and dividing the total by 12, should be used instead of the year-end value. If month-end balances are unavailable, the average can be approximated by dividing the sum of the beginning-of-year and end-of-year balances by 2. These approaches ensure a ratio that on the average better reflects the firm's circumstances. Because the data needed to find averages are generally unavailable to the external analyst, year-end values are frequently used to calculate activity ratios for current accounts.

Applying this relationship to Bartlett Company in 2003 yields

$$\text{Inventory turnover} = \frac{\$2{,}088{,}000}{\$289{,}000} = 7.2$$

The resulting turnover is meaningful only when it is compared with that of other firms in the same industry or to the firm's past inventory turnover. An inventory turnover of 20.0 would not be unusual for a grocery store, whereas a common inventory turnover for an aircraft manufacturer is 4.0.

average age of inventory
Average number of days' sales in inventory.

Inventory turnover can be easily converted into an **average age of inventory** by dividing it into 360—the assumed number of days in a year.[8] For Bartlett Company, the average age of inventory in 2003 is 50.0 days (360 ÷ 7.2). This value can also be viewed as the average number of days' sales in inventory.

Average Collection Period

average collection period
The average amount of time needed to collect accounts receivable.

The **average collection period,** or average age of accounts receivable, is useful in evaluating credit and collection policies.[9] It is arrived at by dividing the average daily sales[10] into the accounts receivable balance:

$$\text{Average collection period} = \frac{\text{Accounts receivable}}{\text{Average sales per day}}$$

$$= \frac{\text{Accounts receivable}}{\dfrac{\text{Annual sales}}{360}}$$

The average collection period for Bartlett Company in 2003 is

$$\frac{\$503{,}000}{\dfrac{\$3{,}074{,}000}{360}} = \frac{\$503{,}000}{\$8{,}539} = 58.9 \text{ days}$$

On the average, it takes the firm 58.9 days to collect an account receivable.

The average collection period is meaningful only in relation to the firm's credit terms. If Bartlett Company extends 30-day credit terms to customers, an average collection period of 58.9 days may indicate a poorly managed credit or collection department, or both. It is also possible that the lengthened collection period resulted from an intentional relaxation of credit-term enforcement in response to competitive pressures. If the firm had extended 60-day credit terms, the 58.9-day average collection period would be quite acceptable. Clearly, additional information is needed to evaluate the effectiveness of the firm's credit and collection policies.

---

8. Unless otherwise specified, a 360-day year consisting of twelve 30-day months is assumed throughout this textbook. This assumption simplifies the calculations used to illustrate key concepts.

9. The average collection period is sometimes called the *days' sales outstanding (DSO)*. A discussion of the evaluation and establishment of credit and collection policies is presented in Chapter 13.

10. The formula as presented assumes, for simplicity, that all sales are made on a credit basis. If this is not the case, *average credit sales per day* should be substituted for average sales per day.

Average Payment Period

average payment period
The average amount of time needed to pay accounts payable.

The **average payment period,** or average age of accounts payable, is calculated in the same manner as the average collection period:

$$\text{Average payment period} = \frac{\text{Accounts payable}}{\text{Average purchases per day}}$$

$$= \frac{\text{Accounts payable}}{\frac{\text{Annual purchases}}{360}}$$

The difficulty in calculating this ratio stems from the need to find annual purchases,[11] a value not available in published financial statements. Ordinarily, purchases are estimated as a given percentage of cost of goods sold. If we assume that Bartlett Company's purchases equaled 70 percent of its cost of goods sold in 2003, its average payment period is

$$\frac{\$382{,}000}{\frac{0.70 \times \$2{,}088{,}000}{360}} = \frac{\$382{,}000}{\$4{,}060} = 94.1 \text{ days}$$

This figure is meaningful only in relation to the average credit terms extended to the firm. If Bartlett Company's suppliers have extended, on average, 30-day credit terms, an analyst would give Bartlett a low credit rating. Prospective lenders and suppliers of trade credit are most interested in the average payment period because it provides insight into the firm's bill-paying patterns.

Total Asset Turnover

total asset turnover
Indicates the efficiency with which the firm uses its assets to generate sales.

The **total asset turnover** indicates the efficiency with which the firm uses its assets to generate sales. Total asset turnover is calculated as follows:

$$\text{Total asset turnover} = \frac{\text{Sales}}{\text{Total assets}}$$

The value of Bartlett Company's total asset turnover in 2003 is

$$\frac{\$3{,}074{,}000}{\$3{,}597{,}000} = 0.85$$

This means the company turns over its assets 0.85 times a year.

Generally, the higher a firm's total asset turnover, the more efficiently its assets have been used. This measure is probably of greatest interest to management, because it indicates whether the firm's operations have been financially efficient.

Review Question

2–8 To assess the firm's average collection period and average payment period ratios, what additional information is needed, and why?

11. Technically, annual *credit* purchases—rather than annual purchases—should be used in calculating this ratio. For simplicity, this refinement is ignored here.

LG4

Debt Ratios

The *debt position* of a firm indicates the amount of other people's money being used to generate profits. In general, the financial analyst is most concerned with long-term debts, because these commit the firm to a stream of payments over the long run. Because creditors' claims must be satisfied before the earnings can be distributed to shareholders, present and prospective shareholders pay close attention to the firm's ability to repay debts. Lenders are also concerned about the firm's indebtedness. Management obviously must be concerned with indebtedness.

In general, the more debt a firm uses in relation to its total assets, the greater its *financial leverage*. **Financial leverage** is the magnification of risk and return introduced through the use of fixed-cost financing, such as debt and preferred stock. The more fixed-cost debt a firm uses, the greater will be its expected risk and return.

financial leverage
The magnification of risk and return introduced through the use of fixed-cost financing, such as debt and preferred stock.

EXAMPLE

Patty Akers is in the process of incorporating her new business. After much analysis she determined that an initial investment of $50,000—$20,000 in current assets and $30,000 in fixed assets—is necessary. These funds can be obtained in either of two ways. The first is the *no-debt plan,* under which she would invest the full $50,000 without borrowing. The other alternative, the *debt plan,* involves investing $25,000 and borrowing the balance of $25,000 at 12% annual interest.

Regardless of which alternative she chooses, Patty expects sales to average $30,000, costs and operating expenses to average $18,000, and earnings to be taxed at a 40% rate. Projected balance sheets and income statements associated with the two plans are summarized in Table 2.6. The no-debt plan results in after-tax profits of $7,200, which represent a 14.4% rate of return on Patty's $50,000 investment. The debt plan results in $5,400 of after-tax profits, which represent a 21.6% rate of return on Patty's investment of $25,000. The debt plan provides Patty with a higher rate of return, but the risk of this plan is also greater, because the annual $3,000 of interest must be paid before receipt of earnings.

The example demonstrates that *with increased debt comes greater risk as well as higher potential return.* Therefore, the greater the financial leverage, the greater the potential risk and return. A detailed discussion of the impact of debt on the firm's risk, return, and value is included in Chapter 12. Here, we emphasize the use of financial debt ratios to assess externally a firm's debt position.

There are two general types of debt measures: measures of the degree of indebtedness and measures of the ability to service debts. The **degree of indebtedness** measures the amount of debt relative to other significant balance sheet amounts. A popular measure of the degree of indebtedness is the debt ratio.

The second type of debt measure, the **ability to service debts,** reflects a firm's ability to make the payments required on a scheduled basis over the life of a debt.[12] The firm's ability to pay certain fixed charges is measured using **coverage ratios.** Typically, higher coverage ratios are preferred, but too high a ratio (above industry norms) may result in unnecessarily low risk and return. In general, the

degree of indebtedness
Measures the amount of debt relative to other significant balance sheet amounts.

ability to service debts
The ability of a firm to make the payments required on a scheduled basis over the life of a debt.

coverage ratios
Ratios that measure the firm's ability to pay certain fixed charges.

12. The term *service* refers to the payment of interest and repayment of principal associated with a firm's debt obligations. When a firm services its debts, it pays—or fulfills—these obligations.

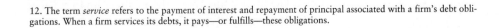

TABLE 2.6 Financial Statements Associated with Patty's Alternatives

	No-debt plan		Debt plan	
Balance Sheets				
Current assets	$20,000		$20,000	
Fixed assets	30,000		30,000	
Total assets	$50,000		$50,000	
Debt (12% interest)	$ 0		$25,000	
(1) Equity	50,000		25,000	
Total liabilities and equity	$50,000		$50,000	
Income Statements				
Sales	$30,000		$30,000	
Less: Costs and operating expenses	18,000		18,000	
Operating profits	$12,000		$12,000	
Less: Interest expense	0		0.12 × $25,000 = 3,000	
Net profit before taxes	$12,000		$ 9,000	
Less: Taxes (rate = 40%)	4,800		3,600	
(2) Net profit after taxes	$ 7,200		$ 5,400	
Return on equity [(2) ÷ (1)]	$\frac{\$7,200}{\$50,000}$	= 14.4%	$\frac{\$5,400}{\$25,000}$	= 21.6%

lower the firm's coverage ratios, the less certain it is to be able to pay fixed obligations. If a firm is unable to pay these obligations, its creditors may seek immediate repayment, which in most instances would force a firm into bankruptcy. Two popular coverage ratios are the times interest earned ratio and the fixed-payment coverage ratio.

Debt Ratio

debt ratio
Measures the proportion of total assets financed by the firm's creditors.

The **debt ratio** measures the proportion of total assets financed by the firm's creditors. The higher this ratio, the greater the amount of other people's money being used to generate profits. The ratio is calculated as follows:

$$\text{Debt ratio} = \frac{\text{Total liabilities}}{\text{Total assets}}$$

The debt ratio for Bartlett Company in 2003 is

$$\frac{\$1,643,000}{\$3,597,000} = 0.457 = 45.7\%$$

This value indicates that the company has financed close to half of its assets with debt. The higher this ratio, the greater the firm's degree of indebtedness and the more financial leverage it has.

Times Interest Earned Ratio

times interest earned ratio
Measures the firm's ability to make contractual interest payments; sometimes called the *interest coverage ratio.*

The **times interest earned ratio,** sometimes called the *interest coverage ratio,* measures the firm's ability to make contractual interest payments. The higher its value, the better able the firm is to fulfill its interest obligations. The times interest earned ratio is calculated as follows:

$$\text{Times interest earned ratio} = \frac{\text{Earnings before interest and taxes}}{\text{Interest}}$$

The figure for *earnings before interest and taxes* is the same as that for *operating profits* shown in the income statement. Applying this ratio to Bartlett Company yields the following 2003 value:

$$\text{Times interest earned ratio} = \frac{\$418{,}000}{\$93{,}000} = 4.5$$

The times interest earned ratio for Bartlett Company seems acceptable. A value of at least 3.0—and preferably closer to 5.0—is often suggested. The firm's earnings before interest and taxes could shrink by as much as 78 percent $[(4.5 - 1.0) \div 4.5]$, and the firm would still be able to pay the $93,000 in interest it owes. Thus it has a good margin of safety.

Fixed-Payment Coverage Ratio

fixed-payment coverage ratio
Measures the firm's ability to meet all fixed-payment obligations.

The **fixed-payment coverage ratio** measures the firm's ability to meet all fixed-payment obligations, such as loan interest and principal, lease payments, and preferred stock dividends.[13] As is true of the times interest earned ratio, the higher this value, the better. The formula for the fixed-payment coverage ratio is

$$\text{Fixed-payment coverage ratio} = \frac{\text{Earnings before interest and taxes} + \text{Lease payments}}{\text{Interest} + \text{Lease payments} + \{(\text{Principal payments} + \text{Preferred stock dividends}) \times [1/(1-T)]\}}$$

where T is the corporate tax rate applicable to the firm's income. The term $1/(1-T)$ is included to adjust the after-tax principal and preferred stock dividend payments back to a before-tax equivalent that is consistent with the before-tax values of all other terms. Applying the formula to Bartlett Company's 2003 data yields

$$\text{Fixed-payment coverage ratio} = \frac{\$418{,}000 + \$35{,}000}{\$93{,}000 + \$35{,}000 + \{(\$71{,}000 + \$10{,}000) \times [1/(1-0.29)]\}}$$

$$= \frac{\$453{,}000}{\$242{,}000} = 1.9$$

Because the earnings available are nearly twice as large as its fixed-payment obligations, the firm appears safely able to meet the latter.

Like the times interest earned ratio, the fixed-payment coverage ratio measures risk. The lower the ratio, the greater the risk to both lenders and owners;

13. Although preferred stock dividends, which are stated at the time of issue, can be "passed" (not paid) at the option of the firm's directors, it is generally believed that the payment of such dividends is necessary. *This text therefore treats the preferred stock dividend as a contractual obligation, to be paid as a fixed amount, as scheduled.*

the greater the ratio, the lower the risk. This ratio allows interested parties to assess the firm's ability to meet additional fixed-payment obligations without being driven into bankruptcy.

Review Questions

2–9 What is *financial leverage?*

2–10 What ratio measures the firm's *degree of indebtedness*? What ratios assesses the firm's *ability to service debts?*

LG5

Profitability Ratios

There are many measures of profitability. As a group, these measures enable the analyst to evaluate the firm's profits with respect to a given level of sales, a certain level of assets, or the owners' investment. Without profits, a firm could not attract outside capital. Owners, creditors, and management pay close attention to boosting profits because of the great importance placed on earnings in the marketplace.

Common-Size Income Statements

common-size income statement
An income statement in which each item is expressed as a percentage of sales.

A popular tool for evaluating profitability in relation to sales is the **common-size income statement.** Each item on this statement is expressed as a percentage of sales. Common-size income statements are especially useful in comparing performance across years. Three frequently cited ratios of profitability that can be read directly from the common-size income statement are (1) the gross profit margin, (2) the operating profit margin, and (3) the net profit margin.

Common-size income statements for 2003 and 2002 for Bartlett Company are presented and evaluated in Table 2.7. These statements reveal that the firm's cost of goods sold increased from 66.7 percent of sales in 2002 to 67.9 percent in 2003, resulting in a worsening gross profit margin. However, thanks to a decrease in total operating expenses, the firm's net profit margin rose from 5.4 percent of sales in 2002 to 7.2 percent in 2003. The decrease in expenses more than compensated for the increase in the cost of goods sold. A decrease in the firm's 2003 interest expense (3.0 percent of sales versus 3.5 percent in 2002) added to the increase in 2003 profits.

Gross Profit Margin

gross profit margin
Measures the percentage of each sales dollar remaining after the firm has paid for its goods.

The **gross profit margin** measures the percentage of each sales dollar remaining after the firm has paid for its goods. The higher the gross profit margin, the better (that is, the lower the relative cost of merchandise sold). The gross profit margin is calculated as follows:

$$\text{Gross profit margin} = \frac{\text{Sales} - \text{Cost of goods sold}}{\text{Sales}} = \frac{\text{Gross profits}}{\text{Sales}}$$

TABLE 2.7 Bartlett Company Common-Size Income Statements

	For the years ended December 31		Evaluation[a]
	2003	2002	2002–2003
Sales revenue	100.0%	100.0%	same
Less: Cost of goods sold	67.9	66.7	worse
(1) Gross profit margin	32.1%	33.3%	worse
Less: Operating expenses			
Selling expense	3.3%	4.2%	better
General and administrative expenses	6.8	6.7	better
Lease expense	1.1	1.3	better
Depreciation expense	7.3	9.3	better
Total operating expense	18.5%	21.5%	better
(2) Operating profit margin	13.6%	11.8%	better
Less: Interest expense	3.0	3.5	better
Net profits before taxes	10.6%	8.3%	better
Less: Taxes	3.1	2.5	worse[b]
Net profits after taxes	7.5%	5.8%	better
Less: Preferred stock dividends	0.3	0.4	better
(3) Net profit margin	7.2%	5.4%	better

[a]Subjective assessments based on data provided.

[b]Taxes as a percent of sales increased noticeably between 2002 and 2003 because of differing costs and expenses, whereas the average tax rates (taxes ÷ net profits before taxes) for 2002 and 2003 remained about the same—30% and 29%, respectively.

Bartlett Company's gross profit margin for 2003 is

$$\frac{\$3{,}074{,}000 - \$2{,}088{,}000}{\$3{,}074{,}000} = \frac{\$986{,}000}{\$3{,}074{,}000} = 32.1\%$$

This value is labeled (1) on the common-size income statement in Table 2.7.

Operating Profit Margin

operating profit margin
Measures the percentage of each sales dollar remaining after all costs and expenses *other than* interest, taxes, and preferred stock dividends are deducted; the "pure profits" earned on each sales dollar.

The **operating profit margin** measures the percentage of each sales dollar remaining after all costs and expenses *other than* interest, taxes, and preferred stock dividends are deducted. It represents the "pure profits" earned on each sales dollar. Operating profits are "pure" because they measure only the profits earned on operations and ignore interest, taxes, and preferred stock dividends. A high operating profit margin is preferred. The operating profit margin is calculated as follows:

$$\text{Operating profit margin} = \frac{\text{Operating profits}}{\text{Sales}}$$

Bartlett Company's operating profit margin for 2003 is

$$\frac{\$418{,}000}{\$3{,}074{,}000} = 13.6\%$$

This value is labeled (2) on the common-size income statement in Table 2.7.

Net Profit Margin

net profit margin
Measures the percentage of each sales dollar remaining after all costs and expenses, *including* interest, taxes, and preferred stock dividends, have been deducted.

The **net profit margin** measures the percentage of each sales dollar remaining after all costs and expenses, *including* interest, taxes, and preferred stock dividends, have been deducted. The higher the firm's net profit margin, the better. The net profit margin is calculated as follows:

$$\text{Net profit margin} = \frac{\text{Earnings available for common stockholders}}{\text{Sales}}$$

Bartlett Company's net profit margin for 2003 is

$$\frac{\$221{,}000}{\$3{,}074{,}000} = 7.2\%$$

This value is labeled (3) on the common-size income statement in Table 2.7.

The net profit margin is a commonly cited measure of the firm's success with respect to earnings on sales. "Good" net profit margins differ considerably across industries. A net profit margin of 1 percent or less would not be unusual for a grocery store, whereas a net profit margin of 10 percent would be low for a retail jewelry store.

Earnings per Share (EPS)

The firm's *earnings per share (EPS)* is generally of interest to present or prospective stockholders and management. As we noted earlier, EPS represents the number of dollars earned during the period on behalf of each outstanding share of common stock. Earnings per share is calculated as follows:

$$\text{Earnings per share} = \frac{\text{Earnings available for common stockholders}}{\text{Number of shares of common stock outstanding}}$$

Bartlett Company's earnings per share in 2003 is

$$\frac{\$221{,}000}{76{,}262} = \$2.90$$

This figure represents the dollar amount earned on behalf of each share. The dollar amount of cash *actually distributed* to each shareholder is the *dividend per share (DPS),* which as noted Bartlett Company's income statement (Table 2.1), rose to \$1.29 in 2003 from \$0.75 in 2002. EPS is closely watched by the investing public and is considered an important indicator of corporate success.

Return on Total Assets (ROA)

return on total assets (ROA) Measures the overall effectiveness of management in generating profits with its available assets; also called the *return on investment (ROI).*

The **return on total assets (ROA),** often called the *return on investment (ROI),* measures the overall effectiveness of management in generating profits with its available assets. The higher the firm's return on total assets, the better. The return on total assets is calculated as follows:

$$\text{Return on total assets} = \frac{\text{Earnings available for common stockholders}}{\text{Total assets}}$$

Bartlett Company's return on total assets in 2003 is

$$\frac{\$221{,}000}{\$3{,}597{,}000} = 6.1\%$$

This value indicates that the firm earned 6.1 cents on each dollar of asset investment.

Return on Common Equity (ROE)

return on common equity (ROE) Measures the return earned on the common stockholders' investment in the firm.

The **return on common equity** (ROE) measures the return earned on the common stockholders' investment in the firm. Generally, the higher this return, the better off are the owners. Return on common equity is calculated as follows:

$$\text{Return on common equity} = \frac{\text{Earnings available for common stockholders}}{\text{Common stock equity}}$$

This ratio for Bartlett Company in 2003 is

$$\frac{\$221{,}000}{\$1{,}754{,}000} = 12.6\%$$

Note that the value for common stock equity ($1,754,000) was found by subtracting the $200,000 of preferred stock equity from the total stockholders' equity of $1,954,000 (see Bartlett Company's 2003 balance sheet in Table 2.2). The calculated ROE of 12.6 percent indicates that during 2003 Bartlett earned 12.6 cents on each dollar of common stock equity.

Review Questions

2–11 What three ratios of profitability are found on a *common-size income statement?*

2–12 What would explain a firm's having a high gross profit margin and a low net profit margin?

2–13 Which measure of profitability is probably of greatest interest to the investing public? Why?

LG5

Market Ratios

market ratios
Relate a firm's market value, as measured by its current share price, to certain accounting values.

Market ratios relate the firm's market value, as measured by its current share price, to certain accounting values. These ratios give insight into how well investors in the marketplace feel the firm is doing in terms of risk and return. They tend to reflect, on a relative basis, the common stockholders' assessment of all aspects of the firm's past and expected future performance. Here we consider two popular market ratios, one that focuses on earnings and another that considers book value.

Price/Earnings (P/E) Ratio

price/earnings (P/E) ratio
Measures the amount that investors are willing to pay for each dollar of a firm's earnings; the higher the P/E ratio, the greater is investor confidence.

The **price/earnings (P/E) ratio** measures the amount that investors are willing to pay for each dollar of a firm's earnings. The level of the price/earnings ratio indicates the degree of confidence that investors have in the firm's future performance. The higher the P/E ratio, the greater is investor confidence. The P/E ratio is calculated as follows:

$$\text{Price/earnings (P/E) ratio} = \frac{\text{Market price per share of common stock}}{\text{Earnings per share}}$$

If Bartlett Company's common stock at the end of 2003 was selling at \$32.25, using the EPS of \$2.90, the P/E ratio at year-end 2003 is

$$\frac{\$32.25}{\$2.90} = 11.1$$

This figure indicates that investors were paying \$11.10 for each \$1.00 of earnings. The P/E ratio is most informative when applied in cross-sectional analysis using an industry average P/E ratio or the P/E ratio of a benchmark firm.

Market/Book (M/B) Ratio

market/book (M/B) ratio
Provides an assessment of how investors view the firm's performance. Firms expected to earn high returns relative to their risk typically sell at higher M/B multiples.

The **market/book (M/B) ratio** provides an assessment of how investors view the firm's performance. It relates the market value of the firm's shares to their book—strict accounting—value. To calculate the firm's M/B ratio, we first need to find the *book value per share of common stock:*

$$\text{Book value per share of common stock} = \frac{\text{Common stock equity}}{\text{Number of shares of common stock outstanding}}$$

Substituting the appropriate values for Bartlett Company from its 2003 balance sheet, we get

$$\text{Book value per share of common stock} = \frac{\$1{,}754{,}000}{76{,}262} = \$23.00$$

The formula for the market/book ratio is

$$\text{Market/book (M/B) ratio} = \frac{\text{Market price per share of common stock}}{\text{Book value per share of common stock}}$$

Substituting Bartlett Company's end of 2003 common stock price of \$32.25 and its \$23.00 book value per share of common stock (calculated above) into the M/B ratio formula, we get

$$\text{Market/book (M/B) ratio} = \frac{\$32.25}{\$23.00} = 1.40$$

This M/B ratio means that investors are currently paying \$1.40 for each \$1.00 of book value of Bartlett Company's stock.

The stocks of firms that are expected to perform well—improve profits, increase their market share, or launch successful products—typically sell at higher M/B ratios than the stocks of firms with less attractive outlooks. Simply stated, firms expected to earn high returns relative to their risk typically sell at higher M/B multiples. Clearly, Bartlett's future prospects are being viewed favorably by investors, who are willing to pay more than its book value for the firm's shares. Like P/E ratios, M/B ratios are typically assessed cross-sectionally, to get a feel for the firm's risk and return compared to peer firms.

Review Question

2–14 How do the *price/earnings (P/E) ratio* and the *market/book (M/B) ratio* provide a feel for the firm's risk and return?

LG6

A Complete Ratio Analysis

Analysts frequently wish to take an overall look at the firm's financial performance and status. Here we consider two popular approaches to a complete ratio analysis: (1) summarizing all ratios and (2) the DuPont system of analysis. The summary analysis approach tends to view *all aspects* of the firm's financial activities to isolate key areas of responsibility. The DuPont system acts as a search technique aimed at finding the *key areas* responsible for the firm's financial condition.

Summarizing All Ratios

We can use Bartlett Company's ratios to perform a complete ratio analysis using both cross-sectional and time-series analysis approaches. The 2003 ratio values calculated earlier and the ratio values calculated for 2001 and 2002 for Bartlett Company, along with the industry average ratios for 2003, are summarized in Table 2.8, which also shows the formula used to calculate each ratio. Using these data, we can discuss the five key aspects of Bartlett's performance—liquidity, activity, debt, profitability, and market.

Liquidity

The overall liquidity of the firm seems to exhibit a reasonably stable trend, having been maintained at a level that is relatively consistent with the industry average in 2003. The firm's liquidity seems to be good.

TABLE 2.8 Summary of Bartlett Company Ratios (2001–2003, Including 2003 Industry Averages)

Ratio	Formula	Year			Industry average	Evaluation[d]		
		2001[a]	2002[b]	2003[b]	2003[c]	Cross-sectional 2003	Time-series 2001–2003	Overall
Liquidity								
Current ratio	$\frac{\text{Current assets}}{\text{Current liabilities}}$	2.04	2.08	1.97	2.05	OK	OK	OK
Quick (acid-test) ratio	$\frac{\text{Current assets} - \text{Inventory}}{\text{Current liabilities}}$	1.32	1.46	1.51	1.43	OK	good	good
Activity								
Inventory turnover	$\frac{\text{Cost of goods sold}}{\text{Inventory}}$	5.1	5.7	7.2	6.6	good	good	good
Average collection period	$\frac{\text{Accounts receivable}}{\text{Average sales per day}}$	43.9 days	51.2 days	58.9 days	44.3 days	poor	poor	poor
Average payment period	$\frac{\text{Accounts payable}}{\text{Average purchases per day}}$	75.8 days	81.2 days	94.1 days	66.5 days	poor	poor	poor
Total asset turnover	$\frac{\text{Sales}}{\text{Total assets}}$	0.94	0.79	0.85	0.75	OK	OK	OK
Debt								
Debt ratio	$\frac{\text{Total liabilities}}{\text{Total assets}}$	36.8%	44.3%	45.7%	40.0%	OK	OK	OK
Times interest earned ratio	$\frac{\text{Earnings before interest and taxes}}{\text{Interest}}$	5.6	3.3	4.5	4.3	good	OK	OK
Fixed-payment coverage ratio	$\frac{\text{Earnings before interest and taxes} + \text{Lease payments}}{\text{Int.} + \text{Lease pay.} + \{(\text{Prin.} + \text{Pref. div.}) \times [1/(1-T)]\}}$	2.4	1.4	1.9	1.5	good	OK	good

Ratio	Formula	Year			Industry average	Evaluation[d]		
		2001[a]	2002[b]	2003[b]	2003[c]	Cross-sectional 2003	Time-series 2001–2003	Overall
Profitability								
Gross profit margin	$\frac{\text{Gross profits}}{\text{Sales}}$	31.4%	33.3%	32.1%	30.0%	OK	OK	OK
Operating profit margin	$\frac{\text{Operating profits}}{\text{Sales}}$	14.6%	11.8%	13.6%	11.0%	good	OK	good
Net profit margin	$\frac{\text{Earnings available for common stockholders}}{\text{Sales}}$	8.2%	5.4%	7.2%	6.2%	good	OK	good
Earnings per share (EPS)	$\frac{\text{Earnings available for common stockholders}}{\text{Number of shares of common stock outstanding}}$	$3.26	$1.81	$2.90	$2.26	good	OK	good
Return on total assets (ROA)	$\frac{\text{Earnings available for common stockholders}}{\text{Total assets}}$	7.8%	4.2%	6.1%	4.6%	good	OK	good
Return on common equity (ROE)	$\frac{\text{Earnings available for common stockholders}}{\text{Common stock equity}}$	13.7%	8.5%	12.6%	8.5%	good	OK	good
Market								
Price/earnings (P/E) ratio	$\frac{\text{Market price per share of common stock}}{\text{Earnings per share}}$	10.5	10.0[e]	11.1	12.5	OK	OK	OK
Market/book (M/B) ratio	$\frac{\text{Market price per share of common stock}}{\text{Book value per share of common stock}}$	1.25	0.85[e]	1.40	1.30	OK	OK	OK

[a]Calculated from data not included in the chapter.
[b]Calculated by using the financial statements presented in Tables 2.1 and 2.2.
[c]Obtained from sources not included in this chapter.
[d]Subjective assessments based on data provided.
[e]The market price per share at the end of 2002 was $18.06.

Activity

Bartlett Company's inventory appears to be in good shape. Its inventory management seems to have improved, and in 2003 it performed at a level above that of the industry. The firm may be experiencing some problems with accounts receivable. The average collection period seems to have crept up above that of the industry. Bartlett also appears to be slow in paying its bills; it pays nearly 30 days slower than the industry average. This could adversely affect the firm's credit standing. Although overall liquidity appears to be good, the management of receivables and payables should be examined. Bartlett's total asset turnover reflects a decline in the efficiency of total asset utilization between 2001 and 2002. Although in 2003 it rose to a level considerably above the industry average, it appears that the pre-2002 level of efficiency has not yet been achieved.

Debt

Bartlett Company's indebtedness increased over the 2001–2003 period and is currently above the industry average. Although this increase in the debt ratio could be cause for alarm, the firm's ability to meet interest and fixed-payment obligations improved, from 2002 to 2003, to a level that outperforms the industry. The firm's increased indebtedness in 2002 apparently caused a deterioration in its ability to pay debt adequately. However, Bartlett has evidently improved its income in 2003 so that it is able to meet its interest and fixed-payment obligations at a level consistent with the average in the industry. In summary, it appears that although 2002 was an off year, the company's ability to pay debts in 2003 compensates for its increased degree of indebtedness.

Profitability

Bartlett's profitability relative to sales in 2003 was better than the average company in the industry, although it did not match the firm's 2001 performance. Although the *gross* profit margin was better in 2002 and 2003 than in 2001, higher levels of operating and interest expenses in 2002 and 2003 appear to have caused the 2003 *net* profit margin to fall below that of 2001. However, Bartlett Company's 2003 net profit margin is quite favorable when compared to the industry average.

The firm's earnings per share, return on total assets, and return on common equity behaved much as its net profit margin did over the 2001–2003 period. Bartlett appears to have experienced either a sizable drop in sales between 2001 and 2002 or a rapid expansion in assets during that period. The exceptionally high 2003 level of return on common equity suggests that the firm is performing quite well. The firm's above-average returns—net profit margin, EPS, ROA, and ROE—may be attributable to the fact that it is more risky than average. A look at market ratios is helpful in assessing risk.

Market

Investors have greater confidence in the firm in 2003 than in the prior two years, as reflected in the price/earnings (P/E) ratio of 11.1. However, this ratio is below the industry average. The P/E ratio suggests that the firm's risk has declined but remains above that of the average firm in its industry. The firm's market/book (M/B) ratio has increased over the 2001–2003 period, and in 2003 it exceeds the industry average. This implies that investors are optimistic about the firm's future performance. The P/E and M/B ratios reflect the firm's increased profitability over the 2001–2003 period: Investors expect to earn high future returns as compensation for the firm's above-average risk.

In summary, the firm appears to be growing and has recently undergone an expansion in assets, financed primarily through the use of debt. The 2002–2003 period seems to reflect a phase of adjustment and recovery from the rapid growth in assets. Bartlett's sales, profits, and other performance factors seem to be growing with the increase in the size of the operation. In addition, the market response to these accomplishments appears to have been positive. In short, the firm seems to have done well in 2003.

DuPont System of Analysis

DuPont system of analysis
System used to dissect the firm's financial statements and to assess its financial condition.

The **DuPont system of analysis** is used to dissect the firm's financial statements and to assess its financial condition. It merges the income statement and balance sheet into two summary measures of profitability: return on total assets (ROA) and return on common equity (ROE). Figure 2.2 depicts the basic DuPont system with Bartlett Company's 2003 monetary and ratio values. The upper portion of the chart summarizes the income statement activities; the lower portion summarizes the balance sheet activities.

DuPont formula
Multiplies the firm's *net profit margin* by its *total asset turnover* to calculate the firm's *return on total assets (ROA).*

The DuPont system first brings together the *net profit margin,* which measures the firm's profitability on sales, with its *total asset turnover,* which indicates how efficiently the firm has used its assets to generate sales. In the **DuPont formula,** the product of these two ratios results in the *return on total assets (ROA)*:

$$\text{ROA} = \text{Net profit margin} \times \text{Total asset turnover}$$

Substituting the appropriate formulas into the equation and simplifying results in the formula given earlier,

$$\text{ROA} = \frac{\text{Earnings available for common stockholders}}{\text{Sales}} \times \frac{\text{Sales}}{\text{Total assets}} = \frac{\text{Earnings available for common stockholders}}{\text{Total assets}}$$

When the 2003 values of the net profit margin and total asset turnover for Bartlett Company, calculated earlier, are substituted into the DuPont formula, the result is

$$\text{ROA} = 7.2\% \times 0.85 = 6.1\%$$

This value is the same as that calculated directly in an earlier section (page 59). The DuPont formula enables the firm to break down its return into profit-on-sales and efficiency-of-asset-use components. Typically, a firm with a low net profit margin has a high total asset turnover, which results in a reasonably good return on total assets. Often, the opposite situation exists.

modified DuPont formula
Relates the firm's *return on total assets (ROA)* to its *return on common equity (ROE)* using the *financial leverage multiplier (FLM).*

The second step in the DuPont system employs the **modified DuPont formula.** This formula relates the firm's *return on total assets (ROA)* to its *return on common equity (ROE)*. The latter is calculated by multiplying the return on total

FIGURE 2.2 **DuPont System of Analysis**
The DuPont system of analysis with application to Bartlett Company (2003)

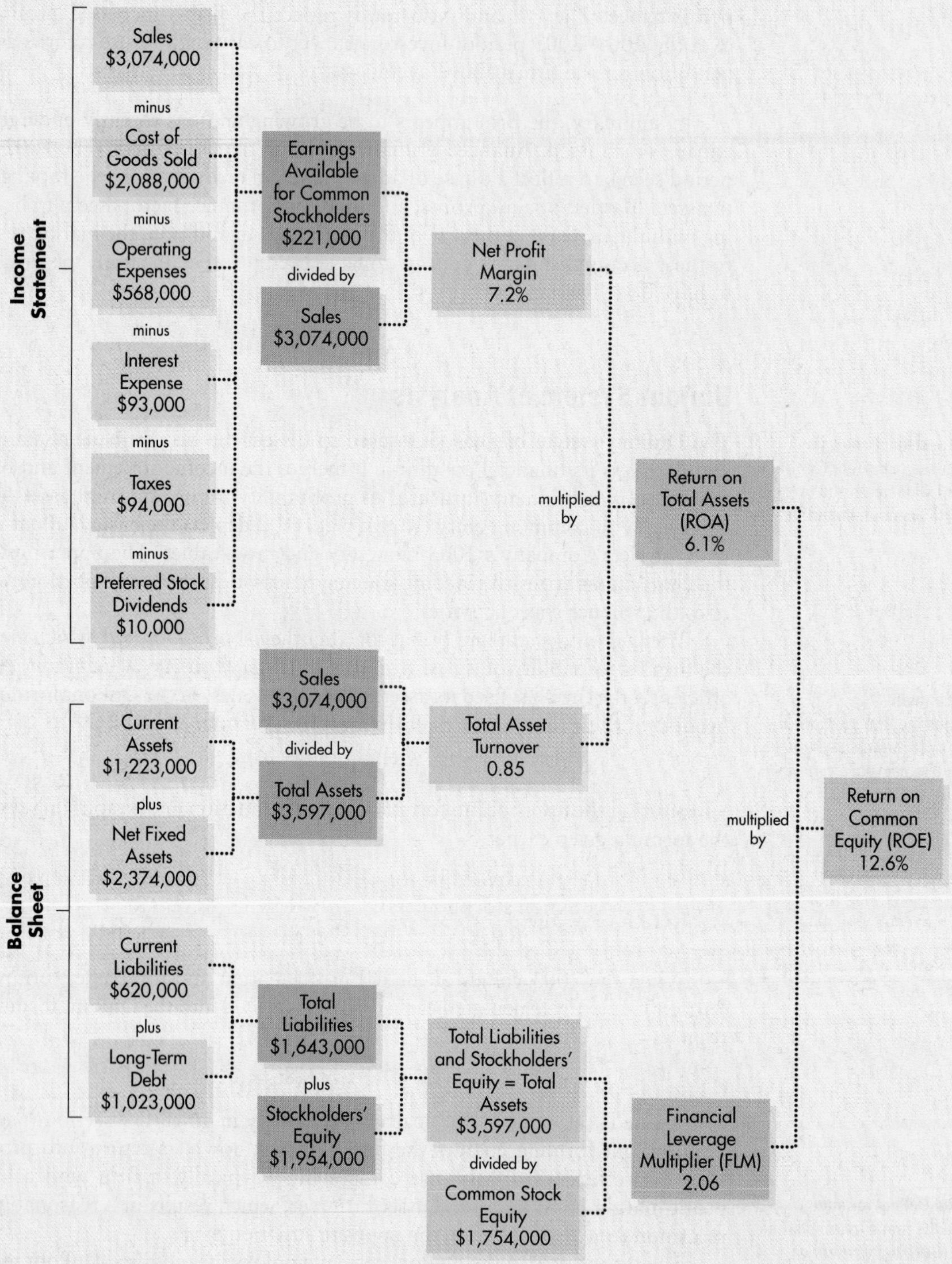

financial leverage multiplier (FLM)
The ratio of the firm's total assets to its common stock equity.

assets (ROA) by the **financial leverage multiplier (FLM)**, which is the ratio of total assets to common stock equity:

$$\text{ROE} = \text{ROA} \times \text{FLM}$$

Substituting the appropriate formulas into the equation and simplifying results in the formula given earlier,

$$\text{ROE} = \frac{\text{Earnings available for common stockholders}}{\text{Total assets}} \times \frac{\text{Total assets}}{\text{Common stock equity}} = \frac{\text{Earnings available for common stockholders}}{\text{Common stock equity}}$$

Use of the financial leverage multiplier (FLM) to convert the ROA into the ROE reflects the impact of financial leverage on owners' return. Substituting the values for Bartlett Company's ROA of 6.1 percent, calculated earlier, and Bartlett's FLM of 2.06 ($3,597,000 total assets ÷ $1,754,000 common stock equity) into the modified DuPont formula yields

$$\text{ROE} = 6.1\% \times 2.06 = 12.6\%$$

The 12.6 percent ROE calculated by using the modified DuPont formula is the same as that calculated directly (page 59).

The advantage of the DuPont system is that it allows the firm to break its return on equity into a profit-on-sales component (net profit margin), an efficiency-of-asset-use component (total asset turnover), and a use-of-financial-leverage component (financial leverage multiplier). The total return to owners therefore can be analyzed in these important dimensions.

The use of the DuPont system of analysis as a diagnostic tool is best explained using Figure 2.2. Beginning with the rightmost value—the ROE—the financial analyst moves to the left, dissecting and analyzing the inputs to the formula in order to isolate the probable cause of the resulting above-average (or below-average) value. For the sake of discussion, let's assume that Bartlett's ROE of 12.6 percent is actually below the industry average. Moving to the left, we would examine the inputs to the ROE—the ROA and the FLM—relative to the industry averages. Let's assume that the FLM is in line with the industry average, but the ROA is below the industry average. Moving farther to the left, we examine the two inputs to the ROA—the net profit margin and total asset turnover. Assume that the net profit margin is in line with the industry average, but the total asset turnover is below the industry average. Moving still farther to the left, we find that whereas the firm's sales are consistent with the industry value, Bartlett's total assets have grown significantly during the past year. Looking farther to the left, we would review the firm's activity ratios for current assets. Let's say that whereas the firm's inventory turnover is in line with the industry average, its average collection period is well above the industry average.

Clearly, we can trace the possible problem back to its cause: Bartlett's low ROE is primarily the consequence of slow collections of accounts receivable, which resulted in high levels of receivables and therefore high levels of total assets. The high total assets slowed Bartlett's total asset turnover, driving down its ROA, which then drove down its ROE. By using the DuPont system of analysis to dissect Bartlett's overall returns as measured by its ROE, we found that slow collections of receivables caused the below-industry-average ROE. Clearly, the firm needs to manage its credit operations better.

Review Questions

2–15 Financial ratio analysis is often divided into five areas: *liquidity, activity, debt, profitability,* and *market* ratios. Differentiate each of these areas of analysis from the others. Which is of the greatest concern to creditors?

2–16 Describe how you would use a large number of ratios to perform a complete ratio analysis of the firm.

2–17 What three areas of analysis are combined in the *modified DuPont formula?* Explain how the *DuPont system of analysis* is used to dissect the firm's results and isolate their causes.

SUMMARY

FOCUS ON VALUE

Financial managers review and analyze the firm's financial statements periodically, both to uncover developing problems and to assess the firm's progress toward achieving its goals. These actions are aimed at **preserving and creating value for the firm's owners.** Financial ratios enable financial managers to monitor the pulse of the firm and its progress toward its strategic goals. Although financial statements and financial ratios rely on accrual concepts, they can provide useful insights into important aspects of risk and return (cash flow) that affect share price, which management is attempting to maximize.

REVIEW OF LEARNING GOALS

LG1 **Review the contents of the stockholders' report and the procedures for consolidating international financial statements.** The annual stockholders' report, which publicly owned corporations are required to provide to stockholders, documents the firm's financial activities during the past year. It includes the letter to stockholders and various subjective and factual information, as well as four key financial statements: the income statement, the balance sheet, the statement of retained earnings, and the statement of cash flows. Notes describing the technical aspects of the financial statements follow them. Financial statements of companies that have operations whose cash flows are denominated in one or more foreign currencies must be translated into dollars in accordance with *FASB Standard No. 52.*

LG2 **Understand who uses financial ratios, and how.** Ratio analysis enables present and prospective stockholders and lenders and the firm's management to evaluate the firm's financial performance. It can be performed on a cross-sectional or a time-series basis. Benchmarking is a popular type of cross-sectional analysis. Key cautions for applying financial ratios are: (1) Ratios with large deviations from the norm only indicate symptoms of a problem. (2) A single ratio does not generally provide sufficient information. (3) The ratios being compared should be calculated using financial statements dated at the same point in time during the year. (4) Audited financial statements should be used. (5) Data should be checked for consistency of accounting treatment. (6) Inflation and different asset ages can distort ratio comparisons.

LG3 **Use ratios to analyze a firm's liquidity and activity.** Liquidity, or ability of the firm to pay its bills as they come due, can be measured by the current ratio and the quick (acid-test) ratio. Activity ratios measure the speed with which accounts are converted into sales or cash—inflows or outflows. The activity of inventory can be measured by its turnover, that of accounts receivable by the average collection period, and that of accounts payable by the average payment period. Total asset turnover measures the efficiency with which the firm uses its assets to generate sales. Formulas for these liquidity and activity ratios are summarized in Table 2.8.

LG4 **Discuss the relationship between debt and financial leverage and the ratios used to analyze a firm's debt.** The more debt a firm uses, the greater its financial leverage, which magnifies both risk and return. Financial debt ratios measure both the degree of indebtedness and the ability to service debts. A common measure of indebtedness is the debt ratio. The ability to pay fixed charges can be measured by times interest earned and fixed-payment coverage ratios. Formulas for these debt ratios are summarized in Table 2.8.

LG5 **Use ratios to analyze a firm's profitability and its market value.** The common-size income statement, which shows all items as a percentage of sales, can be used to determine gross profit margin, operating profit margin, and net profit margin. Other measures of profitability include earnings per share, return on total assets, and return on common equity. Market ratios include the price/earnings ratio and the market/book ratio. Formulas for these profitability and market ratios are summarized in Table 2.8.

LG6 **Use a summary of financial ratios and the DuPont system of analysis to perform a complete ratio analysis.** A summary of all ratios—liquidity, activity, debt, profitability, and market—as shown in Table 2.8 can be used to perform a complete ratio analysis using cross-sectional and time-series analysis approaches. The DuPont system of analysis, summarized in Figure 2.2, is a diagnostic tool used to find the key areas responsible for the firm's financial performance. It enables the firm to break the return on common equity into three components: profit on sales, efficiency of asset use, and use of leverage. The DuPont system of analysis makes it possible to assess all aspects of the firm's activities in order to isolate key areas of responsibility.

SELF-TEST PROBLEMS (Solutions in Appendix B)

LG3 LG4 LG5 ST 2–1 **Ratio formulas and interpretations** Without referring to the text, indicate for each of the following ratios the formula for calculating it and the kinds of problems, if any, the firm is likely to have if that ratio is too high relative to the industry average. What if the ratio is too low relative to the industry? Create a table similar to the one that follows and fill in the empty blocks.

Ratio	Too high	Too low
Current ratio =		
Inventory turnover =		
Times interest earned =	X	
Gross profit margin =		
Return on total assets =	X	

LG3 LG4 LG5 ST 2–2 **Balance sheet completion using ratios** Complete the 2003 balance sheet for O'Keefe Industries using the information that follows it.

O'Keefe Industries
Balance Sheet
December 31, 2003

Assets		Liabilities and Stockholders' Equity	
Cash	$30,000	Accounts payable	$120,000
Marketable securities	25,000	Notes payable	______
Accounts receivable	______	Accruals	20,000
Inventories	______	Total current liabilities	______
Total current assets	______	Long-term debt	______
Net fixed assets	______	Stockholders' equity	$600,000
Total assets	$	Total liabilities and stockholders' equity	$

The following financial data for 2003 are also available:

(1) Sales totaled $1,800,000.
(2) The gross profit margin was 25%.
(3) Inventory turnover was 6.0.
(4) There are 360 days in the year.
(5) The average collection period was 40 days.
(6) The current ratio was 1.60.
(7) The total asset turnover ratio was 1.20.
(8) The debt ratio was 60%.

PROBLEMS

LG1 **2–1 Reviewing basic financial statements** The income statement for the year ended December 31, 2003, the balance sheets for December 31, 2003 and 2002, and the statement of retained earnings for the year ended December 31, 2003, for Technica, Inc., are given here. Briefly discuss the form and informational content of each of these statements.

Technica, Inc.
Income Statement
for the Year Ended December 31, 2003

Sales revenue		$600,000
Less: Cost of goods sold		460,000
Gross profits		$140,000
Less: Operating expenses		
General and administrative expense	$30,000	
Depreciation expense	30,000	
Total operating expense		60,000
Operating profits		$ 80,000
Less: Interest expense		10,000
Net profits before taxes		$ 70,000
Less: Taxes		27,100
Earnings available for common stockholders		$ 42,900
Earnings per share (EPS)		$2.15

Technica, Inc.
Balance Sheets

Assets	December 31 2003	December 31 2002
Cash	$ 15,000	$ 16,000
Marketable securities	7,200	8,000
Accounts receivable	34,100	42,200
Inventories	82,000	50,000
Total current assets	$138,300	$116,200
Land and buildings	$150,000	$150,000
Machinery and equipment	200,000	190,000
Furniture and fixtures	54,000	50,000
Other	11,000	10,000
Total gross fixed assets	$415,000	$400,000
Less: Accumulated depreciation	145,000	115,000
Net fixed assets	$270,000	$285,000
Total assets	$408,300	$401,200
Liabilities and Stockholders' Equity		
Accounts payable	$ 57,000	$ 49,000
Notes payable	13,000	16,000
Accruals	5,000	6,000
Total current liabilities	$ 75,000	$ 71,000
Long-term debt	$150,000	$160,000
Stockholders' equity		
Common stock equity (shares outstanding: 19,500 in 2003 and 20,000 in 2002)	$110,200	$120,000
Retained earnings	73,100	50,200
Total stockholders' equity	$183,300	$170,200
Total liabilities and stockholders' equity	$408,300	$401,200

Technica, Inc.
Statement of Retained Earnings
for the Year Ended December 31, 2003

Retained earnings balance (January 1, 2003)	$50,200
Plus: Net profits after taxes (for 2003)	42,900
Less: Cash dividends (paid during 2003)	(20,000)
Retained earnings balance (December 31, 2003)	$73,100

LG1 **2–2 Financial statement account identification** Mark each of the accounts listed in the following table as follows:

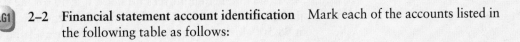

a. In column (1), indicate in which statement—income statement (IS) or balance sheet (BS)—the account belongs.

b. In column (2), indicate whether the account is a current asset (CA), current liability (CL), expense (E), fixed asset (FA), long-term debt (LTD), revenue (R), or stockholders' equity (SE).

Account name	(1) Statement	(2) Type of account
Accounts payable	______	______
Accounts receivable	______	______
Accruals	______	______
Accumulated depreciation	______	______
Administrative expense	______	______
Buildings	______	______
Cash	______	______
Common stock (at par)	______	______
Cost of goods sold	______	______
Depreciation	______	______
Equipment	______	______
General expense	______	______
Interest expense	______	______
Inventories	______	______
Land	______	______
Long-term debts	______	______
Machinery	______	______
Marketable securities	______	______
Notes payable	______	______
Operating expense	______	______
Paid-in capital in excess of par	______	______
Preferred stock	______	______
Preferred stock dividends	______	______
Retained earnings	______	______
Sales revenue	______	______
Selling expense	______	______
Taxes	______	______
Vehicles	______	______

LG1 2–3 **Income statement preparation** On December 31, 2003, Cathy Chen, a self-employed certified public accountant (CPA), completed her first full year in business. During the year, she billed $180,000 for her accounting services. She had two employees: a bookkeeper and a clerical assistant. In addition to her *monthly* salary of $4,000, Ms. Chen paid *annual* salaries of $24,000 and $18,000 to the bookkeeper and the clerical assistant, respectively. Employment taxes and benefit costs for Ms. Chen and her employees totaled $17,300 for the year. Expenses for office supplies, including postage, totaled $5,200 for the year. In addition, Ms. Chen spent $8,500 during the year on tax-deductible travel and entertainment associated with client visits and new business development. Lease payments for the office space rented (a tax-deductible expense) were $1,350 *per month*. Depreciation expense on the office furniture and fixtures was $7,800 for the year. During the year, Ms. Chen paid interest of $7,500 on the $60,000 borrowed to start the business. She paid an average tax rate of 30 percent during 2003.

a. Prepare an income statement for Cathy Chen, CPA, for the year ended December 31, 2003.

b. Evaluate her 2003 financial performance.

LG1 2–4 **Calculation of EPS and retained earnings** Philagem, Inc., ended 2003 with net profit *before* taxes of $218,000. The company is subject to a 40% tax rate and must pay $32,000 in preferred stock dividends before distributing any earnings on the 85,000 shares of common stock currently outstanding.

a. Calculate Philagem's 2003 earnings per share (EPS).

b. If the firm paid common stock dividends of $0.80 per share, how many dollars would go to retained earnings?

LG1 2–5 **Balance sheet preparation** Use the *appropriate items* from the following list to prepare in good form Owen Davis Company's balance sheet at December 31, 2003.

Item	Value ($000) at December 31, 2003
Accounts payable	$ 220
Accounts receivable	450
Accruals	55
Accumulated depreciation	265
Buildings	225
Cash	215
Common stock (at par)	90
Cost of goods sold	2,500
Depreciation expense	45
Equipment	140
Furniture and fixtures	170
General expense	320
Inventories	375
Land	100
Long-term debts	420
Machinery	420
Marketable securities	75
Notes payable	475
Paid-in capital in excess of par	360
Preferred stock	100
Retained earnings	210
Sales revenue	3,600
Vehicles	25

LG1 **2–6 Initial sale price of common stock** Beck Corporation has one issue of preferred stock and one issue of common stock outstanding. Given Beck's stockholders' equity account that follows, determine the original price per share at which the firm sold its single issue of common stock.

Stockholders' Equity ($000)	
Preferred stock	$ 125
Common stock ($0.75 par, 300,000 shares outstanding)	225
Paid-in capital in excess of par on common stock	2,625
Retained earnings	900
Total stockholders' equity	$3,875

LG1 **2–7 Statement of retained earnings** Hayes Enterprises began 2003 with a retained earnings balance of $928,000. During 2003, the firm earned $377,000 after taxes. From this amount, preferred stockholders were paid $47,000 in dividends. At year-end 2003, the firm's retained earnings totaled $1,048,000. The firm had 140,000 shares of common stock outstanding during 2003.

a. Prepare a statement of retained earnings for the year ended December 31, 2003, for Hayes Enterprises. (*Note:* Be sure to calculate and include the amount of cash dividends paid in 2003.)

b. Calculate the firm's 2003 earnings per share (EPS).

c. How large a per-share cash dividend did the firm pay on common stock during 2003?

LG2 LG3 LG4 LG5 **2–8 Ratio comparisons** Robert Arias recently inherited a stock portfolio from his uncle. Wishing to learn more about the companies that he is now invested in, Robert performs a ratio analysis on each one and decides to compare them to each other. Some of his ratios are listed below.

Ratio	Island Electric Utility	Burger Heaven	Fink Software	Roland Motors
Current ratio	1.10	1.3	6.8	4.5
Quick ratio	0.90	0.82	5.2	3.7
Debt ratio	0.68	0.46	0	0.35
Net profit margin	6.2%	14.3%	28.5%	8.4%

Assuming that his uncle was a wise investor who assembled the portfolio with care, Robert finds the wide differences in these ratios confusing. Help him out.

a. What problems might Robert encounter in comparing these companies to one another on the basis of their ratios?

b. Why might the current and quick ratios for the electric utility and the fast-food stock be so much lower than the same ratios for the other companies?

c. Why might it be all right for the electric utility to carry a large amount of debt, but not the software company?
d. Why wouldn't investors invest all of their money in software companies instead of in less profitable companies? (Focus on risk and return.)

LG3 **2–9 Liquidity management** Bauman Company's total current assets, total current liabilities, and inventory for each of the past 4 years follow:

Item	2000	2001	2002	2003
Total current assets	$16,950	$21,900	$22,500	$27,000
Total current liabilities	9,000	12,600	12,600	17,400
Inventory	6,000	6,900	6,900	7,200

a. Calculate the firm's current and quick ratios for each year. Compare the resulting time series for these measures of liquidity.
b. Comment on the firm's liquidity over the 2000–2003 period.
c. If you were told that Bauman Company's inventory turnover for each year in the 2000–2003 period and the industry averages were as follows, would this information support or conflict with your evaluation in part **b**? Why?

Inventory turnover	2000	2001	2002	2003
Bauman Company	6.3	6.8	7.0	6.4
Industry average	10.6	11.2	10.8	11.0

LG3 **2–10 Inventory management** Wilkins Manufacturing has sales of $4 million and a gross profit margin of 40%. Its *end-of-quarter inventories* are

Quarter	Inventory
1	$ 400,000
2	800,000
3	1,200,000
4	200,000

a. Find the average quarterly inventory and use it to calculate the firm's inventory turnover and the average age of inventory.
b. Assuming that the company is in an industry with an average inventory turnover of 2.0, how would you evaluate the activity of Wilkins' inventory?

LG3 **2–11 Accounts receivable management** An evaluation of the books of Blair Supply, which follows, gives the end-of-year accounts receivable balance, which is believed to consist of amounts originating in the months indicated. The company had annual sales of $2.4 million. The firm extends 30-day credit terms.

Month of origin	Amounts receivable
July	$ 3,875
August	2,000
September	34,025
October	15,100
November	52,000
December	193,000
Year-end accounts receivable	$300,000

a. Use the year-end total to evaluate the firm's collection system.
b. If 70% of the firm's sales occur between July and December, would this affect the validity of your conclusion in part **a**? Explain.

LG4 **2–12 Debt analysis** Springfield Bank is evaluating Creek Enterprises, which has requested a $4,000,000 loan, to assess the firm's financial leverage and financial risk. On the basis of the debt ratios for Creek, along with the industry averages and Creek's recent financial statements (which follow), evaluate and recommend appropriate action on the loan request.

Creek Enterprises
Balance Sheet
December 31, 2003

Assets		Liabilities and Stockholders' Equity	
Current assets		Current liabilities	
Cash	$ 1,000,000	Accounts payable	$ 8,000,000
Marketable securities	3,000,000	Notes payable	8,000,000
Accounts receivable	12,000,000	Accruals	500,000
Inventories	7,500,000	Total current liabilities	$16,500,000
Total current assets	$23,500,000	Long-term debt (includes financial leases)[b]	$20,000,000
Gross fixed assets (at cost)[a]		Stockholders' equity	
Land and buildings	$11,000,000	Preferred stock (25,000 shares,	
Machinery and equipment	20,500,000	$4 dividend)	$ 2,500,000
Furniture and fixtures	8,000,000	Common stock (1 million shares at $5 par)	5,000,000
Gross fixed assets	$39,500,000	Paid-in capital in excess of par value	4,000,000
Less: Accumulated depreciation	13,000,000	Retained earnings	2,000,000
Net fixed assets	$26,500,000	Total stockholders' equity	$13,500,000
Total assets	$50,000,000	Total liabilities and stockholders' equity	$50,000,000

[a]The firm has a 4-year financial lease requiring annual beginning-of-year payments of $200,000. Three years of the lease have yet to run.
[b]Required annual principal payments are $800,000.

Creek Enterprises Income Statement for the Year Ended December 31, 2003		
Sales revenue		$30,000,000
Less: Cost of goods sold		21,000,000
Gross profits		$ 9,000,000
Less: Operating expenses		
Selling expense	$3,000,000	
General and administrative expenses	1,800,000	
Lease expense	200,000	
Depreciation expense	1,000,000	
Total operating expense		6,000,000
Operating profits		$ 3,000,000
Less: Interest expense		1,000,000
Net profits before taxes		$ 2,000,000
Less: Taxes (rate = 40%)		800,000
Net profits after taxes		$ 1,200,000
Less: Preferred stock dividends		100,000
Earnings available for common stockholders		$ 1,100,000

Industry averages	
Debt ratio	0.51
Times interest earned ratio	7.30
Fixed-payment coverage ratio	1.85

LG5 **2–13 Common-size statement analysis** A common-size income statement for Creek Enterprises' 2002 operations follows. Using the firm's 2003 income statement presented in problem 2–12, develop the 2003 common-size income statement and compare it to the 2002 statement. Which areas require further analysis and investigation?

Creek Enterprises Common-size Income Statement for the Year Ended December 31, 2002		
Sales revenue ($35,000,000)		100.0%
Less: Cost of goods sold		65.9
Gross profits		34.1%
Less: Operating expenses		
Selling expense	12.7%	
General and administrative expenses	6.3	
Lease expense	0.6	
Depreciation expense	3.6	
Total operating expense		23.2
Operating profits		10.9%
Less: Interest expense		1.5
Net profits before taxes		9.4%
Less: Taxes (rate = 40%)		3.8
Net profits after taxes		5.6%
Less: Preferred stock dividends		0.1
Earnings available for common stockholders		5.5%

LG6 **2–14 Dupont system of analysis** Use the following ratio information for Johnson International and the industry averages for Johnson's line of business to:

a. Construct the DuPont system of analysis for both Johnson and the industry.
b. Evaluate Johnson (and the industry) over the 3-year period.
c. Indicate in which areas Johnson requires further analysis. Why?

	2001	2002	2003
Johnson			
Financial leverage multiplier	1.75	1.75	1.85
Net profit margin	0.059	0.058	0.049
Total asset turnover	2.11	2.18	2.34
Industry Averages			
Financial leverage multiplier	1.67	1.69	1.64
Net profit margin	0.054	0.047	0.041
Total asset turnover	2.05	2.13	2.15

LG6 **2–15 Cross-sectional ratio analysis** Use the following financial statements for Fox Manufacturing Company for the year ended December 31, 2003, along with the industry average ratios also given in what follows, to:

a. Prepare and interpret a complete ratio analysis of the firm's 2003 operations.
b. Summarize your findings and make recommendations.

Fox Manufacturing Company
Income Statement
for the Year Ended December 31, 2003

Sales revenue		$600,000
Less: Cost of goods sold		460,000
Gross profits		$140,000
Less: Operating expenses		
General and administrative expenses	$30,000	
Depreciation expense	30,000	
Total operating expense		60,000
Operating profits		$ 80,000
Less: Interest expense		10,000
Net profits before taxes		$ 70,000
Less: Taxes		27,100
Net profits after taxes (earnings available for common stockholders)		$ 42,900
Earnings per share (EPS)		$2.15

Fox Manufacturing Company Balance Sheet December 31, 2003	
Assets	
Cash	$ 15,000
Marketable securities	7,200
Accounts receivable	34,100
Inventories	82,000
Total current assets	$138,300
Net fixed assets	$270,000
Total assets	$408,300
Liabilities and Stockholders' Equity	
Accounts payable	$ 57,000
Notes payable	13,000
Accruals	5,000
Total current liabilities	$ 75,000
Long-term debt	$150,000
Stockholders' equity	
Common stock equity (20,000 shares outstanding)	$110,200
Retained earnings	73,100
Total stockholders' equity	$183,300
Total liabilities and stockholders' equity	$408,300

Ratio	Industry average, 2003
Current ratio	2.35
Quick ratio	0.87
Inventory turnover[a]	4.55
Average collection period[a]	35.3 days
Total asset turnover	1.09
Debt ratio	0.300
Times interest earned ratio	12.3
Gross profit margin	0.202
Operating profit margin	0.135
Net profit margin	0.091
Return on total assets (ROA)	0.099
Return on common equity (ROE)	0.167
Earnings per share (EPS)	$3.10

[a]Based on a 360-day year and on end-of-year figures.

LG6 **2–16 Financial statement analysis** The financial statements of Zach Industries for the year ended December 31, 2003, follow.

Zach Industries Income Statement for the Year Ended December 31, 2003	
Sales revenue	$160,000
Less: Cost of goods sold	106,000
Gross profits	$ 54,000
Less: Operating expenses	
Selling expense	$ 16,000
General and administrative expenses	10,000
Lease expense	1,000
Depreciation expense	10,000
Total operating expense	$ 37,000
Operating profits	$ 17,000
Less: Interest expense	6,100
Net profits before taxes	$ 10,900
Less: Taxes	4,360
Net profits after taxes	$ 6,540

Zach Industries Balance Sheet December 31, 2003	
Assets	
Cash	$ 500
Marketable securities	1,000
Accounts receivable	25,000
Inventories	45,500
Total current assets	$ 72,000
Land	$ 26,000
Buildings and equipment	90,000
Less: Accumulated depreciation	38,000
Net fixed assets	$ 78,000
Total assets	$150,000
Liabilities and Stockholders' Equity	
Accounts payable	$ 22,000
Notes payable	47,000
Total current liabilities	$ 69,000
Long-term debt	$ 22,950
Common stock[a]	$ 31,500
Retained earnings	$ 26,550
Total liabilities and stockholders' equity	$150,000

[a]The firm's 3,000 outstanding shares of common stock closed 2003 at a price of $25 per share.

a. Use the preceding financial statements to complete the following table. Assume that the industry averages given in the table are applicable for both 2002 and 2003.

Ratio	Industry average	Actual 2002	Actual 2003
Current ratio	1.80	1.84	____
Quick ratio	0.70	0.78	____
Inventory turnover[a]	2.50	2.59	____
Average collection period[a]	37 days	36 days	____
Debt ratio	65%	67%	____
Times interest earned ratio	3.8	4.0	____
Gross profit margin	38%	40%	____
Net profit margin	3.5%	3.6%	____
Return on total assets	4.0%	4.0%	____
Return on common equity	9.5%	8.0%	____
Market/book ratio	1.1	1.2	____

[a]Based on a 360-day year and on end-of-year figures.

b. Analyze Zach Industries' financial condition as it is related to (1) liquidity, (2) activity, (3) debt, (4) profitability, and (5) market. Summarize the company's overall financial condition.

LG6 **2–17 Integrative—Complete ratio analysis** Given the following financial statements, historical ratios, and industry averages, calculate Sterling Company's financial ratios for the most recent year. Analyze its overall financial situation from both a cross-sectional and a time-series viewpoint. Break your analysis into evaluations of the firm's liquidity, activity, debt, profitability, and market.

Sterling Company
Income Statement
for the Year Ended December 31, 2003

Sales revenue		$10,000,000
Less: Cost of goods sold		7,500,000
Gross profits		$ 2,500,000
Less: Operating expenses		
Selling expense	$300,000	
General and administrative expenses	650,000	
Lease expense	50,000	
Depreciation expense	200,000	
Total operating expense		1,200,000
Operating profits		$ 1,300,000
Less: Interest expense		200,000
Net profits before taxes		$ 1,100,000
Less: Taxes (rate = 40%)		440,000
Net profits after taxes		$ 660,000
Less: Preferred stock dividends		50,000
Earnings available for common stockholders		$ 610,000
Earnings per share (EPS)		$3.05

Sterling Company
Balance Sheet
December 31, 2003

Assets		
Current assets		
Cash		$ 200,000
Marketable securities		50,000
Accounts receivable		800,000
Inventories		950,000
Total current assets		$ 2,000,000
Gross fixed assets (at cost)[a]	$12,000,000	
Less: Accumulated depreciation	3,000,000	
Net fixed assets		$ 9,000,000
Other assets		$ 1,000,000
Total assets		$12,000,000

Liabilities and Stockholders' Equity	
Current liabilities	
Accounts payable[b]	$ 900,000
Notes payable	200,000
Accruals	100,000
Total current liabilities	$ 1,200,000
Long-term debt (includes financial leases)[c]	$ 3,000,000
Stockholders' equity	
Preferred stock (25,000 shares, $2 dividend)	$ 1,000,000
Common stock (200,000 shares at $3 par)[d]	600,000
Paid-in capital in excess of par value	5,200,000
Retained earnings	1,000,000
Total stockholders' equity	$ 7,800,000
Total liabilities and stockholders' equity	$12,000,000

[a]The firm has an 8-year financial lease requiring annual beginning-of-year payments of $50,000. Five years of the lease have yet to run.
[b]Annual credit purchases of $6,200,000 were made during the year.
[c]The annual principal payment on the long-term debt is $100,000.
[d]On December 31, 2003, the firm's common stock closed at $39.50 per share.

Historical and Industry Average Ratios for Sterling Company

Ratio	Actual 2001	Actual 2002	Industry average, 2003
Current ratio	1.40	1.55	1.85
Quick ratio	1.00	0.92	1.05
Inventory turnover	9.52	9.21	8.60
Average collection period	45.0 days	36.4 days	35.0 days
Average payment period	58.5 days	60.8 days	45.8 days
Total asset turnover	0.74	0.80	0.74
Debt ratio	0.20	0.20	0.30
Times interest earned ratio	8.2	7.3	8.0
Fixed-payment coverage ratio	4.5	4.2	4.2
Gross profit margin	0.30	0.27	0.25
Operating profit margin	0.12	0.12	0.10
Net profit margin	0.062	0.062	0.053
Return on total assets (ROA)	0.045	0.050	0.040
Return on common equity (ROE)	0.061	0.067	0.066
Earnings per share (EPS)	$1.75	$2.20	$1.50
Price/earnings (P/E) ratio	12.0	10.5	11.2
Market/book (M/B) ratio	1.20	1.05	1.10

CHAPTER 2 CASE

Assessing Martin Manufacturing's Current Financial Position

Terri Spiro, an experienced budget analyst at Martin Manufacturing Company, has been charged with assessing the firm's financial performance during 2003 and its financial position at year-end 2003. To complete this assignment, she gathered the firm's 2003 financial statements, which follow. In addition, Terri obtained the firm's ratio values for 2001 and 2002, along with the 2003 industry average ratios (also applicable to 2001 and 2002). These are presented in the table on page 84.

Martin Manufacturing Company
Balance Sheets

	December 31	
Assets	**2003**	**2002**
Current assets		
Cash	$ 25,000	$ 24,100
Accounts receivable	805,556	763,900
Inventories	700,625	763,445
Total current assets	$1,531,181	$1,551,445
Gross fixed assets (at cost)	$2,093,819	$1,691,707
Less: Accumulated depreciation	500,000	348,000
Net fixed assets	$1,593,819	$1,343,707
Total assets	$3,125,000	$2,895,152
Liabilities and Stockholders' Equity		
Current liabilities		
Accounts payable	$ 230,000	$ 400,500
Notes payable	311,000	370,000
Accruals	75,000	100,902
Total current liabilities	$ 616,000	$ 871,402
Long-term debt	$1,165,250	$ 700,000
Total liabilities	$1,781,250	$1,571,402
Stockholders' equity		
Preferred stock (2,500 shares, $1.20 dividend)	$ 50,000	$ 50,000
Common stock (100,000 shares at $4 par)[a]	400,000	400,000
Paid-in capital in excess of par value	593,750	593,750
Retained earnings	300,000	280,000
Total stockholders' equity	$1,343,750	$1,323,750
Total liabilities and stockholders' equity	$3,125,000	$2,895,152

[a]The firm's 100,000 outstanding shares of common stock closed 2003 at a price of $11.38 per share.

Martin Manufacturing Company Income Statement for the Year Ended December 31, 2003		
Sales revenue		$5,075,000
Less: Cost of goods sold		3,704,000
Gross profits		$1,371,000
Less: Operating expenses		
Selling expense	$650,000	
General and administrative expenses	416,000	
Depreciation expense	152,000	
Total operating expense		1,218,000
Operating profits		$ 153,000
Less: Interest expense		93,000
Net profits before taxes		$ 60,000
Less: Taxes (rate = 40%)		24,000
Net profits after taxes		$ 36,000
Less: Preferred stock dividends		3,000
Earnings available for common stockholders		$ 33,000
Earnings per share (EPS)		$0.33

Martin Manufacturing Company
Historical ratios

Ratio	Actual 2001	Actual 2002	Actual 2003	Industry average 2003
Current ratio	1.7	1.8	_____	1.5
Quick ratio	1.0	0.9	_____	1.2
Inventory turnover (times)	5.2	5.0	_____	10.2
Average collection period	50 days	55 days	_____	46 days
Total asset turnover (times)	1.5	1.5	_____	2.0
Debt ratio	45.8%	54.3%	_____	24.5%
Times interest earned ratio	2.2	1.9	_____	2.5
Gross profit margin	27.5%	28.0%	_____	26.0%
Net profit margin	1.1%	1.0%	_____	1.2%
Return on total assets (ROA)	1.7%	1.5%	_____	2.4%
Return on common equity (ROE)	3.1%	3.3%	_____	3.2%
Price/earnings (P/E) ratio	33.5	38.7	_____	43.4
Market/book (M/B) ratio	1.0	1.1	_____	1.2

Required

a. Calculate the firm's 2003 financial ratios, and then fill in the preceding table.
b. Analyze the firm's current financial position from both a cross-sectional and a time-series viewpoint. Break your analysis into evaluations of the firm's liquidity, activity, debt, profitability, and market.

c. Summarize the firm's overall financial position on the basis of your findings in part **b.**

WEB EXERCISE

Go to Web site *www.yahoo.com*. On the left side of the Yahoo! home page screen, click on the Finance category under **Business and Economy.** On the next screen click on **Y! Finance.**

Using this screen, click on **Symbol Lookup** and find the symbol for Southwest Airlines. Click on this symbol to find the latest trading data for Southwest Airlines.

1. What was the selling price for the last sale of Southwest's common stock? How much in dollars per share was the change?
2. What was the number of shares sold in this trade?

In the **More Info** box, you will see **Profile.** Click on it, and scroll down to **Statistics at a Glance.**

3. What was the amount of Southwest's sales? What was its after-tax income?
4. What were Southwest's earnings per share? What was its book value per share?
5. How many shares of stock does Southwest have outstanding?
6. What were the values of the following ratios for Southwest?
   a. Current ratio
   b. Operating profit margin
   c. Debt/equity ratio
   d. Return on equity
   e. What other information would you need to evaluate Southwest's financial performance on the basis of these ratios?
7. Find **More from Market Guide** and click on **Ratio Comparisons.** Using these data, summarize Southwest's performance.

Remember to check the book's Web site at

www.aw.com/gitman

for additional resources, including additional Web exercises.

Chapter

3

Cash Flow and Financial Planning

LEARNING GOALS

LG1 Understand the effect of depreciation on the firm's cash flows, the depreciable value of an asset, its depreciable life, and tax depreciation methods.

LG2 Discuss the firm's statement of cash flows, operating cash flow, and free cash flow.

LG3 Understand the financial planning process, including long-term (strategic) financial plans and short-term (operating) financial plans.

LG4 Discuss the cash-planning process and the preparation, evaluation, and use of the cash budget.

LG5 Explain the simplified procedures used to prepare and evaluate the pro forma income statement and the pro forma balance sheet.

LG6 Cite the weaknesses of the simplified approaches to pro forma financial statement preparation and the common uses of pro forma statements.

Across the Disciplines
Why This Chapter Matters To You

Accounting: You need to understand how depreciation is used for both tax and financial reporting purposes; how to develop the statement of cash flows; the primacy of cash flows, rather than accruals, in financial decision making; and how pro forma financial statements are used within the firm.

Information systems: You need to understand the data that must be kept to record depreciation for tax and financial reporting; the information needs for strategic and operating plans; and what data are needed as inputs for cash-planning and profit-planning modules.

Management: You need to understand the difference between strategic and operating plans, and the role of each; the importance of focusing on the firm's cash flows; and how use of pro forma statements can head off trouble for the firm.

Marketing: You need to understand the central role that marketing plays in formulating the firm's long-term, strategic plans, and the importance of the sales forecast as the key input for both cash planning and profit planning.

Operations: You need to understand how depreciation affects the value of the firm's plant assets; how the results of operations are captured in the statement of cash flows; that operations are monitored primarily in the firm's short-term financial plans; and the distinction between fixed and variable operating costs.

Cash flow is the primary focus of financial management. The goal is twofold: to meet the firm's financial obligations and to generate positive cash flow for its owners. Financial planning focuses on the firm's cash and profits—both of which are key elements of continued financial success, and even survival. This chapter outlines how the firm analyzes its cash flows, including the effect of depreciation, and the use of cash budgets and pro forma statements as tools of financial planning.

LG1 LG2

Analyzing the Firm's Cash Flow

Cash flow, the lifeblood of the firm, is the primary focus of the financial manager both in managing day-to-day finances and in planning and making strategic decisions aimed at creation of shareholder value. An important factor affecting a firm's cash flow is depreciation (and any other noncash charges). From an accounting perspective, a firm's cash flows can be summarized in the statement of cash flows, which was described in Chapter 2. From a strict financial perspective, firms often focus on both *operating cash flow,* which is used in managerial decision making, and *free cash flow,* which is closely watched by participants in the capital market. We begin our analysis of cash flow by considering the key aspects of depreciation, which is closely related to the firm's cash flow.

Depreciation

depreciation
The systematic charging of a portion of the costs of fixed assets against annual revenues over time.

modified accelerated cost recovery system (MACRS)
System used to determine the depreciation of assets for tax purposes.

Business firms are permitted for tax and financial reporting purposes to charge a portion of the costs of fixed assets systematically against annual revenues. This allocation of historical cost over time is called **depreciation.** For tax purposes, the depreciation of business assets is regulated by the Internal Revenue Code. Because the objectives of financial reporting are sometimes different from those of tax legislation, firms often use different depreciation methods for financial reporting than those required for tax purposes. Tax laws are used to accomplish economic goals such as providing incentives for business investment in certain types of assets, whereas the objectives of financial reporting are of course quite different. Keeping two different sets of records for these two different purposes is legal.

Depreciation for tax purposes is determined by using the **modified accelerated cost recovery system (MACRS)**; a variety of depreciation methods are available for financial reporting purposes. Before we discuss the methods of depreciating an asset, you must understand the depreciable value of an asset and the depreciable life of an asset.

Depreciable Value of an Asset

Under the basic MACRS procedures, the depreciable value of an asset (the amount to be depreciated) is its *full* cost, including outlays for installation.[1] No adjustment is required for expected salvage value.

1. Land values are *not* depreciable. Therefore, to determine the depreciable value of real estate, the value of the land is subtracted from the cost of real estate. In other words, only buildings and other improvements are depreciable.

EXAMPLE Baker Corporation acquired a new machine at a cost of $38,000, with installation costs of $2,000. Regardless of its expected salvage value, the depreciable value of the machine is $40,000: $38,000 cost + $2,000 installation cost.

Depreciable Life of an Asset

depreciable life
Time period over which an asset is depreciated.

recovery period
The appropriate depreciable life of a particular asset as determined by MACRS.

The time period over which an asset is depreciated—its **depreciable life**—can significantly affect the pattern of cash flows. The shorter the depreciable life, the more quickly the cash flow created by the depreciation write-off will be received. Given the financial manager's preference for faster receipt of cash flows, a shorter depreciable life is preferred to a longer one. However, the firm must abide by certain Internal Revenue Service (IRS) requirements for determining depreciable life. These MACRS standards, which apply to both new and used assets, require the taxpayer to use as an asset's depreciable life the appropriate MACRS **recovery period.**[2] There are six MACRS recovery periods—3, 5, 7, 10, 15, and 20 years—excluding real estate. It is customary to refer to the property classes, in accordance with their recovery periods, as 3-, 5-, 7-, 10-, 15-, and 20-year property. The first four property classes—those routinely used by business—are defined in Table 3.1.

Depreciation Methods

For *financial reporting purposes,* a variety of depreciation methods (straight-line, double-declining balance, and sum-of-the-years'-digits[3]) can be used. For *tax purposes,* using MACRS recovery periods, assets in the first four property classes are depreciated by the double-declining balance (200 percent) method, using the half-year convention and switching to straight-line when advantageous. Although tables of depreciation percentages are not provided by law, the *approximate percentages* (rounded to the nearest whole percent) written off each year for the first four property classes are shown in Table 3.2. Rather than using the percentages in the table, the firm can either use straight-line depreciation over the asset's recovery period with the half-year convention or use the alternative depreciation system. For purposes of this text, we will use the MACRS depreciation percentages, because they generally provide for the fastest write-off and therefore the best cash flow effects for the profitable firm.

TABLE 3.1 First Four Property Classes Under MACRS

Property class (recovery period)	Definition
3 years	Research equipment and certain special tools.
5 years	Computers, typewriters, copiers, duplicating equipment, cars, light-duty trucks, qualified technological equipment, and similar assets.
7 years	Office furniture, fixtures, most manufacturing equipment, railroad track, and single-purpose agricultural and horticultural structures.
10 years	Equipment used in petroleum refining or in the manufacture of tobacco products and certain food products.

2. An exception occurs in the case of assets depreciated under the *alternative depreciation system.* For convenience, in this text we ignore the depreciation of assets under this system.

3. For a review of these depreciation methods as well as other aspects of financial reporting, see any recently published financial accounting text.

TABLE 3.2 Rounded Depreciation Percentages by Recovery Year Using MACRS for First Four Property Classes

Recovery year	Percentage by recovery year[a]			
	3 years	5 years	7 years	10 years
1	33%	20%	14%	10%
2	45	32	25	18
3	15	19	18	14
4	7	12	12	12
5		12	9	9
6		5	9	8
7			9	7
8			4	6
9				6
10				6
11				4
Totals	100%	100%	100%	100%

[a]These percentages have been rounded to the nearest whole percent to simplify calculations while retaining realism. To calculate the *actual* depreciation for tax purposes, be sure to apply the actual unrounded percentages or directly apply double-declining balance (200%) depreciation using the half-year convention.

Because MACRS requires use of the half-year convention, assets are assumed to be acquired in the middle of the year, and therefore only one-half of the first year's depreciation is recovered in the first year. As a result, the final half-year of depreciation is recovered in the year immediately following the asset's stated recovery period. In Table 3.2, the depreciation percentages for an n-year class asset are given for $n + 1$ years. For example, a 5-year asset is depreciated over 6 recovery years. The application of the tax depreciation percentages given in Table 3.2 can be demonstrated by a simple example.

EXAMPLE Baker Corporation acquired, for an installed cost of $40,000, a machine having a recovery period of 5 years. Using the applicable percentages from Table 3.2, Baker calculates the depreciation in each year as follows:

Year	Cost (1)	Percentages (from Table 3.2) (2)	Depreciation [(1) × (2)] (3)
1	$40,000	20%	$ 8,000
2	40,000	32	12,800
3	40,000	19	7,600
4	40,000	12	4,800
5	40,000	12	4,800
6	40,000	5	2,000
Totals		100%	$40,000

Column 3 shows that the full cost of the asset is written off over 6 recovery years.

Because financial managers focus primarily on cash flows, *only tax depreciation methods will be utilized throughout this textbook.*

Developing the Statement of Cash Flows

The *statement of cash flows,* introduced in Chapter 2, summarizes the firm's cash flow over a given period of time. Before discussing the statement and its interpretation, we will review the cash flow through the firm and the classification of inflows and outflows of cash.

The Firm's Cash Flows

operating flows
Cash flows directly related to sale and production of the firm's products and services.

investment flows
Cash flows associated with purchase and sale of both fixed assets and business interests.

financing flows
Cash flows that result from debt and equity financing transactions; includes incurrence and repayment of debt, cash inflow from the sale of stock, and cash outflows to pay cash dividends or repurchase stock.

Figure 3.1 illustrates the firm's cash flows. Note that marketable securities are considered the same as cash because of their highly liquid nature. Both cash and marketable securities represent a reservoir of liquidity that is *increased by cash inflows* and *decreased by cash outflows.* Also note that the firm's cash flows can be divided into (1) operating flows, (2) investment flows, and (3) financing flows. The **operating flows** are cash inflows and outflows directly related to sale and production of the firm's products and services. **Investment flows** are cash flows associated with purchase and sale of both fixed assets and business interests. Clearly, purchase transactions would result in cash outflows, whereas sales transactions would generate cash inflows. The **financing flows** result from debt and equity financing transactions. Incurring (or repaying) either short-term or long-term debt would result in a corresponding cash inflow (or outflow). Similarly, the sale of stock would result in a cash inflow; the payment of cash dividends or repurchase of stock would result in a financing outflow. In combination, the firm's operating, investment, and financing cash flows during a given period affect the firm's cash and marketable securities balances.

Classifying Inflows and Outflows of Cash

The statement of cash flows in effect summarizes the inflows and outflows of cash during a given period. Table 3.3 (on page 92) classifies the basic inflows (sources) and outflows (uses) of cash. For example, if a firm's accounts payable increased by $1,000 during the year, the change would be an *inflow of cash.* If the firm's inventory increased by $2,500, the change would be an *outflow of cash.*

A few additional points can be made with respect to the classification scheme in Table 3.3:

1. A *decrease* in an asset, such as the firm's cash balance, is an *inflow of cash,* because cash that has been tied up in the asset is released and can be used for some other purpose, such as repaying a loan. On the other hand, an *increase* in the firm's cash balance is an *outflow of cash,* because additional cash is being tied up in the firm's cash balance.
2. Depreciation (like amortization and depletion) is a **noncash charge**—an expense that is deducted on the income statement but does not involve the actual outlay of cash during the period. Because it shields the firm from taxes by lowering taxable income, the noncash charge is considered a cash inflow. From a strict accounting perspective, adding depreciation back to the firm's net profits after taxes gives cash flow from operations:

noncash charge
An expense deducted on the income statement but does not involve the actual outlay of cash during the period; includes depreciation, amortization, and depletion.

$$\text{Cash flow from operations} = \text{Net profits after taxes} + \text{Depreciation and other noncash charges} \quad (3.1)$$

FIGURE 3.1 **Cash Flows**
The firm's cash flows

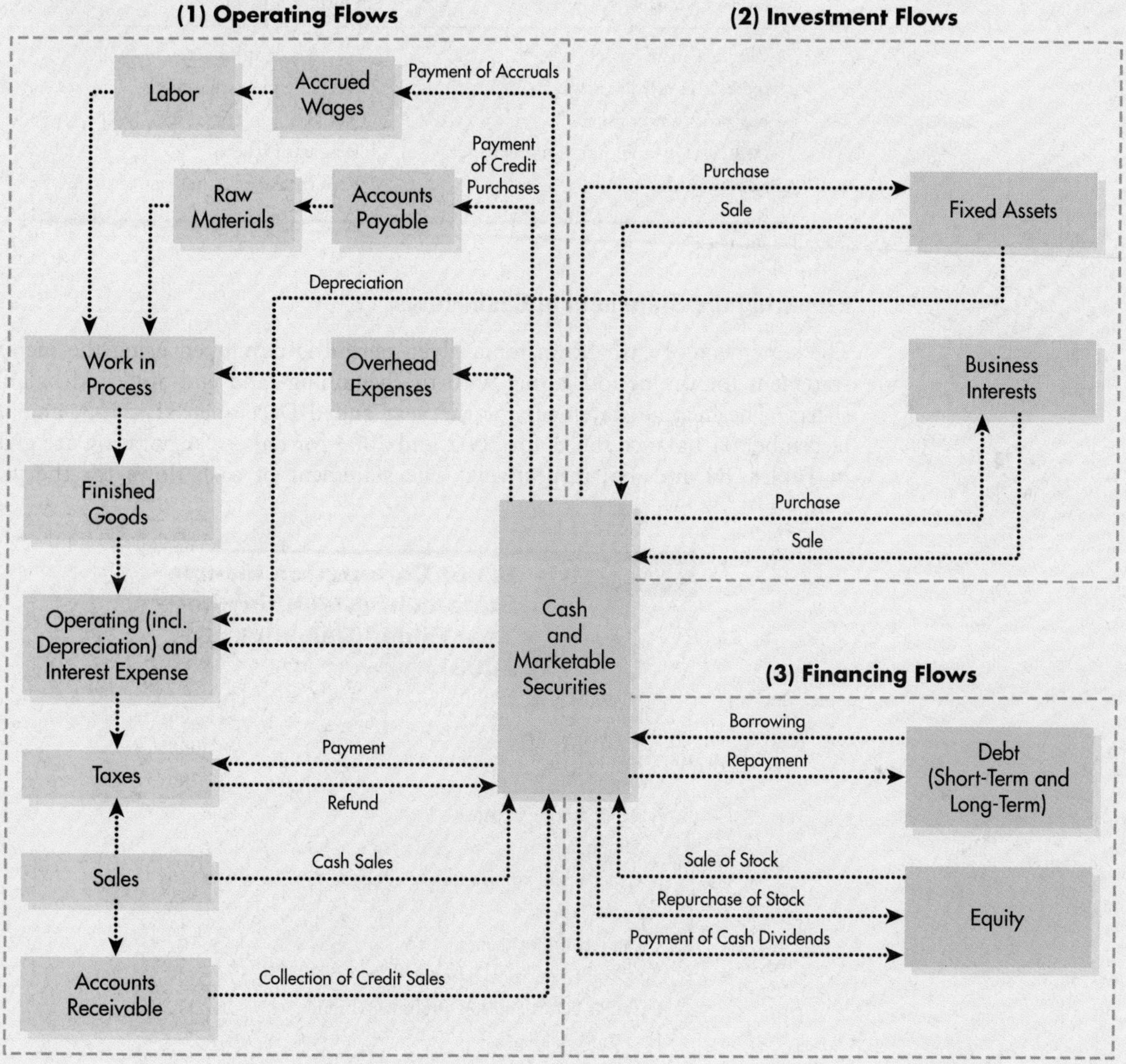

Note that a firm can have a *net loss* (negative net profits after taxes) and still have positive cash flow from operations when depreciation (and other noncash charges) during the period are greater than the net loss. In the statement of cash flows, net profits after taxes (or net losses) and depreciation (and other noncash charges) are therefore treated as separate entries.

3. Because depreciation is treated as a separate cash inflow, only *gross* rather than *net* changes in fixed assets appear on the statement of cash flows. This treatment avoids the potential double counting of depreciation.
4. Direct entries of changes in retained earnings are not included on the statement of cash flows. Instead, entries for items that affect retained earnings appear as net profits or losses after taxes and dividends paid.

TABLE 3.3 The Inflows and Outflows of Cash

Inflows (sources)	Outflows (uses)
Decrease in any asset	Increase in any asset
Increase in any liability	Decrease in any liability
Net profits after taxes	Net loss
Depreciation and other noncash charges	Dividends paid
Sale of stock	Repurchase or retirement of stock

Preparing the Statement of Cash Flows

The statement of cash flows for a given period is developed using the income statement for the period, along with the beginning- and end-of-period balance sheets. The income statement for the year ended December 31, 2003, and the December 31 balance sheets for 2002 and 2003 for Baker Corporation are given in Tables 3.4 and 3.5, respectively. The statement of cash flows for the year

TABLE 3.4 Baker Corporation Income Statement ($000) for the Year Ended December 31, 2003

Sales revenue	$1,700
Less: Cost of goods sold	1,000
Gross profits	$ 700
Less: Operating expenses	
Selling expense	$ 70
General and administrative expense	120
Lease expense[a]	40
Depreciation expense	100
Total operating expense	330
Earnings before interest and taxes (EBIT)	$ 370
Less: Interest expense	70
Net profits before taxes	$ 300
Less: Taxes (rate = 40%)	120
Net profits after taxes	$ 180
Less: Preferred stock dividends	10
Earnings available for common stockholders	$ 170
Earnings per share (EPS)[b]	$1.70

[a]Lease expense is shown here as a separate item rather than included as interest expense as specified by the FASB for financial-reporting purposes. The approach used here is consistent with tax-reporting rather than financial-reporting procedures.

[b]Calculated by dividing the earnings available for common stockholders by the number of shares of common stock outstanding ($170,000 ÷ 100,000 shares = $1.70 per share).

TABLE 3.5 Baker Corporation Balance Sheets ($000)

	December 31	
Assets	**2003**	**2002**
Current assets		
Cash	$ 400	$ 300
Marketable securities	600	200
Accounts receivable	400	500
Inventories	600	900
Total current assets	$2,000	$1,900
Gross fixed assets (at cost)		
Land and buildings	$1,200	$1,050
Machinery and equipment	850	800
Furniture and fixtures	300	220
Vehicles	100	80
Other (includes certain leases)	50	50
Total gross fixed assets (at cost)	$2,500	$2,200
Less: Accumulated depreciation	1,300	1,200
Net fixed assets	$1,200	$1,000
Total assets	$3,200	$2,900
Liabilities and Stockholders' Equity		
Current liabilities		
Accounts payable	$ 700	$ 500
Notes payable	600	700
Accruals	100	200
Total current liabilities	$1,400	$1,400
Long-term debt	$ 600	$ 400
Total liabilities	$2,000	$1,800
Stockholders' equity		
Preferred stock	$ 100	$ 100
Common stock—$1.20 par, 100,000 shares outstanding in 2003 and 2002	120	120
Paid-in capital in excess of par on common stock	380	380
Retained earnings	600	500
Total stockholders' equity	$1,200	$1,100
Total liabilities and stockholders' equity	$3,200	$2,900

ended December 31, 2003, for Baker Corporation is presented in Table 3.6. Note that all cash inflows as well as net profits after taxes and depreciation are treated as positive values. All cash outflows, any losses, and dividends paid are treated as negative values. The items in each category—operating, investment, and financing—are totaled, and the three totals are added to get the "Net

TABLE 3.6 Baker Corporation Statement of Cash Flows ($000) for the Year Ended December 31, 2003

Cash Flow from Operating Activities		
Net profits after taxes	$180	
Depreciation	100	
Decrease in accounts receivable	100	
Decrease in inventories	300	
Increase in accounts payable	200	
Decrease in accruals	(100)[a]	
Cash provided by operating activities		$780
Cash Flow from Investment Activities		
Increase in gross fixed assets	($300)	
Changes in business interests	0	
Cash provided by investment activities		(300)
Cash Flow from Financing Activities		
Decrease in notes payable	($100)	
Increase in long-term debts	200	
Changes in stockholders' equity[b]	0	
Dividends paid	(80)	
Cash provided by financing activities		20
Net increase in cash and marketable securities		$500

[a]As is customary, parentheses are used to denote a negative number, which in this case is a cash outflow.

[b]Retained earnings are excluded here, because their change is actually reflected in the combination of the "Net profits after taxes" and "Dividends paid" entries.

increase (decrease) in cash and marketable securities" for the period. As a check, this value should reconcile with the actual change in cash and marketable securities for the year, which is obtained from the beginning- and end-of-period balance sheets.

Interpreting the Statement

The statement of cash flows allows the financial manager and other interested parties to analyze the firm's cash flow. The manager should pay special attention both to the major categories of cash flow and to the individual items of cash inflow and outflow, to assess whether any developments have occurred that are contrary to the company's financial policies. In addition, the statement can be used to evaluate progress toward projected goals or to isolate inefficiencies. For example, increases in accounts receivable or inventories resulting in major cash outflows may signal credit or inventory problems, respectively. The financial manager also can prepare a statement of cash flows developed from projected financial statements. This approach can be used to determine whether planned actions are desirable in view of the resulting cash flows.

An understanding of the basic financial principles presented throughout this text is absolutely essential to the effective interpretation of the statement of cash flows.

Operating Cash Flow

operating cash flow (OCF)
The cash flow a firm generates from its normal operations; calculated as EBIT − taxes + depreciation.

A firm's **operating cash flow (OCF)** is the cash flow it generates from its normal operations—producing and selling its output of goods or services. A variety of definitions of OCF can be found in the financial literature. We've already been introduced to the simple accounting definition of cash flow from operations in Equation 3.1. Here we refine this definition to estimate cash flows more accurately. Unlike the earlier definition, we exclude interest and taxes in order to focus on the true cash flow resulting from operations without regard to financing costs and taxes. Operating cash flow (OCF) is defined in Equation 3.2.

$$\text{OCF} = \text{EBIT} - \text{Taxes} + \text{Depreciation} \tag{3.2}$$

EXAMPLE ▼ Substituting the values for Baker Corporation from its income statement (Table 3.4) into Equation 3.2, we get

$$\text{OCF} = \$370 - \$120 + \$100 = \$350$$

Baker Corporation during 2003 generated $350,000 of cash flow from producing and selling its output. Because Baker's operating cash flow is positive, we can conclude that the firm's operations are generating positive cash flows. ▲

Comparing Equations 3.1 and 3.2, we can see that the key difference between the accounting and finance definitions of operating cash flow is that the finance definition excludes interest as an operating flow, whereas the accounting definition in effect includes it as an operating flow. In the unlikely case that a firm had no interest expense, the accounting (Equation 3.1) and finance (Equation 3.2) definitions of operating cash flow would be the same.

Free Cash Flow

free cash flow (FCF)
The amount of cash flow available to investors (creditors and owners) after the firm has met all operating needs and paid for investments in net fixed assets and net current assets.

The firm's **free cash flow (FCF)** represents the amount of cash flow available to investors—the providers of debt (creditors) and equity (owners)—after the firm has met all operating needs and paid for investments in net fixed assets and net current assets. It is called "free" not because it is "without cost" but because it is "available" to investors. It represents the summation of the net amount of cash flow available to creditors and owners during the period. Free cash flow can be defined by Equation 3.3.

$$\text{FCF} = \text{OCF} - \text{Net fixed asset investment (NFAI)} - \text{Net current asset investment (NCAI)} \tag{3.3}$$

The *net fixed asset investment* (*NFAI*) can be calculated as shown in Equation 3.4.

$$\text{NFAI} = \text{Change in net fixed assets} + \text{Depreciation} \tag{3.4}$$

EXAMPLE ▼ Using the Baker Corporation's balance sheets in Table 3.5, we see that its change in net fixed assets between 2002 and 2003 was +$200 ($1,200 in 2003 − $1,000 in 2002). Substituting this value and the $100 of depreciation for 2003 into Equation 3.4, we get Baker's net fixed asset investment (NFAI) for 2003:

$$\text{NFAI} = \$200 + \$100 = \$300$$

Baker Corporation therefore invested a net $300,000 in fixed assets during 2003. This amount would, of course, represent a net cash outflow to acquire fixed assets during 2003. ▲

Looking at Equation 3.4, we can see that if the depreciation during a year is less than the *decrease* during that year in net fixed assets, the NFAI would be negative. A negative NFAI represents a net cash *inflow* attributable to the fact that the firm sold more assets than it acquired during the year.

The final variable in the FCF equation, *net current asset investment (NCAI)*, represents the net investment made by the firm in its current (operating) assets. "Net" refers to the difference between current assets and spontaneous current liabilities, which typically include accounts payable and accruals. (Because they are a negotiated source of short-term financing, notes payable are not included in the NCAI calculation. Instead, they serve as a creditor claim on the firm's free cash flow.) Equation 3.5 shows the NCAI calculation.

$$\text{NCAI} = \text{Change in current assets} - \text{Change in spontaneous current liabilities (Accounts payable + Accruals)} \quad (3.5)$$

EXAMPLE Looking at the Baker Corporation's balance sheets for 2002 and 2003 in Table 3.5, we see that the change in current assets between 2002 and 2003 is +\$100 (\$2,000 in 2003 − \$1,900 in 2002). The difference between Baker's accounts payable plus accruals of \$800 in 2003 (\$700 in accounts payable + \$100 in accruals) and of \$700 in 2002 (\$500 in accounts payable + \$200 in accruals) is +\$100 (\$800 in 2003 − \$700 in 2002). Substituting into Equation 3.5 the change in current assets and the change in the sum of accounts payable plus accruals for Baker Corporation, we get its 2003 NCAI:

$$\text{NCAI} = \$100 - \$100 = \$0$$

This means that during 2003 Baker Corporation made no investment (\$0) in its current assets net of spontaneous current liabilities.

Now we can substitute Baker Corporation's 2003 operating cash flow (OCF) of \$350, its net fixed asset investment (NFAI) of \$300, and its net current asset investment (NCAI) of \$0 into Equation 3.3 to find its free cash flow (FCF):

$$\text{FCF} = \$350 - \$300 - \$0 = \$50$$

We can see that during 2003 Baker generated \$50,000 of free cash flow, which it can use to pay its investors—creditors (payment of interest) and owners (payment of dividends). Thus, the firm generated adequate cash flow to cover all of its operating costs and investments and had free cash flow available to pay investors.

Further analysis of free cash flow is beyond the scope of this initial introduction to cash flow. Clearly, cash flow is the lifeblood of the firm. We next consider various aspects of financial planning for cash flow and profit.

Review Questions

3–1 Briefly describe the first four modified accelerated cost recovery system (MACRS) property classes and recovery periods. Explain how the depreciation percentages are determined by using the MACRS recovery periods.

3–2 Describe the overall cash flow through the firm in terms of operating flows, investments flows, and financing flows.

3–3 Explain why a decrease in cash is classified as a *cash inflow (source)* and why an increase in cash is classified as a *cash outflow (use)* in preparing the statement of cash flows.

3–4 Why is depreciation (as well as amortization and depletion) considered a *noncash charge?* How do accountants estimate *cash flow from operations?*

3–5 Describe the general format of the statement of cash flows. How are cash inflows differentiated from cash outflows on this statement?

3–6 From a strict financial perspective, define and differentiate between a firm's *operating cash flow (OCF)* and its *free cash flow (FCF).*

LG3

The Financial Planning Process

Financial planning is an important aspect of the firm's operations because it provides road maps for guiding, coordinating, and controlling the firm's actions to achieve its objectives. Two key aspects of the financial planning process are *cash planning* and *profit planning.* Cash planning involves preparation of the firm's cash budget. Profit planning involves preparation of pro forma statements. Both the cash budget and the pro forma statements are useful for internal financial planning; they also are routinely required by existing and prospective lenders.

financial planning process
Planning that begins with long-term, or *strategic,* financial plans that in turn guide the formulation of short-term, or *operating,* plans and budgets.

The **financial planning process** begins with long-term, or *strategic,* financial plans. These in turn guide the formulation of short-term, or *operating,* plans and budgets. Generally, the short-term plans and budgets implement the firm's long-term strategic objectives. Although the remainder of this chapter places primary emphasis on short-term financial plans and budgets, a few preliminary comments on long-term financial plans are in order.

Long-Term (Strategic) Financial Plans

long-term (strategic) financial plans
Lay out a company's planned financial actions and the anticipated impact of those actions over periods ranging from 2 to 10 years.

Long-term (strategic) financial plans lay out a company's planned financial actions and the anticipated impact of those actions over periods ranging from 2 to 10 years. Five-year strategic plans, which are revised as significant new information becomes available, are common. Generally, firms that are subject to high degrees of operating uncertainty, relatively short production cycles, or both, tend to use shorter planning horizons.

Long-term financial plans are part of an integrated strategy that, along with production and marketing plans, guides the firm toward strategic goals. Those long-term plans consider proposed outlays for fixed assets, research and development activities, marketing and product development actions, capital structure, and major sources of financing. Also included would be termination of existing projects, product lines, or lines of business; repayment or retirement of outstanding debts; and any planned acquisitions. Such plans tend to be supported by a series of annual budgets and profit plans.

Short-Term (Operating) Financial Plans

short-term (operating) financial plans
Specify short-term financial actions and the anticipated impact of those actions.

Short-term (operating) financial plans specify short-term financial actions and the anticipated impact of those actions. These plans most often cover a 1- to 2-year period. Key inputs include the sales forecast and various forms of operating and

FIGURE 3.2 **Short-Term Financial Planning**
The short-term (operating) financial planning process

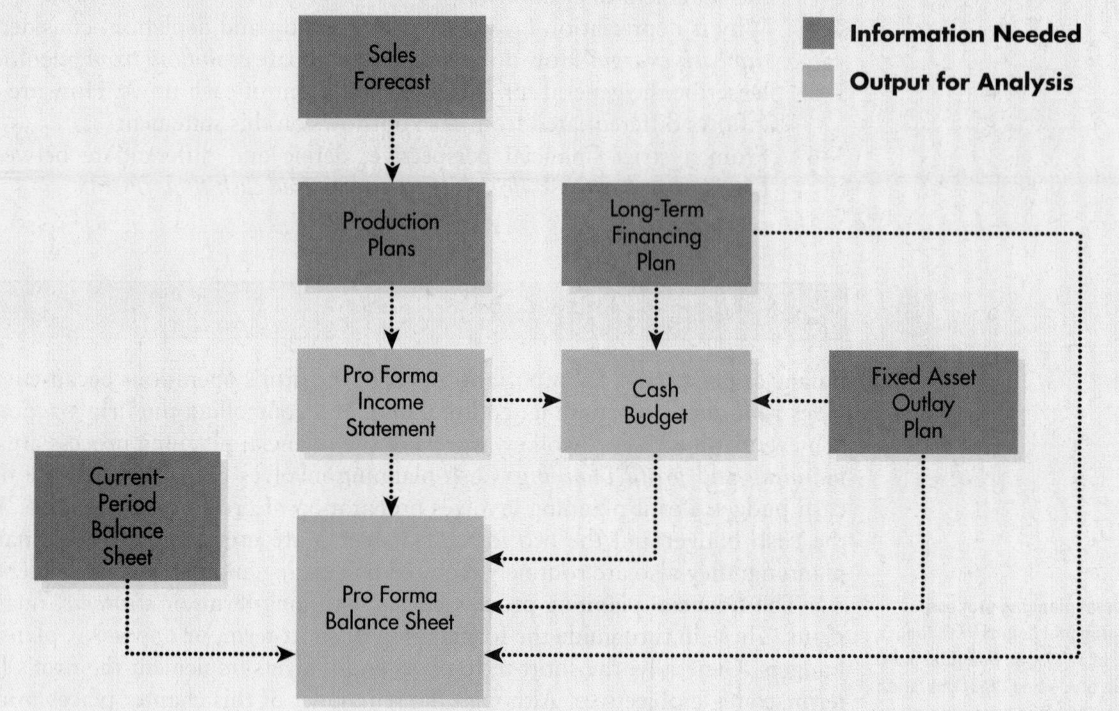

financial data. Key outputs include a number of operating budgets, the cash budget, and pro forma financial statements. The entire short-term financial planning process is outlined in Figure 3.2.

Short-term financial planning begins with the sales forecast. From it, production plans are developed that take into account lead (preparation) times and include estimates of the required raw materials. Using the production plans, the firm can estimate direct labor requirements, factory overhead outlays, and operating expenses. Once these estimates have been made, the firm's pro forma income statement and cash budget can be prepared. With the basic inputs (pro forma income statement, cash budget, fixed asset outlay plan, long-term financing plan, and current-period balance sheet), the pro forma balance sheet can finally be developed.

Throughout the remainder of this chapter, we will concentrate on the key outputs of the short-term financial planning process: the cash budget, the pro forma income statement, and the pro forma balance sheet.

Review Questions

3–7 What is the *financial planning process?* Contrast *long-term (strategic) financial plans* and *short-term (operating) financial plans.*

3–8 Which three statements result as part of the short-term (operating) financial planning process?

LG4

Cash Planning: Cash Budgets

cash budget (cash forecast)
A statement of the firm's planned inflows and outflows of cash that is used to estimate its short-term cash requirements.

The **cash budget,** or **cash forecast,** is a statement of the firm's planned inflows and outflows of cash. It is used by the firm to estimate its short-term cash requirements, with particular attention to planning for surplus cash and for cash shortages.

Typically, the cash budget is designed to cover a 1-year period, divided into smaller time intervals. The number and type of intervals depend on the nature of the business. The more seasonal and uncertain a firm's cash flows, the greater the number of intervals. Because many firms are confronted with a seasonal cash flow pattern, the cash budget is quite often presented on a monthly basis. Firms with stable patterns of cash flow may use quarterly or annual time intervals.

The Sales Forecast

sales forecast
The prediction of the firm's sales over a given period, based on external and/or internal data; used as the key input to the short-term financial planning process.

The key input to the short-term financial planning process is the firm's **sales forecast.** This prediction of the firm's sales over a given period is ordinarily prepared by the marketing department. On the basis of the sales forecast, the financial manager estimates the monthly cash flows that will result from projected sales receipts and from outlays related to production, inventory, and sales. The manager also determines the level of fixed assets required and the amount of financing, if any, needed to support the forecast level of sales and production. In practice, obtaining good data is the most difficult aspect of forecasting. The sales forecast may be based on an analysis of external data, internal data, or a combination of the two.

external forecast
A sales forecast based on the relationships observed between the firm's sales and certain key external economic indicators.

An **external forecast** is based on the relationships observed between the firm's sales and certain key external economic indicators such as the gross domestic product (GDP), new housing starts, consumer confidence, and disposable personal income. Forecasts containing these indicators are readily available. Because the firm's sales are often closely related to some aspect of overall national economic activity, a forecast of economic activity should provide insight into future sales.

internal forecast
A sales forecast based on a buildup, or consensus, of sales forecasts through the firm's own sales channels.

Internal forecasts are based on a buildup, or consensus, of sales forecasts through the firm's own sales channels. Typically, the firm's salespeople in the field are asked to estimate how many units of each type of product they expect to sell in the coming year. These forecasts are collected and totaled by the sales manager, who may adjust the figures using knowledge of specific markets or of the salesperson's forecasting ability. Finally, adjustments may be made for additional internal factors, such as production capabilities.

Firms generally use a combination of external and internal forecast data to make the final sales forecast. The internal data provide insight into sales expectations, and the external data provide a means of adjusting these expectations to

In Practice

FOCUS ON PRACTICE Cash Forecasts Needed, "Rain or Shine"

Given the importance of cash to sound financial management, it is surprising how many companies ignore the cash-forecasting process. Three reasons come up most often: Cash forecasts are always wrong, they're hard to do, and managers don't see the benefits of these forecasts unless the company is already in a cash crunch. In addition, each company has its own methodology for cash forecasting. If the firm's cash inflows and outflows don't form a pattern that managers can graph, it's tough to develop successful forecasts.

Yet the reasons to forecast cash are equally compelling: Cash forecasts provide for reliable liquidity, enable a company to minimize borrowing costs or maximize investment income, and help financial executives manage currency exposures more accurately. In times of tight credit, lenders expect borrowers to monitor cash carefully and will favor a company that prepares good cash forecasts. When cash needs and the forecasted cash position don't match, financial managers can plan for borrowed funds to close the gap.

New York City–based men's apparel manufacturer **Salant Corp.** closely integrates its financial plans and forecasts. "Our biggest challenge is to keep the cash forecast and the projected profit and loss in sync with the balance sheet and vice versa," says William R. Bennett, vice president and treasurer. "We learned that the hard way and developed our own spreadsheet-based model." Although complicated to build, the model is easy for managers to use.

Salant is a capital-intensive operation, so its liquidity is linked to its assets. Bennett uses the forecast of inventory and receivables as the forecast for borrowing capacity required to meet its operating needs.

Like Salant, many companies are using technology to demystify cash forecasts. Software can apply statistical techniques, graph historical data, or build models based on each customer's payment patterns. It can also tap corporate databases for the firm's purchases and associated payment information and order shipments to customers and the associated payment terms. These data increase forecast accuracy.

Sources: Adapted from Richard H. Gamble, "Cash Forecast: Cloudy But Clearing," *Business Finance* (May 2001), downloaded from *www.businessfinancemag.com;* "Profile: Salant Corp.," *Yahoo! Finance, www.biz.yahoo.com,* downloaded November 19, 2001.

take into account general economic factors. The nature of the firm's product also often affects the mix and types of forecasting methods used.

Preparing the Cash Budget

The general format of the cash budget is presented in Table 3.7. We will discuss each of its components individually.

Cash Receipts

cash receipts
All of a firm's inflows of cash in a given financial period.

Cash receipts include all of a firm's inflows of cash in a given financial period. The most common components of cash receipts are cash sales, collections of accounts receivable, and other cash receipts.

EXAMPLE Coulson Industries, a defense contractor, is developing a cash budget for October, November, and December. Coulson's sales in August and September were \$100,000 and \$200,000, respectively. Sales of \$400,000, \$300,000, and \$200,000 have been forecast for October, November, and December, respec-

TABLE 3.7 The General Format of the Cash Budget

	Jan.	Feb.	...	Nov.	Dec.
Cash receipts	$XXX	$XXG		$XXM	$XXT
Less: Cash disbursements	XXA	XXH	...	XXN	XXU
Net cash flow	$XXB	$XXI		$XXO	$XXV
Add: Beginning cash	XXC	↗ XXD	↗ XXJ	↗ XXP	↗ XXQ
Ending cash	$XXD	$XXJ		$XXQ	$XXW
Less: Minimum cash balance	XXE	XXK	...	XXR	XXY
Required total financing		$XXL		$XXS	
Excess cash balance	$XXF				$XXZ

tively. Historically, 20% of the firm's sales have been for cash, 50% have generated accounts receivable collected after 1 month, and the remaining 30% have generated accounts receivable collected after 2 months. Bad-debt expenses (uncollectible accounts) have been negligible.[4] In December, the firm will receive a $30,000 dividend from stock in a subsidiary. The schedule of expected cash receipts for the company is presented in Table 3.8. It contains the following items:

Forecast sales This initial entry is *merely informational.* It is provided as an aid in calculating other sales-related items.

Cash sales The cash sales shown for each month represent 20% of the total sales forecast for that month.

Collections of A/R These entries represent the collection of accounts receivable (A/R) resulting from sales in earlier months.

Lagged 1 month These figures represent sales made in the preceding month that generated accounts receivable collected in the current month. Because 50% of the current month's sales are collected 1 month later, the collections of A/R with a 1-month lag shown for September represent 50% of the sales in August, collections for October represent 50% of September sales, and so on.

Lagged 2 months These figures represent sales made 2 months earlier that generated accounts receivable collected in the current month. Because 30% of sales are collected 2 months later, the collections with a 2-month lag shown for October represent 30% of the sales in August, and so on.

Other cash receipts These are cash receipts expected from sources other than sales. Interest received, dividends received, proceeds from the sale of equipment, stock and bond sale proceeds, and lease receipts may show up

4. Normally, it would be expected that the collection percentages would total slightly less than 100%, because some of the accounts receivable would be uncollectible. In this example, the sum of the collection percentages is 100% (20% + 50% + 30%), which reflects the fact that all sales are assumed to be collected.

TABLE 3.8 A Schedule of Projected Cash Receipts for Coulson Industries ($000)

Forecast sales	Aug. $100	Sept. $200	Oct. $400	Nov. $300	Dec. $200
Cash sales (0.20)	$20	$40	$ 80	$ 60	$ 40
Collections of A/R:					
Lagged 1 month (0.50)		50	100	200	150
Lagged 2 months (0.30)			30	60	120
Other cash receipts			—	—	30
Total cash receipts			$210	$320	$340

here. For Coulson Industries, the only other cash receipt is the $30,000 dividend due in December.

Total cash receipts This figure represents the total of all the cash receipts listed for each month. For Coulson Industries, we are concerned only with October, November, and December, as shown in Table 3.8.

Cash Disbursements

cash disbursements
All outlays of cash by the firm during a given financial period.

Cash disbursements include all outlays of cash by the firm during a given financial period. The most common cash disbursements are

Cash purchases	Fixed-asset outlays
Payments of accounts payable	Interest payments
Rent (and lease) payments	Cash dividend payments
Wages and salaries	Principal payments (loans)
Tax payments	Repurchases or retirements of stock

It is important to recognize that *depreciation and other noncash charges are NOT included in the cash budget,* because they merely represent a scheduled write-off of an earlier cash outflow. The impact of depreciation, as we noted earlier, is reflected in the reduced cash outflow for tax payments.

EXAMPLE Coulson Industries has gathered the following data needed for the preparation of a cash disbursements schedule for October, November, and December.

Purchases The firm's purchases represent 70% of sales. Of this amount, 10% is paid in cash, 70% is paid in the month immediately following the month of purchase, and the remaining 20% is paid 2 months following the month of purchase.[5]

Rent payments Rent of $5,000 will be paid each month.

5. Unlike the collection percentages for sales, the total of the payment percentages should equal 100%, because it is expected that the firm will pay off all of its accounts payable.

Wages and salaries Fixed salary cost for the year is $96,000, or $8,000 per month. In addition, wages are estimated as 10% of monthly sales.

Tax payments Taxes of $25,000 must be paid in December.

Fixed-asset outlays New machinery costing $130,000 will be purchased and paid for in November.

Interest payments An interest payment of $10,000 is due in December.

Cash dividend payments Cash dividends of $20,000 will be paid in October.

Principal payments (loans) A $20,000 principal payment is due in December.

Repurchases or retirements of stock No repurchase or retirement of stock is expected between October and December.

The firm's cash disbursements schedule, using the preceding data, is shown in Table 3.9. Some items in the table are explained in greater detail below.

Purchases This entry is *merely informational.* The figures represent 70% of the forecast sales for each month. They have been included to facilitate calculation of the cash purchases and related payments.

Cash purchases The cash purchases for each month represent 10% of the month's purchases.

Payments of A/P These entries represent the payment of accounts payable (A/P) resulting from purchases in earlier months.

TABLE 3.9 A Schedule of Projected Cash Disbursements for Coulson Industries ($000)

Purchases (0.70 × sales)	Aug. $70	Sept. $140	Oct. $280	Nov. $210	Dec. $140
Cash purchases (0.10)	$7	$14	$ 28	$ 21	$ 14
Payments of A/P:					
Lagged 1 month (0.70)		49	98	196	147
Lagged 2 months (0.20)			14	28	56
Rent payments			5	5	5
Wages and salaries			48	38	28
Tax payments					25
Fixed-asset outlays				130	
Interest payments					10
Cash dividend payments			20		
Principal payments					20
Total cash disbursements			$213	$418	$305

net cash flow
The mathematical difference between the firm's cash receipts and its cash disbursements in each period.

ending cash
The sum of the firm's beginning cash and its net cash flow for the period.

required total financing
Amount of funds needed by the firm if the ending cash for the period is less than the desired minimum cash balance; typically represented by notes payable.

excess cash balance
The (excess) amount available for investment by the firm if the period's ending cash is greater than the desired minimum cash balance; assumed to be invested in marketable securities.

Lagged 1 month These figures represent purchases made in the preceding month that are paid for in the current month. Because 70% of the firm's purchases are paid for 1 month later, the payments with a 1-month lag shown for September represent 70% of the August purchases, payments for October represent 70% of September purchases, and so on.

Lagged 2 months These figures represent purchases made 2 months earlier that are paid for in the current month. Because 20% of the firm's purchases are paid for 2 months later, the payments with a 2-month lag for October represent 20% of the August purchases, and so on.

Wages and salaries These amounts were obtained by adding $8,000 to 10% of the *sales* in each month. The $8,000 represents the salary component; the rest represents wages.

▲ The remaining items on the cash disbursements schedule are self-explanatory.

Net Cash Flow, Ending Cash, Financing, and Excess Cash

Look back at the general-format cash budget in Table 3.7. We have inputs for the first two entries, and we now continue calculating the firm's cash needs. The firm's **net cash flow** is found by subtracting the cash disbursements from cash receipts in each period. Then we add beginning cash to the firm's net cash flow to determine the **ending cash** for each period. Finally, we subtract the desired minimum cash balance from ending cash to find the **required total financing** or the **excess cash balance**. If the ending cash is less than the minimum cash balance, *financing* is required. Such financing is typically viewed as short-term and is therefore represented by notes payable. If the ending cash is greater than the minimum cash balance, *excess cash* exists. Any excess cash is assumed to be invested in a liquid, short-term, interest-paying vehicle—that is, in marketable securities.

EXAMPLE ▼ Table 3.10 presents Coulson Industries' cash budget, based on the data already developed. At the end of September, Coulson's cash balance was $50,000, and its notes payable and marketable securities equaled $0. The company wishes to maintain, as a reserve for unexpected needs, a minimum cash balance of $25,000.

For Coulson Industries to maintain its required $25,000 ending cash balance, it will need total borrowing of $76,000 in November and $41,000 in December. In October the firm will have an excess cash balance of $22,000, which can be held in an interest-earning marketable security. The required total financing figures in the cash budget refer to *how much will be owed at the end of the month;* they do *not* represent the monthly changes in borrowing.

The monthly changes in borrowing and in excess cash can be found by further analyzing the cash budget. In October the $50,000 beginning cash, which becomes $47,000 after the $3,000 net cash outflow, results in a $22,000 excess cash balance once the $25,000 minimum cash is deducted. In November the $76,000 of required total financing resulted from the $98,000 net cash outflow less the $22,000 of excess cash from October. The $41,000 of required total financing in December resulted from reducing November's $76,000 of required total financing by the $35,000 of net cash inflow during December. Summarizing, the financial activities for each month would be as follows:

TABLE 3.10 A Cash Budget for Coulson Industries ($000)

	Oct.	Nov.	Dec.
Total cash receipts[a]	$210	$320	$340
Less: Total cash disbursements[b]	213	418	305
Net cash flow	($ 3)	($ 98)	$ 35
Add: Beginning cash	50	47	(51)
Ending cash	$ 47 ↗	($ 51) ↗	($ 16)
Less: Minimum cash balance	25	25	25
Required total financing (notes payable)[c]	—	$ 76	$ 41
Excess cash balance (marketable securities)[d]	$ 22	—	—

[a]From Table 3.8.
[b]From Table 3.9.
[c]Values are placed in this line when the ending cash is less than the desired minimum cash balance. These amounts are typically financed short-term and therefore are represented by notes payable.
[d]Values are placed in this line when the ending cash is greater than the desired minimum cash balance. These amounts are typically assumed to be invested short-term and therefore are represented by marketable securities.

October: Invest the $22,000 excess cash balance in marketable securities.

November: Liquidate the $22,000 of marketable securities and borrow $76,000 (notes payable).

December: Repay $35,000 of notes payable to leave $41,000 of outstanding required total financing.

Evaluating the Cash Budget

The cash budget indicates whether a cash shortage or surplus is expected in each of the months covered by the forecast. Each month's figure is based on the internally imposed requirement of a minimum cash balance and *represents the total balance at the end of the month.*

At the end of each of the 3 months, Coulson expects the following balances in cash, marketable securities, and notes payable:

	End-of-month balance ($000)		
Account	Oct.	Nov.	Dec.
Cash	$25	$25	$25
Marketable securities	22	0	0
Notes payable	0	76	41

Note that the firm is assumed first to liquidate its marketable securities to meet deficits and then to borrow with notes payable if additional financing is needed. As a result, it will not have marketable securities and notes payable on its books at the same time.

Because it may be necessary to borrow up to $76,000 for the 3-month period, the financial manager should be certain that some arrangement is made to ensure the availability of these funds.

Coping with Uncertainty in the Cash Budget

Aside from careful estimation of cash budget inputs, there are two ways of coping with the uncertainty of the cash budget.[6] One is to prepare several cash budgets—based on pessimistic, most likely, and optimistic forecasts. From this range of cash flows, the financial manager can determine the amount of financing necessary to cover the most adverse situation. The use of several cash budgets, based on differing assumptions, also should give the financial manager a sense of the riskiness of various alternatives. This *sensitivity analysis,* or "what if" approach, is often used to analyze cash flows under a variety of circumstances. Computers and electronic spreadsheets simplify the process of performing sensitivity analysis.

EXAMPLE Table 3.11 presents the summary of Coulson Industries' cash budget prepared for each month of concern using pessimistic, most likely, and optimistic estimates of total cash receipts and disbursements. The most likely estimate is based on the expected outcomes presented earlier.

TABLE 3.11 A Sensitivity Analysis of Coulson Industries' Cash Budget ($000)

	October			November			December		
	Pessimistic	Most likely	Optimistic	Pessimistic	Most likely	Optimistic	Pessimistic	Most likely	Optimistic
Total cash receipts	$160	$210	$285	$210	$320	$ 410	$275	$340	$422
Less: Total cash disbursements	200	213	248	380	418	467	280	305	320
Net cash flow	($ 40)	($ 3)	$ 37	($170)	($ 98)	($ 57)	($ 5)	$ 35	$102
Add: Beginning cash	50	50	50	10	47	87	(160)	(51)	30
Ending cash	$ 10	$ 47	$ 87	($160)	($ 51)	$ 30	($165)	($ 16)	$132
Less: Minimum cash balance	25	25	25	25	25	25	25	25	25
Required total financing	$ 15	—	—	$185	$ 76	—	$190	$ 41	—
Excess cash balance	—	$ 22	$ 62	—	—	$ 5	—	—	$107

6. The term *uncertainty* is used here to refer to the variability of the cash flow outcomes that may actually occur.

During October, Coulson will, at worst, need a maximum of \$15,000 of financing and, at best, will have a \$62,000 excess cash balance. During November, its financing requirement will be between \$0 and \$185,000, or it could experience an excess cash balance of \$5,000. The December projections show maximum borrowing of \$190,000 with a possible excess cash balance of \$107,000. By considering the extreme values in the pessimistic and optimistic outcomes, Coulson Industries should be better able to plan its cash requirements. For the 3-month period, the peak borrowing requirement under the worst circumstances would be \$190,000, which happens to be considerably greater than the most likely estimate of \$76,000 for this period.

A second and much more sophisticated way of coping with uncertainty in the cash budget is *simulation* (discussed in Chapter 9). By simulating the occurrence of sales and other uncertain events, the firm can develop a probability distribution of its ending cash flows for each month. The financial decision maker can then use the probability distribution to determine the amount of financing needed to protect the firm adequately against a cash shortage.

Review Questions

3–9 What is the purpose of the *cash budget?* What role does the sales forecast play in its preparation?

3–10 Briefly describe the basic format of the cash budget.

3–11 How can the two "bottom lines" of the cash budget be used to determine the firm's short-term borrowing and investment requirements?

3–12 What is the cause of uncertainty in the cash budget, and what two techniques can be used to cope with this uncertainty?

LG5

Profit Planning: Pro Forma Statements

pro forma statements
Projected, or forecast, income statements and balance sheets.

Whereas cash planning focuses on forecasting cash flows, *profit planning* relies on accrual concepts to project the firm's profit and overall financial position. Shareholders, creditors, and the firm's management pay close attention to the **pro forma statements,** which are projected, or forecast, income statements and balance sheets. The basic steps in the short-term financial planning process were shown in the flow diagram of Figure 3.2. Various approaches for estimating the pro forma statements are based on the belief that the financial relationships reflected in the firm's past financial statements will not change in the coming period. The commonly used simplified approaches are presented in subsequent discussions.

Two inputs are required for preparing pro forma statements: (1) financial statements for the preceding year and (2) the sales forecast for the coming year. A variety of assumptions must also be made. The company that we will use to illustrate the simplified approaches to pro forma preparation is Vectra Manufacturing, which manufactures and sells one product. It has two basic product models—X and Y—which are produced by the same process but require different amounts of raw material and labor.

TABLE 3.12 Vectra Manufacturing's Income Statement for the Year Ended December 31, 2003

Sales revenue		
Model X (1,000 units at $20/unit)	$20,000	
Model Y (2,000 units at $40/unit)	80,000	
Total sales		$100,000
Less: Cost of goods sold		
Labor	$28,500	
Material A	8,000	
Material B	5,500	
Overhead	38,000	
Total cost of goods sold		80,000
Gross profits		$ 20,000
Less: Operating expenses		10,000
Operating profits		$ 10,000
Less: Interest expense		1,000
Net profits before taxes		$ 9,000
Less: Taxes (0.15 × $9,000)		1,350
Net profits after taxes		$ 7,650
Less: Common stock dividends		4,000
To retained earnings		$ 3,650

Preceding Year's Financial Statements

The income statement for the firm's 2003 operations is given in Table 3.12. It indicates that Vectra had sales of $100,000, total cost of goods sold of $80,000, net profits before taxes of $9,000, and net profits after taxes of $7,650. The firm paid $4,000 in cash dividends, leaving $3,650 to be transferred to retained earnings. The firm's balance sheet for 2003 is given in Table 3.13.

TABLE 3.13 Vectra Manufacturing's Balance Sheet, December 31, 2003

Assets		Liabilities and Stockholders' Equity	
Cash	$ 6,000	Accounts payable	$ 7,000
Marketable securities	4,000	Taxes payable	300
Accounts receivable	13,000	Notes payable	8,300
Inventories	16,000	Other current liabilities	3,400
Total current assets	$39,000	Total current liabilities	$19,000
Net fixed assets	$51,000	Long-term debt	$18,000
Total assets	$90,000	Stockholders' equity	
		Common stock	$30,000
		Retained earnings	$23,000
		Total liabilities and stockholders' equity	$90,000

TABLE 3.14 2004 Sales Forecast for Vectra Manufacturing

Unit sales	
Model X	1,500
Model Y	1,950
Dollar sales	
Model X ($25/unit)	$ 37,500
Model Y ($50/unit)	97,500
Total	$135,000

Sales Forecast

Just as for the cash budget, the key input for pro forma statements is the sales forecast. Vectra Manufacturing's sales forecast for the coming year, based on both external and internal data, is presented in Table 3.14. The unit sale prices of the products reflect an increase from $20 to $25 for model X and from $40 to $50 for model Y. These increases are necessary to cover anticipated increases in costs.

Review Question

3–13 What is the purpose of *pro forma statements?* What inputs are required for preparing them using the simplified approaches?

LG5

Preparing the Pro Forma Income Statement

percent-of-sales method
A simple method for developing the pro forma income statement; it forecasts sales and then expresses the various income statement items as percentages of projected sales.

A simple method for developing a pro forma income statement is the **percent-of-sales method.** It forecasts sales and then expresses the various income statement items as percentages of projected sales. The percentages used are likely to be the percentages of sales for those items in the previous year. By using dollar values taken from Vectra's 2003 income statement (Table 3.12), we find that these percentages are

$$\frac{\text{Cost of goods sold}}{\text{Sales}} = \frac{\$80{,}000}{\$100{,}000} = 80.0\%$$

$$\frac{\text{Operating expenses}}{\text{Sales}} = \frac{\$10{,}000}{\$100{,}000} = 10.0\%$$

$$\frac{\text{Interest expense}}{\text{Sales}} = \frac{\$1{,}000}{\$100{,}000} = 1.0\%$$

Applying these percentages to the firm's forecast sales of $135,000 (developed in Table 3.14), we get the 2004 pro forma income statement shown in Table 3.15. We have assumed that Vectra will pay $4,000 in common stock dividends, so the

TABLE 3.15 A Pro Forma Income Statement, Using the Percent-of-Sales Method, for Vectra Manufacturing for the Year Ended December 31, 2004

Sales revenue	$135,000
Less: Cost of goods sold (0.80)	108,000
Gross profits	$ 27,000
Less: Operating expenses (0.10)	13,500
Operating profits	$ 13,500
Less: Interest expense (0.01)	1,350
Net profits before taxes	$ 12,150
Less: Taxes (0.15 × $12,150)	1,823
Net profits after taxes	$ 10,327
Less: Common stock dividends	4,000
To retained earnings	$ 6,327

expected contribution to retained earnings is $6,327. This represents a considerable increase over $3,650 in the preceding year (see Table 3.12).

Considering Types of Costs and Expenses

The technique that is used to prepare the pro forma income statement in Table 3.15 assumes that all the firm's costs and expenses are *variable*. That is, we assumed that for a given percentage increase in sales, the same percentage increase in cost of goods sold, operating expenses, and interest expense would result. For example, as Vectra's sales increased by 35 percent (from $100,000 in 2003 to $135,000 projected for 2004), we assumed that its costs of goods sold also increased by 35 percent (from $80,000 in 2003 to $108,000 in 2004). On the basis of this assumption, the firm's net profits before taxes also increased by 35 percent (from $9,000 in 2003 to $12,150 projected for 2004).

This approach implies that the firm will not receive the benefits that result from fixed costs when sales are increasing.[7] Clearly, though, if the firm has fixed costs, these costs do not change when sales increase; the result is increased profits. But by remaining unchanged when sales decline, these costs tend to lower profits. Therefore, the use of past cost and expense ratios generally *tends to understate profits when sales are increasing*. (Likewise, it *tends to overstate profits when sales are decreasing*.) The best way to adjust for the presence of fixed

7. The potential returns as well as risks resulting from use of fixed (operating and financial) costs to create "leverage" are discussed in Chapter 11. The key point to recognize here is that when the firm's revenue is *increasing*, fixed costs can magnify returns.

costs when preparing a pro forma income statement is to break the firm's historical costs and expenses into *fixed* and *variable* components.

EXAMPLE Vectra Manufacturing's 2003 actual and 2004 pro forma income statements, broken into fixed and variable cost and expense components, follow:

Vectra Manufacturing
Income Statements

	2003 Actual	2004 Pro forma
Sales revenue	$100,000	$135,000
Less: Cost of good sold		
Fixed cost	40,000	40,000
Variable cost (0.40 × sales)	40,000	54,000
Gross profits	$ 20,000	$ 41,000
Less: Operating expenses		
Fixed expense	5,000	5,000
Variable expense (0.05 × sales)	5,000	6,750
Operating profits	$ 10,000	$ 29,250
Less: Interest expense (all fixed)	1,000	1,000
Net profits before taxes	$ 9,000	$ 28,250
Less: Taxes (0.15 × net profits before taxes)	1,350	4,238
Net profits after taxes	$ 7,650	$ 24,012

Breaking Vectra's costs and expenses into fixed and variable components provides a more accurate projection of its pro forma profit. By assuming that *all* costs are variable (as shown in Table 3.15), we find that projected net profits before taxes would continue to equal 9 percent of sales (in 2003, $9,000 net profits before taxes ÷ $100,000 sales). Therefore, the 2004 net profits before taxes would have been $12,150 (0.09 × $135,000 projected sales) instead of the $28,250 obtained by using the firm's fixed-cost–variable-cost breakdown.

Clearly, when using a simplified approach to prepare a pro forma income statement, we should break down costs and expenses into fixed and variable components.

Review Questions

3–14 How is the *percent-of-sales method* used to prepare pro forma income statements?

3–15 Why does the presence of fixed costs cause the percent-of-sales method of pro forma income statement preparation to fail? What is a better method?

LG5

Preparing the Pro Forma Balance Sheet

judgmental approach
A simplified approach for preparing the pro forma balance sheet under which the values of certain balance sheet accounts are estimated and the firm's external financing is used as a balancing, or "plug," figure.

A number of simplified approaches are available for preparing the pro forma balance sheet. Probably the best and most popular is the **judgmental approach,**[8] under which the values of certain balance sheet accounts are estimated and the firm's external financing is used as a balancing, or "plug," figure. To apply the judgmental approach to prepare Vectra Manufacturing's 2004 pro forma balance sheet, a number of assumptions must be made about levels of various balance sheet accounts:

1. A minimum cash balance of $6,000 is desired.
2. Marketable securities are assumed to remain unchanged from their current level of $4,000.
3. Accounts receivable on average represent 45 days of sales. Because Vectra's annual sales are projected to be $135,000, accounts receivable should average $16,875 (1/8 × $135,000). (Forty-five days expressed fractionally is one-eighth of a year: 45/360 = 1/8.)
4. The ending inventory should remain at a level of about $16,000, of which 25 percent (approximately $4,000) should be raw materials and the remaining 75 percent (approximately $12,000) should consist of finished goods.
5. A new machine costing $20,000 will be purchased. Total depreciation for the year is $8,000. Adding the $20,000 acquisition to the existing net fixed assets of $51,000 and subtracting the depreciation of $8,000 yield net fixed assets of $63,000.
6. Purchases are expected to represent approximately 30% of annual sales, which in this case is approximately $40,500 (0.30 × $135,000). The firm estimates that it can take 72 days on average to satisfy its accounts payable. Thus accounts payable should equal one-fifth (72 days ÷ 360 days) of the firm's purchases, or $8,100 (1/5 × $40,500).
7. Taxes payable are expected to equal one-fourth of the current year's tax liability, which equals $455 (one-fourth of the tax liability of $1,823 shown in the pro forma income statement in Table 3.15).
8. Notes payable are assumed to remain unchanged from their current level of $8,300.
9. No change in other current liabilities is expected. They remain at the level of the previous year: $3,400.
10. The firm's long-term debt and its common stock are expected to remain unchanged at $18,000 and $30,000, respectively; no issues, retirements, or repurchases of bonds or stocks are planned.
11. Retained earnings will increase from the beginning level of $23,000 (from the balance sheet dated December 31, 2003, in Table 3.13) to $29,327. The increase of $6,327 represents the amount of retained earnings calculated in the year-end 2004 pro forma income statement in Table 3.15.

external financing required ("plug" figure)
Under the judgmental approach for developing a pro forma balance sheet, the amount of external financing needed to bring the statement into balance.

A 2004 pro forma balance sheet for Vectra Manufacturing based on these assumptions is presented in Table 3.16. A **"plug" figure**—called the **external fi-**

8. The judgmental approach represents an improved version of the often discussed *percent-of-sales approach* to pro forma balance sheet preparation. Because the judgmental approach requires only slightly more information and should yield better estimates than the somewhat naive percent-of-sales approach, it is presented here.

TABLE 3.16 A Pro Forma Balance Sheet, Using the Judgmental Approach, for Vectra Manufacturing (December 31, 2004)

Assets			Liabilities and Stockholders' Equity	
Cash		$ 6,000	Accounts payable	$ 8,100
Marketable securities		4,000	Taxes payable	455
Accounts receivable		16,875	Notes payable	8,300
Inventories			Other current liabilities	3,400
Raw materials	$ 4,000		Total current liabilities	$ 20,255
Finished goods	12,000		Long-term debt	$ 18,000
Total inventory		16,000	Stockholders' equity	
Total current assets		$ 42,875	Common stock	$ 30,000
Net fixed assets		$ 63,000	Retained earnings	$ 29,327
Total assets		$105,875	Total	$ 97,582
			External financing required[a]	$ 8,293
			Total liabilities and stockholders' equity	$105,875

[a]The amount of external financing needed to force the firm's balance sheet to balance. Because of the nature of the judgmental approach, the balance sheet is not expected to balance without some type of adjustment.

nancing required—of $8,293 is needed to bring the statement into balance. This means that the firm will have to obtain about $8,293 of additional external financing to support the increased sales level of $135,000 for 2004.

A *positive* value for "external financing required," like that shown in Table 3.16, means that to support the forecast level of operation, the firm must raise funds externally using debt and/or equity financing or by reducing dividends. Once the form of financing is determined, the pro forma balance sheet is modified to replace "external financing required" with the planned increases in the debt and/or equity accounts.

A *negative* value for "external financing required" indicates that the firm's forecast financing is in excess of its needs. In this case, funds are available for use in repaying debt, repurchasing stock, or increasing dividends. Once the specific actions are determined, "external financing required" is replaced in the pro forma balance sheet with the planned reductions in the debt and/or equity accounts. Obviously, besides being used to prepare the pro forma balance sheet, the judgmental approach is also frequently used specifically to estimate the firm's financing requirements.

Review Questions

3–16 Describe the *judgmental approach* for simplified preparation of the pro forma balance sheet.

3–17 What is the significance of the "plug" figure, *external financing required?* Differentiate between strategies associated with positive and with negative values for external financing required.

Evaluation of Pro Forma Statements

LG6

It is difficult to forecast the many variables involved in preparing pro forma statements. As a result, investors, lenders, and managers frequently use the techniques presented in this chapter to make rough estimates of pro forma financial statements. However, it is important to recognize the basic weaknesses of these simplified approaches. The weaknesses lie in two assumptions: (1) that the firm's past financial condition is an accurate indicator of its future, and (2) that certain variables (such as cash, accounts receivable, and inventories) can be forced to take on certain "desired" values. These assumptions cannot be justified solely on the basis of their ability to simplify the calculations involved. Despite their weaknesses, the simplified approaches to pro forma statement preparation are likely to remain popular because of their relative simplicity. Eventually, the use of computers to streamline financial planning will become the norm.

However pro forma statements are prepared, analysts must understand how to use them to make financial decisions. Both financial managers and lenders can use pro forma statements to analyze the firm's inflows and outflows of cash, as well as its liquidity, activity, debt, profitability, and market value. Various ratios can be calculated from the pro forma income statement and balance sheet to evaluate performance. Cash inflows and outflows can be evaluated by preparing a pro forma statement of cash flows. After analyzing the pro forma statements, the financial manager can take steps to adjust planned operations to achieve short-term financial goals. For example, if projected profits on the pro forma income statement are too low, a variety of pricing and/or cost-cutting actions might be initiated. If the projected level of accounts receivable on the pro forma balance sheet is too high, changes in credit or collection policy may be called for. Pro forma statements are therefore of great importance in solidifying the firm's financial plans for the coming year.

Review Questions

3–18 What are the two key weaknesses of the simplified approaches to preparing pro forma statements?

3–19 What is the financial manager's objective in evaluating pro forma statements?

SUMMARY

FOCUS ON VALUE

Cash flow, the lifeblood of the firm, is a key determinant of the value of the firm. The financial manager must plan and manage—create, allocate, conserve, and monitor—the firm's cash flow. The goal is to ensure the firm's solvency by meeting financial obligations in a timely manner and to generate positive cash flow for the firm's owners. Both the magnitude and the risk of the cash flows generated on behalf of the owners determine the firm's value.

In order to carry out the responsibility **to create value for owners,** the financial manager uses tools such as cash budgets and pro forma financial statements as part of the process of generating positive cash flow. Good financial plans should result in large free cash flows that fully satisfy creditor claims and produce positive cash flows on behalf of owners. Clearly, the financial manager must use deliberate and careful planning and management of the firm's cash flows in order to achieve the firm's goal of maximizing share price.

REVIEW OF LEARNING GOALS

LG1 **Understand the effect of depreciation on the firm's cash flows, the depreciable value of an asset, its depreciable life, and tax depreciation methods.** Depreciation is an important factor affecting a firm's cash flow. The depreciable value of an asset and its depreciable life are determined by using the modified accelerated cost recovery system (MACRS) standards in the federal tax code. MACRS groups assets (excluding real estate) into six property classes based on length of recovery period—3, 5, 7, 10, 15, and 20 years—and can be applied over the appropriate period by using a schedule of yearly depreciation percentages for each period.

LG2 **Discuss the firm's statement of cash flows, operating cash flow, and free cash flow.** The statement of cash flows is divided into operating, investment, and financing flows. It reconciles changes in the firm's cash flows with changes in cash and marketable securities for the period. Interpreting the statement of cash flows requires an understanding of basic financial principles and involves both the major categories of cash flow and the individual items of cash inflow and outflow. From a strict financial point of view, a firm's operating cash flows, the cash flow it generates from normal operations, is defined to exclude interest and taxes; the simpler accounting view does not make these exclusions. Of greater importance is a firm's free cash flow, which is the amount of cash flow available to investors—the providers of debt (creditors) and equity (owners).

LG3 **Understand the financial planning process, including long-term (strategic) financial plans and short-term (operating) financial plans.** The two key aspects of the financial planning process are cash planning and profit planning. Cash planning involves the cash budget or cash forecast. Profit planning relies on the pro forma income statement and balance sheet. Long-term (strategic) financial plans act as a guide for preparing short-term (operating) financial plans. Long-term plans tend to cover periods ranging from 2 to 10 years and are updated periodically. Short-term plans most often cover a 1- to 2-year period.

LG4 **Discuss the cash-planning process and the preparation, evaluation, and use of the cash budget.** The cash planning process uses the cash budget, based on a sales forecast, to estimate short-term cash surpluses and shortages. The cash budget is typically prepared for a 1-year period divided into months. It nets cash receipts and disbursements for each period to calculate net cash flow. Ending cash is estimated by adding beginning cash to the net cash flow. By subtracting the desired minimum cash balance from the ending cash, the financial manager can determine required total financing (typically borrowing with notes payable) or the excess cash balance (typically investing in marketable securities). To cope with uncertainty in the cash budget, sensitivity analysis or simulation can be used.

LG5 **Explain the simplified procedures used to prepare and evaluate the pro forma income statement and the pro forma balance sheet.** A pro forma income statement can be developed by calculating past percentage relationships between certain cost and expense items and the firm's sales and then applying these percentages to forecasts. Because this approach implies that all costs and expenses are variable, it tends to understate profits when sales are increasing and to overstate profits when sales are decreasing. This problem can be avoided by breaking down costs and expenses into fixed and variable components. In this case, the fixed components remain unchanged from the most recent year, and the variable costs and expenses are forecast on a percent-of-sales basis.

Under the judgmental approach, the values of certain balance sheet accounts are estimated and others are calculated, frequently on the basis of their relationship to sales. The firm's external financing is used as a balancing, or "plug," figure. A positive value for "external financing required" means that the firm must raise funds externally or reduce dividends; a negative value indicates that funds are available for use in repaying debt, repurchasing stock, or increasing dividends.

LG6 **Cite the weaknesses of the simplified approaches to pro forma financial statement preparation and the common uses of pro forma statements.** Simplified approaches for preparing pro forma statements, although popular, can be criticized for assuming that the firm's past financial condition is an accurate indicator of the future and that certain variables can be forced to take on certain "desired" values. Pro forma statements are commonly used to forecast and analyze the firm's level of profitability and overall financial performance so that adjustments can be made to planned operations in order to achieve short-term financial goals.

SELF-TEST PROBLEMS (Solutions in Appendix B)

LG1 LG2 **ST 3–1 Depreciation and cash flow** A firm expects to have earnings before interest and taxes (EBIT) of $160,000 in each of the next 6 years. It pays annual interest of $1,500. The firm is considering the purchase of an asset that costs $140,000, requires $10,000 in installation cost, and has a recovery period of 5 years. It will be the firm's only asset, and the asset's depreciation is already reflected in its EBIT estimates.

a. Calculate the annual depreciation for the asset purchase using the MACRS depreciation percentages in Table 3.2 on page 89.

b Calculate the annual operating cash flows for each of the 6 years, using both the accounting and the finance definitions of *operating cash flow*. Assume that the firm is subject to a 40% ordinary tax rate.

c. Say the firm's net fixed assets, current assets, accounts payable, and accruals had the following values at the start and end of the final year (year 6). Calculate the firm's free cash flow (FCF) for that year.

Account	Year 6 Start	Year 6 End
Net fixed assets	$ 7,500	$ 0
Current assets	90,000	110,000
Accounts payable	40,000	45,000
Accruals	8,000	7,000

d. Compare and discuss the significance of each value calculated in parts **b** and **c.**

LG4 LG5 **ST 3–2** **Cash budget and pro forma balance sheet inputs** Jane McDonald, a financial analyst for Carroll Company, has prepared the following sales and cash disbursement estimates for the period February–June of the current year.

Month	Sales	Cash disbursements
February	$500	$400
March	600	300
April	400	600
May	200	500
June	200	200

Ms. McDonald notes that historically, 30% of sales have been for cash. Of *credit sales,* 70% are collected 1 month after the sale, and the remaining 30% are collected 2 months after the sale. The firm wishes to maintain a minimum ending balance in its cash account of $25. Balances above this amount would be invested in short-term government securities (marketable securities), whereas any deficits would be financed through short-term bank borrowing (notes payable). The beginning cash balance at April 1 is $115.

a. Prepare a cash budget for April, May, and June.

b. How much financing, if any, at a maximum would Carroll Company require to meet its obligations during this 3-month period?

c. A pro forma balance sheet dated at the end of June is to be prepared from the information presented. Give the size of each of the following: cash, notes payable, marketable securities, and accounts receivable.

LG5 **ST 3–3** **Pro forma income statement** Euro Designs, Inc., expects sales during 2004 to rise from the 2003 level of $3.5 million to $3.9 million. Because of a scheduled large loan payment, the interest expense in 2004 is expected to drop to $325,000. The firm plans to increase its cash dividend payments during 2004 to $320,000. The company's year-end 2003 income statement follows.

Euro Designs, Inc.
Income Statement
for the Year Ended December 31, 2003

Sales revenue	$3,500,000
Less: Cost of goods sold	1,925,000
Gross profits	$1,575,000
Less: Operating expenses	420,000
Operating profits	$1,155,000
Less: Interest expense	400,000
Net profits before taxes	$ 755,000
Less: Taxes (rate = 40%)	302,000
Net profits after taxes	$ 453,000
Less: Cash dividends	250,000
To retained earnings	$ 203,000

a. Use the *percent-of-sales method* to prepare a 2004 pro forma income statement for Euro Designs, Inc.
b. Explain why the statement may underestimate the company's actual 2004 pro forma income.

PROBLEMS

LG1 **3–1 Depreciation** On March 20, 2003, Norton Systems acquired two new assets. Asset A was research equipment costing $17,000 and having a 3-year recovery period. Asset B was duplicating equipment having an installed cost of $45,000 and a 5-year recovery period. Using the MACRS depreciation percentages in Table 3.2 on page 89, prepare a depreciation schedule for each of these assets.

LG2 **3–2 Accounting cash flow** A firm had earnings after taxes of $50,000 in 2003. Depreciation charges were $28,000, and a $2,000 charge for amortization of a bond discount was incurred. What was the firm's accounting *cash flow from operations* (see Equation 3.1) during 2003?

LG1 LG2 **3–3 Depreciation and accounting cash flow** A firm in the third year of depreciating its only asset, which originally cost $180,000 and has a 5-year MACRS recovery period, has gathered the following data relative to the current year's operations.

Accruals	$ 15,000
Current assets	120,000
Interest expense	15,000
Sales revenue	400,000
Inventory	70,000
Total costs before depreciation, interest, and taxes	290,000
Tax rate on ordinary income	40%

a. Use the *relevant data* to determine the accounting *cash flow from operations* (see Equation 3.1) for the current year.
b. Explain the impact that depreciation, as well as any other noncash charges, has on a firm's cash flows.

LG2 **3–4 Classifying inflows and outflows of cash** Classify each of the following items as an inflow (I) or an outflow (O) of cash, or as neither (N).

Item	Change ($)	Item	Change ($)
Cash	+100	Accounts receivable	−700
Accounts payable	−1,000	Net profits	+600
Notes payable	+500	Depreciation	+100
Long-term debt	−2,000	Repurchase of stock	+600
Inventory	+200	Cash dividends	+800
Fixed assets	+400	Sale of stock	+1,000

LG2 **3–5 Finding operating and free cash flows** Given the balance sheets and selected data from the income statement of Keith corporation that follow:

a. Calculate the firm's accounting *cash flow from operations* for the year ended December 31, 2003, using Equation 3.1.

b. Calculate the firm's *operating cash flow* (*OCF*) for the year ended December 31, 2003, using Equation 3.2.

c. Calculate the firm's *free cash flow* (*FCF*) for the year ended December 31, 2003, using Equation 3.3.

d. Interpret, compare, and contrast your cash flow estimates in parts **a, b,** and **c.**

Keith Corporation
Balance Sheets

	December 31	
Assets	**2003**	**2002**
Cash	$ 1,500	$ 1,000
Marketable securities	1,800	1,200
Accounts receivable	2,000	1,800
Inventories	2,900	2,800
Total current assets	$ 8,200	$ 6,800
Gross fixed assets	$29,500	$28,100
Less: Accumulated depreciation	14,700	13,100
Net fixed assets	$14,800	$15,000
Total assets	$23,000	$21,800
Liabilities and Stockholders' Equity		
Accounts payable	$ 1,600	$ 1,500
Notes payable	2,800	2,200
Accruals	200	300
Total current liabilities	$ 4,600	$ 4,000
Long-term debt	$ 5,000	$ 5,000
Common stock	$10,000	$10,000
Retained earnings	3,400	2,800
Total stockholders' equity	$13,400	$12,800
Total liabilities and stockholders' equity	$23,000	$21,800

Income Statement Data (2003)	
Depreciation expense	$11,600
Earnings before interest and taxes (EBIT)	2,700
Taxes	933
Net profits after taxes	1,400

LG4 **3–6 Cash receipts** A firm has actual sales of $65,000 in April and $60,000 in May. It expects sales of $70,000 in June and $100,000 in July and in August. Assuming that sales are the only source of cash inflows and that half of them are for cash and the remainder are collected evenly over the following 2 months, what are the firm's expected cash receipts for June, July, and August?

LG4 **3–7 Cash budget—Basic** Grenoble Enterprises had sales of $50,000 in March and $60,000 in April. Forecast sales for May, June, and July are $70,000, $80,000, and $100,000, respectively. The firm has a cash balance of $5,000 on May 1 and wishes to maintain a minimum cash balance of $5,000. Given the following data, prepare and interpret a cash budget for the months of May, June, and July.

(1) The firm makes 20% of sales for cash, 60% are collected in the next month, and the remaining 20% are collected in the second month following sale.
(2) The firm receives other income of $2,000 per month.
(3) The firm's actual or expected purchases, all made for cash, are $50,000, $70,000, and $80,000 for the months of May through July, respectively.
(4) Rent is $3,000 per month.
(5) Wages and salaries are 10% of the previous month's sales.
(6) Cash dividends of $3,000 will be paid in June.
(7) Payment of principal and interest of $4,000 is due in June.
(8) A cash purchase of equipment costing $6,000 is scheduled in July.
(9) Taxes of $6,000 are due in June.

LG4 **3–8 Cash budget—Advanced** The actual sales and purchases for Xenocore, Inc., for September and October 2003, along with its forecast sales and purchases for the period November 2003 through April 2004, follow.

Year	Month	Sales	Purchases
2003	September	$210,000	$120,000
2003	October	250,000	150,000
2003	November	170,000	140,000
2003	December	160,000	100,000
2004	January	140,000	80,000
2004	February	180,000	110,000
2004	March	200,000	100,000
2004	April	250,000	90,000

The firm makes 20% of all sales for cash and collects on 40% of its sales in each of the 2 months following the sale. Other cash inflows are expected to be $12,000 in September and April, $15,000 in January and March, and $27,000 in February. The firm pays cash for 10% of its purchases. It pays for 50% of its purchases in the following month and for 40% of its purchases 2 months later.

Wages and salaries amount to 20% of the preceding month's sales. Rent of $20,000 per month must be paid. Interest payments of $10,000 are due in January and April. A principal payment of $30,000 is also due in April. The firm expects to pay cash dividends of $20,000 in January and April. Taxes of $80,000 are due in April. The firm also intends to make a $25,000 cash purchase of fixed assets in December.

a. Assuming that the firm has a cash balance of $22,000 at the beginning of November, determine the end-of-month cash balances for each month, November through April.

b. Assuming that the firm wishes to maintain a $15,000 minimum cash balance, determine the required total financing or excess cash balance for each month, November through April.

c. If the firm were requesting a line of credit to cover needed financing for the period November to April, how large would this line have to be? Explain your answer.

LG4 3–9 **Cash flow concepts** The following represent financial transactions that Johnsfield & Co. will be undertaking in the next planning period. For each transaction, check the statement or statements that will be affected immediately.

	Statement		
Transaction	Cash budget	Pro forma income statement	Pro forma balance sheet
Cash sale			
Credit sale			
Accounts receivable are collected			
Asset with 5-year life is purchased			
Depreciation is taken			
Amortization of goodwill is taken			
Sale of common stock			
Retirement of outstanding bonds			
Fire insurance premium is paid for the next 3 years			

LG4 3–10 **Multiple cash budgets—Sensitivity analysis** Brownstein, Inc., expects sales of $100,000 during each of the next 3 months. It will make monthly purchases of $60,000 during this time. Wages and salaries are $10,000 per month plus 5% of sales. Brownstein expects to make a tax payment of $20,000 in the next month and a $15,000 purchase of fixed assets in the second month and to receive $8,000 in cash from the sale of an asset in the third month. All sales and purchases are for cash. Beginning cash and the minimum cash balance are assumed to be zero.

a. Construct a cash budget for the next 3 months.

b. Brownstein is unsure of the sales levels, but all other figures are certain. If the most pessimistic sales figure is $80,000 per month and the most optimistic is $120,000 per month, what are the monthly minimum and maximum ending cash balances that the firm can expect for each of the 1-month periods?

c. Briefly discuss how the financial manager can use the data in parts **a** and **b** to plan for financing needs.

LG5 **3–11 Pro forma income statement** The marketing department of Metroline Manufacturing estimates that its sales in 2004 will be $1.5 million. Interest expense is expected to remain unchanged at $35,000, and the firm plans to pay $70,000 in cash dividends during 2004. Metroline Manufacturing's income statement for the year ended December 31, 2003, is given below, along with a breakdown of the firm's cost of goods sold and operating expenses into their fixed and variable components.

Metroline Manufacturing
Income Statement
for the Year Ended December 31, 2003

Sales revenue	$1,400,000
Less: Cost of goods sold	910,000
Gross profits	$ 490,000
Less: Operating expenses	120,000
Operating profits	$ 370,000
Less: Interest expense	35,000
Net profits before taxes	$ 335,000
Less: Taxes (rate = 40%)	134,000
Net profits after taxes	$ 201,000
Less: Cash dividends	66,000
To retained earnings	$ 135,000

Metroline Manufacturing
Breakdown of
Costs and Expenses
into Fixed and Variable
Components for the
Year Ended December 31, 2003

Cost of goods sold	
Fixed cost	$210,000
Variable cost	700,000
Total cost	$910,000
Operating expenses	
Fixed expenses	$ 36,000
Variable expenses	84,000
Total expenses	$120,000

a. Use the *percent-of-sales method* to prepare a pro forma income statement for the year ended December 31, 2004.
b. Use *fixed and variable cost data* to develop a pro forma income statement for the year ended December 31, 2004.
c. Compare and contrast the statements developed in parts **a** and **b**. Which statement probably provides the better estimate of 2004 income? Explain why.

LG5 **3–12 Pro forma balance sheet—Basic** Leonard Industries wishes to prepare a pro forma balance sheet for December 31, 2004. The firm expects 2004 sales to total $3,000,000. The following information has been gathered.

(1) A minimum cash balance of $50,000 is desired.
(2) Marketable securities are expected to remain unchanged.
(3) Accounts receivable represent 10% of sales.
(4) Inventories represent 12% of sales.
(5) A new machine costing $90,000 will be acquired during 2004. Total depreciation for the year will be $32,000.
(6) Accounts payable represent 14% of sales.
(7) Accruals, other current liabilities, long-term debt, and common stock are expected to remain unchanged.
(8) The firm's net profit margin is 4%, and it expects to pay out $70,000 in cash dividends during 2004.
(9) The December 31, 2003, balance sheet follows.

Leonard Industries
Balance Sheet
December 31, 2003

Assets		**Liabilities and Stockholders' Equity**	
Cash	$ 45,000	Accounts payable	$ 395,000
Marketable securities	15,000	Accruals	60,000
Accounts receivable	255,000	Other current liabilities	30,000
Inventories	340,000	Total current liabilities	$ 485,000
Total current assets	$ 655,000	Long-term debt	$ 350,000
Net fixed assets	$ 600,000	Common stock	$ 200,000
Total assets	$1,255,000	Retained earnings	$ 220,000
		Total liabilities and stockholders' equity	$1,255,000

a. Use the *judgmental approach* to prepare a pro forma balance sheet dated December 31, 2004, for Leonard Industries.

b. How much, if any, additional financing will Leonard Industries require in 2004? Discuss.

c. Could Leonard Industries adjust its planned 2004 dividend to avoid the situation described in part **b**? Explain how.

LG5 **3–13 Pro forma balance sheet** Peabody & Peabody has 2003 sales of $10 million. It wishes to analyze expected performance and financing needs for 2005—2 years ahead. Given the following information, respond to parts **a** and **b**.

(1) The percents of sales for items that vary directly with sales are as follows:

Accounts receivable, 12%
Inventory, 18%
Accounts payable, 14%
Net profit margin, 3%

(2) Marketable securities and other current liabilities are expected to remain unchanged.
(3) A minimum cash balance of $480,000 is desired.
(4) A new machine costing $650,000 will be acquired in 2004, and equipment costing $850,000 will be purchased in 2005. Total depreciation in 2004 is forecast as $290,000, and in 2005 $390,000 of depreciation will be taken.
(5) Accruals are expected to rise to $500,000 by the end of 2005.
(6) No sale or retirement of long-term debt is expected.
(7) No sale or repurchase of common stock is expected.
(8) The dividend payout of 50% of net profits is expected to continue.
(9) Sales are expected to be $11 million in 2004 and $12 million in 2005.
(10) The December 31, 2003, balance sheet follows.

Peabody & Peabody
Balance Sheet
December 31, 2003
($000)

Assets		Liabilities and Stockholders' Equity	
Cash	$ 400	Accounts payable	$1,400
Marketable securities	200	Accruals	400
Accounts receivable	1,200	Other current liabilities	80
Inventories	1,800	Total current liabilities	$1,880
Total current assets	$3,600	Long-term debt	$2,000
Net fixed assets	$4,000	Common equity	$3,720
Total assets	$7,600	Total liabilities and stockholders' equity	$7,600

a. Prepare a pro forma balance sheet dated December 31, 2005.
b. Discuss the financing changes suggested by the statement prepared in part **a.**

LG5 3–14 **Integrative—Pro forma statements** Red Queen Restaurants wishes to prepare financial plans. Use the financial statements (on page 125) and the other information provided in what follows to prepare the financial plans. The following financial data are also available:
(1) The firm has estimated that its sales for 2004 will be $900,000.
(2) The firm expects to pay $35,000 in cash dividends in 2004.
(3) The firm wishes to maintain a minimum cash balance of $30,000.
(4) Accounts receivable represent approximately 18% of annual sales.
(5) The firm's ending inventory will change directly with changes in sales in 2004.

(6) A new machine costing $42,000 will be purchased in 2004. Total depreciation for 2004 will be $17,000.
(7) Accounts payable will change directly in response to changes in sales in 2004.
(8) Taxes payable will equal one-fourth of the tax liability on the pro forma income statement.
(9) Marketable securities, other current liabilities, long-term debt, and common stock will remain unchanged.

Red Queen Restaurants
Income Statement for the Year Ended December 31, 2003

Sales revenue	$800,000
Less: Cost of goods sold	600,000
Gross profits	$200,000
Less: Operating expenses	100,000
Net profits before taxes	$100,000
Less: Taxes (rate = 40%)	40,000
Net profits after taxes	$ 60,000
Less: Cash dividends	20,000
To retained earnings	$ 40,000

Red Queen Restaurants
Balance Sheet
December 31, 2003

Assets		Liabilities and Stockholders' Equity	
Cash	$ 32,000	Accounts payable	$100,000
Marketable securities	18,000	Taxes payable	20,000
Accounts receivable	150,000	Other current liabilities	5,000
Inventories	100,000	Total current liabilities	$125,000
Total current assets	$300,000	Long-term debt	$200,000
Net fixed assets	$350,000	Common stock	$150,000
Total assets	$650,000	Retained earnings	$175,000
		Total liabilities and stockholders' equity	$650,000

a. Prepare a pro forma income statement for the year ended December 31, 2004, using the *percent-of-sales method*.
b. Prepare a pro forma balance sheet dated December 31, 2004, using the *judgmental approach*.
c. Analyze these statements, and discuss the resulting *external financing required*.

CHAPTER 3 CASE Preparing Martin Manufacturing's 2004 Pro Forma Financial Statements

To improve its competitive position, Martin Manufacturing is planning to implement a major equipment modernization program. Included will be replacement and modernization of key manufacturing equipment at a cost of $400,000 in 2004. The planned program is expected to lower the variable cost per unit of finished product. Terri Spiro, an experienced budget analyst, has been charged with preparing a forecast of the firm's 2004 financial position, assuming replacement and modernization of manufacturing equipment. She plans to use the 2003 financial statements presented on pages 83 and 84, along with the key projected financial data summarized in the following table.

Martin Manufacturing Company
Key Projected Financial Data (2004)

Data item	Value
Sales revenue	$6,500,000
Minimum cash balance	$25,000
Inventory turnover (times)	7.0
Average collection period	50 days
Fixed-asset purchases	$400,000
Dividend payments	$20,000
Depreciation expense	$185,000
Interest expense	$97,000
Accounts payable increase	20%
Accruals and long-term debt	Unchanged
Notes payable, preferred and common stock	Unchanged

Required

a. Use the historical and projected financial data provided to prepare a pro forma income statement for the year ended December 31, 2004. (*Hint:* Use the *percent-of-sales method* to estimate all values *except* depreciation expense and interest expense, which have been estimated by management and included in the table.)

b. Use the projected financial data along with relevant data from the pro forma income statement prepared in part **a** to prepare the pro forma balance sheet at December 31, 2004. (*Hint:* Use the *judgmental approach.*)

c. Will Martin Manufacturing Company need to obtain *external financing* to fund the proposed equipment modernization program? Explain.

WEB EXERCISE

Go to the **Best Depreciation Calculator** at the Fixed Asset Info. site, *www.fixedassetinfo.com/defaultCalc.asp*. Use this calculator to determine the straight-line, declining balance (using 200%), and MACRS depreciation schedules for the following items, using half-year averaging (the half-year convention).

Item	Date placed in service	Cost
Office furnishings	2/15/2002	$22,500
Laboratory equipment	5/27/2001	$14,375
Fleet vehicles	9/5/2000	$45,863

Make a chart comparing the depreciation amounts that these three methods yield for the years 2002 to 2007. Discuss the implications of these differences.

Remember to check the book's Web site at

www.aw.com/gitman

for additional resources, including additional Web exercises.

Part 2

Important Financial Concepts

Chapter

4

Time Value of Money

LEARNING GOALS

- LG1 Discuss the role of time value in finance, the use of computational tools, and the basic patterns of cash flow.
- LG2 Understand the concepts of future and present value, their calculation for single amounts, and the relationship of present value to future value.
- LG3 Find the future value and the present value of an ordinary annuity, and find the present value of a perpetuity.
- LG4 Calculate both the future value and the present value of a mixed stream of cash flows.
- LG5 Understand the effect that compounding interest more frequently than annually has on future value and on the effective annual rate of interest.
- LG6 Describe the procedures involved in (1) determining deposits to accumulate a future sum, (2) loan amortization, (3) finding interest or growth rates, and (4) finding an unknown number of periods.

Across the Disciplines

Why This Chapter Matters To You

Accounting: You need to understand time-value-of-money calculations in order to account for certain transactions such as loan amortization, lease payments, and bond interest rates.

Information systems: You need to understand time-value-of-money calculations in order to design systems that optimize the firm's cash flows.

Management: You need to understand time-value-of-money calculations so that you can plan cash collections and disbursements in a way that will enable the firm to get the greatest value from its money.

Marketing: You need to understand time value of money because funding for new programs and products must be justified financially using time-value-of-money techniques.

Operations: You need to understand time value of money because investments in new equipment, in inventory, and in production quantities will be affected by time-value-of-money techniques.

Because we view the firm as a going concern, we assess the decisions of its financial managers, and ultimately the value of the firm itself, in light of its cash flows. The opportunity to earn interest on the firm's funds makes the timing of its cash flows important, because a dollar received in the future in not the same as a dollar received today. Thus, money has a time value, which affects every-one—individuals, businesses, and government. In this chapter we explore the concepts related to the time value of money.

LG1

The Role of Time Value in Finance

Financial managers and investors are always confronted with opportunities to earn positive rates of return on their funds, whether through investment in attractive projects or in interest-bearing securities or deposits. Therefore, the timing of cash outflows and inflows has important economic consequences, which financial managers explicitly recognize as the *time value of money*. Time value is based on the belief that a dollar today is worth more than a dollar that will be received at some future date. We begin our study of time value in finance by considering the two views of time value—future value and present value, the computational tools used to streamline time value calculations, and the basic patterns of cash flow.

Future Value versus Present Value

Financial values and decisions can be assessed by using either future value or present value techniques. Although these techniques will result in the same decisions, they view the decision differently. Future value techniques typically measure cash flows at the *end* of a project's life. Present value techniques measure cash flows at the *start* of a project's life (time zero). *Future value* is cash you will receive at a given future date, and *present value* is just like cash in hand today.

time line
A horizontal line on which time zero appears at the leftmost end and future periods are marked from left to right; can be used to depict investment cash flows.

A **time line** can be used to depict the cash flows associated with a given investment. It is a horizontal line on which time zero appears at the leftmost end and future periods are marked from left to right. A line covering five periods (in this case, years) is given in Figure 4.1. The cash flow occurring at time zero and that at the end of each year are shown above the line; the negative values represent *cash outflows* ($10,000 at time zero) and the positive values represent *cash inflows* ($3,000 inflow at the end of year 1, $5,000 inflow at the end of year 2, and so on).

FIGURE 4.1

Time Line

Time line depicting an investment's cash flows

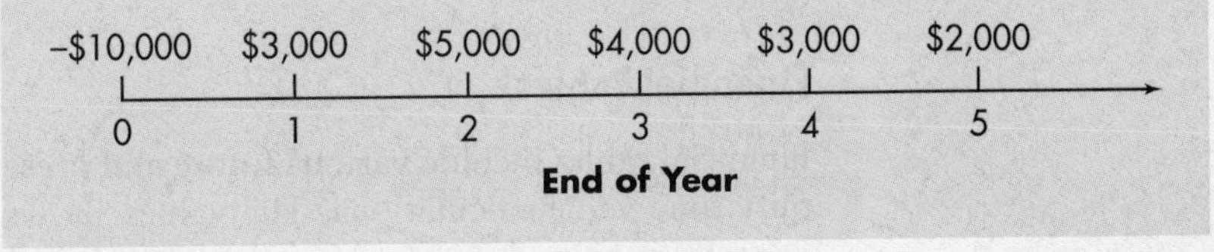

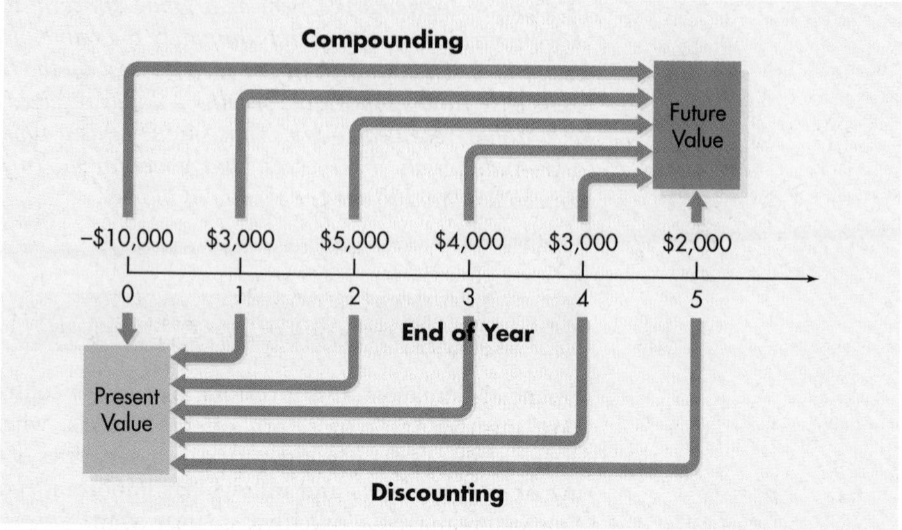

FIGURE 4.2

Compounding and Discounting
Time line showing compounding to find future value and discounting to find present value

Because money has a time value, all of the cash flows associated with an investment, such as those in Figure 4.1, must be measured at the same point in time. Typically, that point is either the end or the beginning of the investment's life. The future value technique uses *compounding* to find the *future value* of each cash flow at the end of the investment's life and then sums these values to find the investment's future value. This approach is depicted above the time line in Figure 4.2. The figure shows that the future value of each cash flow is measured at the end of the investment's 5-year life. Alternatively, the present value technique uses *discounting* to find the *present value* of each cash flow at time zero and then sums these values to find the investment's value today. Application of this approach is depicted below the time line in Figure 4.2.

The meaning and mechanics of compounding to find future value and of discounting to find present value are covered in this chapter. Although future value and present value result in the same decisions, *financial managers—because they make decisions at time zero—tend to rely primarily on present value techniques.*

Computational Tools

Time-consuming calculations are often involved in finding future and present values. Although you should understand the concepts and mathematics underlying these calculations, the application of time value techniques can be streamlined. We focus on the use of financial tables, hand-held financial calculators, and computers and spreadsheets as aids in computation.

Financial Tables

Financial tables include various future and present value interest factors that simplify time value calculations. The values shown in these tables are easily developed from formulas, with various degrees of rounding. The tables are typically

FIGURE 4.3

Financial Tables
Layout and use of a financial table

	Interest Rate							
Period	1%	2%	⋯	10%	⋯	**20%** ↓	⋯	50%
1			⋯		⋯	⋮	⋯	
2			⋯		⋯	⋮	⋯	
3			⋯		⋯	⋮	⋯	
⋮	⋮	⋮	⋯	⋮	⋯	⋮	⋯	⋮
→ **10**	⋯	⋯	⋯	⋯	⋯	**X.XXX**	⋯	⋯
⋮	⋮	⋮	⋯	⋮	⋯	⋮	⋯	⋮
20			⋯		⋯		⋯	
⋮	⋮	⋮	⋯	⋮	⋯	⋮	⋯	⋮
50			⋯		⋯		⋯	

indexed by the interest rate (in columns) and the number of periods (in rows). Figure 4.3 shows this general layout. The interest factor at a 20 percent interest rate for 10 years would be found at the intersection of the 20% column and the 10-period row, as shown by the dark blue box. A full set of the four basic financial tables is included in Appendix A at the end of the book. These tables are described more fully later in the chapter.

Financial Calculators

Financial calculators also can be used for time value computations. Generally, *financial calculators* include numerous preprogrammed financial routines. This chapter and those that follow show the keystrokes for calculating interest factors and making other financial computations. For convenience, we use the important financial keys, labeled in a fashion consistent with most major financial calculators.

We focus primarily on the keys pictured and defined in Figure 4.4. We typically use four of the first five keys shown in the left column, along with the compute (**CPT**) key. One of the four keys represents the unknown value being

FIGURE 4.4

Calculator Keys
Important financial keys on the typical calculator

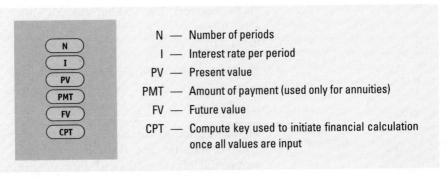

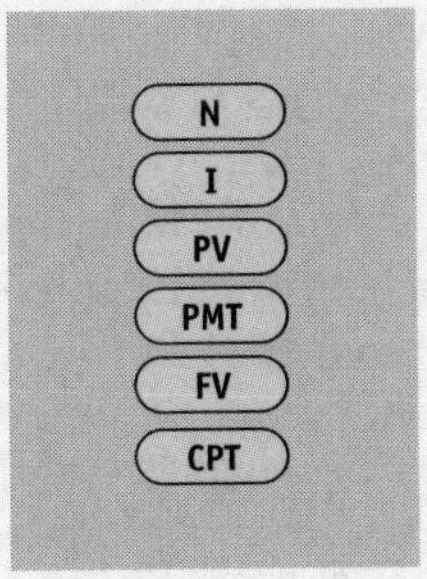

N — Number of periods
I — Interest rate per period
PV — Present value
PMT — Amount of payment (used only for annuities)
FV — Future value
CPT — Compute key used to initiate financial calculation once all values are input

calculated. (Occasionally, all five of the keys are used, with one representing the unknown value.) The keystrokes on some of the more sophisticated calculators are menu-driven: After you select the appropriate routine, the calculator prompts you to input each value; on these calculators, a compute key is not needed to obtain a solution. Regardless, any calculator with the basic future and present value functions can be used in lieu of financial tables. The keystrokes for other financial calculators are explained in the reference guides that accompany them.

Once you understand the basic underlying concepts, you probably will want to use a calculator to streamline routine financial calculations. With a little practice, you can increase both the speed and the accuracy of your financial computations. Note that because of a calculator's greater precision, slight differences are likely to exist between values calculated by using financial tables and those found with a financial calculator. Remember that *conceptual understanding of the material is the objective.* An ability to solve problems with the aid of a calculator does not necessarily reflect such an understanding, so don't just settle for answers. Work with the material until you are sure you also understand the concepts.

Computers and Spreadsheets

Like financial calculators, computers and spreadsheets have built-in routines that simplify time value calculations. We provide in the text a number of spreadsheet solutions that identify the cell entries for calculating time values. The value for each variable is entered in a cell in the spreadsheet, and the calculation is programmed using an equation that links the individual cells. If values of the variables are changed, the solution automatically changes as a result of the equation linking the cells. In the spreadsheet solutions in this book, the equation that determines the calculation is shown at the bottom of the spreadsheet.

The ability to use spreadsheets has become a prime skill for today's managers. As the saying goes, "Get aboard the bandwagon, or get run over." The spreadsheet solutions we present in this book will help you climb up onto that bandwagon!

Basic Patterns of Cash Flow

The cash flow—both inflows and outflows—of a firm can be described by its general pattern. It can be defined as a single amount, an annuity, or a mixed stream.

Single amount: A lump-sum amount either currently held or expected at some future date. Examples include $1,000 today and $650 to be received at the end of 10 years.

Annuity: A level periodic stream of cash flow. For our purposes, we'll work primarily with *annual* cash flows. Examples include either paying out or receiving $800 at the end of each of the next 7 years.

Mixed stream: A stream of cash flow that is *not* an annuity; a stream of unequal periodic cash flows that reflect no particular pattern. Examples include the following two cash flow streams A and B.

	Mixed cash flow stream	
End of year	A	B
1	$ 100	−$ 50
2	800	100
3	1,200	80
4	1,200	− 60
5	1,400	
6	300	

Note that neither cash flow stream has equal, periodic cash flows and that A is a 6-year mixed stream and B is a 4-year mixed stream.

In the next three sections of this chapter, we develop the concepts and techniques for finding future and present values of single amounts, annuities, and mixed streams, respectively. Detailed demonstrations of these cash flow patterns are included.

Review Questions

4–1 What is the difference between *future value* and *present value?* Which approach is generally preferred by financial managers? Why?

4–2 Define and differentiate among the three basic patterns of cash flow: (1) a single amount, (2) an annuity, and (3) a mixed stream.

LG2

Single Amounts

The most basic future value and present value concepts and computations concern single amounts, either present or future amounts. We begin by considering the future value of present amounts. Then we will use the underlying concepts to learn how to determine the present value of future amounts. You will see that although future value is more intuitively appealing, present value is more useful in financial decision making.

Future Value of a Single Amount

Imagine that at age 25 you began making annual purchases of $2,000 of an investment that earns a guaranteed 5 percent annually. At the end of 40 years, at age 65, you would have invested a total of $80,000 (40 years × $2,000 per year). Assuming that all funds remain invested, how much would you have accumulated at the end of the fortieth year? $100,000? $150,000? $200,000? No, your $80,000 would have grown to $242,000! Why? Because the time value of money allowed your investments to generate returns that built on each other over the 40 years.

compound interest
Interest that is earned on a given deposit and has become part of the principal at the end of a specified period.

principal
The amount of money on which interest is paid.

future value
The value of a present amount at a future date, found by applying *compound interest* over a specified period of time.

The Concept of Future Value

We speak of **compound interest** to indicate that the amount of interest earned on a given deposit has become part of the principal at the end of a specified period. The term **principal** refers to the amount of money on which the interest is paid. Annual compounding is the most common type.

The **future value** of a present amount is found by applying *compound interest* over a specified period of time. Savings institutions advertise compound interest returns at a rate of x percent, or x percent interest, compounded annually, semiannually, quarterly, monthly, weekly, daily, or even continuously. The concept of future value with annual compounding can be illustrated by a simple example.

EXAMPLE

If Fred Moreno places \$100 in a savings account paying 8% interest compounded annually, at the end of 1 year he will have \$108 in the account—the initial principal of \$100 plus 8% (\$8) in interest. The future value at the end of the first year is calculated by using Equation 4.1:

$$\text{Future value at end of year 1} = \$100 \times (1 + 0.08) = \$108 \tag{4.1}$$

If Fred were to leave this money in the account for another year, he would be paid interest at the rate of 8% on the new principal of \$108. At the end of this second year there would be \$116.64 in the account. This amount would represent the principal at the beginning of year 2 (\$108) plus 8% of the \$108 (\$8.64) in interest. The future value at the end of the second year is calculated by using Equation 4.2:

$$\begin{aligned}\text{Future value at end of year 2} &= \$108 \times (1 + 0.08) \\ &= \$116.64\end{aligned} \tag{4.2}$$

Substituting the expression between the equals signs in Equation 4.1 for the \$108 figure in Equation 4.2 gives us Equation 4.3:

$$\begin{aligned}\text{Future value at end of year 2} &= \$100 \times (1 + 0.08) \times (1 + 0.08) \\ &= \$100 \times (1 + 0.08)^2 \\ &= \$116.64\end{aligned} \tag{4.3}$$

The equations in the preceding example lead to a more general formula for calculating future value.

The Equation for Future Value

The basic relationship in Equation 4.3 can be generalized to find the future value after any number of periods. We use the following notation for the various inputs:

FV_n = future value at the end of period n
PV = initial principal, or present value
i = annual rate of interest paid. (*Note:* On financial calculators, **I** is typically used to represent this rate.)
n = number of periods (typically years) that the money is left on deposit

The general equation for the future value at the end of period n is

$$FV_n = PV \times (1 + i)^n \tag{4.4}$$

A simple example will illustrate how to apply Equation 4.4.

EXAMPLE

Jane Farber places $800 in a savings account paying 6% interest compounded annually. She wants to know how much money will be in the account at the end of 5 years. Substituting $PV = \$800$, $i = 0.06$, and $n = 5$ into Equation 4.4 gives the amount at the end of year 5.

$$FV_5 = \$800 \times (1 + 0.06)^5 = \$800 \times (1.338) = \$1{,}070.40$$

This analysis can be depicted on a time line as follows:

Time line for future value of a single amount ($800 initial principal, earning 6%, at the end of 5 years)

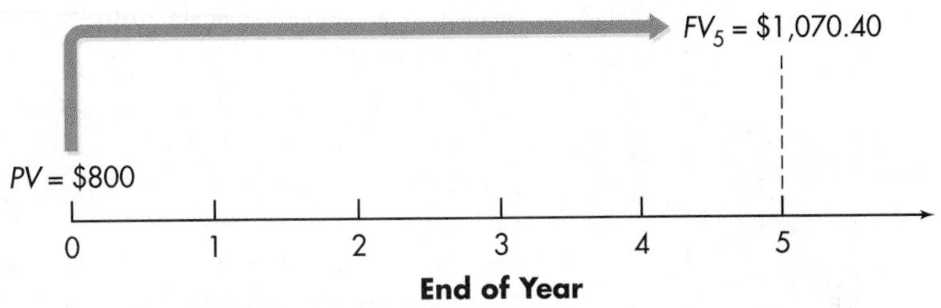

Using Computational Tools to Find Future Value

future value interest factor
The multiplier used to calculate, at a specified interest rate, the future value of a present amount as of a given time.

Solving the equation in the preceding example involves raising 1.06 to the fifth power. Using a future value interest table or a financial calculator or a computer and spreadsheet greatly simplifies the calculation. A table that provides values for $(1 + i)^n$ in Equation 4.4 is included near the back of the book in Appendix Table A–1.[1] The value in each cell of the table is called the **future value interest factor.** This factor is the multiplier used to calculate, at a specified interest rate, the future value of a present amount as of a given time. The future value interest factor for an initial principal of $1 compounded at i percent for n periods is referred to as $FVIF_{i,n}$.

$$\text{Future value interest factor} = FVIF_{i,n} = (1 + i)^n \tag{4.5}$$

By finding the intersection of the annual interest rate, i, and the appropriate periods, n, you will find the future value interest factor that is relevant to a particular problem.[2] Using $FVIF_{i,n}$ as the appropriate factor, we can rewrite the general equation for future value (Equation 4.4) as follows:

$$FV_n = PV \times (FVIF_{i,n}) \tag{4.6}$$

This expression indicates that to find the future value at the end of period n of an initial deposit, we have merely to multiply the initial deposit, PV, by the appropriate future value interest factor.[3]

1. This table is commonly referred to as a "compound interest table" or a "table of the future value of one dollar." As long as you understand the source of the table values, the various names attached to it should not create confusion, because you can always make a trial calculation of a value for one factor as a check.

2. Although we commonly deal with years rather than periods, financial tables are frequently presented in terms of periods to provide maximum flexibility.

3. Occasionally, you may want to estimate roughly how long a given sum must earn at a given annual rate to double the amount. The *Rule of 72* is used to make this estimate; dividing the annual rate of interest into 72 results in the approximate number of periods it will take to double one's money at the given rate. For example, to double one's money at a 10% annual rate of interest will take about 7.2 years ($72 \div 10 = 7.2$). Looking at Table A–1, we can see that the future value interest factor for 10% and 7 years is slightly below 2 (1.949); this approximation therefore appears to be reasonably accurate.

EXAMPLE ▼

In the preceding example, Jane Farber placed $800 in her savings account at 6% interest compounded annually and wishes to find out how much will be in the account at the end of 5 years.

Table Use The future value interest factor for an initial principal of $1 on deposit for 5 years at 6% interest compounded annually, $FVIF_{6\%,\ 5yrs}$, found in Table A–1, is 1.338. Using Equation 4.6, $800 × 1.338 = $1,070.40. Therefore, the future value of Jane's deposit at the end of year 5 will be $1,070.40.

Calculator Use[4] The financial calculator can be used to calculate the future value directly.[5] First punch in $800 and depress **PV**; next punch in 5 and depress **N**; then punch in 6 and depress **I** (which is equivalent to "*i*" in our notation)[6]; finally, to calculate the future value, depress **CPT** and then **FV**. The future value of $1,070.58 should appear on the calculator display as shown at the left. On many calculators, this value will be preceded by a minus sign (−1,070.58). *If a minus sign appears on your calculator, ignore it here as well as in all other "Calculator Use" illustrations in this text.*[7]

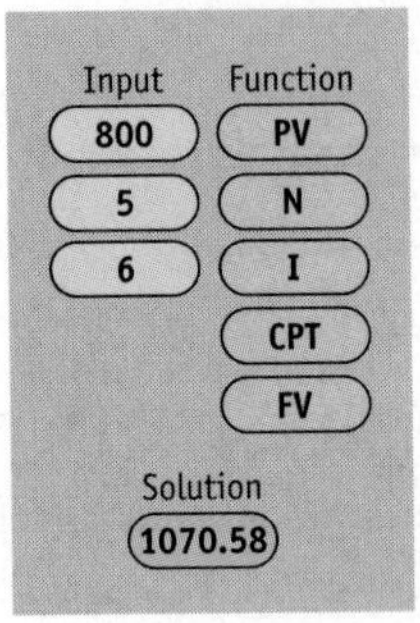

Because the calculator is more accurate than the future value factors, which have been rounded to the nearest 0.001, a slight difference—in this case, $0.18—will frequently exist between the values found by these alternative methods. Clearly, the improved accuracy and ease of calculation tend to favor the use of the calculator. (*Note:* In future examples of calculator use, we will use only a display similar to that shown at the left. If you need a reminder of the procedures involved, go back and review the preceding paragraph.)

Spreadsheet Use The future value of the single amount also can be calculated as shown on the following Excel spreadsheet.

Input	Function
800	PV
5	N
6	I
	CPT
	FV

Solution
1070.58

	A	B
1	**FUTURE VALUE OF A SINGLE AMOUNT**	
2	Present value	$800
3	Interest rate, pct per year compounded annually	6%
4	Number of years	5
5	Future value	$1,070.58

Entry in Cell B5 is =FV(B3,B4,0,−B2,0).
The minus sign appears before B2 because the present value
is an outflow (i.e., a deposit made by Jane Farber).

4. Many calculators allow the user to set the number of payments per year. Most of these calculators are preset for monthly payments—12 payments per year. Because we work primarily with annual payments—one payment per year—it is important *to be sure that your calculator is set for one payment per year.* And although most calculators are preset to recognize that all payments occur at the end of the period, it is important to *make sure that your calculator is correctly set on the END mode.* Consult the reference guide that accompanies your calculator for instructions for setting these values.

5. To avoid including previous data in current calculations, *always clear all registers of your calculator before inputting values and making each computation.*

6. The known values *can be punched into the calculator in any order;* the order specified in this as well as other demonstrations of calculator use included in this text merely reflects convenience and personal preference.

7. The calculator differentiates inflows from outflows by preceding the outflows with a negative sign. For example, in the problem just demonstrated, the $800 present value (PV), because it was keyed as a positive number (800), is considered an inflow or deposit. Therefore, the calculated future value (FV) of −1,070.58 is preceded by a minus sign to show that it is the resulting outflow or withdrawal. Had the $800 present value been keyed in as a negative number (−800), the future value of $1,070.58 would have been displayed as a positive number (1,070.58). Simply stated, *the cash flows—present value (PV) and future value (FV)—will have opposite signs.*

A Graphical View of Future Value

Remember that we measure future value at the *end* of the given period. Figure 4.5 illustrates the relationship among various interest rates, the number of periods interest is earned, and the future value of one dollar. The figure shows that (1) the higher the interest rate, the higher the future value, and (2) the longer the period of time, the higher the future value. Note that for an interest rate of 0 percent, the future value always equals the present value ($1.00). But for any interest rate greater than zero, the future value is greater than the present value of $1.00.

Present Value of a Single Amount

present value
The current dollar value of a future amount—the amount of money that would have to be invested today at a given interest rate over a specified period to equal the future amount.

It is often useful to determine the value today of a future amount of money. For example, how much would I have to deposit today into an account paying 7 percent annual interest in order to accumulate $3,000 at the end of 5 years? **Present value** is the current dollar value of a future amount—the amount of money that would have to be invested today at a given interest rate over a specified period to equal the future amount. Present value depends largely on the investment opportunities and the point in time at which the amount is to be received. This section explores the present value of a single amount.

The Concept of Present Value

discounting cash flows
The process of finding present values; the inverse of compounding interest.

The process of finding present values is often referred to as **discounting cash flows.** It is concerned with answering the following question: "If I can earn *i* percent on my money, what is the most I would be willing to pay now for an opportunity to receive FV_n dollars *n* periods from today?"

This process is actually the inverse of compounding interest. Instead of finding the future value of present dollars invested at a given rate, discounting determines the present value of a future amount, assuming an opportunity to earn a certain return on the money. This annual rate of return is variously referred to

FIGURE 4.5

Future Value Relationship

Interest rates, time periods, and future value of one dollar

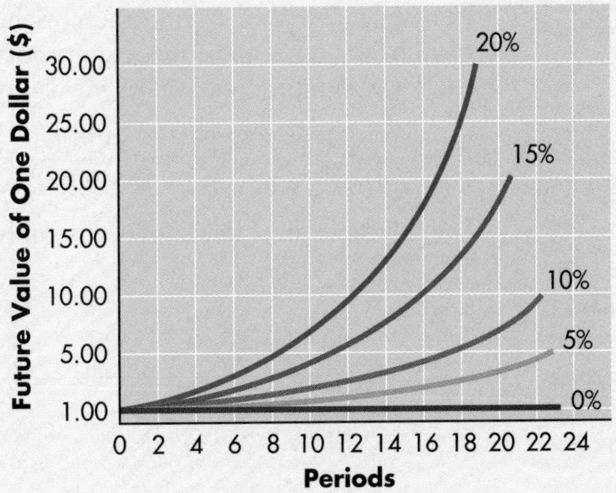

as the *discount rate, required return, cost of capital,* and *opportunity cost.* These terms will be used interchangeably in this text.

EXAMPLE Paul Shorter has an opportunity to receive \$300 one year from now. If he can earn 6% on his investments in the normal course of events, what is the most he should pay now for this opportunity? To answer this question, Paul must determine how many dollars he would have to invest at 6% today to have \$300 one year from now. Letting PV equal this unknown amount and using the same notation as in the future value discussion, we have

$$PV \times (1 + 0.06) = \$300 \tag{4.7}$$

Solving Equation 4.7 for PV gives us Equation 4.8:

$$PV = \frac{\$300}{(1 + 0.06)} = \$283.02 \tag{4.8}$$

The value today ("present value") of \$300 received one year from today, given an opportunity cost of 6%, is \$283.02. That is, investing \$283.02 today at the 6% opportunity cost would result in \$300 at the end of one year.

The Equation for Present Value

The present value of a future amount can be found mathematically by solving Equation 4.4 for PV. In other words, the present value, PV, of some future amount, FV_n, to be received n periods from now, assuming an opportunity cost of i, is calculated as follows:

$$PV = \frac{FV_n}{(1 + i)^n} = FV_n \times \left[\frac{1}{(1 + i)^n}\right] \tag{4.9}$$

Note the similarity between this general equation for present value and the equation in the preceding example (Equation 4.8). Let's use this equation in an example.

EXAMPLE Pam Valenti wishes to find the present value of \$1,700 that will be received 8 years from now. Pam's opportunity cost is 8%. Substituting $FV_8 = \$1,700$, $n = 8$, and $i = 0.08$ into Equation 4.9 yields Equation 4.10:

$$PV = \frac{\$1,700}{(1 + 0.08)^8} = \frac{\$1,700}{1.851} = \$918.42 \tag{4.10}$$

The following time line shows this analysis.

Time line for present value of a single amount (\$1,700 future amount, discounted at 8%, from the end of 8 years)

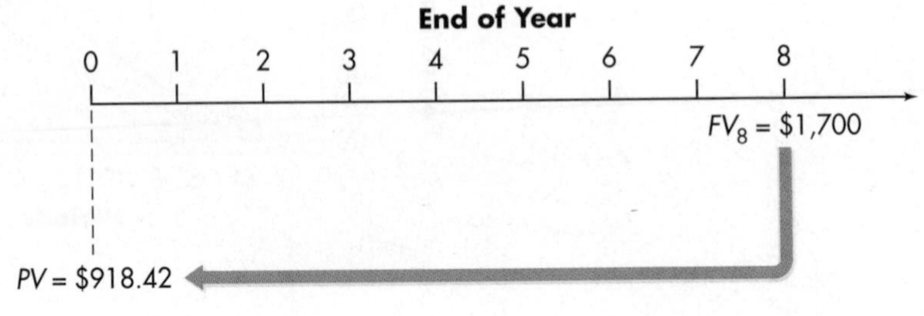

Using Computational Tools to Find Present Value

present value interest factor
The multiplier used to calculate, at a specified discount rate, the present value of an amount to be received in a future period.

The present value calculation can be simplified by using a **present value interest factor.** This factor is the multiplier used to calculate, at a specified discount rate, the present value of an amount to be received in a future period. The present value interest factor for the present value of \$1 discounted at i percent for n periods is referred to as $PVIF_{i,n}$.

$$\text{Present value interest factor} = PVIF_{i,n} = \frac{1}{(1+i)^n} \tag{4.11}$$

Appendix Table A–2 presents present value interest factors for \$1. By letting $PVIF_{i,n}$ represent the appropriate factor, we can rewrite the general equation for present value (Equation 4.9) as follows:

$$PV = FV_n \times (PVIF_{i,n}) \tag{4.12}$$

This expression indicates that to find the present value of an amount to be received in a future period, n, we have merely to multiply the future amount, FV_n, by the appropriate present value interest factor.

EXAMPLE

Input	Function
1700	FV
8	N
8	I
	CPT
	PV

Solution
918.46

As noted, Pam Valenti wishes to find the present value of \$1,700 to be received 8 years from now, assuming an 8% opportunity cost.

Table Use The present value interest factor for 8% and 8 years, $PVIF_{8\%,\,8\text{ yrs}}$, found in Table A–2, is 0.540. Using Equation 4.12, \$1,700 × 0.540 = \$918. The present value of the \$1,700 Pam expects to receive in 8 years is \$918.

Calculator Use Using the calculator's financial functions and the inputs shown at the left, you should find the present value to be \$918.46. The value obtained with the calculator is more accurate than the values found using the equation or the table, although for the purposes of this text, these differences are insignificant.

Spreadsheet Use The present value of the single future amount also can be calculated as shown on the following Excel spreadsheet.

	A	B
1	PRESENT VALUE OF A SINGLE FUTURE AMOUNT	
2	Future value	\$1,700
3	Interest rate, pct per year compounded annually	8%
4	Number of years	8
5	Present value	\$918.46

Entry in Cell B5 is =–PV(B3,B4,0,B2).
The minus sign appears before PV to change the present value to a positive amount.

A Graphical View of Present Value

Remember that present value calculations assume that the future values are measured at the *end* of the given period. The relationships among the factors in a present value calculation are illustrated in Figure 4.6. The figure clearly shows that, everything else being equal, (1) the higher the discount rate, the lower the

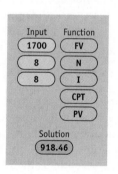

FIGURE 4.6

Present Value Relationship
Discount rates, time periods, and present value of one dollar

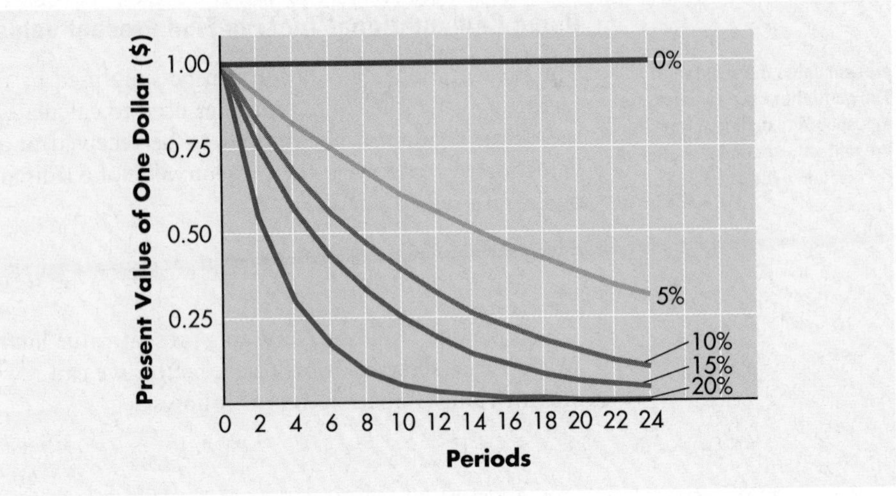

present value, and (2) the longer the period of time, the lower the present value. Also note that given a discount rate of 0 percent, the present value always equals the future value ($1.00). But for any discount rate greater than zero, the present value is less than the future value of $1.00.

Comparing Present Value and Future Value

We will close this section with some important observations about present values. One is that the expression for the present value interest factor for i percent and n periods, $1/(1+i)^n$, is the *inverse* of the future value interest factor for i percent and n periods, $(1+i)^n$. You can confirm this very simply: Divide a present value interest factor for i percent and n periods, $PVIF_{i,n}$, given in Table A–2, into 1.0, and compare the resulting value to the future value interest factor given in Table A–1 for i percent and n periods, $FVIF_{i,n}$. The two values should be equivalent.

Second, because of the relationship between present value interest factors and future value interest factors, we can find the present value interest factors given a table of future value interest factors, and vice versa. For example, the future value interest factor (from Table A–1) for 10 percent and 5 periods is 1.611. Dividing this value into 1.0 yields 0.621, which is the present value interest factor (given in Table A–2) for 10 percent and 5 periods.

Review Questions

4–3 How is the *compounding process* related to the payment of interest on savings? What is the general equation for future value?

4–4 What effect would a *decrease* in the interest rate have on the future value of a deposit? What effect would an *increase* in the holding period have on future value?

4–5 What is meant by "the present value of a future amount"? What is the general equation for present value?

4–6 What effect does *increasing* the required return have on the present value of a future amount? Why?

4–7 How are present value and future value calculations related?

LG3

Annuities

How much will you have at the end of 5 years if your employer withholds and invests $1,000 of your year-end bonus at the end of *each* of the next 5 years, guaranteeing you a 9 percent annual rate of return? How much would you pay today, given that you can earn 7 percent on low-risk investments, to receive a guaranteed $3,000 at the end of *each* of the next 20 years? To answer these questions, you need to understand the application of the time value of money to *annuities.*

annuity
A stream of equal periodic cash flows, over a specified time period. These cash flows can be *inflows* of returns earned on investments or *outflows* of funds invested to earn future returns.

An **annuity** is a stream of equal periodic cash flows, over a specified time period. These cash flows are usually annual but can occur at other intervals, such as monthly (rent, car payments). The cash flows in an annuity can be *inflows* (the $3,000 received at the end of each of the next 20 years) or *outflows* (the $1,000 invested at the end of each of the next 5 years).

ordinary annuity
An annuity for which the cash flow occurs at the *end* of each period.

annuity due
An annuity for which the cash flow occurs at the *beginning* of each period.

Types of Annuities

There are two basic types of annuities. For an **ordinary annuity,** the cash flow occurs at the *end* of each period. For an **annuity due,** the cash flow occurs at the *beginning* of each period.

EXAMPLE

Fran Abrams is choosing which of two annuities to receive. Both are 5-year, $1,000 annuities; annuity A is an ordinary annuity, and annuity B is an annuity due. To better understand the difference between these annuities, she has listed their cash flows in Table 4.1. Note that the amount of each annuity totals $5,000. The two annuities differ in the timing of their cash flows: The cash flows are received sooner with the annuity due than with the ordinary annuity.

Although the cash flows of both annuities in Table 4.1 total $5,000, the annuity due would have a higher future value than the ordinary annuity, because each of its five annual cash flows can earn interest for one year more than each of the ordinary annuity's cash flows. Similarly, the present value of the annuity due would be greater than that of the ordinary annuity, because each annuity due cash flow is discounted back one less year than for the ordinary annuity. In general, *both the future value and the present value of an annuity due are always greater than the future value and the present value, respectively, of an otherwise identical ordinary annuity.*

Because ordinary annuities are more frequently used in finance, unless otherwise specified, the term *annuity* is used throughout this book to refer to ordinary annuities. In addition, discussions of annuities in this book concentrate on ordinary annuities. For discussion and computations of annuities due, see the book's Web site at *www.aw.com/gitman.*

TABLE 4.1 Comparison of Ordinary Annuity and Annuity Due Cash Flows ($1,000, 5 Years)

	Annual cash flows	
End of year[a]	Annuity A (*ordinary*)	Annuity B (*annuity due*)
0	$ 0	$1,000
1	1,000	1,000
2	1,000	1,000
3	1,000	1,000
4	1,000	1,000
5	1,000	0
Totals	$5,000	$5,000

[a]The ends of years 0, 1, 2, 3, 4, and 5 are equivalent to the beginnings of years 1, 2, 3, 4, 5, and 6, respectively.

Finding the Future Value of an Ordinary Annuity

The calculations required to find the future value of an ordinary annuity are illustrated in the following example.

EXAMPLE Fran Abrams wishes to determine how much money she will have at the end of 5 years if he chooses annuity A, the ordinary annuity. It represents deposits of $1,000 annually, at the *end of each* of the next 5 years, into a savings account paying 7% annual interest. This situation is depicted on the following time line:

Time line for future value of an ordinary annuity ($1,000 end-of-year deposit, earning 7%, at the end of 5 years)

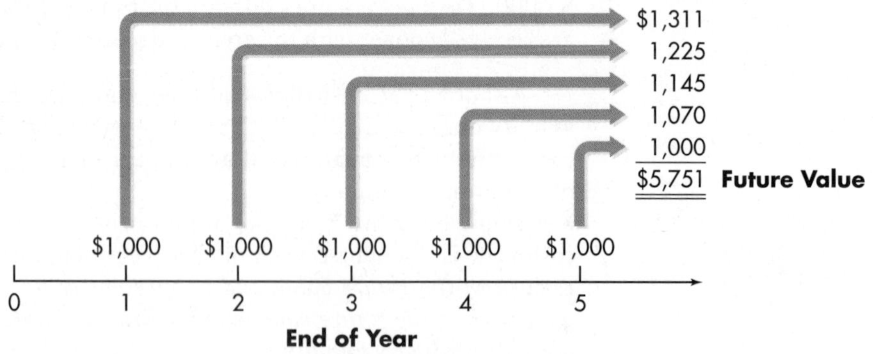

As the figure shows, at the end of year 5, Fran will have $5,751 in her account. Note that because the deposits are made at the end of the year, the first deposit will earn interest for 4 years, the second for 3 years, and so on.

Using Computational Tools to Find the Future Value of an Ordinary Annuity

Annuity calculations can be simplified by using an interest table or a financial calculator or a computer and spreadsheet. A table for the future value of a $1 *ordinary annuity* is given in Appendix Table A–3. The factors in the table are derived by summing the future value interest factors for the appropriate number of years. For example, the factor for the annuity in the preceding example is the sum of the factors for the five years (years 4 through 0): 1.311 + 1.225 + 1.145 + 1.070 + 1.000 = 5.751. Because the deposits occur at the end of each year, they will earn interest from the end of the year in which each occurs to the end of year 5. Therefore, the first deposit earns interest for 4 years (end of year 1 through end of year 5), and the last deposit earns interest for zero years. The future value interest factor for zero years at any interest rate, $FVIF_{i,0}$, is 1.000, as we have noted. The formula for the **future value interest factor for an ordinary annuity** when interest is compounded annually at i percent for n periods, $FVIFA_{i,n}$, is[8]

future value interest factor for an ordinary annuity
The multiplier used to calculate the future value of an *ordinary annuity* at a specified interest rate over a given period of time.

$$FVIFA_{i,n} = \sum_{t=1}^{n} (1+i)^{t-1} \qquad (4.13)$$

This factor is the multiplier used to calculate the future value of an *ordinary annuity* at a specified interest rate over a given period of time.

Using FVA_n for the future value of an n-year annuity, PMT for the amount to be deposited annually at the *end* of each year, and $FVIFA_{i,n}$ for the appropriate *future value interest factor for a one-dollar ordinary annuity compounded at* i *percent for* n *years,* we can express the relationship among these variables alternatively as

$$FVA_n = PMT \times (FVIFA_{i,n}) \qquad (4.14)$$

The following example illustrates this calculation using a table, a calculator, and a spreadsheet.

EXAMPLE

Input	Function
1000	PMT
5	N
7	I
	CPT
	FV

Solution
5750.74

As noted earlier, Fran Abrams wishes to find the future value (FVA_n) at the end of 5 years (n) of an annual *end-of-year deposit* of $1,000 ($PMT$) into an account paying 7% annual interest (i) during the next 5 years.

Table Use The future value interest factor for an ordinary 5-year annuity at 7% ($FVIFA_{7\%,5\text{yrs}}$), found in Table A–3, is 5.751. Using Equation 4.14, the $1,000 deposit × 5.751 results in a future value for the annuity of $5,751.

Calculator Use Using the calculator inputs shown at the left, you will find the future value of the ordinary annuity to be $5,750.74, a slightly more precise answer than that found using the table.

---

8. A mathematical expression that can be applied to calculate the future value interest factor for an ordinary annuity more efficiently is

$$FVIFA_{i,n} = \frac{1}{i} \times [(1+i)^n - 1] \qquad (4.13a)$$

The use of this expression is especially attractive in the absence of the appropriate financial tables and of any financial calculator or personal computer and spreadsheet.

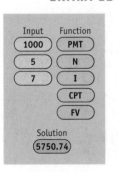

Spreadsheet Use The future value of the ordinary annuity also can be calculated as shown on the following Excel spreadsheet.

	A	B
1	**FUTURE VALUE OF AN ORDINARY ANNUITY**	
2	Annual payment	$1,000
3	Annual rate of interest, compounded annually	7%
4	Number of years	5
5	Future value of an ordinary annuity	$5,750.74
	Entry in Cell B5 is =FV(B3,B4,–B2) The minus sign appears before B2 because the annual payment is a cash outflow.	

Finding the Present Value of an Ordinary Annuity

Quite often in finance, there is a need to find the present value of a *stream* of cash flows to be received in future periods. An annuity is, of course, a stream of equal periodic cash flows. (We'll explore the case of mixed streams of cash flows in a later section.) The method for finding the present value of an ordinary annuity is similar to the method just discussed. There are long and short methods for making this calculation.

EXAMPLE Braden Company, a small producer of plastic toys, wants to determine the most it should pay to purchase a particular ordinary annuity. The annuity consists of cash flows of $700 at the end of each year for 5 years. The firm requires the annuity to provide a minimum return of 8%. This situation is depicted on the following time line:

Time line for present value of an ordinary annuity ($700 end-of-year cash flows, discounted at 8%, over 5 years)

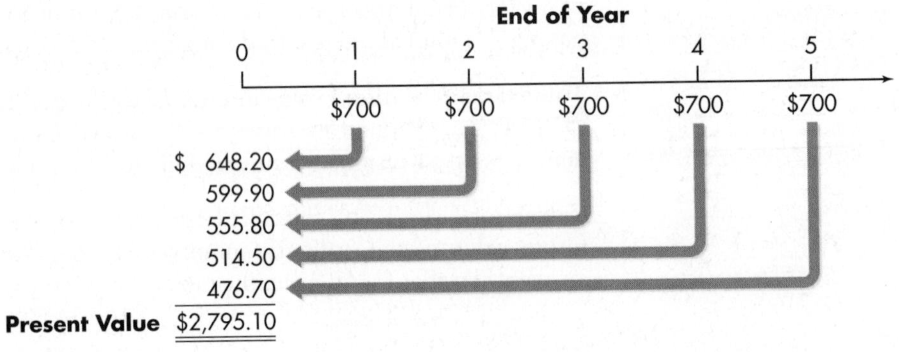

Table 4.2 shows the long method for finding the present value of the annuity. This method involves finding the present value of each payment and summing them. This procedure yields a present value of $2,795.10.

TABLE 4.2 The Long Method for Finding the Present Value of an Ordinary Annuity

Year (n)	Cash flow (1)	$PVIF_{8\%,n}$[a] (2)	Present value [(1) × (2)] (3)
1	$700	0.926	$ 648.20
2	700	0.857	599.90
3	700	0.794	555.80
4	700	0.735	514.50
5	700	0.681	476.70
		Present value of annuity	$2,795.10

[a] Present value interest factors at 8% are from Table A–2.

Using Computational Tools to Find the Present Value of an Ordinary Annuity

present value interest factor for an ordinary annuity
The multiplier used to calculate the present value of an *ordinary annuity* at a specified discount rate over a given period of time.

Annuity calculations can be simplified by using an interest table for the present value of an annuity, a financial calculator, or a computer and spreadsheet. The values for the present value of a $1 ordinary annuity are given in Appendix Table A–4. The factors in the table are derived by summing the present value interest factors (in Table A–2) for the appropriate number of years at the given discount rate. The formula for the **present value interest factor for an ordinary annuity** with cash flows that are discounted at i percent for n periods, $PVIFA_{i,n}$, is[9]

$$PVIFA_{i,n} = \sum_{t=1}^{n} \frac{1}{(1+i)^t} \tag{4.15}$$

This factor is the multiplier used to calculate the present value of an *ordinary annuity* at a specified discount rate over a given period of time.

By letting PVA_n equal the present value of an n-year *ordinary annuity*, letting PMT equal the amount to be received annually at the *end* of each year, and letting $PVIFA_{i,n}$ represent the appropriate *present value interest factor for a one-dollar ordinary annuity discounted at* i *percent for* n *years,* we can express the relationship among these variables as

$$PVA_n = PMT \times (PVIFA_{i,n}) \tag{4.16}$$

9. A mathematical expression that can be applied to calculate the present value interest factor for an ordinary annuity more efficiently is

$$PVIFA_{i,n} = \frac{1}{i} \times \left[1 - \frac{1}{(1+i)^n}\right] \tag{4.15a}$$

The use of this expression is especially attractive in the absence of the appropriate financial tables and of any financial calculator or personal computer and spreadsheet.

The following example illustrates this calculation using a table, a calculator, and a spreadsheet.

EXAMPLE Braden Company, as we have noted, wants to find the present value of a 5-year ordinary annuity of \$700, assuming an 8% opportunity cost.

Input	Function
700	PMT
5	N
8	I
	CPT
	PV

Solution
2794.90

Table Use The present value interest factor for an ordinary annuity at 8% for 5 years ($PVIFA_{8\%,5\text{yrs}}$), found in Table A–4, is 3.993. If we use Equation 4.16, \$700 annuity × 3.993 results in a present value of \$2,795.10.

Calculator Use Using the calculator's inputs shown at the left, you will find the present value of the ordinary annuity to be \$2,794.90. The value obtained with the calculator is more accurate than those found using the equation or the table.

Spreadsheet Use The present value of the ordinary annuity also can be calculated as shown on the following Excel spreadsheet.

	A	B
1	PRESENT VALUE OF AN ORDINARY ANNUITY	
2	Annual payment	\$700
3	Annual rate of interest, compounded annually	8%
4	Number of years	5
5	Present value of an ordinary annuity	\$2,794.90

Entry in Cell B5 is =PV(B3,B4,–B2).
The minus sign appears before B2 because the annual payment is a cash outflow.

Finding the Present Value of a Perpetuity

perpetuity
An annuity with an infinite life, providing continual annual cash flow.

A **perpetuity** is an annuity with an infinite life—in other words, an annuity that never stops providing its holder with a cash flow at the end of each year (for example, the right to receive \$500 at the end of each year forever).

It is sometimes necessary to find the present value of a perpetuity. The present value interest factor for a perpetuity discounted at the rate i is

$$PVIFA_{i,\infty} = \frac{1}{i} \tag{4.17}$$

As the equation shows, the appropriate factor, $PVIFA_{i,\infty}$, is found simply by dividing the discount rate, i (stated as a decimal), into 1. The validity of this method can be seen by looking at the factors in Table A–4 for 8, 10, 20, and 40 percent: As the number of periods (typically years) approaches 50, these factors approach the values calculated using Equation 4.17: $1 \div 0.08 = 12.50$; $1 \div 0.10 = 10.00$; $1 \div 0.20 = 5.00$; and $1 \div 0.40 = 2.50$.

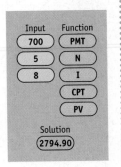

EXAMPLE Ross Clark wishes to endow a chair in finance at his alma mater. The university indicated that it requires \$200,000 per year to support the chair, and the endowment would earn 10% per year. To determine the amount Ross must give the university to fund the chair, we must determine the present value of a \$200,000 perpetuity discounted at 10%. The appropriate present value interest factor can be found by dividing 1 by 0.10, as noted in Equation 4.17. Substituting the resulting factor, 10, and the amount of the perpetuity, $PMT = \$200{,}000$, into Equation 4.16 results in a present value of $2,000,000 for the perpetuity. In other words, to generate $200,000 every year for an indefinite period requires $2,000,000 today if Ross Clark's alma mater can earn 10% on its investments. If the university earns 10% interest annually on the $2,000,000, it can withdraw $200,000 a year indefinitely without touching the initial $2,000,000, which would never be drawn upon.

Review Questions

4–8 What is the difference between an *ordinary annuity* and an *annuity due?* Which always has greater future value and present value for identical annuities and interest rates? Why?

4–9 What are the most efficient ways to calculate the present value of an ordinary annuity? What is the relationship between the *PVIF* and *PVIFA* interest factors given in Tables A–2 and A–4, respectively?

4–10 What is a *perpetuity?* How can the present value interest factor for such a stream of cash flows be determined?

LG4

Mixed Streams

mixed stream
A stream of unequal periodic cash flows that reflect no particular pattern.

Two basic types of cash flow streams are possible: the annuity and the mixed stream. Whereas an *annuity* is a pattern of equal periodic cash flows, a **mixed stream** is a stream of unequal periodic cash flows that reflect no particular pattern. Financial managers frequently need to evaluate opportunities that are expected to provide mixed streams of cash flows. Here we consider both the future value and the present value of mixed streams.

Future Value of a Mixed Stream

Determining the future value of a mixed stream of cash flows is straightforward. We determine the future value of each cash flow at the specified future date and then add all the individual future values to find the total future value.

EXAMPLE

Shrell Industries, a cabinet manufacturer, expects to receive the following mixed stream of cash flows over the next 5 years from one of its small customers.

End of year	Cash flow
1	$11,500
2	14,000
3	12,900
4	16,000
5	18,000

If Shrell expects to earn 8% on its investments, how much will it accumulate by the end of year 5 if it immediately invests these cash flows when they are received? This situation is depicted on the following time time:

Time line for future value of a mixed stream (end-of-year cash flows, compounded at 8% to the end of year 5)

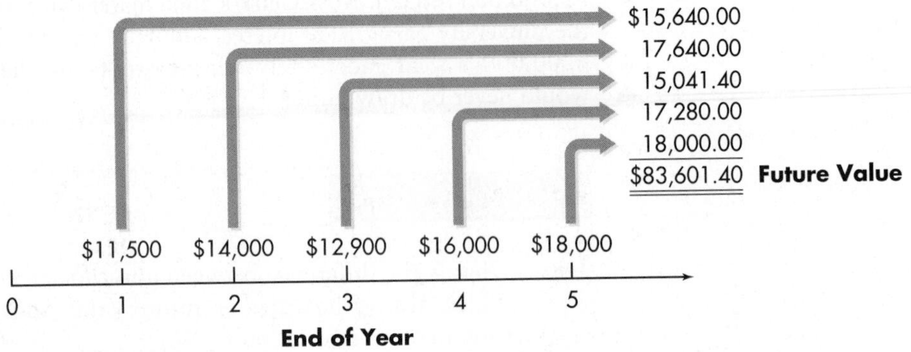

Table Use To solve this problem, we determine the future value of each cash flow compounded at 8% for the appropriate number of years. Note that the first cash flow of $11,500, received at the end of year 1, will earn interest for 4 years (end of year 1 through end of year 5); the second cash flow of $14,000, received at the end of year 2, will earn interest for 3 years (end of year 2 through end of year 5); and so on. The sum of the individual end-of-year-5 future values is the future value of the mixed cash flow stream. The future value interest factors required are those shown in Table A–1. Table 4.3 presents the calculations needed to find the future value of the cash flow stream, which turns out to be $83,601.40.

Calculator Use You can use your calculator to find the future value of each individual cash flow, as demonstrated earlier (page 138), and then sum the future values, to get the future value of the stream. Unfortunately, unless you can program your calculator, most calculators lack a function that would allow you to

TABLE 4.3 Future Value of a Mixed Stream of Cash Flows

Year	Cash flow (1)	Number of years earning interest (n) (2)	$FVIF_{8\%,n}$[a] (2)	Future value [(1) × (3)] (4)
1	$11,500	$5-1=4$	1.360	$15,640.00
2	14,000	$5-2=3$	1.260	17,640.00
3	12,900	$5-3=2$	1.166	15,041.40
4	16,000	$5-4=1$	1.080	17,280.00
5	18,000	$5-5=0$	1.000[b]	18,000.00
			Future value of mixed stream	$83,601.40

[a]Future value interest factors at 8% are from Table A–1.
[b]The future value of the end-of-year-5 deposit at the end of year 5 is its present value because it earns interest for zero years and $(1+0.08)^0 = 1.000$.

input *all of the cash flows,* specify the interest rate, and directly calculate the future value of the entire cash flow stream. Had you used your calculator to find the individual cash flow future values and then summed them, the future value of Shrell Industries' cash flow stream at the end of year 5 would have been $83,608.15, a more precise value than the one obtained by using a financial table.

Spreadsheet Use The future value of the mixed stream also can be calculated as shown on the following Excel spreadsheet.

	A	B
1	FUTURE VALUE OF A MIXED STREAM	
2	Interest rate, pct/year	8%
3	Year	Year-End Cash Flow
4	1	$11,500
5	2	$14,000
6	3	$12,900
7	4	$16,000
8	5	$18,000
9	Future value	$83,608.15
	Entry in Cell B9 is =-FV(B2,A8,0,NPV(B2,B4:B8)). The minus sign appears before FV to convert the future value to a positive amount.	

If Shrell Industries invests at 8% interest the cash flows received from its customer over the next 5 years, the company will accumulate about $83,600 by the end of year 5.

Present Value of a Mixed Stream

Finding the present value of a mixed stream of cash flows is similar to finding the future value of a mixed stream. We determine the present value of each future amount and then add all the individual present values together to find the total present value.

EXAMPLE Frey Company, a shoe manufacturer, has been offered an opportunity to receive the following mixed stream of cash flows over the next 5 years:

End of year	Cash flow
1	$400
2	800
3	500
4	400
5	300

If the firm must earn at least 9% on its investments, what is the most it should pay for this opportunity? This situation is depicted on the following time line:

Time line for present value of a mixed stream (end-of-year cash flows, discounted at 9% over the corresponding number of years)

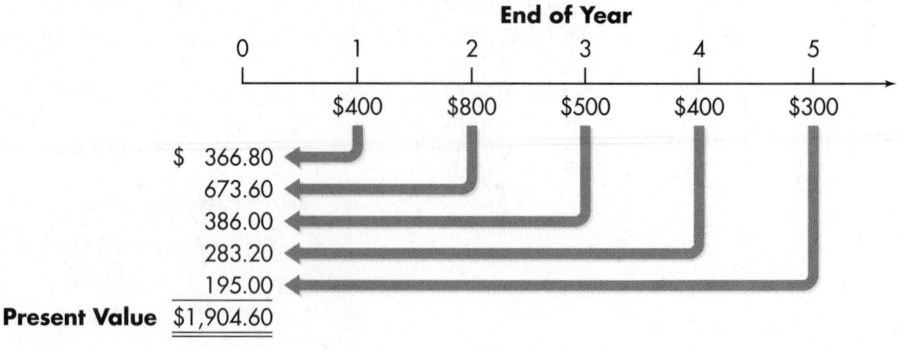

Table Use To solve this problem, determine the present value of each cash flow discounted at 9% for the appropriate number of years. The sum of these individual values is the present value of the total stream. The present value interest factors required are those shown in Table A–2. Table 4.4 presents the calculations needed to find the present value of the cash flow stream, which turns out to be $1,904.60.

Calculator Use You can use a calculator to find the present value of each individual cash flow, as demonstrated earlier (page 141), and then sum the present values, to get the present value of the stream. However, most financial calculators have a function that allows you to punch in *all cash flows,* specify the discount rate, and then directly calculate the present value of the entire cash flow stream. Because calculators provide solutions more precise than those based on rounded table factors, the present value of Frey Company's cash flow stream found using a calculator is $1,904.76, which is close to the $1,904.60 value calculated before.

TABLE 4.4 Present Value of a Mixed Stream of Cash Flows

Year (n)	Cash flow (1)	$PVIF_{9\%,n}$ [a] (2)	Present value [(1) × (2)] (3)
1	$400	0.917	$ 366.80
2	800	0.842	673.60
3	500	0.772	386.00
4	400	0.708	283.20
5	300	0.650	195.00
		Present value of mixed stream	$1,904.60

[a] Present value interest factors at 9% are from Table A–2.

Spreadsheet Use The present value of the mixed stream of future cash flows also can be calculated as shown on the following Excel spreadsheet.

	A	B
1	PRESENT VALUE OF A MIXED STREAM OF FUTURE CASH FLOWS	
2	Interest Rate, pct/year	9%
3	Year	Year-End Cash Flow
4	1	$400
5	2	$800
6	3	$500
7	4	$400
8	5	$300
9	Present value	$1,904.76
	Entry in Cell B9 is =NPV(B2,B4:B8).	

Paying about $1,905 would provide exactly a 9% return. Frey should pay no more than that amount for the opportunity to receive these cash flows.

Review Question

4–11 How is the future value of a mixed stream of cash flows calculated? How is the present value of a mixed stream of cash flows calculated?

LG5

Compounding Interest More Frequently Than Annually

Interest is often compounded more frequently than once a year. Savings institutions compound interest semiannually, quarterly, monthly, weekly, daily, or even continuously. This section discusses various issues and techniques related to these more frequent compounding intervals.

Semiannual Compounding

semiannual compounding
Compounding of interest over two periods within the year.

Semiannual compounding of interest involves two compounding periods within the year. Instead of the stated interest rate being paid once a year, one-half of the stated interest rate is paid twice a year.

EXAMPLE Fred Moreno has decided to invest $100 in a savings account paying 8% interest *compounded semiannually*. If he leaves his money in the account for 24 months (2 years), he will be paid 4% interest compounded over four periods, each of

TABLE 4.5 The Future Value from Investing $100 at 8% Interest Compounded Semiannually Over 24 Months (2 Years)

Period	Beginning principal (1)	Future value interest factor (2)	Future value at end of period [(1) × (2)] (3)
6 months	$100.00	1.04	$104.00
12 months	104.00	1.04	108.16
18 months	108.16	1.04	112.49
24 months	112.49	1.04	116.99

which is 6 months long. Table 4.5 uses interest factors to show that at the end of 12 months (1 year) with 8% semiannual compounding, Fred will have $108.16; at the end of 24 months (2 years), he will have $116.99.

Quarterly Compounding

quarterly compounding Compounding of interest over four periods within the year.

Quarterly compounding of interest involves four compounding periods within the year. One-fourth of the stated interest rate is paid four times a year.

EXAMPLE Fred Moreno has found an institution that will pay him 8% interest *compounded quarterly*. If he leaves his money in this account for 24 months (2 years), he will be paid 2% interest compounded over eight periods, each of which is 3 months long. Table 4.6 uses interest factors to show the amount Fred

TABLE 4.6 The Future Value from Investing $100 at 8% Interest Compounded Quarterly Over 24 Months (2 Years)

Period	Beginning principal (1)	Future value interest factor (2)	Future value at end of period [(1) × (2)] (3)
3 months	$100.00	1.02	$102.00
6 months	102.00	1.02	104.04
9 months	104.04	1.02	106.12
12 months	106.12	1.02	108.24
15 months	108.24	1.02	110.40
18 months	110.40	1.02	112.61
21 months	112.61	1.02	114.86
24 months	114.86	1.02	117.16

TABLE 4.7 The Future Value at the End of Years 1 and 2 from Investing $100 at 8% Interest, Given Various Compounding Periods

	Compounding period		
End of year	Annual	Semiannual	Quarterly
1	$108.00	$108.16	$108.24
2	116.64	116.99	117.16

will have at the end of each period. At the end of 12 months (1 year), with 8% quarterly compounding, Fred will have $108.24; at the end of 24 months (2 years), he will have $117.16.

Table 4.7 compares values for Fred Moreno's $100 at the end of years 1 and 2 given annual, semiannual, and quarterly compounding periods at the 8 percent rate. As shown, *the more frequently interest is compounded, the greater the amount of money accumulated.* This is true for *any interest rate* for *any period of time.*

A General Equation for Compounding More Frequently Than Annually

The formula for annual compounding (Equation 4.4) can be rewritten for use when compounding takes place more frequently. If m equals the number of times per year interest is compounded, the formula for annual compounding can be rewritten as

$$FV_n = PV \times \left(1 + \frac{i}{m}\right)^{m \times n} \tag{4.18}$$

If $m = 1$, Equation 4.18 reduces to Equation 4.4. Thus, if interest is compounded annually (once a year), Equation 4.18 will provide the same result as Equation 4.4. The general use of Equation 4.18 can be illustrated with a simple example.

EXAMPLE The preceding examples calculated the amount that Fred Moreno would have at the end of 2 years if he deposited $100 at 8% interest compounded semiannually and compounded quarterly. For semiannual compounding, m would equal 2 in Equation 4.18; for quarterly compounding, m would equal 4. Substituting the appropriate values for semiannual and quarterly compounding into Equation 4.18, we find that

1. *For semiannual compounding:*

$$FV_2 = \$100 \times \left(1 + \frac{0.08}{2}\right)^{2 \times 2} = \$100 \times (1 + 0.04)^4 = \$116.99$$

2. *For quarterly compounding:*

$$FV_2 = \$100 \times \left(1 + \frac{0.08}{4}\right)^{4\times 2} = \$100 \times (1 + 0.02)^8 = \$117.16$$

▲ These results agree with the values for FV_2 in Tables 4.5 and 4.6.

If the interest were compounded monthly, weekly, or daily, m would equal 12, 52, or 365, respectively.

Using Computational Tools for Compounding More Frequently Than Annually

We can use the future value interest factors for one dollar, given in Table A–1, when interest is compounded m times each year. Instead of indexing the table for i percent and n years, as we do when interest is compounded annually, we index it for $(i \div m)$ percent and $(m \times n)$ periods. However, the table is less useful, because it includes only selected rates for a limited number of periods. Instead, a financial calculator or a computer and spreadsheet is typically required.

EXAMPLE ▼ Fred Moreno wished to find the future value of $100 invested at 8% interest compounded both semiannually and quarterly for 2 years. The number of compounding periods, m, the interest rate, and the number of periods used in each case, along with the future value interest factor, are as follows:

Compounding period	m	Interest rate $(i \div m)$	Periods $(m \times n)$	Future value interest factor from Table A–1
Semiannual	2	$8\% \div 2 = 4\%$	$2 \times 2 = 4$	1.170
Quarterly	4	$8\% \div 4 = 2\%$	$4 \times 2 = 8$	1.172

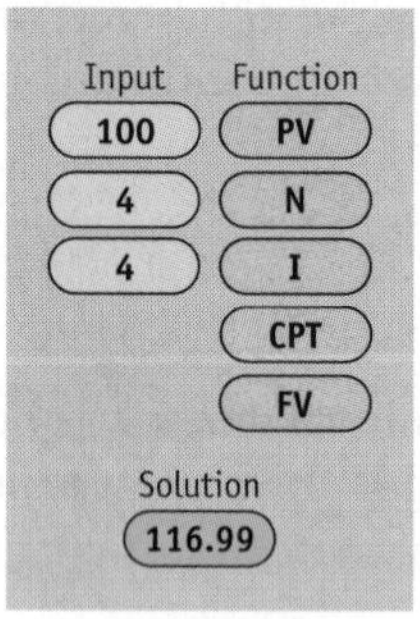

Table Use Multiplying each of the future value interest factors by the initial $100 deposit results in a value of $117.00 (1.170 × $100) for semiannual compounding and a value of $117.20 (1.172 × $100) for quarterly compounding.

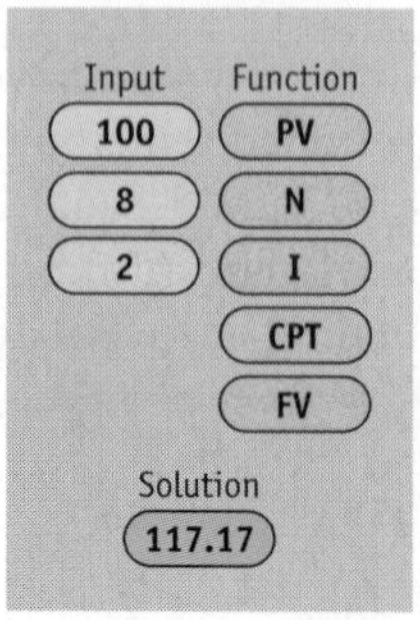

Calculator Use If the calculator were used for the semiannual compounding calculation, the number of periods would be 4 and the interest rate would be 4%. The future value of $116.99 will appear on the calculator display as shown in the first display at the left.

For the quarterly compounding case, the number of periods would be 8 and the interest rate would be 2%. The future value of $117.17 will appear on the calculator display as shown in the second display at the left.

Spreadsheet Use The future value of the single amount with semiannual and quarterly compounding also can be calculated as shown on the following Excel spreadsheet.

	A	B
1	**FUTURE VALUE OF A SINGLE AMOUNT WITH SEMIANNUAL AND QUARTERLY COMPOUNDING**	
2	Present value	$100
3	Interest rate, pct per year compounded semiannually	8%
4	Number of years	2
5	Future value with semiannual compounding	$116.99
6	Present value	$100
7	Interest rate, pct per year compounded quarterly	8%
8	Number of years	2
9	Future value with quarterly compounding	$117.17
	Entry in Cell B5 is =FV(B3/2,B4*2,0,–B2,0). Entry in Cell B9 is =FV(B7/4,B8*4,0,–B2,0). The minus sign appears before B2 because the present value is a cash outflow (i.e., a deposit made by Fred Moreno).	

Comparing the calculator, table, and spreadsheet values, we can see that the calculator and spreadsheet values agree generally with the values in Table 4.7 but are more precise because the table factors have been rounded.

Continuous Compounding

continuous compounding
Compounding of interest an infinite number of times per year at intervals of microseconds.

In the extreme case, interest can be compounded continuously. **Continuous compounding** involves compounding over every microsecond—the smallest time period imaginable. In this case, m in Equation 4.18 would approach infinity. Through the use of calculus, we know that as m approaches infinity, the equation becomes

$$FV_n \text{ (continuous compounding)} = PV \times (e^{i \times n}) \qquad (4.19)$$

where e is the exponential function[10], which has a value of 2.7183. The future value interest factor for continuous compounding is therefore

$$FVIF_{i,n} \text{ (continuous compounding)} = e^{i \times n} \qquad (4.20)$$

EXAMPLE To find the value at the end of 2 years ($n = 2$) of Fred Moreno's $100 deposit ($PV = \$100$) in an account paying 8% annual interest ($i = 0.08$) compounded continuously, we can substitute into Equation 4.19:

$$\begin{aligned} FV_2 \text{ (continuous compounding)} &= \$100 \times e^{0.08 \times 2} \\ &= \$100 \times 2.7183^{0.16} \\ &= \$100 \times 1.1735 = \$117.35 \end{aligned}$$

Calculator Use To find this value using the calculator, you need first to find the value of $e^{0.16}$ by punching in 0.16 and then pressing **2nd** and then **e^x** to get 1.1735.

10. Most calculators have the exponential function, typically noted by e^x, built into them. The use of this key is especially helpful in calculating future value when interest is compounded continuously.

Input Function
0.16 2nd
e^x
1.1735
×
100 =
Solution
117.35

Next multiply this value by \$100 to get the future value of \$117.35 as shown at the left. (*Note:* On some calculators, you may not have to press **2nd** before pressing **e^x**.)

Spreadsheet Use The future value of the single amount with continuous compounding also can be calculated as shown on the following Excel spreadsheet.

	A	B
1	FUTURE VALUE OF A SINGLE AMOUNT WITH CONTINUOUS COMPOUNDING	
2	Present value	\$100
3	Annual rate of interest, compounded continuously	8%
4	Number of years	2
5	Future value with continuous compounding	\$117.35
	Entry in Cell B5 is =B2*EXP(B3*B4).	

The future value with continuous compounding therefore equals \$117.35. As expected, the continuously compounded value is larger than the future value of interest compounded semiannually (\$116.99) or quarterly (\$117.16). Continuous compounding offers the largest amount that would result from compounding interest more frequently than annually.

Nominal and Effective Annual Rates of Interest

Both businesses and investors need to make objective comparisons of loan costs or investment returns over different compounding periods. In order to put interest rates on a common basis, to allow comparison, we distinguish between nominal and effective annual rates. The **nominal,** or **stated, annual rate** is the contractual annual rate of interest charged by a lender or promised by a borrower. The **effective,** or **true, annual rate (EAR)** is the annual rate of interest actually paid or earned. The effective annual rate reflects the impact of compounding frequency, whereas the nominal annual rate does not.

nominal (stated) annual rate
Contractual annual rate of interest charged by a lender or promised by a borrower.

effective (true) annual rate (EAR)
The annual rate of interest actually paid or earned.

Using the notation introduced earlier, we can calculate the effective annual rate, EAR, by substituting values for the nominal annual rate, i, and the compounding frequency, m, into Equation 4.21:

$$EAR = \left(1 + \frac{i}{m}\right)^m - 1 \qquad (4.21)$$

We can apply this equation using data from preceding examples.

EXAMPLE

Fred Moreno wishes to find the effective annual rate associated with an 8% nominal annual rate ($i = 0.08$) when interest is compounded (1) annually ($m = 1$); (2) semiannually ($m = 2$); and (3) quarterly ($m = 4$). Substituting these values into Equation 4.21, we get

1. *For annual compounding:*

$$EAR = \left(1 + \frac{0.08}{1}\right)^1 - 1 = (1 + 0.08)^1 - 1 = 1 + 0.08 - 1 = 0.08 = 8\%$$

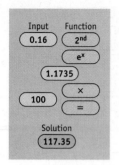

2. *For semiannual compounding:*

$$EAR = \left(1 + \frac{0.08}{2}\right)^2 - 1 = (1 + 0.04)^2 - 1 = 1.0816 - 1 = 0.0816 = 8.16\%$$

3. *For quarterly compounding:*

$$EAR = \left(1 + \frac{0.08}{4}\right)^4 - 1 = (1 + 0.02)^4 - 1 = 1.0824 - 1 = 0.0824 = 8.24\%$$

These values demonstrate two important points: The first is that nominal and effective annual rates are equivalent for annual compounding. The second is that the effective annual rate increases with increasing compounding frequency, up to a limit that occurs with *continuous compounding.*[11]

annual percentage rate (APR) The *nominal annual rate* of interest, found by multiplying the periodic rate by the number of periods in 1 year, that must be disclosed to consumers on credit cards and loans as a result of "truth-in-lending laws."

annual percentage yield (APY) The *effective annual rate* of interest that must be disclosed to consumers by banks on their savings products as a result of "truth-in-savings laws."

At the consumer level, "truth-in-lending laws" require disclosure on credit card and loan agreements of the **annual percentage rate (APR).** The APR is the *nominal annual rate* found by multiplying the periodic rate by the number of periods in one year. For example, a bank credit card that charges 1 1/2 percent per month (the periodic rate) would have an APR of 18% (1.5% per month × 12 months per year).

"Truth-in-savings laws," on the other hand, require banks to quote the **annual percentage yield (APY)** on their savings products. The APY is the *effective annual rate* a savings product pays. For example, a savings account that pays 0.5 percent per month would have an APY of 6.17 percent $[(1.005)^{12} - 1]$.

Quoting loan interest rates at their lower nominal annual rate (the APR) and savings interest rates at the higher effective annual rate (the APY) offers two advantages: It tends to standardize disclosure to consumers, and it enables financial institutions to quote the most attractive interest rates: low loan rates and high savings rates.

Review Questions

4–12 What effect does compounding interest more frequently than annually have on (**a**) future value and (**b**) the *effective annual rate (EAR)*? Why?

4–13 How does the future value of a deposit subject to continuous compounding compare to the value obtained by annual compounding?

4–14 Differentiate between a *nominal annual rate* and an *effective annual rate (EAR)*. Define *annual percentage rate (APR)* and *annual percentage yield (APY)*.

---

11. The effective annual rate for this extreme case can be found by using the following equation:

$$\text{EAR (continuous compounding)} = e^k - 1 \qquad (4.21a)$$

For the 8% nominal annual rate ($k = 0.08$), substitution into Equation 4.21a results in an effective annual rate of

$$e^{0.08} - 1 = 1.0833 - 1 = 0.0833 = 8.33\%$$

in the case of continuous compounding. This is the highest effective annual rate attainable with an 8% nominal rate.

LG6

Special Applications of Time Value

Future value and present value techniques have a number of important applications in finance. We'll study four of them in this section: (1) deposits needed to accumulate a future sum, (2) loan amortization, (3) interest or growth rates, and (4) finding an unknown number of periods.

Deposits Needed to Accumulate a Future Sum

Suppose you want to buy a house 5 years from now, and you estimate that an initial down payment of \$20,000 will be required at that time. To accumulate the \$20,000, you will wish to make equal annual end-of-year deposits into an account paying annual interest of 6 percent. The solution to this problem is closely related to the process of finding the future value of an annuity. You must determine what size annuity will result in a single amount equal to \$20,000 at the end of year 5.

Earlier in the chapter we found the future value of an n-year ordinary annuity, FVA_n, by multiplying the annual deposit, PMT, by the appropriate interest factor, $FVIFA_{i,n}$. The relationship of the three variables was defined by Equation 4.14, which is repeated here as Equation 4.22:

$$FVA_n = PMT \times (FVIFA_{i,n}) \tag{4.22}$$

We can find the annual deposit required to accumulate FVA_n dollars by solving Equation 4.22 for PMT. Isolating PMT on the left side of the equation gives us

$$PMT = \frac{FVA_n}{FVIFA_{i,n}} \tag{4.23}$$

Once this is done, we have only to substitute the known values of FVA_n and $FVIFA_{i,n}$ into the right side of the equation to find the annual deposit required.

EXAMPLE As just stated, you want to determine the equal annual end-of-year deposits required to accumulate \$20,000 at the end of 5 years, given an interest rate of 6%.

Input	Function
20,000	FV
5	N
6	I
	CPT
	PMT
Solution	
3547.93	

Table Use Table A–3 indicates that the future value interest factor for an ordinary annuity at 6% for 5 years ($FVIFA_{6\%,5\text{yrs}}$) is 5.637. Substituting $FVA_5 = \$20{,}000$ and $FVIFA_{6\%,5\text{yrs}} = 5.637$ into Equation 4.23 yields an annual required deposit, PMT, of \$3,547.99. Thus if \$3,547.99 is deposited at the end of each year for 5 years at 6% interest, there will be \$20,000 in the account at the end of the 5 years.

Calculator Use Using the calculator inputs shown at the left, you will find the annual deposit amount to be \$3,547.93. Note that this value, except for a slight rounding difference, agrees with the value found by using Table A–3.

Spreadsheet Use The annual deposit needed to accumulate the future sum also can be calculated as shown on the following Excel spreadsheet.

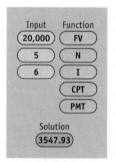

	A	B
1	ANNUAL DEPOSIT NEEDED TO ACCUMULATE A FUTURE SUM	
2	Future value	\$20,000
3	Number of years	5
4	Annual rate of interest	6%
5	Annual deposit	\$3,547.93
	Entry in Cell B5 is =–PMT(B4,B3,0,B2). The minus sign appears before PMT because the annual deposits are cash outflows.	

Loan Amortization

loan amortization
The determination of the equal periodic loan payments necessary to provide a lender with a specified interest return and to repay the loan principal over a specified period.

loan amortization schedule
A schedule of equal payments to repay a loan. It shows the allocation of each loan payment to interest and principal.

The term **loan amortization** refers to the computation of equal periodic loan payments. These payments provide a lender with a specified interest return and repay the loan principal over a specified period. The loan amortization process involves finding the future payments, over the term of the loan, whose present value at the loan interest rate equals the amount of initial principal borrowed. Lenders use a **loan amortization schedule** to determine these payment amounts and the allocation of each payment to interest and principal. In the case of home mortgages, these tables are used to find the equal *monthly* payments necessary to *amortize,* or pay off, the mortgage at a specified interest rate over a 15- to 30-year period.

Amortizing a loan actually involves creating an annuity out of a present amount. For example, say you borrow \$6,000 at 10 percent and agree to make equal annual end-of-year payments over 4 years. To find the size of the payments, the lender determines the amount of a 4-year annuity discounted at 10 percent that has a present value of \$6,000. This process is actually the inverse of finding the present value of an annuity.

Earlier in the chapter, we found the present value, PVA_n, of an n-year annuity by multiplying the annual amount, PMT, by the present value interest factor for an annuity, $PVIFA_{i,n}$. This relationship, which was originally expressed as Equation 4.16, is repeated here as Equation 4.24:

$$PVA_n = PMT \times (PVIFA_{i,n}) \qquad (4.24)$$

To find the equal annual payment required to pay off, or amortize, the loan, PVA_n, over a certain number of years at a specified interest rate, we need to solve Equation 4.24 for PMT. Isolating PMT on the left side of the equation gives us

$$PMT = \frac{PVA_n}{PVIFA_{i,n}} \qquad (4.25)$$

Once this is done, we have only to substitute the known values into the righthand side of the equation to find the annual payment required.

EXAMPLE

As just stated, you want to determine the equal annual end-of-year payments necessary to amortize fully a \$6,000, 10% loan over 4 years.

TABLE 4.8 Loan Amortization Schedule ($6,000 Principal, 10% Interest, 4-Year Repayment Period)

End of year	Beginning-of-year principal (1)	Loan payment (2)	Payments: Interest [0.10 × (2)] (3)	Payments: Principal [(1) − (3)] (4)	End-of-year principal [(2) − (4)] (5)
1	$6,000.00	$1,892.74	$600.00	$1,292.74	$4,707.26
2	4,707.26	1,892.74	470.73	1,422.01	3,285.25
3	3,285.25	1,892.74	328.53	1,564.21	1,721.04
4	1,721.04	1,892.74	172.10	1,720.64	—[a]

[a]Because of rounding, a slight difference ($0.40) exists between the beginning-of-year-4 principal (in column 1) and the year-4 principal payment (in column 4).

Table Use Table A–4 indicates that the present value interest factor for an annuity corresponding to 10% and 4 years ($PVIFA_{10\%,4yrs}$) is 3.170. Substituting $PVA_4 = \$6{,}000$ and $PVIFA_{10\%,4yrs} = 3.170$ into Equation 4.25 and solving for PMT yield an annual loan payment of $1,892.74. Thus to repay the interest and principal on a $6,000, 10%, 4-year loan, equal annual end-of-year payments of $1,892.74 are necessary.

Input	Function
6000	PV
4	N
10	I
	CPT
	PMT

Solution
1892.82

Calculator Use Using the calculator inputs shown at the left, you will find the annual payment amount to be $1,892.82. Except for a slight rounding difference, this value agrees with the table solution.

The allocation of each loan payment to interest and principal can be seen in columns 3 and 4 of the *loan amortization schedule* in Table 4.8. The portion of each payment that represents interest (column 3) declines over the repayment period, and the portion going to principal repayment (column 4) increases. This pattern is typical of amortized loans; as the principal is reduced, the interest component declines, leaving a larger portion of each subsequent loan payment to repay principal.

Spreadsheet Use The annual payment to repay the loan also can be calculated as shown on the first Excel spreadsheet. The amortization schedule allocating each loan payment to interest and principal also can be calculated precisely as shown on the second spreadsheet.

	A	B
1	ANNUAL PAYMENT TO REPAY A LOAN	
2	Loan principal (present value)	$6,000
3	Annual rate of interest	10%
4	Number of years	4
5	Annual payment	$1,892.82

Entry in Cell B5 is =-PMT(B3,B4,B2).
The minus sign appears before PMT because the annual payments are cash outflows.

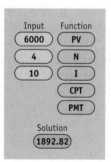

	A	B	C	D	E
1	LOAN AMORTIZATION SCHEDULE				
2		Data: Loan principal		$6,000	
3		Annual rate of interest		10%	
4		Number of years		4	
5		Annual Payments			
6	Year	Total	To Interest	To Principal	Year-End Principal
7	0				$ 6,000.00
8	1	$1,892.82	$600.00	$1,292.82	4,707.18
9	2	$1,892.82	$470.72	$1,422.11	3,285.07
10	3	$1,892.82	$328.51	$1,564.32	1,720.75
11	4	$1,892.82	$172.07	$1,720.75	0.00

Key Cell Entries
Cell B8: =-PMT(D3,D4,D2), copy to B9:B11
Cell C8: =-CUMIPMT(D3,D4,D2,A8,A8,0), copy to C9:C11
Cell D8: =-CUMPRINC(D3,D4,D2,A8,A8,0), copy to D9:D11
Cell E8: =E7-D8, copy to E9:E11
The minus signs appear before the entries in Cells B8, C8, and D8 because these are cash outflows.

Interest or Growth Rates

It is often necessary to calculate the compound annual interest or *growth rate* (that is, the annual rate of change in values) of a series of cash flows. Examples include finding the interest rate on a loan, the rate of growth in sales, and the rate of growth in earnings. In doing this, we can use either future value or present value interest factors. The use of present value interest factors is described in this section. The simplest situation is one in which a person wishes to find the rate of interest or growth in a *series of cash flows*.[12]

EXAMPLE Ray Noble wishes to find the rate of interest or growth reflected in the stream of cash flows he received from a real estate investment over the period 1999 through 2003. The following table lists those cash flows:

Year	Cash flow	
2003	$1,520	
		4
2002	1,440	
		3
2001	1,370	
		2
2000	1,300	
		1
1999	1,250	

By using the first year (1999) as a base year, we see that interest has been earned (or growth experienced) for 4 years.

12. Because the calculations required for finding interest rates and growth rates, given the series of cash flows, are the same, this section refers to the calculations as those required to find interest *or* growth rates.

In Practice

FOCUS ON PRACTICE Time Is on Your Side

For many years, the 30-year fixed-rate mortgage was the traditional choice of home buyers. In recent years, however, more homeowners are choosing fixed-rate mortgages with a 15-year term when they buy a new home or refinance their current residence. They are often pleasantly surprised to discover that they can pay off the loan in half the time with a monthly payment that is only about 25 percent higher. Not only will they own the home free and clear sooner, but they pay considerably less interest over the life of the loan.

For example, assume you need a $200,000 mortgage and can borrow at fixed rates. The shorter loan would carry a lower rate (because it presents less risk for the lender). The accompanying table shows how the two mortgages compare: The extra $431 a month, or a total of $77,580, saves $157,765 in interest payments over the life of the loan, for net savings of $80,185!

Term	Rate	Monthly principal and interest	Total interest paid over the term of the loan
15 years	6.50%	$1,742	$113,625
30 years	6.85%	$1,311	$271,390

Why isn't everyone rushing to take out a shorter mortgage? Many homeowners either can't afford the higher monthly payment or would rather have the extra spending money now. Others hope to do even better by investing the difference themselves. Suppose you invested $431 each month in a mutual fund with an average annual return of 7 percent. At the end of 15 years, your $77,580 investment would have grown to $136,611, or $59,031 more than you contributed! However, many people lack the self-discipline to save rather than spend that money. For them, the 15-year mortgage represents forced savings.

Yet another option is to make additional principal payments whenever possible. This shortens the life of the loan without committing you to the higher payments. By paying just $100 more each month, you can shorten the life of a 30-year mortgage to 24 1/4 years, with attendant interest savings.

Sources: Daniela Deane, "Adding Up Pros, Cons of 15-Year Loans," *Washington Post* (October 13, 2001), p. H7; Henry Savage, "Is 15-Year Loan Right for You?" *Washington Times* (June 22, 2001), p. F22; Carlos Tejada, "Sweet Fifteen: Shorter Mortgages Are Gaining Support," *Wall Street Journal* (September 17, 1998), p. C1; Ann Tergesen, "It's Time to Refinance . . . Again," *Business Week* (November 2, 1998), pp. 134–135.

Table Use The first step in finding the interest or growth rate is to divide the amount received in the earliest year (PV) by the amount received in the latest year (FV_n). Looking back at Equation 4.12, we see that this results in the present value interest factor for a *single amount* for 4 years, $PVIF_{i,4\text{yrs}}$, which is 0.822 ($1,250 ÷ $1,520). The interest rate in Table A–2 associated with the factor closest to 0.822 for 4 years is the interest or growth rate of Ray's cash flows. In the row for year 4 in Table A–2, the factor for 5 percent is 0.823—almost exactly the 0.822 value. Therefore, the interest or growth rate of the given cash flows is approximately (to the nearest whole percent) 5%.[13]

Calculator Use Using the calculator, we treat the earliest value as a present value, PV, and the latest value as a future value, FV_n. (*Note:* Most calculators

13. To obtain more precise estimates of interest or growth rates, *interpolation*—a mathematical technique for estimating unknown intermediate values—can be applied. For information on how to interpolate a more precise answer in this example, see the book's home page at *www.aw.com/gitman*.

Input	Function
1250	PV
−1520	FV
4	N
	CPT
	I

Solution: 5.01

require *either* the *PV* or the *FV* value to be input as a negative number to calculate an unknown interest or growth rate. That approach is used here.) Using the inputs shown at the left, you will find the interest or growth rate to be 5.01%, which is consistent with, but more precise than, the value found using Table A–2.

Spreadsheet Use The interest or growth rate for the series of cash flows also can be calculated as shown on the following Excel spreadsheet.

	A	B
1	INTEREST OR GROWTH RATE – SERIES OF CASH FLOWS	
2	Year	Cash Flow
3	2003	$1,520
4	2002	$1,440
5	2001	$1,370
6	2000	$1,300
7	1999	$1,250
8	Annual growth rate	5.01%

Entry in Cell B8 is
=RATE((A3–A7),0,B7,–B3,0).
The expression A3–A7 in the entry calculates the number of years of growth.
The minus sign appears before B3 because the investment in 2003 is treated as a cash outflow.

Another type of interest-rate problem involves finding the interest rate associated with an *annuity,* or equal-payment loan.

EXAMPLE Jan Jacobs can borrow $2,000 to be repaid in equal annual end-of-year amounts of $514.14 for the next 5 years. She wants to find the interest rate on this loan.

Table Use Substituting $PVA_5 = \$2{,}000$ and $PMT = \$514.14$ into Equation 4.24 and rearranging the equation to solve for $PVIFA_{i,5\text{yrs}}$, we get

$$PVIFA_{i,5yrs} = \frac{PVA_5}{PMT} = \frac{\$2{,}000}{\$514.14} = 3.890 \qquad (4.26)$$

Input	Function
514.14	PMT
−2000	PV
5	N
	CPT
	I

Solution: 9.00

The interest rate for 5 years associated with the annuity factor closest to 3.890 in Table A–4 is 9%. Therefore, the interest rate on the loan is approximately (to the nearest whole percent) 9%.

Calculator Use (*Note:* Most calculators require *either* the *PMT* or the *PV* value to be input as a negative number in order to calculate an unknown interest rate on an equal-payment loan. That approach is used here.) Using the inputs shown at the left, you will find the interest rate to be 9.00%, which is consistent with the value found using Table A–4.

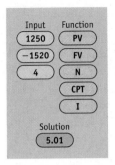

Spreadsheet Use The interest or growth rate for the annuity also can be calculated as shown on the following Excel spreadsheet.

	A	B
1	INTEREST OR GROWTH RATE – ANNUITY	
2	Present value (loan principal)	$2,000
3	Number of years	5
4	Annual payment	$514.14
5	Annual interest rate	9.00%
	Entry in Cell B5 is =RATE(B3,B4,–B2). The minus sign appears before B2 because the loan principal is treated as a cash outflow.	

Finding an Unknown Number of Periods

Sometimes it is necessary to calculate the number of time periods needed to generate a given amount of cash flow from an initial amount. Here we briefly consider this calculation for both single amounts and annuities. This simplest case is when a person wishes to determine the number of periods, n, it will take for an initial deposit, PV, to grow to a specified future amount, FV_n, given a stated interest rate, i.

EXAMPLE Ann Bates wishes to determine the number of years it will take for her initial \$1,000 deposit, earning 8% annual interest, to grow to equal \$2,500. Simply stated, at an 8% annual rate of interest, how many years, n, will it take for Ann's \$1,000, PV, to grow to \$2,500, FV_n?

Table Use In a manner similar to our approach above to finding an unknown interest or growth rate in a series of cash flows, we begin by dividing the amount deposited in the earliest year by the amount received in the latest year. This results in the present value interest factor for 8% and n years, $PVIF_{8\%,n}$, which is 0.400 (\$1,000 ÷ \$2,500). The number of years (periods) in Table A–2 associated with the factor closest to 0.400 for an 8% interest rate is the number of years required for \$1,000 to grow into \$2,500 at 8%. In the 8% column of Table A–2, the factor for 12 years is 0.397—almost exactly the 0.400 value. Therefore, the number of years necessary for the \$1,000 to grow to a future value of \$2,500 at 8% is approximately (to the nearest year) 12.

Input	Function
1000	PV
–2500	FV
8	I
	CPT
	N

Solution
11.91

Calculator Use Using the calculator, we treat the initial value as the present value, PV, and the latest value as the future value, FV_n. (*Note:* Most calculators require *either* the PV or the FV value to be input as a negative number to calculate an unknown number of periods. That approach is used here.) Using the inputs shown at the left, we find the number of periods to be 11.91 years, which is consistent with, but more precise than, the value found above using Table A–2.

Spreadsheet Use The number of years for the present value to grow to a specified future value also can be calculated as shown on the following Excel spreadsheet.

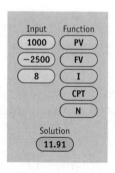

	A	B
1	YEARS FOR A PRESENT VALUE TO GROW TO A SPECIFIED FUTURE VALUE	
2	Present value (deposit)	$1,000
3	Annual rate of interest, compounded annually	8%
4	Future value	$2,500
5	Number of years	11.91
	Entry in Cell B5 is =NPER(B3,0,B2,–B4). The minus sign appears before B4 because the future value is treated as a cash outflow.	

Another type of number-of-periods problem involves finding the number of periods associated with an *annuity*. Occasionally we wish to find the unknown life, n, of an annuity, PMT, that is intended to achieve a specific objective, such as repaying a loan of a given amount, PVA_n, with a stated interest rate, i.

EXAMPLE Bill Smart can borrow $25,000 at an 11% annual interest rate; equal, annual end-of-year payments of $4,800 are required. He wishes to determine how long it will take to fully repay the loan. In other words, he wishes to determine how many years, n, it will take to repay the $25,000, 11% loan, PVA_n, if the payments of $4,800, PMT, are made at the end of each year.

Table Use Substituting $PVA_n = \$25{,}000$ and $PMT = \$4{,}800$ into Equation 4.24 and rearranging the equation to solve $PVIFA_{11\%,n\,yrs}$, we get

$$PVIFA_{11\%,n\,yrs} = \frac{PVA_n}{PMT} = \frac{\$25{,}000}{\$4{,}800} = 5.208 \qquad (4.27)$$

Input	Function
−4800	PMT
25000	PV
11	I
	CPT
	N
Solution	
8.15	

The number of periods for an 11% interest rate associated with the annuity factor closest to 5.208 in Table A–4 is 8 years. Therefore, the number of periods necessary to repay the loan fully is approximately (to the nearest year) 8 years.

Calculator Use (*Note:* Most calculators require *either* the PV or the PMT value to be input as a negative number in order to calculate an unknown number of periods. That approach is used here.) Using the inputs shown at the left, you will find the number of periods to be 8.15, which is consistent with the value found using Table A–4.

Spreadsheet Use The number of years to pay off the loan also can be calculated as shown on the following Excel spreadsheet.

	A	B
1	YEARS TO PAY OFF A LOAN	
2	Annual payment	$4,800
3	Annual rate of interest, compounded annually	11%
4	Present value (loan principal)	$25,000
5	Number of years to pay off the loan	8.15
	Entry in Cell B5 is =NPER(B3,–B2,B4). The minus sign appears before B2 because the payments are treated as cash outflows.	

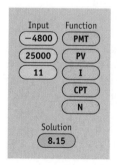

Review Questions

4–15 How can you determine the size of the equal annual end-of-period deposits necessary to accumulate a certain future sum at the end of a specified future period at a given annual interest rate?

4–16 Describe the procedure used to amortize a loan into a series of equal periodic payments.

4–17 Which present value interest factors would be used to find (**a**) the growth rate associated with a series of cash flows and (**b**) the interest rate associated with an equal-payment loan?

4–18 How can you determine the unknown number of periods when you know the present and future values—single amount or annuity—and the applicable rate of interest?

SUMMARY

FOCUS ON VALUE

Time value of money is an important tool that financial managers and other market participants use to assess the impact of proposed actions. Because firms have long lives and their important decisions affect their long-term cash flows, the effective application of time-value-of-money techniques is extremely important. Time value techniques enable financial managers to evaluate cash flows occurring at different times in order to combine, compare, and evaluate them and link them to the firm's **overall goal of share price maximization.** It will become clear in Chapters 6 and 7 that the application of time value techniques is a key part of the value determination process. Using them, we can measure the firm's value and evaluate the impact that various events and decisions might have on it. Clearly, an understanding of time-value-of-money techniques and an ability to apply them are needed in order to make intelligent value-creating decisions.

REVIEW OF LEARNING GOALS

LG1 **Discuss the role of time value in finance, the use of computational tools, and the basic patterns of cash flow.** Financial managers and investors use time-value-of-money techniques when assessing the value of the expected cash flow streams associated with investment alternatives. Alternatives can be assessed by either compounding to find future value or discounting to find present value. Because they are at time zero when making decisions, financial managers rely primarily on present value techniques. Financial tables, financial calculators, and computers and spreadsheets can streamline the application of time value techniques. The cash flow of a firm can be described by its pattern—single amount, annuity, or mixed stream.

LG2 **Understand the concepts of future and present value, their calculation for single amounts, and**

the relationship of present value to future value. Future value relies on compound interest to measure future amounts: The initial principal or deposit in one period, along with the interest earned on it, becomes the beginning principal of the following period. The present value of a future amount is the amount of money today that is equivalent to the given future amount, considering the return that can be earned on the current money. Present value is the inverse future value. The interest factor formulas and basic equations for both the future value and the present value of a single amount are given in Table 4.9.

LG3 **Find the future value and the present value of an ordinary annuity and find the present value of a perpetuity.** An annuity is a pattern of equal periodic cash flows. For an ordinary annuity, the cash flows occur at the end of the period. For an annuity due, cash flows occur at the beginning of the period. Only ordinary annuities are considered in this book. The future value of an ordinary annuity can be found by using the future value interest factor for an annuity; the present value of an ordinary annuity can be found by using the present value interest factor for an annuity. The present value of a perpetuity—an infinite-lived annuity—is found using 1 divided by the discount rate to represent the present value interest factor. The interest factor formulas and basic equations for the future value and the present value of an ordinary annuity and the present value of a perpetuity, are given in Table 4.9.

LG4 **Calculate both the future value and the present value of a mixed stream of cash flows.** A mixed stream of cash flows is a stream of unequal periodic cash flows that reflect no particular pattern. The future value of a mixed stream of cash flows is the sum of the future values of each individual cash flow. Similarly, the present value of a mixed stream of cash flows is the sum of the present values of the individual cash flows.

LG5 **Understand the effect that compounding interest more frequently than annually has on future value and on the effective annual rate of interest.** Interest can be compounded at intervals ranging from annually to daily, and even continuously. The more often interest is compounded, the larger the future amount that will be accumulated, and the higher the effective, or true, annual rate (EAR). The annual percentage rate (APR)—a nominal annual rate—is quoted on credit cards and loans. The annual percentage yield (APY)—an effective annual rate—is quoted on savings products. The interest factor formulas for compounding more frequently than annually are given in Table 4.9.

LG6 **Describe the procedures involved in (1) determining deposits to accumulate a future sum, (2) loan amortization, (3) finding interest or growth rates, and (4) finding an unknown number of periods.** The periodic deposit to accumulate a given future sum can be found by solving the equation for the future value of an annuity for the annual payment. A loan can be amortized into equal periodic payments by solving the equation for the present value of an annuity for the periodic payment. Interest or growth rates can be estimated by finding the unknown interest rate in the equation for the present value of a single amount or an annuity. Similarly, an unknown number of periods can be estimated by finding the unknown number of periods in the equation for the present value of a single amount or an annuity.

SELF-TEST PROBLEMS (Solutions in Appendix B)

LG2 LG5 ST 4–1 **Future values for various compounding frequencies** Delia Martin has $10,000 that she can deposit in any of three savings accounts for a 3-year period. Bank A compounds interest on an annual basis, bank B compounds interest twice each year, and bank C compounds interest each quarter. All three banks have a stated annual interest rate of 4%.

TABLE 4.9 Summary of Key Definitions, Formulas, and Equations for Time Value of Money

Definitions of variables

e = exponential function = 2.7183
EAR = effective annual rate
FV_n = future value or amount at the end of period n
FVA_n = future value of an n-year annuity
i = annual rate of interest
m = number of times per year interest is compounded
n = number of periods—typically years—over which money earns a return
PMT = amount deposited or received annually at the end of each year
PV = initial principal or present value
PVA_n = present value of an n-year annuity
t = period number index

Interest factor formulas

Future value of a single amount with annual compounding:

$$FVIF_{i,n} = (1+i)^n$$ [Eq. 4.5; factors in Table A–1]

Present value of a single amount:

$$PVIF_{i,n} = \frac{1}{(1+i)^n}$$ [Eq. 4.11; factors in Table A–2]

Future value of an ordinary annuity:

$$FVIFA_{i,n} = \sum_{t=1}^{n} (1+i)^{t-1}$$ [Eq. 4.13; factors in Table A–3]

Present value of an ordinary annuity:

$$PVIFA_{i,n} = \sum_{t=1}^{n} \frac{1}{(1+i)^t}$$ [Eq. 4.15; factors in Table A–4]

Present value of a perpetuity:

$$PVIFA_{i,\infty} = \frac{1}{i}$$ [Eq. 4.17]

Future value with compounding more frequently than annually:

$$FVIF_{i,n} = \left(1+\frac{i}{m}\right)^{m\times n}$$ [Eq. 4.18]

for continuous compounding, $m = \infty$:

$$FVIF_{i,n} \text{ (continuous compounding)} = e^{i\times n}$$ [Eq. 4.20]

to find the effective annual rate:

$$EAR = \left(1+\frac{i}{m}\right)^{m} - 1$$ [Eq. 4.21]

Basic equations

Future value (single amount):	$FV_n = PV \times (FVIF_{i,n})$	[Eq. 4.6]
Present value (single amount):	$PV = FV_n \times (PVIF_{i,n})$	[Eq. 4.12]
Future value (annuity):	$FVA_n = PMT \times (FVIFA_{i,n})$	[Eq. 4.14]
Present value (annuity):	$PVA_n = PMT \times (PVIFA_{i,n})$	[Eq. 4.16]

a. What amount would Ms. Martin have at the end of the third year, leaving all interest paid on deposit, in each bank?
b. What *effective annual rate* (*EAR*) would she earn in each of the banks?
c. On the basis of your findings in parts **a** and **b**, which bank should Ms. Martin deal with? Why?
d. If a fourth bank (bank D), also with a 4% stated interest rate, compounds interest continuously, how much would Ms. Martin have at the end of the third year? Does this alternative change your recommendation in part **c**? Explain why or why not.

LG3

ST 4–2 **Future values of annuities** Ramesh Abdul wishes to choose the better of two equally costly cash flow streams: annuity X and annuity Y. X provides a cash inflow of $9,000 at the end of each of the next 6 years. Y provides a cash inflow of $10,000 at the end of each of the next 6 years. Assume that Ramesh can earn 15% on annuity X and 11% on annuity Y.
a. On a purely subjective basis, which annuity do you think is more attractive? Why?
b. Find the future value at the end of year 6, FVA_6, for both annuity X and annuity Y.
c. Use your finding in part **b** to indicate which annuity is more attractive. Compare your finding to your subjective response in part **a**.

LG2 LG3 LG4

ST 4–3 **Present values of single amounts and streams** You have a choice of accepting either of two 5-year cash flow streams or single amounts. One cash flow stream is an ordinary annuity, and the other is a mixed stream. You may accept alternative A or B—either as a cash flow stream or as a single amount. Given the cash flow stream and single amounts associated with each (see the accompanying table), and assuming a 9% opportunity cost, which alternative (A or B) and in which form (cash flow stream or single amount) would you prefer?

	Cash flow stream	
End of year	Alternative A	Alternative B
1	$700	$1,100
2	700	900
3	700	700
4	700	500
5	700	300
	Single amount	
At time zero	$2,825	$2,800

LG6

ST 4–4 **Deposits needed to accumulate a future sum** Judi Janson wishes to accumulate $8,000 by the end of 5 years by making equal annual end-of-year deposits over the next 5 years. If Judi can earn 7% on her investments, how much must she deposit at the *end of each year* to meet this goal?

PROBLEMS

LG1 **4–1** **Using a time line** The financial manager at Starbuck Industries is considering an investment that requires an initial outlay of $25,000 and is expected to result in cash inflows of $3,000 at the end of year 1, $6,000 at the end of years 2 and 3, $10,000 at the end of year 4, $8,000 at the end of year 5, and $7,000 at the end of year 6.

a. Draw and label a time line depicting the cash flows associated with Starbuck Industries' proposed investment.

b. Use arrows to demonstrate, on the time line in part **a,** how compounding to find future value can be used to measure all cash flows at the end of year 6.

c. Use arrows to demonstrate, on the time line in part **b,** how discounting to find present value can be used to measure all cash flows at time zero.

d. Which of the approaches—future value or present value—do financial managers rely on most often for decision making? Why?

LG2 **4–2** **Future value calculation** *Without referring to tables or to the preprogrammed function on your financial calculator,* use the basic formula for future value along with the given interest rate, *i,* and the number of periods, *n,* to calculate the future value interest factor in each of the cases shown in the following table. Compare the calculated value to the value in Appendix Table A–1.

Case	Interest rate, *i*	Number of periods, *n*
A	12%	2
B	6	3
C	9	2
D	3	4

LG2 **4–3** **Future value tables** Use the future value interest factors in Appendix Table A–1 in each of the cases shown in the following table to estimate, to the nearest year, how long it would take an initial deposit, assuming no withdrawals,

a. To double.

b. To quadruple.

Case	Interest rate
A	7%
B	40
C	20
D	10

LG2 **4–4** **Future values** For each of the cases shown in the following table, calculate the future value of the single cash flow deposited today that will be available at the end of the deposit period if the interest is compounded annually at the rate specified over the given period.

Case	Single cash flow	Interest rate	Deposit period (years)
A	$ 200	5%	20
B	4,500	8	7
C	10,000	9	10
D	25,000	10	12
E	37,000	11	5
F	40,000	12	9

LG2 **4–5 Future value** You have $1,500 to invest today at 7% interest compounded annually.

a. Find how much you will have accumulated in the account at the end of (1) 3 years, (2) 6 years, and (3) 9 years.

b. Use your findings in part **a** to calculate the amount of interest earned in (1) the first 3 years (years 1 to 3), (2) the second 3 years (years 4 to 6), and (3) the third 3 years (years 7 to 9).

c. Compare and contrast your findings in part **b.** Explain why the amount of interest earned increases in each succeeding 3-year period.

LG2 **4–6 Inflation and future value** As part of your financial planning, you wish to purchase a new car exactly 5 years from today. The car you wish to purchase costs $14,000 today, and your research indicates that its price will increase by 2% to 4% per year over the next 5 years.

a. Estimate the price of the car at the end of 5 years if inflation is (1) 2% per year, and (2) 4% per year.

b. How much more expensive will the car be if the rate of inflation is 4% rather than 2%?

LG2 **4–7 Future value and time** You can deposit $10,000 into an account paying 9% annual interest either today or exactly 10 years from today. How much better off will you be at the end of 40 years if you decide to make the initial deposit today rather than 10 years from today?

LG2 **4–8 Single-payment loan repayment** A person borrows $200 to be repaid in 8 years with 14% annually compounded interest. The loan may be repaid at the end of any earlier year with no prepayment penalty.

a. What amount will be due if the loan is repaid at the end of year 1?

b. What is the repayment at the end of year 4?

c. What amount is due at the end of the eighth year?

LG2 **4–9 Present value calculation** *Without referring to tables or to the preprogrammed function on your financial calculator,* use the basic formula for present value, along with the given opportunity cost, *i,* and the number of periods, *n,* to calculate the present value interest factor in each of the cases shown in the accompanying table. Compare the calculated value to the table value.

Case	Opportunity cost, i	Number of periods, n
A	2%	4
B	10	2
C	5	3
D	13	2

LG2 **4–10 Present values** For each of the cases shown in the following table, calculate the present value of the cash flow, discounting at the rate given and assuming that the cash flow is received at the end of the period noted.

Case	Single cash flow	Discount rate	End of period (years)
A	$ 7,000	12%	4
B	28,000	8	20
C	10,000	14	12
D	150,000	11	6
E	45,000	20	8

LG2 **4–11 Present value concept** Answer each of the following questions.

a. What single investment made today, earning 12% annual interest, will be worth $6,000 at the end of 6 years?

b. What is the present value of $6,000 to be received at the end of 6 years if the discount rate is 12%?

c. What is the most you would pay today for a promise to repay you $6,000 at the end of 6 years if your opportunity cost is 12%?

d. Compare, contrast, and discuss your findings in parts **a** through **c**.

LG2 **4–12 Present value** Jim Nance has been offered a future payment of $500 three years from today. If his opportunity cost is 7% compounded annually, what value should he place on this opportunity today? What is the most he should pay to purchase this payment today?

LG2 **4–13 Present value** An Iowa state savings bond can be converted to $100 at maturity 6 years from purchase. If the state bonds are to be competitive with U.S. Savings Bonds, which pay 8% annual interest (compounded annually), at what price must the state sell its bonds? Assume no cash payments on savings bonds prior to redemption.

LG2 **4–14 Present value and discount rates** You just won a lottery that promises to pay you $1,000,000 exactly 10 years from today. Because the $1,000,000 payment is guaranteed by the state in which you live, opportunities exist to sell the claim today for an immediate single cash payment.

a. What is the least you will sell your claim for if you can earn the following rates of return on similar-risk investments during the 10-year period?

(1) 6% (2) 9% (3) 12%

b. Rework part **a** under the assumption that the $1,000,000 payment will be received in 15 rather than 10 years.

c. On the basis of your findings in parts **a** and **b**, discuss the effect of both the size of the rate of return and the time until receipt of payment on the present value of a future sum.

LG2 4–15 **Present value comparisons of single amounts** In exchange for a $20,000 payment today, a well-known company will allow you to choose *one* of the alternatives shown in the following table. Your opportunity cost is 11%.

Alternative	Single amount
A	$28,500 at end of 3 years
B	$54,000 at end of 9 years
C	$160,000 at end of 20 years

a. Find the value today of each alternative.

b. Are all the alternatives acceptable, i.e., worth $20,000 today?

c. Which alternative, if any, will you take?

LG2 4–16 **Cash flow investment decision** Tom Alexander has an opportunity to purchase any of the investments shown in the following table. The purchase price, the amount of the single cash inflow, and its year of receipt are given for each investment. Which purchase recommendations would you make, assuming that Tom can earn 10% on his investments?

Investment	Price	Single cash inflow	Year of receipt
A	$18,000	$30,000	5
B	600	3,000	20
C	3,500	10,000	10
D	1,000	15,000	40

LG3 4–17 **Future value of an annuity** For each of the cases shown in the following table, calculate the future value of the annuity at the end of the deposit period, assuming that the annuity cash flows occur at the end of each year.

Case	Amount of annuity	Interest rate	Deposit period (years)
A	$ 2,500	8%	10
B	500	12	6
C	30,000	20	5
D	11,500	9	8
E	6,000	14	30

LG3 **4–18 Present value of an annuity** For each of the cases shown in the table below, calculate the present value of the annuity, assuming that the annuity cash flows occur at the end of each year.

Case	Amount of annuity	Interest rate	Period (years)
A	$ 12,000	7%	3
B	55,000	12	15
C	700	20	9
D	140,000	5	7
E	22,500	10	5

LG3 **4–19 Future value of a retirement annuity** Hal Thomas, a 25-year-old college graduate, wishes to retire at age 65. To supplement other sources of retirement income, he can deposit $2,000 each year into a tax-deferred individual retirement arrangement (IRA). The IRA will be invested to earn an annual return of 10%, which is assumed to be attainable over the next 40 years.

a. If Hal makes annual end-of-year $2,000 deposits into the IRA, how much will he have accumulated by the end of his 65th year?

b. If Hal decides to wait until age 35 to begin making annual end-of-year $2,000 deposits into the IRA, how much will he have accumulated by the end of his 65th year?

c. Using your findings in parts **a** and **b**, discuss the impact of delaying making deposits into the IRA for 10 years (age 25 to age 35) on the amount accumulated by the end of Hal's 65th year.

LG3 **4–20 Present value of a retirement annuity** An insurance agent is trying to sell you an immediate-retirement annuity, which for a single amount paid today will provide you with $12,000 at the end of each year for the next 25 years. You currently earn 9% on low-risk investments comparable to the retirement annuity. Ignoring taxes, what is the most you would pay for this annuity?

LG2 LG3 **4–21 Funding your retirement** You plan to retire in exactly 20 years. Your goal is to create a fund that will allow you to receive $20,000 at the end of each year for the 30 years between retirement and death (a psychic told you would die after 30 years). You know that you will be able to earn 11% per year during the 30-year retirement period.

a. How large a fund will you need *when you retire* in 20 years to provide the 30-year, $20,000 retirement annuity?

b. How much will you need *today* as a single amount to provide the fund calculated in part **a** if you earn only 9% per year during the 20 years preceding retirement?

c. What effect would an increase in the rate you can earn both during and prior to retirement have on the values found in parts **a** and **b**? Explain.

LG2 LG3

4–22 **Present value of an annuity versus a single amount** Assume that you just won the state lottery. Your prize can be taken either in the form of $40,000 at the end of each of the next 25 years (i.e., $1,000,000 over 25 years) or as a single amount of $500,000 paid immediately.

a. If you expect to be able to earn 5% annually on your investments over the next 25 years, ignoring taxes and other considerations, which alternative should you take? Why?

b. Would your decision in part **a** change if you could earn 7% rather than 5% on your investments over the next 25 years? Why?

c. On a strictly economic basis, at approximately what earnings rate would you be indifferent between the two plans?

LG3

4–23 **Perpetuities** Consider the data in the following table.

Perpetuity	Annual amount	Discount rate
A	$ 20,000	8%
B	100,000	10
C	3,000	6
D	60,000	5

Determine, for each of the perpetuities:

a. The appropriate present value interest factor.

b. The present value.

LG3

4–24 **Creating an endowment** Upon completion of her introductory finance course, Marla Lee was so pleased with the amount of useful and interesting knowledge she gained that she convinced her parents, who were wealthy alums of the university she was attending, to create an endowment. The endowment is to allow three needy students to take the introductory finance course each year in perpetuity. The guaranteed annual cost of tuition and books for the course is $600 per student. The endowment will be created by making a single payment to the university. The university expects to earn exactly 6% per year on these funds.

a. How large an initial single payment must Marla's parents make to the university to fund the endowment?

b. What amount would be needed to fund the endowment if the university could earn 9% rather than 6% per year on the funds?

LG4 **4–25 Future value of a mixed stream** For each of the mixed streams of cash flows shown in the following table, determine the future value at the end of the final year if deposits are made at the *beginning of each year* into an account paying annual interest of 12%, assuming that no withdrawals are made during the period.

	Cash flow stream		
Year	A	B	C
1	$ 900	$30,000	$1,200
2	1,000	25,000	1,200
3	1,200	20,000	1,000
4		10,000	1,900
5		5,000	

LG4 **4–26 Future value of a single amount versus a mixed stream** Gina Vitale has just contracted to sell a small parcel of land that she inherited a few years ago. The buyer is willing to pay $24,000 at the closing of the transaction or will pay the amounts shown in the following table at the *beginning* of each of the next 5 years. Because Gina doesn't really need the money today, she plans to let it accumulate in an account that earns 7% annual interest. Given her desire to buy a house at the end of 5 years after closing on the sale of the lot, she decides to choose the payment alternative—$24,000 single amount or the mixed stream of payments in the following table—that provides the higher future value at the end of 5 years.

Mixed stream	
Beginning of year	Cash flow
1	$ 2,000
2	4,000
3	6,000
4	8,000
5	10,000

a. What is the future value of the single amount at the end of year 5?
b. What is the future value of the mixed stream at the end of year 5?
c. On the basis of your findings in parts **a** and **b**, which alternative should Gina take?
d. If Gina could earn 10% rather than 7% on the funds, would your recommendation in part c change? Explain.

LG4 **4–27 Present value—Mixed streams** Find the present value of the streams of cash flows shown in the following table. Assume that the firm's opportunity cost is 12%.

A		B		C	
Year	Cash flow	Year	Cash flow	Year	Cash flow
1	−$2,000	1	$10,000	1–5	$10,000/yr
2	3,000	2–5	5,000/yr	6–10	8,000/yr
3	4,000	6	7,000		
4	6,000				
5	8,000				

LG4 **4–28 Present value—Mixed streams** Consider the mixed streams of cash flows shown in the following table.

	Cash flow stream	
Year	A	B
1	$ 50,000	$ 10,000
2	40,000	20,000
3	30,000	30,000
4	20,000	40,000
5	10,000	50,000
Totals	$150,000	$150,000

a. Find the present value of each stream using a 15% discount rate.
b. Compare the calculated present values and discuss them in light of the fact that the undiscounted cash flows total $150,000 in each case.

LG1 LG4 **4–29 Present value of a mixed stream** Harte Systems, Inc., a maker of electronic surveillance equipment, is considering selling to a well-known hardware chain the rights to market its home security system. The proposed deal calls for payments of $30,000 and $25,000 at the end of years 1 and 2 and for annual year-end payments of $15,000 in years 3 through 9. A final payment of $10,000 would be due at the end of year 10.
a. Lay out the cash flows involved in the offer on a time line.
b. If Harte applies a required rate of return of 12% to them, what is the present value of this series of payments?
c. A second company has offered Harte a one-time payment of $100,000 for the rights to market the home security system. Which offer should Harte accept?

LG4 **4–30 Funding budget shortfalls** As part of your personal budgeting process, you have determined that in each of the next 5 years you will have budget shortfalls. In other words, you will need the amounts shown in the following table at the end of the given year to balance your budget—that is, to make inflows equal outflows. You expect to be able to earn 8% on your investments during the next 5 years and wish to fund the budget shortfalls over the next 5 years with a single amount.

End of year	Budget shortfall
1	$ 5,000
2	4,000
3	6,000
4	10,000
5	3,000

a. How large must the single deposit today into an account paying 8% annual interest be to provide for full coverage of the anticipated budget shortfalls?
b. What effect would an increase in your earnings rate have on the amount calculated in part **a**? Explain.

LG4 4–31 **Relationship between future value and present value—Mixed stream** Using *only* the information in the accompanying table, answer the questions that follow.

Year (t)	Cash flow	Future value interest factor at 5% ($FVIF_{5\%,t}$)
1	$ 800	1.050
2	900	1.102
3	1,000	1.158
4	1,500	1.216
5	2,000	1.276

a. Determine the *present value* of the mixed stream of cash flows using a 5% discount rate.
b. How much would you be willing to pay for an opportunity to buy this stream, assuming that you can at best earn 5% on your investments?
c. What effect, if any, would a 7% rather than a 5% opportunity cost have on your analysis? (Explain verbally.)

LG5 4–32 **Changing compounding frequency** Using annual, semiannual, and quarterly compounding periods, for each of the following: (1) Calculate the future value if $5,000 is initially deposited, and (2) determine the *effective annual rate (EAR)*.
a. At 12% annual interest for 5 years.
b. At 16% annual interest for 6 years.
c. At 20% annual interest for 10 years.

LG5 4–33 **Compounding frequency, future value, and effective annual rates** For each of the cases in the following table:
a. Calculate the future value at the end of the specified deposit period.
b. Determine the *effective annual rate, EAR*.
c. Compare the nominal annual rate, i, to the effective annual rate, EAR. What relationship exists between compounding frequency and the nominal and effective annual rates.

Case	Amount of initial deposit	Nominal annual rate, i	Compounding frequency, m (times/year)	Deposit period (years)
A	$ 2,500	6%	2	5
B	50,000	12	6	3
C	1,000	5	1	10
D	20,000	16	4	6

LG5 **4–34 Continuous compounding** For each of the cases in the following table, find the future value at the end of the deposit period, assuming that interest is compounded continuously at the given nominal annual rate.

Case	Amount of initial deposit	Nominal annual rate, i	Deposit period (years), n
A	$1,000	9%	2
B	600	10	10
C	4,000	8	7
D	2,500	12	4

LG5 **4–35 Compounding frequency and future value** You plan to invest $2,000 in an individual retirement arrangement (IRA) today at a *nominal annual rate* of 8%, which is expected to apply to all future years.

a. How much will you have in the account at the end of 10 years if interest is compounded (1) annually? (2) semiannually? (3) daily (assume a 360-day year)? (4) continuously?

b. What is the *effective annual rate, EAR,* for each compounding period in part **a**?

c. How much greater will your IRA account balance be at the end of 10 years if interest is compounded continuously rather than annually?

d. How does the compounding frequency affect the future value and effective annual rate for a given deposit? Explain in terms of your findings in parts **a** through **c**.

LG5 **4–36 Comparing compounding periods** René Levin wishes to determine the future value at the end of 2 years of a $15,000 deposit made today into an account paying a nominal annual rate of 12%.

a. Find the future value of René's deposit, assuming that interest is compounded (1) annually, (2) quarterly, (3) monthly, and (4) continuously.

b. Compare your findings in part **a**, and use them to demonstrate the relationship between compounding frequency and future value.

c. What is the maximum future value obtainable given the $15,000 deposit, the 2-year time period, and the 12% nominal annual rate? Use your findings in part **a** to explain.

LG3 LG5 4–37 **Annuities and compounding** Janet Boyle intends to deposit $300 per year in a credit union for the next 10 years, and the credit union pays an annual interest rate of 8%.

a. Determine the future value that Janet will have at the end of 10 years, given that end-of-period deposits are made and no interest is withdrawn, if
(1) $300 is deposited annually and the credit union pays interest annually.
(2) $150 is deposited semiannually and the credit union pays interest semiannually.
(3) $75 is deposited quarterly and the credit union pays interest quarterly.

b. Use your finding in part **a** to discuss the effect of more frequent deposits and compounding of interest on the future value of an annuity.

LG6 4–38 **Deposits to accumulate future sums** For each of the cases shown in the following table, determine the amount of the equal annual end-of-year deposits necessary to accumulate the given sum at the end of the specified period, assuming the stated annual interest rate.

Case	Sum to be accumulated	Accumulation period (years)	Interest rate
A	$ 5,000	3	12%
B	100,000	20	7
C	30,000	8	10
D	15,000	12	8

LG6 4–39 **Creating a retirement fund** To supplement your planned retirement in exactly 42 years, you estimate that you need to accumulate $220,000 by the end of 42 years from today. You plan to make equal annual end-of-year deposits into an account paying 8% annual interest.

a. How large must the annual deposits be to create the $220,000 fund by the end of 42 years?

b. If you can afford to deposit only $600 per year into the account, how much will you have accumulated by the end of the 42nd year?

LG6 4–40 **Accumulating a growing future sum** A retirement home at Deer Trail Estates now costs $85,000. Inflation is expected to cause this price to increase at 6% per year over the 20 years before C. L. Donovan retires. How large an equal annual end-of-year deposit must be made each year into an account paying an annual interest rate of 10% for Donovan to have the cash to purchase a home at retirement?

LG3 LG6 4–41 **Deposits to create a perpetuity** You have decided to endow your favorite university with a scholarship. It is expected to cost $6,000 per year to attend the university into perpetuity. You expect to give the university the endowment in

10 years and will accumulate it by making annual (end-of-year) deposits into an account. The rate of interest is expected to be 10% for all future time periods.

a. How large must the endowment be?

b. How much must you deposit at the end of each of the next 10 years to accumulate the required amount?

LG6 4–42 **Loan payment** Determine the equal annual end-of-year payment required each year, over the life of the loans shown in the following table, to repay them fully during the stated term of the loan.

Loan	Principal	Interest rate	Term of loan (years)
A	$12,000	8%	3
B	60,000	12	10
C	75,000	10	30
D	4,000	15	5

LG6 4–43 **Loan amortization schedule** Joan Messineo borrowed $15,000 at a 14% annual rate of interest to be repaid over 3 years. The loan is amortized into three equal annual end-of-year payments.

a. Calculate the annual end-of-year loan payment.

b. Prepare a loan amortization schedule showing the interest and principal breakdown of each of the three loan payments.

c. Explain why the interest portion of each payment declines with the passage of time.

LG6 4–44 **Loan interest deductions** Liz Rogers just closed a $10,000 business loan that is to be repaid in three equal annual end-of-year payments. The interest rate on the loan is 13%. As part of her firm's detailed financial planning, Liz wishes to determine the annual interest deduction attributable to the loan. (Because it is a business loan, the interest portion of each loan payment is tax-deductible to the business.)

a. Determine the firm's annual loan payment.

b. Prepare an amortization schedule for the loan.

c. How much interest expense will Liz's firm have in *each* of the next 3 years as a result of this loan?

LG6 4–45 **Monthly loan payments** Tim Smith is shopping for a used car. He has found one priced at $4,500. The dealer has told Tim that if he can come up with a down payment of $500, the dealer will finance the balance of the price at a 12% annual rate over 2 years (24 months).

a. Assuming that Tim accepts the dealer's offer, what will his *monthly* (end-of-month) payment amount be?

b. Use a financial calculator or Equation 4.15a (found in footnote 9) to help you figure out what Tim's *monthly* payment would be if the dealer were willing to finance the balance of the car price at a 9% yearly rate.

LG6 **4–46 Growth rates** You are given the series of cash flows shown in the following table.

Year	Cash flows A	Cash flows B	Cash flows C
1	$500	$1,500	$2,500
2	560	1,550	2,600
3	640	1,610	2,650
4	720	1,680	2,650
5	800	1,760	2,800
6		1,850	2,850
7		1,950	2,900
8		2,060	
9		2,170	
10		2,280	

a. Calculate the compound annual growth rate associated with each cash flow stream.
b. If year-1 values represent initial deposits in a savings account paying annual interest, what is the annual rate of interest earned on each account?
c. Compare and discuss the growth rate and interest rate found in parts **a** and **b**, respectively.

LG6 **4–47 Rate of return** Rishi Singh has $1,500 to invest. His investment counselor suggests an investment that pays no stated interest but will return $2,000 at the end of 3 years.
a. What annual rate of return will Mr. Singh earn with this investment?
b. Mr. Singh is considering another investment, of equal risk, that earns an annual return of 8%. Which investment should he make, and why?

LG6 **4–48 Rate of return and investment choice** Clare Jaccard has $5,000 to invest. Because she is only 25 years old, she is not concerned about the length of the investment's life. What she is sensitive to is the rate of return she will earn on the investment. With the help of her financial advisor, Clare has isolated the four equally risky investments, each providing a single amount at the end of its life, as shown in the following table. All of the investments require an initial $5,000 payment.

Investment	Single amount	Investment life (years)
A	$ 8,400	6
B	15,900	15
C	7,600	4
D	13,000	10

a. Calculate, to the nearest 1%, the rate of return on each of the four investments available to Clare.
b. Which investment would you recommend to Clare, given her goal of maximizing the rate of return?

LG6 4–49 **Rate of return—Annuity** What is the rate of return on an investment of $10,606 if the company will receive $2,000 each year for the next 10 years?

LG6 4–50 **Choosing the best annuity** Raina Herzig wishes to choose the best of four immediate-retirement annuities available to her. In each case, in exchange for paying a single premium today, she will receive equal annual end-of-year cash benefits for a specified number of years. She considers the annuities to be equally risky and is not concerned about their differing lives. Her decision will be based solely on the rate of return she will earn on each annuity. The key terms of each of the four annuities are shown in the following table.

Annuity	Premium paid today	Annual benefit	Life (years)
A	$30,000	$3,100	20
B	25,000	3,900	10
C	40,000	4,200	15
D	35,000	4,000	12

a. Calculate to the nearest 1% the rate of return on each of the four annuities Raina is considering.
b. Given Raina's stated decision criterion, which annuity would you recommend?

LG6 4–51 **Interest rate for an annuity** Anna Waldheim was seriously injured in an industrial accident. She sued the responsible parties and was awarded a judgment of $2,000,000. Today, she and her attorney are attending a settlement conference with the defendants. The defendants have made an initial offer of $156,000 per year for 25 years. Anna plans to counteroffer at $255,000 per year for 25 years. Both the offer and the counteroffer have a present value of $2,000,000, the amount of the judgment. Both assume payments at the end of each year.
a. What interest rate assumption have the defendants used in their offer (rounded to the nearest whole percent)?
b. What interest rate assumption have Anna and her lawyer used in their counteroffer (rounded to the nearest whole percent)?
c. Anna is willing to settle for an annuity that carries an interest rate assumption of 9%. What annual payment would be acceptable to her?

LG6 4–52 **Loan rates of interest** John Flemming has been shopping for a loan to finance the purchase of a used car. He has found three possibilities that seem attractive and wishes to select the one with the lowest interest rate. The information available with respect to each of the three $5,000 loans is shown in the following table.

Loan	Principal	Annual payment	Term (years)
A	$5,000	$1,352.81	5
B	5,000	1,543.21	4
C	5,000	2,010.45	3

a. Determine the interest rate associated with each of the loans.
b. Which loan should Mr. Flemming take?

LG6 **4–53 Number of years—Single amounts** For each of the following cases, determine the number of years it will take for the initial deposit to grow to equal the future amount at the given interest rate.

Case	Initial deposit	Future amount	Interest rate
A	$ 300	$ 1,000	7%
B	12,000	15,000	5
C	9,000	20,000	10
D	100	500	9
E	7,500	30,000	15

LG6 **4–54 Time to accumulate a given sum** Manuel Rios wishes to determine how long it will take an initial deposit of $10,000 to double.

a. If Manuel earns 10% annual interest on the deposit, how long will it take for him to double his money?
b. How long will it take if he earns only 7% annual interest?
c. How long will it take if he can earn 12% annual interest?
d. Reviewing your findings in parts **a, b,** and **c,** indicate what relationship exists between the interest rate and the amount of time it will take Manuel to double his money?

LG6 **4–55 Number of years—Annuities** In each of the following cases, determine the number of years that the given annual *end-of-year* cash flow must continue in order to provide the given rate of return on the given initial amount.

Case	Initial amount	Annual cash flow	Rate of return
A	$ 1,000	$ 250	11%
B	150,000	30,000	15
C	80,000	10,000	10
D	600	275	9
E	17,000	3,500	6

LG6 **4–56 Time to repay installment loan** Mia Salto wishes to determine how long it will take to repay a loan with initial proceeds of $14,000 where annual *end-of-year* installment payments of $2,450 are required.

a. If Mia can borrow at a 12% annual rate of interest, how long will it take for her to repay the loan fully?

b. How long will it take if she can borrow at a 9% annual rate?

c. How long will it take if she has to pay 15% annual interest?

d. Reviewing your answers in parts **a, b,** and **c,** describe the general relationship between the interest rate and the amount of time it will take Mia to repay the loan fully.

CHAPTER 4 CASE Finding Jill Moran's Retirement Annuity

Sunrise Industries wishes to accumulate funds to provide a retirement annuity for its vice president of research, Jill Moran. Ms. Moran by contract will retire at the end of exactly 12 years. Upon retirement, she is entitled to receive an annual end-of-year payment of $42,000 for exactly 20 years. If she dies prior to the end of the 20-year period, the annual payments will pass to her heirs. During the 12-year "accumulation period" Sunrise wishes to fund the annuity by making equal annual end-of-year deposits into an account earning 9% interest. Once the 20-year "distribution period" begins, Sunrise plans to move the accumulated monies into an account earning a guaranteed 12% per year. At the end of the distribution period, the account balance will equal zero. Note that the first deposit will be made at the end of year 1 and that the first distribution payment will be received at the end of year 13.

Required

a. Draw a time line depicting all of the cash flows associated with Sunrise's view of the retirement annuity.

b. How large a sum must Sunrise accumulate by the end of year 12 to provide the 20-year, $42,000 annuity?

c. How large must Sunrise's equal annual end-of-year deposits into the account be over the 12-year accumulation period to fund fully Ms. Moran's retirement annuity?

d. How much would Sunrise have to deposit annually during the accumulation period if it could earn 10% rather than 9% during the accumulation period?

e. How much would Sunrise have to deposit annually during the accumulation period if Ms. Moran's retirement annuity were a perpetuity and all other terms were the same as initially described?

WEB EXERCISE

Go to Web site *www.arachnoid.com/lutusp/finance_old.html*. Page down to the portion of this screen that contains the financial calculator.

1. To determine the FV of a fixed amount, enter the following:

   Into **PV**, enter −1000; into **np**, enter 1; into **pmt**, enter 0; and, into **ir**, enter 8.

Now click on **Calculate FV**, and 1080.00 should appear in the **FV** window.

2. Determine FV for each of the following compounding periods by changing *only* the following:
   a. **np** to 2, and **ir** to 8/2
   b. **np** to 12, and **ir** to 8/12
   c. **np** to 52, and **ir** to 8/52
3. To determine the PV of a fixed amount, enter the following:

   Into **FV**, 1080; into **np**, 1; into **pmt**, 0; and, into **ir**, 8. Now click on **Calculate PV**. What is the PV?
4. To determine the FV of an annuity, enter the following:

   Into **PV**, 0; into **FV**, 0; into **np**, 12; into **pmt**, 1000; and, into **ir**, 8. Now click on **Calculate FV**. What is the FV?
5. To determine the **PV** of an annuity, change only the **FV** setting to 0; keep the other entries the same as in question 4. Click on **Calculate PV**. What is the PV?
6. Check your answers for questions 4 and 5 by using the techniques discussed in this chapter.

Go to Web site *www.homeowners.com/*. Click on **Calculators** in the left column. Click on **Mortgage Calculator**.

7. Enter the following into the mortgage calculator: **Loan amount**, 100000; **duration in years**, 30; and **interest rate**, 10. Click on **compute payment**. What is the monthly payment?
8. Calculate the monthly payment for $100,000 loans for 30 years at 8%, 6%, 4%, and 2%.
9. Calculate the monthly payment for $100,000 loans at 8% for 30 years, 20 years, 10 years, and 5 years.

Remember to check the book's Web site at

www.aw.com/gitman

for additional resources, including additional Web exercises.

Across the Disciplines
Why This Chapter Matters To You

Accounting: You need to understand the relationship between risk and return because of the effect that riskier projects will have on the firm's annual net income and on your efforts to stabilize net income.

Information systems: You need to understand how to do sensitivity and correlation analyses in order to build decision packages that help management analyze the risk and return of various business opportunities.

Management: You need to understand the relationship between risk and return, and how to measure that relationship in order to evaluate data that come from finance personnel and translate those data into decisions that increase the value of the firm.

Marketing: You need to understand that although higher-risk projects may produce higher returns, they may not be the best choice for the firm if they produce an erratic earnings pattern and do not optimize the value of the firm.

Operations: You need to understand how investments in plant assets and purchases of supplies will be measured by the firm and to recognize that decisions about such investments will be made by evaluating the effects of both risk and return on the value of the firm.

Chapter 5
Risk and Return

LEARNING GOALS

LG1 Understand the meaning and fundamentals of risk, return, and risk aversion.

LG2 Describe procedures for assessing and measuring the risk of a single asset.

LG3 Discuss risk measurement for a single asset using the standard deviation and coefficient of variation.

LG4 Understand the risk and return characteristics of a portfolio in terms of correlation and diversification, and the impact of international assets on a portfolio.

LG5 Review the two types of risk and the derivation and role of beta in measuring the relevant risk of both an individual security and a portfolio.

LG6 Explain the capital asset pricing model (CAPM) and its relationship to the security market line (SML).

The concept that return should increase if risk increases is fundamental to modern management and finance. This relationship is regularly observed in the financial markets, and important clarification of it has led to Nobel prizes. In this chapter we discuss these two key factors in finance—risk and return—and introduce some quantitative tools and techniques used to measure risk and return for individual assets and for groups of assets.

LG1

Risk and Return Fundamentals

portfolio
A collection, or group, of assets.

To maximize share price, the financial manager must learn to assess two key determinants: risk and return. Each financial decision presents certain risk and return characteristics, and the unique combination of these characteristics has an impact on share price. Risk can be viewed as it is related either to a single asset or to a **portfolio**—a collection, or group, of assets. We will look at both, beginning with the risk of a single asset. First, though, it is important to introduce some fundamental ideas about risk, return, and risk aversion.

Risk Defined

risk
The chance of financial loss or, more formally, the *variability of returns associated with a given asset.*

In the most basic sense, **risk** is the chance of financial loss. Assets having greater chances of loss are viewed as more risky than those with lesser chances of loss. More formally, the term *risk* is used interchangeably with *uncertainty* to refer to the *variability of returns associated with a given asset.* A \$1,000 government bond that guarantees its holder \$100 interest after 30 days has no risk, because there is no variability associated with the return. A \$1,000 investment in a firm's common stock, which over the same period may earn anywhere from \$0 to \$200, is very risky because of the high variability of its return. The more nearly certain the return from an asset, the less variability and therefore the less risk.

Some risks directly affect both financial managers and shareholders. Table 5.1 briefly describes the common sources of risk that affect both firms and their shareholders. As you can see, business risk and financial risk are more firm-specific and therefore are of greatest interest to financial managers. Interest rate, liquidity, and market risks are more shareholder-specific and therefore are of greatest interest to stockholders. Event, exchange rate, purchasing-power, and tax risk directly affect both firms and shareholders. The box on page 193 focuses on another risk that affects both firms and shareholders—moral risk.

return
The total gain or loss experienced on an investment over a given period of time; calculated by dividing the asset's cash distributions during the period, plus change in value, by its beginning-of-period investment value.

Return Defined

Obviously, if we are going to assess risk on the basis of variability of return, we need to be certain we know what *return* is and how to measure it. The **return** is the total gain or loss experienced on an investment over a given period of time. It is commonly measured as cash distributions during the period plus the change in value, expressed as a percentage of the beginning-of-period investment value. The

TABLE 5.1 Popular Sources of Risk Affecting Financial Managers and Shareholders

Source of risk	Description
Firm-Specific Risks	
Business risk	The chance that the firm will be unable to cover its operating costs. Level is driven by the firm's revenue stability and the structure of its operating costs (fixed vs. variable).
Financial risk	The chance that the firm will be unable to cover its financial obligations. Level is driven by the predictability of the firm's operating cash flows and its fixed-cost financial obligations.
Shareholder-Specific Risks	
Interest rate risk	The chance that changes in interest rates will adversely affect the value of an investment. Most investments lose value when the interest rate rises and increase in value when it falls.
Liquidity risk	The chance that an investment cannot be easily liquidated at a reasonable price. Liquidity is significantly affected by the size and depth of the market in which an investment is customarily traded.
Market risk	The chance that the value of an investment will decline because of market factors that are independent of the investment (such as economic, political, and social events). In general, the more a given investment's value responds to the market, the greater its risk; and the less it responds, the smaller its risk.
Firm and Shareholder Risks	
Event risk	The chance that a totally unexpected event will have a significant effect on the value of the firm or a specific investment. These infrequent events, such as government-mandated withdrawal of a popular prescription drug, typically affect only a small group of firms or investments.
Exchange rate risk	The exposure of future expected cash flows to fluctuations in the currency exchange rate. The greater the chance of undesirable exchange rate fluctuations, the greater the risk of the cash flows and therefore the lower the value of the firm or investment.
Purchasing-power risk	The chance that changing price levels caused by inflation or deflation in the economy will adversely affect the firm's or investment's cash flows and value. Typically, firms or investments with cash flows that move with general price levels have a low purchasing-power risk, and those with cash flows that do not move with general price levels have high purchasing-power risk.
Tax risk	The chance that unfavorable changes in tax laws will occur. Firms and investments with values that are sensitive to tax law changes are more risky.

expression for calculating the rate of return earned on any asset over period *t*, k_t, is commonly defined as

$$k_t = \frac{C_t + P_t - P_{t-1}}{P_{t-1}} \qquad (5.1)$$

where

$k_t =$ actual,expected, or required rate of return during period t
$C_t =$ cash (flow) received from the asset investment in the time period $t-1$ to t
$P_t =$ price (value) of asset at time t
$P_{t-1} =$ price (value) of asset at time $t-1$

The return, k_t, reflects the combined effect of cash flow, C_t, and changes in value, $P_t - P_{t-1}$, over period t.

Equation 5.1 is used to determine the rate of return over a time period as short as 1 day or as long as 10 years or more. However, in most cases, t is 1 year, and k therefore represents an annual rate of return.

EXAMPLE Robin's Gameroom, a high-traffic video arcade, wishes to determine the return on two of its video machines, Conqueror and Demolition. Conqueror was purchased 1 year ago for \$20,000 and currently has a market value of \$21,500. During the year, it generated \$800 of after-tax cash receipts. Demolition was purchased 4 years ago; its value in the year just completed declined from \$12,000 to \$11,800. During the year, it generated \$1,700 of after-tax cash receipts. Substituting into Equation 5.1, we can calculate the annual rate of return, k, for each video machine.

$$\text{Conqueror (C): } k_C = \frac{\$800 + \$21{,}500 - \$20{,}000}{\$20{,}000} = \frac{\$2{,}300}{\$20{,}000} = \underline{\underline{11.5\%}}$$

$$\text{Demolition (D): } k_D = \frac{\$1{,}700 + \$11{,}800 - \$12{,}000}{\$12{,}000} = \frac{\$1{,}500}{\$12{,}000} = \underline{\underline{12.5\%}}$$

Although the market value of Demolition declined during the year, its cash flow caused it to earn a higher rate of return than Conqueror earned during the same period. Clearly, the combined impact of cash flow and changes in value, measured by the rate of return, is important.

Historical Returns

Investment returns vary both over time and between different types of investments. By averaging historical returns over a long period of time, it is possible to eliminate the impact of market and other types of risk. This enables the financial decision maker to focus on the differences in return that are attributable primarily to the types of investment. Table 5.2 shows the average annual rates of return

TABLE 5.2 Historical Returns for Selected Security Investments (1926–2000)

Investment	Average annual return
Large-company stocks	13.0%
Small-company stocks	17.3
Long-term corporate bonds	6.0
Long-term government bonds	5.7
U.S. Treasury bills	3.9
Inflation	3.2%

Source: Stocks, Bonds, Bills, and Inflation, 2001 Yearbook (Chicago: Ibbotson Associates, Inc., 2001).

In Practice

FOCUS ON ETHICS What About Moral Risk?

The poster boy for "moral risk," the devastating effects of unethical behavior for a company's investors, has to be Nick Leeson. This 28-year-old trader violated his bank's investing rules while secretly placing huge bets on the direction of the Japanese stock market. When those bets proved to be wrong, the $1.24-billion losses resulted in the demise of the centuries-old **Barings Bank**.

More than any other single episode in world financial history, Leeson's misdeeds underscored the importance of character in the financial industry. Forty-one percent of surveyed CFOs admit ethical problems in their organizations (self-reported percents are probably low), and 48 percent of surveyed employees admit to engaging in unethical practices such as cheating on expense accounts and forging signatures. We are reminded again that shareholder wealth maximization has to be ethically constrained.

What can companies do to instill and maintain ethical corporate practices? They can start by building awareness through a code of ethics. Nearly all Fortune 500 companies and about half of all companies have an ethics code spelling out general principles of right and wrong conduct. Companies such as **Halliburton** and **Texas Instruments** have gone into specifics, because ethical codes are often faulted for being too vague and abstract.

Ethical organizations also reveal their commitments through the following activities: talking about ethical values periodically; including ethics in required training for mid-level managers (as at **Procter & Gamble**); modeling ethics throughout top management and the board (termed "tone at the top," especially notable at **Johnson & Johnson**); promoting openness for employees with concerns; weeding out employees who do not share the company's ethics values before those employees can harm the company's reputation or culture; assigning an individual the role of ethics director; and evaluating leaders' ethics in performance reviews (as at **Merck & Co.**).

The Leeson saga underscores the difficulty of dealing with the "moral hazard" problem, when the consequences of an individual's actions are largely borne by others. John Boatright argues in his book *Ethics in Finance* that the best antidote is to attract loyal, hardworking employees. Ethicists Rae and Wong tell us that debating issues is fruitless if we continue to ignore the character traits that empower people for moral behavior.

for a number of popular security investments (and inflation) over the 75-year period January 1, 1926, through December 31, 2000. Each rate represents the average annual rate of return an investor would have realized had he or she purchased the investment on January 1, 1926, and sold it on December 31, 2000. You can see that significant differences exist between the average annual rates of return realized on the various types of stocks, bonds, and bills shown. Later in this chapter, we will see how these differences in return can be linked to differences in the risk of each of these investments.

Risk Aversion

risk-averse
The attitude toward risk in which an increased return is required for an increase in risk.

Financial managers generally seek to avoid risk. Most managers are **risk-averse**—for a given increase in risk they require an increase in return. This attitude is believed consistent with that of the owners for whom the firm is being managed. Managers generally tend to be conservative rather than aggressive when accepting risk. Accordingly, *a risk-averse financial manager requiring higher return for greater risk is assumed throughout this text.*

Review Questions

5–1 What is *risk* in the context of financial decision making?
5–2 Define *return,* and describe how to find the rate of return on an investment.
5–3 Describe the attitude toward risk of a *risk-averse* financial manager.

LG2 LG3

Risk of a Single Asset

The concept of risk can be developed by first considering a single asset held in isolation. We can look at expected-return behaviors to assess risk, and statistics can be used to measure it.

Risk Assessment

Sensitivity analysis and probability distributions can be used to assess the general level of risk embodied in a given asset.

Sensitivity Analysis

sensitivity analysis
An approach for assessing risk that uses several possible-return estimates to obtain a sense of the variability among outcomes.

range
A measure of an asset's risk, which is found by subtracting the pessimistic (worst) outcome from the optimistic (best) outcome.

Sensitivity analysis uses several possible-return estimates to obtain a sense of the variability among outcomes. One common method involves making pessimistic (worst), most likely (expected), and optimistic (best) estimates of the returns associated with a given asset. In this case, the asset's risk can be measured by the range of returns. The **range** is found by subtracting the pessimistic outcome from the optimistic outcome. The greater the range, the more variability, or risk, the asset is said to have.

EXAMPLE

Norman Company, a custom golf equipment manufacturer, wants to choose the better of two investments, A and B. Each requires an initial outlay of $10,000, and each has a *most likely* annual rate of return of 15%. Management has made *pessimistic* and *optimistic* estimates of the returns associated with each. The three estimates for each asset, along with its range, are given in Table 5.3. Asset A appears to be less risky than asset B; its range of 4% (17% − 13%) is less than the range of 16% (23% − 7%) for asset B. The risk-averse decision maker would prefer asset A over asset B, because A offers the same most likely return as B (15%) with lower risk (smaller range).

Although the use of sensitivity analysis and the range is rather crude, it does give the decision maker a feel for the behavior of returns, which can be used to estimate the risk involved.

Probability Distributions

probability
The *chance* that a given outcome will occur.

Probability distributions provide a more quantitative insight into an asset's risk. The **probability** of a given outcome is its *chance* of occurring. An outcome with an 80 percent probability of occurrence would be expected to occur 8 out of 10

TABLE 5.3 Assets A and B

	Asset A	Asset B
Initial investment	\$10,000	\$10,000
Annual rate of return		
Pessimistic	13%	7%
Most likely	15%	15%
Optimistic	17%	23%
Range	4%	16%

times. An outcome with a probability of 100 percent is certain to occur. Outcomes with a probability of zero will never occur.

EXAMPLE

Norman Company's past estimates indicate that the probabilities of the pessimistic, most likely, and optimistic outcomes are 25%, 50%, and 25%, respectively. Note that the sum of these probabilities must equal 100%; that is, they must be based on all the alternatives considered.

probability distribution
A model that relates probabilities to the associated outcomes.

bar chart
The simplest type of probability distribution; shows only a limited number of outcomes and associated probabilities for a given event.

continuous probability distribution
A probability distribution showing all the possible outcomes and associated probabilities for a given event.

A **probability distribution** is a model that relates probabilities to the associated outcomes. The simplest type of probability distribution is the **bar chart,** which shows only a limited number of outcome–probability coordinates. The bar charts for Norman Company's assets A and B are shown in Figure 5.1. Although both assets have the same most likely return, the range of return is much greater, or more dispersed, for asset B than for asset A—16 percent versus 4 percent.

If we knew all the possible outcomes and associated probabilities, we could develop a **continuous probability distribution.** This type of distribution can be thought of as a bar chart for a very large number of outcomes. Figure 5.2 presents continuous probability distributions for assets A and B. Note that although assets A and B have the same most likely return (15 percent), the distribution of returns

FIGURE 5.1

Bar Charts

Bar charts for asset A's and asset B's returns

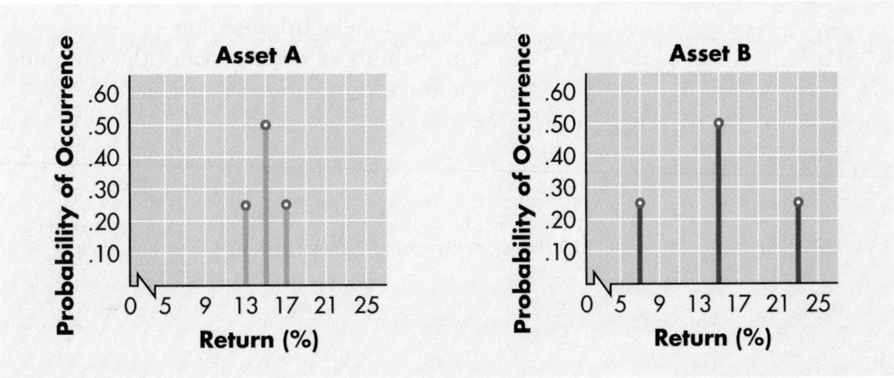

FIGURE 5.2

Continuous Probability Distributions

Continuous probability distributions for asset A's and asset B's returns

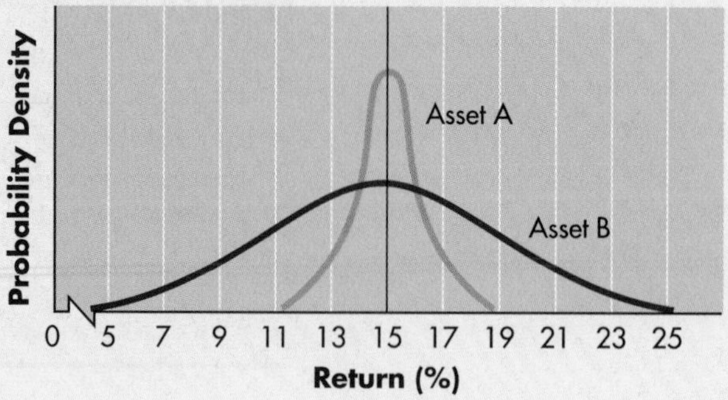

for asset B has much greater *dispersion* than the distribution for asset A. Clearly, asset B is more risky than asset A.

Risk Measurement

In addition to considering its *range,* the risk of an asset can be measured quantitatively by using statistics. Here we consider two statistics—the standard deviation and the coefficient of variation—that can be used to measure the variability of asset returns.

Standard Deviation

standard deviation (σ_k) The most common statistical indicator of an asset's risk; it measures the dispersion around the *expected value.*

expected value of a return ($\bar{k}$) The most likely return on a given asset.

The most common statistical indicator of an asset's risk is the **standard deviation,** $\boldsymbol{\sigma_k}$, which measures the dispersion around the *expected value.* The **expected value of a return, $\bar{k}$,** is the most likely return on an asset. It is calculated as follows:[1]

$$\bar{k} = \sum_{j=1}^{n} k_j \times Pr_j \tag{5.2}$$

where

k_j = return for the jth outcome
Pr_j = probability of occurrence of the jth outcome
n = number of outcomes considered

1. The formula for finding the expected value of return, $\bar{k}$, when all of the outcomes, k_j, are known *and* their related probabilities are assumed to be equal, is a simple arithmetic average:

$$\bar{k} = \frac{\sum_{j=1}^{n} k_j}{n} \tag{5.2a}$$

where n is the number of observations. Equation 5.2 is emphasized in this chapter because returns and related probabilities are often available.

TABLE 5.4 Expected Values of Returns for Assets A and B

Possible outcomes	Probability (1)	Returns (2)	Weighted value [(1) × (2)] (3)
		Asset A	
Pessimistic	.25	13%	3.25%
Most likely	.50	15	7.50
Optimistic	.25	17	4.25
Total	1.00	Expected return	15.00%
		Asset B	
Pessimistic	.25	7%	1.75%
Most likely	.50	15	7.50
Optimistic	.25	23	5.75
Total	1.00	Expected return	15.00%

EXAMPLE The expected values of returns for Norman Company's assets A and B are presented in Table 5.4. Column 1 gives the Pr_j's and column 2 gives the k_j's. In each case n equals 3. The expected value for each asset's return is 15%.

The expression for the *standard deviation of returns,* σ_k, is[2]

$$\sigma_k = \sqrt{\sum_{j=1}^{n} (k_j - \bar{k})^2 \times Pr_j} \qquad (5.3)$$

In general, the higher the standard deviation, the greater the risk.

EXAMPLE Table 5.5 presents the standard deviations for Norman Company's assets A and B, based on the earlier data. The standard deviation for asset A is 1.41%, and the standard deviation for asset B is 5.66%. The higher risk of asset B is clearly reflected in its higher standard deviation.

Historical Returns and Risk We can now use the standard deviation as a measure of risk to assess the historical (1926–2000) investment return data in Table 5.2. Table 5.6 repeats the historical returns and shows the standard devia-

2. The formula that is commonly used to find the standard deviation of returns, σ_k, in a situation in which *all* outcomes are known *and* their related probabilities are assumed equal, is

$$\sigma_k = \sqrt{\frac{\sum_{j=1}^{n} (k_j - \bar{k})^2}{n-1}} \qquad (5.3a)$$

where n is the number of observations. Equation 5.3 is emphasized in this chapter because returns and related probabilities are often available.

TABLE 5.5 The Calculation of the Standard Deviation of the Returns for Assets A and B[a]

i	k_j	$\bar{k}$	$k_j - \bar{k}$	$(k_j - \bar{k})^2$	Pr_j	$(k_j - \bar{k})^2 \times Pr_j$
			Asset A			
1	13%	15%	−2%	4%	.25	1%
2	15	15	0	0	.50	0
3	17	15	2	4	.25	1

$$\sum_{j=1}^{3}(k_j - \bar{k})^2 \times Pr_j = 2\%$$

$$\sigma_{k_A} = \sqrt{\sum_{j=1}^{3}(k_j - \bar{k})^2 \times Pr_j} = \sqrt{2\%} = 1.41\%$$

i	k_j	$\bar{k}$	$k_j - \bar{k}$	$(k_j - \bar{k})^2$	Pr_j	$(k_j - \bar{k})^2 \times Pr_j$
			Asset B			
1	7%	15%	−8%	64%	.25	16%
2	15	15	0	0	.50	0
3	23	15	8	64	.25	16

$$\sum_{j=1}^{3}(k_j - \bar{k})^2 \times Pr_j = 32\%$$

$$\sigma_{k_B} = \sqrt{\sum_{j=1}^{3}(k_j - \bar{k})^2 \times Pr_j} = \sqrt{32\%} = 5.66\%$$

[a]Calculations in this table are made in percentage form rather than decimal form—e.g., 13% rather than 0.13. As a result, some of the intermediate computations may appear to be inconsistent with those that would result from using decimal form. Regardless, the resulting standard deviations are correct and identical to those that would result from using decimal rather than percentage form.

tions associated with each of them. A close relationship can be seen between the investment returns and the standard deviations: Investments with higher returns have higher standard deviations. Because higher standard deviations are associated with greater risk, the historical data confirm the existence of a positive relationship between risk and return. That relationship reflects *risk aversion* by market participants, who require higher returns as compensation for greater risk. The historical data in Table 5.6 clearly show that during the 1926–2000 period, investors were rewarded with higher returns on higher-risk investments.

Coefficient of Variation

coefficient of variation (*CV*) A measure of relative dispersion that is useful in comparing the risks of assets with differing expected returns.

The **coefficient of variation, *CV*,** is a measure of relative dispersion that is useful in comparing the risks of assets with differing expected returns. Equation 5.4 gives the expression for the coefficient of variation:

$$CV = \frac{\sigma_k}{\bar{k}} \qquad (5.4)$$

The higher the coefficient of variation, the greater the risk.

TABLE 5.6 Historical Returns and Standard Deviations for Selected Security Investments (1926–2000)

Investment	Average annual return	Standard deviation
Large-company stocks	13.0%	20.2%
Small-company stocks	17.3	33.4
Long-term corporate bonds	6.0	8.7
Long-term government bonds	5.7	9.4
U.S. Treasury bills	3.9	3.2
Inflation	3.2%	4.4%

Source: Stocks, Bonds, Bills, and Inflation, 2001 Yearbook (Chicago: Ibbotson Associates, Inc., 2001).

EXAMPLE When the standard deviations (from Table 5.5) and the expected returns (from Table 5.4) for assets A and B are substituted into Equation 5.4, the coefficients of variation for A and B are 0.094 (1.41% ÷ 15%) and 0.377 (5.66% ÷ 15%), respectively. Asset B has the higher coefficient of variation and is therefore more risky than asset A—which we already know from the standard deviation. (Because both assets have the same expected return, the coefficient of variation has not provided any new information.)

The real utility of the coefficient of variation comes in comparing the risks of assets that have *different* expected returns.

EXAMPLE A firm wants to select the less risky of two alternative assets—X and Y. The expected return, standard deviation, and coefficient of variation for each of these assets' returns are

Statistics	Asset X	Asset Y
(1) Expected return	12%	20%
(2) Standard deviation	9%[a]	10%
(3) Coefficient of variation [(2) ÷ (1)]	0.75	0.50[a]

[a]Preferred asset using the given risk measure.

Judging solely on the basis of their standard deviations, the firm would prefer asset X, which has a lower standard deviation than asset Y (9% versus 10%). However, management would be making a serious error in choosing asset X over asset Y, because the dispersion—the risk—of the asset, as reflected in the coefficient of variation, is lower for Y (0.50) than for X (0.75). Clearly, using the coefficient of variation to compare asset risk is effective because it also considers the relative size, or expected return, of the assets.

Review Questions

5–4 Explain how the *range* is used in sensitivity analysis.
5–5 What does a plot of the *probability distribution* of outcomes show a decision maker about an asset's risk?
5–6 What relationship exists between the size of the *standard deviation* and the degree of asset risk?
5–7 When is the *coefficient of variation* preferred over the standard deviation for comparing asset risk?

LG4

Risk of a Portfolio

In real-world situations, the risk of any single investment would not be viewed independently of other assets. (We did so for teaching purposes.) New investments must be considered in light of their impact on the risk and return of the *portfolio* of assets. The financial manager's goal is to create an **efficient portfolio,** one that maximizes return for a given level of risk or minimizes risk for a given level of return. The statistical concept of *correlation* underlies the process of diversification that is used to develop an efficient portfolio.

efficient portfolio
A portfolio that maximizes return for a given level of risk or minimizes risk for a given level of return.

Correlation

Correlation is a statistical measure of the relationship between any two series of numbers. The numbers may represent data of any kind, from returns to test scores. If two series move in the same direction, they are **positively correlated.** If the series move in opposite directions, they are **negatively correlated.**

The degree of correlation is measured by the **correlation coefficient,** which ranges from +1 for **perfectly positively correlated** series to −1 for **perfectly negatively correlated** series. These two extremes are depicted for series M and N in Figure 5.3. The perfectly positively correlated series move exactly together; the perfectly negatively correlated series move in exactly opposite directions.

correlation
A statistical measure of the relationship between any two series of numbers representing data of any kind.

positively correlated
Describes two series that move in the same direction.

negatively correlated
Describes two series that move in opposite directions.

correlation coefficient
A measure of the degree of correlation between two series.

Diversification

The concept of correlation is essential to developing an efficient portfolio. To reduce overall risk, it is best to combine, or add to the portfolio, assets that have a negative (or a low positive) correlation. Combining negatively correlated assets can reduce the overall variability of returns. Figure 5.4 shows that a portfolio containing the negatively correlated assets F and G, both of which have the same expected return, $\bar{k}$, also has that same return $\bar{k}$ but has less risk (variability) than either of the individual assets. Even if assets are not negatively correlated, the lower the positive correlation between them, the lower the resulting risk.

Some assets are **uncorrelated**—that is, there is no interaction between their returns. Combining uncorrelated assets can reduce risk, not so effectively as combining negatively correlated assets, but more effectively than combining positively correlated assets. The correlation coefficient for uncorrelated assets is close

perfectly positively correlated
Describes two *positively correlated* series that have a *correlation coefficient* of +1.

perfectly negatively correlated
Describes two *negatively correlated* series that have a *correlation coefficient* of −1.

uncorrelated
Describes two series that lack any interaction and therefore have a *correlation coefficient* close to zero.

FIGURE 5.3

Correlations
The correlation between series M and series N

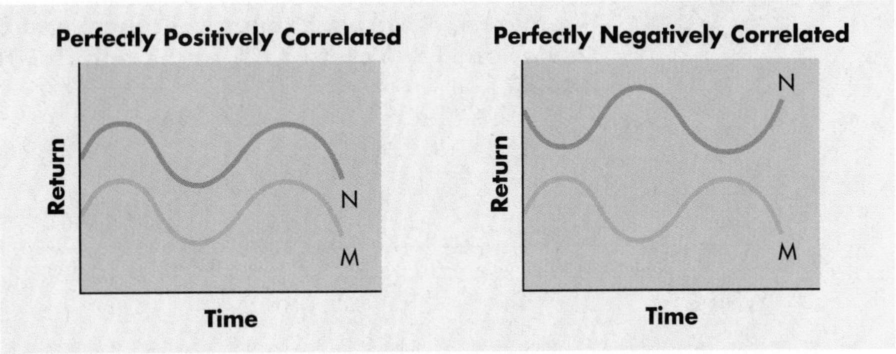

to zero and acts as the midpoint between perfect positive and perfect negative correlation.

The creation of a portfolio that combines two assets with perfectly positively correlated returns results in overall portfolio risk that at minimum equals that of the least risky asset and at maximum equals that of the most risky asset. However, a portfolio combining two assets with less than perfectly positive correlation *can* reduce total risk to a level below that of either of the components, which in certain situations may be zero. For example, assume that you manufacture machine tools. The business is very *cyclical,* with high sales when the economy is expanding and low sales during a recession. If you acquired another machine-tool company, with sales positively correlated with those of your firm, the combined sales would still be cyclical and risk would remain the same. Alternatively, however, you could acquire a sewing machine manufacturer, whose sales are *countercyclical.* It typically has low sales during economic expansion and high sales during recession (when consumers are more likely to make their own clothes). Combination with the sewing machine manufacturer, which has negatively correlated sales, should reduce risk.

EXAMPLE ▼ Table 5.7 presents the forecasted returns from three different assets—X, Y, and Z—over the next 5 years, along with their expected values and standard deviations. Each of the assets has an expected value of return of 12% and a standard deviation of 3.16%. The assets therefore have equal return and equal risk. The return patterns of assets X and Y are perfectly negatively correlated. They move

FIGURE 5.4

Diversification
Combining negatively correlated assets to diversify risk

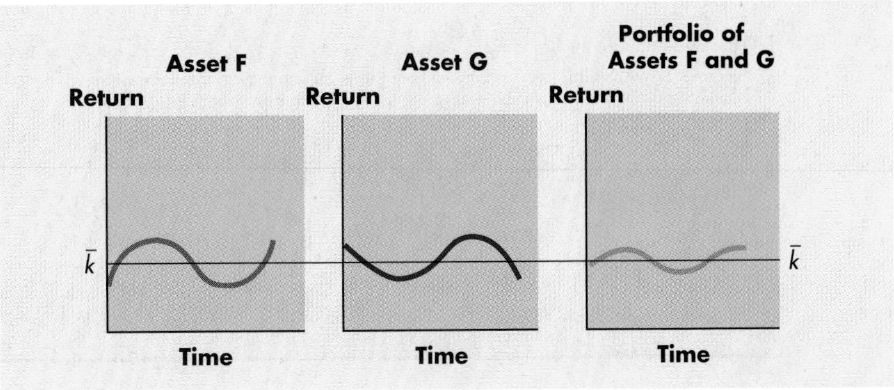

TABLE 5.7 **Forecasted Returns, Expected Values, and Standard Deviations for Assets X, Y, and Z and Portfolios XY and XZ**

	Assets			Portfolios	
Year	X	Y	Z	XY[a] (50%X + 50%Y)	XZ[b] (50%X + 50%Z)
2004	8%	16%	8%	12%	8%
2005	10	14	10	12	10
2006	12	12	12	12	12
2007	14	10	14	12	14
2008	16	8	16	12	16
Statistics:[c]					
Expected value	12%	12%	12%	12%	12%
Standard deviation[d]	3.16%	3.16%	3.16%	0%	3.16%

[a]Portfolio XY, which consists of 50% of asset X and 50% of asset Y, illustrates *perfect negative correlation* because these two return streams behave in completely opposite fashion over the 5-year period. Its return values are calculated as shown in the following table.

	Forecasted return			
Year	Asset X (1)	Asset Y (2)	Portfolio return calculation (3)	Expected portfolio return, k_p (4)
2004	8%	16%	(.50 × 8%) + (.50 × 16%) =	12%
2005	10	14	(.50 × 10%) + (.50 × 14%) =	12
2006	12	12	(.50 × 12%) + (.50 × 12%) =	12
2007	14	10	(.50 × 14%) + (.50 × 10%) =	12
2008	16	8	(.50 × 16%) + (.50 × 8%) =	12

[b]Portfolio XZ, which consists of 50% of asset X and 50% of asset Z, illustrates *perfect positive correlation* because these two return streams behave identically over the 5-year period. Its return values are calculated using the same method demonstrated in note *a* above for portfolio XY.

[c]Because the probabilities associated with the returns are not given, the general equation, Equation 5.2a in footnote 1, is used to calculate expected values as demonstrated below for portfolio XY.

$$\bar{k}_{xy} = \frac{12\% + 12\% + 12\% + 12\% + 12\%}{5} = \frac{60\%}{5} = \underline{\underline{12\%}}$$

The same formula is applied to find the expected value of return for assets X, Y, and Z, and portfolio XZ.

[d]Because the probabilities associated with the returns are not given, the general equation, Equation 5.3a in footnote 2, is used to calculate the standard deviations as demonstrated below for portfolio XY.

$$\sigma_{k_{xy}} = \sqrt{\frac{(12\% - 12\%)^2 + (12\% - 12\%)^2 + (12\% - 12\%)^2 + (12\% - 12\%)^2 + (12\% - 12\%)^2}{5 - 1}}$$

$$= \sqrt{\frac{0\% + 0\% + 0\% + 0\% + 0\%}{4}} = \sqrt{\frac{0}{4}}\% = \underline{\underline{0\%}}$$

The same formula is applied to find the standard deviation of returns for assets X, Y, and Z, and portfolio XZ.

in exactly opposite directions over time. The returns of assets X and Z are perfectly positively correlated. They move in precisely the same direction. (*Note:* The returns for X and Z are identical.)[3]

Portfolio XY Portfolio XY (shown in Table 5.7) is created by combining equal portions of assets X and Y, the perfectly negatively correlated assets.[4] The risk in this portfolio, as reflected by its standard deviation, is reduced to 0%, and the expected return value remains at 12%. Because both assets have the same expected return values, are combined in equal parts, and are perfectly negatively correlated, the combination results in the complete elimination of risk. Whenever assets are perfectly negatively correlated, an optimal combination (similar to the 50–50 mix in the case of assets X and Y) exists for which the resulting standard deviation will equal 0.

Portfolio XZ Portfolio XZ (shown in Table 5.7) is created by combining equal portions of assets X and Z, the perfectly positively correlated assets. The risk in this portfolio, as reflected by its standard deviation, is unaffected by this combination. Risk remains at 3.16%, and the expected return value remains at 12%. Whenever perfectly positively correlated assets such as X and Y are combined, the standard deviation of the resulting portfolio cannot be reduced *below that of the least risky asset;* the maximum portfolio standard deviation will be that of the riskiest asset. Because assets X and Z have the same standard deviation (3.16%), the minimum and maximum standard deviations are the same (3.16%), which is the only value that could be taken on by a combination of these assets. This result can be attributed to the unlikely situation that X and Z are identical assets.

Correlation, Diversification, Risk, and Return

In general, the lower the correlation between asset returns, the greater the potential diversification of risk. (This should be clear from the behaviors illustrated in Table 5.7.) For each pair of assets, there is a combination that will result in the lowest risk (standard deviation) possible. How much risk can be reduced by this combination depends on the degree of correlation. Many potential combinations (assuming divisibility) could be made, but only one combination of the infinite number of possibilities will minimize risk.

Three possible correlations—perfect positive, uncorrelated, and perfect negative—illustrate the effect of correlation on the diversification of risk and return. Table 5.8 summarizes the impact of correlation on the range of return and risk for various two-asset portfolio combinations. The table shows that as we move from perfect positive correlation to uncorrelated assets to perfect negative correlation, the ability to reduce risk is improved. Note that in no case will a portfolio of assets be riskier than the riskiest asset included in the portfolio. Further discussion of these relationships is included at the text's Web site (*www.aw.com/gitman*).

3. Identical return streams are used in this example to permit clear illustration of the concepts, but it is *not* necessary for return streams to be identical for them to be perfectly positively correlated. Any return streams that move (i.e., vary) exactly together—regardless of the relative magnitude of the returns—are perfectly positively correlated.

4. For illustrative purposes it has been assumed that each of the assets—X, Y, and Z—can be divided up and combined with other assets to create portfolios. This assumption is made only to permit clear illustration of the concepts. The assets are not actually divisible.

TABLE 5.8 Correlation, Return, and Risk for Various Two-Asset Portfolio Combinations

Correlation coefficient	Range of return	Range of risk
+1 (perfect positive)	Between returns of two assets held in isolation	Between risk of two assets held in isolation
0 (uncorrelated)	Between returns of two assets held in isolation	Between risk of most risky asset and an amount less than risk of least risky asset but greater than 0
−1 (perfect negative)	Between returns of two assets held in isolation	Between risk of most risky asset and 0

International Diversification

The ultimate example of portfolio diversification involves including foreign assets in a portfolio. The inclusion of assets from countries with business cycles that are not highly correlated with the U.S. business cycle reduces the portfolio's responsiveness to market movements and to foreign currency fluctuations.

Returns from International Diversification

Over long periods, returns from internationally diversified portfolios tend to be superior to those of purely domestic ones. This is particularly so if the U.S. economy is performing relatively poorly and the dollar is depreciating in value against most foreign currencies. At such times, the dollar returns to U.S. investors on a portfolio of foreign assets can be very attractive. However, over any single short or intermediate period, international diversification can yield subpar returns, particularly during periods when the dollar is appreciating in value relative to other currencies. When the U.S. currency gains in value, the dollar value of a foreign-currency-denominated portfolio of assets declines. Even if this portfolio yields a satisfactory return in local currency, the return to U.S. investors will be reduced when translated into dollars. Subpar local currency portfolio returns, coupled with an appreciating dollar, can yield truly dismal dollar returns to U.S. investors.

Overall, though, the logic of international portfolio diversification assumes that these fluctuations in currency values and relative performance will average out over long periods. Compared to similar, purely domestic portfolios, an internationally diversified portfolio will tend to yield a comparable return at a lower level of risk.

political risk
Risk that arises from the possibility that a host government will take actions harmful to foreign investors or that political turmoil in a country will endanger investments there.

Risks of International Diversification

U.S. investors should also be aware of the potential dangers of international investing. In addition to the risk induced by currency fluctuations, several other financial risks are unique to international investing. Most important is **political risk**, which arises from the possibility that a host government will take actions harmful to foreign investors or that political turmoil in a country will endanger investments there. Political risks are particularly acute in developing countries, where unstable or ideologically motivated governments may attempt to block return of profits by foreign investors or even seize (nationalize) their assets in the host country. An example of political risk was the heightened concern after Desert Storm in the early 1990s that Saudi Arabian fundamentalists would take over and nationalize the U.S. oil facilities located there.

Even where governments do not impose exchange controls or seize assets, international investors may suffer if a shortage of hard currency prevents payment of dividends or interest to foreigners. When governments are forced to allocate scarce foreign exchange, they rarely give top priority to the interests of foreign investors. Instead, hard-currency reserves are typically used to pay for necessary imports such as food, medicine, and industrial materials and to pay interest on the government's debt. Because most of the debt of developing countries is held by banks rather than individuals, foreign investors are often badly harmed when a country experiences political or economic problems.

Review Questions

5–8 Why must assets be evaluated in a portfolio context? What is an *efficient portfolio?*

5–9 Why is the *correlation* between asset returns important? How does diversification allow risky assets to be combined so that the risk of the portfolio is less than the risk of the individual assets in it?

5–10 How does international diversification enhance risk reduction? When might international diversification result in subpar returns? What are *political risks,* and how do they affect international diversification?

LG5 LG6

Risk and Return: The Capital Asset Pricing Model (CAPM)

capital asset pricing model (CAPM)
The basic theory that links risk and return for all assets.

The most important aspect of risk is the *overall risk* of the firm as viewed by investors in the marketplace. Overall risk significantly affects investment opportunities and—even more important—the owners' wealth. The basic theory that links risk and return for all assets is the **capital asset pricing model (CAPM).**[5] We will use CAPM to understand the basic risk–return tradeoffs involved in all types of financial decisions.

5. The initial development of this theory is generally attributed to William F. Sharpe, "Capital Asset Prices: A Theory of Market Equilibrium Under Conditions of Risk," *Journal of Finance* 19 (September 1964), pp. 425–442, and John Lintner, "The Valuation of Risk Assets and the Selection of Risky Investments in Stock Portfolios and Capital Budgets," *Review of Economics and Statistics* 47 (February 1965), pp 13–37. A number of authors subsequently advanced, refined, and tested this now widely accepted theory.

FIGURE 5.5

Risk Reduction
Portfolio risk and diversification

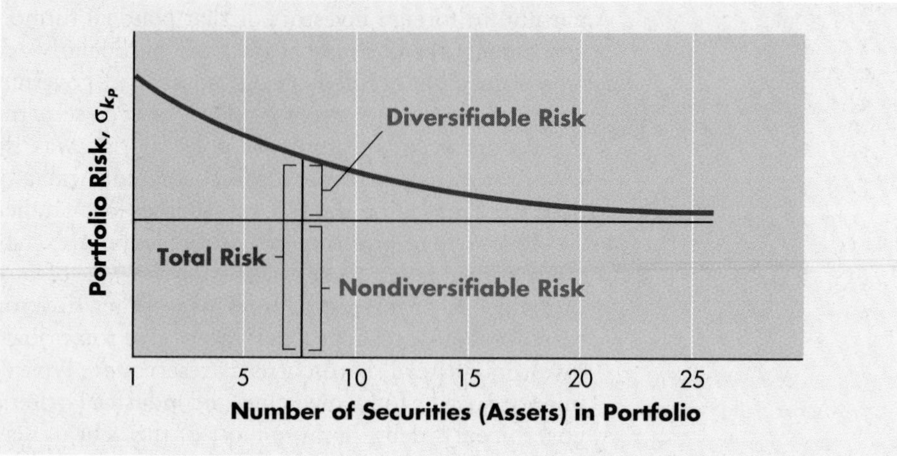

Types of Risk

To understand the basic types of risk, consider what happens to the risk of a portfolio consisting of a single security (asset), to which we add securities randomly selected from, say, the population of all actively traded securities. Using the standard deviation of return, σ_{k_p}, to measure the total portfolio risk, Figure 5.5 depicts the behavior of the total portfolio risk (y axis) as more securities are added (x axis). With the addition of securities, the total portfolio risk declines, as a result of the effects of diversification, and tends to approach a lower limit. Research has shown that, on average, most of the risk-reduction benefits of diversification can be gained by forming portfolios containing 15 to 20 randomly selected securities.

The **total risk** of a security can be viewed as consisting of two parts:

total risk
The combination of a security's *nondiversifiable risk* and *diversifiable risk.*

$$\text{Total security risk} = \text{Nondiversifiable risk} + \text{Diversifiable risk} \quad (5.5)$$

diversifiable risk
The portion of an asset's risk that is attributable to firm-specific, random causes; can be eliminated through diversification. Also called *unsystematic risk.*

nondiversifiable risk
The relevant portion of an asset's risk attributable to market factors that affect all firms; cannot be eliminated through diversification. Also called *systematic risk.*

Diversifiable risk (sometimes called *unsystematic risk*) represents the portion of an asset's risk that is associated with random causes that can be eliminated through diversification. It is attributable to firm-specific events, such as strikes, lawsuits, regulatory actions, and loss of a key account. **Nondiversifiable risk** (also called *systematic risk*) is attributable to market factors that affect all firms; it cannot be eliminated through diversification. (It is the shareholder-specific *market risk* described in Table 5.1.) Factors such as war, inflation, international incidents, and political events account for nondiversifiable risk.

Because any investor can create a portfolio of assets that will eliminate virtually all diversifiable risk, *the only relevant risk is nondiversifiable risk.* Any investor or firm therefore must be concerned solely with nondiversifiable risk. The measurement of nondiversifiable risk is thus of primary importance in selecting assets with the most desired risk–return characteristics.

The Model: CAPM

The capital asset pricing model (CAPM) links nondiversifiable risk and return for all assets. We will discuss the model in four sections. The first deals with the beta coefficient, which is a measure of nondiversifiable risk. The second section presents an equation of the model itself, and the third graphically describes the relationship between risk and return. The final section offers some comments on the CAPM.

Beta Coefficient

beta coefficient (b)
A relative measure of nondiversifiable risk. An *index* of the degree of movement of an asset's return in response to a change in the *market return.*

market return
The return on the market portfolio of all traded securities.

The **beta coefficient, b,** is a relative measure of nondiversifiable risk. It is an *index* of the degree of movement of an asset's return in response to a change in the *market return.* An asset's historical returns are used in finding the asset's beta coefficient. The **market return** is the return on the market portfolio of all traded securities. The *Standard & Poor's 500 Stock Composite Index* or some similar stock index is commonly used as the market return. Betas for actively traded stocks can be obtained from a variety of sources, but you should understand how they are derived and interpreted and how they are applied to portfolios.

Deriving Beta from Return Data An asset's historical returns are used in finding the asset's beta coefficient. Figure 5.6 plots the relationship between the returns of two assets—R and S—and the market return. Note that the horizontal (x) axis measures the historical market returns and that the vertical (y) axis measures the individual asset's historical returns. The first step in deriving beta involves plotting the coordinates for the market return and asset returns from various points in time. Such annual "market return–asset return" coordinates are shown *for asset S only* for the years 1996 through 2003. For example, in 2003, asset S's return was 20 percent when the market return was 10 percent. By use of

FIGURE 5.6

Beta Derivation[a]
Graphical derivation of beta for assets R and S

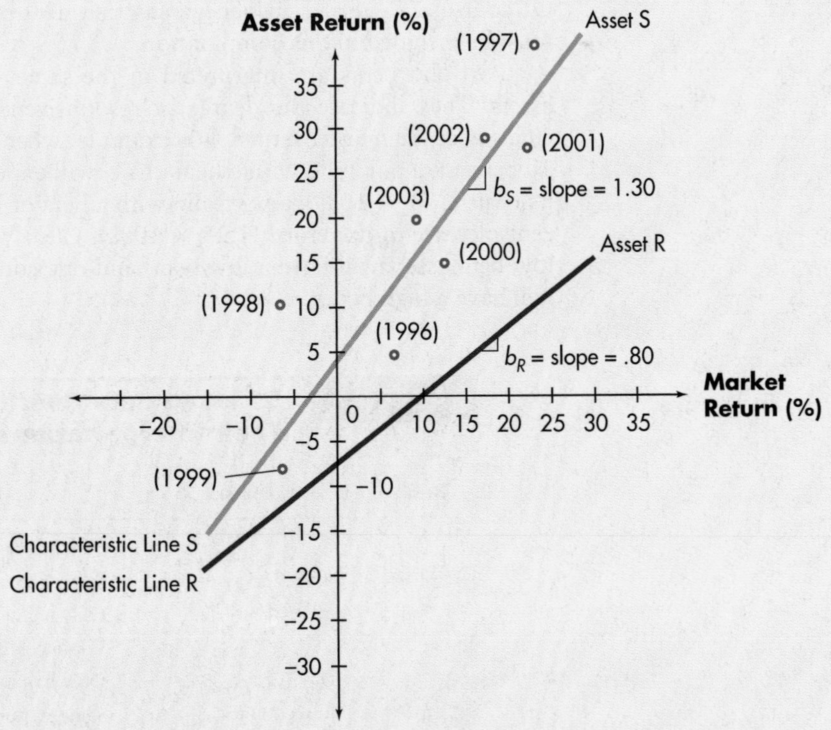

[a] All data points shown are associated with asset S. No data points are shown for asset R.

statistical techniques, the "characteristic line" that best explains the relationship between the asset return and the market return coordinates is fit to the data points. The slope of this line is *beta.* The beta for asset R is about .80 and that for asset S is about 1.30. Asset S's higher beta (steeper characteristic line slope) indicates that its return is more responsive to changing market returns. *Therefore asset S is more risky than asset R.*

Interpreting Betas The beta coefficient for the market is considered to be equal to 1.0. All other betas are viewed in relation to this value. Asset betas may be positive or negative, but positive betas are the norm. The majority of beta coefficients fall between .5 and 2.0. The return of a stock that is half as responsive as the market ($b = .5$) is expected to change by 1/2 percent for each 1 percent change in the return of the market portfolio. A stock that is twice as responsive as the market ($b = 2.0$) is expected to experience a 2 percent change in its return for each 1 percent change in the return of the market portfolio. Table 5.9 provides various beta values and their interpretations. Beta coefficients for actively traded stocks can be obtained from published sources such as *Value Line Investment Survey,* via the Internet, or through brokerage firms. Betas for some selected stocks are given in Table 5.10.

Portfolio Betas The beta of a portfolio can be easily estimated by using the betas of the individual assets it includes. Letting w_j represent the proportion of the portfolio's total dollar value represented by asset j, and letting b_j equal the beta of asset j, we can use Equation 5.6 to find the portfolio beta, b_p:

$$b_p = (w_1 \times b_1) + (w_2 \times b_2) + \cdots + (w_n \times b_n) = \sum_{j=1}^{n} w_j \times b_j \qquad (5.6)$$

Of course, $\sum_{j=1}^{n} w_j = 1$, which means that 100 percent of the portfolio's assets must be included in this computation.

Portfolio betas are interpreted in the same way as the betas of individual assets. They indicate the degree of responsiveness of the *portfolio's* return to changes in the market return. For example, when the market return increases by 10 percent, a portfolio with a beta of .75 will experience a 7.5 percent increase in its return (.75 × 10%); a portfolio with a beta of 1.25 will experience a 12.5 percent increase in its return (1.25 × 10%). Clearly, a portfolio containing mostly low-beta assets will have a low beta, and one containing mostly high-beta assets will have a high beta.

TABLE 5.9 Selected Beta Coefficients and Their Interpretations

Beta	Comment	Interpretation
2.0	Move in same direction as market	Twice as responsive as the market
1.0		Same response as the market
.5		Only half as responsive as the market
0		Unaffected by market movement
− .5	Move in opposite direction to market	Only half as responsive as the market
−1.0		Same response as the market
−2.0		Twice as responsive as the market

TABLE 5.10 Beta Coefficients for Selected Stocks (March 8, 2002)

Stock	Beta	Stock	Beta
Amazon.com	1.95	Int'l Business Machines	1.05
Anheuser-Busch	.60	Merrill Lynch & Co.	1.85
Bank One Corp.	1.25	Microsoft	1.20
Daimler Chrysler AG	1.25	NIKE, Inc.	.90
Disney	1.05	PepsiCo, Inc.	.70
eBay	2.20	Qualcomm	1.30
Exxon Mobil Corp.	.80	Sempra Energy	.60
Gap (The), Inc.	1.60	Wal-Mart Stores	1.15
General Electric	1.30	Xerox	1.25
Intel	1.30	Yahoo! Inc.	2.00

Source: Value Line Investment Survey (New York: Value Line Publishing, March 8, 2002).

EXAMPLE The Austin Fund, a large investment company, wishes to assess the risk of two portfolios it is considering assembling—V and W. Both portfolios contain five assets, with the proportions and betas shown in Table 5.11. The betas for the two portfolios, b_v and b_w, can be calculated by substituting data from the table into Equation 5.6:

$$b_v = (.10 \times 1.65) + (.30 \times 1.00) + (.20 \times 1.30) + (.20 \times 1.10) + (.20 \times 1.25)$$
$$= .165 + .300 + .260 + .220 + .250 = 1.195 \approx \underline{\underline{1.20}}$$

$$b_w = (.10 \times .80) + (.10 \times 1.00) + (.20 \times .65) + (.10 \times .75) + (.50 \times 1.05)$$
$$= .080 + .100 + .130 + .075 + .525 = \underline{\underline{.91}}$$

Portfolio V's beta is 1.20, and portfolio W's is .91. These values make sense, because portfolio V contains relatively high-beta assets, and portfolio W contains relatively low-beta assets. Clearly, portfolio V's returns are more responsive to changes in market returns and are therefore more risky than portfolio W's.

TABLE 5.11 Austin Fund's Portfolios V and W

	Portfolio V		Portfolio W	
Asset	Proportion	Beta	Proportion	Beta
1	.10	1.65	.10	.80
2	.30	1.00	.10	1.00
3	.20	1.30	.20	.65
4	.20	1.10	.10	.75
5	.20	1.25	.50	1.05
Totals	1.00		1.00	

The Equation

Using the beta coefficient to measure nondiversifiable risk, the *capital asset pricing model (CAPM)* is given in Equation 5.7:

$$k_j = R_F + [b_j \times (k_m - R_F)] \tag{5.7}$$

where

k_j = required return on asset j
R_F = risk-free rate of return, commonly measured by the return on a U.S. Treasury bill
b_j = beta coefficient or index of nondiversifiable risk for asset j
k_m = market return; return on the market portfolio of assets

risk-free rate of interest, R_F
The required return on a *risk-free asset,* typically a 3-month *U.S. Treasury bill.*

U.S. Treasury bills (T-bills)
Short-term IOUs issued by the U.S. Treasury; considered the *risk-free asset.*

The CAPM can be divided into two parts: (1) **risk-free of interest, R_F,** which is the required return on a *risk-free asset,* typically a 3-month **U.S. Treasury bill (T-bill),** a short-term IOU issued by the U.S. Treasury, and (2) the *risk premium.* These are, respectively, the two elements on either side of the plus sign in Equation 5.7. The $(k_m - R_F)$ portion of the risk premium is called the *market risk premium,* because it represents the premium the investor must receive for taking the average amount of risk associated with holding the market portfolio of assets.[6]

Historical Risk Premiums Using the historical return data for selected security investments for the 1926–2000 period shown in Table 5.2, we can calculate the risk premiums for each investment category. The calculation (consistent with Equation 5.7) involves merely subtracting the historical U.S. Treasury bill's average return from the historical average return for a given investment:

Investment	Risk premium[a]
Large-company stocks	13.0% − 3.9% = 9.1%
Small company stocks	17.3 − 3.9 = 13.4
Long-term corporate bonds	6.0 − 3.9 = 2.1
Long-term government bonds	5.7 − 3.9 = 1.8
U.S. Treasury bills	3.9 − 3.9 = 0.0

[a]Return values obtained from Table 5.2.

Reviewing the risk premiums calculated above, we can see that the risk premium is highest for small-company stocks, followed by large-company stocks, long-term corporate bonds, and long-term government bonds. This outcome makes sense intuitively because small-company stocks are riskier than large-company stocks, which are riskier than long-term corporate bonds (equity is riskier than debt investment). Long-term corporate bonds are riskier than long-term government bonds (because the government is less likely to renege on debt). And of

6. Although CAPM has been widely accepted, a broader theory, *arbitrage pricing theory (APT),* first described by Stephen A. Ross, "The Arbitrage Theory of Capital Asset Pricing," *Journal of Economic Theory* (December 1976), pp. 341–360, has received a great deal of attention in the financial literature. The theory suggests that the risk premium on securities may be better explained by a number of factors underlying and in place of the market return used in CAPM. The CAPM in effect can be viewed as being derived from APT. Although testing of APT theory confirms the importance of the market return, it has thus far failed to identify other risk factors clearly. As a result of this failure, as well as APT's lack of practical acceptance and usage, we concentrate our attention here on CAPM.

course, U.S. Treasury bills, because of their lack of default risk and their very short maturity, are virtually risk-free, as indicated by their lack of any risk premium.

EXAMPLE

Benjamin Corporation, a growing computer software developer, wishes to determine the required return on an asset Z, which has a beta of 1.5. The risk-free rate of return is 7%; the return on the market portfolio of assets is 11%. Substituting $b_z = 1.5$, $R_F = 7\%$, and $k_m = 11\%$ into the capital asset pricing model given in Equation 5.7 yields a required return of

$$k_z = 7\% + [1.5 \times (11\% - 7\%)] = 7\% + 6\% = \underline{\underline{13}}\%$$

The market risk premium of 4% (11% − 7%), when adjusted for the asset's index of risk (beta) of 1.5, results in a risk premium of 6% (1.5 × 4%). That risk premium, when added to the 7% risk-free rate, results in a 13% required return.

Other things being equal, *the higher the beta, the higher the required return, and the lower the beta, the lower the required return.*

The Graph: The Security Market Line (SML)

security market line (SML)
The depiction of the *capital asset pricing model* (*CAPM*) as a graph that reflects the required return in the marketplace for each level of nondiversifiable risk (beta).

When the capital asset pricing model (Equation 5.7) is depicted graphically, it is called the **security market line** (SML). The SML will, in fact, be a straight line. It reflects the required return in the marketplace for each level of nondiversifiable risk (beta). In the graph, risk as measured by beta, b, is plotted on the x axis, and required returns, k, are plotted on the y axis. The risk–return tradeoff is clearly represented by the SML.

EXAMPLE

In the preceding example for Benjamin Corporation, the risk-free rate, R_F, was 7%, and the market return, k_m, was 11%. The SML can be plotted by using the two sets of coordinates for the betas associated with R_F and k_m, b_{R_F} and b_m (that is, $b_{R_F} = 0$,[7] $R_F = 7\%$; and $b_m = 1.0$, $k_m = 11\%$). Figure 5.7 presents the resulting security market line. As traditionally shown, the security market line in Figure 5.7 presents the required return associated with all positive betas. The market risk premium of 4% (k_m of 11% − R_F of 7%) has been highlighted. For a beta for asset Z, b_z, of 1.5, its corresponding required return, k_z, is 13%. Also shown in the figure is asset Z's risk premium of 6% (k_z of 13% − R_F of 7%). It should be clear that for assets with betas greater than 1, the risk premium is greater than that for the market; for assets with betas less than 1, the risk premium is less than that for the market.

Some Comments on CAPM

The capital asset pricing model generally relies on historical data. The betas may or may not actually reflect the *future* variability of returns. Therefore, the required returns specified by the model can be viewed only as rough approximations. Users of betas commonly make subjective adjustments to the historically determined betas to reflect their expectations of the future.

7. Because R_F is the rate of return on a risk-free asset, the beta associated with the risk-free asset, b_{R_F}, would equal 0. The 0 beta on the risk-free asset reflects not only its absence of risk but also that the asset's return is unaffected by movements in the market return.

FIGURE 5.7

Security Market Line
Security market line (SML) with Benjamin Corporation's asset Z data shown

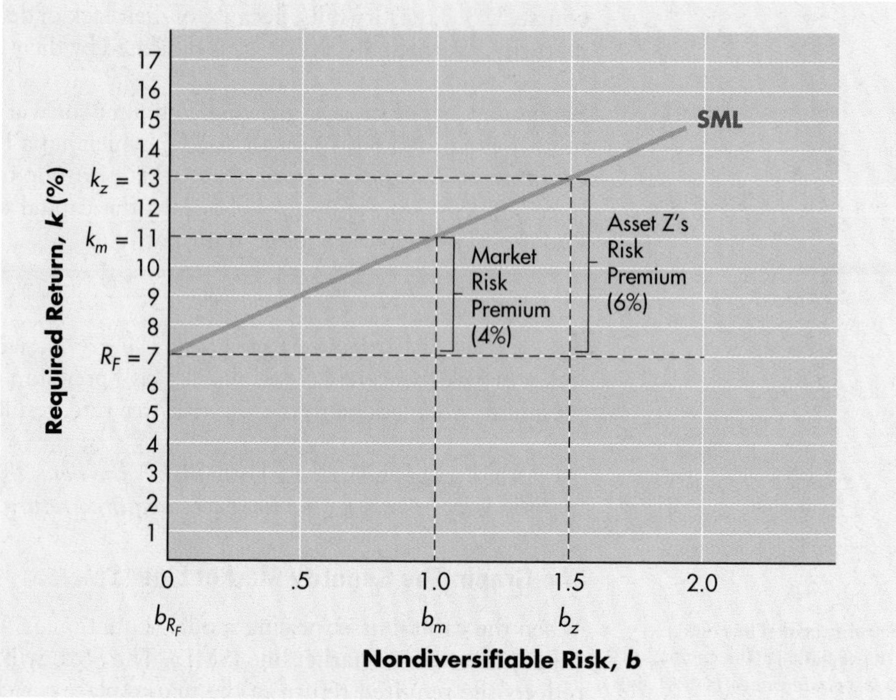

efficient market
A market with the following characteristics: many small investors, all having the same information and expectations with respect to securities; no restrictions on investment, no taxes, and no transaction costs; and rational investors, who view securities similarly and are risk-averse, preferring higher returns and lower risk.

The CAPM was developed to explain the behavior of security prices and provide a mechanism whereby investors could assess the impact of a proposed security investment on their portfolio's overall risk and return. It is based on an assumed **efficient market** with the following characteristics: many small investors, all having the same information and expectations with respect to securities; no restrictions on investment, no taxes, and no transaction costs; and rational investors, who view securities similarly and are risk-averse, preferring higher returns and lower risk.

Although the perfect world of the efficient market appears to be unrealistic, studies have provided support for the existence of the expectational relationship described by CAPM in active markets such as the New York Stock Exchange.[8] In the case of real corporate assets, such as plant and equipment, research thus far has failed to prove the general applicability of CAPM because of indivisibility, relatively large size, limited number of transactions, and absence of an efficient market for such assets.

Despite the limitations of CAPM, it provides a useful conceptual framework for evaluating and linking risk and return. An awareness of this tradeoff and an attempt to consider risk as well as return in financial decision making should help financial managers achieve their goals.

8. A study by Eugene F. Fama and Kenneth R. French, "The Cross-Section of Expected Stock Returns," *Journal of Finance* 47 (June 1992), pp. 427–465, raised serious questions about the validity of CAPM. The study failed to find a significant relationship between the *historical* betas and *historical* returns on over 2,000 stocks during 1963–1990. In other words, it found that the magnitude of a stock's *historical* beta had no relationship to the level of its *historical* return. Although Fama and French's study continues to receive attention, CAPM has not been abandoned because its rejection as a *historical* model fails to discredit its validity as an *expectational* model. Therefore, in spite of this challenge, CAPM continues to be viewed as a logical and useful framework—both conceptually and operationally—for linking *expected* nondiversifiable risk and return.

Review Questions

5–11 How are total risk, nondiversifiable risk, and diversifiable risk related? Why is nondiversifiable risk the *only relevant risk?*

5–12 What risk does *beta* measure? How can you find the beta of a portfolio?

5–13 Explain the meaning of each variable in the *capital asset pricing model (CAPM)* equation. What is the *security market line (SML)?*

5–14 Why do financial managers have some difficulty applying CAPM in financial decision making? Generally, what benefit does CAPM provide them?

SUMMARY

FOCUS ON VALUE

A firm's risk and expected return directly affect its share price. As we shall see in Chapter 7, risk and return are the two key determinants of the firm's value. It is therefore the financial manager's responsibility to assess carefully the risk and return of all major decisions in order to make sure that the expected returns justify the level of risk being introduced.

The way the financial manager can expect to achieve **the firm's goal of increasing its share price** (and thereby benefiting its owners) is to take only those actions that earn returns at least commensurate with their risk. Clearly, financial managers need to recognize, measure, and evaluate risk–return tradeoffs in order to ensure that their decisions contribute to the creation of value for owners.

REVIEW OF LEARNING GOALS

LG1 **Understand the meaning and fundamentals of risk, return, and risk aversion.** Risk is the chance of loss or, more formally, the variability of returns. A number of sources of firm-specific and shareholder-specific risks exists. Return is any cash distributions plus the change in value expressed as a percentage of the initial value. Investment returns vary both over time and between different types of investments. The equation for the rate of return is given in Table 5.12. Most financial managers are risk-averse: They require higher expected returns as compensation for taking greater risk.

LG2 **Describe procedures for assessing and measuring the risk of a single asset.** The risk of a single asset is measured in much the same way as the risk of a portfolio, or collection, of assets. Sensitivity analysis and probability distributions can be used to assess risk. Sensitivity analysis uses a number of possible return estimates to assess the variability of outcomes. Probability distributions, both bar charts and continuous distributions, provide a more quantitative insight into an asset's risk.

LG3 **Discuss risk measurement for a single asset using the standard deviation and coefficient of variation.** In addition to the range, which is the optimistic (best) outcome minus the pessimistic (worst) outcome, the standard deviation and the coefficient of variation can be used to measure risk quantitatively. The standard deviation measures the dispersion around an asset's expected value, and the

TABLE 5.12 Summary of Key Definitions and Formulas for Risk and Return

Definitions of variables

b_j = beta coefficient or index of nondiversifiable risk for asset j
b_p = portfolio beta
C_t = cash received from the asset investment in the time period $t-1$ to t
CV = coefficient of variation
$\bar{k}$ = expected value of a return
k_j = return for the jth outcome; return on asset j; required return on asset j
k_m = market return; the return on the market portfolio of assets
k_t = actual, expected, or required rate of return during period t
n = number of outcomes considered
P_t = price (value) of asset at time t
P_{t-1} = price (value) of asset at time $t-1$
Pr_j = probability of occurrence of the jth outcome
R_F = risk-free rate of return
σ_k = standard deviation of returns
w_j = proportion of total portfolio dollar value represented by asset j

Risk and return formulas

Rate of return during period t:

$$k_t = \frac{C_t + P_t - P_{t-1}}{P_{t-1}} \quad \text{[Eq. 5.1]}$$

Expected value of a return:
for probabilistic data:

$$\bar{k} = \sum_{j=1}^{n} k_j \times Pr_j \quad \text{[Eq. 5.2]}$$

general formula:

$$\bar{k} = \frac{\sum_{j=1}^{n} k_j}{n} \quad \text{[Eq. 5.2a]}$$

Standard deviation of return:
for probabilistic data:

$$\sigma_k = \sqrt{\sum_{j=1}^{n} (k_j - \bar{k})^2 \times Pr_j} \quad \text{[Eq. 5.3]}$$

general formula:

$$\sigma_k = \sqrt{\frac{\sum_{j=1}^{n} (k_j - \bar{k})^2}{n-1}} \quad \text{[Eq. 5.3a]}$$

Coefficient of variation:

$$CV = \frac{\sigma_k}{\bar{k}} \quad \text{[Eq. 5.4]}$$

Total security risk = Nondiversifiable risk + Diversifiable risk [Eq. 5.5]

Portfolio beta:

$$b_p = \sum_{j=1}^{n} w_j \times b_j \quad \text{[Eq. 5.6]}$$

Capital asset pricing model (CAPM):

$$k_j = R_F + [b_j \times (k_m - R_F)] \quad \text{[Eq. 5.7]}$$

coefficient of variation uses the standard deviation to measure dispersion on a relative basis. The key equations for the expected value of a return, the standard deviation of return, and the coefficient of variation are summarized in Table 5.12.

LG4 **Understand the risk and return characteristics of a portfolio in terms of correlation and diversification, and the impact of international assets on a portfolio.** The financial manager's goal is to create an efficient portfolio that maximizes return for a given level of risk or minimizes risk for a given level of return. The risk of a portfolio of assets may be reduced through diversification. New investments must be considered in light of their effect on the risk and return of the portfolio. Correlation, which is the statistical relationship between asset returns, affects the diversification process. The more negative (or less positive) the correlation between asset returns, the greater the risk-reducing benefits of diversification. International diversification can be used to reduce a portfolio's risk further. With foreign assets come the risk of currency fluctuation and political risks.

LG5 **Review the two types of risk and the derivation and role of beta in measuring the relevant risk of both an individual security and a portfolio.** The total risk of a security consists of nondiversifiable and diversifiable risk. Nondiversifiable risk is the only relevant risk; diversifiable risk can be eliminated through diversification. Nondiversifiable risk is measured by the beta coefficient, which is a relative measure of the relationship between an asset's return and the market return. Beta is derived by finding the slope of the "characteristic line" that best explains the historical relationship between the asset's return and the market return. The beta of a portfolio is a weighted average of the betas of the individual assets that it includes. The equations for total risk and the portfolio beta are given in Table 5.12.

LG6 **Explain the capital asset pricing model (CAPM), and its relationship to the security market line (SML).** The capital asset pricing model (CAPM) uses beta to relate an asset's risk relative to the market to the asset's required return. The equation for CAPM is given in Table 5.12. The graphical depiction of CAPM is the security market line (SML). Although it has some shortcomings, CAPM provides a useful conceptual framework for evaluating and linking risk and return.

SELF-TEST PROBLEMS (Solutions in Appendix B)

LG3 LG4 **ST 5–1 Portfolio analysis** You have been asked for your advice in selecting a portfolio of assets and have been given the following data:

	Expected return		
Year	Asset A	Asset B	Asset C
2004	12%	16%	12%
2005	14	14	14
2006	16	12	16

No probabilities have been supplied. You have been told that you can create two portfolios—one consisting of assets A and B and the other consisting of assets A and C—by investing equal proportions (50%) in each of the two component assets.

a. What is the expected return for each asset over the 3-year period?

b. What is the standard deviation for each asset's return?

c. What is the expected return for each of the two portfolios?
d. How would you characterize the correlations of returns of the two assets making up each of the two portfolios identified in part **c**?
e. What is the standard deviation for each portfolio?
f. Which portfolio do you recommend? Why?

LG5 LG6 ST 5–2 **Beta and CAPM** Currently under consideration is a project with a beta, b, of 1.50. At this time, the risk-free rate of return, R_F, is 7%, and the return on the market portfolio of assets, k_m, is 10%. The project is actually *expected* to earn an annual rate of return of 11%.
a. If the return on the market portfolio were to increase by 10%, what would you expect to happen to the project's *required return*? What if the market return were to decline by 10%?
b. Use the capital asset pricing model (CAPM) to find the *required return* on this investment.
c. On the basis of your calculation in part **b**, would you recommend this investment? Why or why not?
d. Assume that as a result of investors becoming less risk-averse, the market return drops by 1% to 9%. What impact would this change have on your responses in parts **b** and **c**?

PROBLEMS

LG1 5–1 **Rate of return** Douglas Keel, a financial analyst for Orange Industries, wishes to estimate the rate of return for two similar-risk investments, X and Y. Keel's research indicates that the immediate past returns will serve as reasonable estimates of future returns. A year earlier, investment X had a market value of \$20,000, investment Y of \$55,000. During the year, investment X generated cash flow of \$1,500 and investment Y generated cash flow of \$6,800. The current market values of investments X and Y are \$21,000 and \$55,000, respectively.
a. Calculate the expected rate of return on investments X and Y using the most recent year's data.
b. Assuming that the two investments are equally risky, which one should Keel recommend? Why?

LG1 5–2 **Return calculations** For each of the investments shown in the following table, calculate the rate of return earned over the unspecified time period.

Investment	Cash flow during period	Beginning-of-period value	End-of-period value
A	−\$ 100	\$ 800	\$ 1,100
B	15,000	120,000	118,000
C	7,000	45,000	48,000
D	80	600	500
E	1,500	12,500	12,400

LG1 5–3 **Risk aversion** Sharon Smith, the financial manager for Barnett Corporation, wishes to evaluate three prospective investments: X, Y, and Z. Currently, the firm earns 12% on its investments, which have a risk index of 6%. The three investments under consideration are profiled in terms of expected return and expected risk in the following table. If Sharon Smith is risk-averse, which investment, if any, will she select? Explain why.

Investment	Expected return	Expected risk index
X	14%	7%
Y	12	8
Z	10	9

LG2 **5–4 Risk analysis** Solar Designs is considering an investment in an expanded product line. Two possible types of expansion are being considered. After investigating the possible outcomes, the company made the estimates shown in the following table

	Expansion A	Expansion B
Initial investment	$12,000	$12,000
Annual rate of return		
Pessimistic	16%	10%
Most likely	20%	20%
Optimistic	24%	30%

a. Determine the *range* of the rates of return for each of the two projects.
b. Which project is less risky? Why?
c. If you were making the investment decision, which one would you choose? Why? What does this imply about your feelings toward risk?
d. Assume that expansion B's most likely outcome is 21% per year and that all other facts remain the same. Does this change your answer to part c? Why?

LG2 **5–5 Risk and probability** Micro-Pub, Inc., is considering the purchase of one of two microfilm cameras, R and S. Both should provide benefits over a 10-year period, and each requires an initial investment of $4,000. Management has constructed the following table of estimates of rates of return and probabilities for pessimistic, most likely, and optimistic results:

	Camera R		Camera S	
	Amount	Probability	Amount	Probability
Initial investment	$4,000	1.00	$4,000	1.00
Annual rate of return				
Pessimistic	20%	.25	15%	.20
Most likely	25%	.50	25%	.55
Optimistic	30%	.25	35%	.25

a. Determine the *range* for the rate of return for each of the two cameras.
b. Determine the *expected value* of return for each camera.
c. Purchase of which camera is riskier? Why?

LG2 **5–6 Bar charts and risk** Swan's Sportswear is considering bringing out a line of designer jeans. Currently, it is negotiating with two different well-known designers. Because of the highly competitive nature of the industry, the two lines of jeans have been given code names. After market research, the firm has established the expectations shown in the following table about the annual rates of return

		Annual rate of return	
Market acceptance	Probability	Line J	Line K
Very poor	.05	.0075	.010
Poor	.15	.0125	.025
Average	.60	.0850	.080
Good	.15	.1475	.135
Excellent	.05	.1625	.150

Use the table to:
a. Construct a bar chart for each line's annual rate of return.
b. Calculate the *expected value* of return for each line.
c. Evaluate the relative riskiness for each jean line's rate of return using the bar charts.

LG3 **5–7 Coefficient of variation** Metal Manufacturing has isolated four alternatives for meeting its need for increased production capacity. The data gathered relative to each of these alternatives is summarized in the following table.

Alternative	Expected return	Standard deviation of return
A	20%	7.0%
B	22	9.5
C	19	6.0
D	16	5.5

a. Calculate the *coefficient of variation* for each alternative.
b. If the firm wishes to minimize risk, which alternative do you recommend? Why?

LG2 LG3 **5–8 Assessing return and risk** Swift Manufacturing must choose between two asset purchases. The annual rate of return and the related probabilities given in the following table summarize the firm's analysis to this point.

Project 257		Project 432	
Rate of return	Probability	Rate of return	Probability
− 10%	.01	10%	.05
10	.04	15	.10
20	.05	20	.10
30	.10	25	.15
40	.15	30	.20
45	.30	35	.15
50	.15	40	.10
60	.10	45	.10
70	.05	50	.05
80	.04		
100	.01		

a. For each project, compute:
(1) The range of possible rates of return.
(2) The expected value of return.
(3) The standard deviation of the returns.
(4) The coefficient of variation of the returns.

b. Construct a bar chart of each distribution of rates of return.

c. Which project would you consider less risky? Why?

LG3 5–9 **Integrative—Expected return, standard deviation, and coefficient of variation** Three assets—F, G, and H—are currently being considered by Perth Industries. The probability distributions of expected returns for these assets are shown in the following table.

	Asset F		Asset G		Asset H	
j	Pr_j	Return, k_j	Pr_j	Return, k_j	Pr_j	Return, k_j
1	.10	40%	.40	35%	.10	40%
2	.20	10	.30	10	.20	20
3	.40	0	.30	−20	.40	10
4	.20	−5			.20	0
5	.10	−10			.10	−20

a. Calculate the expected value of return, $\bar{k}$, for each of the three assets. Which provides the largest expected return?

b. Calculate the standard deviation, σ_k, for each of the three assets' returns. Which appears to have the greatest risk?

c. Calculate the coefficient of variation, CV, for each of the three assets' returns. Which appears to have the greatest *relative* risk?

LG4 5–10 **Portfolio return and standard deviation** Jamie Wong is considering building a portfolio containing two assets, L and M. Asset L will represent 40% of the dollar value of the portfolio, and asset M will account for the other 60%. The expected returns over the next 6 years, 2004–2009, for each of these assets, are shown in the following table.

	Expected return	
Year	Asset L	Asset M
2004	14%	20%
2005	14	18
2006	16	16
2007	17	14
2008	17	12
2009	19	10

a. Calculate the expected portfolio return, k_p, for *each* of the 6 years.
b. Calculate the expected value of portfolio returns, $\bar{k}_p$, over the 6-year period.
c. Calculate the standard deviation of expected portfolio returns, σ_{k_p}, over the 6-year period.
d. How would you characterize the correlation of returns of the two assets L and M?
e. Discuss any benefits of diversification achieved through creation of the portfolio.

LG4 5–11 **Portfolio analysis** You have been given the return data shown in the first table on three assets—F, G, and H—over the period 2004–2007.

		Expected return	
Year	Asset F	Asset G	Asset H
2004	16%	17%	14%
2005	17	16	15
2006	18	15	16
2007	19	14	17

Using these assets, you have isolated the three investment alternatives shown in the following table:

Alternative	Investment
1	100% of asset F
2	50% of asset F and 50% of asset G
3	50% of asset F and 50% of asset H

a. Calculate the expected return over the 4-year period for each of the three alternatives.
b. Calculate the standard deviation of returns over the 4-year period for each of the three alternatives.

c. Use your findings in parts **a** and **b** to calculate the coefficient of variation for each of the three alternatives.

d. On the basis of your findings, which of the three investment alternatives do you recommend? Why?

LG4 5–12 **Correlation, risk, and return** Matt Peters wishes to evaluate the risk and return behaviors associated with various combinations of assets V and W under three assumed degrees of correlation: perfect positive, uncorrelated, and perfect negative. The expected return and risk values calculated for each of the assets are shown in the following table.

Asset	Expected return, $\bar{k}$	Risk (standard deviation), σ_k
V	8%	5%
W	13	10

a. If the returns of assets V and W are *perfectly positively correlated* (correlation coefficient = +1), describe the *range* of (1) expected return and (2) risk associated with all possible portfolio combinations.

b. If the returns of assets V and W are *uncorrelated* (correlation coefficient = 0), describe the *approximate range* of (1) expected return and (2) risk associated with all possible portfolio combinations.

c. If the returns of assets V and W are *perfectly negatively correlated* (correlation coefficient = −1), describe the *range* of (1) expected return and (2) risk associated with all possible portfolio combinations.

LG5 5–13 **Total, nondiversifiable, and diversifiable risk** David Talbot randomly selected securities from all those listed on the New York Stock Exchange for his portfolio. He began with a single security and added securities one by one until a total of 20 securities were held in the portfolio. After each security was added, David calculated the portfolio standard deviation, σ_{k_p}. The calculated values are shown in the following table.

Number of securities	Portfolio risk, σ_{k_p}	Number of securities	Portfolio risk, σ_{k_p}
1	14.50%	11	7.00%
2	13.30	12	6.80
3	12.20	13	6.70
4	11.20	14	6.65
5	10.30	15	6.60
6	9.50	16	6.56
7	8.80	17	6.52
8	8.20	18	6.50
9	7.70	19	6.48
10	7.30	20	6.47

a. On a set of "number of securities in portfolio (*x* axis)–portfolio risk (*y* axis)" axes, plot the portfolio risk data given in the preceding table.
b. Divide the total portfolio risk in the graph into its *nondiversifiable* and *diversifiable* risk components and label each of these on the graph.
c. Describe which of the two risk components is the *relevant risk,* and explain why it is relevant. How much of this risk exists in David Talbot's portfolio?

LG5 **5–14 Graphical derivation of beta** A firm wishes to estimate graphically the betas for two assets, A and B. It has gathered the return data shown in the following table for the market portfolio and for both assets over the last ten years, 1994–2003.

	Actual return		
Year	Market portfolio	Asset A	Asset B
1994	6%	11%	16%
1995	2	8	11
1996	−13	−4	−10
1997	−4	3	3
1998	−8	0	−3
1999	16	19	30
2000	10	14	22
2001	15	18	29
2002	8	12	19
2003	13	17	26

a. On a set of "market return (*x* axis)–asset return (*y* axis)" axes, use the data given to draw the characteristic line for asset A and for asset B.
b. Use the characteristic lines from part **a** to estimate the betas for assets A and B.
c. Use the betas found in part **b** to comment on the relative risks of assets A and B.

LG5 **5–15 Interpreting beta** A firm wishes to assess the impact of changes in the market return on an asset that has a beta of 1.20.
a. If the market return increased by 15%, what impact would this change be expected to have on the asset's return?
b. If the market return decreased by 8%, what impact would this change be expected to have on the asset's return?
c. If the market return did not change, what impact, if any, would be expected on the asset's return?
d. Would this asset be considered more or less risky than the market? Explain.

LG5 **5–16 Betas** Answer the following questions for assets A to D shown in the following table.

Asset	Beta
A	.50
B	1.60
C	−.20
D	.90

a. What impact would a *10% increase* in the market return be expected to have on each asset's return?
b. What impact would a *10% decrease* in the market return be expected to have on each asset's return?
c. If you were certain that the market return would *increase* in the near future, which asset would you prefer? Why?
d. If you were certain that the market return would *decrease* in the near future, which asset would you prefer? Why?

LG5 5–17 **Betas and risk rankings** Stock A has a beta of .80, stock B has a beta of 1.40, and stock C has a beta of −.30.
a. Rank these stocks from the most risky to the least risky.
b. If the return on the market portfolio increased by 12%, what change would you expect in the return for each of the stocks?
c. If the return on the market portfolio decreased by 5%, what change would you expect in the return for each of the stocks?
d. If you felt that the stock market was just ready to experience a significant decline, which stock would you probably add to your portfolio? Why?
e. If you anticipated a major stock market rally, which stock would you add to your portfolio? Why?

LG5 5–18 **Portfolio betas** Rose Berry is attempting to evaluate two possible portfolios, which consist of the same five assets held in different proportions. She is particularly interested in using beta to compare the risks of the portfolios, so she has gathered the data shown in the following table.

		Portfolio weights	
Asset	Asset beta	Portfolio A	Portfolio B
1	1.30	10%	30%
2	.70	30	10
3	1.25	10	20
4	1.10	10	20
5	.90	40	20
Totals		100%	100%

a. Calculate the betas for portfolios A and B.
b. Compare the risks of these portfolios to the market as well as to each other. Which portfolio is more risky?

LG6 **5–19 Capital asset pricing model (CAPM)** For each of the cases shown in the following table, use the capital asset pricing model to find the required return.

Case	Risk-free rate, R_F	Market return, k_m	Beta, b
A	5%	8%	1.30
B	8	13	.90
C	9	12	−.20
D	10	15	1.00
E	6	10	.60

LG5 LG6 **5–20 Beta coefficients and the capital asset pricing model** Katherine Wilson is wondering how much risk she must undertake in order to generate an acceptable return on her portfolio. The risk-free return currently is 5%. The return on the average stock (market return) is 16%. Use the CAPM to calculate the beta coefficient associated with each of the following portfolio returns.

a. 10%
b. 15%
c. 18%
d. 20%
e. Katherine is risk-averse. What is the highest return she can expect if she is unwilling to take more than an average risk?

LG6 **5–21 Manipulating CAPM** Use the basic equation for the capital asset pricing model (CAPM) to work each of the following problems.

a. Find the *required return* for an asset with a beta of .90 when the risk-free rate and market return are 8% and 12%, respectively.
b. Find the *risk-free rate* for a firm with a required return of 15% and a beta of 1.25 when the market return is 14%.
c. Find the *market return* for an asset with a required return of 16% and a beta of 1.10 when the risk-free rate is 9%.
d. Find the *beta* for an asset with a required return of 15% when the risk-free rate and market return are 10% and 12.5%, respectively.

LG6 **5–22 Security market line, SML** Assume that the risk-free rate, R_F, is currently 9% and that the market return, k_m, is currently 13%.

a. Draw the security market line (SML) on a set of "nondiversifiable risk (x axis)–required return (y axis)" axes.
b. Calculate and label the *market risk premium* on the axes in part **a.**
c. Given the previous data, calculate the required return on asset A having a beta of .80 and asset B having a beta of 1.30.
d. Draw in the betas and required returns from part **c** for assets A and B on the axes in part **a.** Label the *risk premium* associated with each of these assets, and discuss them.

LG6 **5–23 Integrative—Risk, return, and CAPM** Wolff Enterprises must consider several investment projects, A through E, using the capital asset pricing model (CAPM) and its graphical representation, the security market line (SML). Relevant information is presented in the following table.

Item	Rate of return	Beta, *b*
Risk-free asset	9%	0
Market portfolio	14	1.00
Project A	—	1.50
Project B	—	.75
Project C	—	2.00
Project D	—	0
Project E	—	− .50

a. Calculate the required rate of return and risk premium for each project, given its level of nondiversifiable risk.
b. Use your findings in part a to draw the security market line (required return relative to nondiversifiable risk).
c. Discuss the relative nondiversifiable risk of projects A through E.

CHAPTER 5 CASE Analyzing Risk and Return on Chargers Products' Investments

Junior Sayou, a financial analyst for Chargers Products, a manufacturer of stadium benches, must evaluate the risk and return of two assets, X and Y. The firm is considering adding these assets to its diversified asset portfolio. To assess the return and risk of each asset, Junior gathered data on the annual cash flow and beginning- and end-of-year values of each asset over the immediately preceding 10 years, 1994–2003. These data are summarized in the accompanying table. Junior's investigation suggests that both assets, on average, will tend to perform in the future just as they have during the past 10 years. He therefore believes that the expected annual return can be estimated by finding the average annual return for each asset over the past 10 years.

Junior believes that each asset's risk can be assessed in two ways: in isolation and as part of the firm's diversified portfolio of assets. The risk of the assets in isolation can be found by using the standard deviation and coefficient of variation of returns over the past 10 years. The capital asset pricing model (CAPM) can be used to assess the asset's risk as part of the firm's portfolio of assets. Applying some sophisticated quantitative techniques, Junior estimated betas for assets X and Y of 1.60 and 1.10, respectively. In addition, he found that the risk-free rate is currently 7% and that the market return is 10%.

Return Data for Assets X and Y, 1994–2003

	Asset X			Asset Y		
		Value			Value	
Year	Cash flow	Beginning	Ending	Cash flow	Beginning	Ending
1994	$1,000	$20,000	$22,000	$1,500	$20,000	$20,000
1995	1,500	22,000	21,000	1,600	20,000	20,000
1996	1,400	21,000	24,000	1,700	20,000	21,000
1997	1,700	24,000	22,000	1,800	21,000	21,000
1998	1,900	22,000	23,000	1,900	21,000	22,000
1999	1,600	23,000	26,000	2,000	22,000	23,000
2000	1,700	26,000	25,000	2,100	23,000	23,000
2001	2,000	25,000	24,000	2,200	23,000	24,000
2002	2,100	24,000	27,000	2,300	24,000	25,000
2003	2,200	27,000	30,000	2,400	25,000	25,000

Required

a. Calculate the annual rate of return for each asset in *each* of the 10 preceding years, and use those values to find the average annual return for each asset over the 10-year period.

b. Use the returns calculated in part **a** to find (1) the standard deviation and (2) the coefficient of variation of the returns for each asset over the 10-year period 1994–2003.

c. Use your findings in parts **a** and **b** to evaluate and discuss the return and risk associated with each asset. Which asset appears to be preferable? Explain.

d. Use the CAPM to find the required return for each asset. Compare this value with the average annual returns calculated in part **a.**

e. Compare and contrast your findings in parts **c** and **d.** What recommendations would you give Junior with regard to investing in either of the two assets? Explain to Junior why he is better off using beta rather than the standard deviation and coefficient of variation to assess the risk of each asset.

WEB EXERCISE

Go to the RiskGrades Web site, *www.riskgrades.com*. This site, from RiskMetrics Group, provides another way to assess the riskiness of stocks and mutual funds. RiskGrades provide a way to compare investment risk across all asset classes, regions, and currencies. They vary over time to reflect asset-specific information (such as the price of a stock reacting to an earnings release) and general market conditions. RiskGrades operate differently from traditional risk measures, such as standard deviation and beta.

1. First, learn more about RiskGrades by clicking on **RiskGrades Help Center** and reviewing the material. How are RiskGrades calculated? What differ-

ences can you identify when you compare them to standard deviation and beta techniques? What are the advantages and disadvantages of this measure, in your opinion?

2. Get RiskGrades for the following stocks using the **Get RiskGrade** pull-down menu at the site's upper right corner. You can enter multiple symbols separated by commas. Select **all dates** to get a historical view.

Company	Symbol
Citigroup	C
Intel	INTC
Microsoft	MSFT
Washington Mutual	WM

What do the results tell you?

3. Select one of the foregoing stocks and find other stocks with similar risk grades. Click on **By RiskGrade** to pull up a list.

4. How much risk can you tolerate? Use a hypothetical portfolio to find out. Click on **Grade Yourself,** take a short quiz, and get your personal RiskGrade measure. Did the results surprise you?

Remember to check the book's Web site at

www.aw.com/gitman

for additional resources, including additional Web exercises.

Chapter

6

Interest Rates and Bond Valuation

LEARNING GOALS

LG1 Describe interest rate fundamentals, the term structure of interest rates, and risk premiums.

LG2 Review the legal aspects of bond financing and bond cost.

LG3 Discuss the general features, quotations, ratings, popular types, and international issues of corporate bonds.

LG4 Understand the key inputs and basic model used in the valuation process.

LG5 Apply the basic valuation model to bonds and describe the impact of required return and time to maturity on bond values.

LG6 Explain yield to maturity (YTM), its calculation, and the procedure used to value bonds that pay interest semiannually.

Across the Disciplines

Why This Chapter Matters To You

Accounting: You need to understand interest rates and the various types of bonds in order to be able to account properly for amortization of bond premiums and discounts and for bond purchases and retirements.

Information systems: You need to understand the data that you will need to track in bond amortization schedules and bond valuation.

Management: You need to understand the behavior of interest rates and how they will affect the types of funds the firm can raise and the timing and cost of bond issues and retirements.

Marketing: You need to understand how the interest rate level and the firm's ability to issue bonds may affect the availability of financing for marketing research projects and new-product development.

Operations: You need to understand how the interest rate level may affect the firm's ability to raise funds to maintain and increase the firm's production capacity.

The interactions of suppliers and demanders of funds in the financial markets affect interest rates. The interest rates (returns) required by suppliers of funds also depend on the perceived risk of an asset. In this chapter, we apply the concepts of risk and return in a process called valuation. This chapter discusses interest rates, describes the key aspects of corporate bonds, and demonstrates the valuation process for the easiest financial asset to value, bonds.

LG1

Interest Rates and Required Returns

As noted in Chapter 1, financial institutions and markets create the mechanism through which funds flow between savers (funds suppliers) and investors (funds demanders). The level of funds flow between suppliers and demanders can significantly affect economic growth. Growth results from the interaction of a variety of economic factors (such as the money supply, trade balances, and economic policies) that affect the cost of money—the interest rate or required return. The interest rate level acts as a regulating device that controls the flow of funds between suppliers and demanders. The *Board of Governors of the Federal Reserve System* regularly assesses economic conditions and, when necessary, initiates actions to raise or lower interest rates to control inflation and economic growth. Generally, the lower the interest rate, the greater the funds flow and therefore the greater the economic growth; the higher the interest rate, the lower the funds flow and economic growth.

interest rate
The compensation paid by the borrower of funds to the lender; from the borrower's point of view, the cost of borrowing funds.

required return
The cost of funds obtained by selling an ownership interest; it reflects the funds supplier's level of expected return.

liquidity preferences
General preferences of investors for shorter-term securities.

real rate of interest
The rate that creates an equilibrium between the supply of savings and the demand for investment funds in a perfect world, without inflation, where funds suppliers and demanders are indifferent to the term of loans or investments and have no liquidity preference, and where all outcomes are certain.

Interest Rate Fundamentals

The interest rate or required return represents the cost of money. It is the compensation that a demander of funds must pay a supplier. When funds are lent, the cost of borrowing the funds is the **interest rate.** When funds are obtained by selling an ownership interest—as in the sale of stock—the cost to the issuer (demander) is commonly called the **required return,** which reflects the funds supplier's level of expected return. In both cases the supplier is compensated for providing funds. Ignoring risk factors, the cost of funds results from the *real rate of interest* adjusted for inflationary expectations and **liquidity preferences**—general preferences of investors for shorter-term securities.

The Real Rate of Interest

Assume a *perfect world* in which there is no inflation and in which funds suppliers and demanders are indifferent to the term of loans or investments because they have no liquidity preference and all outcomes are certain.[1] At any given point in time in that perfect world, there would be one cost of money—the **real rate of interest.** The real rate of interest creates an equilibrium between the supply of savings and the demand for investment funds. It represents the most basic cost of

1. These assumptions are made to describe the most basic interest rate, the *real rate of interest.* Subsequent discussions relax these assumptions to develop the broader concept of the interest rate and required return.

FIGURE 6.1

Supply–Demand Relationship

Supply of savings and demand for investment funds

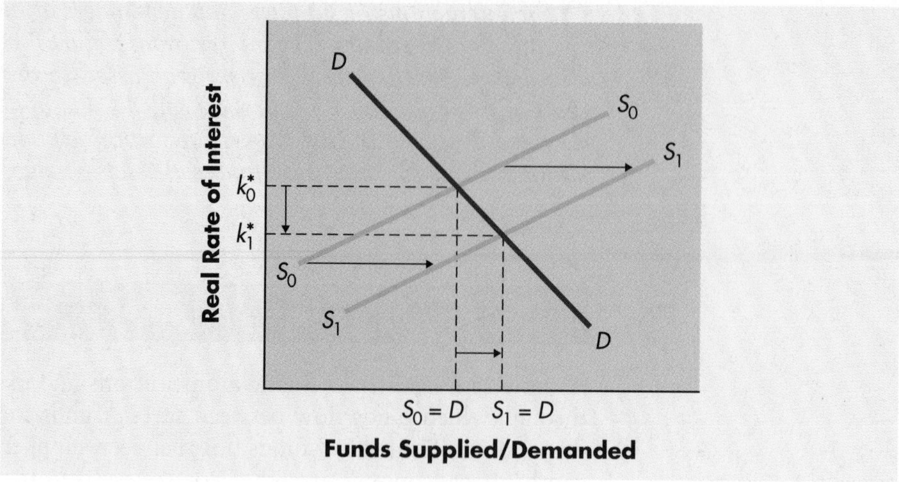

money. The real rate of interest in the United States is assumed to be stable and equal to around 1 percent.[2] This supply–demand relationship is shown in Figure 6.1 by the supply function (labeled S_0) and the demand function (labeled D). An equilibrium between the supply of funds and the demand for funds ($S_0 = D$) occurs at a rate of interest k_0^*, the real rate of interest.

Clearly, the real rate of interest changes with changing economic conditions, tastes, and preferences. A trade surplus could result in an increased supply of funds, causing the supply function in Figure 6.1 to shift to, say, S_1. This could result in a lower real rate of interest, k_1^*, at equilibrium ($S_1 = D$). Likewise, a change in tax laws or other factors could affect the demand for funds, causing the real rate of interest to rise or fall to a new equilibrium level.

Inflation and the Cost of Money

risk-free rate of interest, R_F
The required return on a risk-free asset, typically a 3-month *U.S. Treasury bill.*

Ignoring risk factors, the cost of funds—the interest rate or required return—is closely tied to inflationary expectations. This can be demonstrated by using the **risk-free rate of interest, R_F,** which was defined in Chapter 5 as the required return on the risk-free asset. The risk-free asset is typically considered to be a 3-month *U.S. Treasury bill (T-bill)*, which is a short-term IOU issued regularly by the U.S. Treasury. Figure 6.2 illustrates the movement of the rate of inflation and the risk-free rate of interest during the period 1978–2001. During this period the two rates tended to move in a similar fashion. Between 1978 and the early 1980s, inflation and interest rates were quite high, peaking at over 13 percent in 1980–1981. Since 1981 these rates have declined. The historical data clearly illustrate the significant impact of inflation on the actual rate of interest for the risk-free asset.

2. Data in *Stocks, Bonds, Bills and Inflation, 2001 Yearbook* (Chicago: Ibbotson Associates, Inc., 2001), show that over the period 1926–2000, U.S. Treasury bills provided an average annual real rate of return of about 0.7 percent. Because of certain major economic events that occurred during the 1926–2000 period, many economists believe that the real rate of interest during recent years has been about 1 percent.

FIGURE 6.2

Impact of Inflation

Relationship between annual rate of inflation and 3-month U.S. Treasury bill average annual returns, 1978–2001

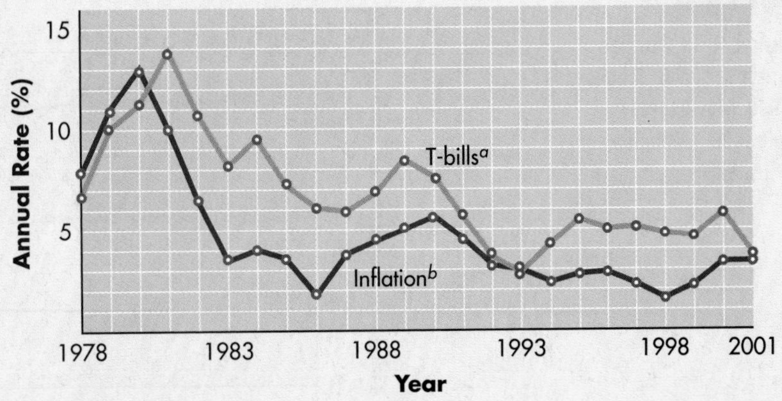

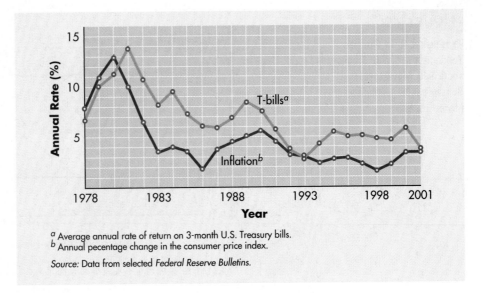

[a] Average annual rate of return on 3-month U.S. Treasury bills.
[b] Annual pecentage change in the consumer price index.

Source: Data from selected *Federal Reserve Bulletins.*

term structure of interest rates
The relationship between the interest rate or rate of return and the time to maturity.

yield to maturity
Annual rate of return earned on a debt security purchased on a given day and held to maturity.

yield curve
A graph of the relationship between the debt's remaining time to maturity (*x* axis) and its yield to maturity (*y* axis); it shows the pattern of annual returns on debts of equal quality and different maturities. Graphically depicts the *term structure of interest rates.*

inverted yield curve
A *downward-sloping* yield curve that indicates generally cheaper long-term borrowing costs than short-term borrowing costs.

normal yield curve
An *upward-sloping* yield curve that indicates generally cheaper short-term borrowing costs than long-term borrowing costs.

flat yield curve
A yield curve that reflects relatively similar borrowing costs for both short- and longer-term loans.

Term Structure of Interest Rates

For any class of similar-risk securities, the **term structure of interest rates** relates the interest rate or rate of return to the time to maturity. For convenience we will use Treasury securities as an example, but other classes could include securities that have similar overall quality or risk. The riskless nature of Treasury securities also provides a laboratory in which to develop the term structure.

Yield Curves

A debt security's **yield to maturity** (discussed later in this chapter) represents the annual rate of return earned on a security purchased on a given day and held to maturity. At any point in time, the relationship between the debt's remaining time to maturity and its yield to maturity is represented by the **yield curve.** The yield curve shows the yield to maturity for debts of equal quality and different maturities; it is a graphical depiction of the *term structure of interest rates.* Figure 6.3 shows three yield curves for all U.S. Treasury securities: one at May 22, 1981, a second at September 29, 1989, and a third at March 15, 2002. Note that both the position and the shape of the yield curves change over time. The yield curve of May 22, 1981, indicates that short-term interest rates at that time were above longer-term rates. This curve is described as *downward-sloping,* reflecting long-term borrowing costs generally cheaper than short-term borrowing costs. Historically, the downward-sloping yield curve, which is often called an **inverted yield curve,** has been the exception. More frequently, yield curves similar to that of March 15, 2002, have existed. These *upward-sloping* or **normal yield curves** indicate that short-term borrowing costs are below long-term borrowing costs. Sometimes, a **flat yield curve,** similar to that of September 29, 1989, exists. It reflects relatively similar borrowing costs for both short- and longer-term loans.

FIGURE 6.3

Treasury Yield Curves
Yield curves for U.S. Treasury securities: May 22, 1981; September 29, 1989; and March 15, 2002

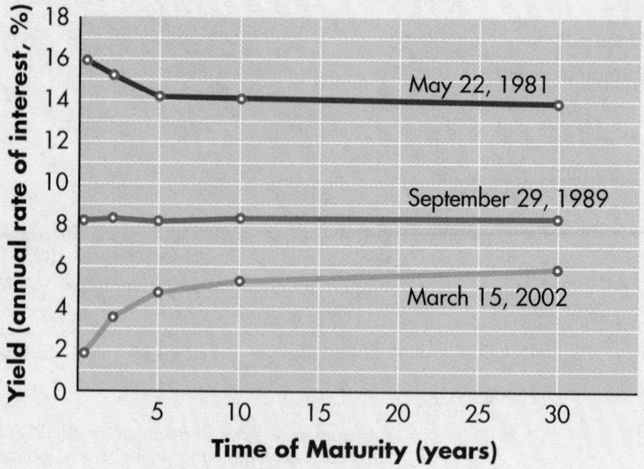

Sources: Data from *Federal Reserve Bulletins* (June 1981), p. A25 and (December 1989), p. A24; and *U.S. Financial Data,* Federal Reserve Bank of St. Louis (March 14, 2002), p. 7.

The shape of the yield curve may affect the firm's financing decisions. A financial manager who faces a downward-sloping yield curve is likely to rely more heavily on cheaper, long-term financing; when the yield curve is upward-sloping, the manager is more likely to use cheaper, short-term financing. Although a variety of other factors also influence the choice of loan maturity, the shape of the yield curve provides useful insights into future interest rate expectations.

Theories of Term Structure

Three theories are frequently cited to explain the general shape of the yield curve. They are the expectations theory, liquidity preference theory, and market segmentation theory.

expectations theory
The theory that the yield curve reflects investor expectations about future interest rates; an increasing inflation expectation results in an upward-sloping yield curve, and a decreasing inflation expectation results in a downward-sloping yield curve

Expectations Theory One theory of the term structure of interest rates, the **expectations theory,** suggests that the yield curve reflects investor expectations about future interest rates and inflation. Higher future rates of expected inflation will result in higher long-term interest rates; the opposite occurs with lower future rates. This widely accepted explanation of the term structure can be applied to the securities of any issuer.

Generally, under the expectations theory, an increasing inflation expectation results in an upward-sloping yield curve; a decreasing inflation expectation results in a downward-sloping yield curve; and a stable inflation expectation results in a flat yield curve. Although, as we'll see, other theories exist, the observed strong relationship between inflation and interest rates (see Figure 6.2) supports this widely accepted theory.

liquidity preference theory
Theory suggesting that for any given issuer, long-term interest rates tend to be higher than short-term rates because (1) lower liquidity and higher responsiveness to general interest rate movements of longer-term securities exists and (2) borrower willingness to pay a higher rate for long-term financing; causes the yield curve to be upward-sloping.

Liquidity Preference Theory The tendency for yield curves to be upward-sloping can be further explained by **liquidity preference theory.** This theory holds that for a given issuer, such as the U.S. Treasury, long-term rates tend to be higher than short-term rates. This belief is based on two behavioral facts:

1. Investors perceive less risk in short-term securities than in longer-term securities and are therefore willing to accept lower yields on them. The reason is that shorter-term securities are more liquid and less responsive to general interest rate movements.[3]
2. Borrowers are generally willing to pay a higher rate for long-term than for short-term financing. By locking in funds for a longer period of time, they can eliminate the potential adverse consequences of having to roll over short-term debt at unknown costs to obtain long-term financing.

Investors (lenders) tend to require a premium for tying up funds for longer periods, whereas borrowers are generally willing to pay a premium to obtain longer-term financing. These preferences of lenders and borrowers cause the yield curve to tend to be upward-sloping. Simply stated, longer maturities tend to have higher interest rates than shorter maturities.

market segmentation theory
Theory suggesting that the market for loans is segmented on the basis of maturity and that the supply of and demand for loans within each segment determine its prevailing interest rate; the slope of the yield curve is determined by the general relationship between the prevailing rates in each segment.

Market Segmentation Theory The **market segmentation theory** suggests that the market for loans is segmented on the basis of maturity and that the supply of and demand for loans within each segment determine its prevailing interest rate. In other words, the equilibrium between suppliers and demanders of short-term funds, such as seasonal business loans, would determine prevailing short-term interest rates, and the equilibrium between suppliers and demanders of long-term funds, such as real estate loans, would determine prevailing long-term interest rates. The slope of the yield curve would be determined by the general relationship between the prevailing rates in each market segment. Simply stated, low rates in the short-term segment and high rates in the long-term segment cause the yield curve to be upward-sloping. The opposite occurs for high short-term rates and low long-term rates.

All three theories of term structure have merit. From them we can conclude that at any time, the slope of the yield curve is affected by (1) inflationary expectations, (2) liquidity preferences, and (3) the comparative equilibrium of supply and demand in the short- and long-term market segments. Upward-sloping yield curves result from higher future inflation expectations, lender preferences for shorter-maturity loans, and greater supply of short-term loans than of long-term loans relative to demand. The opposite behaviors would result in a downward-sloping yield curve. At any time, the interaction of these three forces determines the prevailing slope of the yield curve.

Risk Premiums: Issuer and Issue Characteristics

risk premium
The amount by which the interest rate or required return on a security exceeds the risk-free rate of interest, R_F; it varies with specific issuer and issue characteristics.

So far we have considered only risk-free U.S. Treasury securities. We now add the element of risk, in order to assess what effect it has on the cost of funds. The amount by which the interest rate or required return exceeds the risk-free rate of interest, R_F, is a security's **risk premium.** The risk premium varies with specific issuer and issue characteristics. It causes securities that have similar maturities to have differing rates of interest.

3. Later in this chapter we demonstrate that debt instruments with longer maturities are more sensitive to changing market interest rates. For a given change in market rates, the price or value of longer-term debts will be more significantly changed (up or down) than the price or value of debts with shorter maturities.

TABLE 6.1 Debt-Specific Issuer- and Issue-Related Risk Premium Components

Component	Description
Default risk	The possibility that the issuer of debt will not pay the contractual interest or principal as scheduled. The greater the uncertainty as to the borrower's ability to meet these payments, the greater the risk premium. High bond ratings reflect low default risk, and low bond ratings reflect high default risk.
Maturity risk	The fact that the longer the maturity, the more the value of a security will change in response to a given change in interest rates. If interest rates on otherwise similar-risk securities suddenly rise as a result of a change in the money supply, the prices of long-term bonds will decline by more than the prices of short-term bonds, and vice versa.[a]
Contractual provision risk	Conditions that are often included in a debt agreement or a stock issue. Some of these reduce risk, whereas others may increase risk. For example, a provision allowing a bond issuer to retire its bonds prior to their maturity under favorable terms increases the bond's risk.

[a]A detailed discussion of the effects of interest rates on the price or value of bonds and other fixed-income securities is presented later in this chapter.

The risk premium consists of a number of issuer- and issue-related components, including interest rate risk, liquidity risk, and tax risk, which were defined in Table 5.1 on page 191, and the purely debt-specific risks—default risk, maturity risk, and contractual provision risk, briefly defined in Table 6.1. In general, the highest risk premiums and therefore the highest returns result from securities issued by firms with a high risk of default and from long-term maturities that have unfavorable contractual provisions.

Review Questions

6–1 What is the *real rate of interest?* Differentiate it from the *risk-free rate of interest* for a 3-month U.S. Treasury bill.

6–2 What is the *term structure of interest rates,* and how is it related to the *yield curve?*

6–3 For a given class of similar-risk securities, what does each of the following yield curves reflect about interest rates: (**a**) downward-sloping; (**b**) upward-sloping; and (**c**) flat? Which form has been historically dominant?

6–4 Briefly describe the following theories of the general shape of the yield curve: (**a**) expectations theory; (**b**) liquidity preference theory; and (**c**) market segmentation theory.

6–5 List and briefly describe the potential issuer- and issue-related risk components that are embodied in the risk premium. Which are the purely debt-specific risks?

LG1 LG4

Corporate Bonds

corporate bond
A long-term debt instrument indicating that a corporation has borrowed a certain amount of money and promises to repay it in the future under clearly defined terms.

coupon interest rate
The percentage of a bond's par value that will be paid annually, typically in two equal semiannual payments, as interest.

A **corporate bond** is a long-term debt instrument indicating that a corporation has borrowed a certain amount of money and promises to repay it in the future under clearly defined terms. Most bonds are issued with maturities of 10 to 30 years and with a par value, or face value, of $1,000. The **coupon interest rate** on a bond represents the percentage of the bond's par value that will be paid annually, typically in two equal semiannual payments, as interest. The bondholders, who are the lenders, are promised the semiannual interest payments and, at maturity, repayment of the principal amount.

Legal Aspects of Corporate Bonds

Certain legal arrangements are required to protect purchasers of bonds. Bondholders are protected primarily through the indenture and the trustee.

Bond Indenture

bond indenture
A legal document that specifies both the rights of the bondholders and the duties of the issuing corporation.

A **bond indenture** is a legal document that specifies both the rights of the bondholders and the duties of the issuing corporation. Included in the indenture are descriptions of the amount and timing of all interest and principal payments, various standard and restrictive provisions, and, frequently, sinking-fund requirements and security interest provisions.

standard debt provisions
Provisions in a *bond indenture* specifying certain record-keeping and general business practices that the bond issuer must follow; normally, they do not place a burden on a financially sound business.

Standard Provisions The **standard debt provisions** in the bond indenture specify certain record-keeping and general business practices that the bond issuer must follow. Standard debt provisions do not normally place a burden on a financially sound business.

The borrower commonly must (1) *maintain satisfactory accounting records* in accordance with generally accepted accounting principles (GAAP); (2) periodically *supply audited financial statements;* (3) *pay taxes and other liabilities when due;* and (4) *maintain all facilities in good working order.*

restrictive covenants
Provisions in a *bond indenture* that place operating and financial constraints on the borrower.

Restrictive Provisions Bond indentures also normally include certain **restrictive covenants,** which place operating and financial constraints on the borrower. These provisions help protect the bondholder against increases in borrower risk. Without them, the borrower could increase the firm's risk but not have to pay increased interest to compensate for the increased risk.

The most common restrictive covenants do the following:

1. Require a *minimum level of liquidity,* to ensure against loan default.
2. *Prohibit the sale of accounts receivable* to generate cash. Selling receivables could cause a long-run cash shortage if proceeds were used to meet current obligations.
3. Impose *fixed-asset restrictions.* The borrower must maintain a specified level of fixed assets to guarantee its ability to repay the bonds.
4. *Constrain subsequent borrowing.* Additional long-term debt may be prohibited, or additional borrowing may be *subordinated* to the original loan.

subordination
In a bond indenture, the stipulation that subsequent creditors agree to wait until all claims of the *senior debt* are satisfied.

Subordination means that subsequent creditors agree to wait until all claims of the *senior debt* are satisfied.

5. *Limit the firm's annual cash dividend payments* to a specified percentage or amount.

Other restrictive covenants are sometimes included in bond indentures.

The violation of any standard or restrictive provision by the borrower gives the bondholders the right to demand immediate repayment of the debt. Generally, bondholders evaluate any violation to determine whether it jeopardizes the loan. They may then decide to demand immediate repayment, continue the loan, or alter the terms of the bond indenture.

sinking-fund requirement
A restrictive provision often included in a bond indenture, providing for the systematic retirement of bonds prior to their maturity.

Sinking-Fund Requirements Another common restrictive provision is a **sinking-fund requirement.** Its objective is to provide for the systematic retirement of bonds prior to their maturity. To carry out this requirement, the corporation makes semiannual or annual payments that are used to retire bonds by purchasing them in the marketplace.

Security Interest The bond indenture identifies any collateral pledged against the bond and specifies how it is to be maintained. The protection of bond collateral is crucial to guarantee the safety of a bond issue.

Trustee

trustee
A paid individual, corporation, or commercial bank trust department that acts as the third party to a bond indenture and can take specified actions on behalf of the bondholders if the terms of the indenture are violated.

A **trustee** is a third party to a bond indenture. The trustee can be an individual, a corporation, or (most often) a commercial bank trust department. The trustee is paid to act as a "watchdog" on behalf of the bondholders and can take specified actions on behalf of the bondholders if the terms of the indenture are violated.

Cost of Bonds to the Issuer

The cost of bond financing is generally greater than the issuer would have to pay for short-term borrowing. The major factors that affect the cost, which is the rate of interest paid by the bond issuer, are the bond's maturity, the size of the offering, the issuer's risk, and the basic cost of money.

Impact of Bond Maturity on Bond Cost

Generally, as we noted earlier, long-term debt pays higher interest rates than short-term debt. In a practical sense, the longer the maturity of a bond, the less accuracy there is in predicting future interest rates, and therefore the greater the bondholders' risk of giving up an opportunity to lend money at a higher rate. In addition, the longer the term, the greater the chance that the issuer might default.

Impact of Offering Size on Bond Cost

The size of the bond offering also affects the interest cost of borrowing, but in an inverse manner: Bond flotation and administration costs per dollar borrowed are likely to decrease with increasing offering size. On the other hand, the risk to

In Practice

FOCUS ON PRACTICE Ford Cruises the Debt Markets

Ford and Ford Motor Credit Co. (FMCC), its finance unit, were frequent visitors to the corporate debt markets in 2001, selling over $22 billion in long-term notes and bonds. Despite the problems in the auto industry, investors nervous about stock market volatility were willing to accept the credit risk to get higher yields. The company's 2001 offerings had something for all types of investors, ranging from 2- to 10-year notes to 30-year bonds. Demand for Ford's debt was so high that in January the company increased the size of its issue from $5 billion to $7.8 billion, and October's plan to issue $3 billion turned into a $9.4 billion offering.

The world's second largest auto manufacturer joined other corporate bond issuers to take advantage of strengthening bond markets. Even though the Federal Reserve began cutting short-term rates, interest rates for the longer maturities remained attractively low for corporations. Unlike some other auto companies who limited the size of their debt offerings, FMCC decided to borrow as much as possible to lock in the very wide spread between its lower borrowing costs and what its auto loans yielded.

All this debt came at a price, however. Both major bond-rating agencies—Moody's Investors Service and Standard & Poor's (S&P)—downgraded Ford's debt quality ratings in October 2001. Moody's lowered Ford's long-term debt rating by one rating class but did not change FMCC's quality rating. Ford spokesman Todd Nissen was pleased that Moody's confirmed the FMCC ratings. "It will help us keep our costs of borrowing down, which benefits Ford Credit and ultimately Ford Motor," he said. S&P's outlook for Ford was more negative; the agency cut ratings on all Ford and FMCC debt one rating class. The lower ratings contributed to the higher yields on Ford's October debt. For example, in April FMCC's 10-year notes yielded 7.1 percent, about 2 points above U.S. Treasury bonds. In October, 10-year FMCC notes yielded 7.3 percent, or 2.7 points above U.S. Treasury bonds.

For corporations like Ford, deciding when to issue debt and selecting the best maturities requires knowledge of interest rate fundamentals, risk premiums, issuance costs, ratings, and similar features of corporate bonds.

Sources: Adapted from Jonathan Stempel, "'Buy My Product, Buy My Bonds,' U.S.Companies Say," *Reuters,* April 10, 2001, "Ford Sells $9.4 Bln Bonds, Offers Big Yields, *Reuters,* October 22, 2001, and "Moodys Cuts Ford, but Not Ford Credit, Ratings," *Reuters Business Report,* October 18, 2001, all downloaded from eLibrary, ask.elibrary.com; Ed Zwirn, "Ford to Issue $7.8 Billion and Counting," *CFO.com,* January 24, 2001, and "Full Speed Ahead for Auto Bonds," *CFO.com,* January 19, 2001, both downloaded from www. cfo.com.

the bondholders may increase, because larger offerings result in greater risk of default.

Impact of Issuer's Risk

The greater the issuer's *default risk,* the higher the interest rate. Some of this risk can be reduced through inclusion of appropriate restrictive provisions in the bond indenture. Clearly, bondholders must be compensated with higher returns for taking greater risk. Frequently, bond buyers rely on bond ratings (discussed later) to determine the issuer's overall risk.

Impact of the Cost of Money

The cost of money in the capital market is the basis for determining a bond's coupon interest rate. Generally, the rate on U.S. Treasury securities of equal maturity is used as the lowest-risk cost of money. To that basic rate is added a *risk premium* (as described earlier in this chapter) that reflects the factors mentioned above (maturity, offering size, and issuer's risk).

General Features of a Bond Issue

Three features sometimes included in a corporate bond issue are a conversion feature, a call feature, and stock purchase warrants. These features provide the issuer or the purchaser with certain opportunities for replacing or retiring the bond or supplementing it with some type of equity issue.

conversion feature
A feature of *convertible bonds* that allows bondholders to change each bond into a stated number of shares of common stock.

Convertible bonds offer a **conversion feature** that allows bondholders to change each bond into a stated number of shares of common stock. Bondholders convert their bonds into stock only when the market price of the stock is such that conversion will provide a profit for the bondholder. Inclusion of the conversion feature by the issuer lowers the interest cost and provides for automatic conversion of the bonds to stock if future stock prices appreciate noticeably.

call feature
A feature included in nearly all corporate bond issues that gives the issuer the opportunity to repurchase bonds at a stated *call price* prior to maturity.

call price
The stated price at which a bond may be repurchased, by use of a *call feature,* prior to maturity.

call premium
The amount by which a bond's *call price* exceeds its par value.

The **call feature** is included in nearly all corporate bond issues. It gives the issuer the opportunity to repurchase bonds prior to maturity. The **call price** is the stated price at which bonds may be repurchased prior to maturity. Sometimes the call feature can be exercised only during a certain period. As a rule, the call price exceeds the par value of a bond by an amount equal to 1 year's interest. For example, a $1,000 bond with a 10 percent coupon interest rate would be callable for around $1,100 [$\$1{,}000 + (10\% \times \$1{,}000)$]. The amount by which the call price exceeds the bond's par value is commonly referred to as the **call premium.** This premium compensates bondholders for having the bond called away from them; to the issuer, it is the cost of calling the bonds.

The call feature enables an issuer to call an outstanding bond when interest rates fall and issue a new bond at a lower interest rate. When interest rates rise, the call privilege will not be exercised, except possibly to meet sinking-fund requirements. Of course, to sell a callable bond in the first place, the issuer must pay a higher interest rate than on noncallable bonds of equal risk, to compensate bondholders for the risk of having the bonds called away from them.

stock purchase warrants
Instruments that give their holders the right to purchase a certain number of shares of the issuer's common stock at a specified price over a certain period of time.

Bonds occasionally have stock purchase warrants attached as "sweeteners" to make them more attractive to prospective buyers. **Stock purchase warrants** are instruments that give their holders the right to purchase a certain number of shares of the issuer's common stock at a specified price over a certain period of time. Their inclusion typically enables the issuer to pay a slightly lower coupon interest rate than would otherwise be required.

Interpreting Bond Quotations

quotations
Information on bonds, stocks, and other securities, including current price data and statistics on recent price behavior.

The financial manager needs to stay abreast of the market values of the firm's outstanding securities, whether they are traded on an organized exchange, over the counter, or in international markets. Similarly, existing and prospective investors in the firm's securities need to monitor the prices of the securities they own because these prices represent the current value of their investment. Information on bonds, stocks, and other securities is contained in **quotations,** which include current price data along with statistics on recent price behavior. Security price quotations are readily available for actively traded bonds and stocks. The most up-to-date "quotes" can be obtained electronically, via a personal computer. Price information is available from stockbrokers and is widely published in news media. Popular sources of daily security price quotations include financial newspapers, such as the *Wall Street Journal* and *Investor's Business Daily,* and

FIGURE 6.4

Bond Quotations

Selected bond quotations for April 22, 2002

BONDS	CUR YLD	VOL	CLOSE	NET CHG
HuntPly 11¾04f	...	22	20.13	-0.88
IBM 7¼02	7.1	15	101.75	-0.38
IBM 5⅜09	5.6	50	96.63	0.25
IBM 8⅜19	...	20	114.25	0.38
IBM 7s25	7.0	10	100.25	-1.75 ← IBM
IPap dc5⅛12	5.9	20	86.50	1.88
IntShip 9s03	9.0	3	100	...
JPMChse 7½03	7.3	10	103	-0.25
JPMChse 6⅛08	6.1	25	100.88	0.63
JPMChse 6½09	6.5	40	100.13	...
JCPL 6⅜03	6.3	4	101	-0.75
KCS En 8⅞06	11.5	30	76.88	...
K&B Hm 7¾04	7.6	36	102	...
K&B Hm 9⅝06	9.2	65	104.38	-0.25
Koppers 8½04	8.6	16	99	...
Leucadia 7¾13	7.6	25	101.25	0.25
LionCT 6⅜03	6.3	15	101	-4.00
LglsLt 9s22	8.6	40	104.50	-0.50
Lucent 7¼06	8.9	585	81.63	-0.50
Lucent 5½08	7.8	240	70.75	-0.88
Lucent 6½28	10.5	89	62	0.25
Lucent 6.45s29	10.4	145	62.13	-0.38
MBNA 8.28s26	8.7	121	95.50	-0.50
MailWell 5s02	cv	30	98.75	0.25
Malan 9½04	cv	41	92.88	0.88
McDnl 6⅝05	6.5	87	102.13	0.38
Motrla zr13	...	10	73.25	-0.50
NRurU 6.55s18	7.0	50	94	-2.63
NYTel 6¼04	6.1	25	102	-0.25
NYTel 7⅝23	7.6	50	100.63	-1.25
NYTel 6.70s23	7.0	5	95	-1.75
NYTel 7s25	7.2	20	97	-0.63
NYTel 7s33	7.1	7	98.38	0.63
OcciP 10⅛09	8.4	5	121	0.13
OffDep zr07	...	30	90	-2.50

Source: Wall Street Journal, April 23, 2002, p. C14.

the business sections of daily general newspapers. Here we focus on bond quotations; stock quotations are reviewed in Chapter 7.

Figure 6.4 includes an excerpt from the New York Stock Exchange (NYSE) bond quotations reported in the April 23, 2002, *Wall Street Journal* for transactions through the close of trading on Monday, April 22, 2002. We'll look at the corporate bond quotation for IBM, which is highlighted in Figure 6.4. The numbers following the company name—IBM—represent the bond's *coupon interest rate* and the year it matures: "7s25" means that the bond has a stated coupon interest rate of 7 percent and matures sometime in the year 2025. This information allows investors to differentiate between the various bonds issued by the corporation. Note that on the day of this quote, IBM had four bonds listed. The next column, labeled "Cur Yld.," gives the bond's *current yield,* which is found by dividing its annual coupon (7%, or 7.000%) by its closing price (100.25), which in this case turns out to be 7.0 percent ($7.000 \div 100.25 = 0.0698 = 7.0\%$).

The "Vol" column indicates the actual number of bonds that traded on the given day; 10 IBM bonds traded on Monday, April 22, 2002. The final two columns include price information—the closing price and the net change in closing price from the prior trading day. Although most corporate bonds are issued with a *par,* or *face, value* of $1,000, *all bonds are quoted as a percentage of par.* A $1,000-par-value bond quoted at 110.38 is priced at $1,103.80 (110.38% × $1,000). Corporate bonds are quoted in dollars and cents. Thus IBM's closing price of 100.25 for the day was $1,002.50—that is, 100.25% × $1,000. Because a "Net Chg." of −1.75 is given in the final column, the bond must have closed at 102 or $1,020 (102.00% × $1,000) on the prior day. Its price decreased by 1.75, or $17.50 (1.75% × $1,000), on Tuesday, April 22, 2002. Additional information may be included in a bond quotation, but these are the basic elements.

Bond Ratings

Independent agencies such as Moody's and Standard & Poor's assess the riskiness of publicly traded bond issues. These agencies derive the ratings by using financial ratio and cash flow analyses to assess the likely payment of bond interest and principal. Table 6.2 summarizes these ratings. Normally an inverse relationship exists between the quality of a bond and the rate of return that it must provide bondholders: High-quality (high-rated) bonds provide lower returns than lower-quality (low-rated) bonds. This reflects the lender's risk-return tradeoff. When considering bond financing, the financial manager must be concerned with the expected ratings of the bond issue, because these ratings affect salability and cost.

TABLE 6.2 Moody's and Standard & Poor's Bond Ratings[a]

Moody's	Interpretation	Standard & Poor's	Interpretation
Aaa	Prime quality	AAA	Bank investment quality
Aa	High grade	AA	
A	Upper medium grade	A	
Baa	Medium grade	BBB	
Ba	Lower medium grade	BB	Speculative
	or speculative	B	
B	Speculative		
Caa	From very speculative	CCC	
Ca	to near or in default	CC	
C	Lowest grade	C	Income bond
		D	In default

[a]Some ratings may be modified to show relative standing within a major rating category; for example, Moody's uses numerical modifiers (1, 2, 3), whereas Standard & Poor's uses plus (+) and minus (−) signs.

Sources: Moody's Investors Service, Inc. and Standard & Poor's Corporation.

TABLE 6.3 Characteristics and Priority of Lender's Claim of Traditional Types of Bonds

Bond type	Characteristics	Priority of lender's claim
Unsecured Bonds		
Debentures	Unsecured bonds that only creditworthy firms can issue. Convertible bonds are normally debentures.	Claims are the same as those of any general creditor. May have other unsecured bonds subordinated to them.
Subordinated debentures	Claims are not satisfied until those of the creditors holding certain (senior) debts have been fully satisfied.	Claim is that of a general creditor but not as good as a senior debt claim.
Income bonds	Payment of interest is required only when earnings are available. Commonly issued in reorganization of a failing firm.	Claim is that of a general creditor. Are not in default when interest payments are missed, because they are contingent only on earnings being available.
Secured Bonds		
Mortgage bonds	Secured by real estate or buildings.	Claim is on proceeds from sale of mortgaged assets; if not fully satisfied, the lender becomes a general creditor.The *first-mortgage* claim must be fully satisfied before distribution of proceeds to *second-mortgage* holders, and so on. A number of mortgages can be issued against the same collateral.
Collateral trust bonds	Secured by stock and (or) bonds that are owned by the issuer. Collateral value is generally 25% to 35% greater than bond value.	Claim is on proceeds from stock and (or) bond collateral; if not fully satisfied, the lender becomes a general creditor.
Equipment trust certificates	Used to finance "rolling stock"—airplanes, trucks, boats, railroad cars. A trustee buys such an asset with funds raised through the sale of trust certificates and then leases it to the firm, which, after making the final scheduled lease payment, receives title to the asset. A type of leasing.	Claim is on proceeds from the sale of the asset; if proceeds do not satisfy outstanding debt, trust certificate lenders become general creditors.

Popular Types of Bonds

debentures
subordinated debentures
income bonds
mortgage bonds
collateral trust bonds
equipment trust certificates
See Table 6.3

zero- (or low-) coupon bonds
junk bonds
floating-rate bonds
extendible notes
putable bonds
See Table 6.4

Bonds can be classified in a variety of ways. Here we break them into traditional bonds (the basic types that have been around for years) and contemporary bonds (newer, more innovative types). The traditional types of bonds are summarized in terms of their key characteristics and priority of lender's claim in Table 6.3. Note that the first three types—**debentures, subordinated debentures,** and **income bonds**—are unsecured, whereas the last three—**mortgage bonds, collateral trust bonds,** and **equipment trust certificates**—are secured.

Table 6.4 describes the key characteristics of five contemporary types of bonds: **zero-coupon or low-coupon bonds, junk bonds, floating-rate bonds, extendible notes,** and **putable bonds.** These bonds can be either unsecured or secured. Changing capital market conditions and investor preferences have spurred further innovations in bond financing in recent years and will probably continue to do so.

TABLE 6.4 Characteristics of Contemporary Types of Bonds

Bond type	Characteristics[a]
Zero- (or low-) coupon bonds	Issued with no (zero) or a very low coupon (stated interest) rate and sold at a large discount from par. A significant portion (or all) of the investor's return comes from gain in value (i.e., par value minus purchase price). Generally callable at par value. Because the issuer can annually deduct the current year's interest accrual without having to pay the interest until the bond matures (or is called), its cash flow each year is increased by the amount of the tax shield provided by the interest deduction.
Junk bonds	Debt rated Ba or lower by Moody's or BB or lower by Standard & Poor's. Commonly used during the 1980s by rapidly growing firms to obtain growth capital, most often as a way to finance mergers and takeovers. High-risk bonds with high yields—often yielding 2% to 3% more than the best-quality corporate debt.
Floating-rate bonds	Stated interest rate is adjusted periodically within stated limits in response to changes in specified money market or capital market rates. Popular when future inflation and interest rates are uncertain. Tend to sell at close to par because of the automatic adjustment to changing market conditions. Some issues provide for annual redemption at par at the option of the bondholder.
Extendible notes	Short maturities, typically 1 to 5 years, that can be renewed for a similar period at the option of holders. Similar to a floating-rate bond. An issue might be a series of 3-year renewable notes over a period of 15 years; every 3 years, the notes could be extended for another 3 years, at a new rate competitive with market interest rates at the time of renewal.
Putable bonds	Bonds that can be redeemed at par (typically, $1,000) at the option of their holder either at specific dates after the date of issue and every 1 to 5 years thereafter or when and if the firm takes specified actions, such as being acquired, acquiring another company, or issuing a large amount of additional debt. In return for its conferring the right to "put the bond" at specified times or when the firm takes certain actions, the bond's yield is lower than that of a nonputable bond.

[a]The claims of lenders (i.e., bondholders) against issuers of each of these types of bonds vary, depending on the bonds' other features. Each of these bonds can be unsecured or secured.

International Bond Issues

Companies and governments borrow internationally by issuing bonds in two principal financial markets: the Eurobond market and the foreign bond market. Both give borrowers the opportunity to obtain large amounts of long-term debt financing quickly, in the currency of their choice and with flexible repayment terms.

Eurobond
A bond issued by an international borrower and sold to investors in countries with currencies other than the currency in which the bond is denominated.

A **Eurobond** is issued by an international borrower and sold to investors in countries with currencies other than the currency in which the bond is denominated. An example is a dollar-denominated bond issued by a U.S. corporation and sold to Belgian investors. From the founding of the Eurobond market in the 1960s until the mid-1980s, "blue chip" U.S. corporations were the largest single class of Eurobond issuers. Some of these companies were able to borrow in this market at interest rates below those the U.S. government paid on Treasury bonds. As the market matured, issuers became able to choose the currency in which they borrowed, and European and Japanese borrowers rose to prominence. In more recent years, the Eurobond market has become much more balanced in terms of the mix of borrowers, total issue volume, and currency of denomination.

foreign bond
A bond issued in a host country's financial market, in the host country's currency, by a foreign borrower.

In contrast, a **foreign bond** is issued in a host country's financial market, in the host country's currency, by a foreign borrower. A Swiss-franc–denominated bond issued in Switzerland by a U.S. company is an example of a foreign bond. The three largest foreign-bond markets are Japan, Switzerland, and the United States.

Review Questions

6–6 What are typical maturities, denominations, and interest payments of a corporate bond? What mechanisms protect bondholders?

6–7 Differentiate between *standard debt provisions* and *restrictive covenants* included in a bond indenture. What are the consequences of violation of them by the bond issuer?

6–8 How is the cost of bond financing typically related to the cost of short-term borrowing? In addition to a bond's maturity, what other major factors affect its cost to the issuer?

6–9 What is a *conversion feature?* A *call feature? Stock purchase warrants?*

6–10 What information is found in a bond *quotation?* How are bonds rated, and why?

6–11 Compare the basic characteristics of *Eurobonds* and *foreign bonds.*

LG4

Valuation Fundamentals

valuation
The process that links risk and return to determine the worth of an asset.

Valuation is the process that links risk and return to determine the worth of an asset. It is a relatively simple process that can be applied to *expected* streams of benefits from bonds, stocks, income properties, oil wells, and so on. To determine an asset's worth at a given point in time, a financial manager uses the time-value-of-money techniques presented in Chapter 4 and the concepts of risk and return developed in Chapter 5.

Key Inputs

There are three key inputs to the valuation process: (1) cash flows (returns), (2) timing, and (3) a measure of risk, which determines the required return. Each is described below.

Cash Flows (Returns)

The value of any asset depends on the cash flow(s) it is *expected* to provide over the ownership period. To have value, an asset does not have to provide an annual cash flow; it can provide an intermittent cash flow or even a single cash flow over the period.

EXAMPLE ▼ Celia Sargent, financial analyst for Groton Corporation, a diversified holding company, wishes to estimate the value of three of its assets: common stock in Michaels Enterprises, an interest in an oil well, and an original painting by a well-known artist. Her cash flow estimates for each are as follows:

Stock in Michaels Enterprises *Expect* to receive cash dividends of $300 per year indefinitely.

Oil well *Expect* to receive cash flow of $2,000 at the end of year 1, $4,000 at the end of year 2, and $10,000 at the end of year 4, when the well is to be sold.

Original painting *Expect* to be able to sell the painting in 5 years for $85,000.

With these cash flow estimates, Celia has taken the first step toward placing a value on each of the assets.

Timing

In addition to making cash flow estimates, we must know the timing of the cash flows.[4] For example, Celia expects the cash flows of $2,000, $4,000, and $10,000 for the oil well to occur at the ends of years 1, 2, and 4, respectively. The combination of the cash flow and its timing fully defines the return expected from the asset.

Risk and Required Return

The level of risk associated with a given cash flow can significantly affect its value. In general, the greater the risk of (or the less certain) a cash flow, the lower its value. Greater risk can be incorporated into a valuation analysis by using a higher required return or discount rate. As in the previous chapter, the higher the risk, the greater the required return, and the lower the risk, the less the required return.

EXAMPLE Let's return to Celia Sargent's task of placing a value on Groton Corporation's original painting and consider two scenarios.

Scenario 1—Certainty A major art gallery has contracted to buy the painting for $85,000 at the end of 5 years. Because this is considered a certain situation, Celia views this asset as "money in the bank." She thus would use the prevailing risk-free rate of 9% as the required return when calculating the value of the painting.

Scenario 2—High Risk The values of original paintings by this artist have fluctuated widely over the past 10 years. Although Celia expects to be able to get $85,000 for the painting, she realizes that its sale price in 5 years could range between $30,000 and $140,000. Because of the high uncertainty surrounding the painting's value, Celia believes that a 15% required return is appropriate.

These two estimates of the appropriate required return illustrate how this rate captures risk. The often subjective nature of such estimates is also clear.

The Basic Valuation Model

Simply stated, the value of any asset is *the present value of all future cash flows it is expected to provide over the relevant time period.* The time period can be any length, even infinity. The value of an asset is therefore determined by discounting the expected cash flows back to their present value, using the required return commensurate with the asset's risk as the appropriate discount rate. Utilizing the present value techniques explained in Chapter 4, we can express the value of any asset at time zero, V_0, as

4. Although cash flows can occur at any time during a year, for computational convenience as well as custom, we will assume they occur at the *end of the year* unless otherwise noted.

$$V_0 = \frac{CF_1}{(1+k)^1} + \frac{CF_2}{(1+k^2)} + \cdots + \frac{CF_n}{(1+k)^n} \quad (6.1)$$

where

V_0 = value of the asset at time zero
CF_t = cash flow *expected* at the end of year t
k = appropriate required return (discount rate)
n = relevant time period

Using present value interest factor notation, $PVIF_{k,n}$ from Chapter 4, Equation 6.1 can be rewritten as

$$V_0 = [CF_1 \times (PVIF_{k,1})] + [CF_2 \times (PVIF_{k,2})] + \cdots + [CF_n \times (PVIF_{k,n})] \quad (6.2)$$

We can use Equation 6.2 to determine the value of any asset.

EXAMPLE Celia Sargent used Equation 6.2 to calculate the value of each asset (using present value interest factors from Table A–2), as shown in Table 6.5. Michaels Enterprises stock has a value of $2,500, the oil well's value is $9,262, and the original painting has a value of $42,245. Note that regardless of the pattern of the expected cash flow from an asset, the basic valuation equation can be used to determine its value.

TABLE 6.5 Valuation of Groton Corporation's Assets by Celia Sargent

Asset	Cash flow, *CF*	Appropriate required return	Valuation[a]
Michaels Enterprises stock[b]	$300/year indefinitely	12%	$V_0 = \$300 \times (PVIFA_{12\%,\infty})$ $= \$300 \times \frac{1}{0.12} = \underline{\underline{\$2,500}}$
Oil well[c]	Year (t) / CF_t: 1 — $ 2,000 2 — 4,000 3 — 0 4 — 10,000	20%	$V_0 = [\$2,000 \times (PVIF_{20\%,1})]$ $+ [\$4,000 \times (PVIF_{20\%,2})]$ $+ [\$0 \times (PVIF_{20\%,3})]$ $+ [\$10,000 \times (PVIF_{20\%,4})]$ $= [\$2,000 \times (0.833)]$ $+ [\$4,000 \times (0.694)]$ $+ [\$0 \times (0.579)]$ $+ [\$10,000 \times (0.482)]$ $= \$1,666 + \$2,776$ $+ \$0 + \$4,820$ $= \underline{\underline{\$9,262}}$
Original painting[d]	$85,000 at end of year 5	15%	$V_0 = \$85,000 \times (PVIF_{15\%,5})$ $= \$85,000 \times (0.497)$ $= \underline{\underline{\$42,245}}$

[a]Based on *PVIF* interest factors from Table A–2. If calculated using a calculator, the values of the oil well and original painting would have been $9,266.98 and $42,260.03, respectively.
[b]This is a perpetuity (infinite-lived annuity), and therefore the present value interest factor given in Equation 4.19 is applied.
[c]This is a mixed stream of cash flows and therefore requires a number of *PVIF*s, as noted.
[d]This is a single-amount cash flow and therefore requires a single *PVIF*.

Review Questions

6–12 Why is it important for financial managers to understand the valuation process?
6–13 What are the three key inputs to the valuation process?
6–14 Does the valuation process apply only to assets that provide an annual cash flow? Explain.
6–15 Define and specify the general equation for the value of any asset, V_0.

LG5 LG6

Bond Valuation

The basic valuation equation can be customized for use in valuing specific securities: bonds, common stock, and preferred stock. Bond valuation is described in this chapter, and valuation of common stock and preferred stock is discussed in Chapter 7.

Bond Fundamentals

As noted earlier in this chapter, *bonds* are long-term debt instruments used by business and government to raise large sums of money, typically from a diverse group of lenders. Most corporate bonds pay interest *semiannually* (every 6 months) at a stated *coupon interest rate,* have an initial *maturity* of 10 to 30 years, and have a *par value,* or *face value,* of $1,000 that must be repaid at maturity.

EXAMPLE Mills Company, a large defense contractor, on January 1, 2004, issued a 10% coupon interest rate, 10-year bond with a $1,000 par value that pays interest semiannually. Investors who buy this bond receive the contractual right to two cash flows: (1) $100 annual interest (10% coupon interest rate × $1,000 par value) distributed as $50 (1/2 × $100) at the end of each 6 months, and (2) the $1,000 par value at the end of the tenth year.

We will use data for Mills's bond issue to look at basic bond valuation.

Basic Bond Valuation

The value of a bond is the present value of the payments its issuer is contractually obligated to make, from the current time until it matures. The basic model for the value, B_0, of a bond is given by Equation 6.3:

$$B_0 = I \times \left[\sum_{t=1}^{n} \frac{1}{(1+k_d)^t}\right] + M \times \left[\frac{1}{(1+k_d)^n}\right] \quad (6.3)$$

$$= I \times (PVIFA_{k_d,n}) + M \times (PVIF_{k_d,n}) \quad (6.3a)$$

where

B_0 = value of the bond at time zero
I = *annual* interest paid in dollars[5]
n = number of years to maturity
M = par value in dollars
k_d = required return on a bond

We can calculate bond value using Equation 6.3a and the appropriate financial tables (A–2 and A–4) or by using a financial calculator.

EXAMPLE

Assuming that interest on the Mills Company bond issue is paid annually and that the required return is equal to the bond's coupon interest rate, $I = \$100$, $k_d = 10\%$, $M = \$1{,}000$, and $n = 10$ years.

The computations involved in finding the bond value are depicted graphically on the following time line.

Time line for bond valuation (Mills Company's 10% coupon interest rate, 10-year maturity, $1,000 par, January 1, 2004, issue paying annual interest; required return = 10%)

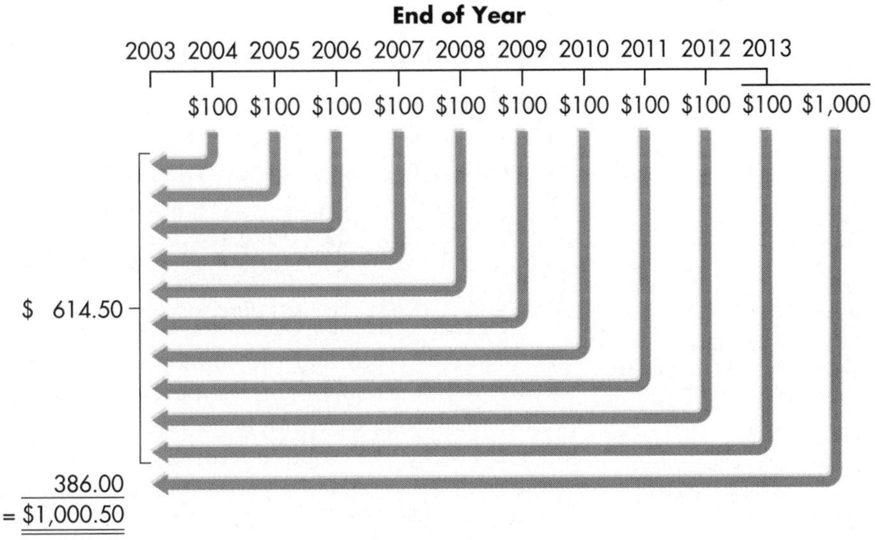

Table Use Substituting the values noted above into Equation 6.3a yields

$$\begin{aligned} B_0 &= \$100 \times (PVIFA_{10\%,10\text{yrs}}) + \$1{,}000 \times (PVIF_{10\%,10\text{yrs}}) \\ &= \$100 \times (6.145) + \$1{,}000 \times (0.386) \\ &= \$614.50 + \$386.00 = \underline{\underline{\$1{,}000.50}} \end{aligned}$$

The bond therefore has a value of approximately $1,000.[6]

---

5. The payment of annual rather than semiannual bond interest is assumed throughout the following discussion. This assumption simplifies the calculations involved, while maintaining the conceptual accuracy of the valuation procedures presented.

6. Note that a slight rounding error ($0.50) results here from the use of the table factors, which are rounded to the nearest thousandth.

Input	Function
10	N
10	I
100	PMT
1000	FV
	CPT
	PV

Solution
1000

Calculator Use Using the Mills Company's inputs shown at the left, you should find the bond value to be exactly $1,000. Note that *the calculated bond value is equal to its par value; this will always be the case when the required return is equal to the coupon interest rate.*

Bond Value Behavior

In practice, the value of a bond in the marketplace is rarely equal to its par value. In bond quotations (see Figure 6.4), the closing prices of bonds often differ from their par values of 100 (100 percent of par). Some bonds are valued below par (quoted below 100), and others are valued above par (quoted above 100). A variety of forces in the economy, as well as the passage of time, tend to affect value. Although these external forces are in no way controlled by bond issuers or investors, it is useful to understand the impact that required return and time to maturity have on bond value.

Required Returns and Bond Values

Whenever the required return on a bond differs from the bond's coupon interest rate, the bond's value will differ from its par value. The required return is likely to differ from the coupon interest rate because either (1) economic conditions have changed, causing a shift in the basic cost of long-term funds, or (2) the firm's risk has changed. Increases in the basic cost of long-term funds or in risk will raise the required return; decreases in the cost of funds or in risk will lower the required return.

discount
The amount by which a bond sells at a value that is less than its par value.

premium
The amount by which a bond sells at a value that is greater than its par value.

Regardless of the exact cause, what is important is the relationship between the required return and the coupon interest rate: When the required return is greater than the coupon interest rate, the bond value, B_0, will be less than its par value, M. In this case, the bond is said to sell at a **discount,** which will equal $M - B_0$. When the required return falls below the coupon interest rate, the bond value will be greater than par. In this situation, the bond is said to sell at a **premium,** which will equal $B_0 - M$.

EXAMPLE The preceding example showed that when the required return equaled the coupon interest rate, the bond's value equaled its $1,000 par value. If for the same bond the required return were to rise or fall, its value would be found as follows (using Equation 6.3a):

Table Use

Required Return = 12%	Required Return = 8%
$B_0 = \$100 \times (PVIFA_{12\%,10\text{yrs}}) + \$1{,}000 \times (PVIF_{12\%,10\text{yrs}})$	$B_0 = \$100 \times (PVIFA_{8\%,10\text{yrs}}) + \$1{,}000 \times (PVIF_{8\%,10\text{yrs}})$
$= \underline{\underline{\$887.00}}$	$= \underline{\underline{\$1{,}134.00}}$

Calculator Use Using the inputs shown on the next page for the two different required returns, you will find the value of the bond to be below or above par. At

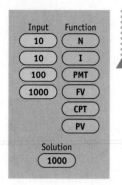

TABLE 6.6 Bond Values for Various Required Returns (Mills Company's 10% Coupon Interest Rate, 10-Year Maturity, \$1,000 Par, January 1, 2004, Issue Paying Annual Interest)

Required return, k_d	Bond value, B_0	Status
12%	\$ 887.00	Discount
10	1,000.00	Par value
8	1,134.00	Premium

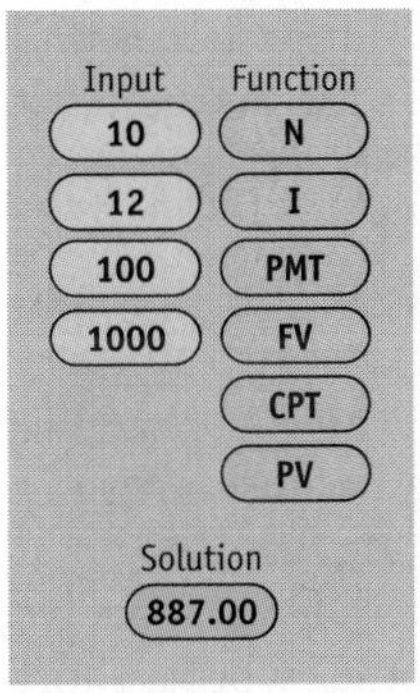

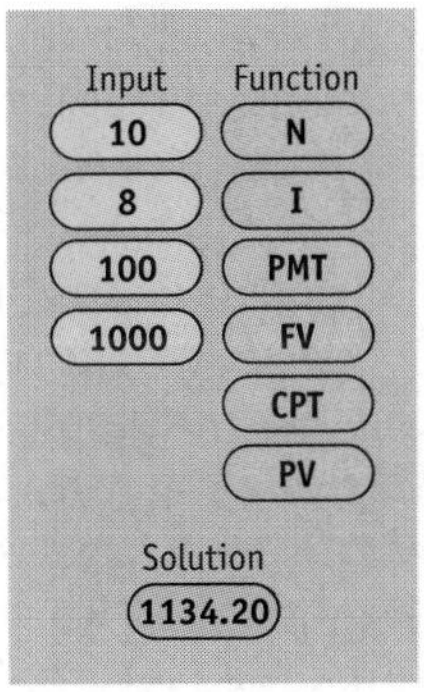

a 12% required return, the bond would sell at a *discount* of \$113.00 (\$1,000 par value − \$887.00 value). At the 8% required return, the bond would sell for a *premium* of about \$134.00 (\$1,134.00 value − \$1,000 par value). The results of this and earlier calculations for Mills Company's bond values are summarized in Table 6.6 and graphically depicted in Figure 6.5. The inverse relationship between bond value and required return is clearly shown in the figure.

FIGURE 6.5

Bond Values and Required Returns

Bond values and required returns (Mills Company's 10% coupon interest rate, 10-year maturity, \$1,000 par, January 1, 2004, issue paying annual interest)

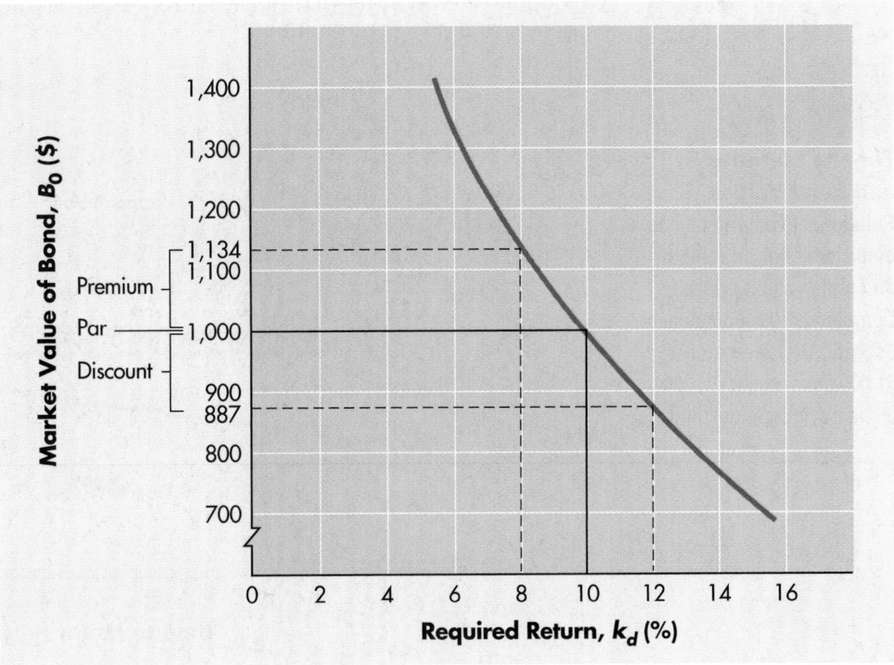

Time to Maturity and Bond Values

Whenever the required return is different from the coupon interest rate, the amount of time to maturity affects bond value. An additional factor is whether required returns are constant or changing over the life of the bond.

Constant Required Returns When the required return is different from the coupon interest rate and is assumed to be *constant until maturity,* the value of the bond will approach its par value as the passage of time moves the bond's value closer to maturity. (Of course, when the required return *equals* the coupon interest rate, the bond's value will remain at par until it matures.)

EXAMPLE Figure 6.6 depicts the behavior of the bond values calculated earlier and presented in Table 6.6 for Mills Company's 10% coupon interest rate bond paying annual interest and having 10 years to maturity. Each of the three required returns—12%, 10%, and 8%—is assumed to remain constant over the 10 years to the bond's maturity. The bond's value at both 12% and 8% approaches and ultimately equals the bond's $1,000 par value at its maturity, as the discount (at 12%) or premium (at 8%) declines with the passage of time.

interest rate risk
The chance that interest rates will change and thereby change the required return and bond value. Rising rates, which result in decreasing bond values, are of greatest concern.

Changing Required Returns The chance that interest rates will change and thereby change the required return and bond value is called **interest rate risk.** (This was described as a shareholder-specific risk in Chapter 5, Table 5.1.) Bondholders are typically more concerned with rising interest rates because a rise in interest rates, and therefore in the required return, causes a decrease in bond value. The shorter the amount of time until a bond's maturity, the less responsive is its market value to a given change in the required return. In other words, short maturities have less interest rate risk than long maturities when all other features (coupon interest rate, par value, and interest payment frequency) are the same.

FIGURE 6.6

Time to Maturity and Bond Values

Relationship among time to maturity, required returns, and bond values (Mills Company's 10% coupon interest rate, 10-year maturity, $1,000 par, January 1, 2004, issue paying annual interest)

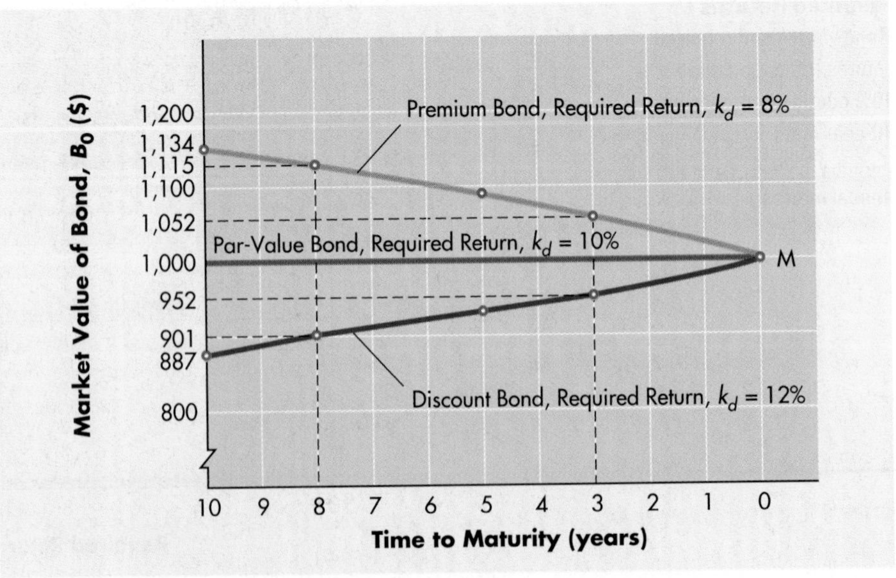

This is because of the mathematics of time value; the present values of short-term cash flows change far less than the present values of longer-term cash flows in response to a given change in the discount rate (required return).

EXAMPLE The effect of changing required returns on bonds of differing maturity can be illustrated by using Mills Company's bond and Figure 6.6. If the required return rises from 10% to 12% (see the dashed line at 8 years), the bond's value decreases from \$1,000 to \$901—a 9.9% decrease. If the same change in required return had occurred with only 3 years to maturity (see the dashed line at 3 years), the bond's value would have dropped to just \$952—only a 4.8% decrease. Similar types of responses can be seen for the change in bond value associated with decreases in required returns. The shorter the time to maturity, the less the impact on bond value caused by a given change in the required return.

Yield to Maturity (YTM)

yield to maturity (YTM)
The rate of return that investors earn if they buy a bond at a specific price and hold it until maturity. (Assumes that the issuer makes all scheduled interest and principal payments as promised.)

When investors evaluate bonds, they commonly consider **yield to maturity (YTM)**. This is the rate of return that investors earn if they buy the bond at a specific price and hold it until maturity. (The measure assumes, of course, that the issuer makes all scheduled interest and principal payments as promised.) The yield to maturity on a bond with a current price equal to its par value (that is, $B_0 = M$) will always equal the coupon interest rate. When the bond value differs from par, the yield to maturity will differ from the coupon interest rate.

Assuming that interest is paid annually, the yield to maturity on a bond can be found by solving Equation 6.3 for k_d. In other words, the current value, the annual interest, the par value, and the years to maturity are known, and the required return must be found. The required return is the bond's yield to maturity. The YTM can be found by trial and error or by use of a financial calculator. The calculator provides accurate YTM values with minimum effort.

EXAMPLE The Mills Company bond, which currently sells for \$1,080, has a 10% coupon interest rate and \$1,000 par value, pays interest annually, and has 10 years to maturity. Because $B_0 = \$1,080$, $I = \$100$ $(0.10 \times \$1,000)$, $M = \$1,000$, and $n = 10$ years, substituting into Equation 6.3a yields

$$\$1,080 = \$100 \times (PVIFA_{k_d,10\text{yrs}}) + \$1,000 \times (PVIF_{k_d,10\text{yrs}})$$

Our objective is to solve the equation for k_d, the YTM.

Trial and Error Because we know that a required return, k_d, of 10% (which equals the bond's 10% coupon interest rate) would result in a value of \$1,000, the discount rate that would result in \$1,080 must be less than 10%. (Remember that the lower the discount rate, the higher the present value, and the higher the discount rate, the lower the present value.) Trying 9%, we get

$$\begin{aligned} &\$100 \times (PVIFA_{9\%,10\text{yrs}}) + \$1,000 \times (PVIF_{9\%,10\text{yrs}}) \\ &= \$100 \times (6.418) + \$1,000 \times (0.422) \\ &= \$641.80 + \$422.00 \\ &= \$1,063.80 \end{aligned}$$

Because the 9% rate is not quite low enough to bring the value up to \$1,080, we next try 8% and get

$$\begin{aligned} &\$100 \times (PVIFA_{8\%,10\text{yrs}}) + \$1{,}000 \times (PVIF_{8\%,10\text{yrs}}) \\ &= \$100 \times (6.710) + \$1{,}000 \times (0.463) \\ &= \$671.00 + \$463.00 \\ &= \$1{,}134.00 \end{aligned}$$

Input	Function
10	N
−1080	PV
100	PMT
1000	FV
	CPT
	I
Solution	
8.766	

Because the value at the 8% rate is higher than \$1,080 and the value at the 9% rate is lower than \$1,080, the bond's yield to maturity must be between 8% and 9%. Because the \$1,063.80 is closer to \$1,080, the YTM to the nearest whole percent is 9%. (By using *interpolation,* we could eventually find the more precise YTM value to be 8.77%.)[7]

Calculator Use [*Note:* Most calculators require *either* the present value (B_0 in this case) or the future values (I and M in this case) to be input as negative numbers to calculate yield to maturity. That approach is employed here.] Using the inputs shown at the left, you should find the YTM to be 8.766%.

Semiannual Interest and Bond Values

The procedure used to value bonds paying interest semiannually is similar to that shown in Chapter 4 for compounding interest more frequently than annually, except that here we need to find present value instead of future value. It involves

1. Converting annual interest, I, to semiannual interest by dividing I by 2.
2. Converting the number of years to maturity, n, to the number of 6-month periods to maturity by multiplying n by 2.
3. Converting the required stated (rather than effective) annual return for similar-risk bonds that also pay semiannual interest from an annual rate, k_d, to a semiannual rate by dividing k_d by 2.

Substituting these three changes into Equation 6.3 yields

$$B_0 = \frac{I}{2} \times \left[\sum_{i=1}^{2n} \frac{1}{\left(1+\frac{k_d}{2}\right)^t}\right] + M \times \left[\frac{1}{\left(1+\frac{k_d}{2}\right)^{2n}}\right] \tag{6.4}$$

$$= \frac{I}{2} \times (PVIFA_{k_d/2,2n}) + M \times (PVIF_{k_d/2,2n}) \tag{6.4a}$$

EXAMPLE Assuming that the Mills Company bond pays interest semiannually and that the required stated annual return, k_d, is 12% for similar-risk bonds that also pay semiannual interest, substituting these values into Equation 6.4a yields

$$B_0 = \frac{\$100}{2} \times (PVIFA_{12\%/2,2\times10\text{yrs}}) + \$1{,}000 \times (PVIF_{12\%/2,2\times10\text{yrs}})$$

7. For information on how to interpolate to get a more precise answer, see the book's home page at *www.aw.com/gitman*

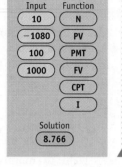

Table Use

$$B_0 = \$50 \times (PVIFA_{6\%,20\text{periods}}) + \$1{,}000 \times (PVIF_{6\%,20\text{periods}})$$
$$= \$50 \times (11.470) + \$1{,}000 \times (0.312) = \underline{\underline{\$885.50}}$$

Input	Function
20	N
6	I
50	PMT
1000	FV
	CPT
	PV

Solution
885.30

Calculator Use In using a calculator to find bond value when interest is paid semiannually, we must double the number of periods and divide both the required stated annual return and the annual interest by 2. For the Mills Company bond, we would use 20 periods (2 × 10 years), a required return of 6% (12% ÷ 2), and an interest payment of \$50 (\$100 ÷ 2). Using these inputs, you should find the bond value with semiannual interest to be \$885.30, as shown at the left. Note that this value is more precise than the value calculated using the rounded financial-table factors.

Comparing this result with the \$887.00 value found earlier for annual compounding (see Table 6.6), we can see that the bond's value is lower when semiannual interest is paid. *This will always occur when the bond sells at a discount.* For bonds selling at a premium, the opposite will occur: The value with semiannual interest will be greater than with annual interest.

Review Questions

6–16 What basic procedure is used to value a bond that pays annual interest? Semiannual interest?

6–17 What relationship between the required return and the coupon interest rate will cause a bond to sell at a *discount?* At a *premium?* At its *par value?*

6–18 If the required return on a bond differs from its coupon interest rate, describe the behavior of the bond value over time as the bond moves toward maturity.

6–19 As a risk-averse investor, would you prefer bonds with short or long periods until maturity? Why?

6–20 What is a bond's *yield to maturity (YTM)?* Briefly describe both the trial-and-error approach and the use of a financial calculator for finding YTM.

SUMMARY

FOCUS ON VALUE

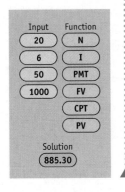

Interest rates and required returns embody the real cost of money, inflationary expectations, and issuer and issue risk. They reflect the level of return required by market participants as compensation for the risk perceived in a specific security or asset investment. Because these returns are affected by economic expectations, they vary as a function of time, typically rising for longer-term maturities or transactions. The yield curve reflects such market expectations at any point in time.

The value of an asset can be found by calculating the present value of its expected cash flows, using the required return as the discount rate. Bonds are the easiest financial assets to value, because both the amounts and the timing of their cash flows are known with certainty. The financial manager needs to understand how to apply valuation techniques to bonds in order to make decisions that are consistent with the firm's **share price maximization goal.**

REVIEW OF LEARNING GOALS

LG1 **Describe interest rate fundamentals, the term structure of interest rates, and risk premiums.** The flow of funds between savers (suppliers) and investors (demanders) is regulated by the interest rate or required return. In a perfect, inflation-free, certain world there would be one cost of money—the real rate of interest. For any class of similar-risk securities, the term structure of interest rates reflects the relationship between the interest rate, or rate of return, and the time to maturity. Yield curves can be downward-sloping (inverted), upward-sloping (normal), or flat. Three theories—expectations theory, liquidity preference theory, and market segmentation theory—are cited to explain the general shape of the yield curve. Risk premiums for non-Treasury debt issues result from interest rate risk, liquidity risk, tax risk, default risk, maturity risk, and contractual provision risk.

LG2 **Review the legal aspects of bond financing and bond cost.** Corporate bonds are long-term debt instruments indicating that a corporation has borrowed an amount that it promises to repay in the future under clearly defined terms. Most bonds are issued with maturities of 10 to 30 years and a par value of $1,000. The bond indenture, enforced by a trustee, states all conditions of the bond issue. It contains both standard debt provisions and restrictive covenants, which may include a sinking-fund requirement and/or a security interest. The cost of bonds to an issuer depends on its maturity, offering size, and issuer risk and on the basic cost of money.

LG3 **Discuss the general features, quotations, ratings, popular types, and international issues of corporate bonds.** A bond issue may include a conversion feature, a call feature, or stock purchase warrants. Bond quotations, published regularly in the financial press, provide information on bonds, including current price data and statistics on recent price behavior. Bond ratings by independent agencies indicate the risk of a bond issue. Various types of traditional and contemporary bonds are available. Eurobonds and foreign bonds enable established creditworthy companies and governments to borrow large amounts internationally.

LG4 **Understand the key inputs and basic model used in the valuation process.** Key inputs to the valuation process include cash flows (returns), timing, and risk and the required return. The value of any asset is equal to the present value of all future cash flows it is *expected* to provide over the relevant time period. The basic valuation formula for any asset is summarized in Table 6.7.

LG5 **Apply the basic valuation model to bonds and describe the impact of required return and time to maturity on bond values.** The value of a bond is the present value of its interest payments plus the present value of its par value. The basic valuation model for a bond is summarized in Table 6.7. The discount rate used to determine bond value is the required return, which may differ from the bond's coupon interest rate. A bond can sell at a discount, at par, or at a premium, depending on whether the required return is greater than, equal to, or less than its coupon interest rate. The amount of time to maturity affects bond values. Even if the required return remains constant, the value of a bond will approach its par value as the bond moves closer to maturity. The chance that interest rates will change and thereby change the required return and bond value is called interest rate risk. The shorter the amount of time until a bond's maturity, the less responsive is its market value to a given change in the required return.

TABLE 6.7 Summary of Key Valuation Definitions and Formulas for Any Asset and for Bonds

Definitions of variables

B_0 = bond value

CF_t = cash flow *expected* at the end of year t

I = annual interest on a bond

k = appropriate required return (discount rate)

k_d = required return on a bond

M = par, or face, value of a bond

n = relevant time period, or number of years to maturity

V_0 = value of the asset at time zero

Valuation formulas

Value of any asset:

$$V_0 = \frac{CF_1}{(1+k)^1} + \frac{CF_2}{(1+k)^2} + \cdots + \frac{CF_n}{(1+k)^n} \quad \text{[Eq. 6.1]}$$

$$= [CF_1 \times (PVIF_{k,1})] + [CF_2 \times (PVIF_{k,2})] + \cdots + [CF_n \times (PVIF_{k,n})] \quad \text{[Eq. 6.2]}$$

Bond value:

$$B_0 = I \times \left[\sum_{t=1}^{n} \frac{1}{(1+k_d)^t}\right] + M \times \left[\frac{1}{(1+k_d)^n}\right] \quad \text{[Eq. 6.3]}$$

$$= I \times (PVIFA_{k_d,n}) + M \times (PVIF_{k_d,n}) \quad \text{[Eq. 6.3a]}$$

LG6 **Explain yield to maturity (YTM), its calculation, and the procedure used to value bonds that pay interest semiannually.** Yield to maturity (YTM) is the rate of return investors earn if they buy a bond at a specific price and hold it until maturity. YTM can be calculated by trial and error or financial calculator. Bonds that pay interest semiannually are valued by using the same procedure used to value bonds paying annual interest, except that the interest payments are one-half of the annual interest payments, the number of periods is twice the number of years to maturity, and the required return is one-half of the stated annual required return on similar-risk bonds.

SELF-TEST PROBLEMS (Solutions in Appendix B)

LG5 LG6 **ST 6–1 Bond valuation** Lahey Industries has outstanding a $1,000 par-value bond with an 8% coupon interest rate. The bond has 12 years remaining to its maturity date.

a. If interest is paid *annually,* find the value of the bond when the required return is (1) 7%, (2) 8%, and (3) 10%?

b. Indicate for each case in part **a** whether the bond is selling at a discount, at a premium, or at its par value.

c. Using the 10% required return, find the bond's value when interest is paid *semiannually.*

LG6 **ST 6–2 Yield to maturity** Elliot Enterprises' bonds currently sell for $1,150, have an 11% coupon interest rate and a $1,000 par value, pay interest *annually,* and have 18 years to maturity.

a. Calculate the bonds' yield to maturity (YTM).

b. Compare the YTM calculated in part **a** to the bonds' coupon interest rate, and use a comparison of the bonds' current price and their par value to explain this difference.

PROBLEMS

LG1 **6–1 Yield curve** A firm wishing to evaluate interest rate behavior has gathered yield data on five U.S. Treasury securities, each having a different maturity and all measured at the same point in time. The summarized data follow.

U.S. Treasury security	Time to maturity	Yield
A	1 year	12.6%
B	10 years	11.2
C	6 months	13.0
D	20 years	11.0
E	5 years	11.4

a. Draw the yield curve associated with these data.

b. Describe the resulting yield curve in part **a,** and explain the general expectations embodied in it.

LG1 **6–2 Term structure of interest rates** The following yield data for a number of highest quality corporate bonds existed at each of the three points in time noted.

	Yield		
Time to maturity (years)	5 years ago	2 years ago	Today
1	9.1%	14.6%	9.3%
3	9.2	12.8	9.8
5	9.3	12.2	10.9
10	9.5	10.9	12.6
15	9.4	10.7	12.7
20	9.3	10.5	12.9
30	9.4	10.5	13.5

a. On the same set of axes, draw the yield curve at each of the three given times.

b. Label each curve in part **a** with its general shape (downward-sloping, upward-sloping, flat).

c. Describe the general inflationary and interest rate expectation existing at each of the three times.

LG1 **6–3 Risk-free rate and risk premiums** The real rate of interest is currently 3%; the inflation expectation and risk premiums for a number of securities follow.

Security	Inflation expectation premium	Risk premium
A	6%	3%
B	9	2
C	8	2
D	5	4
E	11	1

a. Find the risk-free rate of interest, R_F, that is applicable to each security.
b. Although not noted, what factor must be the cause of the differing risk-free rates found in part **a**?
c. Find the actual rate of interest for each security.

LG1 **6–4 Risk premiums** Eleanor Burns is attempting to find the actual rate of interest for each of two securities—A and B—issued by different firms at the same point in time. She has gathered the following data:

Characteristic	Security A	Security B
Time to maturity	3 years	15 years
Inflation expectation premium	9.0%	7.0%
Risk premium for:		
Liquidity risk	1.0%	1.0%
Default risk	1.0%	2.0%
Maturity risk	0.5%	1.5%
Other risk	0.5%	1.5%

a. If the real rate of interest is currently 2%, find the risk-free rate of interest applicable to each security.
b. Find the total risk premium attributable to each security's issuer and issue characteristics.
c. Calculate the actual rate of interest for each security. Compare and discuss your findings.

LG2 **6–5 Bond interest payments before and after taxes** Charter Corp. has issued 2,500 debentures with a total principal value of $2,500,000. The bonds have a coupon interest rate of 7%.
a. What dollar amount of interest per bond can an investor expect to receive each year from Charter Corp.?
b. What is Charter's total interest expense per year associated with this bond issue?
c. Assuming that Charter is in a 35% corporate tax bracket, what is the company's net after-tax interest cost associated with this bond issue?

LG3 **6–6 Bond quotation** Assume that the following quote for the Financial Management Corporation's $1,000-par-value bond was found in the Wednesday, November 8, issue of the *Wall Street Journal.*

Fin Mgmt 8.75 05 8.7 558 100.25 −0.63

Given this information, answer the following questions.

a. On what day did the trading activity occur?
b. At what price did the bond close at the end of the day on November 7?
c. In what year does the bond mature?
d. How many bonds were traded on the day quoted?
e. What is the bond's coupon interest rate?
f. What is the bond's *current yield*? Explain how this value was calculated.
g. How much of a change, if any, in the bond's closing price took place between the day quoted and the day before? At what price did the bond close on the day before?

LG4 6–7 **Valuation fundamentals** Imagine that you are trying to evaluate the economics of purchasing an automobile. You expect the car to provide annual after-tax cash benefits of $1,200 at the end of each year, and assume that you can sell the car for after-tax proceeds of $5,000 at the end of the planned 5-year ownership period. All funds for purchasing the car will be drawn from your savings, which are currently earning 6% after taxes.

a. Identify the cash flows, their timing, and the required return applicable to valuing the car.
b. What is the maximum price you would be willing to pay to acquire the car? Explain.

LG4 6–8 **Valuation of assets** Using the information provided in the following table, find the value of each asset.

	Cash flow		
Asset	End of year	Amount	Appropriate required return
A	1	$ 5,000	18%
	2	5,000	
	3	5,000	
B	1 through ∞	$ 300	15%
C	1	$ 0	16%
	2	0	
	3	0	
	4	0	
	5	35,000	
D	1 through 5	$ 1,500	12%
	6	8,500	
E	1	$ 2,000	14%
	2	3,000	
	3	5,000	
	4	7,000	
	5	4,000	
	6	1,000	

LG4 **6–9 Asset valuation and risk** Laura Drake wishes to estimate the value of an asset expected to provide cash inflows of $3,000 per year at the end of years 1 through 4 and $15,000 at the end of year 5. Her research indicates that she must earn 10% on low-risk assets, 15% on average-risk assets, and 22% on high-risk assets.

a. Determine what is the most Laura should pay for the asset if it is classified as (1) low-risk, (2) average-risk, and (3) high-risk.

b. Say Laura is unable to assess the risk of the asset and wants to be certain she's making a good deal. On the basis of your findings in part **a**, what is the most she should pay? Why?

c. All else being the same, what effect does increasing risk have on the value of an asset? Explain in light of your findings in part **a**.

LG5 **6–10 Basic bond valuation** Complex Systems has an outstanding issue of $1,000-par-value bonds with a 12% coupon interest rate. The issue pays interest *annually* and has 16 years remaining to its maturity date.

a. If bonds of similar risk are currently earning a 10% rate of return, how much should the Complex Systems bond sell for today?

b. Describe the *two* possible reasons why similar-risk bonds are currently earning a return below the coupon interest rate on the Complex Systems bond.

c. If the required return were at 12% instead of 10%, what would the current value of Complex Systems' bond be? Contrast this finding with your findings in part **a** and discuss.

LG5 **6–11 Bond valuation—Annual interest** Calculate the value of each of the bonds shown in the following table, all of which pay interest *annually*.

Bond	Par value	Coupon interest rate	Years to maturity	Required return
A	$1,000	14%	20	12%
B	1,000	8	16	8
C	100	10	8	13
D	500	16	13	18
E	1,000	12	10	10

LG5 **6–12 Bond value and changing required returns** Midland Utilities has outstanding a bond issue that will mature to its $1,000 par value in 12 years. The bond has a coupon interest rate of 11% and pays interest *annually*.

a. Find the value of the bond if the required return is (1) 11%, (2) 15%, and (3) 8%.

b. Plot your findings in part **a** on a set of "required return (x axis)–market value of bond (*y* axis)" axes.

c. Use your findings in parts **a** and **b** to discuss the relationship between the coupon interest rate on a bond and the required return and the market value of the bond relative to its par value.

d. What *two* possible reasons could cause the required return to differ from the coupon interest rate?

LG5 **6–13 Bond value and time—Constant required returns** Pecos Manufacturing has just issued a 15-year, 12% coupon interest rate, $1,000-par bond that pays interest *annually*. The required return is currently 14%, and the company is certain it will remain at 14% until the bond matures in 15 years.

a. Assuming that the required return does remain at 14% until maturity, find the value of the bond with (1) 15 years, (2) 12 years, (3) 9 years, (4) 6 years, (5) 3 years, and (6) 1 year to maturity.

b. Plot your findings on a set of "time to maturity (*x* axis)–market value of bond (*y* axis)" axes constructed similarly to Figure 6.6.

c. All else remaining the same, when the required return differs from the coupon interest rate and is assumed to be constant to maturity, what happens to the bond value as time moves toward maturity? Explain in light of the graph in part **b.**

LG5 **6–14 Bond value and time—Changing required returns** Lynn Parsons is considering investing in either of two outstanding bonds. The bonds both have $1,000 par values and 11% coupon interest rates and pay *annual* interest. Bond A has exactly 5 years to maturity, and bond B has 15 years to maturity.

a. Calculate the value of bond A if the required return is (1) 8%, (2) 11%, and (3) 14%.

b. Calculate the value of bond B if the required return is (1) 8%, (2) 11%, and (3) 14%.

c. From your findings in parts **a** and **b,** complete the following table, and discuss the relationship between time to maturity and changing required returns.

Required return	Value of bond A	Value of bond B
8%	?	?
11	?	?
14	?	?

d. If Lynn wanted to minimize *interest rate risk,* which bond should she purchase? Why?

LG6 **6–15 Yield to maturity** The relationship between a bond's yield to maturity and coupon interest rate can be used to predict its pricing level. For each of the bonds listed, state whether the price of the bond will be at a premium to par, at par, or at a discount to par.

Bond	Coupon interest rate	Yield to maturity	Price
A	6%	10%	______
B	8	8	______
C	9	7	______
D	7	9	______
E	12	10	______

LG6 **6–16 Yield to maturity** The Salem Company bond currently sells for $955, has a 12% coupon interest rate and a $1,000 par value, pays interest *annually*, and has 15 years to maturity.

a. Calculate the *yield to maturity* (*YTM*) on this bond.

b. Explain the relationship that exists between the coupon interest rate and yield to maturity and the par value and market value of a bond.

LG6 **6–17 Yield to maturity** Each of the bonds shown in the following table pays interest *annually*.

Bond	Par value	Coupon interest rate	Years to maturity	Current value
A	$1,000	9%	8	$ 820
B	1,000	12	16	1,000
C	500	12	12	560
D	1,000	15	10	1,120
E	1,000	5	3	900

a. Calculate the *yield to maturity* (*YTM*) for each bond.

b. What relationship exists between the coupon interest rate and yield to maturity and the par value and market value of a bond? Explain.

LG6 **6–18 Bond valuation—Semiannual interest** Find the value of a bond maturing in 6 years, with a $1,000 par value and a coupon interest rate of 10% (5% paid semiannually) if the required return on similar-risk bonds is 14% annual interest (7% paid semiannually).

LG6 **6–19 Bond valuation—Semiannual interest** Calculate the value of each of the bonds shown in the following table, all of which pay interest *semiannually*.

Bond	Par value	Coupon interest rate	Years to maturity	Required stated annual return
A	$1,000	10%	12	8%
B	1,000	12	20	12
C	500	12	5	14
D	1,000	14	10	10
E	100	6	4	14

LG6 **6–20 Bond valuation—Quarterly interest** Calculate the value of a $5,000-par-value bond paying quarterly interest at an annual coupon interest rate of 10% and having 10 years until maturity if the required return on similar-risk bonds is currently a 12% annual rate paid *quarterly*.

CHAPTER 6 CASE Evaluating Annie Hegg's Proposed Investment in Atilier Industries Bonds

Annie Hegg has been considering investing in the bonds of Atilier Industries. The bonds were issued 5 years ago at their $1,000 par value and have exactly 25 years remaining until they mature. They have an 8% coupon interest rate, are convertible into 50 shares of common stock, and can be called any time at $1,080. The bond is rated Aa by Moody's. Atilier Industries, a manufacturer of sporting goods, recently acquired a small athletic-wear company that was in financial distress. As a result of the acquisition, Moody's and other rating agencies are considering a rating change for Atilier bonds. Recent economic data suggest that inflation, currently at 5% annually, is likely to increase to a 6% annual rate.

Annie remains interested in the Atilier bond but is concerned about inflation, a potential rating change, and maturity risk. In order to get a feel for the potential impact of these factors on the bond value, she decided to apply the valuation techniques she learned in her finance course.

Required

a. If the price of the common stock into which the bond is convertible rises to $30 per share after 5 years and the issuer calls the bonds at $1,080, should Annie let the bond be called away from her or should she convert it into common stock?

b. For each of the following required returns, calculate the bond's value, assuming annual interest. Indicate whether the bond will sell at a discount, at a premium, or at par value.
(1) Required return is 6%.
(2) Required return is 8%.
(3) Required return is 10%.

c. Repeat the calculations in part **b**, assuming that interest is paid *semiannually* and that the semiannual required returns are one-half of those shown. Compare and discuss differences between the bond values for each required return calculated here and in part **b** under the annual versus semiannual payment assumptions.

d. If Annie strongly believes that inflation will rise by 1% during the next 6 months, what is the most she should pay for the bond, assuming annual interest?

e. If the Atilier bonds are downrated by Moody's from Aa to A, and if such a rating change will result in an increase in the required return from 8% to 8.75%, what impact will this have on the bond value, assuming annual interest?

f. If Annie buys the bond today at its $1,000 par value and holds it for exactly 3 years, at which time the required return is 7%, how much of a gain or loss will she experience in the value of the bond (ignoring interest already received and assuming annual interest)?

g. Rework part **f**, assuming that Annie holds the bond for 10 years and sells it when the required return is 7%. Compare your finding to that in part **f**, and comment on the bond's *maturity risk*.

h. Assume that Annie buys the bond at its current closing price of 98.38 and holds it until maturity. What will her *yield to maturity* (*YTM*) be, assuming annual interest?

i. After evaluating all of the issues raised above, what recommendation would you give Annie with regard to her proposed investment in the Atilier Industries bonds?

WEB EXERCISE

Go to the Web site *www.smartmoney.com*. Click on **Economy & Bonds.** Then click on **Bond Calculator,** which is located down the page under the column **Bond Tools.** Read the instructions on how to use the bond calculator. Using the bond calculator:

1. Calculate the *yield to maturity* (*YTM*) for a bond whose coupon rate is 7.5% with maturity date of July 31, 2030, which you bought for 95.
2. What is the YTM of the above bond if you bought it for 105? For 100?
3. Change the yield % box to 8.5. What would be the price of this bond?
4. Change the yield % box to 9.5. What is this bond's price?
5. Change the maturity date to 2006 and reset yield % to 6.5. What is the price of this bond?
6. Why is the price of the bond in Question 5 higher than the price of the bond in Question 4?
7. Explore the other bond-related resources at the site. Using **Bond Market Update,** comment on current interest rate levels and the yield curve.

Remember to check the book's Web site at

www.aw.com/gitman

for additional resources, including additional Web exercises.

Chapter

7

Stock Valuation

LEARNING GOALS

- LG1 Differentiate between debt and equity capital.
- LG2 Discuss the rights, characteristics, and features of both common and preferred stock.
- LG3 Describe the process of issuing common stock, including in your discussion venture capital, going public, the investment banker's role, and stock quotations.
- LG4 Understand the concept of market efficiency and basic common stock valuation under the zero-growth and constant-growth models.
- LG5 Discuss the free cash flow valuation model and the use of book value, liquidation value, and price/earnings (P/E) multiples to estimate common stock values.
- LG6 Explain the relationships among financial decisions, return, risk, and the firm's value.

Across the Disciplines
Why This Chapter Matters To You

Accounting: You need to understand the difference between debt and equity in terms of tax treatment; the ownership claims of capital providers, including venture capitalists and stockholders; and why book value per share is not a sophisticated basis for common stock valuation.

Information systems: You need to understand the procedures used to issue common stock; the sources and types of information that impact stock value; and how such information can be used in stock valuation models to link proposed actions to share price.

Management: You need to understand the difference between debt and equity capital; the rights and claims of stockholders; the process of raising funds from venture capitalists and through initial public offerings; and how the market will use various stock valuation models to value the firm's common stock.

Marketing: You need to understand that the firm's ideas for products and services will greatly affect the willingness of venture capitalists and stockholders to contribute capital to the firm and also that a perceived increase in risk as a result of new projects may negatively affect the firm's stock value.

Operations: You need to understand that the amount of capital the firm has to invest in plant assets and inventory will depend on the evaluations of venture capitalists and would-be investors; the better the prospects look for growth, the more money the firm will have for operations.

Owning corporate stock is a popular investment activity. Each weekday, the news media report on the movements of stock prices in the financial markets. The price of each share of a firm's common stock is driven by the cash flows (dividends) owners expect to receive from owning the stock and the perceived riskiness of those forecasted cash flows. This chapter describes the key aspects of corporate stock and continues our discussion of the valuation process—this time, of the valuation of stock.

LG1

Differences Between Debt and Equity Capital

capital
The long-term funds of a firm; all items on the right-hand side of the firm's balance sheet, *excluding current liabilities.*

debt capital
All long-term borrowing incurred by a firm, including bonds.

equity capital
The long-term funds provided by the firm's owners, the stockholders.

The term **capital** denotes the long-term funds of a firm. All items on the right-hand side of the firm's balance sheet, *excluding current liabilities,* are sources of capital. **Debt capital** includes all long-term borrowing incurred by a firm, including bonds, which were discussed in Chapter 6. **Equity capital** consists of long-term funds provided by the firm's owners, the stockholders. A firm can obtain equity capital either *internally,* by retaining earnings rather than paying them out as dividends to its stockholders, or *externally,* by selling common or preferred stock. The key differences between debt and equity capital are summarized in Table 7.1 and discussed below.

Voice in Management

Unlike creditors (lenders), holders of equity capital (common and preferred stockholders) are owners of the firm. Holders of common stock have voting rights that permit them to select the firm's directors and to vote on special issues. In contrast, debtholders and preferred stockholders may receive voting privileges only when the firm has violated its stated contractual obligations to them.

TABLE 7.1 Key Differences Between Debt and Equity Capital

	Type of capital	
Characteristic	Debt	Equity
Voice in management[a]	No	Yes
Claims on income and assets	Senior to equity	Subordinate to debt
Maturity	Stated	None
Tax treatment	Interest deduction	No deduction

[a]In the event that the issuer violates its stated contractual obligations to them, debtholders and preferred stockholders *may* receive a voice in management; otherwise, only common stockholders have voting rights.

Claims on Income and Assets

Holders of equity have claims on both income and assets that are secondary to the claims of creditors. Their *claims on income* cannot be paid until the claims of all creditors (including both interest and scheduled principal payments) have been satisfied. After satisfying these claims, the firm's board of directors decides whether to distribute dividends to the owners.

The equity holders' *claims on assets* also are secondary to the claims of creditors. If the firm fails, its assets are sold, and the proceeds are distributed in this order: employees and customers, the government, creditors, and (finally) equity holders. Because equity holders are the last to receive any distribution of assets, they expect greater returns from dividends and/or increases in stock price.

As is explained in Chapter 10, the costs of equity financing are generally higher than debt costs. One reason is that the suppliers of equity capital take more risk because of their subordinate claims on income and assets. Despite being more costly, equity capital is necessary for a firm to grow. All corporations must initially be financed with some common stock equity.

Maturity

Unlike debt, equity capital is a *permanent form* of financing for the firm. It does not "mature" so repayment is not required. Because equity is liquidated only during bankruptcy proceedings, stockholders must recognize that although a ready market may exist for their shares, the price that can be realized may fluctuate. This fluctuation of the market price of equity makes the overall returns to a firm's stockholders even more risky.

Tax Treatment

Interest payments to debtholders are treated as tax-deductible expenses by the issuing firm, whereas dividend payments to a firm's common and preferred stockholders are not tax-deductible. The tax deductibility of interest lowers the cost of debt financing, further causing it to be lower than the cost of equity financing.

Review Question

7–1 What are the key differences between *debt capital* and *equity capital?*

LG2 LG3

Common and Preferred Stock

A firm can obtain equity, or ownership, capital by selling either common or preferred stock. All corporations initially issue common stock to raise equity capital. Some of these firms later issue either additional common stock or preferred stock to raise more equity capital. Although both common and preferred stock are forms of equity capital, preferred stock has some similarities to debt capital that significantly differentiate it from common stock. Here we first consider the key features and behaviors of both common and preferred stock and then describe the process of issuing common stock, including the use of venture capital.

Common Stock

The true owners of business firms are the common stockholders. Common stockholders are sometimes referred to as *residual owners* because they receive what is left—the residual—after all other claims on the firm's income and assets have been satisfied. They are assured of only one thing: that they cannot lose any more than they have invested in the firm. As a result of this generally uncertain position, common stockholders expect to be compensated with adequate dividends and, ultimately, capital gains.

Ownership

privately owned (stock)
All common stock of a firm owned by a single individual.

closely owned (stock)
All common stock of a firm owned by a small group of investors (such as a family).

publicly owned (stock)
Common stock of a firm owned by a broad group of unrelated individual or institutional investors.

The common stock of a firm can be **privately owned** by a single individual, **closely owned** by a small group of investors (such as a family), or **publicly owned** by a broad group of unrelated individual or institutional investors. Typically, small corporations are privately or closely owned; if their shares are traded, this occurs infrequently and in small amounts. Large corporations, which are emphasized in the following discussions, are publicly owned, and their shares are generally actively traded on the major securities exchanges described in Chapter 1.

Par Value

par value (stock)
A relatively useless value for a stock established for legal purposes in the firm's corporate charter.

Unlike bonds, which always have a par value, common stock may be sold with or without a par value. The **par value** of a common stock is a relatively useless value established for legal purposes in the firm's corporate charter. It is generally quite low, about $1.

Firms often issue stock with no par value, in which case they may assign the stock a value or record it on the books at the price at which it is sold. A low par value may be advantageous in states where certain corporate taxes are based on the par value of stock; if a stock has no par value, the tax may be based on an arbitrarily determined per-share figure.

Preemptive Rights

preemptive right
Allows common stockholders to maintain their *proportionate* ownership in the corporation when new shares are issued.

dilution of ownership
Occurs when a new stock issue results in each present shareholder having a claim on a *smaller* part of the firm's earnings than previously.

rights
Financial instruments that permit stockholders to purchase additional shares at a price below the market price, in direct proportion to their number of owned shares.

The **preemptive right** allows common stockholders to maintain their *proportionate* ownership in the corporation when new shares are issued. It allows existing shareholders to maintain voting control and protects them against the dilution of their ownership. **Dilution of ownership** usually results in the dilution of earnings, because each present shareholder has a claim on a *smaller* part of the firm's earnings than previously.

In a *rights offering,* the firm grants **rights** to its shareholders. These financial instruments permit stockholders to purchase additional shares at a price below the market price, in direct proportion to their number of owned shares. Rights are used primarily by smaller corporations whose shares are either *closely owned* or *publicly owned* and not actively traded. In these situations, rights are an important financing tool without which shareholders would run the risk of losing their proportionate control of the corporation.

From the firm's viewpoint, the use of rights offerings to raise new equity capital may be less costly and may generate more interest than a public offering of stock. An example may help to clarify the use of rights.

EXAMPLE

Dominic Company, a regional advertising firm, currently has 100,000 shares of common stock outstanding and is contemplating a rights offering of an additional 10,000 shares. Each existing shareholder will receive one right per share, and each right will entitle the shareholder to purchase one-tenth of a share of new common stock (10,000 ÷ 100,000), so 10 rights will be required to purchase one share of the stock. The holder of 1,000 shares (1 percent) of the outstanding common stock will receive 1,000 rights, each permitting the purchase of one-tenth of a share of new common stock, for a total of 100 new shares. If the shareholder exercises the rights, he or she will end up with a total of 1,100 share of common stock, or 1 percent of the total number of shares then outstanding (110,000). Thus, the shareholder maintains the same proportion of ownership he or she had prior to the rights offering.

authorized shares
The number of shares of common stock that a firm's corporate charter allows it to issue.

outstanding shares
The number of shares of common stock held by the public.

treasury stock
The number of shares of outstanding stock that have been repurchased by the firm.

issued shares
The number of shares of common stock that have been put into circulation; the sum of outstanding shares and treasury stock.

Authorized, Outstanding, and Issued Shares

A firm's corporate charter indicates how many **authorized shares** it can issue. The firm cannot sell more shares than the charter authorizes without obtaining approval through a shareholder vote. To avoid later having to amend the charter, firms generally attempt to authorize more shares than they initially plan to issue.

Authorized shares become **outstanding shares** when they are held by the public. If the *firm* repurchases any of its outstanding shares, these shares are recorded as **treasury stock** and are no longer considered to be outstanding shares. **Issued shares** are the shares of common stock that have been put into circulation; they represent the sum of outstanding shares and treasury stock.

EXAMPLE

Golden Enterprises, a producer of medical pumps, has the following stockholders' equity account on December 31:

Stockholders' Equity	
Common stock—$0.80 par value:	
Authorized 35,000,000 shares; issued 15,000,000 shares	$ 12,000,000
Paid-in capital in excess of par	63,000,000
Retained earnings	31,000,000
	$106,000,000
Less: Cost of treasury stock (1,000,000 shares)	4,000,000
Total stockholders' equity	$102,000,000

How many shares of additional common stock can Golden sell without gaining approval from its shareholders? The firm has 35 million authorized shares, 15 million issued shares, and 1 million shares of treasury stock. Thus 14 million shares are outstanding (15 million issued shares − 1 million shares of treasury stock), and Golden can issue 21 million additional shares (35 million authorized shares − 14 million outstanding shares) without seeking shareholder approval. This total includes the treasury shares currently held, which the firm can reissue to the public without obtaining shareholder approval.

Voting Rights

Generally, each share of common stock entitles its holder to one vote in the election of directors and on special issues. Votes are generally assignable and may be cast at the annual stockholders' meeting.

In recent years, many firms have issued two or more classes of common stock; they differ mainly in having unequal voting rights. A firm can use different classes of stock as a defense against a *hostile takeover* in which an outside group, without management support, tries to gain voting control of the firm by buying its shares in the marketplace. **Supervoting shares** of stock give each owner multiple votes. When supervoting shares are issued to "insiders," an outside group, whose shares have only one vote each typically cannot obtain enough votes to gain control of the firm. At other times, a class of **nonvoting common stock** is issued when the firm wishes to raise capital through the sale of common stock but does not want to give up its voting control.

supervoting shares
Stock that carries with it multiple votes per share rather than the single vote per share typically given on regular shares of common stock.

nonvoting common stock
Common stock that carries no voting rights; issued when the firm wishes to raise capital through the sale of common stock but does not want to give up its voting control.

When different classes of common stock are issued on the basis of unequal voting rights, class A common is typically—but not universally—designated as nonvoting, and class B common has voting rights. Generally, higher classes of shares (class A, for example) are given preference in the distribution of earnings (dividends) and assets; lower-class shares, in exchange, receive voting rights. Treasury stock, which is held within the corporation, generally *does not* have voting rights, *does not* earn dividends, and *does not* have a claim on assets in liquidation.

Because most small stockholders do not attend the annual meeting to vote, they may sign a **proxy statement** giving their votes to another party. The solicitation of proxies from shareholders is closely controlled by the Securities and Exchange Commission to ensure that proxies are not being solicited on the basis of false or misleading information. Existing management generally receives the stockholders' proxies, because it is able to solicit them at company expense.

proxy statement
A statement giving the votes of a stockholder to another party.

proxy battle
The attempt by a nonmanagement group to gain control of the management of a firm by soliciting a sufficient number of proxy votes.

Occasionally, when the firm is widely owned, outsiders may wage a **proxy battle** to unseat the existing management and gain control. To win a corporate election, votes from a majority of the shares voted are required. However, the odds of a nonmanagement group winning a proxy battle are generally slim.

Dividends

The payment of dividends to the firm's shareholders is at the discretion of the corporation's board of directors. Most corporations pay dividends quarterly. Dividends may be paid in cash, stock, or merchandise. Cash dividends are the most common, merchandise dividends the least.

Common stockholders are not promised a dividend, but they come to expect certain payments on the basis of the historical dividend pattern of the firm. Before dividends are paid to common stockholders, the claims of the government, all creditors, and preferred stockholders must be satisfied. Because of the importance of the dividend decision to the growth and valuation of the firm, dividends are discussed in greater detail in Chapter 12.

International Stock Issues

Although the international market for common stock is not so large as the international market for bonds, cross-border issuance and trading of common stock have increased dramatically in the past 20 years.

Some corporations *issue stock in foreign markets.* For example, the stock of General Electric trades in Frankfurt, London, Paris, and Tokyo; the stocks of AOL Time Warner and Microsoft trade in Frankfurt; and the stock of McDonald's trades in Frankfurt and Paris. The London, Frankfurt, and Tokyo markets are the most popular. Issuing stock internationally broadens the ownership base and also helps a company to integrate itself into the local business scene. A listing on a foreign stock exchange both increases local business press coverage and serves as effective corporate advertising. Having locally traded stock can also facilitate corporate acquisitions, because shares can be used as an acceptable method of payment.

Foreign corporations have also discovered the benefits of trading their stock in the United States. The disclosure and reporting requirements mandated by the U.S. Securities and Exchange Commission have historically discouraged all but the largest foreign firms from directly listing their shares on the New York Stock Exchange or the American Stock Exchange. For example, in 1993, Daimler-Benz (now Daimler Chrysler) became the first large German company to be listed on the NYSE.

American depositary receipts (ADRs)
Claims issued by U.S. banks representing ownership of shares of a foreign company's stock held on deposit by the U.S. bank in the foreign market and issued in dollars to U.S. investors.

Alternatively, most foreign companies tap the U.S. market through **American depositary receipts (ADRs).** These are claims issued by U.S. banks representing ownership of shares of a foreign company's stock held on deposit by the U.S. bank in the foreign market. Because ADRs are issued, in dollars, by a U.S. bank to U.S. investors, they are subject to U.S. securities laws. Yet they still give investors the opportunity to diversify their portfolios internationally.

Preferred Stock

par-value preferred stock
Preferred stock with a stated face value that is used with the specified dividend percentage to determine the annual dollar dividend.

no-par preferred stock
Preferred stock with no stated face value but with a stated annual dollar dividend.

Preferred stock gives its holders certain privileges that make them senior to common stockholders. Preferred stockholders are promised a fixed periodic dividend, which is stated either as a percentage or as a dollar amount. How the dividend is specified depends on whether the preferred stock has a *par value,* which, as in common stock, is a relatively useless stated value established for legal purposes. **Par-value preferred stock** has a stated face value, and its annual dividend is specified as a percentage of this value. **No-par preferred stock** has no stated face value, but its annual dividend is stated in dollars. Preferred stock is most often issued by public utilities, by acquiring firms in merger transactions, and by firms that are experiencing losses and need additional financing.

Basic Rights of Preferred Stockholders

The basic rights of preferred stockholders are somewhat more favorable than the rights of common stockholders. Preferred stock is often considered *quasi-debt* because, much like interest on debt, it specifies a fixed periodic payment (dividend). Of course, as ownership, preferred stock is unlike debt in that it has no maturity date. Because they have a fixed claim on the firm's income that takes precedence over the claim of common stockholders, preferred stockholders are exposed to less risk. They are consequently *not normally given a voting right.*

Preferred stockholders have *preference over common stockholders in the distribution of earnings.* If the stated preferred stock dividend is "passed" (not paid) by the board of directors, the payment of dividends to common stockholders is prohibited. It is this preference in dividend distribution that makes common stockholders the true risk takers.

Preferred stockholders are also usually given *preference over common stockholders in the liquidation of assets* in a legally bankrupt firm, although they must "stand in line" behind creditors. The amount of the claim of preferred stockholders in liquidation is normally equal to the par or stated value of the preferred stock.

Features of Preferred Stock

A number of features are generally included as part of a preferred stock issue. These features, along with the stock's par value, the amount of dividend payments, the dividend payment dates, and any restrictive covenants, are specified in an agreement similar to a *bond indenture.*

Restrictive Covenants The restrictive covenants in a preferred stock issue are aimed at ensuring the firm's continued existence and regular payment of the dividend. These covenants include provisions about passing dividends, the sale of senior securities, mergers, sales of assets, minimum liquidity requirements, and repurchases of common stock. The violation of preferred stock covenants usually permits preferred stockholders either to obtain representation on the firm's board of directors or to force the retirement of their stock at or above its par or stated value.

cumulative preferred stock
Preferred stock for which all passed (unpaid) dividends in arrears, along with the current dividend, must be paid before dividends can be paid to common stockholders.

noncumulative preferred stock
Preferred stock for which passed (unpaid) dividends do not accumulate.

Cumulation Most preferred stock is **cumulative** with respect to any dividends passed. That is, all dividends in arrears, along with the current dividend, must be paid before dividends can be paid to common stockholders. If preferred stock is **noncumulative,** passed (unpaid) dividends do not accumulate. In this case, only the current dividend must be paid before dividends can be paid to common stockholders. Because the common stockholders can receive dividends only after the dividend claims of preferred stockholders have been satisfied, it is in the firm's best interest to pay preferred dividends when they are due.[1]

---

1. Most preferred stock is cumulative, because it is difficult to sell noncumulative stock. Common stockholders obviously prefer issuance of noncumulative preferred stock, because it does not place them in quite so risky a position. But it is often in the best interest of the firm to sell cumulative preferred stock because of its lower cost.

EXAMPLE Utley Corporation, a manufacturer of specialty automobiles, currently has outstanding an issue of $6 preferred stock on which quarterly dividends of $1.50 are to be paid. Because of a cash shortage, the last two quarterly dividends were passed. The directors of the company have been receiving a large number of complaints from common stockholders, who have, of course, not received any dividends in the past two quarters either. If the preferred stock is *cumulative,* the company will have to pay its preferred stockholders $4.50 per share ($3.00 of dividends in arrears plus the current $1.50 dividend) prior to paying dividends to its common stockholders. If the preferred stock is *noncumulative,* the firm must pay only the current $1.50 dividend to its preferred stockholders prior to paying dividends to its common stockholders.

Other Features Preferred stock is generally *callable*—the issuer can retire outstanding stock within a certain period of time at a specified price. The call option generally cannot be exercised until a specified date. The call price is normally set above the initial issuance price, but it may decrease as time passes. Making preferred stock callable provides the issuer with a way to bring the fixed-payment commitment of the preferred issue to an end if conditions in the financial markets make it desirable to do so.

conversion feature (preferred stock)
A feature of *convertible preferred stock* that allows holders to change each share into a stated number of shares of common stock.

Preferred stock quite often contains a **conversion feature** that allows *holders of convertible preferred stock* to change each share into a stated number of shares of common stock. Sometimes the number of shares of common stock that the preferred stock can be exchanged for changes according to a prespecified formula.

Issuing Common Stock

Because of the high risk associated with a business startup, a firm's initial financing typically comes from its founders in the form of a common stock investment. Until the founders have made an equity investment, it is highly unlikely that others will contribute either equity or debt capital. Early-stage investors in the firm's equity, as well as lenders who provide debt capital, want to be assured that they are taking no more risk than the founding owner(s). In addition, they want confirmation that the founders are confident enough in their vision for the firm that they are willing to risk their own money.

The initial nonfounder financing for business startups with attractive growth prospects comes from private equity investors. Then, as the firm establishes the viability of its product or service offering and begins to generate revenues, cash flow, and profits, it will often "go public" by issuing shares of common stock to a much broader group of investors.

Before we consider the initial *public* sales of equity, let's review some of the key aspects of early-stage equity financing in firms that have attractive growth prospects.

venture capital
Privately raised external equity capital used to fund early-stage firms with attractive growth prospects.

venture capitalists (VCs)
Providers of venture capital; typically, formal businesses that maintain strong oversight over the firms they invest in and that have clearly defined exit strategies.

Venture Capital

The initial external equity financing privately raised by firms, typically early-stage firms with attractive growth prospects, is called **venture capital.** Those who provide venture capital are known as **venture capitalists (VCs).** They typically are formal business entities that maintain strong oversight over the firms they invest in and that have clearly defined exit strategies. Less visible early-stage investors

TABLE 7.2 Organization of Institutional Venture Capital Investors

Organization	Description
Small business investment companies (SBICs)	Corporations chartered by the federal government that can borrow at attractive rates from the U.S. Treasury and use the funds to make venture capital investments in private companies.
Financial VC funds	Subsidiaries of financial institutions, particularly banks, set up to help young firms grow and, it is hoped, become major customers of the institution.
Corporate VC funds	Firms, sometimes subsidiaries, established by nonfinancial firms, typically to gain access to new technologies that the corporation can access to further its own growth.
VC limited partnerships	Limited partnerships organized by professional VC firms, who serve as the general partner and organize, invest, and manage the partnership using the limited partners' funds; the professional VCs ultimately liquidate the partnership and distribute the proceeds to all partners.

angel capitalists (angels)
Wealthy individual investors who do not operate as a business but invest in promising early-stage companies in exchange for a portion of the firm's equity.

called **angel capitalists** (or **angels**) tend to be investors who do not actually operate as a business; they are often wealthy individual investors who are willing to invest in promising early-stage companies in exchange for a portion of the firm's equity. Although angels play a major role in early-stage equity financing, we will focus on VCs because of their more formal structure and greater public visibility.

Organization and Investment Stages Institutional venture capital investors tend to be organized in one of four basic ways, as described in Table 7.2. The *VC limited partnership* is by far the dominant structure. These funds have as their sole objective to earn high returns, rather than to obtain access to the companies in order to sell or buy other products or services.

VCs can invest in early-stage companies, later-stage companies, or buyouts and acquisitions. Generally, about 40 to 50 percent of VC investments are devoted to early-stage companies (for startup funding and expansion) and a similar percentage to later-stage companies (for marketing, production expansion, and preparation for public offering); the remaining 5 to 10 percent are devoted to the buyout or acquisition of other companies. Generally, VCs look for compound rates of return ranging from 20 to 50 percent or more, depending on both the development stage and the attributes of each company. Earlier-stage investments tend to demand higher returns than later-stage financing because of the higher risk associated with the earlier stages of a firm's growth.

Deal Structure and Pricing Regardless of the development stage, venture capital investments are made under a legal contract that clearly allocates responsibilities and ownership interests between existing owners (founders) and the VC fund or limited partnership. The terms of the agreement will depend on numerous factors related to the founders; the business structure, stage of development, and outlook; and other market and timing issues. The specific financial terms will depend on the value of the enterprise, the amount of funding, and the perceived risk. To control the VC's risk, various covenants are included in the agreement, and the actual funding may be pegged to the achievement of measurable milestones. The contract will have an explicit exit strategy for the VC that may be tied both to measurable milestones and to time.

Each VC investment is unique. The amount of equity to which the VC is entitled will depend on the value of the firm, the terms of the contract, the exit terms, and the minimum compound rate of return required by the VC on its investment. The transaction will be structured to provide the VC with a high rate of return that is consistent with the typically high risk of such transactions. The exit strategy of most VC investments is to take the firm public through an initial public offering.

Going Public

When a firm wishes to sell its stock in the primary market, it has three alternatives. It can make (1) a *public offering,* in which it offers its shares for sale to the general public; (2) a *rights offering,* in which new shares are sold to existing stockholders; or (3) a *private placement,* in which the firm sells new securities directly to an investor or group of investors. Here we focus on public offerings, particularly the **initial public offering (IPO),** which is the first public sale of a firm's stock. IPOs are typically made by small, rapidly growing companies that either require additional capital to continue expanding or have met a milestone for going public that was established in a contract signed earlier in order to obtain VC funding.

initial public offering (IPO)
The first public sale of a firm's stock.

To go public, the firm must first obtain the approval of its current shareholders, the investors who own its privately issued stock. Next, the company's auditors and lawyers must certify that all documents for the company are legitimate. The company then finds an investment bank willing to *underwrite* the offering. This underwriter is responsible for promoting the stock and facilitating the sale of the company's IPO shares. The underwriter often brings in other investment banking firms as participants. We'll discuss the role of the investment banker in more detail in the next section.

The company files a registration statement with the SEC. One portion of the registration statement is called the **prospectus.** It describes the key aspects of the issue, the issuer, and its management and financial position. During the waiting period between the statement's filing and its approval, prospective investors can receive a preliminary prospectus. This preliminary version is called a **red herring,** because a notice printed in red on the front cover indicates the tentative nature of the offer. The cover of the preliminary prospectus describing the 2002 stock issue of Ribapharm, Inc. is shown in Figure 7.1. Note the red herring printed vertically on its left edge.

prospectus
A portion of a security registration statement that describes the key aspects of the issue, the issuer, and its management and financial position.

red herring
A preliminary prospectus made available to prospective investors during the waiting period between the registration statement's filing with the SEC and its approval.

After the SEC approves the registration statement, the investment community can begin analyzing the company's prospects. However, from the time it files until at least one month after the IPO is complete, the company must observe a *quiet period,* during which there are restrictions on what company officials may say about the company. The purpose of the quiet period is to make sure that all potential investors have access to the same information about the company—the information presented in the preliminary prospectus—and not to any unpublished data that might give them an unfair advantage.

FIGURE 7.1

Cover of a Preliminary Prospectus for a Stock Issue

Some of the key factors related to the 2002 common stock issue by Ribapharm, Inc. are summarized on the cover of the prospectus. The type printed vertically on the left edge is normally red, which explains its name "red herring." (*Source:* Ribapharm, Inc., March 21, 2002, p. 1.)

The information in this preliminary prospectus is not complete and may be changed. We may not sell these securities until the registration statement filed with the Securities and Exchange Commission is effective. This preliminary prospectus is not an offer to sell these securities and it is not soliciting an offer to buy these securities in any state where the offer or sale is not permitted.

PRELIMINARY PROSPECTUS Subject to completion March 21, 2002

26,000,000 Shares

Ribapharm

Common Stock

This is an initial public offering of shares of our common stock. ICN Pharmaceuticals, Inc. is selling all of these shares of our common stock and will receive all of the proceeds of this offering. We expect the public offering price to be between $13.00 and $15.00 per share.

Upon completion of this offering, ICN will own approximately 82.67% of our outstanding shares of common stock, assuming no exercise of the over-allotment option referred to below. If the over-allotment option referred to below is exercised, ICN will own approximately 80.07% of our outstanding shares of common stock.

Our common stock is approved for listing on the New York Stock Exchange under the symbol "RNA," subject to official notice of issuance.

Before buying any shares you should read the discussion of material risks of investing in our common stock in "Risk factors" beginning on page 11.

Neither the Securities and Exchange Commission nor any state securities commission has approved or disapproved of these securities or passed upon the adequacy or accuracy of this prospectus. Any representation to the contrary is a criminal offense.

	Per share	Total
Public offering price	$	$
Underwriting discounts and commissions	$	$
Proceeds, before expenses, to ICN	$	$

The underwriters may also purchase up to an additional 3,900,000 shares of our common stock from ICN at the public offering price, less the underwriting discounts and commissions, within 30 days from the date of this prospectus. The underwriters may exercise this option only to cover over-allotments, if any. If the underwriters exercise the option in full, the total underwriting discounts and commissions will be $ and the total proceeds to ICN, before expenses, will be $.

The underwriters are offering the common stock as set forth under "Underwriting." Delivery of the shares will be made on or about , 2002.

UBS Warburg **CIBC World Markets** **SG Cowen**

The investment bankers and company executives promote the company's stock offering through a *road show*, a series of presentations to potential investors around the country and sometimes overseas. In addition to providing investors with information about the new issue, road show sessions help the investment bankers gauge the demand for the offering and set an expected pricing range. After the underwriter sets terms and prices the issue, the SEC must approve the offering.

investment banker
Financial intermediary that specializes in selling new security issues and advising firms with regard to major financial transactions.

The Investment Banker's Role

Most public offerings are made with the assistance of an **investment banker.** The investment banker is a financial intermediary (such as Salomon Brothers or Goldman, Sachs) that specializes in selling new security issues and advising firms

underwriting
The role of the *investment banker* in bearing the risk of reselling, at a profit, the securities purchased from an issuing corporation at an agreed-on price.

underwriting syndicate
A group formed by an investment banker to share the financial risk associated with *underwriting* new securities.

selling group
A large number of brokerage firms that join the originating investment banker(s); each accepts responsibility for selling a certain portion of a new security issue on a commission basis.

with regard to major financial transactions. The main activity of the investment banker is **underwriting.** This process involves purchasing the security issue from the issuing corporation at an agreed-on price and bearing the risk of reselling it to the public at a profit. The investment banker also provides the issuer with advice about pricing and other important aspects of the issue.

In the case of very large security issues, the investment banker brings in other bankers as partners to form an **underwriting syndicate.** The syndicate shares the financial risk associated with buying the entire issue from the issuer and reselling the new securities to the public. The originating investment banker and the syndicate members put together a **selling group,** normally made up of themselves and a large number of brokerage firms. Each member of the selling group accepts the responsibility for selling a certain portion of the issue and is paid a commission on the securities it sells. The selling process for a large security issue is depicted in Figure 7.2.

Compensation for underwriting and selling services typically comes in the form of a discount on the sale price of the securities. For example, an investment banker may pay the issuing firm $24 per share for stock that will be sold for $26 per share. The investment banker may then sell the shares to members of the selling group for $25.25 per share. In this case, the original investment banker earns $1.25 per share ($25.25 sale price − $24 purchase price). The members of the selling group earn 75 cents for each share they sell ($26 sale price − $25.25 purchase price). Although some primary security offerings are directly placed by the issuer, the majority of new issues are sold through public offering via the mechanism just described.

FIGURE 7.2

The Selling Process for a Large Security Issue
The investment banker hired by the issuing corporation may form an underwriting syndicate. The underwriting syndicate buys the entire security issue from the issuing corporation at an agreed-on price. The underwriter then has the opportunity (and bears the risk) of reselling the issue to the public at a profit. Both the originating investment banker and the other syndicate members put together a selling group to sell the issue on a commission basis to investors.

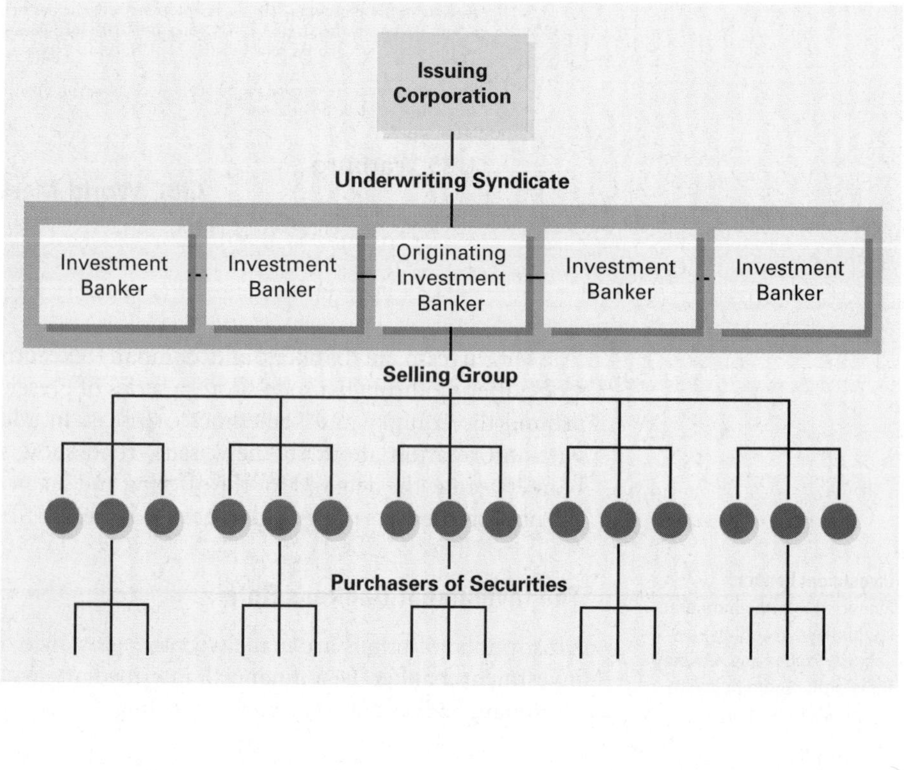

Interpreting Stock Quotations

The financial manager needs to stay abreast of the market values of the firm's outstanding stock, whether it is traded on an organized exchange, over the counter, or in international markets. Similarly, existing and prospective stockholders need to monitor the prices of the securities they own because these prices represent the current value of their investments. Price *quotations,* which include current price data along with statistics on recent price behavior, are readily available for actively traded stocks. The most up-to-date "quotes" can be obtained electronically, via a personal computer. Price information is available from stockbrokers and is widely published in news media. Popular sources of daily security price quotations include financial newspapers, such as the *Wall Street Journal* and *Investor's Business Daily,* and the business sections of daily general newspapers.

Figure 7.3 includes an excerpt from the NYSE quotations, reported in the *Wall Street Journal* of March 18, 2002, for transactions through the close of trading on Friday, March 15, 2002. We'll look at the quotations for common stock for McDonalds, highlighted in the figure. The quotations show that stock prices are quoted in dollars and cents.

The first column gives the percent change in the stock's closing price for the calendar year to date. You can see that McDonalds' price has increased 8.5 percent (+8.5) since the start of 2002. The next two columns, labeled "HI" and "LO," show the highest and lowest prices at which the stock sold during the preceding 52 weeks. McDonalds common stock, for example, traded between \$24.75 and \$31.00 during the 52-week period that ended March 15, 2002. Listed to the right of the company's name is its *stock symbol;* McDonalds goes by "MCD." The figure listed right after the stock symbol under "DIV" is the annual cash dividend paid on each share of stock. The dividend for McDonalds was \$0.23 per share. The next item, labeled "YLD%," is the *dividend yield,* which is found by dividing the stated dividend by the last share price. The dividend yield for McDonalds is 0.8 percent ($0.23 \div 28.72 = 0.0080 = 0.8\%$).

The price/earnings (P/E) ratio, labeled "PE," is next. It is calculated by dividing the closing market price by the firm's most recent annual earnings per share (EPS). The price/earnings (P/E) ratio, as noted in Chapter 2, measures the amount investors are willing to pay for each dollar of the firm's earnings. McDonalds' P/E ratio was 23—the stock was trading at 23 times it earnings. The P/E ratio is believed to reflect investor expectations concerning the firm's future prospects: Higher P/E ratios reflect investor optimism and confidence; lower P/E ratios reflect investor pessimism and concern.

The daily volume, labeled "VOL 100s," follows the P/E ratio. Here the day's sales are quoted in lots of 100 shares. The value 59195 for McDonalds indicates that 5,919,500 shares of its common stock were traded on March 15, 2002. The next column, labeled "LAST," contains the last price at which the stock sold on the given day. The value for McDonalds was \$28.72. The final column, "NET CHG," indicates the change in the closing price from that on the prior trading day. McDonalds closed up \$0.57 from March 14, 2002, which means the closing price on that day was \$28.15.

Similar quotations systems are used for stocks that trade on other exchanges such as the American Stock Exchange (AMEX) and for the over-the-counter (OTC) exchange's Nasdaq National Market Issues. Also note that when a stock

FIGURE 7.3

Stock Quotations
Selected stock quotations for March 15, 2002

YTD	52 WEEKS				YLD		VOL		NET	
% CHG	HI	LO	STOCK (SYM)	DIV	%	PE	100S	LAST	CHG	
− 5.6	15.70	9.40	Masisa ADS **MYS**	.41e	3.4	...	361	12.20	− 0.05	
▲+ 23.8	15	4.95	MasoniteIntl **MHM**		...	18	37	15.12	+ 0.31	
− 20.6	28.95	12.25	MasseyEngy **MEE**	.16	1.0	dd	3883	16.45	+ 0.70	
− 12.7	**19.45**	**3.98**	**MasTec MTZ**		**...**	**dd**	**590**	**6.07**	**− 0.44**	
+ 4.9	19.04	10.85	Matav **MTA**	.17e	1.0	...	34	17.83	− 0.01	
+ 2.2	10.96	6.64	MaterlSci **MSC**		...	dd	166	10.34	− 0.19	
+ 7.4	19.47	11.14	MatsuElec **MC**	.08e	.6	...	2312	13.53	− 0.03	
▲+ 16.5	**19.92**	**14.25**	**Mattel MAT**	**.05**	**.2**	**28**	**51657**	**20.04**	**+ 1.21**	
+ 10.4	27.20	8.47	♣MavrckTube **MVK**		...	17	2724	14.30	+ 0.15	
+ 4.7	8.38	3.30	Maxtor **MXO**		...	dd	11416	6.64	− 0.18	
+ 1.7	39.65	27	MayDeptStrs **MAY**	.95f	2.5	17	13201	37.60	+ 0.58	
+ 44.4	45.58	22.25	Maytag **MYG**	.72	1.6	65	8034	44.80	+ 0.05	
+ 21.1	59.40	36.50	McClatchy A **MNI**	.40	.7	45	394	56.93	+ 0.77	
+ 15.3	49.57	36.50	McCrmkCo **MKC**	.84	1.7	...	3337	48.41	+ 1.14	
+ 14.0	49	40.80	McCrmkCo Vtg **MKCV** n	.21	.4	...	10	48.60	+ 0.75	
+ 18.3	15.17	7.31	McDermInt **MDR**	.15j	...	dd	3621	14.51	+ 0.26	
+ 8.5	31	24.75	McDonalds **MCD**	.23f	.8	23	59195	28.72	+ 0.57	← McDonalds
+ 11.5	70.87	48.70	McGrawH **MHP**	1.02f	1.5	35	10305	67.99	+ 0.48	
− 0.5	41.50	23.40	McKesson **MCK**	.24	.6	98	24513	37.22	+ 0.95	
− 21.4	15	3.20	McMoRanExpl **MMR**		...	dd	762	4.55	+ 0.16	
+ 48.2	4.10	1.66	♣MdwbrkInsGp **MIG**	.12	4.1	dd	43	2.95	+ 0.05	
+ 14.1	36.50	23.71	MeadWstVaco **MWV**		...	dd	14191	35.25	− 0.51	
+ 20.2	4.85	1.88	MediaArts **MDA**		...	dd	277	3.16	+ 0.03	
+ 15.4	59.10	38.45	MediaGen A **MEG**	.72f	1.3	73	973	57.51	+ 0.51	
− 20.4	35.75	18.50	MedOne PIES II	3.04	14.1	...	16	21.60	+ 0.13	
− 12.5	64.60	31	MedicisPhrm **MRX**		...	36	2123	56.50	+ 0.60	
− 10.0	51.68	36.64	Medtronic **MDT**	.23	.5	54	56604	46.08	+ 0.98	
+ 6.6	47.25	27.75	MellonFnl **MEL**	.48	1.2	15	22026	40.09	+ 0.72	
+ 21.5	30	17	MensWearhs **MW**		...	24	1572	25.10	+ 0.79	
+ 1.6	**80.85**	**56.71**	**Merck MRK**	**1.40**	**2.3**	**19**	**266814**	**59.75**	**− 3.69**	
− 0.4	44.50	32	♣MercuryGen **MCY**	1.20f	2.8	22	675	43.48	− 0.12	
+ 17.8	42.27	26.50	Meredith **MDP**	.36	.9	45	1648	41.98	+ 0.03	
+ 9.4	14.78	5.75	MeridnGld **MDG**		...	22	3804	11.30	− 0.25	
+ 2.8	7.98	2.65	MeridnRes **TMR**		...	11	2376	4.10	− 0.09	

Source: Wall Street Journal, March 18, 2002, p. C4.

(or bond) issue is not traded on a given day, it generally is not quoted in the financial and business press.

Review Questions

7–2 What risks do common stockholders take that other suppliers of long-term capital do not?

7–3 How does a rights offering protect a firm's stockholders against the *dilution of ownership?*

7–4 Explain the relationships among authorized shares, outstanding shares, treasury stock, and issued shares.

7–5 What are the advantages to both U.S.-based and foreign corporations of issuing stock outside their home markets? What are *American depositary receipts (ADRs)*?

7–6 What claims do preferred stockholders have with respect to distribution of earnings (dividends) and assets?

7–7 Explain the *cumulative feature* of preferred stock. What is the purpose of a *call feature* in a preferred stock issue?

7–8 What is the difference between a *venture capitalist* (*VC*) and an *angel capitalist* (*angel*)?

7–9 Into what bodies are institutional VCs most commonly organized? How are their deals structured and priced?

7–10 What general procedures must a private firm go through in order to go public via an *initial public offering* (*IPO*)?

7–11 What role does an *investment banker* play in a public offering? Explain the sequence of events in the issuing of stock.

7–12 Describe the key items of information included in a stock *quotation*. What information does the stock's price/earnings (P/E) ratio provide?

LG4 LG5

Common Stock Valuation

Common stockholders expect to be rewarded through periodic cash dividends and an increasing—or at least nondeclining—share value. Like current owners, prospective owners and security analysts frequently estimate the firm's value. Investors purchase the stock when they believe that it is *undervalued*—when its true value is greater than its market price. They sell the stock when they feel that it is *overvalued*—when its market price is greater than its true value.

In this section, we will describe specific stock valuation techniques. First, though, we will look at the concept of an efficient market, which questions whether the prices of actively traded stocks can differ from their true values.

Market Efficiency

Economically rational buyers and sellers use their assessment of an asset's risk and return to determine its value. To a buyer, the asset's value represents the maximum price that he or she would pay to acquire it; a seller views the asset's value as a minimum sale price. In competitive markets with many active participants, such as the New York Stock Exchange, the interactions of many buyers and sellers result in an equilibrium price—the *market value*—for each security. This price reflects the collective actions that buyers and sellers take on the basis of all available information. Buyers and sellers are assumed to digest new information immediately as it becomes available and, through their purchase and sale activities, to create a new market equilibrium price quickly.

efficient-market hypothesis
Theory describing the behavior of an assumed "perfect" market in which (1) securities are typically in equilibrium, (2) security prices fully reflect all public information available and react swiftly to new information, and, (3) because stocks are fairly priced, investors need not waste time looking for mispriced securities.

The Efficient-Market Hypothesis

As noted in Chapter 1, active markets such as the New York Stock Exchange are *efficient*—they are made up of many rational investors who react quickly and objectively to new information. The **efficient-market hypothesis,** which is the basic theory describing the behavior of such a "perfect" market, specifically states that

1. Securities are typically in equilibrium, which means that they are fairly priced and that their expected returns equal their required returns.

2. At any point in time, security prices fully reflect all public information available about the firm and its securities,[2] and these prices react swiftly to new information.
3. Because stocks are fully and fairly priced, investors need not waste their time trying to find and capitalize on mispriced (undervalued or overvalued) securities.

Not all market participants are believers in the efficient-market hypothesis. Some feel that it is worthwhile to search for undervalued or overvalued securities and to trade them to profit from market inefficiencies. Others argue that it is mere luck that would allow market participants to anticipate new information correctly and as a result earn *excess returns*—that is, actual returns greater than required returns. They believe it is unlikely that market participants can *over the long run* earn excess returns. Contrary to this belief, some well-known investors such as Warren Buffett and Peter Lynch *have* over the long run consistently earned excess returns on their portfolios. It is unclear whether their success is the result of their superior ability to anticipate new information or of some form of market inefficiency.

Throughout this text we ignore the disbelievers and continue to assume market efficiency. This means that *the terms "expected return" and "required return" are used interchangeably,* because they should be equal in an efficient market. This also means that stock prices accurately reflect true value based on risk and return. In other words, we will operate under the assumption that the market price at any point in time is the best estimate of value. We're now ready to look closely at the mechanics of stock valuation.

The Basic Stock Valuation Equation

Like the value of a bond, which we discussed in Chapter 6, *the value of a share of common stock is equal to the present value of all future cash flows (dividends) that it is expected to provide over an infinite time horizon.* Although a stockholder can earn capital gains by selling stock at a price above that originally paid, what is really sold is the right to all future dividends. What about stocks that are not expected to pay dividends in the foreseeable future? Such stocks have a value attributable to a distant dividend expected to result from sale of the company or liquidation of its assets. Therefore, *from a valuation viewpoint, only dividends are relevant.*

By redefining terms, the basic valuation model in Equation 6.1 can be specified for common stock, as given in Equation 7.1:

$$P_0 = \frac{D_1}{(1+k_s)^1} + \frac{D_2}{(1+k_s)^2} + \cdots + \frac{D_\infty}{(1+k_s)^\infty} \tag{7.1}$$

2. Those market participants who have nonpublic—*inside*—information may have an unfair advantage that enables them to earn an excess return. Since the mid-1980s disclosure of the insider-trading activities of a number of well-known financiers and investors, major national attention has been focused on the "problem" of insider trading and its resolution. Clearly, those who trade securities on the basis of inside information have an unfair and illegal advantage. Empirical research has confirmed that those with inside information do indeed have an opportunity to earn an excess return. Here we ignore this possibility, given its illegality and that given enhanced surveillance and enforcement by the securities industry and the government have in recent years (it appears) significantly reduced insider trading. We, in effect, assume that all relevant information is public and that therefore the market is efficient.

where

P_0 = value of common stock
D_t = per-share dividend *expected* at the end of year t
k_s = required return on common stock

The equation can be simplified somewhat by redefining each year's dividend, D_t, in terms of anticipated growth. We will consider two models here: zero-growth and constant-growth.

Zero-Growth Model

zero-growth model
An approach to dividend valuation that assumes a constant, nongrowing dividend stream.

The simplest approach to dividend valuation, the **zero-growth model**, assumes a constant, nongrowing dividend stream. In terms of the notation already introduced,

$$D_1 = D_2 = \cdots = D_\infty$$

When we let D_1 represent the amount of the annual dividend, Equation 7.1 under zero growth reduces to

$$P_0 = D_1 \times \sum_{t=1}^{\infty} \frac{1}{(1+k_s)^t} = D_1 \times (PVIFA_{k_s,\infty}) = D_1 \times \frac{1}{k_s} = \frac{D_1}{k_s} \quad (7.2)$$

The equation shows that with zero growth, the value of a share of stock would equal the present value of a perpetuity of D_1 dollars discounted at a rate k_s. (Perpetuities were introduced in Chapter 4; see Equation 4.17 and the related discussion.)

EXAMPLE The dividend of Denham Company, an established textile producer, is expected to remain constant at $3 per share indefinitely. If the required return on its stock is 15%, the stock's value is $20 ($3 ÷ 0.15) per share.

Preferred Stock Valuation Because preferred stock typically provides its holders with a fixed annual dividend over its assumed infinite life, *Equation 7.2 can be used to find the value of preferred stock*. The value of preferred stock can be estimated by substituting the stated dividend on the preferred stock for D_1 and the required return for k_s in Equation 7.2. For example, a preferred stock paying a $5 stated annual dividend and having a required return of 13 percent would have a value of $38.46 ($5 ÷ 0.13) per share.

Constant-Growth Model

constant-growth model
A widely cited dividend valuation approach that assumes that dividends will grow at a constant rate, but a rate that is less than the required return.

The most widely cited dividend valuation approach, the **constant-growth model,** assumes that dividends will grow at a constant rate, but a rate that is less than the required return. (The assumption that the constant rate of growth, g, is less than the required return, k_s, is a necessary mathematical condition for deriving this model.) By letting D_0 represent the most recent dividend, we can rewrite Equation 7.2 as follows:

$$P_0 = \frac{D_0 \times (1+g)^1}{(1+k_s)^1} + \frac{D_0 \times (1+g)^2}{(1+k_s)^2} + \cdots + \frac{D_0 \times (1+g)^\infty}{(1+k_s)^\infty} \quad (7.3)$$

If we simplify Equation 7.3, it can be rewritten as[3]

Gordon model
A common name for the *constant-growth model* that is widely cited in dividend valuation.

$$P_0 = \frac{D_1}{k_s - g} \tag{7.4}$$

The constant-growth model in Equation 7.4 is commonly called the **Gordon model.** An example will show how it works.

EXAMPLE

Lamar Company, a small cosmetics company, from 1998 through 2003 paid the following per-share dividends:

Year	Dividend per share
2003	$1.40
2002	1.29
2001	1.20
2000	1.12
1999	1.05
1998	1.00

We assume that the historical compound annual growth rate of dividends is an accurate estimate of the future constant annual rate of dividend growth, g. Using Appendix Table A–2 or a financial calculator, we find that the historical compound annual growth rate of Lamar Company dividends equals 7%.[4] The com-

3. For the interested reader, the calculations necessary to derive Equation 7.4 from Equation 7.3 follow. The first step is to multiply each side of Equation 7.3 by $(1+k_s)/(1+g)$ and subtract Equation 7.3 from the resulting expression. This yields

$$\frac{P_0 \times (1+k_s)}{1+g} - P_0 = D_0 - \frac{D_0 \times (1+g)^\infty}{(1+k_s)^\infty} \tag{1}$$

Because k_s is assumed to be greater than g, the second term on the right side of Equation 1 should be zero. Thus

$$P_0 \times \left(\frac{1+k_s}{1+g} - 1\right) = D_0 \tag{2}$$

Equation 2 is simplified as follows:

$$P_0 \times \left[\frac{(1+k_s)-(1+g)}{1+g}\right] = D_0 \tag{3}$$

$$P_0 + (k_s - g) = D_0 \times (1+g) \tag{4}$$

$$P_0 = \frac{D_1}{k_s - g} \tag{5}$$

Equation 5 equals Equation 7.4.

4. The technique involves solving the following equation for g:

$$D_{2003} = D_{1998} \times (1+g)^5$$

$$\frac{D_{1998}}{D_{2003}} = \frac{1}{(1+g)^5} = PVIF_{g,5}$$

To do so, we can use financial tables or a financial calculator.

Two basic steps can be followed using the present value table. First, dividing the earliest dividend (D_{1998} = \$1.00) by the most recent dividend (D_{2003} = \$1.40) yields a factor for the present value of one dollar, *PVIF*, of 0.714 (\$1.00 ÷ \$1.40). Although six dividends are shown, *they reflect only 5 years of growth.* (The number of years of growth can also be found by subtracting the earliest year from the most recent year—that is, 2003–1998 = *5 years of growth.*) By looking across the Appendix Table A–2 at the *PVIF* for 5 years, we find that the factor closest to 0.714 occurs at 7% (0.713). Therefore, the growth rate of the dividends, rounded to the nearest whole percent, is 7%.

Alternatively, a financial calculator can be used. (*Note:* Most calculators require *either* the *PV* or *FV* value to be input as a negative number to calculate an unknown interest or growth rate. That approach is used here.) Using the inputs shown at the left, you should find the growth rate to be 6.96%, which we round to 7%.

Input	Function
1.00	PV
−1.40	FV
5	N
	CPT
	I

Solution
6.96

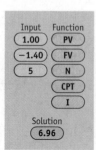

In Practice

FOCUS ON e-FINANCE What's the Value of the American Dream?

For many people, owning their own business represents the dream of a lifetime. But how much should this dream cost? To get an idea of how to value a small business, check out the "Business for Sale" column in *Inc.*, a magazine that focuses on smaller emerging businesses. Each month the column describes the operations, financial situation, industry outlook, price rationale, and pros and cons of a small business offered for sale. For example, columns featured in 2000 and 2001 included such diverse companies as a distributor of semiprecious stones, a software developer, a Christmas tree grower, a small chain of used-book stores, and a baseball camp, with prices ranging from $200,000 to $9 million. Most valuations are based on a multiple of cash flow or annual sales, with accepted guidelines for different industries. That number is just a starting point, however, and must be adjusted for other factors.

For example, food distributors typically sell for about 30 percent of annual sales. A Southeastern seafood distributor was recently offered for $2.25 million, a discount from the $3.9 million price you'd get strictly on the basis of annual sales. The reason? The new owner would have to buy or lease a warehouse facility, freezers, and other equipment.

Because valuing a small business is difficult, many owners make use of reasonably priced valuation software such as BallPark Business Valuation and VALUware. These programs offer buyers and sellers a quick way to estimate the business's value and to answer such questions as:

- How much cash will my business generate or consume?
- What will my balance sheet, income statement, and cash flow statement look like in 5 years?
- Should I seek debt or equity to finance growth?
- What impact will capital purchases have on my venture?
- How much ownership in my business should I give up for a $2 million equity contribution?

Once the negotiators decide to move forward, however, they usually should hire an experienced valuation professional to develop a formal valuation.

Sources: "About Ballpark Business Valuation," *Bullet Proof Business Plans,* downloaded from *www.bulletproofbizplans.com/BallPark/About_/about_.html*; Jill Andresky Fraser, "Business for Sale: Southeastern Seafood Distributor," *Inc.* (October 1, 2000), downloaded from *www.inc.com*; *VALUware, www.bizbooksoftware.com/VALUWARE.HTM.*

pany estimates that its dividend in 2004, D_1, will equal \$1.50. The required return, k_s, is assumed to be 15%. By substituting these values into Equation 7.4, we find the value of the stock to be

$$P_0 = \frac{\$1.50}{0.15 - 0.07} = \frac{\$1.50}{0.08} = \underline{\underline{\$18.75}} \text{ per share}$$

Assuming that the values of D_1, k_s, and g are accurately estimated, Lamar Company's stock value is \$18.75 per share.

Free Cash Flow Valuation Model

free cash flow valuation model
A model that determines the value of an entire company as the present value of its expected free cash flows discounted at the firm's *weighted average cost of capital,* which is its expected average future cost of funds over the long run.

As an alternative to the dividend valuation models presented above, a firm's value can be estimated by using its projected *free cash flows* (*FCFs*). This approach is appealing when one is valuing firms that have no dividend history or are startups or when one is valuing an operating unit or division of a larger public company. Although dividend valuation models are widely used and accepted, in these situations it is preferable to use a more general free cash flow valuation model.

The **free cash flow valuation model** is based on the same basic premise as dividend valuation models: The value of a share of common stock is the present value of all future cash flows it is expected to provide over an infinite time horizon.

However, in the free cash flow valuation model, instead of valuing the firm's expected dividends, we value the firm's expected *free cash flows,* defined in Equation 3.3 (page 95). They represent the amount of cash flow available to investors—the providers of debt (creditors) and equity (owners)—after all other obligations have been met.

The free cash flow valuation model estimates the value of the entire company by finding the present value of its expected free cash flows discounted at its *weighted average cost of capital,* which is its expected average future cost of funds over the long run (see Chapter 10), as specified in Equation 7.5.

$$V_C = \frac{FCF_1}{(1+k_a)^1} + \frac{FCF_2}{(1+k_a)^2} + \cdots + \frac{FCF_\infty}{(1+k_a)^\infty} \tag{7.5}$$

where

V_C = value of the entire company
FCF_t = free cash flow *expected* at the end of year t
k_a = the firm's weighted average cost of capital

Note the similarity between Equations 7.5 and 7.1, the general stock valuation equation.

Because the value of the entire company, V_C, is the market value of the entire enterprise (that is, of all assets), to find common stock value, V_S, we must subtract the market value of all of the firm's debt, V_D, and the market value of preferred stock, V_P, from V_C.

$$V_S = V_C - V_D - V_P \tag{7.6}$$

Because it is difficult to forecast a firm's free cash flow, specific annual cash flows are typically forecast for only about 5 years, beyond which a constant growth rate is assumed. Here we assume that the first 5 years of free cash flows are explicitly forecast and that a constant rate of free cash flow growth occurs beyond the end of year 5 to infinity. This model therefore requires a number of steps to calculate and combine the forecast values of the early-year free cash flows with those of the later-year constant-growth free cash flows. Its application is best demonstrated with an example.

EXAMPLE Dewhurst Inc. wishes to determine the value of its stock by using the free cash flow valuation model. In order to apply the model, the firm's CFO developed the data given in Table 7.3. Application of the model can be performed in four steps.

Step 1 Calculate the present value of the free cash flow occurring from the end of 2009 to infinity, measured at the beginning of 2009 (that is, at the end of 2008). Because a constant rate of growth in FCF is forecast beyond 2008, we can use the constant-growth dividend valuation model (Equation 7.4) to calculate the value of the free cash flows from the end of 2009 to infinity.

$$\text{Value of } FCF_{2009\to\infty} = \frac{FCF_{2009}}{k_a - g_{FCF}}$$
$$= \frac{\$600{,}000 \times (1+0.03)}{0.09-0.03}$$
$$= \frac{\$618{,}000}{0.06} = \underline{\underline{\$10{,}300{,}000}}$$

TABLE 7.3 Dewhurst Inc.'s Data for Free Cash Flow Valuation Model

Free cash flow		
Year (t)	$(FCF_t)^a$	Other data
2004	\$400,000	Growth rate of FCF, beyond 2008 to infinity, $g_{FCF} = 3\%$
2005	450,000	Weighted average cost of capital, $k_a = 9\%$
2006	520,000	Market value of all debt, $V_D = \$3,100,000$
2007	560,000	Market value of preferred stock, $V_P = \$800,000$
2008	600,000	Number of shares of common stock outstanding = 300,000

[a]Developed using Equations 3.2 and 3.3 (page 95).

Note that to calculate the FCF in 2009, we had to increase the 2008 FCF value of \$600,000 by the 3% FCF growth rate, g_{FCF}.

Step 2 Add the present value of the FCF from 2009 to infinity, which is measured at the end of 2008, to the 2008 FCF value to get the total FCF in 2008.

$$\text{Total } FCF_{2008} = \$600,000 + \$10,300,000 = \$10,900,000$$

Step 3 Find the sum of the present values of the FCFs for 2004 through 2008 to determine the value of the entire company, V_C. This calculation is shown in Table 7.4, using present value interest factors, *PVIF*s, from Appendix Table A–2.

Step 4 Calculate the value of the common stock using Equation 7.6. Substituting the value of the entire company, V_C, calculated in Step 3, and the market values of debt, V_D, and preferred stock, V_P, given in Table 7.3, yields the value of the common stock, V_S:

$$V_S = \$8,628,620 - \$3,100,000 - \$800,000 = \underline{\underline{\$4,728,620}}$$

The value of Dewhurst's common stock is therefore estimated to be \$4,728,620. By dividing this total by the 300,000 shares of common

TABLE 7.4 Calculation of the Value of the Entire Company for Dewhurst Inc.

Year (t)	FCF_t (1)	$PVIF_{9\%,t}$ (2)	Present value of FCF_t [(1) × (2)] (3)
2004	\$ 400,000	0.917	\$ 366,800
2005	450,000	0.842	378,900
2006	520,000	0.772	401,440
2007	560,000	0.708	396,480
2008	10,900,000[a]	0.650	7,085,000
		Value of entire company, V_C =	\$8,628,620

[a]This amount is the sum of the FCF_{2008} of \$600,000 from Table 7.3 and the \$10,300,000 value of the $FCF_{2009 \to \infty}$ calculated in Step 1.

stock that the firm has outstanding, we get a common stock value of *$15.76 per share* ($4,728,620 ÷ 300,000).

It should now be clear that the free cash flow valuation model is consistent with the dividend valuation models presented earlier. The appeal of this approach is its focus on the free cash flow estimates rather than on forecast dividends, which are far more difficult to estimate, given that they are paid at the discretion of the firm's board. The more general nature of the free cash flow model is responsible for its growing popularity, particularly with CFOs and other financial managers.

Other Approaches to Common Stock Valuation

Many other approaches to common stock valuation exist. The more popular approaches include book value, liquidation value, and some type of price/earnings multiple.

Book Value

book value per share
The amount per share of common stock that would be received if all of the firm's assets were *sold for their exact book (accounting) value* and the proceeds remaining after paying all liabilities (including preferred stock) were divided among the common stockholders.

Book value per share is simply the amount per share of common stock that would be received if all of the firm's assets were *sold for their exact book (accounting) value* and the proceeds remaining after paying all liabilities (including preferred stock) were divided among the common stockholders. This method lacks sophistication and can be criticized on the basis of its reliance on historical balance sheet data. It ignores the firm's expected earnings potential and generally lacks any true relationship to the firm's value in the marketplace. Let us look at an example.

EXAMPLE

At year-end 2003, Lamar Company's balance sheet shows total assets of $6 million, total liabilities (including preferred stock) of $4.5 million, and 100,000 shares of common stock outstanding. Its book value per share therefore would be

$$\frac{\$6{,}000{,}000 - \$4{,}500{,}000}{100{,}000 \text{ shares}} = \underline{\underline{\$15}} \text{ per share}$$

Because this value assumes that assets could be sold for their book value, it may not represent the minimum price at which shares are valued in the marketplace. As a matter of fact, although most stocks sell above book value, it is not unusual to find stocks selling below book value when investors believe either that assets are overvalued or that the firm's liabilities are understated.

Liquidation Value

liquidation value per share
The *actual amount* per share of common stock that would be received if all of the firm's assets were *sold for their market value,* liabilities (including preferred stock) were paid, and any remaining money were divided among the common stockholders.

Liquidation value per share is the *actual amount* per share of common stock that would be received if all of the firm's assets were *sold for their market value,* liabilities (including preferred stock) were paid, and any remaining money were divided among the common stockholders.[5] This measure is more realistic than book

5. In the event of liquidation, creditors' claims must be satisfied first, then those of the preferred stockholders. Anything left goes to common stockholders.

value—because it is based on the current market value of the firm's assets—but it still fails to consider the earning power of those assets. An example will illustrate.

EXAMPLE Lamar Company found upon investigation that it could obtain only \$5.25 million if it sold its assets today. The firm's liquidation value per share therefore would be

$$\frac{\$5{,}250{,}000 - \$4{,}500{,}000}{100{,}000 \text{ shares}} = \underline{\underline{\$7.50}} \text{ per share}$$

Ignoring liquidation expenses, this amount would be the firm's minimum value.

Price/Earnings (P/E) Multiples

The *price/earnings (P/E) ratio,* introduced in Chapter 2, reflects the amount investors are willing to pay for each dollar of earnings. The average P/E ratio in a particular industry can be used as the guide to a firm's value—if it is assumed that investors value the earnings of that firm in the same way they do the "average" firm in the industry. The **price/earnings multiple approach** is a popular technique used to estimate the firm's share value; it is calculated by multiplying the firm's expected earnings per share (EPS) by the average price/earnings (P/E) ratio for the industry. The average P/E ratio for the industry can be obtained from a source such as *Standard & Poor's Industrial Ratios.*

price/earnings multiple approach
A popular technique used to estimate the firm's share value; calculated by multiplying the firm's expected earnings per share (EPS) by the average price/earnings (P/E) ratio for the industry.

The use of P/E multiples is especially helpful in valuing firms that are not publicly traded, whereas market price quotations can be used to value publicly traded firms. In any case, the price/earnings multiple approach is considered superior to the use of book or liquidation values because it considers *expected* earnings. An example will demonstrate the use of price/earnings multiples.

EXAMPLE Lamar Company is expected to earn \$2.60 per share next year (2004). This expectation is based on an analysis of the firm's historical earnings trend and of expected economic and industry conditions. The average price/earnings (P/E) ratio for firms in the same industry is 7. Multiplying Lamar's expected earnings per share (EPS) of \$2.60 by this ratio gives us a value for the firm's shares of \$18.20, assuming that investors will continue to measure the value of the average firm at 7 times its earnings.

So how much is Lamar Company's stock really worth? That's a trick question, because there's no one right answer. It is important to recognize that the answer depends on the assumptions made and the techniques used. Professional securities analysts typically use a variety of models and techniques to value stocks. For example, an analyst might use the constant-growth model, liquidation value, and price/earnings (P/E) multiples to estimate the worth of a given stock. If the analyst feels comfortable with his or her estimates, the stock would be valued at no more than the largest estimate. Of course, should the firm's estimated liquidation value per share exceed its "going concern" value per share, estimated by using one of the valuation models (zero- or constant-growth or free cash flow) or the P/E multiple approach, the firm would be viewed as being "worth more dead than alive." In such an event, the firm would lack sufficient earning power to justify its existence and should probably be liquidated.

Review Questions

7–13 What does the *efficient-market hypothesis* say about (**a**) securities prices, (**b**) their reaction to new information, and (**c**) investor opportunities to profit?

7–14 Describe, compare, and contrast the following common stock dividend valuation models: (**a**) zero-growth and (**b**) constant-growth.

7–15 Describe the *free cash flow valuation model* and explain how it differs from the dividend valuation models. What is the appeal of this model?

7–16 Explain each of the three other approaches to common stock valuation: (**a**) book value, (**b**) liquidation value, and (**c**) price/earnings (P/E) multiples. Which of these is considered the best?

LG6

Decision Making and Common Stock Value

Valuation equations measure the stock value at a point in time based on expected return and risk. Any decisions of the financial manager that affect these variables can cause the value of the firm to change. Figure 7.4 depicts the relationship among financial decisions, return, risk, and stock value.

Changes in Expected Return

Assuming that economic conditions remain stable, any management action that would cause current and prospective stockholders to raise their dividend expectations should increase the firm's value. In Equation 7.4, we can see that P_0 will increase for any increase in D_1 or g. Any action of the financial manager that will increase the level of expected returns without changing risk (the required return) should be undertaken, because it will positively affect owners' wealth.

EXAMPLE Using the constant-growth model, we found Lamar Company to have a share value of $18.75. On the following day, the firm announced a major technological breakthrough that would revolutionize its industry. Current and prospective stockholders would not be expected to adjust their required return of 15%, but

FIGURE 7.4

Decision Making and Stock Value

Financial decisions, return, risk, and stock value

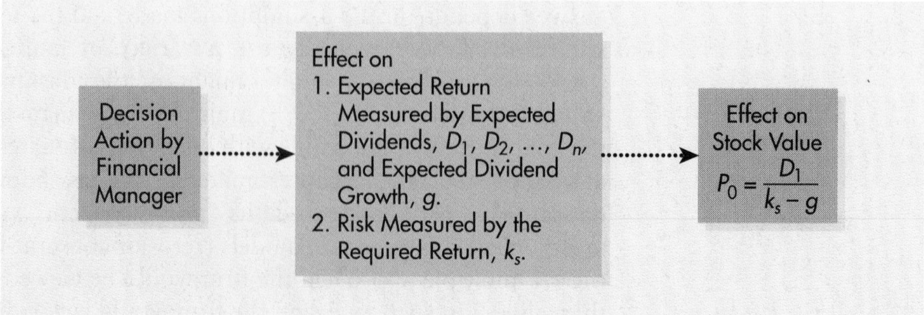

they would expect that future dividends will increase. Specifically, they expect that although the dividend next year, D_1, will remain at \$1.50, the expected rate of growth thereafter will increase from 7% to 9%. If we substitute $D_1 = \$1.50$, $k_s = 0.15$, and $g = 0.09$ into Equation 7.4, the resulting value is \$25 [\$1.50 ÷ (0.15 − 0.09)]. The increased value therefore resulted from the higher expected future dividends reflected in the increase in the growth rate.

Changes in Risk

Although k_s is defined as the required return, we know from Chapter 5 that it is directly related to the nondiversifiable risk, which can be measured by beta. The *capital asset pricing model (CAPM)* given in Equation 5.7 is restated here as Equation 7.7:

$$k_s = R_F + [b \times (k_m - R_F)] \tag{7.7}$$

With the risk-free rate, R_F, and the market return, k_m, held constant, the required return, k_s, depends directly on beta. Any action taken by the financial manager that increases risk (beta) will also increase the required return. In Equation 7.4, we can see that with everything else constant, an increase in the required return, k_s, will reduce share value, P_0. Likewise, a decrease in the required return will increase share value. Thus any action of the financial manager that increases risk contributes to a reduction in value, and any action that decreases risk contributes to an increase in value.

EXAMPLE Assume that Lamar Company's 15% required return resulted from a risk-free rate of 9%, a market return of 13%, and a beta of 1.50. Substituting into the capital asset pricing model, Equation 7.7, we get a required return, k_s, of 15%:

$$k_s = 9\% + [1.50 \times (13\% - 9\%)] = \underline{\underline{15}}\%$$

With this return, the value of the firm was calculated in the example above to be \$18.75.

Now imagine that the financial manager makes a decision that, without changing expected dividends, causes the firm's beta to increase to 1.75. Assuming that R_F and k_m remain at 9% and 13%, respectively, the required return will increase to 16% (9% + [1.75 × (13% − 9%)]) to compensate stockholders for the increased risk. Substituting $D_1 = \$1.50$, $k_s = 0.16$, and $g = 0.07$ into the valuation equation, Equation 7.4, results in a share value of \$16.67 [\$1.50 ÷ (0.16 − 0.07)]. As expected, raising the required return, without any corresponding increase in expected return, causes the firm's stock value to decline. Clearly, the financial manager's action was not in the owners' best interest.

Combined Effect

A financial decision rarely affects return and risk independently; most decisions affect both factors. In terms of the measures presented, with an increase in risk (b) one would expect an increase in return (D_1 or g, or both), assuming that R_F and k_m remain unchanged. The net effect on value depends on the size of the changes in these variables.

EXAMPLE If we assume that the two changes illustrated for Lamar Company in the preceding examples occur simultaneously, key variable values would be $D_1 = \$1.50$, $k_s = 0.16$, and $g = 0.09$. Substituting into the valuation model, we obtain a share price of \$21.43 [$\$1.50 \div (0.16 - 0.09)$]. The net result of the decision, which increased return (*g*, from 7% to 9%) as well as risk (*b*, from 1.50 to 1.75 and therefore k_s from 15% to 16%), is positive: The share price increased from \$18.75 to \$21.43. The decision appears to be in the best interest of the firm's owners, because it increases their wealth.

Review Questions

7–17 Explain the linkages among financial decisions, return, risk, and stock value.

7–18 Assuming that all other variables remain unchanged, what impact would *each* of the following have on stock price? (**a**) The firm's beta increases. (**b**) The firm's required return decreases. (**c**) The dividend expected next year decreases. (**d**) The rate of growth in dividends is expected to increase.

SUMMARY

FOCUS ON VALUE

The price of each share of a firm's common stock is the value of each ownership interest. Although common stockholders typically have voting rights, which indirectly give them a say in management, their only significant right is their claim on the residual cash flows of the firm. This claim is subordinate to those of vendors, employees, customers, lenders, the government (for taxes), and preferred stockholders. The value of the common stockholders' claim is embodied in the cash flows they are entitled to receive from now to infinity. The present value of those expected cash flows is the firm's share value.

To determine this present value, cash flows are discounted at a rate that reflects the riskiness of the forecast cash flows. Riskier cash flows are discounted at higher rates, resulting in lower present values. The value of the firm's common stock is therefore driven by its expected cash flows (returns) and risk (certainty of the expected cash flows).

In pursuing the firm's goal of **maximizing the stock price**, the financial manager must carefully consider the balance of return and risk associated with each proposal and must undertake only those that create value for owners. By focusing on value creation and by managing and monitoring the firm's cash flows and risk, the financial manager should be able to achieve the firm's goal of share price maximization.

REVIEW OF LEARNING GOALS

LG1 **Differentiate between debt and equity capital.** Holders of equity capital (common and preferred stock) are owners of the firm. Typically, only common stockholders have a voice in management through their voting rights. Equity holders have claims on income and assets that are secondary to the claims of creditors, there is no maturity date, and the firm does not benefit from tax deductibility of dividends paid to stockholders, as is the case for interest paid to debtholders.

LG2 **Discuss the rights, characteristics, and features of both common and preferred stock.** The common stock of a firm can be privately owned, closely owned, or publicly owned. It can be sold with or without a par value. Preemptive rights allow common stockholders to avoid dilution of ownership when new shares are issued. Not all shares authorized in the corporate charter are outstanding. If a firm has treasury stock, it will have issued more shares than are outstanding. Some firms have two or more classes of common stock that differ mainly in having unequal voting rights. Proxies transfer voting rights from one party to another. Dividend distributions to common stockholders are made at the discretion of the firm's board of directors. Firms can issue stock in foreign markets. The stock of many foreign corporations is traded in the form of American depositary receipts (ADRs) in U.S. markets.

Preferred stockholders have preference over common stockholders with respect to the distribution of earnings and assets and so are normally not given voting privileges. Preferred stock issues may have certain restrictive covenants, cumulative dividends, a call feature, and a conversion feature.

LG3 **Describe the process of issuing common stock, including in your discussion venture capital, going public, the investment banker's role, and stock quotations.** The initial nonfounder financing for business startups with attractive growth prospects typically comes from private equity investors. These investors can be either angel capitalists or venture capitalists (VCs), which are more formal business entities. Institutional VCs can be organized in a number of ways, but the VC limited partnership is the most common. VCs usually invest in both early-stage and later-stage companies that they hope to take public in order to cash out their investments.

The first public issue of a firm's stock is called an initial public offering (IPO). The company selects an investment banker to advise it and to sell the securities. The lead investment banker may form a selling syndicate with other investment bankers to sell the issue. The IPO process includes filing a registration statement with the Securities and Exchange Commission (SEC), getting SEC approval, promoting the offering to investors, pricing the issue, and selling the shares.

Stock quotations, published regularly in the financial media, provide information on stocks, including calendar year change in price, 52-week high and low, dividend, dividend yield, P/E ratio, volume, latest price, and net price change from the prior trading day.

LG4 **Understand the concept of market efficiency and basic common stock valuation under the zero-growth and constant-growth models.** Market efficiency suggests that rational investors react quickly to new information, causing the market value of common stock to adjust quickly upward or downward. The efficient-market hypothesis suggests that securities are fairly priced, that they reflect fully all publicly available information, and that investors should therefore not waste time trying to find and capitalize on mispriced securities. The value of a share of common stock is the present value of all future dividends it is expected to provide over an infinite time horizon. The basic stock valuation equation and the zero-growth and constant-growth valuation models are summarized in Table 7.5. The most widely cited model is the constant-growth model.

LG5 **Discuss the free cash flow valuation model and the use of book value, liquidation value, and price/earnings (P/E) multiples to estimate common stock values.** The free cash flow valuation model is appealing when one is valuing firms that have no dividend history, startups, or operating units or divisions of a larger public company. The model finds the value of the entire company by discounting the firm's expected free cash flow at its weighted

TABLE 7.5 Summary of Key Valuation Definitions and Formulas for Common Stock

Definitions of variables

D_t = per-share dividend *expected* at the end of year t

FCF_t = free cash flow *expected* at the end of year t

g = constant rate of growth in dividends

k_a = weighted average cost of capital

k_s = required return on common stock

P_0 = value of common stock

V_C = value of the entire company

V_D = market value of all the firm's debt

V_P = market value of preferred stock

V_S = value of common stock

Valuation formulas

Basic stock value:

$$P_0 = \frac{D_1}{(1+k_s)^1} + \frac{D_2}{(1+k_s)^2} + \cdots + \frac{D_\infty}{(1+k_s)^\infty} \quad \text{[Eq. 7.1]}$$

Common stock value:

Zero-growth:

$$P_0 = \frac{D_1}{k_s} \text{ (also used to value preferred stock)} \quad \text{[Eq. 7.2]}$$

Constant-growth:

$$P_0 = \frac{D_1}{k_s - g} \quad \text{[Eq. 7.4]}$$

FCF value of entire company:

$$V_C = \frac{FCF_1}{(1+k_a)^1} + \frac{FCF_2}{(1+k_a)^2} + \cdots + \frac{FCF_\infty}{(1+k_a)^\infty} \quad \text{[Eq. 7.5]}$$

FCF common stock value:

$$V_S = V_C - V_D - V_P \quad \text{[Eq. 7.6]}$$

average cost of capital. The common stock value is found by subtracting the market values of the firm's debt and preferred stock from the value of the entire company. The two equations involved in this model are summarized in Table 7.5.

Book value per share is the amount per share of common stock that would be received if all of the firm's assets were *sold for their book (accounting) value* and the proceeds remaining after paying all liabilities (including preferred stock) were divided among the common stockholders. Liquidation value per share is the *actual amount* per share of common stock that would be received if all of the firm's assets were *sold for their market value*, liabilities (including preferred stock) were paid, and the remaining money were divided among the common stockholders. The price/earnings (P/E) multiples approach estimates stock value by multiplying the firm's expected earnings per share (EPS) by the average price/earnings (P/E) ratio for the industry.

LG6 **Explain the relationships among financial decisions, return, risk, and the firm's value.** In a stable economy, any action of the financial manager that increases the level of expected return without changing risk should increase share value, and any action that reduces the level of expected return without changing risk should reduce share value. Similarly, any action that increases risk (required return) will reduce share value, and any action that reduces risk will increase share value. Because most financial decisions affect both return and risk, an assessment of their combined effect on stock value must be part of the financial decision-making process.

SELF-TEST PROBLEMS (Solutions in Appendix B)

LG4 **ST 7–1 Common stock valuation** Perry Motors' common stock currently pays an annual dividend of $1.80 per share. The required return on the common stock is 12%. Estimate the value of the common stock under each of the following assumptions about the dividend.

a. Dividends are expected to grow at an annual rate of 0% to infinity.
b. Dividends are expected to grow at a constant annual rate of 5% to infinity.

LG5 **ST 7–2 Free cash flow valuation** Erwin Footwear wishes to assess the value of its Active Shoe Division. This division has debt with a market value of $12,500,000 and no preferred stock. Its weighted average cost of capital is 10%. The Active Shoe Division's estimated free cash flow each year from 2004 through 2007 is given in the accompanying table. Beyond 2007 to infinity, the firm expects its free cash flow to grow at 4% annually.

Year (t)	Free cash flow (FCF_t)
2004	$ 800,000
2005	1,200,000
2006	1,400,000
2007	1,500,000

a. Use the *free cash flow valuation model* to estimate the value of Erwin's Active Shoe Division.
b. Use your finding in part **a** along with the data provided above to find this division's common stock value.
c. If the Active Shoe Division as a public company will have 500,000 shares outstanding, use your finding in part **b** to calculate its value per share.

PROBLEMS

LG2 **7–1 Authorized and available shares** Aspin Corporation's charter authorizes issuance of 2,000,000 shares of common stock. Currently, 1,400,000 shares are outstanding and 100,000 shares are being held as treasury stock. The firm wishes to raise $48,000,000 for a plant expansion. Discussions with its investment bankers indicate that the sale of new common stock will net the firm $60 per share.

a. What is the maximum number of new shares of common stock that the firm can sell without receiving further authorization from shareholders?

b. Judging on the basis of the data given and your finding in part **a**, will the firm be able to raise the needed funds without receiving further authorization?

c. What must the firm do to obtain authorization to issue more than the number of shares found in part **a**?

LG2 7–2 **Preferred dividends** Slater Lamp Manufacturing has an outstanding issue of preferred stock with an $80 par value and an 11% annual dividend.

a. What is the annual dollar dividend? If it is paid quarterly, how much will be paid each quarter?

b. If the preferred stock is *noncumulative* and the board of directors has passed the preferred dividend for the last 3 quarters, how much must be paid to preferred stockholders before dividends are paid to common stockholders?

c. If the preferred stock is *cumulative* and the board of directors has passed the preferred dividend for the last 3 quarters, how much must be paid to preferred stockholders before dividends are paid to common stockholders?

LG2 7–3 **Preferred dividends** In each case in the following table, how many dollars of preferred dividends per share must be paid to preferred stockholders before common stock dividends are paid?

Case	Type	Par value	Dividend per share per period	Periods of dividends passed
A	Cumulative	$ 80	$5	2
B	Noncumulative	110	8%	3
C	Noncumulative	100	$11	1
D	Cumulative	60	8.5%	4
E	Cumulative	90	9%	0

LG2 7–4 **Convertible preferred stock** Valerian Corp. convertible preferred stock has a fixed conversion ratio of 5 common shares per 1 share of preferred stock. The preferred stock pays a dividend of $10.00 per share per year. The common stock currently sells for $20.00 per share and pays a dividend of $1.00 per share per year.

a. Judging on the basis of the conversion ratio and the price of the common shares, what is the current conversion value of each preferred share?

b. If the preferred shares are selling at $96.00 each, should an investor convert the preferred shares to common shares?

c. What factors might cause an investor not to convert from preferred to common?

LG2 **7–5 Stock quotation** Assume that the following quote for the Advanced Business Machines stock (traded on the NYSE) was found in the Thursday, December 14, issue of the *Wall Street Journal.*

+3.2 84.13 51.25 AdvBusMach ABM 1.32 1.6 23 12432 81.75 +1.63

Given this information, answer the following questions:

a. On what day did the trading activity occur?

b. At what price did the stock sell at the end of the day on Wednesday, December 13?

c. What percentage change has occurred in the stock's last price since the beginning of the calendar year?

d. What is the firm's price/earnings ratio? What does it indicate?

e. What is the last price at which the stock traded on the day quoted?

f. How large a dividend is expected in the current year?

g. What are the highest and the lowest price at which the stock traded during the latest 52-week period?

h. How many shares of stock were traded on the day quoted?

i. How much, if any, of a change in stock price took place between the day quoted and the day before? At what price did the stock close on the day before?

LG4 **7–6 Common stock valuation—Zero growth** Scotto Manufacturing is a mature firm in the machine tool component industry. The firm's most recent common stock dividend was $2.40 per share. Because of its maturity as well as its stable sales and earnings, the firm's management feels that dividends will remain at the current level for the foreseeable future.

a. If the required return is 12%, what will be the value of Scotto's common stock?

b. If the firm's risk as perceived by market participants suddenly increases, causing the required return to rise to 20%, what will be the common stock value?

c. Judging on the basis of your findings in parts **a** and **b,** what impact does risk have on value? Explain.

LG4 **7–7 Common stock value—Zero growth** Kelsey Drums, Inc., is a well-established supplier of fine percussion instruments to orchestras all over the United States. The company's class A common stock has paid a dividend of $5.00 per share per year for the last 15 years. Management expects to continue to pay at that rate for the foreseeable future. Sally Talbot purchased 100 shares of Kelsey class A common 10 years ago at a time when the required rate of return for the stock was 16%. She wants to sell her shares today. The current required rate of return for the stock is 12%. How much capital gain or loss will she have on her shares?

LG4 **7–8 Preferred stock valuation** Jones Design wishes to estimate the value of its outstanding preferred stock. The preferred issue has an $80 par value and pays an annual dividend of $6.40 per share. Similar-risk preferred stocks are currently earning a 9.3% annual rate of return.

a. What is the market value of the outstanding preferred stock?

b. If an investor purchases the preferred stock at the value calculated in part **a,** how much does she gain or lose per share if she sells the stock when the required return on similar-risk preferreds has risen to 10.5%? Explain.

LG4 **7–9 Common stock value—Constant growth** Use the constant-growth model (Gordon model) to find the value of each firm shown in the following table.

Firm	Dividend expected next year	Dividend growth rate	Required return
A	$1.20	8%	13%
B	4.00	5	15
C	0.65	10	14
D	6.00	8	9
E	2.25	8	20

LG4 **7–10 Common stock value—Constant growth** McCracken Roofing, Inc., common stock paid a dividend of $1.20 per share last year. The company expects earnings and dividends to grow at a rate of 5% per year for the foreseeable future.

a. What required rate of return for this stock would result in a price per share of $28?

b. If McCracken had both earnings growth and dividend growth at a rate of 10%, what required rate of return would result in a price per share of $28?

LG4 **7–11 Common stock value—Constant growth** Elk County Telephone has paid the dividends shown in the following table over the past 6 years.

Year	Dividend per share
2003	$2.87
2002	2.76
2001	2.60
2000	2.46
1999	2.37
1998	2.25

The firm's dividend per share next year is expected to be $3.02.

a. If you can earn 13% on similar-risk investments, what is the most you would be willing to pay per share?

b. If you can earn only 10% on similar-risk investments, what is the most you would be willing to pay per share?

c. Compare and contrast your findings in parts **a** and **b**, and discuss the impact of changing risk on share value.

LG4 **7–12 Common stock value—Both growth models** You are evaluating the potential purchase of a small business currently generating $42,500 of after-tax cash flow ($D_0 = \$42,500$). On the basis of a review of similar-risk investment opportunities, you must earn an 18% rate of return on the proposed purchase. Because you are relatively uncertain about future cash flows, you decide to estimate the firm's value using two possible assumptions about the growth rate of cash flows.

a. What is the firm's value if cash flows are expected to grow at an annual rate of 0% from now to infinity?

b. What is the firm's value if cash flows are expected to grow at a constant annual rate of 7% from now to infinity?

LG5 **7–13 Free cash flow valuation** Nabor Industries is considering going public but is unsure of a fair offering price for the company. Before hiring an investment banker to assist in making the public offering, managers at Nabor have decided to make their own estimate of the firm's common stock value. The firm's CFO has gathered data for performing the valuation using the free cash flow valuation model.

The firm's weighted average cost of capital is 11%, and it has $1,500,000 of debt at market value and $400,000 of preferred stock at its assumed market value. The estimated free cash flows over the next 5 years, 2004 through 2008, are given below. Beyond 2008 to infinity, the firm expects its free cash flow to grow by 3% annually.

Year (t)	Free cash flow (FCF_t)
2004	$200,000
2005	250,000
2006	310,000
2007	350,000
2008	390,000

a. Estimate the value of Nabor Industries' entire company by using the *free cash flow valuation model.*

b. Use your finding in part **a**, along with the data provided above, to find Nabor Industries' common stock value.

c. If the firm plans to issue 200,000 shares of common sock, what is its estimated value per share?

LG5 **7–14 Using the free cash flow valuation model to price an IPO** Assume that you have an opportunity to buy the stock of CoolTech, Inc., an IPO being offered for $12.50 per share. Although you are very much interested in owning the company, you are concerned about whether it is fairly priced. In order to determine the value of the shares, you have decided to apply the free cash flow valuation model to the firm's financial data that you've developed from a variety of data sources. The key values you have compiled are summarized in the following table.

Free cash flow		
Year (t)	FCF_t	Other data
2004	$ 700,000	Growth rate of FCF, beyond 2007 to infinity = 2%
2005	800,000	Weighted average cost of capital = 8%
2006	950,000	Market value of all debt = $2,700,000
2007	1,100,000	Market value of preferred stock = $1,000,000
		Number of shares of common stock outstanding = 1,100,000

a. Use the *free cash flow valuation model* to estimate CoolTech's common stock value per share.

b. Judging on the basis of your finding in part **a** and the stock's offering price, should you buy the stock?

c. Upon further analysis, you find that the growth rate in FCF beyond 2007 will be 3% rather than 2%. What effect would this finding have on your responses in parts **a** and **b**?

LG5 7–15 **Book and liquidation value** The balance sheet for Gallinas Industries is as follows.

Gallinas Industries
Balance Sheet
December 31

Assets		Liabilities and Stockholders' Equity	
Cash	$ 40,000	Accounts payable	$100,000
Marketable securities	60,000	Notes payable	30,000
Accounts receivable	120,000	Accrued wages	30,000
Inventories	160,000	Total current liabilities	$160,000
Total current assets	$380,000	Long-term debt	$180,000
Land and buildings (net)	$150,000	Preferred stock	$ 80,000
Machinery and equipment	250,000	Common stock (10,000 shares)	360,000
Total fixed assets (net)	$400,000	Total liabilities and stockholders' equity	$780,000
Total assets	$780,000		

Additional information with respect to the firm is available:
(1) Preferred stock can be liquidated at book value.
(2) Accounts receivable and inventories can be liquidated at 90% of book value.
(3) The firm has 10,000 shares of common stock outstanding.
(4) All interest and dividends are currently paid up.
(5) Land and buildings can be liquidated at 130% of book value.
(6) Machinery and equipment can be liquidated at 70% of book value.
(7) Cash and marketable securities can be liquidated at book value.

Given this information, answer the following:
a. What is Gallinas Industries' book value per share?
b. What is its liquidation value per share?
c. Compare, contrast, and discuss the values found in parts **a** and **b**.

LG5 7–16 **Valuation with price/earnings multiples** For each of the firms shown in the following table, use the data given to estimate their common stock value employing price/earnings (P/E) multiples.

Firm	Expected EPS	Price/earnings multiple
A	$3.00	6.2
B	4.50	10.0
C	1.80	12.6
D	2.40	8.9
E	5.10	15.0

LG6 **7–17 Management action and stock value** REH Corporation's most recent dividend was $3 per share, its expected annual rate of dividend growth is 5%, and the required return is now 15%. A variety of proposals are being considered by management to redirect the firm's activities. Determine the impact on share price for each of the following proposed actions, and indicate the best alternative.

a. Do nothing, which will leave the key financial variables unchanged.
b. Invest in a new machine that will increase the dividend growth rate to 6% and lower the required return to 14%.
c. Eliminate an unprofitable product line, which will increase the dividend growth rate to 7% and raise the required return to 17%.
d. Merge with another firm, which will reduce the growth rate to 4% and raise the required return to 16%.
e. Acquire a subsidiary operation from another manufacturer. The acquisition should increase the dividend growth rate to 8% and increase the required return to 17%.

LG4 LG6 **7–18 Integrative—Valuation and CAPM formulas** Given the following information for the stock of Foster Company, calculate its beta.

Current price per share of common	$50.00
Expected dividend per share next year	$ 3.00
Constant annual dividend growth rate	9%
Risk-free rate of return	7%
Return on market portfolio	10%

LG4 LG6 **7–19 Integrative—Risk and valuation** Giant Enterprises has a beta of 1.20, the risk-free rate of return is currently 10%, and the market return is 14%. The company, which plans to pay a dividend of $2.60 per share in the coming year, anticipates that its future dividends will increase at an annual rate consistent with that experienced over the 1997–2003 period, when the following dividends were paid:

Year	Dividend per share
2003	$2.45
2002	2.28
2001	2.10
2000	1.95
1999	1.82
1998	1.80
1997	1.73

a. Use the capital asset pricing model (CAPM) to determine the required return on Giant's stock.
b. Using the constant-growth model and your finding in part **a**, estimate the value of Giant's stock.
c. Explain what effect, if any, a decrease in beta would have on the value of Giant's stock.

LG4 LG6 **7–20 Integrative—Valuation and CAPM** Hamlin Steel Company wishes to determine the value of Craft Foundry, a firm that it is considering acquiring for cash. Hamlin wishes to use the capital asset pricing model (CAPM) to determine the applicable discount rate to use as an input to the constant-growth valuation model. Craft's stock is not publicly traded. After studying the betas of firms similar to Craft that are publicly traded, Hamlin believes that an appropriate beta for Craft's stock would be 1.25. The risk-free rate is currently 9%, and the market return is 13%. Craft's dividend per share for each of the past 6 years is shown in the following table.

Year	Dividend per share
2003	$3.44
2002	3.28
2001	3.15
2000	2.90
1999	2.75
1998	2.45

a. Given that Craft is expected to pay a dividend of $3.68 next year, determine the maximum cash price that Hamlin should pay for each share of Craft.

b. Discuss the use of the CAPM for estimating the value of common stock, and describe the effect on the resulting value of Craft of:
(1) A decrease in its dividend growth rate of 2% from that exhibited over the 1998–2003 period.
(2) A decrease in its beta to 1.

CHAPTER 7 CASE Assessing the Impact of Suarez Manufacturing's Proposed Risky Investment on Its Stock Value

Early in 2004, Inez Marcus, the chief financial officer for Suarez Manufacturing, was given the task of assessing the impact of a proposed risky investment on the firm's stock value. To perform the necessary analysis, Inez gathered the following information on the firm's stock.

During the immediate past 5 years (1999–2003), the annual dividends paid on the firm's common stock were as follows:

Year	Dividend per share
2003	$1.90
2002	1.70
2001	1.55
2000	1.40
1999	1.30

The firm expects that without the proposed investment, the dividend in 2004 will be $2.09 per share and the historical annual rate of growth (rounded to the nearest whole percent) will continue in the future. Currently, the required return on the common stock is 14%. Inez's research indicates that if the proposed investment is undertaken, the 2004 dividend will rise to $2.15 per share and the annual rate of dividend growth will increase to 13%. As a result of the increased risk associated with the proposed risky investment, the required return on the common stock is expected to increase by 2% to an annual rate of 16%.

Armed with the preceding information, Inez must now assess the impact of the proposed risky investment on the market value of Suarez's stock. To simplify her calculations, she plans to round the historical growth rate in common stock dividends to the nearest whole percent.

Required

a. Find the *current* value per share of Suarez Manufacturing's common stock.

b. Find the value of Suarez's common stock in the event that it *undertakes the proposed risky investment* and assuming that the dividend growth rate stays at 13% forever. Compare this value to that found in part **a**. What effect would the proposed investment have on the firm's stockholders? Explain.

c. On the basis of your findings in part **b**, do the stockholders win or lose as a result of undertaking the proposed risky investment? Should the firm do it? Why?

WEB EXERCISE

To use the price/earnings multiples approach to valuation, you need to find a firm's projected earnings and the P/E multiple. One of the most popular sites to obtain these estimates is Zacks Investment Research, *www.zacks.com*.

1. At the top of the page, locate the area where you can enter a company's ticker symbol and select the desired information.
2. Enter OO for Oakley Inc. and select **estimates** from the pull-down menu.
   - **a.** What is the current mean/consensus estimate for the next fiscal year's earnings?
   - **b.** Using the indicated price/earnings ratio further down on that page, calculate the stock price.
3. Repeat steps **2a** and **b** for the following stocks:
   - **a.** Southwest Airlines: LUV
   - **b.** Microsoft: MSFT
   - **c.** Weight Watchers: WTW

Remember to check the book's Web site at

www.aw.com/gitman

for additional resources, including additional Web exercises.

Part 3

Long-Term Investment Decisions

Chapter

8

Capital Budgeting Cash Flows

LEARNING GOALS

- LG1 Understand the key motives for capital expenditure and the steps in the capital budgeting process.
- LG2 Define basic capital budgeting terminology.
- LG3 Discuss the major components of relevant cash flows, expansion versus replacement cash flows, sunk costs and opportunity costs, and international capital budgeting and long-term investments.
- LG4 Calculate the initial investment associated with a proposed capital expenditure.
- LG5 Determine relevant operating cash inflows using the income statement format.
- LG6 Find the terminal cash flow.

Across the Disciplines
Why This Chapter Matters To You

Accounting: You need to understand capital budgeting cash flows in order to provide revenue, cost, depreciation, and tax data for use both in monitoring existing projects and in developing cash flows for proposed projects.

Information systems: You need to understand capital budgeting cash flows in order to maintain and facilitate the retrieval of cash flow data for both completed and existing projects.

Management: You need to understand capital budgeting cash flows so that you will understand what cash flows are relevant in making decisions about proposals for acquiring additional production facilities, for new products, and for the expansion of existing product lines.

Marketing: You need to understand capital budgeting cash flows so that you can make revenue estimates for proposals for new marketing programs, for new products, and for the expansion of existing product lines.

Operations: You need to understand capital budgeting cash flows so that you can make cost estimates for proposals for the acquisition of new equipment and production facilities.

Before committing resources to expand, replace, or renew fixed assets or to undertake other types of long-term investments, firms carefully estimate and analyze the expected costs and benefits associated with these expenditures. This evaluation and selection process is called capital budgeting. We address this important topic in finance in two chapters. This chapter describes important aspects of the steps in the capital budgeting decision process and explains how the key cash flows that are inputs to it are developed.

LG1 LG2

The Capital Budgeting Decision Process

Long-term investments represent sizable outlays of funds that commit a firm to some course of action. Consequently, the firm needs procedures to analyze and properly select its long-term investments. It must be able to measure cash flows and apply appropriate decision techniques. As time passes, fixed assets may become obsolete or may require an overhaul; at these points, too, financial decisions may be required. **Capital budgeting** is the process of evaluating and selecting long-term investments that are consistent with the firm's goal of maximizing owner wealth. Firms typically make a variety of long-term investments, but the most common for the manufacturing firm is in *fixed assets,* which include property (land), plant, and equipment. These assets, often referred to as *earning assets,* generally provide the basis for the firm's earning power and value.

capital budgeting
The process of evaluating and selecting long-term investments that are consistent with the firm's goal of maximizing owner wealth.

Because firms treat capital budgeting (investment) and financing decisions *separately,* both this and the following chapter concentrate on fixed-asset acquisition without regard to the specific method of financing used. We begin by discussing the motives for capital expenditure.

Motives for Capital Expenditure

A **capital expenditure** is an outlay of funds by the firm that is expected to produce benefits over a period of time *greater than* 1 year. An **operating expenditure** is an outlay resulting in benefits received *within* 1 year. Fixed-asset outlays are capital expenditures, but not all capital expenditures are classified as fixed assets. A $60,000 outlay for a new machine with a usable life of 15 years is a capital expenditure that would appear as a fixed asset on the firm's balance sheet. A $60,000 outlay for advertising that produces benefits over a long period is also a capital expenditure, but would rarely be shown as a fixed asset.

capital expenditure
An outlay of funds by the firm that is expected to produce benefits over a period of time *greater than* 1 year.

operating expenditure
An outlay of funds by the firm resulting in benefits received *within* 1 year.

Capital expenditures are made for many reasons. The basic motives for capital expenditures are to expand, replace, or renew fixed assets or to obtain some other, less tangible benefit over a long period. Table 8.1 briefly describes the key motives for making capital expenditures.

Steps in the Process

The **capital budgeting process** consists of five distinct but interrelated steps.

capital budgeting process
Five distinct but interrelated steps: *proposal generation, review and analysis, decision making, implementation,* and *follow-up.*

1. *Proposal generation.* Proposals are made at all levels within a business organization and are reviewed by finance personnel. Proposals that require large outlays are more carefully scrutinized than less costly ones.

TABLE 8.1 Key Motives for Making Capital Expenditures

Motive	Description
Expansion	The most common motive for a capital expenditure is to expand the level of operations—usually through acquisition of fixed assets. A growing firm often needs to acquire new fixed assets rapidly, as in the purchase of property and plant facilities.
Replacement	As a firm's growth slows and it reaches maturity, most capital expenditures will be made to replace or renew obsolete or worn-out assets. Each time a machine requires a major repair, the outlay for the repair should be compared to the outlay to replace the machine and the benefits of replacement.
Renewal	Renewal, an alternative to replacement, may involve rebuilding, overhauling, or retrofitting an existing fixed asset. For example, an existing drill press could be renewed by replacing its motor and adding a numeric control system, or a physical facility could be renewed by rewiring and adding air conditioning. To improve efficiency, both replacement and renewal of existing machinery may be suitable solutions.
Other purposes	Some capital expenditures do not result in the acquisition or transformation of tangible fixed assets. Instead, they involve a long-term commitment of funds in expectation of a future return. These expenditures include outlays for advertising, research and development, management consulting, and new products. Other capital expenditure proposals—such as the installation of pollution-control and safety devices mandated by the government—are difficult to evaluate because they provide intangible returns rather than clearly measurable cash flows.

2. *Review and analysis.* Formal review and analysis is performed to assess the appropriateness of proposals and evaluate their economic viability. Once the analysis is complete, a summary report is submitted to decision makers.
3. *Decision making.* Firms typically delegate capital expenditure decision making on the basis of dollar limits. Generally, the board of directors must authorize expenditures beyond a certain amount. Often plant managers are given authority to make decisions necessary to keep the production line moving.
4. *Implementation.* Following approval, expenditures are made and projects implemented. Expenditures for a large project often occur in phases.
5. *Follow-up.* Results are monitored, and actual costs and benefits are compared with those that were expected. Action may be required if actual outcomes differ from projected ones.

Each step in the process is important. Review and analysis and decision making (Steps 2 and 3) consume the majority of time and effort, however. Follow-up (Step 5) is an important but often ignored step aimed at allowing the firm to improve the accuracy of its cash flow estimates continuously. Because of their fundamental importance, this and the following chapters give primary consideration to review and analysis and to decision making.

Basic Terminology

Before we develop the concepts, techniques, and practices related to the capital budgeting process, we need to explain some basic terminology. In addition, we will present some key assumptions that are used to simplify the discussion in the remainder of this chapter and in Chapter 9.

Independent versus Mutually Exclusive Projects

independent projects
Projects whose cash flows are unrelated or independent of one another; the acceptance of one *does not eliminate* the others from further consideration.

mutually exclusive projects
Projects that compete with one another, so that the acceptance of one *eliminates* from further consideration all other projects that serve a similar function.

The two most common types of projects are (1) independent projects and (2) mutually exclusive projects. **Independent projects** are those whose cash flows are unrelated or independent of one another; the acceptance of one *does not eliminate* the others from further consideration. **Mutually exclusive projects** are those that have the same function and therefore compete with one another. The acceptance of one *eliminates* from further consideration all other projects that serve a similar function. For example, a firm in need of increased production capacity could obtain it by (1) expanding its plant, (2) acquiring another company, or (3) contracting with another company for production. Clearly, accepting any one option eliminates the need for either of the others.

Unlimited Funds versus Capital Rationing

unlimited funds
The financial situation in which a firm is able to accept all independent projects that provide an acceptable return.

capital rationing
The financial situation in which a firm has only a fixed number of dollars available for capital expenditures, and numerous projects compete for these dollars.

The availability of funds for capital expenditures affects the firm's decisions. If a firm has **unlimited funds** for investment, making capital budgeting decisions is quite simple: All independent projects that will provide an acceptable return can be accepted. Typically, though, firms operate under **capital rationing** instead. This means that they have only a fixed number of dollars available for capital expenditures and that numerous projects will compete for these dollars. Procedures for dealing with capital rationing are presented in Chapter 9. The discussions that follow in this chapter assume unlimited funds.

Accept–Reject versus Ranking Approaches

accept–reject approach
The evaluation of capital expenditure proposals to determine whether they meet the firm's minimum acceptance criterion.

ranking approach
The ranking of capital expenditure projects on the basis of some predetermined measure, such as the rate of return.

Two basic approaches to capital budgeting decisions are available. The **accept–reject approach** involves evaluating capital expenditure proposals to determine whether they meet the firm's minimum acceptance criterion. This approach can be used when the firm has unlimited funds, as a preliminary step when evaluating mutually exclusive projects, or in a situation in which capital must be rationed. In these cases, only acceptable projects should be considered.

The second method, the **ranking approach**, involves ranking projects on the basis of some predetermined measure, such as the rate of return. The project with the highest return is ranked first, and the project with the lowest return is ranked last. Only acceptable projects should be ranked. Ranking is useful in selecting the "best" of a group of mutually exclusive projects and in evaluating projects with a view to capital rationing.

Conventional versus Nonconventional Cash Flow Patterns

conventional cash flow pattern
An initial outflow followed only by a series of inflows.

Cash flow patterns associated with capital investment projects can be classified as *conventional* or *nonconventional*. A **conventional cash flow pattern** consists of an initial outflow followed only by a series of inflows. For example, a firm may

FIGURE 8.1

Conventional Cash Flow
Time line for a conventional cash flow pattern

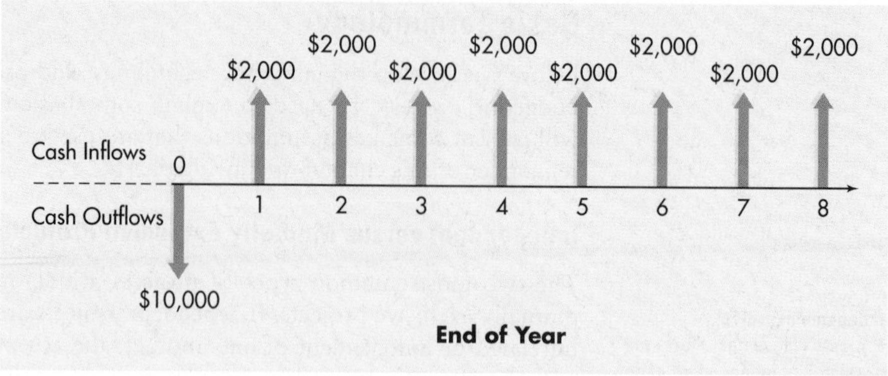

spend $10,000 today and as a result expect to receive equal annual cash inflows (an annuity) of $2,000 each year for the next 8 years, as depicted on the time line in Figure 8.1.[1] A conventional cash flow pattern that provides unequal annual cash inflows is depicted in Figure 8.3 on page 310.

nonconventional cash flow pattern
An initial outflow followed by a series of inflows *and* outflows.

A **nonconventional cash flow pattern** is one in which an initial outflow is followed by a series of inflows *and* outflows. For example, the purchase of a machine may require an initial cash outflow of $20,000 and may generate cash inflows of $5,000 each year for 4 years. In the fifth year after purchase, an outflow of $8,000 may be required to overhaul the machine, after which it generates inflows of $5,000 each year for 5 more years. This nonconventional pattern is illustrated on the time line in Figure 8.2.

Difficulties often arise in evaluating projects with nonconventional patterns of cash flow. *The discussions in the remainder of this chapter and in Chapter 9 are therefore limited to the evaluation of conventional cash flow patterns.*

FIGURE 8.2

Nonconventional Cash Flow
Time line for a nonconventional cash flow pattern

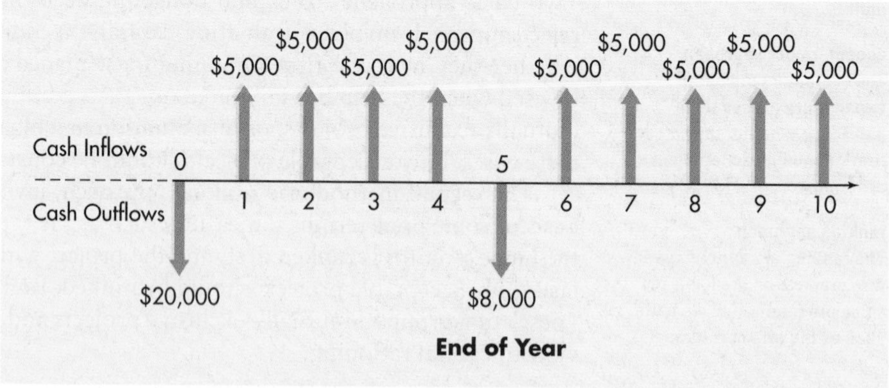

1. Arrows rather than plus or minus signs are frequently used on time lines to distinguish between cash inflows and cash outflows. Upward-pointing arrows represent cash inflows (positive cash flows), and downward-pointing arrows represent cash outflows (negative cash flows).

Review Questions

8–1 What is *capital budgeting?* Do all capital expenditures involve fixed assets? Explain.

8–2 What are the key motives for making capital expenditures? Discuss, compare, and contrast them.

8–3 What are the five steps involved in the capital budgeting process?

8–4 Differentiate between the members of each of the following pairs of capital budgeting terms: (**a**) independent versus mutually exclusive projects; (**b**) unlimited funds versus capital rationing; (**c**) accept–reject versus ranking approaches; and (**d**) conventional versus nonconventional cash flow patterns.

LG3

The Relevant Cash Flows

relevant cash flows
The *incremental cash outflow (investment) and resulting subsequent inflows* associated with a proposed capital expenditure.

incremental cash flows
The *additional* cash flows—outflows or inflows—expected to result from a proposed capital expenditure.

To evaluate capital expenditure alternatives, the firm must determine the **relevant cash flows.** These are the *incremental cash outflow (investment) and resulting subsequent inflows.* The **incremental cash flows** represent the *additional* cash flows—outflows or inflows—expected to result from a proposed capital expenditure. As noted in Chapter 3, cash flows rather than accounting figures are used, because cash flows directly affect the firm's ability to pay bills and purchase assets. The remainder of this chapter is devoted to the procedures for measuring the relevant cash flows associated with proposed capital expenditures.

Major Cash Flow Components

initial investment
The relevant cash outflow for a proposed project at time zero.

operating cash inflows
The incremental after-tax cash inflows resulting from implementation of a project during its life.

terminal cash flow
The after-tax nonoperating cash flow occurring in the final year of a project. It is usually attributable to liquidation of the project.

The cash flows of any project having the *conventional pattern* can include three basic components: (1) an initial investment, (2) operating cash inflows, and (3) terminal cash flow. All projects—whether for expansion, replacement, renewal, or some other purpose—have the first two components. Some, however, lack the final component, terminal cash flow.

Figure 8.3 depicts on a time line the cash flows for a project. The **initial investment** for the proposed project is $50,000. This is the relevant cash outflow at time zero. The **operating cash inflows,** which are the incremental after-tax cash inflows resulting from implementation of the project during its life, gradually increase from $4,000 in its first year to $10,000 in its tenth and final year. The **terminal cash flow** is the after-tax nonoperating cash flow occurring in the final year of the project. It is usually attributable to liquidation of the project. In this case it is $25,000, received at the end of the project's 10-year life. Note that the terminal cash flow does *not* include the $10,000 operating cash inflow for year 10.

Expansion versus Replacement Cash Flows

Developing relevant cash flow estimates is most straightforward in the case of *expansion decisions.* In this case, the initial investment, operating cash inflows, and terminal cash flow are merely the after-tax cash outflow and inflows associated with the proposed capital expenditure.

FIGURE 8.3

Cash Flow Components
Time line for major cash flow components

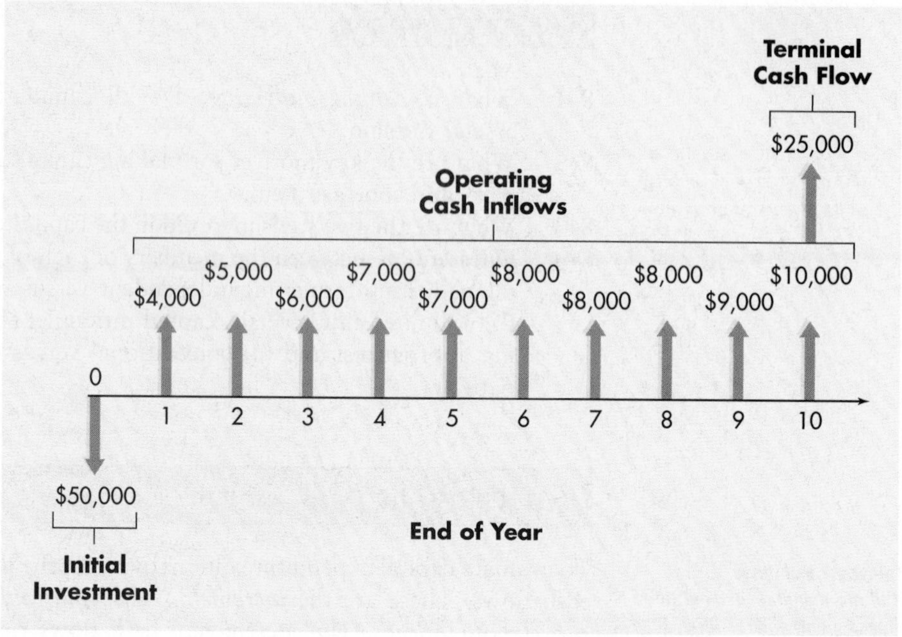

Identifying relevant cash flows for *replacement decisions* is more complicated, because the firm must identify the *incremental* cash outflow and inflows that would result from the proposed replacement. The initial investment in the case of replacement is the difference between the initial investment needed to acquire the new asset and any after-tax cash inflows expected from liquidation of the old asset. The operating cash inflows are the difference between the operating cash inflows from the new asset and those from the old asset. The terminal cash flow is the difference between the after-tax cash flows expected upon termination of the new and the old assets. These relationships are shown in Figure 8.4.

FIGURE 8.4

Relevant Cash Flows for Replacement Decisions
Calculation of the three components of relevant cash flow for a replacement decision

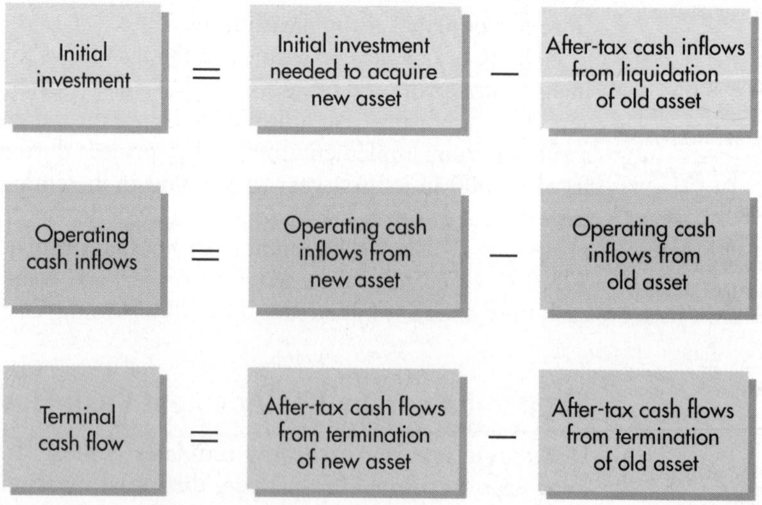

In Practice

FOCUS ON e-FINANCE **Chipping Away at E-Business Investment Analysis**

It should come as no surprise that Intel, the world's largest chip maker and technology pioneer, is also a leader in e-business. Chairman Andy Grove decided in 1998 that Intel would transform itself into a "100 percent e-corporation." Since then, each of the company's new business applications has been based on the Internet or on e-commerce. Leading the Internet initiative was CFO Andy Bryant, whose responsibilities were expanded to include enterprise services.

Bryant was an unlikely choice to lead the company's transformation, because he was skeptical about the value of e-commerce. He quickly changed his tune when he learned that Intel receives over one-quarter of its orders after hours. The flexibility of online ordering added value for customers. Intel has launched more than 300 e-business projects since 1998. In 2001, the company generated 90 percent of its revenue—$31.4 billion—from e-commerce transactions.

Ironically, Bryant's skepticism about e-commerce turned out to be a good thing. He developed methods to analyze e-business proposals to make sure they added value to the company, applying rigorous financial discipline and monitoring returns on investment. "Every project has an ROI," Bryant says. "It isn't always positive, but you still have to measure what you put in and what you get back."

The difficulty comes in deciding what to measure—and how. Like most companies, Intel already had expertise in evaluating new manufacturing facilities and other capital projects. But technology projects also have intangible benefits that aren't easily quantified. One of Bryant's challenges was formalizing financial accountability for e-business applications.

The company's track record has been quite good so far. E-business projects have reduced costs in many areas. For example, an electronic accounts payable (A/P) system was devised to take over many routine transactions so that employees could focus on analysis. Bryant estimates that the present value of this project's cash inflows, less the initial investment, is $8 million. And the company no longer misses opportunities to take advantage of discounts for prompt payments.

Like Intel, every firm must evaluate the costs and returns of projects for expansion, asset replacement or renewal, research and development, advertising, and other areas that require long-term commitments of funds in expectation of future returns. The first step in evaluating projects involves the identification of the relevant cash outflows and inflows that must be considered in making the investment decision.

Sources: Annual Report 2000, Intel Corporation, downloaded from *www.intel.com;* Shari Caudron, "The Tao of E-Business," *Business Finance,* September 2001, downloaded from *www. businessfinance.com;* and Tim Reason, "How E-Business Transformed Intel and CFO Andy Bryant," *CFO,* October 2001, downloaded from *www.cfo.com.*

Actually, all capital budgeting decisions can be viewed as replacement decisions. Expansion decisions are merely replacement decisions in which all cash flows from the old asset are zero. In light of this fact, this chapter focuses primarily on replacement decisions.

Sunk Costs and Opportunity Costs

sunk costs
Cash outlays that have already been made (past outlays) and therefore have no effect on the cash flows relevant to a current decision.

When estimating the relevant cash flows associated with a proposed capital expenditure, the firm must recognize any *sunk costs* and *opportunity costs.* These costs are easy to mishandle or ignore, particularly when determining a project's incremental cash flows. **Sunk costs** are cash outlays that have already been made (past outlays) and therefore have no effect on the cash flows relevant to the current decision. As a result, *sunk costs should not be included in a project's incremental cash flows.*

opportunity costs
Cash flows that could be realized from the best alternative use of an owned asset.

Opportunity costs are cash flows that could be realized from the best alternative use of an owned asset. They therefore represent cash flows that will *not be realized* as a result of employing that asset in the proposed project. Because of this, any *opportunity costs should be included as cash outflows when one is determining a project's incremental cash flows.*

EXAMPLE

Jankow Equipment is considering renewing its drill press X12, which it purchased 3 years earlier for $237,000, by retrofitting it with the computerized control system from an obsolete piece of equipment it owns. The obsolete equipment could be sold today for a high bid of $42,000, but without its computerized control system, it would be worth nothing. Jankow is in the process of estimating the labor and materials costs of retrofitting the system to drill press X12 and the benefits expected from the retrofit. The $237,000 cost of drill press X12 is a *sunk cost* because it represents an earlier cash outlay. It *would not be included* as a cash outflow when determining the cash flows relevant to the retrofit decision. Although Jankow owns the obsolete piece of equipment, the proposed use of its computerized control system represents an *opportunity cost* of $42,000—the highest price at which it could be sold today. This opportunity cost *would be included* as a cash outflow associated with using the computerized control system.

International Capital Budgeting and Long-Term Investments

Although the same basic capital budgeting principles are used for domestic and international projects, several additional factors must be addressed in evaluating foreign investment opportunities. International capital budgeting differs from the domestic version because (1) cash outflows and inflows occur in a foreign currency, and (2) foreign investments entail potentially significant political risk. Both of these risks can be minimized through careful planning.

Companies face both long-term and short-term *currency risks* related to both the invested capital and the cash flows resulting from it. Long-term currency risk can be minimized by financing the foreign investment at least partly in the local capital markets rather than with dollar-denominated capital from the parent company. This step ensures that the project's revenues, operating costs, and financing costs will be in the local currency. Likewise, the dollar value of short-term, local-currency cash flows can be protected by using special securities and strategies such as futures, forwards, and options market instruments.

Political risks can be minimized by using both operating and financial strategies. For example, by structuring the investment as a joint venture and selecting a well-connected local partner, the U.S. company can minimize the risk of its operations being seized or harassed. Companies also can protect themselves from having their investment returns blocked by local governments by structuring the financing of such investments as debt rather than as equity. Debt-service payments are legally enforceable claims, whereas equity returns (such as dividends) are not. Even if local courts do not support the claims of the U.S. company, the company can threaten to pursue its case in U.S. courts.

foreign direct investment
The transfer of capital, managerial, and technical assets to a foreign country.

In spite of the preceding difficulties, **foreign direct investment,** which involves the transfer of capital, managerial, and technical assets to a foreign country, has surged in recent years. This is evident in the growing market values of foreign assets owned by U.S.-based companies and of foreign direct investment in the United States, particularly by British, Canadian, Dutch, German, and Japanese companies. Furthermore, foreign direct investment by U.S. companies seems to be accelerating.

Review Questions

8–5 Why is it important to evaluate capital budgeting projects on the basis of *incremental cash flows?*

8–6 What three components of cash flow may exist for a given project? How can expansion decisions be treated as replacement decisions? Explain.

8–7 What effect do *sunk costs* and *opportunity costs* have on a project's incremental cash flows?

8–8 How can *currency risk* and *political risk* be minimized when one is making *foreign direct investment?*

LG4

Finding the Initial Investment

The term *initial investment* as used here refers to the relevant cash outflows to be considered when evaluating a prospective capital expenditure. Because our discussion of capital budgeting is concerned only with investments that exhibit conventional cash flows, the initial investment occurs at *time zero*—the time at which the expenditure is made. The initial investment is calculated by subtracting all cash inflows occurring at time zero from all cash outflows occurring at time zero.

The basic format for determining the initial investment is given in Table 8.2. The cash flows that must be considered when determining the initial investment associated with a capital expenditure are the installed cost of the new asset, the after-tax proceeds (if any) from the sale of an old asset, and the change (if any) in net working capital. Note that if there are no installation costs and the firm is not

TABLE 8.2 The Basic Format for Determining Initial Investment

	Installed cost of new asset =
	Cost of new asset
	+ Installation costs
−	**After-tax proceeds from sale of old asset =**
	Proceeds from sale of old asset
	∓ Tax on sale of old asset
±	**Change in net working capital**
	Initial investment

replacing an existing asset, then the purchase price of the asset, adjusted for any change in net working capital, is equal to the initial investment.

Installed Cost of New Asset

cost of new asset
The net outflow necessary to acquire a new asset.

installation costs
Any added costs that are necessary to place an asset into operation.

installed cost of new asset
The cost of the asset plus its installation costs; equals the asset's depreciable value.

As shown in Table 8.2, the installed cost of the new asset is found by adding the cost of the new asset to its installation costs. The **cost of new asset** is the net outflow that its acquisition requires. Usually, we are concerned with the acquisition of a fixed asset for which a definite purchase price is paid. **Installation costs** are any added costs that are necessary to place an asset into operation. The Internal Revenue Service (IRS) requires the firm to add installation costs to the purchase price of an asset to determine its depreciable value, which is expensed over a period of years. The **installed cost of new asset,** calculated by adding the cost of the asset to its installation costs, equals its depreciable value.

After-Tax Proceeds from Sale of Old Asset

after-tax proceeds from sale of old asset
The difference between the old asset's sale proceeds and any applicable taxes or tax refunds related to its sale.

proceeds from sale of old asset
The cash inflows, net of any *removal* or *cleanup costs,* resulting from the sale of an existing asset.

tax on sale of old asset
Tax that depends on the relationship among the old asset's sale price, initial purchase price, and *book value,* and on existing government tax rules.

Table 8.2 shows that the **after-tax proceeds from sale of old asset** decrease the firm's initial investment in the new asset. These proceeds are the difference between the old asset's sale proceeds and any applicable taxes or tax refunds related to its sale. The **proceeds from sale of old asset** are the net cash inflows it provides. This amount is net of any costs incurred in the process of removing the asset. Included in these *removal costs* are *cleanup costs,* such as those related to removal and disposal of chemical and nuclear wastes. These costs may not be trivial.

The proceeds from the sale of an old asset are normally subject to some type of tax.[2] This **tax on sale of old asset** depends on the relationship among its sale price, initial purchase price, and *book value,* and on existing government tax rules.

Book Value

book value
The strict accounting value of an asset, calculated by subtracting its accumulated depreciation from its installed cost.

The **book value** of an asset is its strict accounting value. It can be calculated by using the following equation:

$$\text{Book value} = \text{Installed cost of asset} - \text{Accumulated depreciation} \quad (8.1)$$

EXAMPLE

Hudson Industries, a small electronics company, 2 years ago acquired a machine tool with an installed cost of \$100,000. The asset was being depreciated under MACRS using a 5-year recovery period.[3] Table 3.2 (page 89) shows that under MACRS for a 5-year recovery period, 20% and 32% of the installed cost would be depreciated in years 1 and 2, respectively. In other words, 52% (20% + 32%)

2. A brief discussion of the tax treatment of ordinary and capital gains income was presented in Chapter 1.

3. For a review of MACRS, see Chapter 3. Under current tax law, most manufacturing equipment has a 7-year recovery period, as noted in Table 3.1. Using this recovery period results in 8 years of depreciation, which unnecessarily complicates examples and problems. To simplify, *manufacturing equipment is treated as a 5-year asset in this and the following chapter.*

of the \$100,000 cost, or \$52,000 ($0.52 \times$ \$100,000), would represent the accumulated depreciation at the end of year 2. Substituting into Equation 8.1, we get

$$\text{Book value} = \$100{,}000 - \$52{,}000 = \underline{\underline{\$48{,}000}}$$

The book value of Hudson's asset at the end of year 2 is therefore \$48,000.

Basic Tax Rules

Four potential tax situations can occur when an asset is sold. These situations depend on the relationship between the asset's sale price, its initial purchase price, and its book value. The three key forms of taxable income and their associated tax treatments are defined and summarized in Table 8.3. The assumed tax rates used throughout this text are noted in the final column. There are four possible tax situations, which result in one or more forms of taxable income: The asset may be sold (1) for more than its initial purchase price, (2) for more than its book value but less than its initial purchase price, (3) for its book value, or (4) for less than its book value. An example will illustrate.

EXAMPLE The old asset purchased 2 years ago for \$100,000 by Hudson Industries has a current book value of \$48,000. What will happen if the firm now decides to sell the asset and replace it? The tax consequences depend on the sale price. Figure 8.5 on page 316 depicts the taxable income resulting from four possible sale prices in light of the asset's initial purchase price of \$100,000 and its current book value of \$48,000. The taxable consequences of each of these sale prices is described below.

The sale of the asset for more than its initial purchase price If Hudson sells the old asset for \$110,000, it realizes a capital gain of \$10,000, which is taxed as

TABLE 8.3 Tax Treatment on Sales of Assets

Form of taxable income	Definition	Tax treatment	Assumed tax rate
Capital gain	Portion of the sale price that is in excess of the initial purchase price.	Regardless of how long the asset has been held, the total capital gain is taxed as ordinary income.	40%
Recaptured depreciation	Portion of the sale price that is in excess of book value and represents a recovery of previously taken depreciation.	All recaptured depreciation is taxed as ordinary income.	40%
Loss on sale of asset	Amount by which sale price is *less than* book value.	If the asset is depreciable and used in business, loss is deducted from ordinary income.	40% of loss is a tax savings
		If the asset is *not* depreciable or is *not* used in business, loss is deductible only against capital gains.	40% of loss is a tax savings

FIGURE 8.5 **Taxable Income from Sale of Asset**
Taxable income from sale of asset at various sale prices for Hudson Industries

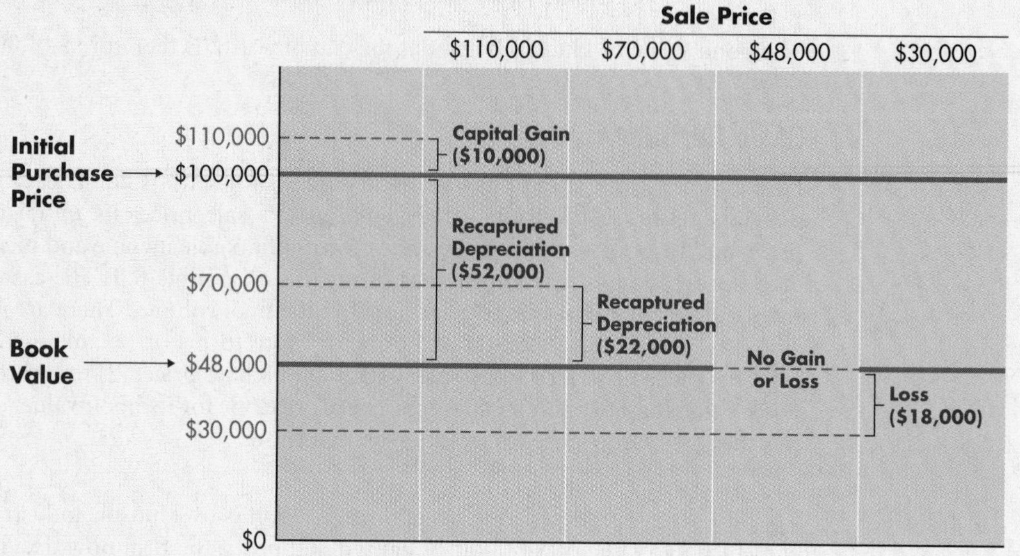

recaptured depreciation
The portion of an asset's sale price that is above its book value and below its initial purchase price.

ordinary income.[4] The firm also experiences ordinary income in the form of **recaptured depreciation,** which is the portion of the sale price that is above book value and below the initial purchase price. In this case there is recaptured depreciation of $52,000 ($100,000 – $48,000). Both the $10,000 capital gain and the $52,000 recaptured depreciation are shown under the $110,000 sale price in Figure 8.5. The taxes on the total gain of $62,000 are calculated as follows:

	Amount (1)	Rate (2)	Tax [(1) × (2)] (3)
Capital gain	$10,000	0.40	$ 4,000
Recaptured depreciation	52,000	0.40	20,800
Totals	$62,000		$24,800

These taxes should be used in calculating the initial investment in the new asset, using the format in Table 8.2. In effect, the taxes raise the amount of the firm's initial investment in the new asset by reducing the proceeds from the sale of the old asset.

4. Although the current tax law requires corporate capital gains to be treated as ordinary income, the structure for corporate capital gains is retained under the law to facilitate a rate differential in the likely event of future tax revisions. Therefore, this distinction is made throughout the text discussions.

The sale of the asset for more than its book value but less than its initial purchase price If Hudson sells the old asset for $70,000, there is no capital gain. However, the firm still experiences a gain in the form of recaptured depreciation of $22,000 ($70,000 – $48,000), as shown under the $70,000 sale price in Figure 8.5. This recaptured depreciation is taxed as ordinary income. Because the firm is assumed to be in the 40% tax bracket, the taxes on the $22,000 gain are $8,800. This amount in taxes should be used in calculating the initial investment in the new asset.

The sale of the asset for its book value If the asset is sold for $48,000, its book value, the firm breaks even. There is no gain or loss, as shown under the $48,000 sale price in Figure 8.5. Because *no tax results from selling an asset for its book value,* there is no tax effect on the initial investment in the new asset.

The sale of the asset for less than its book value If Hudson sells the asset for $30,000, it experiences a loss of $18,000 ($48,000 – $30,000), as shown under the $30,000 sale price in Figure 8.5. If this is a depreciable asset used in the business, the loss may be used to offset ordinary operating income. If the asset is *not* depreciable or is *not* used in the business, the loss can be used only to offset capital gains. In either case, the loss will save the firm $7,200 ($18,000 × 0.40) in taxes. And, if current operating earnings or capital gains are not sufficient to offset the loss, the firm may be able to apply these losses to prior or future years' taxes.[5]

Change in Net Working Capital

net working capital
The amount by which a firm's current assets exceed its current liabilities.

Net working capital is the amount by which a firm's current assets exceed its current liabilities. This topic is treated in depth in Chapter 13, but at this point it is important to note that changes in net working capital often accompany capital expenditure decisions. If a firm acquires new machinery to expand its level of operations, it will experience an increase in levels of cash, accounts receivable, inventories, accounts payable, and accruals. These increases result from the need for more cash to support expanded operations, more accounts receivable and inventories to support increased sales, and more accounts payable and accruals to support increased outlays made to meet expanded product demand. As noted in Chapter 3, increases in cash, accounts receivable, and inventories are *outflows of cash,* whereas increases in accounts payable and accruals are *inflows of cash.*

change in net working capital
The difference between a change in current assets and a change in current liabilities.

The difference between the change in current assets and the change in current liabilities is the **change in net working capital.** Generally, current assets increase by more than current liabilities, resulting in an increased investment in net working capital. This increased investment is treated as an initial outflow. If the change in net working capital were negative, it would be shown as an initial inflow. The change in net working capital—regardless of whether it is an increase or a decrease—*is not taxable* because it merely involves a net buildup or net reduction of current accounts.

EXAMPLE Danson Company, a metal products manufacturer, is contemplating expanding its operations. Financial analysts expect that the changes in current accounts summa-

5. The tax law provides detailed procedures for using *tax loss carrybacks/carryforwards.* Application of such procedures to capital budgeting is beyond the scope of this text, and they are therefore ignored in subsequent discussions.

TABLE 8.4 Calculation of Change in Net Working Capital for Danson Company

Current account	Change in balance	
Cash	+$ 4,000	
Accounts receivable	+ 10,000	
Inventories	+ 8,000	
(1) Current assets		+$22,000
Accounts payable	+$ 7,000	
Accruals	+ 2,000	
(2) Current liabilities		+ 9,000
Change in net working capital [(1) − (2)]		+$13,000

rized in Table 8.4 will occur and will be maintained over the life of the expansion. Current assets are expected to increase by $22,000, and current liabilities are expected to increase by $9,000, resulting in a $13,000 increase in net working capital. In this case, the increase will represent an increased net working capital investment and will be treated as a cash outflow in calculating the initial investment.

Calculating the Initial Investment

A variety of tax and other considerations enter into the initial investment calculation. The following example illustrates calculation of the initial investment according to the format in Table 8.2.

EXAMPLE Powell Corporation, a large, diversified manufacturer of aircraft components, is trying to determine the initial investment required to replace an old machine with a new, more sophisticated model. The machine's purchase price is $380,000, and an additional $20,000 will be necessary to install it. It will be depreciated under MACRS using a 5-year recovery period. The present (old) machine was purchased 3 years ago at a cost of $240,000 and was being depreciated under MACRS using a 5-year recovery period. The firm has found a buyer willing to pay $280,000 for the present machine and to remove it at the buyer's expense. The firm expects that a $35,000 increase in current assets and an $18,000 increase in current liabilities will accompany the replacement; these changes will result in a $17,000 ($35,000 − $18,000) *increase* in net working capital. Both ordinary income and capital gains are taxed at a rate of 40%.

The only component of the initial investment calculation that is difficult to obtain is taxes. Because the firm is planning to sell the present machine for $40,000 more than its initial purchase price, a *capital gain* of $40,000 will be realized. The book value of the present machine can be found by using the depreciation percentages from Table 3.2 (page 89) of 20%, 32%, and 19% for years 1, 2, and 3, respectively. The resulting *book value is $69,600* ($240,000 − [(0.20 + 0.32 + 0.19) × $240,000]). An *ordinary gain* of $170,400 ($240,000 − $69,600) in recaptured depreciation is also realized on the sale. The total taxes on the gain are \$84,160 [(\$40,000 + \$170,400) × 0.40]. Substituting these amounts into the format in Table 8.2 results in an initial investment of \$221,160, which represents the net cash outflow required at time zero.

Installed cost of proposed machine		
Cost of proposed machine	\$380,000	
+ Installation costs	20,000	
Total installed cost—proposed (depreciable value)		\$400,000
− After-tax proceeds from sale of present machine		
Proceeds from sale of present machine	\$280,000	
− Tax on sale of present machine	84,160	
Total after-tax proceeds—present		195,840
+ Change in net working capital		17,000
Initial investment		\$221,160

Review Questions

8–9 Explain how each of the following inputs is used to calculate the *initial investment:* **(a)** cost of new asset, **(b)** installation costs, **(c)** proceeds from sale of old asset, **(d)** tax on sale of old asset, and **(e)** change in net working capital.

8–10 How is the *book value* of an asset calculated? What are the three key forms of taxable income?

8–11 What four tax situations may result from the sale of an asset that is being replaced?

8–12 Referring to the basic format for calculating initial investment, explain how a firm would determine the *depreciable value* of the new asset.

LG5

Finding the Operating Cash Inflows

The benefits expected from a capital expenditure or "project" are embodied in its *operating cash inflows,* which are *incremental after-tax cash inflows.* In this section we use the income statement format to develop clear definitions of the terms *after-tax, cash inflows,* and *incremental.*

Interpreting the Term *After-Tax*

Benefits expected to result from proposed capital expenditures must be measured on an *after-tax basis,* because the firm will not have the use of any benefits until it has satisfied the government's tax claims. These claims depend on the firm's taxable income, so deducting taxes *before* making comparisons between proposed investments is necessary for consistency when evaluating capital expenditure alternatives.

Interpreting the Term *Cash Inflows*

All benefits expected from a proposed project must be measured on a *cash flow basis*. Cash inflows represent dollars that can be spent, not merely "accounting profits." A simple accounting technique for converting after-tax net profits into operating cash inflows was given in Equation 3.1 on page 90. The basic calculation requires adding depreciation and any other *noncash charges* (amortization and depletion) deducted as expenses on the firm's income statement back to net profits after taxes. Because depreciation is commonly found on income statements, it is the only noncash charge we consider.

EXAMPLE Powell Corporation's estimates of its revenue and expenses (excluding depreciation), with and without the proposed new machine described in the preceding example, are given in Table 8.5. Note that both the expected usable life of the proposed machine and the remaining usable life of the present machine are 5 years. The amount to be depreciated with the proposed machine is calculated by summing the purchase price of $380,000 and the installation costs of $20,000. The proposed machine is to be depreciated under MACRS using a 5-year recovery period.[6] The resulting depreciation on this machine for each of the 6 years, as well as the remaining 3 years of depreciation (years 4, 5, and 6) on the present machine, are calculated in Table 8.6.[7]

The operating cash inflows in each year can be calculated by using the income statement format shown in Table 8.7. Substituting the data from Tables 8.5 and 8.6 into this format and assuming a 40% tax rate, we get Table 8.8. It demonstrates the calculation of operating cash inflows for each year for both the proposed and the present machine. Because the proposed machine is depreciated

TABLE 8.5 Powell Corporation's Revenue and Expenses (Excluding Depreciation) for Proposed and Present Machines

With proposed machine			With present machine		
Year	Revenue (1)	Expenses (excl. depr.) (2)	Year	Revenue (1)	Expenses (excl. depr.) (2)
1	$2,520,000	$2,300,000	1	$2,200,000	$1,990,000
2	2,520,000	2,300,000	2	2,300,000	2,110,000
3	2,520,000	2,300,000	3	2,400,000	2,230,000
4	2,520,000	2,300,000	4	2,400,000	2,250,000
5	2,520,000	2,300,000	5	2,250,000	2,120,000

6. As noted in Chapter 3, it takes $n+1$ years to depreciate an n-year class asset under current tax law. Therefore, MACRS percentages are given for each of 6 years for use in depreciating an asset with a 5-year recovery period.

7. It is important to recognize that although both machines will provide 5 years of use, the proposed new machine will be depreciated over the 6-year period, whereas the present machine, as noted in the preceding example, has been depreciated over 3 years and therefore has remaining only its final 3 years (years 4, 5, and 6) of depreciation (12%, 12%, and 5%, respectively, under MACRS).

TABLE 8.6 Depreciation Expense for Proposed and Present Machines for Powell Corporation

Year	Cost (1)	Applicable MACRS depreciation percentages (from Table 3.2) (2)	Depreciation [(1) × (2)] (3)
With proposed machine			
1	$400,000	20%	$ 80,000
2	400,000	32	128,000
3	400,000	19	76,000
4	400,000	12	48,000
5	400,000	12	48,000
6	400,000	5	20,000
Totals		100%	$400,000
With present machine			
1	$240,000	12% (year-4 depreciation)	$28,800
2	240,000	12 (year-5 depreciation)	28,800
3	240,000	5 (year-6 depreciation)	12,000
4	Because the present machine is at the end of the third year of its cost recovery at the time the analysis is performed, it has only the final 3 years of depreciation (as noted above) still applicable.		0
5			0
6			0
Total			$69,600[a]

[a]The total $69,600 represents the book value of the present machine at the end of the third year, as calculated in the preceding example.

TABLE 8.7 Calculation of Operating Cash Inflows Using the Income Statement Format

Revenue
− Expenses (excluding depreciation)
Profits before depreciation and taxes
− Depreciation
Net profits before taxes
− Taxes
Net profits after taxes
+ Depreciation
Operating cash inflows

over 6 years, the analysis must be performed over the 6-year period to capture fully the tax effect of its year-6 depreciation. The resulting operating cash inflows are shown in the final row of Table 8.8 for each machine. The $8,000 year-6 cash inflow for the proposed machine results solely from the tax benefit of its year-6 depreciation deduction.

TABLE 8.8 Calculation of Operating Cash Inflows for Powell Corporation's Proposed and Present Machines

	Year 1	Year 2	Year 3	Year 4	Year 5	Year 6
With proposed machine						
Revenue[a]	$2,520,000	$2,520,000	$2,520,000	$2,520,000	$2,520,000	$ 0
− Expenses (excl. depr.)[b]	2,300,000	2,300,000	2,300,000	2,300,000	2,300,000	0
Profits before depr. and taxes	$ 220,000	$ 220,000	$ 220,000	$ 220,000	$ 220,000	$ 0
− Depreciation[c]	80,000	128,000	76,000	48,000	48,000	20,000
Net profits before taxes	$ 140,000	$ 92,000	$ 144,000	$ 172,000	$ 172,000	−$20,000
− Taxes (rate = 40%)	56,000	36,800	57,600	68,800	68,800	− 8,000
Net profits after taxes	$ 84,000	$ 55,200	$ 86,400	$ 103,200	$ 103,200	−$12,000
+ Depreciation[c]	80,000	128,000	76,000	48,000	48,000	20,000
Operating cash inflows	$ 164,000	$ 183,200	$ 162,400	$ 151,200	$ 151,200	$ 8,000
With present machine						
Revenue[a]	$2,200,000	$2,300,000	$2,400,000	$2,400,000	$2,250,000	$ 0
− Expenses (excl. depr.)[b]	1,990,000	2,110,000	2,230,000	2,250,000	2,120,000	0
Profits before depr. and taxes	$ 210,000	$ 190,000	$ 170,000	$ 150,000	$ 130,000	$ 0
− Depreciation[c]	28,800	28,800	12,000	0	0	0
Net profits before taxes	$ 181,200	$ 161,200	$ 158,000	$ 150,000	$ 130,000	$ 0
− Taxes (rate = 40%)	72,480	64,480	63,200	60,000	52,000	0
Net profits after taxes	$ 108,720	$ 96,720	$ 94,800	$ 90,000	$ 78,000	$ 0
+ Depreciation[c]	28,800	28,800	12,000	0	0	0
Operating cash inflows	$ 137,520	$ 125,520	$ 106,800	$ 90,000	$ 78,000	$ 0

[a]From column 1 of Table 8.5.
[b]From column 2 of Table 8.5.
[c]From column 3 of Table 8.6.

Interpreting the Term *Incremental*

The final step in estimating the operating cash inflows for a proposed project is to calculate the *incremental (relevant)* cash inflows. Incremental operating cash inflows are needed, because our concern is *only* with the change in operating cash inflows that result from the proposed project.

EXAMPLE Table 8.9 demonstrates the calculation of Powell Corporation's incremental (relevant) operating cash inflows for each year. The estimates of operating cash inflows developed in Table 8.8 are given in columns 1 and 2. Column 2 values represent the amount of operating cash inflows that Powell Corporation will receive if it does not replace the present machine. If the proposed machine replaces the present machine, the firm's operating cash inflows for each year will be those shown in column 1. Subtracting the present machine's operating cash inflows from the proposed machine's operating cash inflows, we get the incremental oper-

TABLE 8.9 Incremental (Relevant) Operating Cash Inflows for Powell Corporation

	Operating cash inflows		
Year	Proposed machine[a] (1)	Present machine[a] (2)	Incremental (relevant) [(1) − (2)] (3)
1	$164,000	$137,520	$26,480
2	183,200	125,520	57,680
3	162,400	106,800	55,600
4	151,200	90,000	61,200
5	151,200	78,000	73,200
6	8,000	0	8,000

[a]From final row for respective machine in Table 8.8.

ating cash inflows for each year, shown in column 3. These cash flows represent the amounts by which each respective year's cash inflows will increase as a result of the replacement. For example, in year 1, Powell Corporation's cash inflows would increase by $26,480 if the proposed project were undertaken. Clearly, these are the relevant inflows to be considered when evaluating the benefits of making a capital expenditure for the proposed machine.

Review Questions

8–13 How does depreciation enter into the calculation of operating cash inflows?

8–14 How are the incremental (relevant) *operating cash inflows* that are associated with a replacement decision calculated?

LG6

Finding the Terminal Cash Flow

Terminal cash flow is the cash flow resulting from termination and liquidation of a project at the end of its economic life. It represents the after-tax cash flow, exclusive of operating cash inflows, that occurs in the final year of the project. When it applies, this flow can significantly affect the capital expenditure decision. Terminal cash flow can be calculated for replacement projects by using the basic format presented in Table 8.10.

Proceeds from Sale of Assets

The proceeds from sale of the new and the old asset, often called "salvage value," represent the amount *net of any removal or cleanup costs* expected upon termination of the project. For replacement projects, proceeds from both the new asset

TABLE 8.10 The Basic Format for Determining Terminal Cash Flow

	After-tax proceeds from sale of new asset =
	Proceeds from sale of new asset
	∓ Tax on sale of new asset
−	**After-tax proceeds from sale of old asset =**
	Proceeds from sale of old asset
	∓ Tax on sale of old asset
±	**Change in net working capital**
	Terminal cash flow

and the old asset must be considered. For expansion and renewal types of capital expenditures, the proceeds from the old asset are zero. Of course, it is not unusual for the value of an asset to be zero at the termination of a project.

Taxes on Sale of Assets

Earlier we calculated the tax on sale of old asset (as part of finding the initial investment). Similarly, taxes must be considered on the terminal sale of both the new and the old asset for replacement projects and on only the new asset in other cases. The tax calculations apply whenever an asset is sold for a value different from its book value. If the net proceeds from the sale are expected to exceed book value, a tax payment shown as an *outflow* (deduction from sale proceeds) will occur. When the net proceeds from the sale are less than book value, a tax rebate shown as a cash *inflow* (addition to sale proceeds) will result. For assets sold to net exactly book value, no taxes will be due.

Change in Net Working Capital

When we calculated the initial investment, we took into account any change in net working capital that is attributable to the new asset. Now, when we calculate the terminal cash flow, the change in net working capital represents the reversion of any initial net working capital investment. Most often, this will show up as a cash inflow due to the reduction in net working capital; with termination of the project, the need for the increased net working capital investment is assumed to end. Because the net working capital investment is in no way consumed, the amount recovered at termination will equal the amount shown in the calculation of the initial investment. Tax considerations are not involved.

Calculating the terminal cash flow involves the same procedures as those used to find the initial investment. In the following example, the terminal cash flow is calculated for a replacement decision.

EXAMPLE Continuing with the Powell Corporation example, assume that the firm expects to be able to liquidate the new machine at the end of its 5-year usable life to net $50,000 after paying removal and cleanup costs. The old machine can be liquidated at the end of the 5 years to net $0 because it will then be completely obsolete. The firm expects to recover its $17,000 net working capital investment upon termination of the project. Both ordinary income and capital gains are taxed at a rate of 40%.

From the analysis of the operating cash inflows presented earlier, we can see that the proposed (new) machine will have a book value of $20,000 (equal to the year-6 depreciation) at the end of 5 years. The present (old) machine will be fully depreciated and therefore have a book value of zero at the end of the 5 years. Because the sale price of $50,000 for the proposed (new) machine is below its initial installed cost of $400,000 but greater than its book value of $20,000, taxes will have to be paid only on the recaptured depreciation of $30,000 ($50,000 sale proceeds − $20,000 book value). Applying the ordinary tax rate of 40% to this $30,000 results in a tax of $12,000 (0.40 × $30,000) on the sale of the proposed machine. Its after-tax sale proceeds would therefore equal $38,000 ($50,000 sale proceeds − $12,000 taxes). Because the present machine would net $0 at termination and its book value would be $0, no tax would be due on its sale. Its after-tax sale proceeds would therefore equal $0. Substituting the appropriate values into the format in Table 8.10 results in the terminal cash inflow of $55,000.

After-tax proceeds from sale of proposed machine		
Proceeds from sale of proposed machine	$50,000	
− Tax on sale of proposed machine	12,000	
Total after-tax proceeds—proposed		$38,000
− After-tax proceeds from sale of present machine		
Proceeds from sale of present machine	$ 0	
∓ Tax on sale of present machine	0	
Total after-tax proceeds—present		0
+ Change in net working capital		17,000
Terminal cash flow		$55,000

Review Question

8–15 Explain how the *terminal cash flow* is calculated for replacement projects.

LG4 LG5 LG6

Summarizing the Relevant Cash Flows

The initial investment, operating cash inflows, and terminal cash flow together represent a project's *relevant cash flows.* These cash flows can be viewed as the incremental after-tax cash flows attributable to the proposed project. They represent, in a cash flow sense, how much better or worse off the firm will be if it chooses to implement the proposal.

EXAMPLE The relevant cash flows for Powell Corporation's proposed replacement expenditure can now be shown graphically, on a time line. Note that because the new asset is assumed to be sold at the end of its 5-year usable life, the year-6 incremental operating cash inflow calculated in Table 8.9 has no relevance; the terminal cash flow effectively replaces this value in the analysis. As the following time line shows, the relevant cash flows follow a *conventional cash flow pattern.*

Time line for Powell Corporation's relevant cash flows with the proposed machine

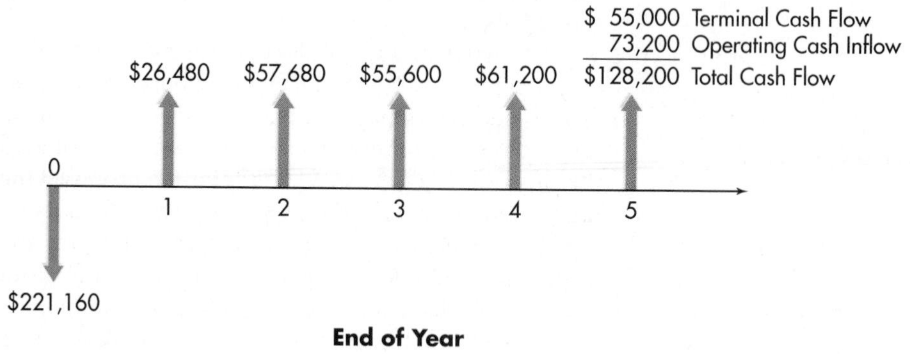

Techniques for analyzing conventional cash flow patterns to determine whether to undertake a proposed capital investment are discussed in Chapter 9.

Review Question

8–16 Diagram and describe the three components of the *relevant cash flows* for a capital budgeting project.

SUMMARY

FOCUS ON VALUE

A key responsibility of financial managers is to review and analyze proposed investment decisions in order to make sure that only those that contribute positively to the value of the firm are undertaken. Utilizing a variety of tools and techniques, financial managers estimate the cash flows that a proposed investment will generate and then apply appropriate decision techniques to assess the investment's impact on the firm's value. The most difficult and important aspect of this capital budgeting process is developing good estimates of the relevant cash flows.

The relevant cash flows are the incremental after-tax cash flows resulting from a proposed investment. These estimates represent the cash flow benefits that are likely to accrue to the firm as a result of implementing the investment. By applying decision techniques that capture time value of money and risk factors, the financial manager can estimate the impact the investment will have on the firm's share price. Clearly, only those investments that can be expected to increase the stock price should be undertaken. Consistent application of capital budgeting procedures to proposed long-term investments should therefore allow the firm to **maximize its stock price.**

REVIEW OF LEARNING GOALS

LG1 **Understand the key motives for capital expenditure and the steps in the capital budgeting process.** Capital budgeting is the process used to evaluate and select capital expenditures consistent with the firm's goal of maximizing owner wealth. Capital expenditures are long-term investments made to expand, replace, or renew fixed assets or to obtain some less tangible benefit. The capital budgeting process includes five distinct but interrelated steps: proposal generation, review and analysis, decision making, implementation, and follow-up.

LG2 **Define basic capital budgeting terminology.** Capital expenditure proposals may be independent or mutually exclusive. Typically, firms have only limited funds for capital investments and must ration them among carefully selected projects. Two basic approaches to capital budgeting decisions are the accept–reject approach and the ranking approach. Conventional cash flow patterns consist of an initial outflow followed by a series of inflows; any other pattern is nonconventional.

LG3 **Discuss the major components of relevant cash flows, expansion versus replacement cash flows, sunk costs and opportunity costs, and international capital budgeting and long-term investments.** The relevant cash flows for capital budgeting decisions are the initial investment, the operating cash inflows, and the terminal cash flow. For replacement decisions, these flows are found by determining the difference between the cash flows of the new asset and the old asset. Expansion decisions are viewed as replacement decisions in which all cash flows from the old asset are zero. When estimating relevant cash flows, one should ignore sunk costs, and opportunity costs should be included as cash outflows. In international capital budgeting, currency risks and political risks can be minimized through careful planning.

LG4 **Calculate the initial investment associated with a proposed capital expenditure.** The initial investment is the initial outflow required, taking into account the installed cost of the new asset, the after-tax proceeds from the sale of the old asset, and any change in net working capital. Finding the after-tax proceeds from sale of the old asset, which reduces the initial investment, involves cost, depreciation, and tax data. The book value of an asset is its accounting value, which is used to determine what taxes are owed as a result of its sale. Any of three forms of taxable income—capital gain, recaptured depreciation, or a loss—can result from sale of an asset. The form of taxable income that applies depends on whether the asset is sold for (1) more than its initial purchase price, (2) more than book value but less than what was initially paid, (3) book value, or (4) less than book value. The change in net working capital is the difference between the change in current assets and the change in current liabilities expected to accompany a given capital expenditure.

LG5 **Determine relevant operating cash inflows using the income statement format.** The operating cash inflows are the incremental after-tax cash inflows expected to result from a project. The income statement format involves adding depreciation back to net profits after taxes and gives the operating cash inflows associated with the proposed and present projects. The relevant (incremental) cash inflows are the difference between the operating cash inflows of the proposed project and those of the present project.

LG6 **Find the terminal cash flow.** The terminal cash flow represents the after-tax cash flow, exclusive of operating cash inflows, that is expected from liquidation of a project. It is calculated by finding the difference between the after-tax proceeds from sale of the new and the old asset at project termination and then adjusting this difference for any change in net working capital. Sale price and depreciation data are used to find the taxes and the after-tax sale proceeds on the new and old assets. The change in net working capital typically represents the reversion of any initial net working capital investment.

SELF-TEST PROBLEMS (Solutions in Appendix B)

LG4

ST 8–1 Book value, taxes, and initial investment Irvin Enterprises is considering the purchase of a new piece of equipment to replace the current equipment. The new equipment costs $75,000 and requires $5,000 in installation costs. It will be depreciated under MACRS using a 5-year recovery period. The old piece of equipment was purchased 4 years ago for an installed cost of $50,000; it was being depreciated under MACRS using a 5-year recovery period. The old equipment can be sold today for $55,000 net of any removal or cleanup costs. As a result of the proposed replacement, the firm's investment in net working capital is expected to increase by $15,000. The firm pays taxes at a rate of 40% on both ordinary income and capital gains. (Table 3.2 on page 89 contains the applicable MACRS depreciation percentages.)

a. Calculate the book value of the old piece of equipment.

b. Determine the taxes, if any, attributable to the sale of the old equipment.

c. Find the initial investment associated with the proposed equipment replacement.

LG4 LG5 LG6

ST 8–2 Determining relevant cash flows A machine currently in use was originally purchased 2 years ago for $40,000. The machine is being depreciated under MACRS using a 5-year recovery period; it has 3 years of usable life remaining. The current machine can be sold today to net $42,000 after removal and cleanup costs. A new machine, using a 3-year MACRS recovery period, can be purchased at a price of $140,000. It requires $10,000 to install and has a 3-year usable life. If the new machine is acquired, the investment in accounts receivable will be expected to rise by $10,000, the inventory investment will increase by $25,000, and accounts payable will increase by $15,000. *Profits before depreciation and taxes* are expected to be $70,000 for each of the next 3 years with the old machine and to be $120,000 in the first year and $130,000 in the second and third years with the new machine. At the end of 3 years, the market value of the old machine will equal zero, but the new machine could be sold to net $35,000 before taxes. Both ordinary corporate income and capital gains are subject to a 40% tax. (Table 3.2 on page 89 contains the applicable MACRS depreciation percentages.)

a. Determine the initial investment associated with the proposed replacement decision.

b. Calculate the incremental operating cash inflows for years 1 to 4 associated with the proposed replacement. (*Note:* Only depreciation cash flows must be considered in year 4.)

c. Calculate the terminal cash flow associated with the proposed replacement decision. (*Note:* This is at the end of year 3.)

d. Depict on a time line the relevant cash flows found in parts **a**, **b**, and **c** that are associated with the proposed replacement decision, assuming that it is terminated at the end of year 3.

PROBLEMS

LG1

8–1 Classification of expenditures Given the following list of outlays, indicate whether each is normally considered a *capital* or an *operating* expenditure. Explain your answers.

a. An initial lease payment of $5,000 for electronic point-of-sale cash register systems.
b. An outlay of $20,000 to purchase patent rights from an inventor.
c. An outlay of $80,000 for a major research and development program.
d. An $80,000 investment in a portfolio of marketable securities.
e. A $300 outlay for an office machine.
f. An outlay of $2,000 for a new machine tool.
g. An outlay of $240,000 for a new building.
h. An outlay of $1,000 for a marketing research report.

LG2 8–2 **Basic terminology** A firm is considering the following three separate situations.

Situation A Build either a small office building or a convenience store on a parcel of land located in a high-traffic area. Adequate funding is available, and both projects are known to be acceptable. The office building requires an initial investment of $620,000 and is expected to provide operating cash inflows of $40,000 per year for 20 years. The convenience store is expected to cost $500,000 and to provide a growing stream of operating cash inflows over its 20-year life. The initial operating cash inflow is $20,000, and it will increase by 5% each year.

Situation B Replace a machine with a new one that requires a $60,000 initial investment and will provide operating cash inflows of $10,000 per year for the first 5 years. At the end of year 5, a machine overhaul costing $20,000 will be required. After it is completed, expected operating cash inflows will be $10,000 in year 6; $7,000 in year 7; $4,000 in year 8; and $1,000 in year 9, at the end of which the machine will be scrapped.

Situation C Invest in any or all of the four machines whose relevant cash flows are given in the following table. The firm has $500,000 budgeted to fund these machines, all of which are known to be acceptable. Initial investment for each machine is $250,000.

	Operating cash inflows			
Year	Machine 1	Machine 2	Machine 3	Machine 4
1	$ 50,000	$70,000	$65,000	$90,000
2	70,000	70,000	65,000	80,000
3	90,000	70,000	80,000	70,000
4	− 30,000	70,000	80,000	60,000
5	100,000	70,000	− 20,000	50,000

For each situation, indicate:
a. Whether the projects involved are independent or mutually exclusive.
b. Whether the availability of funds is unlimited or capital rationing exists.
c. Whether accept–reject or ranking decisions are required.
d. Whether each project's cash flows are conventional or nonconventional.

LG3 **8–3 Relevant cash flow pattern fundamentals** For each of the following projects, determine the *relevant cash flows,* classify the cash flow pattern, and depict the cash flows on a time line.

a. A project that requires an initial investment of $120,000 and will generate annual operating cash inflows of $25,000 for the next 18 years. In each of the 18 years, maintenance of the project will require a $5,000 cash outflow.

b. A new machine with an installed cost of $85,000. Sale of the old machine will yield $30,000 after taxes. Operating cash inflows generated by the replacement will exceed the operating cash inflows of the old machine by $20,000 in each year of a 6-year period. At the end of year 6, liquidation of the new machine will yield $20,000 after taxes, which is $10,000 greater than the after-tax proceeds expected from the old machine had it been retained and liquidated at the end of year 6.

c. An asset that requires an initial investment of $2 million and will yield annual operating cash inflows of $300,000 for each of the next 10 years. Operating cash outlays will be $20,000 for each year except year 6, when an overhaul requiring an additional cash outlay of $500,000 will be required. The asset's liquidation value at the end of year 10 is expected to be $0.

LG3 **8–4 Expansion versus replacement cash flows** Edison Systems has estimated the cash flows over the 5-year lives for two projects, A and B. These cash flows are summarized in the following table.

	Project A	Project B
Initial investment	$40,000	$12,000[a]
Year	**Operating cash inflows**	
1	$10,000	$ 6,000
2	12,000	6,000
3	14,000	6,000
4	16,000	6,000
5	10,000	6,000

[a]After-tax cash inflow expected from liquidation.

a. If project A were actually a *replacement* for project B and if the $12,000 initial investment shown for project B were the after-tax cash inflow expected from liquidating it, what would be the relevant cash flows for this replacement decision?

b. How can an *expansion decision* such as project A be viewed as a special form of a replacement decision? Explain.

LG3 **8–5 Sunk costs and opportunity costs** Covol Industries is developing the relevant cash flows associated with the proposed replacement of an existing machine tool with a new, technologically advanced one. Given the following costs related to the proposed project, explain whether each would be treated as a *sunk cost* or an *opportunity cost* in developing the relevant cash flows associated with the proposed replacement decision.

a. Covol would be able to use the same tooling, which had a book value of $40,000, on the new machine tool as it had used on the old one.
b. Covol would be able to use its existing computer system to develop programs for operating the new machine tool. The old machine tool did not require these programs. Although the firm's computer has excess capacity available, the capacity could be leased to another firm for an annual fee of $17,000.
c. Covol would have to obtain additional floor space to accommodate the larger new machine tool. The space that would be used is currently being leased to another company for $10,000 per year.
d. Covol would use a small storage facility to store the increased output of the new machine tool. The storage facility was built by Covol 3 years earlier at a cost of $120,000. Because of its unique configuration and location, it is currently of no use to either Covol or any other firm.
e. Covol would retain an existing overhead crane, which it had planned to sell for its $180,000 market value. Although the crane was not needed with the old machine tool, it would be used to position raw materials on the new machine tool.

LG4 8–6 **Book value** Find the book value for each of the assets shown in the following table, assuming that MACRS depreciation is being used. (*Note:* See Table 3.2 on page 89 for the applicable depreciation percentages.)

Asset	Installed cost	Recovery period (years)	Elapsed time since purchase (years)
A	$ 950,000	5	3
B	40,000	3	1
C	96,000	5	4
D	350,000	5	1
E	1,500,000	7	5

LG4 8–7 **Book value and taxes on sale of assets** Troy Industries purchased a new machine 3 years ago for $80,000. It is being depreciated under MACRS with a 5-year recovery period using the percentages given in Table 3.2 on page 89. Assume 40% ordinary and capital gains tax rates.
a. What is the book value of the machine?
b. Calculate the firm's tax liability if it sold the machine for each of the following amounts: $100,000; $56,000; $23,200; and $15,000.

LG4 8–8 **Tax calculations** For each of the following cases, describe the various taxable components of the funds received through sale of the asset, and determine the total taxes resulting from the transaction. Assume 40% ordinary and capital gains tax rates. The asset was purchased 2 years ago for $200,000 and is being depreciated under MACRS using a 5-year recovery period. (See Table 3.2 on page 89 for the applicable depreciation percentages.)
a. The asset is sold for $220,000.
b. The asset is sold for $150,000.
c. The asset is sold for $96,000.
d. The asset is sold for $80,000.

LG4 8–9 **Change in net working capital calculation** Samuels Manufacturing is considering the purchase of a new machine to replace one they feel is obsolete. The firm has total current assets of $920,000 and total current liabilities of $640,000. As a result of the proposed replacement, the following *changes* are anticipated in the levels of the current asset and current liability accounts noted.

Account	Change
Accruals	+ $ 40,000
Marketable securities	0
Inventories	− 10,000
Accounts payable	+ 90,000
Notes payable	0
Accounts receivable	+ 150,000
Cash	+ 15,000

a. Using the information given, calculate the change, if any, in net working capital that is expected to result from the proposed replacement action.
b. Explain why a change in these current accounts would be relevant in determining the initial investment for the proposed capital expenditure.
c. Would the change in net working capital enter into any of the other cash flow components that make up the relevant cash flows? Explain.

LG4 8–10 **Calculating initial investment** Vastine Medical, Inc., is considering replacing its existing computer system, which was purchased 2 years ago at a cost of $325,000. The system can be sold today for $200,000. It is being depreciated using MACRS and a 5-year recovery period (see Table 3.2, page 89). A new computer system will cost $500,000 to purchase and install. Replacement of the computer system would not involve any change in net working capital. Assume a 40% tax rate on ordinary income and capital gains.
a. Calculate the book value of the existing computer system.
b. Calculate the after-tax proceeds of its sale for $200,000.
c. Calculate the initial investment associated with the replacement project.

LG4 8–11 **Initial investment—Basic calculation** Cushing Corporation is considering the purchase of a new grading machine to replace the existing one. The existing machine was purchased 3 years ago at an installed cost of $20,000; it was being depreciated under MACRS using a 5-year recovery period. (See Table 3.2 on page 89 for the applicable depreciation percentages.) The existing machine is expected to have a usable life of at least 5 more years. The new machine costs $35,000 and requires $5,000 in installation costs; it will be depreciated using a 5-year recovery period under MACRS. The existing machine can currently be sold for $25,000 without incurring any removal or cleanup costs. The firm pays 40% taxes on both ordinary income and capital gains. Calculate the *initial investment* associated with the proposed purchase of a new grading machine.

LG4 8–12 **Initial investment at various sale prices** Edwards Manufacturing Company is considering replacing one machine with another. The old machine was purchased 3 years ago for an installed cost of $10,000. The firm is depreciating the machine under MACRS, using a 5-year recovery period. (See Table 3.2 on page 89 for the applicable depreciation percentages.) The new machine costs $24,000 and requires $2,000 in installation costs. The firm is subject to a 40% tax rate on both ordinary income and capital gains. In each of the following cases, calculate the initial investment for the replacement.

a. Edwards Manufacturing Company (EMC) sells the old machine for $11,000.
b. EMC sells the old machine for $7,000.
c. EMC sells the old machine for $2,900.
d. EMC sells the old machine for $1,500.

LG5 8–13 **Depreciation** A firm is evaluating the acquisition of an asset that costs $64,000 and requires $4,000 in installation costs. If the firm depreciates the asset under MACRS, using a 5-year recovery period (see Table 3.2 on page 89 for the applicable depreciation percentages), determine the depreciation charge for each year.

LG5 8–14 **Incremental operating cash inflows** A firm is considering renewing its equipment to meet increased demand for its product. The cost of equipment modifications is $1.9 million plus $100,000 in installation costs. The firm will depreciate the equipment modifications under MACRS, using a 5-year recovery period. (See Table 3.2 on page 89 for the applicable depreciation percentages.) Additional sales revenue from the renewal should amount to $1.2 million per year, and additional operating expenses and other costs (excluding depreciation) will amount to 40% of the additional sales. The firm has an ordinary tax rate of 40%. (*Note:* Answer the following questions for each of the next *6 years.*)

a. What incremental earnings before depreciation and taxes will result from the renewal?
b. What incremental earnings after taxes will result from the renewal?
c. What incremental operating cash inflows will result from the renewal?

LG5 8–15 **Incremental operating cash inflows—Expense reduction** Miller Corporation is considering replacing a machine. The replacement will reduce operating expenses (that is, increase revenues) by $16,000 per year for each of the 5 years the new machine is expected to last. Although the old machine has zero book value, it can be used for 5 more years. The depreciable value of the new machine is $48,000. The firm will depreciate the machine under MACRS using a 5-year recovery period (see Table 3.2 on page 89 for the applicable depreciation percentages) and is subject to a 40% tax rate on ordinary income. Estimate the incremental operating cash inflows generated by the replacement. (*Note:* Be sure to consider the depreciation in year 6.)

LG5 8–16 **Incremental operating cash inflows** Strong Tool Company has been considering purchasing a new lathe to replace a fully depreciated lathe that will last 5 more years. The new lathe is expected to have a 5-year life and depreciation charges of $2,000 in year 1; $3,200 in year 2; $1,900 in year 3; $1,200 in both year 4 and year 5; and $500 in year 6. The firm estimates the revenues and expenses (excluding depreciation) for the new and the old lathes to be as shown in the following table. The firm is subject to a 40% tax rate on ordinary income.

	New lathe		Old lathe	
Year	Revenue	Expenses (excl. depr.)	Revenue	Expenses (excl. depr.)
1	$40,000	$30,000	$35,000	$25,000
2	41,000	30,000	35,000	25,000
3	42,000	30,000	35,000	25,000
4	43,000	30,000	35,000	25,000
5	44,000	30,000	35,000	25,000

a. Calculate the operating cash inflows associated with each lathe. (*Note:* Be sure to consider the depreciation in year 6.)
b. Calculate the incremental (relevant) operating cash inflows resulting from the proposed lathe replacement.
c. Depict on a time line the incremental operating cash inflows calculated in part **b.**

LG6 8–17 **Terminal cash flow—Various lives and sale prices** Looner Industries is currently analyzing the purchase of a new machine that costs $160,000 and requires $20,000 in installation costs. Purchase of this machine is expected to result in an increase in net working capital of $30,000 to support the expanded level of operations. The firm plans to depreciate the machine under MACRS using a 5-year recovery period (see Table 3.2 on page 89 for the applicable depreciation percentages) and expects to sell the machine to net $10,000 before taxes at the end of its usable life. The firm is subject to a 40% tax rate on both ordinary and capital gains income.
a. Calculate the terminal cash flow for a usable life of (1) 3 years, (2) 5 years, and (3) 7 years.
b. Discuss the effect of usable life on terminal cash flows using your findings in part **a.**
c. Assuming a 5-year usable life, calculate the terminal cash flow if the machine were sold to net (1) $9,000 or (2) $170,000 (before taxes) at the end of 5 years.
d. Discuss the effect of sale price on terminal cash flow using your findings in part **c.**

LG6 8–18 **Terminal cash flow—Replacement decision** Russell Industries is considering replacing a fully depreciated machine that has a remaining useful life of 10 years with a newer, more sophisticated machine. The new machine will cost $200,000 and will require $30,000 in installation costs. It will be depreciated under MACRS using a 5-year recovery period (see Table 3.2 on page 89 for the applicable depreciation percentages). A $25,000 increase in net working capital will be required to support the new machine. The firm's managers plans to evaluate the potential replacement over a 4-year period. They estimate that the old machine could be sold at the end of 4 years to net $15,000 before taxes; the new machine at the end of 4 years will be worth $75,000 before taxes. Calculate the terminal cash flow at the end of year 4 that is relevant to the proposed purchase of the new machine. The firm is subject to a 40% tax rate on both ordinary and capital gains income.

LG4 LG5 LG6 **8–19 Relevant cash flows for a marketing campaign** Marcus Tube, a manufacturer of high-quality aluminum tubing, has maintained stable sales and profits over the past 10 years. Although the market for aluminum tubing has been expanding by 3% per year, Marcus has been unsuccessful in sharing this growth. To increase its sales, the firm is considering an aggressive marketing campaign that centers on regularly running ads in all relevant trade journals and exhibiting products at all major regional and national trade shows. The campaign is expected to require an *annual* tax-deductible expenditure of $150,000 over the next 5 years. Sales revenue, as shown in the income statement for 2003 (below), totaled $20,000,000. If the proposed marketing campaign is not initiated, sales are expected to remain at this level in each of the next 5 years, 2004–2008. With the marketing campaign, sales are expected to rise to the levels shown in the accompanying table for each of the next 5 years; cost of goods sold is expected to remain at 80% of sales; general and administrative expense (exclusive of any marketing campaign outlays) is expected to remain at 10% of sales; and annual depreciation expense is expected to remain at $500,000. Assuming a 40% tax rate, find the relevant cash flows over the next 5 years associated with the proposed marketing campaign.

Marcus Tube
Income Statement
for the Year Ended December 31, 2003

Sales revenue		$20,000,000
Less: Cost of goods sold (80%)		16,000,000
Gross profits		$ 4,000,000
Less: Operating expenses		
General and administrative expense (10%)	$2,000,000	
Depreciation expense	500,000	
Total operating expense		2,500,000
Net profits before taxes		$ 1,500,000
Less: Taxes (rate = 40%)		600,000
Net profits after taxes		$ 900,000

Marcus Tube
Sales Forecast

Year	Sales revenue
2004	$20,500,000
2005	21,000,000
2006	21,500,000
2007	22,500,000
2008	23,500,000

LG4 LG5 **8–20 Relevant cash flows—No terminal value** Central Laundry and Cleaners is considering replacing an existing piece of machinery with a more sophisticated machine. The old machine was purchased 3 years ago at a cost of $50,000, and this amount was being depreciated under MACRS using a 5-year recovery period. The machine has 5 years of usable life remaining. The new machine that is being considered costs $76,000 and requires $4,000 in installation costs. The new machine would be depreciated under MACRS using a 5-year recovery period. The firm can currently sell the old machine for $55,000 without incurring any removal or cleanup costs. The firm pays a tax rate of 40% on both ordinary income and capital gains. The revenues and expenses (excluding depreciation) associated with the new and the old machine for the next 5 years are given in the table below. (Table 3.2 on page 89 contains the applicable MACRS depreciation percentages.)

	New machine		Old machine	
Year	Revenue	Expenses (excl. depr.)	Revenue	Expenses (excl. depr.)
1	$750,000	$720,000	$674,000	$660,000
2	750,000	720,000	676,000	660,000
3	750,000	720,000	680,000	660,000
4	750,000	720,000	678,000	660,000
5	750,000	720,000	674,000	660,000

a. Calculate the initial investment associated with replacement of the old machine by the new one.

b. Determine the incremental operating cash inflows associated with the proposed replacement. (*Note:* Be sure to consider the depreciation in year 6.)

c. Depict on a time line the relevant cash flows found in parts **a** and **b** associated with the proposed replacement decision.

LG4 LG5 LG6 8–21 **Integrative—Determining relevant cash flows** Lombard Company is contemplating the purchase of a new high-speed widget grinder to replace the existing grinder. The existing grinder was purchased 2 years ago at an installed cost of $60,000; it was being depreciated under MACRS using a 5-year recovery period. The existing grinder is expected to have a usable life of 5 more years. The new grinder costs $105,000 and requires $5,000 in installation costs; it has a 5-year usable life and would be depreciated under MACRS using a 5-year recovery period. Lombard can currently sell the existing grinder for $70,000 without incurring any removal or cleanup costs. To support the increased business resulting from purchase of the new grinder, accounts receivable would increase by $40,000, inventories by $30,000, and accounts payable by $58,000. At the end of 5 years, the existing grinder is expected to have a market value of zero; the new grinder would be sold to net $29,000 after removal and cleanup costs and before taxes. The firm pays taxes at a rate of 40% on both ordinary income and capital gains. The estimated *profits before depreciation and taxes* over the 5 years for both the new and the existing grinder are shown in the following table. (Table 3.2 on page 89 contains the applicable MACRS depreciation percentages.)

	Profits before depreciation and taxes	
Year	New grinder	Existing grinder
1	$43,000	$26,000
2	43,000	24,000
3	43,000	22,000
4	43,000	20,000
5	43,000	18,000

a. Calculate the initial investment associated with the replacement of the existing grinder by the new one.
b. Determine the incremental operating cash inflows associated with the proposed grinder replacement. (*Note:* Be sure to consider the depreciation in year 6.)
c. Determine the terminal cash flow expected at the end of year 5 from the proposed grinder replacement.
d. Depict on a time line the relevant cash flows associated with the proposed grinder replacement decision.

CHAPTER 8 CASE Developing Relevant Cash Flows for Clark Upholstery Company's Machine Renewal or Replacement Decision

Bo Humphries, chief financial officer of Clark Upholstery Company, expects the firm's *net profits after taxes* for the next 5 years to be as shown in the following table.

Year	Net profits after taxes
1	$100,000
2	150,000
3	200,000
4	250,000
5	320,000

Bo is beginning to develop the relevant cash flows needed to analyze whether to renew or replace Clark's *only* depreciable asset, a machine that originally cost $30,000, has a current book value of zero, and can now be sold for $20,000. (*Note:* Because the firm's only depreciable asset is fully depreciated—its book value is zero—its expected net profits after taxes equal its operating cash inflows.) He estimates that at the end of 5 years, the existing machine can be sold to net $2,000 before taxes. Bo plans to use the following information to develop the relevant cash flows for each of the alternatives.

Alternative 1 Renew the existing machine at a total depreciable cost of $90,000. The renewed machine would have a 5-year usable life and would be depreciated under MACRS using a 5-year recovery period. Renewing the machine would result in the following projected revenues and expenses (excluding depreciation):

Year	Revenue	Expenses (excl. depreciation)
1	$1,000,000	$801,500
2	1,175,000	884,200
3	1,300,000	918,100
4	1,425,000	943,100
5	1,550,000	968,100

The renewed machine would result in an increased investment in net working capital of $15,000. At the end of 5 years, the machine could be sold to net $8,000 before taxes.

Alternative 2 Replace the existing machine with a new machine that costs $100,000 and requires installation costs of $10,000. The new machine would have a 5-year usable life and would be depreciated under MACRS using a 5-year recovery period. The firm's projected revenues and expenses (excluding depreciation), if it acquires the machine, would be as follows:

Year	Revenue	Expenses (excl. depreciation)
1	$1,000,000	$764,500
2	1,175,000	839,800
3	1,300,000	914,900
4	1,425,000	989,900
5	1,550,000	998,900

The new machine would result in an increased investment in net working capital of $22,000. At the end of 5 years, the new machine could be sold to net $25,000 before taxes.

The firm is subject to a 40% tax on both ordinary income and capital gains. As noted, the company uses MACRS depreciation. (See Table 3.2 on page 89 for the applicable depreciation percentages.)

Required

a. Calculate the initial investment associated with each of Clark Upholstery's alternatives.

b. Calculate the incremental operating cash inflows associated with each of Clark's alternatives. (*Note:* Be sure to consider the depreciation in year 6.)

c. Calculate the terminal cash flow at the end of year 5 associated with each of Clark's alternatives.

d. Use your findings in parts **a, b,** and **c** to depict on a time line the relevant cash flows associated with each of Clark Upholstery's alternatives.

e. Solely on the basis of your comparison of their relevant cash flows, which alternative appears to be better? Why?

WEB EXERCISE

Go to the Web site *www.reportgallery.com*. Click on **Reports,** at the top of the page, navigate to the listing for Intel Corp., and click on **Annual Report.** This takes you to an investor relations page; select the most recent annual report. Answer the following questions using information in various report sections, such as **Intel Facts and Figures, Financial Summary, Consolidated Balance Sheets,** and **Consolidated Statements of Cash Flow.** (These may change from year to year and may be listed in the left navigation bar.)

1. How much did Intel spend on capital expenditures for each of the past 5 years?
2. Did capital expenditures increase or decrease?
3. Is Intel's capital spending consistent or erratic?
4. What were the major uses of capital spending for the most recent 2 years?
5. What were the account balances for property, plant, and equipment (PP&E) for the most recent 2 years (found on the *Consolidated Balance Sheets*)?
6. What percent of PP&E does Intel replace every year? (*Hint:* For a rough estimate, divide capital expenditures for a year by that year's PP&E balance.)
7. Select *one* of the following companies, and use the *Reportgallery* site to access its annual report. Research its capital spending patterns and compare them to Intel's.
   a. Abbot Laboratories
   b. Southwest Airlines
   c. Ford Motor Company

Remember to check the book's Web site at

www.aw.com/gitman

for additional resources, including additional Web exercises.

Chapter

9

Capital Budgeting Techniques: Certainty and Risk

LEARNING GOALS

LG1 Calculate, interpret, and evaluate the payback period.

LG2 Apply net present value (NPV) and internal rate of return (IRR) to relevant cash flows to choose acceptable capital expenditures.

LG3 Use net present value profiles to compare the NPV and IRR techniques in light of conflicting rankings.

LG4 Discuss two additional considerations in capital budgeting—recognizing real options and choosing projects under capital rationing.

LG5 Recognize sensitivity analysis and scenario analysis, decision trees, and simulation as behavioral approaches for dealing with project risk, and the unique risks that multinational companies face.

LG6 Understand the calculation and practical aspects of risk-adjusted discount rates (RADRs).

Across the Disciplines
Why This Chapter Matters To You

Accounting: You need to understand capital budgeting techniques in order to develop good estimates of the relevant cash flows associated with a proposed capital expenditure and to appreciate how risk may affect the variability of cash flows.

Information systems: You need to understand capital budgeting techniques, including how risk is measured in those techniques, in order to design decision modules that help reduce the amount of work required in analyzing proposed capital projects.

Management: You need to understand capital budgeting techniques in order to understand the decision criteria used to accept or reject proposed projects; how to apply capital budgeting techniques when capital must be rationed; and behavioral and risk-adjustment approaches for dealing with risk, including international risk.

Marketing: You need to understand capital budgeting techniques in order to understand how proposals for new products and expansion of existing product lines will be evaluated by the firm's decision makers and how risk of proposed projects is treated in capital budgeting.

Operations: You need to understand capital budgeting techniques in order to understand how proposals for the acquisition of new equipment and plants will be evaluated by the firm's decision makers, especially when capital must be rationed.

Firms use the relevant cash flows to make decisions about proposed capital expenditures. These decisions can be expressed in the form of project acceptance or rejection or of project rankings. A number of techniques are used in such decision making, some more sophisticated than others. These techniques are the topic of this chapter, wherein we describe the assumptions on which capital budgeting techniques are based, show how they are used in both certain and risky situations, and evaluate their strengths and weaknesses.

LG1 LG2

Capital Budgeting Techniques

When firms have developed relevant cash flows, as demonstrated in Chapter 8, they analyze them to assess whether a project is acceptable or to rank projects. A number of techniques are available for performing such analyses. The preferred approaches integrate time value procedures, risk and return considerations, and valuation concepts to select capital expenditures that are consistent with the firm's goal of maximizing owners' wealth. This section and the following one focus on the use of these techniques in an environment of certainty. Later in the chapter, we will look at capital budgeting under uncertain circumstances.

We will use one basic problem to illustrate all the techniques described in this chapter. The problem concerns Bennett Company, a medium-sized metal fabricator that is currently contemplating two projects: Project A requires an initial investment of $42,000, project B an initial investment of $45,000. The projected relevant operating cash inflows for the two projects are presented in Table 9.1 and depicted on the time lines in Figure 9.1.[1] The projects exhibit *conventional*

TABLE 9.1 Capital Expenditure Data for Bennett Company

	Project A	Project B
Initial investment	$42,000	$45,000
Year	**Operating cash inflows**	
1	$14,000	$28,000
2	14,000	12,000
3	14,000	10,000
4	14,000	10,000
5	14,000	10,000

1. For simplification, these 5-year-lived projects with 5 years of cash inflows are used throughout this chapter. Projects with usable lives equal to the number of years of cash inflows are also included in the end-of-chapter problems. Recall from Chapter 8 that under current tax law, MACRS depreciation results in $n + 1$ years of depreciation for an n-year class asset. This means that projects will commonly have at least 1 year of cash flow beyond their recovery period. In actual practice, the usable lives of projects (and the associated cash inflows) may differ significantly from their depreciable lives. Generally, under MACRS, usable lives are longer than depreciable lives.

FIGURE 9.1

Bennett Company's Projects A and B

Time lines depicting the conventional cash flows of projects A and B

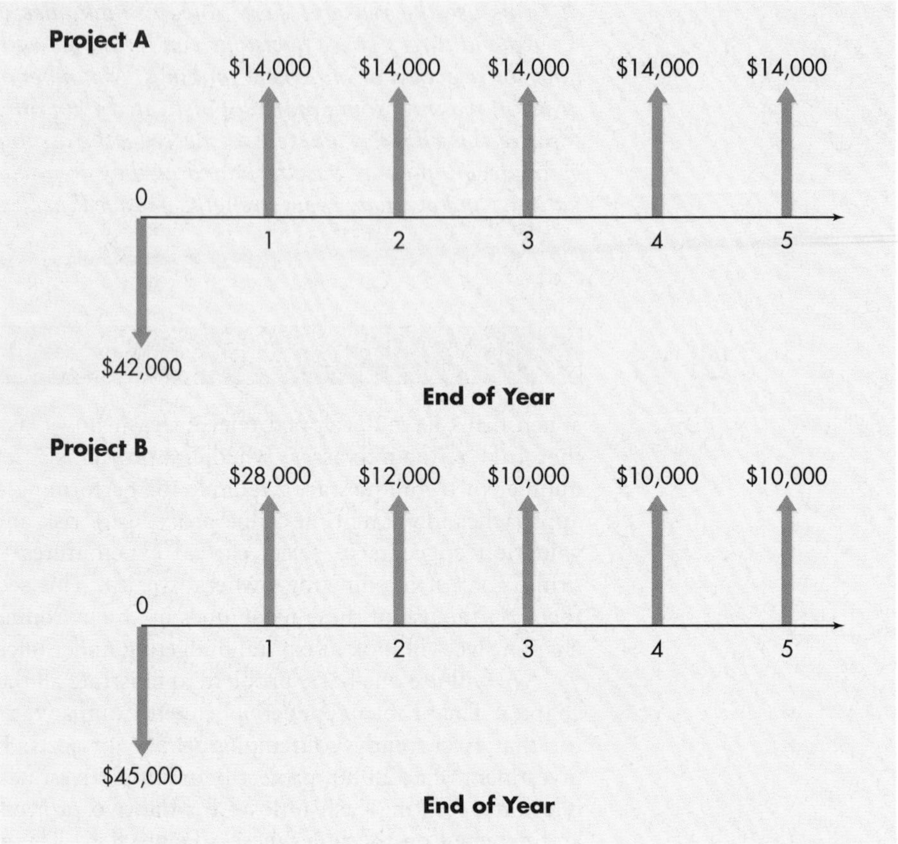

cash flow patterns, which are assumed throughout the text. In addition, we initially assume that all projects' cash flows have the same level of risk, that projects being compared have equal usable lives, and that the firm has unlimited funds. Because very few decisions are actually made under such conditions, some of these simplifying assumptions are relaxed in later sections of this chapter. Here we begin with a look at the three most popular capital budgeting techniques: payback period, net present value, and internal rate of return.[2]

Payback Period

payback period
The amount of time required for a firm to recover its initial investment in a project, as calculated from *cash inflows.*

Payback periods are commonly used to evaluate proposed investments. The **payback period** is the amount of time required for the firm to recover its initial investment in a project, as calculated from *cash inflows*. In the case of an *annuity,*

2. Two other, closely related techniques that are sometimes used to evaluate capital budgeting projects are the *average (or accounting) rate of return (ARR)* and the *profitability index (PI)*. The ARR is an unsophisticated technique that is calculated by dividing a project's average profits after taxes by its average investment. Because it fails to consider cash flows and the time value of money, it is ignored here. The PI, sometimes called the *benefit–cost ratio,* is calculated by dividing the present value of cash inflows by the initial investment. This technique, which does consider the time value of money, is sometimes used as a starting point in the selection of projects under capital rationing; the more popular NPV and IRR methods are discussed here.

the payback period can be found by dividing the initial investment by the annual cash inflow. For a *mixed stream* of cash inflows, the yearly cash inflows must be accumulated until the initial investment is recovered. Although popular, the payback period is generally viewed as an *unsophisticated capital budgeting technique,* because it does not *explicitly* consider the time value of money.

The Decision Criteria

When the payback period is used to make accept–reject decisions, the decision criteria are as follows:

- If the payback period is *less than* the maximum acceptable payback period, *accept* the project.
- If the payback period is *greater than* the maximum acceptable payback period, *reject* the project.

The length of the maximum acceptable payback period is determined by management. This value is set *subjectively* on the basis of a number of factors, including the type of project (expansion, replacement, renewal), the perceived risk of the project, and the perceived relationship between the payback period and the share value. It is simply a value that management feels, on average, will result in value-creating investment decisions.

EXAMPLE We can calculate the payback period for Bennett Company's projects A and B using the data in Table 9.1. For project A, which is an annuity, the payback period is 3.0 years ($42,000 initial investment ÷ $14,000 annual cash inflow). Because project B generates a mixed stream of cash inflows, the calculation of its payback period is not as clear-cut. In year 1, the firm will recover $28,000 of its $45,000 initial investment. By the end of year 2, $40,000 ($28,000 from year 1 + $12,000 from year 2) will have been recovered. At the end of year 3, $50,000 will have been recovered. Only 50% of the year 3 cash inflow of $10,000 is needed to complete the payback of the initial $45,000. The payback period for project B is therefore 2.5 years (2 years + 50% of year 3).

If Bennett's maximum acceptable payback period were 2.75 years, project A would be rejected and project B would be accepted. If the maximum payback were 2.25 years, both projects would be rejected. If the projects were being ranked, B would be preferred over A, because it has a shorter payback period.

Pros and Cons of Payback Periods

The payback period is widely used by large firms to evaluate small projects and by small firms to evaluate most projects. Its popularity results from its computational simplicity and intuitive appeal. It is also appealing in that it considers cash flows rather than accounting profits. By measuring how quickly the firm recovers its initial investment, the payback period also gives *implicit* consideration to the timing of cash flows and therefore to the time value of money. Because it can be viewed as a measure of *risk exposure,* many firms use the payback period as a decision criterion or as a supplement to other decision techniques. The longer the firm must wait to recover its invested funds, the greater the possibility of a calamity. Therefore, the shorter the payback period, the lower the firm's exposure to such risk.

The major weakness of the payback period is that the appropriate payback period is merely a subjectively determined number. It cannot be specified in light of the wealth maximization goal because it is not based on discounting cash flows to determine whether they add to the firm's value. Instead, the appropriate payback period is simply the maximum acceptable period of time over which management decides that a project's cash flows must break even (that is, just equal the initial investment). A second weakness is that this approach fails to take *fully* into account the time factor in the value of money.[3] This weakness can be illustrated by an example.

EXAMPLE DeYarman Enterprises, a small medical appliance manufacturer, is considering two mutually exclusive projects, which it has named projects Gold and Silver. The firm uses only the payback period to choose projects. The relevant cash flows and payback period for each project are given in Table 9.2. Both projects have 3-year payback periods, which would suggest that they are equally desirable. But comparison of the pattern of cash inflows over the first 3 years shows that more of the $50,000 initial investment in project Silver is recovered sooner than is recovered for project Gold. For example, in year 1, $40,000 of the $50,000 invested in project Silver is recovered, whereas only $5,000 of the $50,000 investment in project Gold is recovered. Given the time value of money, project Silver would clearly be preferred over project Gold, in spite of the fact that they both have identical 3-year payback periods. The payback approach does not fully

TABLE 9.2 Relevant Cash Flows and Payback Periods for DeYarman Enterprises' Projects

	Project Gold	Project Silver
Initial investment	$50,000	$50,000
Year	Operating cash inflows	
1	$ 5,000	$40,000
2	5,000	2,000
3	40,000	8,000
4	10,000	10,000
5	10,000	10,000
Payback period	3 years	3 years

3. To consider differences in timing *explicitly* in applying the payback method, the *present value payback period* is sometimes used. It is found by first calculating the present value of the cash inflows at the appropriate discount rate and then finding the payback period by using the present value of the cash inflows.

TABLE 9.3 Calculation of the Payback Period for Rashid Company's Two Alternative Investment Projects

	Project X	Project Y
Initial investment	$10,000	$10,000
Year	Operating cash inflows	
1	$5,000	$3,000
2	5,000	4,000
3	1,000	3,000
4	100	4,000
5	100	3,000
Payback period	2 years	3 years

account for the time value of money, which, if recognized, would cause project Silver to be preferred over project Gold.

A third weakness of payback is its failure to recognize cash flows that occur *after* the payback period.

EXAMPLE Rashid Company, a software developer, has two investment opportunities, X and Y. Data for X and Y are given in Table 9.3. The payback period for project X is 2 years; for project Y it is 3 years. Strict adherence to the payback approach suggests that project X is preferable to project Y. However, if we look beyond the payback period, we see that project X returns only an additional $1,200 ($1,000 in year 3 + $100 in year 4 + $100 in year 5), whereas project Y returns an additional $7,000 ($4,000 in year 4 + $3,000 in year 5). On the basis of this information, project Y appears preferable to X. The payback approach ignored the cash inflows occurring after the end of the payback period.[4]

Net Present Value (NPV)

Because *net present value (NPV)* gives explicit consideration to the time value of money, it is considered a *sophisticated capital budgeting technique.* All such techniques in one way or another discount the firm's cash flows at a specified rate.

4. To get around this weakness, some analysts add a desired dollar return to the initial investment and then calculate the payback period for the increased amount. For example, if the analyst wished to pay back the initial investment plus 20% for projects X and Y in Table 9.3, the amount to be recovered would be $12,000 [$10,000 + (0.20 × $10,000)]. For project X, the payback period would be infinite because the $12,000 would never be recovered; for project Y, the payback period would be 3.50 years [3 years + ($2,000 ÷ $4,000) years]. Clearly, project Y would be preferred.

This rate—often called the *discount rate, required return, cost of capital,* or *opportunity cost*—is the minimum return that must be earned on a project to leave the firm's market value unchanged. In this chapter, we take this rate as a "given." In Chapter 10 we will explore how it is calculated.

net present value (NPV)
A sophisticated capital budgeting technique; found by subtracting a project's initial investment from the present value of its cash inflows discounted at a rate equal to the firm's cost of capital.

The **net present value (NPV)** is found by subtracting a project's initial investment (CF_0) from the present value of its cash inflows (CF_t) discounted at a rate equal to the firm's cost of capital (k).

$$\text{NPV} = \text{Present value of cash inflows} - \text{Initial investment}$$

$$\text{NPV} = \sum_{t=1}^{n} \frac{CF_t}{(1+k)^t} - CF_0 \tag{9.1}$$

$$= \sum_{t=1}^{n} (CF_t \times PVIF_{k,t}) - CF_0 \tag{9.1a}$$

When NPV is used, both inflows and outflows are measured in terms of present dollars. Because we are dealing only with investments that have *conventional cash flow patterns,* the initial investment is automatically stated in terms of today's dollars. If it were not, the present value of a project would be found by subtracting the present value of outflows from the present value of inflows.

The Decision Criteria

When NPV is used to make accept–reject decisions, the decision criteria are as follows:

- If the NPV is *greater than* \$0, *accept* the project.
- If the NPV is *less than* \$0, *reject* the project.

If the NPV is greater than \$0, the firm will earn a return greater than its cost of capital. Such action should enhance the market value of the firm and therefore the wealth of its owners.

EXAMPLE We can illustrate the net present value (NPV) approach by using Bennett Company data presented in Table 9.1. If the firm has a 10% cost of capital, the net present values for projects A (an annuity) and B (a mixed stream) can be calculated as shown on the time lines in Figure 9.2. These calculations result in net present values for projects A and B of \$11,071 and \$10,924, respectively. Both projects are acceptable, because the net present value of each is greater than \$0. If the projects were being ranked, however, project A would be considered superior to B, because it has a higher net present value (\$11,071 versus \$10,924).

Project A

Input	Function
−42000	CF_0
14000	CF_1
5	N
10	I
	NPV

Solution: 11071.01

Project B

Input	Function
−45000	CF_0
28000	CF_1
12000	CF_2
10000	CF_3
3	N
10	I
	NPV

Solution: 10924.40

Calculator Use The preprogrammed NPV function in a financial calculator can be used to simplify the NPV calculation. The keystrokes for project A—the annuity—typically are as shown at left. Note that because project A is an annuity, only its first cash inflow, $CF_1 = 14000$, is input, followed by its frequency, $N = 5$.

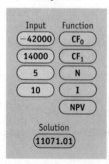

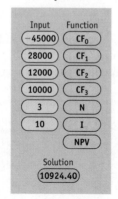

FIGURE 9.2 **Calculation of NPVs for Bennett Company's Capital Expenditure Alternatives**
Time lines depicting the cash flows and NPV calculations for projects A and B

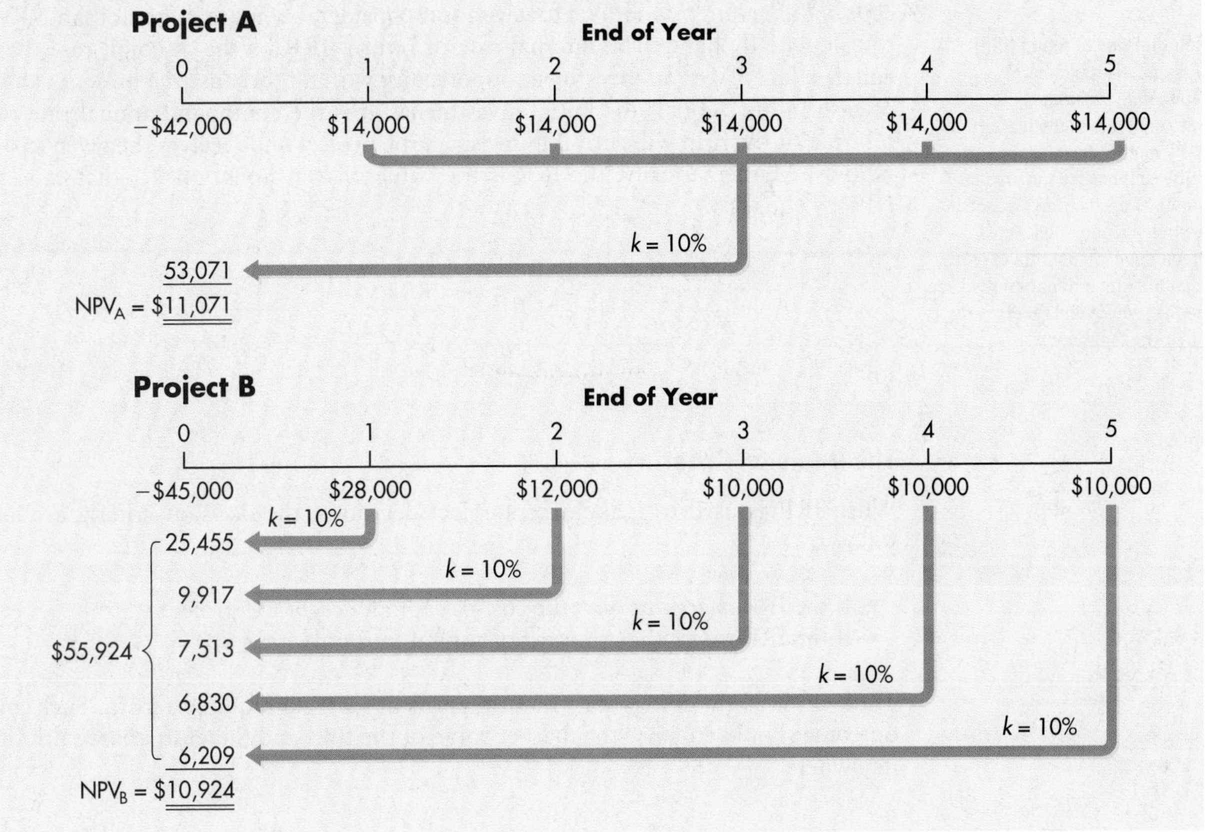

	A	B	C
1	DETERMINING THE NET PRESENT VALUE		
2	Firm's cost of capital		10%
3		Year-End Cash Flow	
4	Year	Project A	Project B
5	0	$ (42,000)	$ (45,000)
6	1	$ 14,000	$ 28,000
7	2	$ 14,000	$ 12,000
8	3	$ 14,000	$ 10,000
9	4	$ 14,000	$ 10,000
10	5	$ 14,000	$ 10,000
11	NPV	$ 11,071	$ 10,924
12	Choice of project		Project A

Entry in Cell B11 is
=NPV(C2,B6:B10)+B5
Copy the entry in Cell B11 to Cell C11.
Entry in Cell C12 is IF(B11>C11,B4,C4).

The keystrokes for project B—the mixed stream—are as shown on page 346. Because the last three cash inflows for project B are the same ($CF_3 = CF_4 = CF_5 = 10000$), after inputting the first of these cash inflows, CF_3, we merely input its frequency, $N = 3$.

The calculated NPVs for projects A and B of $11,071 and $10,924, respectively, agree with the NPVs cited above.

Spreadsheet Use The NPVs can be calculated as shown on the Excel spreadsheet at the left.

Internal Rate of Return (IRR)

internal rate of return (IRR)
A sophisticated capital budgeting technique; the discount rate that equates the NPV of an investment opportunity with \$0 (because the present value of cash inflows equals the initial investment); it is the compound annual rate of return that the firm will earn if it invests in the project and receives the given cash inflows.

The *internal rate of return (IRR)* is probably the most widely used *sophisticated capital budgeting technique*. However, it is considerably more difficult than NPV to calculate by hand. The **internal rate of return (IRR)** is the discount rate that equates the NPV of an investment opportunity with \$0 (because the present value of cash inflows equals the initial investment). It is the compound annual rate of return that the firm will earn if it invests in the project and receives the given cash inflows. Mathematically, the IRR is the value of k in Equation 9.1 that causes NPV to equal \$0.

$$\$0 = \sum_{t=1}^{n} \frac{CF_t}{(1+IRR)^t} - CF_0 \tag{9.2}$$

$$\sum_{t=1}^{n} \frac{CF_t}{(1+IRR)^t} = CF_0 \tag{9.2a}$$

The Decision Criteria

When IRR is used to make accept–reject decisions, the decision criteria are as follows:

- If the IRR is *greater than* the cost of capital, *accept* the project.
- If the IRR is *less than* the cost of capital, *reject* the project.

These criteria guarantee that the firm earns at least its required return. Such an outcome should enhance the market value of the firm and therefore the wealth of its owners.

Calculating the IRR

WWW

The actual calculation by hand of the IRR from Equation 9.2a is no easy chore. It involves a complex trial-and-error technique that is described and demonstrated on this text's Web site: *www.aw.com/gitman*. Fortunately, many financial calculators have a preprogrammed IRR function that can be used to simplify the IRR calculation. With these calculators, you merely punch in all cash flows just as if to calculate NPV and then depress **IRR** to find the internal rate of return. Computer software, including spreadsheets, is also available for simplifying these calculations. All NPV and IRR values presented in this and subsequent chapters are obtained by using these functions on a popular financial calculator.

EXAMPLE

We can demonstrate the internal rate of return (IRR) approach using Bennett Company data presented in Table 9.1. Figure 9.3 uses time lines to depict the framework for finding the IRRs for Bennett's projects A and B, both of which have conventional cash flow patterns. It can be seen in the figure that the IRR is the unknown discount rate that causes the NPV just to equal \$0.

Calculator Use To find the IRR using the preprogrammed function in a financial calculator, the keystrokes for each project are the same as those shown on

FIGURE 9.3 **Calculation of IRRs for Bennett Company's Capital Expenditure Alternatives**
Time lines depicting the cash flows and IRR calculations for projects A and B

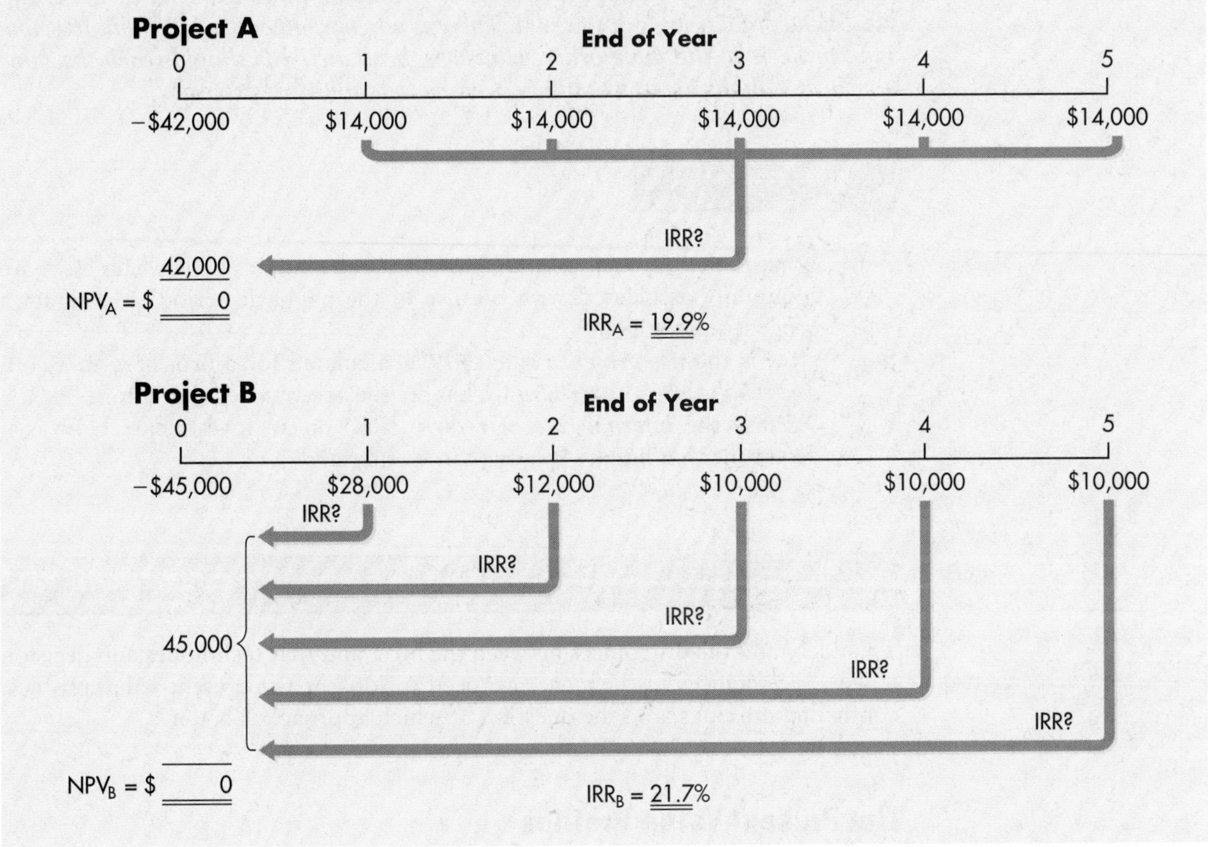

	A	B	C
1	DETERMINING THE INTERNAL RATE OF RETURN		
2		Year-End Cash Flow	
3	Year	Project A	Project B
4	0	$ (42,000)	$ (45,000)
5	1	$ 14,000	$ 28,000
6	2	$ 14,000	$ 12,000
7	3	$ 14,000	$ 10,000
8	4	$ 14,000	$ 10,000
9	5	$ 14,000	$ 10,000
10	IRR	19.9%	21.7%
11	Choice of Project		Project B

Entry in Cell B10 is =IRR(B4:B9).
Copy the entry in Cell B10 to Cell C10.
Entry in Cell C11 is =IF(B10>C10,B3,C3).

page 346 for the NPV calculation, except that the last two NPV keystrokes (punching **I** and then **NPV**) are replaced by a single **IRR** keystroke.

Comparing the IRRs of projects A and B given in Figure 9.3 to Bennett Company's 10% cost of capital, we can see that both projects are acceptable because

$$IRR_A = 19.9\% > 10.0\% \text{ cost of capital}$$
$$IRR_B = 21.7\% > 10.0\% \text{ cost of capital}$$

Comparing the two projects' IRRs, we would prefer project B over project A because $IRR_B = 21.7\% > IRR_A = 19.9\%$. If these projects are mutually exclusive, the IRR decision technique would recommend project B.

Spreadsheet Use The internal rate of return also can be calculated as shown on the Excel spreadsheet at the left.

It is interesting to note in the preceding example that the IRR suggests that project B, which has an IRR of 21.7%, is preferable to project A, which has an IRR of 19.9%. This conflicts with the NPV rankings obtained in an earlier example. Such conflicts are not unusual. *There is no guarantee that NPV and IRR will rank projects in the same order. However, both methods should reach the same conclusion about the acceptability or nonacceptability of projects.*

Review Questions

9–1 What is the *payback period?* How is it calculated? What weaknesses are commonly associated with the use of the payback period to evaluate a proposed investment?

9–2 How is the *net present value (NPV)* calculated for a project with a *conventional cash flow pattern?* What are the acceptance criteria for NPV?

9–3 What is the *internal rate of return (IRR)* on an investment? How is it determined? What are its acceptance criteria?

LG3

Comparing NPV and IRR Techniques

To understand the differences between the NPV and IRR techniques and decision makers' preferences in their use, we need to look at net present value profiles, conflicting rankings, and the question of which approach is better.

Net Present Value Profiles

net present value profile
Graph that depicts a project's NPVs for various discount rates.

Projects can be compared graphically by constructing **net present value profiles** that depict the projects' NPVs for various discount rates. These profiles are useful in evaluating and comparing projects, especially when conflicting rankings exist. They are best demonstrated via an example.

EXAMPLE

To prepare net present value profiles for Bennett Company's two projects, A and B, the first step is to develop a number of "discount rate–net present value" coordinates. Three coordinates can be easily obtained for each project; they are at discount rates of 0%, 10% (the cost of capital, k), and the IRR. The net present value at a 0% discount rate is found by merely adding all the cash inflows and subtracting the initial investment. Using the data in Table 9.1 and Figure 9.1, we get

For project A:

$$(\$14{,}000 + \$14{,}000 + \$14{,}000 + \$14{,}000 + \$14{,}000) - \$42{,}000 = \$28{,}000$$

For project B:

$$(\$28{,}000 + \$12{,}000 + \$10{,}000 + \$10{,}000 + \$10{,}000) - \$45{,}000 = \$25{,}000$$

TABLE 9.4 Discount-Rate–NPV Coordinates for Projects A and B

	Net present value	
Discount rate	Project A	Project B
0 %	$28,000	$25,000
10	11,071	10,924
19.9	0	—
21.7	—	0

FIGURE 9.4

NPV Profiles

Net present value profiles for Bennett Company's projects A and B

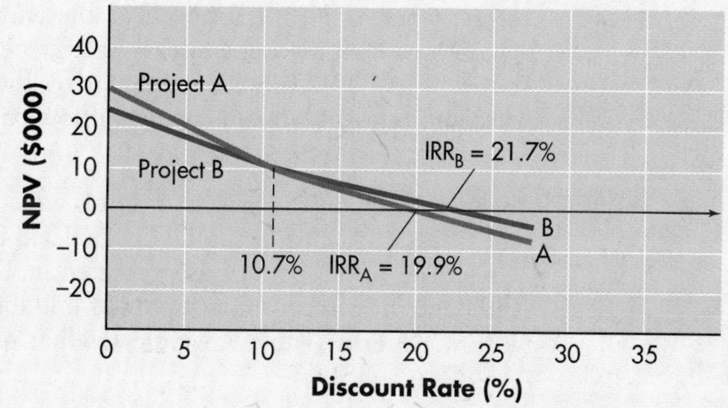

The net present values for projects A and B at the 10% cost of capital are $11,071 and $10,924, respectively (from Figure 9.2). Because the IRR is the discount rate for which net present value equals zero, the IRRs (from Figure 9.3) of 19.9% for project A and 21.7% for project B result in $0 NPVs. The three sets of coordinates for each of the projects are summarized in Table 9.4.

Plotting the data from Table 9.4 results in the net present value profiles for projects A and B shown in Figure 9.4. The figure indicates that for any discount rate less than approximately 10.7%, the NPV for project A is greater than the NPV for project B. Beyond this point, the NPV for project B is greater. Because the net present value profiles for projects A and B cross at a positive NPV, the IRRs for the projects cause conflicting rankings whenever they are compared to NPVs calculated at discount rates below 10.7%.

Conflicting Rankings

Ranking is an important consideration when projects are mutually exclusive or when capital rationing is necessary. When projects are mutually exclusive, ranking enables the firm to determine which project is best from a financial standpoint.

conflicting rankings
Conflicts in the ranking given a project by NPV and IRR, resulting from *differences in the magnitude and timing of cash flows.*

intermediate cash inflows
Cash inflows received prior to the termination of a project.

When capital rationing is necessary, ranking projects will provide a logical starting point for determining what group of projects to accept. As we'll see, **conflicting rankings** using NPV and IRR result from *differences in the magnitude and timing of cash flows.*

The underlying cause of conflicting rankings is different implicit assumptions about the *reinvestment* of **intermediate cash inflows**—cash inflows received prior to the termination of a project. NPV assumes that intermediate cash inflows are reinvested at the cost of capital, whereas IRR assumes that intermediate cash inflows are invested at a rate equal to the project's IRR.[5]

In general, projects with similar-size investments and lower cash inflows in the early years tend to be preferred at lower discount rates. Projects that have higher cash inflows in the early years tend to be preferred at higher discount rates. Why? Because at high discount rates, later-year cash inflows tend to be severely penalized in present value terms. For example, at a high discount rate, say 20 percent, the present value of $1 received at the end of 5 years is about 40 cents, whereas for $1 received at the end of 15 years it is less than 7 cents. Clearly, at high discount rates a project's early-year cash inflows count most in terms of its NPV. Table 9.5 summarizes the preferences associated with extreme discount rates and dissimilar cash inflow patterns.

EXAMPLE Bennett Company's projects A and B were found to have conflicting rankings at the firm's 10% cost of capital (as depicted in Figure 9.4). If we review each project's cash inflow pattern as presented in Table 9.1 and Figure 9.1, we see that although the projects require similar initial investments, they have dissimilar cash inflow patterns. Table 9.5 indicates that project B, which has higher early-year

TABLE 9.5 Preferences Associated with Extreme Discount Rates and Dissimilar Cash Inflow Patterns

	Cash inflow pattern	
Discount rate	Lower early-year cash inflows	Higher early-year cash inflows
Low	Preferred	Not preferred
High	Not preferred	Preferred

5. To eliminate the reinvestment rate assumption of the IRR, some practitioners calculate the *modified internal rate of return (MIRR)*. The MIRR is found by converting each operating cash inflow to its future value measured at the end of the project's life and then summing the future values of all inflows to get the project's *terminal value*. Each future value is found by using the cost of capital, thereby eliminating the reinvestment rate criticism of the traditional IRR. The MIRR represents the discount rate that causes the terminal value just to equal the initial investment. Because it uses the cost of capital as the reinvestment rate, the MIRR is generally viewed as a better measure of a project's true profitability than the IRR. Although this technique is frequently used in commercial real estate valuation and is a preprogrammed function on some sophisticated financial calculators, its failure to resolve the issue of conflicting rankings and its theoretical inferiority to NPV have resulted in the MIRR receiving only limited attention and acceptance in the financial literature. For a thorough analysis of the arguments surrounding IRR and MIRR, see D. Anthony Plath and William F. Kennedy, "Teaching Return-Based Measures of Project Evaluation," *Financial Practice and Education* (Spring/Summer 1994), pp. 77–86.

cash inflows than project A, would be preferred over project A at higher discount rates. Figure 9.4 shows that this is in fact the case. At any discount rate in excess of 10.7%, project B's NPV is above that of project A. Clearly, the magnitude and timing of the projects' cash inflows do affect their rankings.

Which Approach Is Better?

It is difficult to choose one approach over the other, because the theoretical and practical strengths of the approaches differ. It is therefore wise to view both NPV and IRR techniques in each of those dimensions.

Theoretical View

On a purely theoretical basis, NPV is the better approach to capital budgeting as a result of several factors. Most important is that the use of NPV implicitly assumes that any intermediate cash inflows generated by an investment are *reinvested at the firm's cost of capital.* The use of IRR assumes *reinvestment at the often high rate specified by the IRR.* Because the cost of capital tends to be a reasonable estimate of the rate at which the firm could *actually reinvest* intermediate cash inflows, the use of NPV, with its more conservative and realistic reinvestment rate, is in theory preferable.

In addition, certain mathematical properties may cause a project with a nonconventional cash flow pattern to have zero or more than one *real* IRR; this problem does not occur with the NPV approach.

Practical View

Evidence suggests that in spite of the theoretical superiority of NPV, *financial managers prefer to use IRR.*[6] The preference for IRR is due to the general disposition of businesspeople toward *rates of return* rather than actual *dollar returns.* Because interest rates, profitability, and so on are most often expressed as annual rates of return, the use of IRR makes sense to financial decision makers. They tend to find NPV less intuitive because it does not measure benefits *relative to the amount invested.* Because a variety of techniques are available for avoiding the pitfalls of the IRR, its widespread use does not imply a lack of sophistication on the part of financial decision makers.

Review Questions

9–4 Do the net present value (NPV) and internal rate of return (IRR) always agree with respect to accept–reject decisions? With respect to ranking decisions? Explain.

6. For example, see Harold Bierman, Jr., "Capital Budgeting in 1992: A Survey," *Financial Management* (Autumn 1993), p. 24, and Lawrence J. Gitman and Charles E. Maxwell, "A Longitudinal Comparison of Capital Budgeting Techniques Used by Major U.S. Firms: 1986 versus 1976," *Journal of Applied Business Research* (Fall 1987), pp. 41–50, for discussions of evidence with respect to capital budgeting decision-making practices in major U.S. firms.

9–5 How is a *net present value profile* used to compare projects? What causes conflicts in the ranking of projects via net present value and internal rate of return?

9–6 Does the assumption concerning the reinvestment of intermediate cash inflow tend to favor NPV or IRR? In practice, which technique is preferred and why?

LG4

Additional Considerations: Real Options and Capital Rationing

A couple of important issues that often confront the financial manager when making capital budgeting decisions are (1) the potential real options embedded in capital projects and (2) the availability of only limited funding for acceptable projects. Here we briefly consider each of these situations.

Recognizing Real Options

The procedures described in Chapter 8 and thus far in this chapter suggest that to make capital budgeting decisions, we must (1) estimate relevant cash flows and (2) apply an appropriate decision technique such as NPV or IRR to those cash flows. Although this traditional procedure is believed to yield good decisions, a more *strategic approach* to these decisions has emerged in recent years. This more modern view considers any **real options**—opportunities that are embedded in capital projects ("real," rather than financial, asset investments) that enable managers to alter their cash flows and risk in a way that affects project acceptability (NPV). Because these opportunities are more likely to exist in, and be more important to, large "strategic" capital budgeting projects, they are sometimes called *strategic options.*

real options
Opportunities that are embedded in capital projects that enable managers to alter their cash flows and risk in a way that affects project acceptability (NPV). Also called *strategic options.*

Some of the more common types of real options—abandonment, flexibility, growth, and timing—are briefly described in Table 9.6. It should be clear from their descriptions that each of these types of options could be embedded in a capital budgeting decision and that explicit recognition of them would probably alter the cash flow and risk of a project and change its NPV.

By explicitly recognizing these options when making capital budgeting decisions, managers can make improved, more strategic decisions that consider in advance the economic impact of certain contingent actions on project cash flow and risk. The explicit recognition of real options embedded in capital budgeting projects will cause the project's *strategic NPV* to differ from its *traditional NPV* as indicated by Equation 9.3.

$$NPV_{strategic} = NPV_{traditional} + \text{Value of real options} \quad (9.3)$$

Application of this relationship is illustrated in the following example.

EXAMPLE Assume that a strategic analysis of Bennett Company's projects A and B (see cash flows and NPVs in Figure 9.2) finds no real options embedded in project A

TABLE 9.6 Major Types of Real Options

Option type	Description
Abandonment option	The option to abandon or terminate a project prior to the end of its planned life. This option allows management to avoid or minimize losses on projects that turn bad. Explicitly recognizing the abandonment option when evaluating a project often increases its NPV.
Flexibility option	The option to incorporate flexibility into the firm's operations, particularly production. It generally includes the opportunity to design the production process to accept multiple inputs, use flexible production technology to create a variety of outputs by reconfiguring the same plant and equipment, and purchase and retain excess capacity in capital-intensive industries subject to wide swings in output demand and long lead time in building new capacity from scratch. Recognition of this option embedded in a capital expenditure should increase the NPV of the project.
Growth option	The option to develop follow-on projects, expand markets, expand or retool plants, and so on, that would not be possible without implementation of the project that is being evaluated. If a project being considered has the measurable potential to open new doors if successful, then recognition of the cash flows from such opportunities should be included in the initial decision process. Growth opportunities embedded in a project often increase the NPV of the project in which they are embedded.
Timing option	The option to determine when various actions with respect to a given project are taken. This option recognizes the firm's opportunity to delay acceptance of a project for one or more periods, to accelerate or slow the process of implementing a project in response to new information, or to shut down a project temporarily in response to changing product market conditions or competition. As in the case of the other types of options, the explicit recognition of timing opportunities can improve the NPV of a project that fails to recognize this option in an investment decision.

and two real options embedded in project B. The two real options in project B are as follows: (1) The project would have, during the first two years, some downtime that would result in unused production capacity that could be used to perform contract manufacturing for another firm, and (2) the project's computerized control system could, with some modification, control two other machines, thereby reducing labor cost, without affecting operation of the new project.

Bennett's management estimated the NPV of the contract manufacturing over the 2 years following implementation of project B to be \$1,500 and the NPV of the computer control sharing to be \$2,000. Management felt there was a 60% chance that the contract manufacturing option would be exercised and only a 30% chance that the computer control sharing option would be exercised.

The combined value of these two real options would be the sum of their expected values.

$$\text{Value of real options for project B} = (0.60 \times \$1{,}500) + (0.30 \times \$2{,}000)$$
$$= \$900 + \$600 = \$1{,}500$$

Substituting the \$1,500 real options value along with the traditional NPV of \$10,924 for project B (from Figure 9.2) into Equation 9.3, we get the strategic NPV for project B.

$$NPV_{strategic} = \$10{,}924 + \$1{,}500 = \underline{\underline{\$12{,}424}}$$

Bennett Company's project B therefore has a strategic NPV of \$12,424, which is above its traditional NPV and now exceeds project A's NPV of \$11,071. Clearly, recognition of project B's real options improved its NPV (from \$10,924 to \$12,424) and causes it to be preferred over project A (NPV of \$12,424 for B > NPV of \$11,071 for A), which has no real options embedded in it.

It is important to realize that the recognition of attractive real options when determining NPV could cause an otherwise unacceptable project ($NPV_{traditional} < \$0$) to become acceptable ($NPV_{strategic} > \$0$). The failure to recognize the value of real options could therefore cause management to reject projects that are acceptable. Although doing so requires more strategic thinking and analysis, it is important for the financial manager to identify and incorporate real options in the NPV process. The procedures for doing this efficiently are emerging, and the use of the strategic NPV that incorporates real options is expected to become more commonplace in the future.

Choosing Projects under Capital Rationing

Firms commonly operate under *capital rationing*—they have more acceptable independent projects than they can fund. *In theory,* capital rationing should not exist. Firms should accept all projects that have positive NPVs (or IRRs > the cost of capital). However, *in practice,* most firms operate under capital rationing. Generally, firms attempt to isolate and select the best acceptable projects subject to a capital expenditure budget set by management. Research has found that management internally imposes capital expenditure constraints to avoid what it deems to be "excessive" levels of new financing, particularly debt. Although failing to fund all acceptable independent projects is theoretically inconsistent with the goal of maximizing owner wealth, we will discuss capital rationing procedures because they are widely used in practice.

The objective of *capital rationing* is to select the group of projects that provides the *highest overall net present value* and does not require more dollars than are budgeted. As a prerequisite to capital rationing, the best of any mutually exclusive projects must be chosen and placed in the group of independent projects. Two basic approaches to project selection under capital rationing are discussed here.

internal rate of return approach
An approach to capital rationing that involves graphing project IRRs in descending order against the total dollar investment, to determine the group of acceptable projects.

investment opportunities schedule (IOS)
The graph that plots project IRRs in descending order against total dollar investment.

Internal Rate of Return Approach

The **internal rate of return approach** involves graphing project IRRs in descending order against the total dollar investment. This graph, which is discussed in more detail in Chapter 10, is called the **investment opportunities schedule** (IOS). By drawing the cost-of-capital line and then imposing a budget constraint, the financial manager can determine the group of acceptable projects. The problem with this technique is that it does not guarantee the maximum dollar return to the firm. It merely provides a satisfactory solution to capital-rationing problems.

EXAMPLE

Tate Company, a fast-growing plastics company, is confronted with six projects competing for its fixed budget of $250,000. The initial investment and IRR for each project are as follows:

Project	Initial investment	IRR
A	$ 80,000	12%
B	70,000	20
C	100,000	16
D	40,000	8
E	60,000	15
F	110,000	11

The firm has a cost of capital of 10%. Figure 9.5 presents the IOS that results from ranking the six projects in descending order on the basis of their IRRs. According to the schedule, only projects B, C, and E should be accepted.

FIGURE 9.5

Investment Opportunities Schedule
Investment opportunities schedule (IOS) for Tate Company projects

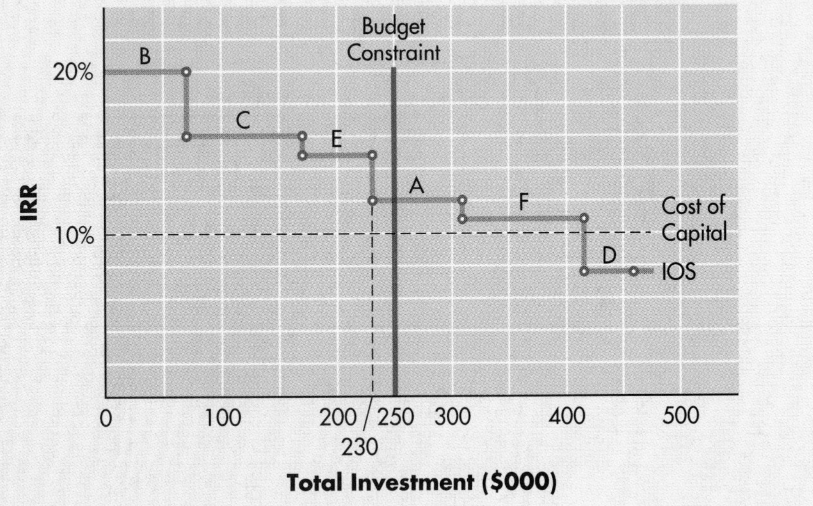

Together they will absorb $230,000 of the $250,000 budget. Projects A and F are acceptable but cannot be chosen because of the budget constraint. Project D is not worthy of consideration; its IRR is less than the firm's 10% cost of capital.

The drawback of this approach is that there is no guarantee that the acceptance of projects B, C, and E will maximize *total dollar returns* and therefore owners' wealth.

Net Present Value Approach

net present value approach
An approach to capital rationing that is based on the use of present values to determine the group of projects that will maximize owners' wealth.

The **net present value approach** is based on the use of present values to determine the group of projects that will maximize owners' wealth. It is implemented by ranking projects on the basis of IRRs and then evaluating the present value of the benefits from each potential project to determine *the combination of projects with the highest overall present value.* This is the same as maximizing net present value, in which the entire budget is viewed as the total initial investment. Any portion of the firm's budget that is not used does not increase the firm's value. At best, the unused money can be invested in marketable securities or returned to the owners in the form of cash dividends. In either case, the wealth of the owners is not likely to be enhanced.

EXAMPLE

The group of projects described in the preceding example is ranked in Table 9.7 on the basis of IRRs. The present value of the cash inflows associated with the projects is also included in the table. Projects B, C, and E, which together require $230,000, yield a present value of $336,000. However, if projects B, C, and A were implemented, the total budget of $250,000 would be used, and the present value of the cash inflows would be $357,000. This is greater than the return expected from selecting the projects on the basis of the highest IRRs. Implementing B, C, and A is preferable, because they maximize the present value for the given budget. *The firm's objective is to use its budget to generate the highest present value of inflows.* Assuming that any unused portion of the budget does not gain or lose money, the total NPV for projects B, C, and E would be $106,000

TABLE 9.7 Rankings for Tate Company Projects

Project	Initial investment	IRR	Present value of inflows at 10%	
B	$ 70,000	20%	$112,000	
C	100,000	16	145,000	
E	60,000	15	79,000	
A	80,000	12	100,000	
F	110,000	11	126,500	Cutoff point
D	40,000	8	36,000	(IRR < 10%)

($336,000 – $230,000), whereas for projects B, C, and A the total NPV would be $107,000 ($357,000 – $250,000). Selection of projects B, C, and A will therefore maximize NPV.

Review Questions

9–7 What are *real options?* What are some major types of real options?

9–8 What is the difference between the *strategic NPV* and the *traditional NPV?* Do they always result in the same accept–reject decisions?

9–9 What is *capital rationing?* In theory, should capital rationing exist? Why does it frequently occur in practice?

9–10 Compare and contrast the *internal rate of return approach* and the *net present value approach* to capital rationing. Which is better? Why?

LG5

Behavioral Approaches for Dealing with Risk

risk (in capital budgeting)
The chance that a project will prove unacceptable or, more formally, the degree of variability of cash flows.

In the context of capital budgeting, the term **risk** refers to the chance that a project will prove unacceptable—that is, NPV < $0 or IRR < cost of capital. More formally, risk in capital budgeting is the degree of variability of cash flows. Projects with a small chance of acceptability and a broad range of expected cash flows are more risky than projects that have a high chance of acceptability and a narrow range of expected cash flows.

In the conventional capital budgeting projects assumed here, risk stems almost entirely from *cash inflows,* because the initial investment is generally known with relative certainty. These inflows, of course, derive from a number of variables related to revenues, expenditures, and taxes. Examples include the level of sales, the cost of raw materials, labor rates, utility costs, and tax rates. We will concentrate on the risk in the cash inflows, but remember that this risk actually results from the interaction of these underlying variables.

Behavioral approaches can be used to get a "feel" for the level of project risk, whereas other approaches explicitly recognize project risk. Here we present a few behavioral approaches for dealing with risk in capital budgeting: sensitivity and scenario analysis, decision trees, and simulation. In addition, some international risk considerations are discussed.

Sensitivity Analysis and Scenario Analysis

Two approaches for dealing with project risk to capture the variability of cash inflows and NPVs are sensitivity analysis and scenario analysis. As noted in Chapter 5, *sensitivity analysis* is a behavioral approach that uses several possible values for a given variable, such as cash inflows, to assess that variable's impact on the firm's return, measured here by NPV. This technique is often useful in getting a feel for the variability of return in response to changes in a key variable. In capital budgeting, one of the most common sensitivity approaches is to estimate

TABLE 9.8 Sensitivity Analysis of Treadwell's Projects A and B

	Project A	Project B
Initial investment	$10,000	$10,000
	Annual cash inflows	
Outcome		
Pessimistic	$1,500	$ 0
Most likely	2,000	2,000
Optimistic	2,500	4,000
Range	$1,000	$ 4,000
	Net present values[a]	
Outcome		
Pessimistic	$1,409	−$10,000
Most likely	5,212	5,212
Optimistic	9,015	20,424
Range	$7,606	$30,424

[a]These values were calculated by using the corresponding annual cash inflows. A 10% cost of capital and a 15-year life for the annual cash inflows were used.

the NPVs associated with pessimistic (worst), most likely (expected), and optimistic (best) estimates of cash inflow. The *range* can be determined by subtracting the pessimistic-outcome NPV from the optimistic-outcome NPV.

EXAMPLE Treadwell Tire Company, a tire retailer with a 10% cost of capital, is considering investing in either of two mutually exclusive projects, A and B. Each requires a $10,000 initial investment, and both are expected to provide equal annual cash inflows over their 15-year lives. The firm's financial manager made pessimistic, most likely, and optimistic estimates of the cash inflows for each project. The cash inflow estimates and resulting NPVs in each case are summarized in Table 9.8. Comparing the ranges of cash inflows ($1,000 for project A and $4,000 for B) and, more important, the ranges of NPVs ($7,606 for project A and $30,424 for B) makes it clear that project A is less risky than project B. Given that both projects have the same most likely NPV of $5,212, the assumed risk-averse decision maker will take project A because it has less risk and no possibility of loss.

scenario analysis
A behavioral approach that evaluates the impact on the firm's return of simultaneous changes in *a number of variables.*

Scenario analysis is a behavioral approach similar to sensitivity analysis but broader in scope. It evaluates the impact on the firm's return of simultaneous changes in *a number of variables,* such as cash inflows, cash outflows, and the cost of capital. For example, the firm could evaluate the impact of both high inflation (scenario 1) and low inflation (scenario 2) on a project's NPV. Each scenario will affect the firm's cash inflows, cash outflows, and cost of capital, thereby resulting in different levels of NPV. The decision maker can use these

NPV estimates to assess the risk involved with respect to the level of inflation. The widespread availability of computer and spreadsheets has greatly enhanced the use of both scenario and sensitivity analysis.

Decision Trees

decision trees
A behavioral approach that uses diagrams to map the various investment decision alternatives and payoffs, along with their probabilities of occurrence.

Decision trees are a behavioral approach that uses diagrams to map the various investment decision alternatives and payoffs, along with their probabilities of occurrence. Their name derives from their resemblance to the branches of a tree (see Figure 9.6). Decision trees rely on estimates of the probabilities associated with the outcomes (payoffs) of competing courses of action. The payoffs of each course of action are weighted by the associated probability; the weighted payoffs are summed; and the expected value of each course of action is then determined. The alternative that provides the highest expected value is preferred.

EXAMPLE ▼ Convoy, Inc., a manufacturer of picture frames, wishes to choose between two equally risky projects, I and J. To make this decision, Convoy's management has gathered the necessary data, which are depicted in the decision tree in Figure 9.6. Project I requires an initial investment of $120,000; a resulting expected present value of cash inflows of $130,000 is shown in column 4. Project I's expected net present value, which is calculated below the decision tree, is therefore $10,000. The expected net present value of project J is determined in a similar fashion. Project J is preferred because it offers a higher NPV—$15,000.

FIGURE 9.6

Decision Tree for NPV
Decision Tree for Convoy, Inc.'s choice between projects I and J

$$\text{Expected NPV}_I = \$130,000 - \$120,000 = \$10,000$$
$$\text{Expected NPV}_J = \$155,000 - \$140,000 = \$15,000$$
Because Expected NPV$_J$ > Expected NPV$_I$, Choose J.

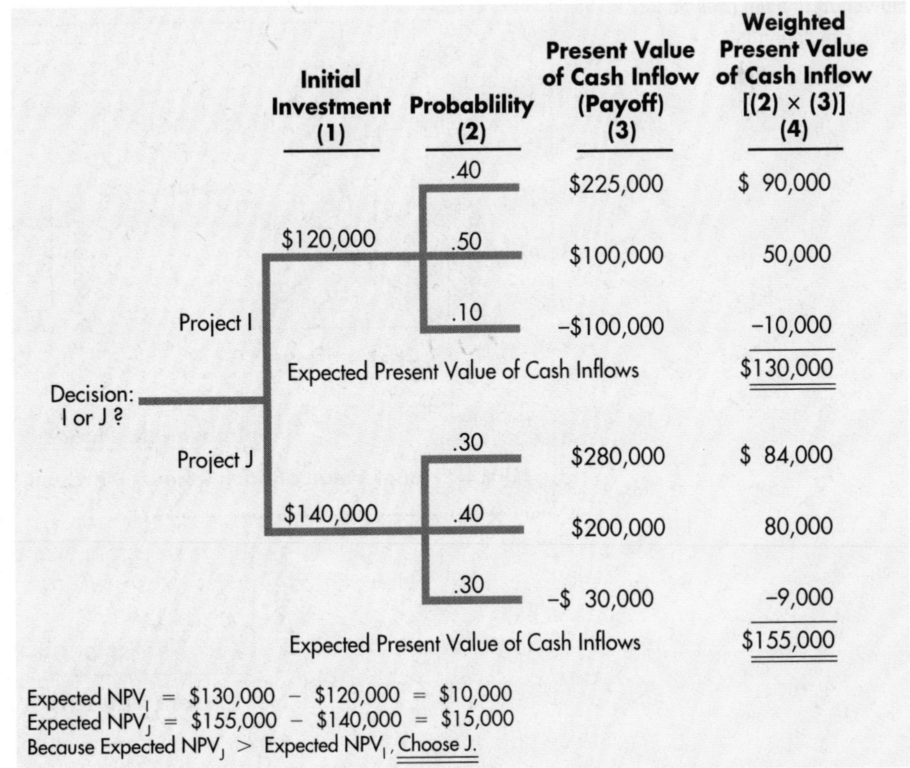

Simulation

simulation
A statistics-based behavioral approach that applies predetermined probability distributions and random numbers to estimate risky outcomes.

Simulation is a statistics-based behavioral approach that applies predetermined probability distributions and random numbers to estimate risky outcomes. By tying the various cash flow components together in a mathematical model and repeating the process numerous times, the financial manager can develop a probability distribution of project returns. Figure 9.7 presents a flowchart of the simulation of the net present value of a project. The process of generating random numbers and using the probability distributions for cash inflows and cash outflows enables the financial manager to determine values for each of these variables. Substituting these values into the mathematical model results in an NPV. By repeating this process perhaps a thousand times, one can create a probability distribution of net present values.

Although only gross cash inflows and cash outflows are simulated in Figure 9.7, more sophisticated simulations using individual inflow and outflow components, such as sales volume, sale price, raw material cost, labor cost, maintenance expense, and so on, are quite common. From the distribution of returns, the decision maker can determine not only the expected value of the return but also the probability of achieving or surpassing a given return. The use of computers has made the simulation approach feasible. The output of simulation provides an

FIGURE 9.7

NPV Simulation

Flowchart of a net present value simulation

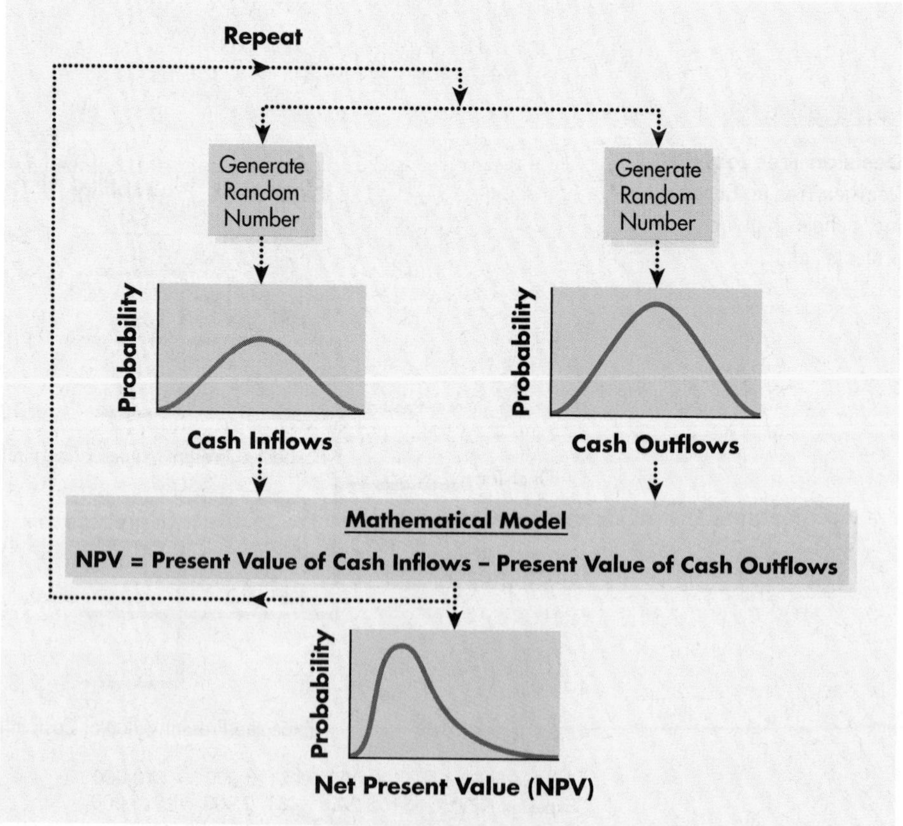

excellent basis for decision making, because it enables the decision maker to view a continuum of risk–return tradeoffs rather than a single-point estimate.

International Risk Considerations

Although the basic techniques of capital budgeting are the same for multinational companies (MNCs) as for purely domestic firms, firms that operate in several countries face risks that are unique to the international arena. Two types of risk are particularly important: exchange rate risk and political risk.

exchange rate risk
The danger that an unexpected change in the exchange rate between the dollar and the currency in which a project's cash flows are denominated will reduce the market value of that project's cash flow.

Exchange rate risk reflects the danger that an unexpected change in the exchange rate between the dollar and the currency in which a project's cash flows are denominated will reduce the market value of that project's cash flow. The dollar value of future cash inflows can be dramatically altered if the local currency depreciates against the dollar. In the short term, specific cash flows can be hedged by using financial instruments such as currency futures and options. Long-term exchange rate risk can best be minimized by financing the project, in whole or in part, in local currency.

Political risk is much harder to protect against. Once a foreign project is accepted, the foreign government can block the return of profits, seize the firm's assets, or otherwise interfere with a project's operation. The inability to manage political risk after the fact makes it even more important that managers account for political risks before making an investment. They can do so either by adjusting a project's expected cash inflows to account for the probability of political interference or by using risk-adjusted discount rates (discussed later in this chapter) in capital budgeting formulas. In general, it is much better to adjust individual project cash flows for political risk subjectively than to use a blanket adjustment for all projects.

In addition to unique risks that MNCs must face, several other special issues are relevant only for international capital budgeting. One of these special issues is *taxes*. Because only after-tax cash flows are relevant for capital budgeting, financial managers must carefully account for taxes paid to foreign governments on profits earned within their borders. They must also assess the impact of these tax payments on the parent company's U.S. tax liability.

transfer prices
Prices that subsidiaries charge each other for the goods and services traded between them.

Another special issue in international capital budgeting is *transfer pricing*. Much of the international trade involving MNCs is, in reality, simply the shipment of goods and services from one of a parent company's subsidiaries to another subsidiary located abroad. The parent company therefore has great discretion in setting **transfer prices,** the prices that subsidiaries charge each other for the goods and services traded between them. The widespread use of transfer pricing in international trade makes capital budgeting in MNCs very difficult unless the transfer prices that are used accurately reflect actual costs and incremental cash flows.

Finally, MNCs often must approach international capital projects from a *strategic point of view,* rather than from a strictly financial perspective. For example, an MNC may feel compelled to invest in a country to ensure continued access, even if the project itself may not have a positive net present value. This motivation was important for Japanese automakers who set up assembly plants in the United States in the early 1980s. For much the same reason, U.S. investment in Europe surged during the years before the market integration of the European Community

In Practice

FOCUS ON PRACTICE Bestfoods' Recipe for Risk

With future volume growth in North America and Western Europe limited to 3 percent at most, executives at Bestfoods (now a unit of the Anglo-Dutch conglomerate Unilever) decided to look for more promising markets. Whereas other food manufacturers were hesitant to take the international plunge, Bestfoods took its popular brands, such as Hellman's/Best Foods, Knorr, Mazola, and Skippy, where the growth was—emerging markets like Latin America, where the company could grow at a rate of 15 percent a year. At the time it was acquired by Unilever, Bestfoods derived about 22 percent of its revenues outside the United States and Western Europe, producing mayonnaise, soups, and other foods for 110 different markets at 130 manufacturing plants worldwide.

Bestfoods' international expansion succeeded because the company developed methods to incorporate the risks and rewards of its foreign investments into project analyses. These risks included exchange rate and political risks, as well as tax and legal considerations and strategic issues. First, it increased its familiarity with the foreign market by partnering with other companies whenever possible and by developing local management and experience. From this knowledge base, Bestfoods was willing to take calculated risks. Working with consultants, the company created its own analytical model to set discount rates for different markets.

Some companies attempt to quantify the risk of foreign projects by arbitrarily assigning a premium to the discount rate they use for domestic projects. Executives who rely on this subjective method may overestimate the costs of doing business overseas and rule out good projects. Unlike these companies, Bestfoods took the time to develop specific costs of capital for international markets. To incorporate the benefits of diversification for a multinational company like Bestfoods, the company adapted the capital asset pricing model (CAPM). The model factors in elements of economic and political risk to obtain the country's risk premium and develops betas for each country on the basis of the local market's volatility and its correlation to the U.S. market. For example, the high volatility of Brazil's market has a low correlation to the U.S. market, so the country beta was .81. With the risk-free rates and country betas, Bestfoods could calculate local and global costs of capital. This more sophisticated approach gave Bestfoods the confidence to pursue an aggressive international strategy that increased shareholder value and resulted in Unilever offering a substantial premium to acquire the company.

Sources: Adapted from Andrew Osterland, "Lowering the Bar," *CFO* (August 1, 2002), downloaded from *www.cfo.com;* Stanley Reed, "Unilever Restocks," *Business Week International* (August 6, 2001), downloaded from Electric Library, *ask.elibrary.com*

in 1992. MNCs often invest in production facilities in the home country of major rivals to deny these competitors an uncontested home market. MNCs also may feel compelled to invest in certain industries or countries to achieve a broad corporate objective such as completing a product line or diversifying raw material sources, even when the project's cash flows may not be sufficiently profitable.

Review Questions

9–11 Define risk in terms of the cash inflows from a capital budgeting project. Briefly describe and compare the following behavioral approaches, explaining how each can be used to deal with project risk: (**a**) sensitivity analysis; (**b**) scenario analysis; (**c**) decision trees; and (**d**) simulation.

9–12 Briefly explain how each of the following considerations affects the capital budgeting decisions of multinational companies: (**a**) exchange rate risk; (**b**) political risk; (**c**) tax law differences; (**d**) transfer pricing; and (**e**) a strategic rather than strictly financial viewpoint.

LG6

Risk-Adjusted Discount Rates

The approaches for dealing with risk that have been presented so far enable the financial manager to get a "feel" for project risk. Unfortunately, they do not explicitly recognize project risk. We will now illustrate the most popular risk-adjustment technique that employs the net present value (NPV) decision method.[7] The NPV decision rule of accepting only those projects with NPVs > \$0 will continue to hold. Close examination of the basic equation for NPV, Equation 9.1, should make it clear that because the initial investment (CF_0) is known with certainty, a project's risk is embodied in the present value of its cash inflows:

$$\sum_{t=1}^{n} \frac{CF_t}{(1+k)^t}$$

Two opportunities to adjust the present value of cash inflows for risk exist: (1) The cash inflows (CF_t) can be adjusted, or (2) the discount rate (k) can be adjusted. Adjusting the cash inflows is highly subjective, so here we describe the more popular process of adjusting the discount rate. In addition, we consider the practical aspects of risk-adjusted discount rates.

Determining Risk-Adjusted Discount Rates (RADRs)

A popular approach for risk adjustment involves the use of *risk-adjusted discount rates (RADRs)*. This approach uses Equation 9.1 but employs a risk-adjusted discount rate, as noted in the following expression:

$$\text{NPV} = \sum_{t=1}^{n} \frac{CF_t}{(1+\text{RADR})^t} - CF_0 \tag{9.4}$$

risk-adjusted discount rate (RADR)
The rate of return that must be earned on a given project to compensate the firm's owners adequately—that is, to maintain or improve the firm's share price.

The **risk-adjusted discount rate (RADR)** is the rate of return that must be earned on a given project to compensate the firm's owners adequately—that is, to maintain or improve the firm's share price. The higher the risk of a project, the higher the RADR, and therefore the lower the net present value for a given stream of cash inflows. The logic underlying the use of RADRs is closely linked to the capital asset pricing model (CAPM) developed in Chapter 5. Because the CAPM is based on an assumed efficient market, which does *not* exist for real corporate (nonfinancial) assets such as plant and equipment, the CAPM is not directly applicable in making capital budgeting decisions. Financial managers therefore assess the *total risk* of a project and use it to determine the risk-adjusted discount rate (RADR), which can be used in Equation 9.4 to find the NPV.

In order not to damage its market value, the firm must use the correct discount rate to evaluate a project. If a firm discounts a risky project's cash inflows at too low a rate and accepts the project, the firm's market price may drop as investors recognize that the firm itself has become more risky. On the other hand, if the firm discounts a project's cash inflows at too high a rate, it will reject acceptable projects. Eventually the firm's market price may drop, because

7. The IRR could just as well have been used, but because NPV is theoretically preferable, it is used instead.

investors who believe that the firm is being overly conservative will sell their stock, putting downward pressure on the firm's market value.

Unfortunately, there is no formal mechanism for linking total project risk to the level of required return. As a result, most firms subjectively determine the RADR by adjusting their existing required return. They adjust it up or down depending on whether the proposed project is more or less risky, respectively, than the average risk of the firm. This CAPM-type of approach provides a "rough estimate" of the project risk and required return because both the project risk measure and the linkage between risk and required return are estimates.

EXAMPLE Bennett Company wishes to use the risk-adjusted discount rate approach to determine, according to NPV, whether to implement project A or project B. In addition to the data presented earlier, Bennett's management after much analysis assigned a "risk index" of 1.6 to project A and of 1.0 to project B. The risk index is merely a numerical scale used to classify project risk: Higher index values are assigned to higher-risk projects, and vice versa. The CAPM-type relationship used by the firm to link risk (measured by the risk index) and the required return (RADR) is shown in the following table.

	Risk index	Required return (RADR)
	0.0	6% (risk-free rate, R_F)
	0.2	7
	0.4	8
	0.6	9
	0.8	10
Project B→	1.0	11
	1.2	12
	1.4	13
Project A→	1.6	14
	1.8	16
	2.0	18

Because project A is riskier than project B, its RADR of 14% is greater than project B's 11%. The net present value of each project, calculated using its RADR, is found as shown on the time lines in Figure 9.8. The results clearly show that project B in preferable, because its risk-adjusted NPV of $9,798 is greater than the $6,063 risk-adjusted NPV for project A. As reflected by the NPVs in Figure 9.2, if the discount rates were not adjusted for risk, project A would be preferred to project B.

Calculator Use We can again use the preprogrammed NPV function in a financial calculator to simplify the NPV calculation. The keystrokes for project A—the annuity—typically are as shown at the top of the next page. The keystrokes for project B—the mixed stream—are also shown at the top of the next page. The calculated NPVs for projects A and B of $6,063 and $9,798, respectively, agree with those shown in Figure 9.8.

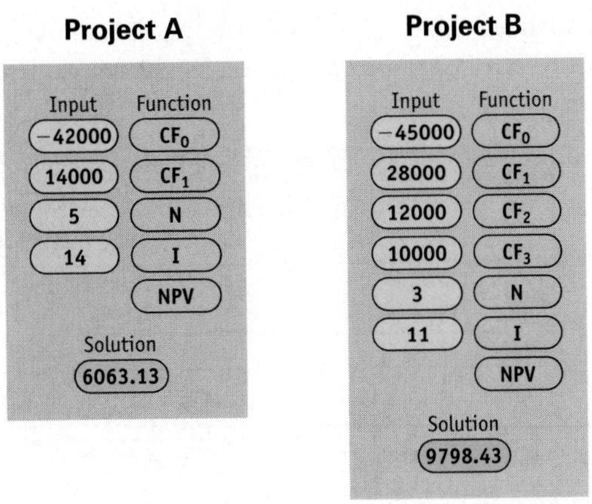

FIGURE 9.8 **Calculation of NPVs for Bennett Company's Capital Expenditure Alternatives using RADRs**

Time lines depicting the cash flows and NPV calculations using RADRs for projects A and B

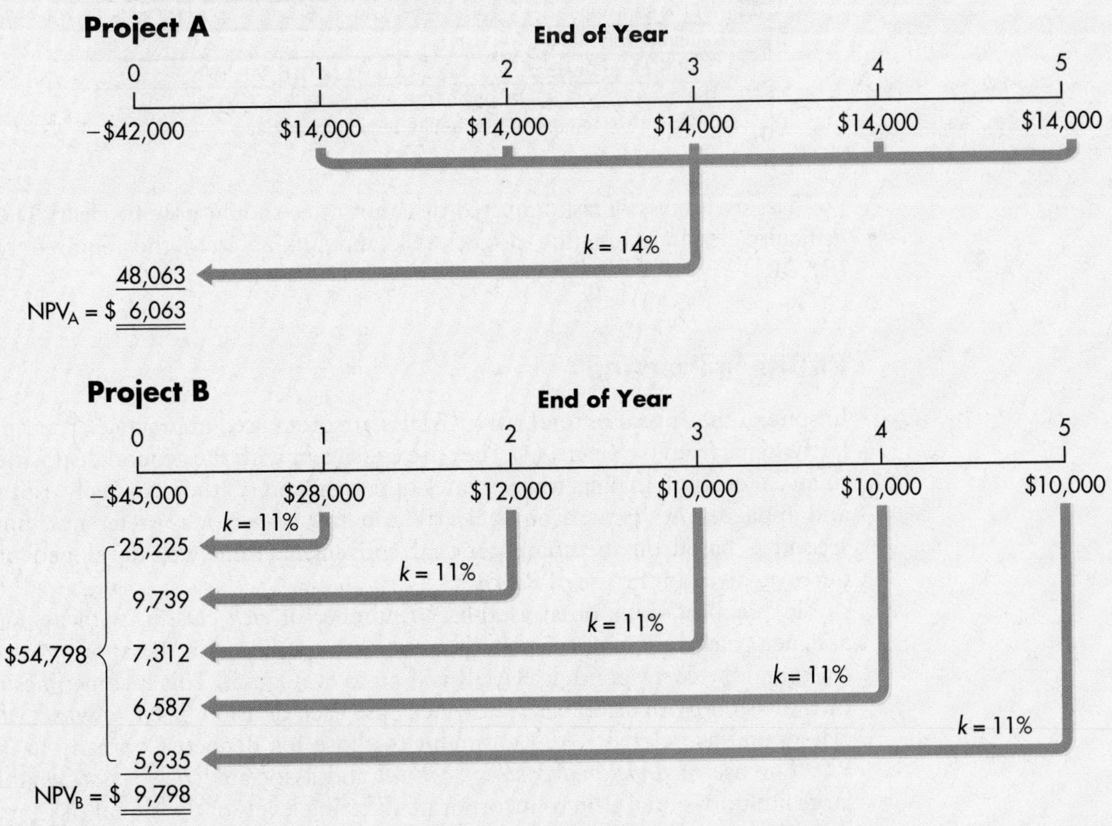

Note: When we use the risk indexes of 1.6 and 1.0 for projects A and B, respectively, along with the table in the middle of the preceding page, a risk-adjusted discount rate (RADR) of 14% results for project A and a RADR of 11% results for project B.

Spreadsheet Use Analysis of projects using risk-adjusted discount rates (RADRs) also can be calculated as shown on the following Excel spreadsheet.

	A	B	C	D
1	ANALYSIS OF PROJECTS USING RISK-ADJUSTED DISCOUNT RATES			
2	Year	Cash Inflow	Present Value	Formulas for Calculated Values in Column C
3	Project A			
4	1-5	$ 14,000	$48,063	-PV(C7,5,B4,0)
5	Initial Investment		$42,000	
6	Net Present Value		**$ 6,063**	C4–C5
7	Required Return (RADR)		14%	
8	Project B			
9	1	$ 28,000	$25,225	-PV(C17,A9,0,B9,0)
10	2	12,000	9,739	-PV(C17,A10,0,B10,0)
11	3	10,000	7,312	-PV(C17,A11,0,B11,0)
12	4	10,000	6,587	-PV(C17,A12,0,B12,0)
13	5	10,000	5,935	-PV(C17,A13,0,B13,0)
14	Present value		$54,798	SUM(C9:C13) or NPV(C17,B9:B13)
15	Initial Investment		$45,000	
16	Net Present Value		**$ 9,798**	C14–C15
17	Required Return (RADR)		11%	
18	**Choice of project**		B	IF(C6>=C16,"A","B")
	The minus signs appear before the entries in Cells C4 and C9:C13 to convert the results to positive values.			

The usefulness of risk-adjusted discount rates should now be clear. The real difficulty lies in estimating project risk and linking it to the required return (RADR).

RADRs in Practice

In spite of the appeal of total risk, RADRs are often used in practice. Their popularity stems from two facts: (1) They are consistent with the general disposition of financial decision makers toward rates of return, and (2) they are easily estimated and applied. The first reason is clearly a matter of personal preference, but the second is based on the computational convenience and well-developed procedures involved in the use of RADRs.

In practice, firms often establish a number of *risk classes,* with an RADR assigned to each. Each project is then subjectively placed in the appropriate risk class, and the corresponding RADR is used to evaluate it. This is sometimes done on a division-by-division basis, in which case each division has its own set of risk classes and associated RADRs, similar to those for Bennett Company in Table 9.9. The use of *divisional costs of capital* and associated risk classes enables a large multidivisional firm to incorporate differing levels of divisional risk into the capital budgeting process and still recognize differences in the levels of individual project risk.

TABLE 9.9 Bennett Company's Risk Classes and RADRs

Risk class	Description	Risk-adjusted discount rate, RADR
I	*Below-average risk:* Projects with low risk. Typically involve routine replacement without renewal of existing activities.	8%
II	*Average risk:* Projects similar to those currently implemented. Typically involve replacement or renewal of existing activities.	10%[a]
III	*Above-average risk:* Projects with higher than normal, but not excessive, risk. Typically involve expansion of existing or similar activities.	14%
IV	*Highest risk:* Projects with very high risk. Typically involve expansion into new or unfamiliar activities.	20%

[a]This RADR is actually the firm's cost of capital, which is discussed in detail in Chapter 10. It represents the firm's required return on its existing portfolio of projects, which is assumed to be unchanged with acceptance of the "average risk" project.

EXAMPLE Assume that the management of Bennett Company decided to use risk classes to analyze projects and so placed each project in one of four risk classes according to its perceived risk. The classes ranged from I for the lowest-risk projects to IV for the highest-risk projects. Associated with each class was an RADR appropriate to the level of risk of projects in the class, as given in Table 9.9. Bennett classified as lower-risk those projects that tend to involve routine replacement or renewal activities; higher-risk projects involve expansion, often into new or unfamiliar activities.

The financial manager of Bennett has assigned project A to class III and project B to class II. The cash flows for project A would be evaluated using a 14% RADR, and project B's would be evaluated using a 10% RADR.[8] The NPV of project A at 14% was calculated in Figure 9.8 to be $6,063, and the NPV for project B at a 10% RADR was shown in Figure 9.2 to be $10,924. Clearly, with RADRs based on the use of risk classes, project B is preferred over project A. As noted earlier, this result is contrary to the preference shown in Figure 9.2, where differing risks of projects A and B were not taken into account.

Review Questions

9–13 Describe the logic involved in using *risk-adjusted discount rates* (*RADRs*). How is this approach related to the *capital asset pricing model* (*CAPM*)? Explain.

9–14 How are risk classes often used to apply RADRs?

8. Note that the 10% RADR for project B using the risk classes in Table 9.9 differs from the 11% RADR used in the preceding example for project B. This difference is attributable to the less precise nature of the use of risk classes.

SUMMARY

FOCUS ON VALUE

After estimating the relevant cash flows, the financial manager must apply appropriate decision techniques to assess whether the project creates value for shareholders. Net present value (NPV) and internal rate of return (IRR) are the generally preferred capital budgeting techniques. Both use the cost of capital as the required return needed to compensate shareholders for undertaking projects with the same risk as that of the firm. Both indicate whether a proposed investment creates or destroys shareholder value. NPV is the theoretically preferred approach, but IRR is preferred in practice because of its intuitive appeal.

Procedures for explicitly recognizing real options embedded in capital projects and procedures for selecting projects under capital rationing enable the financial manager to refine the capital budgeting process further. Not all capital budgeting projects have the same level of risk as the firm's existing portfolio of projects. The financial manager must therefore adjust projects for differences in risk when evaluating their acceptability. Risk-adjusted discount rates (RADRs) provide a mechanism for adjusting the discount rate in a manner consistent with the risk–return preferences of market participants and thereby accepting only value-creating projects. These techniques should enable the financial manager to make capital budgeting decisions that are consistent with the firm's goal of **maximizing stock price.**

REVIEW OF LEARNING GOALS

LG1 **Calculate, interpret, and evaluate the payback period.** The payback period measures the exact amount of time required for the firm to recover its initial investment from cash inflows. The formula and decision criterion for the payback period are summarized in Table 9.10. Shorter payback periods are preferred. In addition to its ease of calculation and simple intuitive appeal, the advantages of the payback period lie in its consideration of cash inflows, the implicit consideration given to timing, and its ability to measure risk exposure. Its weaknesses include its lack of linkage to the wealth maximization goal, failure to explicitly consider time value, and the fact that it ignores cash flows that occur after the payback period.

LG2 **Apply net present value (NPV) and internal rate of return (IRR) to relevant cash flows to choose acceptable capital expenditures.** Sophisticated capital budgeting techniques use the cost of capital to consider the time factor in the value of money. Two such techniques are net present value (NPV) and internal rate of return (IRR). The key formulas and decision criteria for these techniques are summarized in Table 9.10. Both NPV and IRR provide the same accept–reject decisions but often provide conflicting ranks.

LG3 **Use net present value profiles to compare the NPV and IRR techniques in light of conflicting rankings.** Net present value profiles are useful in comparing projects, especially when conflicting

TABLE 9.10 Summary of Key Formulas/Definitions and Decision Criteria for Capital Budgeting Techniques

Technique	Formula/definition	Decision criteria
Payback period[a]	*For annuity:* $\frac{\text{Initial investment}}{\text{Annual cash inflow}}$ *For mixed stream:* Calculate cumulative cash inflows on year-to-year basis until the initial investment is recovered.	*Accept* if < maximum acceptable payback period. *Reject* if > maximum acceptable payback period.
Net present value (NPV)[b]	Present value of cash inflows − Initial investment.	*Accept* if > \$0. *Reject* if < \$0.
Internal rate of return (IRR)[b]	The discount rate that causes NPV = \$0 (present value of cash inflows equals the initial investment).	*Accept* if > the cost of capital. *Reject* if < the cost of capital.

[a]Unsophisticated technique, because it does not give explicit consideration to the time value of money.
[b]Sophisticated technique, because it gives explicit consideration to the time value of money.

rankings exist between NPV and IRR. On a purely theoretical basis, NPV is preferred over IRR, because NPV assumes reinvestment of intermediate cash inflows at the cost of capital and is not subject to the mathematical problems that often arise when one is calculating IRRs for nonconventional cash flows. In practice, the IRR is more commonly used because it is consistent with the general preference toward rates of return.

LG4 **Discuss two additional considerations in capital budgeting—recognizing real options and choosing projects under capital rationing.** By explicitly recognizing real options—opportunities that are embedded in capital projects and that allow managers to alter their cash flow and risk in a way that effects project acceptability (NPV)—the financial manager can find a project's strategic NPV. Some of the more common types of real options are abandonment, flexibility, growth, and timing options. The strategic NPV explicitly recognizes the value of real options and thereby improves the quality of the capital budgeting decision.

Capital rationing commonly occurs in practice. Its objective is to select from all acceptable projects the group that provides the highest overall net present value but does not require more dollars than are budgeted. Of the two basic approaches for choosing projects under capital rationing, the NPV approach better achieves the objective of using the budget to generate the highest present value of cash inflows.

LG5 **Recognize sensitivity analysis and scenario analysis, decision trees, and simulation as behavioral approaches for dealing with project risk, and the unique risks that multinational companies face.** Risk in capital budgeting is concerned with either the chance that a project will prove unacceptable or, more formally, the degree of variability of cash flows. Sensitivity analysis and scenario analysis are two behavioral approaches for dealing with project risk to capture the variability of cash inflows and NPVs. A decision tree is a behavioral approach for dealing with risk that relies on estimates of probabilities associated with the outcomes of competing courses of action to determine the expected values used to select a preferred action. Simulation is a statistics-based behavioral approach that results in a probability distribution of project returns. It usually requires a computer and allows the decision maker to understand the risk–return tradeoffs involved in a proposed investment.

Although the basic capital budgeting techniques are the same for multinational and purely domestic companies, firms that operate in several countries must also deal with both exchange rate and political risks, tax law differences, transfer pricing, and strategic rather than strictly financial considerations.

LG6 **Understand the calculation and practical aspects of risk-adjusted discount rates (RADRs).** The risk adjusted discount rate (RADR) technique involves a market-based adjustment of the discount rate used to calculate NPV. The RADR is closely linked to the CAPM, but because real corporate assets are generally not traded in an efficient market, the CAPM cannot be applied directly to capital budgeting. RADRs are commonly used in practice because decision makers prefer rates of return and find them easy to estimate and apply.

SELF-TEST PROBLEMS (Solutions in Appendix B)

LG1 LG2 LG3

ST 9–1 **All techniques with NPV profile—Mutually exclusive projects** Fitch Industries is in the process of choosing the better of two equal-risk, mutually exclusive capital expenditure projects—M and N. The relevant cash flows for each project are shown in the following table. The firm's cost of capital is 14%.

	Project M	Project N
Initial investment (CF_0)	\$28,500	\$27,000
Year (t)	Cash inflows (CF_t)	
1	\$10,000	\$11,000
2	10,000	10,000
3	10,000	9,000
4	10,000	8,000

a. Calculate each project's payback period.
b. Calculate the net present value (NPV) for each project.
c. Calculate the internal rate of return (IRR) for each project.
d. Summarize the preferences dictated by each measure you calculated, and indicate which project you would recommend. Explain why.
e. Draw the net present value profiles for these projects on the same set of axes, and explain the circumstances under which a conflict in rankings might exist.

LG6

ST 9–2 **Risk-adjusted discount rates** CBA Company is considering two mutually exclusive projects, A and B. The following table shows the CAPM-type relationship between a risk index and the required return (RADR) applicable to CBA Company.

Risk index	Required return (RADR)
0.0	7.0% (risk-free rate, R_F)
0.2	8.0
0.4	9.0
0.6	10.0
0.8	11.0
1.0	12.0
1.2	13.0
1.4	14.0
1.6	15.0
1.8	16.0
2.0	17.0

Project data are shown as follows:

	Project A	Project B
Initial investment (CF_0)	\$15,000	\$20,000
Project life	3 years	3 years
Annual cash inflow (CF)	\$7,000	\$10,000
Risk index	0.4	1.8

a. Ignoring any differences in risk and assuming that the firm's cost of capital is 10%, calculate the net present value (NPV) of each project.
b. Use NPV to evaluate the projects, using *risk-adjusted discount rates* (*RADRs*) to account for risk.
c. Compare, contrast, and explain your findings in parts **a** and **b**.

PROBLEMS

LG1 **9–1 Payback period** Lee Corporation is considering a capital expenditure that requires an initial investment of \$42,000 and returns after-tax cash inflows of \$7,000 per year for 10 years. The firm has a maximum acceptable payback period of 8 years.
a. Determine the payback period for this project.
b. Should the company accept the project? Why or why not?

LG1 **9–2 Payback comparisons** Dallas Tool has a 5-year maximum acceptable payback period. The firm is considering the purchase of a new machine and must choose between two alternative ones. The first machine requires an initial investment of \$14,000 and generates annual after-tax cash inflows of \$3,000 for each of the next 7 years. The second machine requires an initial investment of \$21,000 and provides an annual cash inflow after taxes of \$4,000 for 20 years.
a. Determine the payback period for each machine.

b. Comment on the acceptability of the machines, assuming that they are independent projects.
c. Which machine should the firm accept? Why?
d. Do the machines in this problem illustrate any of the weaknesses of using payback? Discuss.

LG2 9–3 **NPV** Calculate the net present value (NPV) for the following 20-year projects. Comment on the acceptability of each. Assume that the firm has an opportunity cost of 14%.

a. Initial investment is $10,000; cash inflows are $2,000 per year.
b. Initial investment is $25,000; cash inflows are $3,000 per year.
c. Initial investment is $30,000; cash inflows are $5,000 per year.

LG2 9–4 **NPV for varying costs of capital** Cheryl's Beauty Aids is evaluating a new fragrance-mixing machine. The machine requires an initial investment of $24,000 and will generate after-tax cash inflows of $5,000 per year for 8 years. For each of the costs of capital listed, (1) calculate the net present value (NPV), (2) indicate whether to accept or reject the machine, and (3) explain your decision.

a. The cost of capital is 10%.
b. The cost of capital is 12%.
c. The cost of capital is 14%.

LG2 9–5 **Net present value—Independent projects** Using a 14% cost of capital, calculate the net present value for each of the independent projects shown in the following table, and indicate whether each is acceptable.

	Project A	Project B	Project C	Project D	Project E
Initial investment (CF_0)	$26,000	$500,000	$170,000	$950,000	$80,000
Year (t)	Cash inflows (CF_t)				
1	$4,000	$100,000	$20,000	$230,000	$ 0
2	4,000	120,000	19,000	230,000	0
3	4,000	140,000	18,000	230,000	0
4	4,000	160,000	17,000	230,000	20,000
5	4,000	180,000	16,000	230,000	30,000
6	4,000	200,000	15,000	230,000	0
7	4,000		14,000	230,000	50,000
8	4,000		13,000	230,000	60,000
9	4,000		12,000		70,000
10	4,000		11,000		

LG2 9–6 **NPV and maximum return** A firm can purchase a fixed asset for a $13,000 initial investment. The asset generates an annual after-tax cash inflow of $4,000 for 4 years.

a. Determine the net present value (NPV) of the asset, assuming that the firm has a 10% cost of capital. Is the project acceptable?

b. Determine the maximum required rate of return (closest whole-percentage rate) that the firm can have and still accept the asset. Discuss this finding in light of your response in part **a.**

LG2 9–7 **NPV—Mutually exclusive projects** Jackson Enterprises is considering the replacement of one of its old drill presses. Three alternative replacement presses are under consideration. The relevant cash flows associated with each are shown in the following table. The firm's cost of capital is 15%.

	Press A	Press B	Press C
Initial investment (CF_0)	$85,000	$60,000	$130,000
Year (t)	Cash inflows (CF_t)		
1	$18,000	$12,000	$50,000
2	18,000	14,000	30,000
3	18,000	16,000	20,000
4	18,000	18,000	20,000
5	18,000	20,000	20,000
6	18,000	25,000	30,000
7	18,000	—	40,000
8	18,000	—	50,000

a. Calculate the net present value (NPV) of each press.
b. Using NPV, evaluate the acceptability of each press.
c. Rank the presses from best to worst using NPV.

LG2 9–8 **Payback and NPV** McAllister Products has three projects under consideration. The cash flows for each of them are shown in the following table. The firm has a 16% cost of capital.

	Project A	Project B	Project C
Initial investment (CF_0)	$40,000	$40,000	$40,000
Year (t)	Cash inflows (CF_t)		
1	$13,000	$ 7,000	$19,000
2	13,000	10,000	16,000
3	13,000	13,000	13,000
4	13,000	16,000	10,000
5	13,000	19,000	7,000

a. Calculate each project's payback period. Which project is preferred according to this method?
b. Calculate each project's net present value (NPV). Which project is preferred according to this method?

c. Comment on your findings in parts **a** and **b**, and recommend the best project. Explain your recommendation.

LG2 **9–9 Internal rate of return** For each of the projects shown in the following table, calculate the internal rate of return (IRR). Then indicate, for each project, the maximum cost of capital that the firm could have and still find the IRR acceptable.

	Project A	Project B	Project C	Project D
Initial investment (CF_0)	$90,000	$490,000	$20,000	$240,000
Year (t)	Cash inflows (CF_t)			
1	$20,000	$150,000	$7,500	$120,000
2	25,000	150,000	7,500	100,000
3	30,000	150,000	7,500	80,000
4	35,000	150,000	7,500	60,000
5	40,000	—	7,500	—

LG2 **9–10 IRR—Mutually exclusive projects** Paulus Corporation is attempting to choose the better of two mutually exclusive projects for expanding the firm's warehouse capacity. The relevant cash flows for the projects are shown in the following table. The firm's cost of capital is 15%.

	Project X	Project Y
Initial investment (CF_0)	$500,000	$325,000
Year (t)	Cash inflows (CF_t)	
1	$100,000	$140,000
2	120,000	120,000
3	150,000	95,000
4	190,000	70,000
5	250,000	50,000

a. Calculate the IRR to the nearest whole percent for each of the projects.
b. Assess the acceptability of each project on the basis of the IRRs found in part **a**.
c. Which project, on this basis, is preferred?

LG2 **9–11 IRR, investment life, and cash inflows** Cincinnati Machine Tool (CMT) accepts projects earning more than the firm's 15% cost of capital. CMT is currently considering a 10-year project that provides annual cash inflows of $10,000 and requires an initial investment of $61,450. (*Note:* All amounts are after taxes.)
a. Determine the IRR of this project. Is it acceptable?
b. Assuming that the cash inflows continue to be $10,000 per year, how many *additional years* would the flows have to continue to make the project acceptable (that is, to make it have an IRR of 15%)?

c. With the given life, initial investment, and cost of capital, what is the minimum annual cash inflow that the firm should accept?

LG2

9–12 NPV and IRR Lilo Manufacturing has prepared the following estimates for a long-term project it is considering. The initial investment is $18,250, and the project is expected to yield after-tax cash inflows of $4,000 per year for 7 years. The firm has a 10% cost of capital.

a. Determine the net present value (NPV) for the project.
b. Determine the internal rate of return (IRR) for the project.
c. Would you recommend that the firm accept or reject the project? Explain your answer.

LG1 LG2

9–13 Payback, NPV, and IRR Bruce Reed Enterprises is attempting to evaluate the feasibility of investing $95,000 in a piece of equipment that has a 5-year life. The firm has estimated the *cash inflows* associated with the proposal as shown in the following table. The firm has a 12% cost of capital.

Year (t)	Cash inflows (CF_t)
1	$20,000
2	25,000
3	30,000
4	35,000
5	40,000

a. Calculate the payback period for the proposed investment.
b. Calculate the net present value (NPV) for the proposed investment.
c. Calculate the internal rate of return (IRR), rounded to the nearest whole percent, for the proposed investment.
d. Evaluate the acceptability of the proposed investment using NPV and IRR. What recommendation would you make relative to implementation of the project? Why?

LG2 LG3

9–14 NPV, IRR, and NPV profiles Candor Enterprises is considering two mutually exclusive projects. The firm, which has a 12% cost of capital, has estimated its cash flows as shown in the following table.

	Project A	Project B
Initial investment (CF_0)	$130,000	$85,000
Year (t)	Cash inflows (CF_t)	
1	$25,000	$40,000
2	35,000	35,000
3	45,000	30,000
4	50,000	10,000
5	55,000	5,000

a. Calculate the NPV of each project, and assess its acceptability.
b. Calculate the IRR for each project, and assess its acceptability.
c. Draw the NPV profiles for both projects on the same set of axes.
d. Evaluate and discuss the rankings of the two projects on the basis of your findings in parts **a**, **b**, and **c**.
e. Explain your findings in part **d** in light of the pattern of cash inflows associated with each project.

LG1 LG2 LG3

9–15 All techniques—mutually exclusive investment decision Easi Chair Company is attempting to select the best of three mutually exclusive projects. The initial investment and after-tax cash inflows associated with these projects are shown in the following table.

Cash flows	Project A	Project B	Project C
Initial investment (CF_0)	$60,000	$100,000	$110,000
Cash inflows (CF_t), $t = 1$ to 5	$20,000	$ 31,500	$ 32,500

a. Calculate the payback period for each project.
b. Calculate the net present value (NPV) of each project, assuming that the firm has a cost of capital equal to 13%.
c. Calculate the internal rate of return (IRR) for each project.
d. Draw the net present value profiles for these projects on the same set of axes, and discuss any conflict in ranking that may exist between NPV and IRR.
e. Summarize the preferences dictated by each measure, and indicate which project you would recommend. Explain why.

LG1 LG2 LG3

9–16 All techniques with NPV profile—Mutually exclusive projects Projects A and B, of equal risk, are alternatives for expanding the Rosa Company's capacity. The firm's cost of capital is 13%. The cash flows for each project are shown in the following table.

	Project A	Project B
Initial investment (CF_0)	$80,000	$50,000
Year (t)	Cash inflows (CF_t)	
1	$15,000	$15,000
2	20,000	15,000
3	25,000	15,000
4	30,000	15,000
5	35,000	15,000

a. Calculate each project's payback period.
b. Calculate the net present value (NPV) for each project.
c. Calculate the internal rate of return (IRR) for each project.
d. Draw the net present value profiles for these projects on the same set of axes, and discuss any conflict in ranking that may exist between NPV and IRR.

e. Summarize the preferences dictated by each measure, and indicate which project you would recommend. Explain why.

LG1 LG2 **9–17 Integrative—Complete investment decision** Hot Springs Press is considering the purchase of a new printing press. The total installed cost of the press is $2.2 million. This outlay would be partially offset by the sale of an existing press. The old press has zero book value, cost $1 million 10 years ago, and can be sold currently for $1.2 million before taxes. As a result of acquisition of the new press, sales in each of the next 5 years are expected to increase by $1.6 million, but product costs (excluding depreciation) will represent 50% of sales. The new press will not affect the firm's net working capital requirements. The new press will be depreciated under MACRS using a 5-year recovery period (see Table 3.2 on page 89). The firm is subject to a 40% tax rate on both ordinary income and capital gains. Hot Spring Press's cost of capital is 11%. (*Note:* Assume that both the old and the new press will have terminal values of $0 at the end of year 6.)

a. Determine the initial investment required by the new press.
b. Determine the operating cash inflows attributable to the new press. (*Note:* Be sure to consider the depreciation in year 6.)
c. Determine the payback period.
d. Determine the net present value (NPV) and the internal rate of return (IRR) related to the proposed new press.
e. Make a recommendation to accept or reject the new press, and justify your answer.

LG2 **9–18 Integrative—Investment decision** Holliday Manufacturing is considering the replacement of an existing machine. The new machine costs $1.2 million and requires installation costs of $150,000. The existing machine can be sold currently for $185,000 before taxes. It is 2 years old, cost $800,000 new, and has a $384,000 book value and a remaining useful life of 5 years. It was being depreciated under MACRS using a 5-year recovery period (see Table 3.2 on page 89) and therefore has the final 4 years of depreciation remaining. If it is held until the end of 5 years, the machine's market value will be $0. Over its 5-year life, the new machine should reduce operating costs by $350,000 per year. The new machine will be depreciated under MACRS using a 5-year recovery period (see Table 3.2 on page 89). The new machine can be sold for $200,000 net of removal and clean up costs at the end of 5 years. An increased investment in net working capital of $25,000 will be needed to support operations if the new machine is acquired. Assume that the firm has adequate operating income against which to deduct any loss experienced on the sale of the existing machine. The firm has a 9% cost of capital and is subject to a 40% tax rate on both ordinary income and capital gains.

a. Develop the relevant cash flows needed to analyze the proposed replacement.
b. Determine the net present value (NPV) of the proposal.
c. Determine the internal rate of return (IRR) of the proposal.
d. Make a recommendation to accept or reject the replacement proposal, and justify your answer.
e. What is the highest cost of capital that the firm could have and still accept the proposal? Explain.

LG4 **9–19 Real options and the strategic NPV** Jenny Rene, the CFO of Asor Products, Inc., has just completed an evaluation of a proposed capital expenditure for equipment that would expand the firm's manufacturing capacity. Using the traditional NPV methodology, she found the project unacceptable because

$$NPV_{traditional} = -\$1{,}700 < \$0$$

Before recommending rejection of the proposed project, she has decided to assess whether there might be real options embedded in the firm's cash flows. Her evaluation uncovered the following three options.

Option 1: Abandonment—The project could be abandoned at the end of 3 years, resulting in an addition to NPV of $1,200.

Option 2: Expansion—If the projected outcomes occurred, an opportunity to expand the firm's product offerings further would occur at the end of 4 years. Exercise of this option is estimated to add $3,000 to the project's NPV.

Option 3: Delay—Certain phases of the proposed project could be delayed if market and competitive conditions caused the firm's forecast revenues to develop more slowly than planned. Such a delay in implementation at that point has a NPV of $10,000.

Rene estimated that there was a 25% chance that the abandonment option would need to be exercised, a 30% chance the expansion option would be exercised, and only a 10% chance that the implementation of certain phases of the project would have to be delayed.

a. Use the information provided to calculate the strategic NPV, $NPV_{strategic}$, for Asor Products' proposed equipment expenditure.

b. Judging on the basis of your findings in part **a**, what action should Rene recommend to management with regard to the proposed equipment expenditures?

c. In general, how does this problem demonstrate the importance of considering real options when making capital budgeting decisions?

LG4 **9–20 Capital rationing—IRR and NPV approaches** Bromley and Sons is attempting to select the best of a group of independent projects competing for the firm's fixed capital budget of $4.5 million. The firm recognizes that any unused portion of this budget will earn less than its 15% cost of capital, thereby resulting in a present value of inflows that is less than the initial investment. The firm has summarized the key data to be used in selecting the best group of projects in the following table.

Project	Initial investment	IRR	Present value of inflows at 15%
A	$5,000,000	17%	$5,400,000
B	800,000	18	1,100,000
C	2,000,000	19	2,300,000
D	1,500,000	16	1,600,000
E	800,000	22	900,000
F	2,500,000	23	3,000,000
G	1,200,000	20	1,300,000

a. Use the *internal rate of return (IRR) approach* to select the best group of projects.
b. Use the *net present value (NPV) approach* to select the best group of projects.
c. Compare, contrast, and discuss your findings in parts **a** and **b**.
d. Which projects should the firm implement? Why?

LG4 9–21 **Capital rationing—NPV approach** A firm with a 13% cost of capital must select the optimal group of projects from those shown in the following table, given its capital budget of $1 million.

Project	Initial investment	NPV at 13% cost of capital
A	$300,000	$ 84,000
B	200,000	10,000
C	100,000	25,000
D	900,000	90,000
E	500,000	70,000
F	100,000	50,000
G	800,000	160,000

a. Calculate the *present value of cash inflows* associated with each project.
b. Select the optimal group of projects, keeping in mind that unused funds are costly.

LG5 9–22 **Basic sensitivity analysis** Renaissance Pharmaceutical is in the process of evaluating two mutually exclusive additions to its processing capacity. The firm's financial analysts have developed pessimistic, most likely, and optimistic estimates of the annual cash inflows associated with each project. These estimates are shown in the following table.

	Project A	Project B
Initial investment (CF_0)	$8,000	$8,000
Outcome	**Annual cash inflows (CF)**	
Pessimistic	$ 200	$ 900
Most likely	1,000	1,000
Optimistic	1,800	1,100

a. Determine the *range* of annual cash inflows for each of the two projects.
b. Assume that the firm' s cost of capital is 10% and that both projects have 20-year lives. Construct a table similar to this for the NPVs for each project. Include the *range* of NPVs for each project.
c. Do parts **a** and **b** provide consistent views of the two projects? Explain.
d. Which project do you recommend? Why?

LG5 **9–23 Sensitivity analysis** James Secretarial Services is considering the purchase of one of two new personal computers, P and Q. Both are expected to provide benefits over a 10-year period, and each has a required investment of \$3,000. The firm has a 10% cost of capital. Management has constructed the following table of estimates of annual cash inflows for pessimistic, most likely, and optimistic results.

	Computer P	Computer Q
Initial investment (CF_0)	\$3,000	\$3,000
Outcome	**Annual cash inflows (*CF*)**	
Pessimistic	\$ 500	\$ 400
Most likely	750	750
Optimistic	1,000	1,200

a. Determine the *range* of annual cash inflows for each of the two computers.
b. Construct a table similar to this for the NPVs associated with each outcome for both computers.
c. Find the *range* of NPVs, and subjectively compare the risks associated with purchasing these computers.

LG5 **9–24 Decision trees** The Ouija Board-Games Company can bring out one of two new games this season. The *Signs Away* game has a higher initial cost but also a higher expected return. *Monopolistic Competition,* the alternative, has a slightly lower initial cost but also a lower expected return. The present values and probabilities associated with each game are listed in the table.

Game	Initial investment	Present value of cash inflows	Probabilities
Signs Away	\$140,000		1.00
		\$320,000	.30
		220,000	.50
		− 80,000	.20
Monopolistic Competition	\$120,000		1.00
		\$260,000	.20
		200,000	.45
		− 50,000	.35

a. Construct a decision tree to analyze the games.
b. Which game do you recommend (following a decision-tree analysis)?
c. Has your analysis captured the differences in the risks associated with these games? Explain.

LG5 **9–25 Simulation** Wales Castings has compiled the following information on a capital expenditure proposal:

(1) The projected cash *inflows* are normally distributed with a mean of \$36,000 and a standard deviation of \$9,000.

(2) The projected cash *outflows* are normally distributed with a mean of $30,000 and a standard deviation of $6,000.
(3) The firm has an 11% cost of capital.
(4) The probability distributions of cash inflows and cash outflows are not expected to change over the project's 10-year life.

a. Describe how the foregoing data can be used to develop a simulation model for finding the net present value of the project.
b. Discuss the advantages of using a simulation to evaluate the proposed project.

LG6 **9–26 Risk-adjusted discount rates—Basic** Country Wallpapers is considering investing in one of three mutually exclusive projects, E, F, and G. The firm's cost of capital, k, is 15%, and the risk-free rate, R_F, is 10%. The firm has gathered the following basic cash flow and risk index data for each project.

	Project (j)		
	E	F	G
Initial investment (CF_0)	$15,000	$11,000	$19,000
Year (t)	Cash inflows (CF_t)		
1	$ 6,000	$ 6,000	$ 4,000
2	6,000	4,000	6,000
3	6,000	5,000	8,000
4	6,000	2,000	12,000
Risk index (RI_j)	1.80	1.00	0.60

a. Find the net present value (NPV) of each project using the firm's cost of capital. Which project is preferred in this situation?
b. The firm uses the following equation to determine the risk-adjusted discount rate, RADR_j, for each project j:

$$\text{RADR}_j = R_F + [RI_j \times (k - R_F)]$$

where

R_F = risk-free rate of return
RI_j = risk index for project j
k = cost of capital

Substitute each project's risk index into this equation to determine its RADR.
c. Use the RADR for each project to determine its risk-adjusted NPV. Which project is preferable in this situation?
d. Compare and discuss your findings in parts **a** and **c.** Which project do you recommend that the firm accept?

LG6 **9–27 Risk-adjusted discount rates—Tabular** After a careful evaluation of investment alternatives and opportunities, Joely Company has developed a CAPM-type relationship linking a risk index to the required return (RADR), as shown in the following table.

Risk index	Required return (RADR)
0.0	7.0% (risk-free rate, R_F)
0.2	8.0
0.4	9.0
0.6	10.0
0.8	11.0
1.0	12.0
1.2	13.0
1.4	14.0
1.6	15.0
1.8	16.0
2.0	17.0

The firm is considering two mutually exclusive projects, A and B. The following are the data the firm has been able to gather about the projects.

	Project A	Project B
Initial investment (CF_0)	$20,000	$30,000
Project life	5 years	5 years
Annual cash inflow (CF)	$7,000	$10,000
Risk index	0.2	1.4

All the firm's cash inflows have already been adjusted for taxes.

a. Evaluate the projects using *risk-adjusted discount rates.*

b. Discuss your findings in part **a**, and recommend the preferred project.

LG6 **9–28 Risk classes and RADR** Attila Industries is attempting to select the best of three mutually exclusive projects, X, Y, and Z. Though all the projects have 5-year lives, they possess differing degrees of risk. Project X is in class V, the highest-risk class; project Y is in class II, the below-average-risk class; and project Z is in class III, the average-risk class. The basic cash flow data for each project and the risk classes and risk-adjusted discount rates (RADRs) used by the firm are shown in the following tables.

	Project X	Project Y	Project Z
Initial investment (CF_0)	$180,000	$235,000	$310,000
Year (t)	Cash inflows (CF_t)		
1	$ 80,000	$ 50,000	$ 90,000
2	70,000	60,000	90,000
3	60,000	70,000	90,000
4	60,000	80,000	90,000
5	60,000	90,000	90,000

Risk Classes and RADRs		
Risk Class	**Description**	**Risk-adjusted discount rate (RADR)**
I	Lowest risk	10%
II	Below-average risk	13
III	Average risk	15
IV	Above-average risk	19
V	Highest risk	22

a. Find the risk-adjusted NPV for each project.
b. Which project, if any, would you recommend that the firm undertake?

CHAPTER 9 CASE Making Norwich Tool's Lathe Investment Decision

Norwich Tool, a large machine shop, is considering replacing one of its lathes with either of two new lathes—lathe A or lathe B. Lathe A is a highly automated, computer-controlled lathe; lathe B is a less expensive lathe that uses standard technology. To analyze these alternatives, Mario Jackson, a financial analyst, prepared estimates of the initial investment and incremental (relevant) cash inflows associated with each lathe. These are shown in the following table.

	Lathe A	**Lathe B**
Initial investment (CF_0)	**$660,000**	**$360,000**
Year (t)	**Cash inflows (CF_t)**	
1	$128,000	$ 88,000
2	182,000	120,000
3	166,000	96,000
4	168,000	86,000
5	450,000	207,000

Note that Mario plans to analyze both lathes over a 5-year period. At the end of that time, the lathes would be sold, thus accounting for the large fifth-year cash inflows.

One of Mario's dilemmas centered on the risk of the two lathes. He believes that although the two lathes are equally risky, lathe A has a much higher chance of breakdown and repair because of its sophisticated and not fully proven solid-state electronic technology. Mario is unable to quantify this possibility effectively, so he decides to apply the firm's 13% cost of capital when analyzing the lathes. Norwich Tool requires all projects to have a maximum payback period of 4.0 years.

Required

a. Use the payback period to assess the acceptability and relative ranking of each lathe.
b. Assuming equal risk, use the following sophisticated capital budgeting techniques to assess the acceptability and relative ranking of each lathe:
   (1) Net present value (NPV).
   (2) Internal rate of return (IRR).
c. Summarize the preferences indicated by the techniques used in parts **a** and **b**, and indicate which lathe you recommend, if either, (1) if the firm has unlimited funds and (2) if the firm has capital rationing.
d. Repeat part **b** assuming that Mario decides that because of its greater risk, lathe A's cash inflows should be evaluated by using a 15% cost of capital.
e. What effect, if any, does recognition of lathe A's greater risk in part **d** have on our recommendation in part **c**?

WEB EXERCISE

Go to the Web site *www.arachnoid.com/lutusp/finance_old.html*. Page down to the portion of this screen that contains the financial calculator.

1. To determine the internal rate of return (IRR) of a project whose initial investment was $5,000 and whose cash inflows are $1,000 per year for the next 10 years, perform the steps outlined below. By entering various interest rates, you will eventually get a present value of $5,000. When this happens you, have determined the IRR of the project.
   To get started, into **PV**, enter 0; into **FV**, enter 0; into **np**, enter 1000; into **pmt**, enter 10; and then into **ir**, enter 8. Click on **Calculate PV**. This gives you a number much greater than $5,000. Now change **ir** to 20 and then click on **Calculate PV**. Keeping changing the **ir** until PV = $5,000, the same as the initial investment.
2. Try another project. The initial investment is $10,000. The cash inflows are $2,500 per year for the next 6 years. What is its IRR?
3. To calculate the IRR of an investment of $3,000 with a single cash inflow of $4,800 to be received exactly 3 years after the investment, do the following: Into **FV**, enter 4800; into **np**, enter 3; into **pmt**, enter 0; and then into **ir**, enter 8. Then click on **Calculate PV**. As before, keep changing **ir** until the PV is equal to the initial investment of $3,000. What is this investment's IRR?

Remember to check the book's Web site at

www.aw.com/gitman

for additional resources, including additional Web exercises.

Part 4

Long-Term Financial Decisions

Chapter

10

The Cost of Capital

LEARNING GOALS

LG1 Understand the key assumptions that underlie cost of capital, the basic concept of cost of capital, and the specific sources of capital that it includes.

LG2 Determine the cost of long-term debt and the cost of preferred stock.

LG3 Calculate the cost of common stock equity and convert it into the cost of retained earnings and the cost of new issues of common stock.

LG4 Calculate the weighted average cost of capital (WACC) and discuss the alternative weighting schemes.

LG5 Describe the procedures used to determine break points and the weighted marginal cost of capital (WMCC).

LG6 Explain how the weighted marginal cost of capital (WMCC) can be used with the investment opportunities schedule (IOS) to make the firm's financing/investment decisions.

Across the Disciplines

Why This Chapter Matters To You

Accounting: You need to understand the various sources of capital and how their costs are calculated in order to provide data used in determining the firm's overall cost of capital.

Information systems: You need to understand the various sources of capital and how their costs are calculated in order to develop systems that will estimate the costs of those sources of capital, as well as the overall cost of capital.

Management: You need to understand the cost of capital in order to assess the acceptability and relative rankings of proposed long-term investments.

Marketing: You need to understand what the firm's cost of capital is because proposed projects will face rejection if their promised returns are less than the firm's cost of capital.

Operations: You need to understand the cost of capital in order to assess the economic viability of investments in plant and equipment needed to improve or expand the firm's capacity.

The cost of capital is used to select capital investments that increase shareholder value. In applying the net present value and internal rate of return techniques in Chapter 9, we simply assumed a reasonable cost of capital. Now we will demonstrate how the cost of capital is calculated. This chapter considers the costs of long-term debt, preferred stock, common stock, and retained earnings and shows how to combine them to determine cost of capital measures the firm will use in making long-term financing/investment decisions.

LG1

An Overview of the Cost of Capital

cost of capital
The rate of return that a firm must earn on the projects in which it invests to maintain its market value and attract funds.

The **cost of capital** is the rate of return that a firm must earn on the projects in which it invests to maintain the market value of its stock. It can also be thought of as the rate of return required by the market suppliers of capital to attract their funds to the firm. If risk is held constant, projects with a rate of return above the cost of capital will increase the value of the firm, and projects with a rate of return below the cost of capital will decrease the value of the firm.

The cost of capital is an extremely important financial concept. It acts as a major link between the firm's long-term investment decisions (discussed in Part 3) and the wealth of the owners as determined by investors in the marketplace. It is in effect the "magic number" that is used to decide whether a proposed corporate investment will increase or decrease the firm's stock price. Clearly, only those investments that are expected to increase stock price (NPV > $0, or IRR > cost of capital) would be recommended. Because of its key role in financial decision making, the importance of the cost of capital cannot be overemphasized.

Some Key Assumptions

The cost of capital is a dynamic concept affected by a variety of economic and firm-specific factors. To isolate the basic structure of the cost of capital, we make some key assumptions relative to risk and taxes:

business risk
The risk to the firm of being unable to cover operating costs.

financial risk
The risk to the firm of being unable to cover required financial obligations (interest, lease payments, preferred stock dividends).

1. **Business risk**—the risk to the firm of being unable to cover operating costs—*is assumed to be unchanged.* This assumption means that the firm's acceptance of a given project does not affect its ability to meet operating costs.
2. **Financial risk**—the risk to the firm of being unable to cover required financial obligations (interest, lease payments, preferred stock dividends)—*is assumed to be unchanged.* This assumption means that projects are financed in such a way that the firm's ability to meet required financing costs is unchanged.
3. After-tax costs are considered relevant. In other words, *the cost of capital is measured on an after-tax basis.* This assumption is consistent with the framework used to make capital budgeting decisions.

The Basic Concept

The cost of capital is estimated at a given point in time. It reflects the expected average future cost of funds over the long run. Although firms typically raise money in lumps, the cost of capital should reflect the interrelatedness of financing activities. For example, if a firm raises funds with debt (borrowing) today, it is likely that some form of equity, such as common stock, will have to be used the next time it needs funds. Most firms attempt to maintain a desired optimal mix of debt and equity financing. This mix is commonly called a **target capital structure**—a topic that will be addressed in Chapter 11. Here, it is sufficient to say that although firms raise money in lumps, they tend toward some desired *mix of financing.*

target capital structure
The desired optimal mix of debt and equity financing that most firms attempt to maintain.

To capture the interrelatedness of financing assuming the presence of a target capital structure, we need to look at the *overall cost of capital* rather than the cost of the specific source of funds used to finance a given expenditure.

EXAMPLE A firm is *currently* faced with an investment opportunity. Assume the following:

Best project available today

Cost = \$100,000
Life = 20 years
IRR = 7%

Cost of least-cost financing source available

Debt = 6%

Because it can earn 7% on the investment of funds costing only 6%, the firm undertakes the opportunity. Imagine that *1 week later* a new investment opportunity is available:

Best project available 1 week later

Cost = \$100,000
Life = 20 years
IRR = 12%

Cost of least-cost financing source available

Equity = 14%

In this instance, the firm rejects the opportunity, because the 14% financing cost is greater than the 12% expected return.

Were the firm's actions in the best interests of its owners? No; it accepted a project yielding a 7% return and rejected one with a 12% return. Clearly, there should be a better way, and there is: The firm can use a combined cost, which over the long run will yield better decisions. By weighting the cost of each source of financing by its *target proportion* in the firm's capital structure, the firm can obtain a *weighted average cost* that reflects the interrelationship of financing decisions. Assuming that a 50–50 mix of debt and equity is targeted, the weighted average cost here would be 10% [(0.50 × 6% debt) + (0.50 × 14% equity)]. With this cost, the first opportunity would have been rejected (7% IRR < 10% weighted average cost), and the second would have been accepted (12% IRR > 10% weighted average cost). Such an outcome would clearly be more desirable.

The Cost of Specific Sources of Capital

This chapter focuses on finding the costs of specific sources of capital and combining them to determine the weighted average cost of capital. Our concern is only with the *long-term* sources of funds available to a business firm, because these sources supply the permanent financing. Long-term financing supports the firm's fixed-asset investments.[1] We assume throughout the chapter that such investments are selected by using appropriate capital budgeting techniques.

There are four basic sources of long-term funds for the business firm: long-term debt, preferred stock, common stock, and retained earnings. The right-hand side of a balance sheet can be used to illustrate these sources:

Balance Sheet		
	Current liabilities	
	Long-term debt	Sources of long-term funds
Assets	Stockholders' equity Preferred stock Common stock equity Common stock Retained earnings	

Although not every firm will use all of these methods of financing, each firm is expected to have funds from some of these sources in its capital structure.

The *specific cost* of each source of financing is the *after-tax* cost of obtaining the financing *today,* not the historically based cost reflected by the existing financing on the firm's books. Techniques for determining the specific cost of each source of long-term funds are presented on the following pages. Although these techniques tend to develop precisely calculated values, the resulting values are at best *rough approximations* because of the numerous assumptions and forecasts that underlie them. Although we round calculated costs to the nearest 0.1 percent throughout this chapter, it is not unusual for practicing financial managers to use costs rounded to the nearest 1 percent because these values are merely estimates.

Review Questions

10–1 What is the *cost of capital?* What role does it play in long-term investment decisions?

10–2 Why do we assume that *business risk* and *financial risk* are unchanged when evaluating the cost of capital? Discuss the implications of these assumptions on the acceptance and financing of new projects.

10–3 Why is the cost of capital measured on an *after-tax basis?* Why is use of a weighted average cost of capital rather than the cost of the specific source of funds recommended?

10–4 You have just been told, "Because we are going to finance this project with debt, its required rate of return must exceed the cost of debt." Do you agree or disagree? Explain.

1. The role of both long-term and short-term financing in supporting both fixed and current asset investments is addressed in Chapter 13. Suffice it to say that long-term funds are at a minimum used to finance fixed assets.

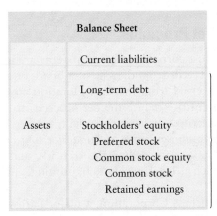

LG2

The Cost of Long-Term Debt

cost of long-term debt, k_i
The after-tax cost today of raising long-term funds through borrowing.

The **cost of long-term debt, k_i**, is the after-tax cost today of raising long-term funds through borrowing. For convenience, we typically assume that the funds are raised through the sale of bonds. In addition, as we did in Chapter 6, we assume that the bonds pay *annual* (rather than *semiannual*) interest.

Net Proceeds

net proceeds
Funds actually received from the sale of a security.

flotation costs
The total costs of issuing and selling a security.

Most corporate long-term debts are incurred through the sale of bonds. The **net proceeds** from the sale of a bond, or any security, are the funds that are actually received from the sale. **Flotation costs**—the total costs of issuing and selling a security—reduce the net proceeds from the sale. These costs apply to all public offerings of securities—debt, preferred stock, and common stock. They include two components: (1) *underwriting costs*—compensation earned by investment bankers for selling the security, and (2) *administrative costs*—issuer expenses such as legal, accounting, printing, and other expenses.

EXAMPLE Duchess Corporation, a major hardware manufacturer, is contemplating selling \$10 million worth of 20-year, 9% coupon (stated *annual* interest rate) bonds, each with a par value of \$1,000. Because similar-risk bonds earn returns greater than 9%, the firm must sell the bonds for \$980 to compensate for the lower coupon interest rate. The flotation costs are 2% of the par value of the bond ($0.02 \times \$1,000$), or \$20. The net proceeds to the firm from the sale of each bond are therefore \$960 (\$980 – \$20).

Before-Tax Cost of Debt

The before-tax cost of debt, k_d, for a bond can be obtained in any of three ways: quotation, calculation, or approximation.

Using Cost Quotations

When the net proceeds from sale of a bond equal its par value, the before-tax cost just equals the coupon interest rate. For example, a bond with a 10 percent coupon interest rate that nets proceeds equal to the bond's \$1,000 par value would have a before-tax cost, k_d, of 10 percent.

A second quotation that is sometimes used is the *yield to maturity* (*YTM*) on a similar-risk bond[2] (see Chapter 6). For example, if a similar-risk bond has a YTM of 9.7 percent, this value can be used as the before-tax cost of debt, k_d.

Calculating the Cost

This approach finds the before-tax cost of debt by calculating the *internal rate of return* (*IRR*) on the bond cash flows. From the issuer's point of view, this value is the *cost to maturity* of the cash flows associated with the debt. The cost to

2. Generally, the yield to maturity of bonds with a similar "rating" is used. Bond ratings, which are published by independent agencies, were discussed in Chapter 6.

In Practice

FOCUS ON e-FINANCE Sold to the Lowest Bidder

In August 2000, **Dow Chemical** became the first industrial corporation to price and distribute bonds online. **WR Hambrecht + Co.**, a pioneer in online equity IPOs, conducted the 2-hour Dutch auction at its OpenBook auction Web site. In a Dutch auction (long used to price and sell Treasury bonds), investors place bids to buy a particular amount of a security at a specific price within a spread set by the issuer before the auction. The underwriter accepts the lowest price at which there is enough demand to sell all the bonds offered (the clearing price). Investors who bid that price or higher get their requested allocations at the clearing price.

Dow's open bond auction of $300 million in 5-year bonds was well received, attracting a broader investor base that could reduce volatility in the secondary market. The interest rate on the issue was similar to what Dow would have paid using the traditional syndication process, but the underwriting fee was over 50 percent lower. "To me, it's a no-brainer," said Dow treasurer Geoffery Merszei.

In the future, market watchers expect Internet auctions to lower issuance costs for debt capital through more efficient pricing that reflects market demand. All bidders have equal access to securities, and investors can see a real-time, fully visible demand curve for a bond issue as it unfolds, resulting in improved distribution and enhanced liquidity.

Despite Dow's success, few corporations have followed it online. **Ford Motor Credit** issued $750 million of 3-year notes in March 2001. In February 2001, government-sponsored residential mortgage agency **Freddie Mac** announced that it would use OpenBook for eight auctions. So far, most major investment bankers have resisted endorsing a method that would undercut their more lucrative traditional underwriting business. However, both proponents and opponents of online Dutch auctions of corporate debt believe that this method works best for large, standard-issue bonds from investment-grade issuers.

Sources: Adapted from Shella Calamba, "Wall St. Ignores Online Bond Deals at Its Peril," *Dow Jones Newswires* (August 18, 2000), downloaded from *www.wrhambrecht.com/inst/openbook/media.html;* Emily S. Plishner, "E-bonds: Will They Fly?" *CFO* (March 1, 2001); and "WR Hambrecht + Co's Core Technology to Support the First Dutch Auction of Freddie Mac Two- and Three-Year Reference Notes," press release from WR Hambrecht + Co. (February 8, 2001), downloaded from *www.wrhambrecht.com/inst/openbook/media.html.*

maturity can be calculated by using either a trial-and-error technique[3] or a financial calculator. It represents the annual before-tax percentage cost of the debt.

EXAMPLE In the preceding example, the net proceeds of a $1,000, 9% coupon interest rate, 20-year bond were found to be $960. The calculation of the annual cost is quite simple. The cash flow pattern is exactly the opposite of a conventional pattern; it consists of an initial inflow (the net proceeds) followed by a series of annual outlays (the interest payments). In the final year, when the debt is retired, an outlay representing the repayment of the principal also occurs. The cash flows associated with Duchess Corporation's bond issue are as follows:

End of year(s)	Cash flow
0	$ 960
1–20	−$ 90
20	−$1,000

WWW

3. The trial-and-error technique is presented at the book's Web site, *www.aw.com/gitman.*

Input	Function
20	N
960	PV
−90	PMT
−1000	FV
	CPT
	I

Solution
9.452

The initial \$960 inflow is followed by annual interest outflows of \$90 (9% coupon interest rate × \$1,000 par value) over the 20-year life of the bond. In year 20, an outflow of \$1,000 (the repayment of the principal) occurs. We can determine the cost of debt by finding the IRR, which is the discount rate that equates the present value of the outflows to the initial inflow.

Calculator Use [*Note:* Most calculators require either the present (net proceeds) or the future (annual interest payments and repayment of principal) values to be input as negative numbers when we calculate cost to maturity. That approach is used here.] Using the calculator and the inputs shown at the left, you should find the before-tax cost (cost to maturity) to be 9.452%.

Approximating the Cost

The before-tax cost of debt, k_d, for a bond with a \$1,000 par value can be approximated by using the following equation:

$$k_d = \frac{I + \dfrac{\$1{,}000 - N_d}{n}}{\dfrac{N_d + \$1{,}000}{2}} \qquad (10.1)$$

where

I = annual interest in dollars
N_d = net proceeds from the sale of debt (bond)
n = number of years to the bond's maturity

EXAMPLE Substituting the appropriate values from the Duchess Corporation example into the approximation formula given in Equation 10.1, we get

$$k_d = \frac{I + \dfrac{\$1{,}000 - \$960}{20}}{\dfrac{\$960 + \$1{,}000}{2}} = \frac{\$90 + 2}{\$980}$$

$$= \frac{\$92}{\$980} = \underline{\underline{9.4\%}}$$

This approximate before-tax cost of debt is close to the 9.452% value calculated precisely in the preceding example.

After-Tax Cost of Debt

However, as indicated earlier, the *specific cost* of financing must be stated on an after-tax basis. Because interest on debt is tax deductible, it reduces the firm's taxable income. The after-tax cost of debt, k_i, can be found by multiplying the before-tax cost, k_d, by 1 minus the tax rate, T, as stated in the following equation:

$$k_i = k_d \times (1 - T) \qquad (10.2)$$

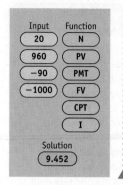

EXAMPLE Duchess Corporation has a 40% tax rate. Using the 9.4% before-tax debt cost calculated above, and applying Equation 10.2, we find an after-tax cost of debt of 5.6% [9.4% × (1 − 0.40)]. Typically, the explicit cost of long-term debt is less than the explicit cost of any of the alternative forms of long-term financing, primarily because of the tax deductibility of interest.

Review Questions

10–5 What are the *net proceeds* from the sale of a bond? What are *flotation costs* and how do they affect a bond's net proceeds?

10–6 What three methods can be used to find the before-tax cost of debt?

10–7 How is the before-tax cost of debt converted into the after-tax cost?

LG2

The Cost of Preferred Stock

Preferred stock represents a special type of ownership interest in the firm. It gives preferred stockholders the right to receive their *stated* dividends before any earnings can be distributed to common stockholders. Because preferred stock is a form of ownership, the proceeds from its sale are expected to be held for an infinite period of time. The key characteristics of preferred stock were described in Chapter 7. However, the one aspect of preferred stock that requires review is dividends.

Preferred Stock Dividends

Most preferred stock dividends are stated as a *dollar amount:* "x dollars per year." When dividends are stated this way, the stock is often referred to as "x-dollar preferred stock." Thus a "$4 preferred stock" is expected to pay preferred stockholders $4 in dividends each year on each share of preferred stock owned.

Sometimes preferred stock dividends are stated as an *annual percentage rate.* This rate represents the percentage of the stock's par value, or face value, that equals the annual dividend. For instance, an 8 percent preferred stock with a $50 par value would be expected to pay an annual dividend of $4 a share (0.08 × $50 par = $4). Before the cost of preferred stock is calculated, any dividends stated as percentages should be converted to annual dollar dividends.

Calculating the Cost of Preferred Stock

cost of preferred stock, k_p
The ratio of the preferred stock dividend to the firm's net proceeds from the sale of preferred stock; calculated by dividing the annual dividend, D_p, by the net proceeds from the sale of the preferred stock, N_p.

The **cost of preferred stock, k_p**, is the ratio of the preferred stock dividend to the firm's net proceeds from the sale of the preferred stock. The net proceeds represents the amount of money to be received minus any flotation costs. Equation 10.3 gives the cost of preferred stock, k_p, in terms of the annual dollar dividend, D_p, and the net proceeds from the sale of the stock, N_p:

$$k_p = \frac{D_p}{N_p} \tag{10.3}$$

Because preferred stock dividends are paid out of the firm's *after-tax* cash flows, a tax adjustment is not required.

EXAMPLE Duchess Corporation is contemplating issuance of a 10% preferred stock that is expected to sell for its \$87-per-share par value. The cost of issuing and selling the stock is expected to be \$5 per share. The first step in finding the cost of the stock is to calculate the dollar amount of the annual preferred dividend, which is \$8.70 ($0.10 \times \$87$). The net proceeds per share from the proposed sale of stock equals the sale price minus the flotation costs ($\$87 - \$5 = \$82$). Substituting the annual dividend, D_p, of \$8.70 and the net proceeds, N_p, of \$82 into Equation 10.3 gives the cost of preferred stock, 10.6% ($\$8.70 \div \$82$).

The cost of Duchess's preferred stock (10.6%) is much greater than the cost of its long-term debt (5.6%). This difference exists primarily because the cost of long-term debt (the interest) is tax deductible.

Review Question

10–8 How would you calculate the cost of preferred stock?

LG3

The Cost of Common Stock

The *cost of common stock* is the return required on the stock by investors in the marketplace. There are two forms of common stock financing: (1) retained earnings and (2) new issues of common stock. As a first step in finding each of these costs, we must estimate the cost of common stock equity.

Finding the Cost of Common Stock Equity

cost of common stock equity, k_s
The rate at which investors discount the expected dividends of the firm to determine its share value.

The **cost of common stock equity, k_s,** is the rate at which investors discount the expected dividends of the firm to determine its share value. Two techniques are used to measure the cost of common stock equity. One relies on the constant-growth valuation model, the other on the capital asset pricing model (CAPM).

Using the Constant-Growth Valuation (Gordon) Model

constant-growth valuation (Gordon) model
Assumes that the value of a share of stock equals the present value of all future dividends (assumed to grow at a constant rate) that it is expected to provide over an infinite time horizon.

In Chapter 7 we found the value of a share of stock to be equal to the present value of all future dividends, which in one model were assumed to grow at a constant annual rate over an infinite time horizon. This is the **constant-growth valuation model,** also known as the **Gordon model.** The key expression derived for this model was presented as Equation 7.4 and is restated here:

$$P_0 = \frac{D_1}{k_s - g} \tag{10.4}$$

where

P_0 = value of common stock
D_1 = per-share dividend *expected* at the end of year 1
k_s = required return on common stock
g = constant rate of growth in dividends

Solving Equation 10.4 for k_s results in the following expression for the *cost of common stock equity:*

$$k_s = \frac{D_1}{P_0} + g \qquad (10.5)$$

Equation 10.5 indicates that the cost of common stock equity can be found by dividing the dividend expected at the end of year 1 by the current price of the stock and adding the expected growth rate. Because common stock dividends are paid from *after-tax* income, no tax adjustment is required.

EXAMPLE Duchess Corporation wishes to determine its cost of common stock equity, k_s. The market price, P_0, of its common stock is \$50 per share. The firm expects to pay a dividend, D_1, of \$4 at the end of the coming year, 2004. The dividends paid on the outstanding stock over the past 6 years (1998–2003) were as follows:

Year	Dividend
2003	\$3.80
2002	3.62
2001	3.47
2000	3.33
1999	3.12
1998	2.97

Using the table for the present value interest factors, *PVIF* (Table A–2), or a financial calculator in conjunction with the technique described for finding growth rates in Chapter 4, we can calculate the annual growth rate of dividends, *g*. It turns out to be approximately 5% (more precisely, it is 5.05%). Substituting $D_1 = \$4$, $P_0 = \$50$, and $g = 5\%$ into Equation 10.5 yields the cost of common stock equity:

$$k_s = \frac{\$4}{\$50} + 0.05 = 0.08 + 0.05 = 0.130, \text{ or } \underline{\underline{13.0}}\%$$

The 13.0% cost of common stock equity represents the return required by *existing* shareholders on their investment. If the actual return is less than that, shareholders are likely to begin selling their stock.

Using the Capital Asset Pricing Model (CAPM)

capital asset pricing model (CAPM)
Describes the relationship between the required return, k_s, and the nondiversifiable risk of the firm as measured by the beta coefficient, *b*.

Recall from Chapter 5 that the **capital asset pricing model (CAPM)** describes the relationship between the required return, k_s, and the nondiversifiable risk of the firm as measured by the beta coefficient, *b*. The basic CAPM is

$$k_s = R_F + [b \times (k_m - R_F)] \qquad (10.6)$$

where

R_F = risk-free rate of return
k_m = market return; return on the market portfolio of assets

Using CAPM indicates that the cost of common stock equity is the return required by investors as compensation for the firm's nondiversifiable risk, measured by beta.

EXAMPLE Duchess Corporation now wishes to calculate its cost of common stock equity, k_s, by using the capital asset pricing model. The firm's investment advisers and its own analyses indicate that the risk-free rate, R_F, equals 7%; the firm's beta, b, equals 1.5; and the market return, k_m, equals 11%. Substituting these values into Equation 10.6, the company estimates the cost of common stock equity, k_s, to be

$$k_s = 7.0\% + [1.5 \times (11.0\% - 7.0\%)] = 7.0\% + 6.0\% = \underline{\underline{13.0}}\%$$

The 13.0% cost of common stock equity represents the required return of investors in Duchess Corporation common stock. It is the same as that found by using the constant-growth valuation model.

The Cost of Retained Earnings

As you know, dividends are paid out of a firm's earnings. Their payment, made in cash to common stockholders, reduces the firm's retained earnings. Let's say a firm needs common stock equity financing of a certain amount; it has two choices relative to retained earnings: It can issue additional common stock in that amount and still pay dividends to stockholders out of retained earnings. Or it can increase common stock equity by retaining the earnings (not paying the cash dividends) in the needed amount. In a strict accounting sense, the retention of earnings increases common stock equity in the same way that the sale of additional shares of common stock does. Thus the **cost of retained earnings, k_r,** to the firm is the same as the cost of an *equivalent fully subscribed issue of additional common stock*. Stockholders find the firm's retention of earnings acceptable only if they expect that it will earn at least their required return on the reinvested funds.

cost of retained earnings, k_r
The same as the cost of an *equivalent fully subscribed issue of additional common stock,* which is equal to the cost of common stock equity, k_s.

Viewing retained earnings as a fully subscribed issue of additional common stock, we can set the firm's cost of retained earnings, k_r, equal to the cost of common stock equity as given by Equations 10.5 and 10.6.[4]

$$k_r = k_s \tag{10.7}$$

It is not necessary to adjust the cost of retained earnings for flotation costs, because by retaining earnings, the firm "raises" equity capital without incurring these costs.

4. Technically, if a stockholder received dividends and wished to invest them in additional shares of the firm's stock, he or she would first have to pay personal taxes on the dividends and then pay brokerage fees before acquiring additional shares. By using *pt* as the average stockholder's personal tax rate and *bf* as the average brokerage fees stated as a percentage, we can specify the cost of retained earnings, k_r, as $k_r = k_s \times (1 - pt) \times (1 - bf)$. Because of the difficulty in estimating *pt* and *bf*, only the simpler definition of k_r given in Equation 10.7 is used here.

EXAMPLE The cost of retained earnings for Duchess Corporation was actually calculated in the preceding examples: It is equal to the cost of common stock equity. Thus k_r equals 13.0%. As we will show in the next section, the cost of retained earnings is always lower than the cost of a new issue of common stock, because it entails no flotation costs.

The Cost of New Issues of Common Stock

cost of a new issue of common stock, k_n
The cost of common stock, net of underpricing and associated flotation costs.

underpriced
Stock sold at a price below its current market price, P_0.

Our purpose in finding the firm's overall cost of capital is to determine the after-tax cost of *new* funds required for financing projects. The **cost of a new issue of common stock, k_n,** is determined by calculating the cost of common stock, net of underpricing and associated flotation costs. Normally, for a new issue to sell, it has to be **underpriced**—sold at a price below its current market price, P_0.

Firms underprice new issues for a variety of reasons. First, when the market is in equilibrium (that is, the demand for shares equals the supply of shares), additional demand for shares can be achieved only at a lower price. Second, when additional shares are issued, each share's percent of ownership in the firm is diluted, thereby justifying a lower share value. Finally, many investors view the issuance of additional shares as a signal that management is using common stock equity financing because it believes that the shares are currently overpriced. Recognizing this information, they will buy shares only at a price below the current market price. Clearly, these and other factors necessitate underpricing of new offerings of common stock. Flotation costs paid for issuing and selling the new issue will further reduce proceeds.

We can use the constant-growth valuation model expression for the cost of existing common stock, k_s, as a starting point. If we let N_n represent the net proceeds from the sale of new common stock after subtracting underpricing and flotation costs, the cost of the new issue, k_n, can be expressed as follows:

$$k_n = \frac{D_1}{N_n} + g \tag{10.8}$$

The net proceeds from sale of new common stock, N_n, will be less than the current market price, P_0. Therefore, the cost of new issues, k_n, will always be greater than the cost of existing issues, k_s, which is equal to the cost of retained earnings, k_r. *The cost of new common stock is normally greater than any other long-term financing cost.* Because common stock dividends are paid from after-tax cash flows, no tax adjustment is required.

EXAMPLE In the constant-growth valuation example, we found Duchess Corporation's cost of common stock equity, k_s, to be 13%, using the following values: an expected dividend, D_1, of \$4; a current market price, P_0, of \$50; and an expected growth rate of dividends, g, of 5%.

To determine its cost of *new* common stock, k_n, Duchess Corporation has estimated that on the average, new shares can be sold for \$47. The \$3-per-share underpricing is due to the competitive nature of the market. A second cost associated with a new issue is flotation costs of \$2.50 per share that would be paid to issue and sell the new shares. The total underpricing and flotation costs per share are therefore expected to be \$5.50.

Subtracting the \$5.50 per share underpricing and flotation cost from the current \$50 share price results in expected net proceeds of \$44.50 per share (\$50.00 − \$5.50). Substituting $D_1 = \$4$, $N_n = \$44.50$, and $g = 5\%$ into Equation 10.8 results in a cost of new common stock, k_n, as follows:

$$k_n = \frac{\$4.00}{\$44.50} + 0.05 = 0.09 + 0.05 = 0.140, \text{ or } \underline{\underline{14.0\%}}$$

Duchess Corporation's cost of new common stock is therefore 14.0%. This is the value to be used in subsequent calculations of the firm's overall cost of capital.

Review Questions

10–9 What premise about share value underlies the constant-growth valuation (Gordon) model that is used to measure the cost of common stock equity, k_s?

10–10 Why is the cost of financing a project with retained earnings less than the cost of financing it with a new issue of common stock?

LG4

The Weighted Average Cost of Capital

weighted average cost of capital (WACC), k_a
Reflects the expected average future cost of funds over the long run; found by weighting the cost of each specific type of capital by its proportion in the firm's capital structure.

Now that we have calculated the cost of specific sources of financing, we can determine the overall cost of capital. As noted earlier, the **weighted average cost of capital (WACC), k_a**, reflects the expected average future cost of funds over the long run. It is found by weighting the cost of each specific type of capital by its proportion in the firm's capital structure.

Calculating the Weighted Average Cost of Capital (WACC)

Calculating the weighted average cost of capital (WACC) is straightforward: Multiply the specific cost of each form of financing by its proportion in the firm's capital structure and sum the weighted values. As an equation, the weighted average cost of capital, k_a, can be specified as follows:

$$k_a = (w_i \times k_i) + (w_p \times k_p) + (w_s \times k_{r \text{ or } n}) \tag{10.9}$$

where

w_i = proportion of long-term debt in capital structure
w_p = proportion of preferred stock in capital structure
w_s = proportion of common stock equity in capital structure
$w_i + w_p + w_s = 1.0$

Three important points should be noted in Equation 10.9:

1. For computational convenience, it is best to convert the weights into decimal form and leave the specific costs in percentage terms.

2. *The sum of the weights must equal 1.0.* Simply stated, all capital structure components must be accounted for.
3. The firm's common stock equity weight, w_s, is multiplied by either the cost of retained earnings, k_r, or the cost of new common stock, k_n. Which cost is used depends on whether the firm's common stock equity will be financed using retained earnings, k_r, or new common stock, k_n.

EXAMPLE In earlier examples, we found the costs of the various types of capital for Duchess Corporation to be as follows:

$$\text{Cost of debt, } k_i = 5.6\%$$
$$\text{Cost of preferred stock, } k_p = 10.6\%$$
$$\text{Cost of retained earnings, } k_r = 13.0\%$$
$$\text{Cost of new common stock, } k_n = 14.0\%$$

The company uses the following weights in calculating its weighted average cost of capital:

Source of capital	Weight
Long-term debt	40%
Preferred stock	10
Common stock equity	50
Total	100%

Because the firm expects to have a sizable amount of retained earnings available ($300,000), it plans to use its cost of retained earnings, k_r, as the cost of common stock equity. Duchess Corporation's weighted average cost of capital is calculated in Table 10.1. The resulting weighted average cost of capital for Duchess is 9.8%. Assuming an unchanged risk level, the firm should accept all projects that will earn a return greater than 9.8%.

TABLE 10.1 Calculation of the Weighted Average Cost of Capital for Duchess Corporation

Source of capital	Weight (1)	Cost (2)	Weighted cost [(1) × (2)] (3)
Long-term debt	0.40	5.6%	2.2%
Preferred stock	0.10	10.6	1.1
Common stock equity	0.50	13.0	6.5
Totals	1.00		9.8%

Weighted average cost of capital = 9.8%

Weighting Schemes

Weights can be calculated on the basis of either *book value* or *market value* and using either *historical* or *target* proportions.

Book Value Versus Market Value

book value weights
Weights that use accounting values to measure the proportion of each type of capital in the firm's financial structure.

market value weights
Weights that use market values to measure the proportion of each type of capital in the firm's financial structure.

Book value weights use accounting values to measure the proportion of each type of capital in the firm's financial structure. **Market value weights** measure the proportion of each type of capital at its market value. Market value weights are appealing, because the market values of securities closely approximate the actual dollars to be received from their sale. Moreover, because the costs of the various types of capital are calculated by using prevailing market prices, it seems reasonable to use market value weights. In addition, the long-term investment cash flows to which the cost of capital is applied are estimated in terms of current as well as future market values. *Market value weights are clearly preferred over book value weights.*

Historical Versus Target

historical weights
Either book or market value weights based on *actual* capital structure proportions.

target weights
Either book or market value weights based on *desired* capital structure proportions.

Historical weights can be either book or market value weights based on *actual* capital structure proportions. For example, past or current book value proportions would constitute a form of historical weighting, as would past or current market value proportions. Such a weighting scheme would therefore be based on real—rather than desired—proportions.

Target weights, which can also be based on either book or market values, reflect the firm's *desired* capital structure proportions. Firms using target weights establish such proportions on the basis of the "optimal" capital structure they wish to achieve. (The development of these proportions and the optimal structure are discussed in detail in Chapter 11 .)

When one considers the somewhat approximate nature of the calculation of weighted average cost of capital, the choice of weights may not be critical. However, from a strictly theoretical point of view, the *preferred weighting scheme is target market value proportions,* and these are assumed throughout this chapter.

Review Questions

10–11 What is the *weighted average cost of capital (WACC),* and how is it calculated?

10–12 Describe the logic underlying the use of *target capital structure weights,* and compare and contrast this approach with the use of *historical weights.* What is the preferred weighting scheme?

LG5 LG6

The Marginal Cost and Investment Decisions

The firm's weighted average cost of capital is a key input to the investment decision-making process. As demonstrated earlier in the chapter, the firm should make only those investments for which the expected return is greater than the weighted average cost of capital. Of course, at any given time, the firm's financing costs and investment returns will be affected by the volume of financing and investment undertaken. The *weighted marginal cost of capital* and the *investment opportunities schedule* are mechanisms whereby financing and investment decisions can be made simultaneously.

The Weighted Marginal Cost of Capital (WMCC)

weighted marginal cost of capital (WMCC)
The firm's weighted average cost of capital (WACC) associated with its *next dollar* of total new financing.

The weighted average cost of capital may vary over time, depending on the volume of financing that the firm plans to raise. *As the volume of financing increases, the costs of the various types of financing will increase, raising the firm's weighted average cost of capital.* Therefore, it is useful to calculate the **weighted marginal cost of capital (WMCC)**, which is simply the firm's weighted average cost of capital (WACC) associated with its *next dollar* of total new financing. This marginal cost is relevant to current decisions.

The costs of the financing components (debt, preferred stock, and common stock) rise as larger amounts are raised. Suppliers of funds require greater returns in the form of interest, dividends, or growth as compensation for the increased risk introduced by larger volumes of *new* financing. The WMCC is therefore an increasing function of the level of total new financing.

Another factor that causes the weighted average cost of capital to increase is the use of common stock equity financing. New financing provided by common stock equity will be taken from available retained earnings until this supply is exhausted and then will be obtained through new common stock financing. Because retained earnings are a less expensive form of common stock equity financing than the sale of new common stock, the weighted average cost of capital will rise with the addition of new common stock.

Finding Break Points

break point
The level of *total* new financing at which the cost of one of the financing components rises, thereby causing an upward shift in the *weighted marginal cost of capital (WMCC)*.

To calculate the WMCC, we must calculate **break points,** which reflect the level of *total* new financing at which the cost of one of the financing components rises. The following general equation can be used to find break points:

$$BP_j = \frac{AF_j}{w_j} \tag{10.10}$$

where

BP_j = break point for financing source j
AF_j = amount of funds available from financing source j at a given cost
w_j = capital structure weight (stated in decimal form) for financing source j

EXAMPLE When Duchess Corporation exhausts its \$300,000 of available retained earnings (at $k_r = 13.0\%$), it must use the more expensive new common stock financing (at $k_n = 14.0\%$) to meet its common stock equity needs. In addition, the firm expects that it can borrow only \$400,000 of debt at the 5.6% cost; additional debt will have an after-tax cost (k_i) of 8.4%. Two break points therefore exist: (1) when the \$300,000 of retained earnings costing 13.0% is exhausted, and (2) when the \$400,000 of long-term debt costing 5.6% is exhausted.

The break points can be found by substituting these values and the corresponding capital structure weights given earlier into Equation 10.10. We get the dollar amounts of *total* new financing at which the costs of the given financing sources rise:

$$BP_{\text{common equity}} = \frac{\$300{,}000}{0.50} = \$600{,}000$$

$$BP_{\text{long-term debt}} = \frac{\$400{,}000}{0.40} = \$1{,}000{,}000$$

Calculating the WMCC

Once the break points have been determined, the next step is to calculate the weighted average cost of capital over the range of total new financing between break points. First, we find the WACC for a level of total new financing between zero and the first break point. Next, we find the WACC for a level of total new financing between the first and second break points, and so on. By definition, for each of the ranges of total new financing between break points, certain component capital costs (such as debt or common equity) will increase. This will cause the weighted average cost of capital to increase to a higher level than that over the preceding range.

weighted marginal cost of capital (WMCC) schedule Graph that relates the firm's weighted average cost of capital to the level of total new financing.

Together, these data can be used to prepare a **weighted marginal cost of capital (WMCC) schedule.** This is a graph that relates the firm's weighted average cost of capital to the level of total new financing.

EXAMPLE Table 10.2 summarizes the calculation of the WACC for Duchess Corporation over the three ranges of total new financing created by the two break points—

TABLE 10.2 Weighted Average Cost of Capital for Ranges of Total New Financing for Duchess Corporation

Range of total new financing	Source of capital (1)	Weight (2)	Cost (3)	Weighted cost [(2) × (3)] (4)
\$0 to \$600,000	Debt	.40	5.6%	2.2%
	Preferred	.10	10.6	1.1
	Common	.50	13.0	6.5
	Weighted average cost of capital			9.8%
\$600,000 to \$1,000,000	Debt	.40	5.6%	2.2%
	Preferred	.10	10.6	1.1
	Common	.50	14.0	7.0
	Weighted average cost of capital			10.3%
\$1,000,000 and above	Debt	.40	8.4%	3.4%
	Preferred	.10	10.6	1.1
	Common	.50	14.0	7.0
	Weighted average cost of capital			11.5%

FIGURE 10.1

WMCC Schedule
Weighted marginal cost of capital (WMCC) schedule for Duchess Corporation

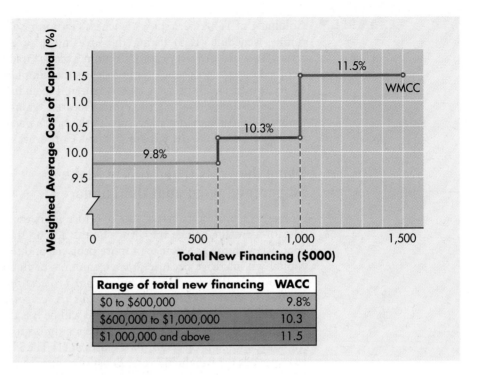

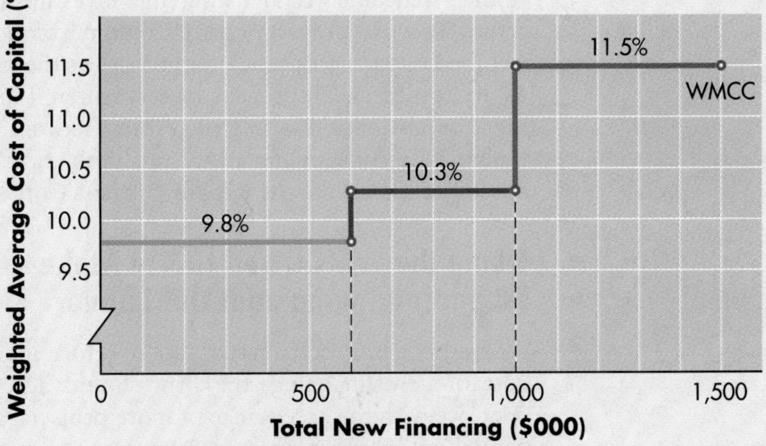

Range of total new financing	WACC
$0 to $600,000	9.8%
$600,000 to $1,000,000	10.3
$1,000,000 and above	11.5

$600,000 and $1,000,000. Comparing the costs in column 3 of the table for each of the three ranges, we can see that the costs in the first range ($0 to $600,000) are those calculated in earlier examples and used in Table 10.1. The second range ($600,000 to $1,000,000) reflects the increase in the common stock equity cost to 14.0%. In the final range, the increase in the long-term debt cost to 8.4% is introduced.

The weighted average costs of capital (WACC) for the three ranges are summarized in the table shown at the bottom of Figure 10.1. These data describe the weighted marginal cost of capital (WMCC), which increases as levels of total new financing increase. Figure 10.1 presents the WMCC schedule. Again, it is clear that the WMCC is an increasing function of the amount of total new financing raised.

The Investment Opportunities Schedule (IOS)

investment opportunities schedule (IOS)
A ranking of investment possibilities from best (highest return) to worst (lowest return).

At any given time, a firm has certain investment opportunities available to it. These opportunities differ with respect to the size of investment, risk, and return.[5] The firm's **investment opportunities schedule** (IOS) is a ranking of investment possibilities from best (highest return) to worst (lowest return). Generally, the first project selected will have the highest return, the next project the second highest, and so on. The return on investments will *decrease* as the firm accepts additional projects.

5. Because the calculated weighted average cost of capital does not apply to risk-changing investments, we assume that all opportunities have equal risk similar to the firm's risk.

EXAMPLE Column 1 of Table 10.3 shows Duchess Corporation's current investment opportunities schedule (IOS) listing the investment possibilities from best (highest return) to worst (lowest return). Column 2 of the table shows the initial investment required by each project. Column 3 shows the cumulative total invested funds necessary to finance all projects better than and including the corresponding investment opportunity. Plotting the project returns against the cumulative investment (column 1 against column 3) results in the firm's investment opportunities schedule (IOS). A graph of the IOS for Duchess Corporation is given in Figure 10.2.

Using the WMCC and IOS to Make Financing/Investment Decisions

As long as a project's internal rate of return is greater than the weighted marginal cost of new financing, the firm should accept the project.[6] The return will decrease with the acceptance of more projects, and the weighted marginal cost of capital will increase because greater amounts of financing will be required. The decision rule therefore would be: *Accept projects up to the point at which the marginal return on an investment equals its weighted marginal cost of capital.* Beyond that point, its investment return will be less than its capital cost.

This approach is consistent with the maximization of net present value (NPV) for conventional projects for two reasons: (1) The NPV is positive as long as the IRR exceeds the weighted average cost of capital, k_a. (2) The larger the difference between the IRR and k_a, the larger the resulting NPV. Therefore, the acceptance of projects beginning with those that have the greatest positive difference between IRR and k_a, down to the point at which IRR just equals k_a, should result in the maximum total NPV for all independent projects accepted. Such an outcome is completely consistent with the firm's goal of maximizing owner wealth.

EXAMPLE Figure 10.2 shows Duchess Corporation's WMCC schedule and IOS on the same set of axes. By raising $1,100,000 of new financing and investing these funds in

TABLE 10.3 Investment Opportunities Schedule (IOS) for Duchess Corporation

Investment opportunity	Internal rate of return (IRR) (1)	Initial investment (2)	Cumulative investment[a] (3)
A	15.0%	$100,000	$ 100,000
B	14.5	200,000	300,000
C	14.0	400,000	700,000
D	13.0	100,000	800,000
E	12.0	300,000	1,100,000
F	11.0	200,000	1,300,000
G	10.0	100,000	1,400,000

[a]The cumulative investment represents the total amount invested in projects with higher returns plus the investment required for the corresponding investment opportunity.

6. Although net present value could be used to make these decisions, the internal rate of return is used here because of the ease of comparison it offers.

FIGURE 10.2

IOS and WMCC Schedules

Using the IOS and WMCC to select projects for Duchess Corporation

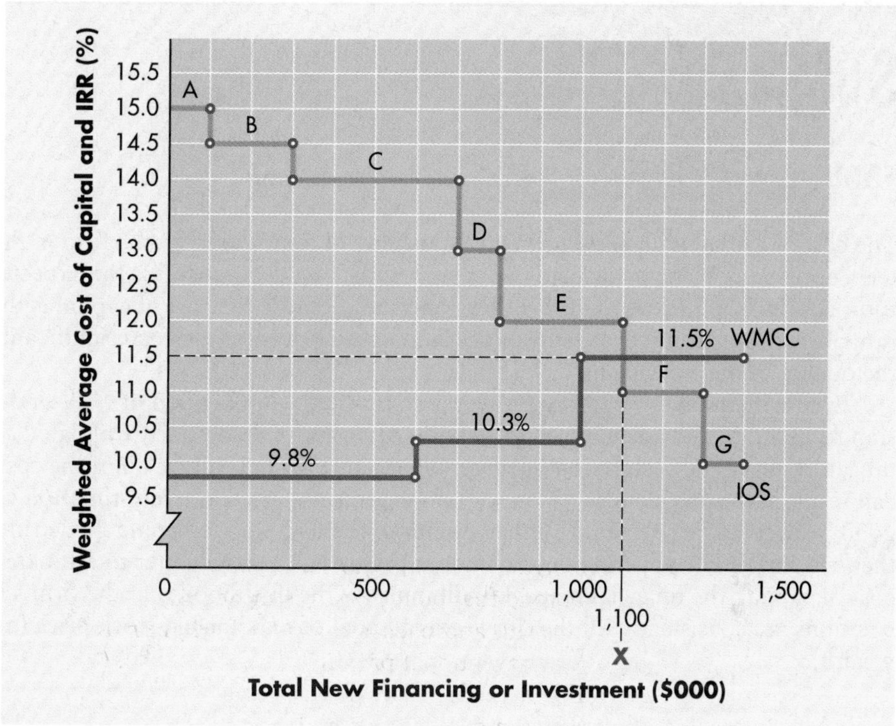

projects A, B, C, D, and E, the firm should maximize the wealth of its owners, because these projects result in the maximum total net present value. Note that the 12.0% return on the last dollar invested (in project E) *exceeds* its 11.5% weighted average cost. Investment in project F is not feasible, because its 11.0% return is *less than* the 11.5% cost of funds available for investment.

The firm's optimal capital budget of $1,100,000 is marked with an **X** in Figure 10.2. At that point, the IRR equals the weighted average cost of capital, and the firm's size as well as its shareholder value will be optimized. In a sense, the size of the firm is determined by the market—the availability of and returns on investment opportunities, and the availability and cost of financing.

In practice, most firms operate under *capital rationing*. That is, management imposes constraints that keep the capital expenditure budget below optimal (where IRR $= k_a$). Because of this, a gap frequently exists between the theoretically optimal capital budget and the firm's actual level of financing/investment.

Review Questions

10–13 What is the *weighted marginal cost of capital (WMCC)?* What does the *WMCC schedule* represent? Why does this schedule increase?

10–14 What is the *investment opportunities schedule (IOS)?* Is it typically depicted as an increasing or a decreasing function? Why?

10–15 How can the WMCC schedule and the IOS be used to find the level of financing/investment that maximizes owner wealth? Why do many firms finance/invest at a level below this optimum?

SUMMARY

FOCUS ON VALUE

The cost of capital is an extremely important rate of return used by the firm in the long-term decision process, particularly in capital budgeting decisions. It is the expected average future cost to the firm of funds over the long run. Because the cost of capital is the pivotal rate of return used in the investment decision process, its accuracy can significantly affect the quality of these decisions.

Even with good estimates of project cash flows, the application of NPV and IRR decision techniques, and adequate consideration of project risk, a poorly estimated cost of capital can result in the destruction of shareholder value. Underestimation of the cost of capital can result in the mistaken acceptance of poor projects, whereas overestimation can cause good projects to be rejected. In either situation, the firm's action could be detrimental to the firm's value. By applying the techniques presented in this chapter to estimate the firm's cost of capital, the financial manager will improve the likelihood that the firm's long-term decisions are consistent with the firm's overall goal of **maximizing stock price (owner wealth).**

REVIEW OF LEARNING GOALS

LG1 **Understand the key assumptions that underlie cost of capital, the basic concept of cost of capital, and the specific sources of capital that it includes.** The cost of capital is the rate of return that a firm must earn on its investments to maintain its market value and attract needed funds. It is affected by business and financial risks, which are assumed to be unchanged. To capture the interrelatedness of financing, a weighted average cost of capital should be used to find the expected average future cost of funds over the long run. The specific costs of the basic sources of capital (long-term debt, preferred stock, retained earnings, and common stock) can be calculated individually.

LG2 **Determine the cost of long-term debt and the cost of preferred stock.** The cost of long-term debt is the after-tax cost today of raising long-term funds through borrowing. Cost quotations, calculation (using either a trial-and-error technique or a financial calculator), or an approximation can be used to find the before-tax cost of debt, which must then be tax-adjusted. The cost of preferred stock is the ratio of the preferred stock dividend to the firm's net proceeds from the sale of preferred stock. The key formulas for the before- and after-tax cost of debt and the cost of preferred stock are given in Table 10.4.

LG3 **Calculate the cost of common stock equity and convert it into the cost of retained earnings and the cost of new issues of common stock.** The cost of common stock equity can be calculated by using the constant-growth valuation (Gordon) model or the CAPM. The cost of retained earnings is equal to the cost of common stock equity. An adjustment in the cost of common stock equity to reflect underpricing and flotation costs is necessary to find the cost of new issues of common stock. The key formulas for the cost of common stock equity, the cost of retained earnings, and the cost of new issues of common stock are given in Table 10.4.

LG4 **Calculate the weighted average cost of capital (WACC) and discuss the alternative weighting schemes.** The firm's WACC reflects the expected

TABLE 10.4 Summary of Key Definitions and Formulas for Cost of Capital

Definitions of variables

AF_j = amount of funds available from financing source j at a given cost

b = beta coefficient or measure of nondiversifiable risk

BP_j = break point for financing source j

D_1 = per share dividend *expected* at the end of year 1

D_p = annual preferred stock dividend (in dollars)

g = constant rate of growth in dividends

I = annual interest in dollars

k_a = weighted average cost of capital

k_d = before-tax cost of debt

k_i = after-tax cost of debt

k_m = required return on the market portfolio

k_n = cost of a new issue of common stock

k_p = cost of preferred stock

k_r = cost of retained earnings

k_s = required return on common stock

n = number of years to the bond's maturity

N_d = net proceeds from the sale of debt (bond)

N_n = net proceeds from the sale of new common stock

N_p = net proceeds from the sale of preferred stock

P_0 = value of common stock

R_F = risk-free rate of return

T = firm's tax rate

w_i = proportion of long-term debt in capital structure

w_j = capital structure proportion (historical or target, stated in decimal form) for financing source j

w_p = proportion of preferred stock in capital structure

w_s = proportion of common stock equity in capital structure

Cost of capital formulas

Before-tax cost of debt (approximation):

$$k_d = \frac{I + \dfrac{\$1{,}000 - N_d}{n}}{\dfrac{N_d + \$1{,}000}{2}} \qquad \text{[Eq. 10.1]}$$

After-tax cost of debt:

$$k_i = k_d \times (1 - T) \qquad \text{[Eq. 10.2]}$$

Cost of preferred stock:

$$k_p = \frac{D_p}{N_p} \qquad \text{[Eq. 10.3]}$$

Cost of common stock equity:

Using constant-growth valuation model:

$$k_s = \frac{D_1}{P_0} + g \qquad \text{[Eq. 10.5]}$$

Using CAPM:

$$k_s = R_F + [b \times (k_m - R_F)] \qquad \text{[Eq. 10.6]}$$

Cost of retained earnings:

$$k_r = k_s \qquad \text{[Eq. 10.7]}$$

Cost of new issues of common stock:

$$k_n = \frac{D_1}{N_n} + g \qquad \text{[Eq. 10.8]}$$

Weighted average cost of capital (WACC):

$$k_a = (w_i \times k_i) + (w_p \times k_p) + (w_s \times k_{r \text{ or } n}) \qquad \text{[Eq. 10.9]}$$

Break point:

$$BP_j = \frac{AF_j}{w_j} \qquad \text{[Eq. 10.10]}$$

average future cost of funds over the long run. It can be determined by combining the costs of specific types of capital after weighting each of them by its proportion using historical book or market value weights, or target book or market value weights. The theoretically preferred approach uses target weights based on market values. The key formula for WACC is given in Table 10.4.

LG5 **Describe the procedures used to determine break points and the weighted marginal cost of capital (WMCC).** As the volume of total new financing increases, the costs of the various types of financing will increase, raising the firm's WACC. The WMCC is the firm's WACC associated with its next dollar of total new financing. Break points represent the level of total new financing at which the cost of one of the financing components rises, causing an upward shift in the WMCC. The general formula for break points is given in Table 10.4. The WMCC schedule relates the WACC to each level of total new financing.

LG6 **Explain how the weighted marginal cost of capital (WMCC) can be used with the investment opportunities schedule (IOS) to make the firm's financing/investment decisions.** The IOS presents a ranking of currently available investments from best (highest return) to worst (lowest return). It is used in combination with the WMCC to find the level of financing/investment that maximizes owner wealth. The firm accepts projects up to the point at which the marginal return on its investment equals its weighted marginal cost of capital.

SELF-TEST PROBLEM (Solution in Appendix B)

LG2 LG3 LG4 LG5 LG6

ST 10–1 **Specific costs, WACC, WMCC, and IOS** Humble Manufacturing is interested in measuring its overall cost of capital. The firm is in the 40% tax bracket. Current investigation has gathered the following data:

Debt The firm can raise an unlimited amount of debt by selling \$1,000-par-value, 10% coupon interest rate, 10-year bonds on which *annual interest* payments will be made. To sell the issue, an average discount of \$30 per bond must be given. The firm must also pay flotation costs of \$20 per bond.

Preferred stock The firm can sell 11% (annual dividend) preferred stock at its \$100-per-share par value. The cost of issuing and selling the preferred stock is expected to be \$4 per share. An unlimited amount of preferred stock can be sold under these terms.

Common stock The firm's common stock is currently selling for \$80 per share. The firm expects to pay cash dividends of \$6 per share next year. The firm's dividends have been growing at an annual rate of 6%, and this rate is expected to continue in the future. The stock will have to be underpriced by \$4 per share, and flotation costs are expected to amount to \$4 per share. The firm can sell an unlimited amount of new common stock under these terms.

Retained earnings The firm expects to have \$225,000 of retained earnings available in the coming year. Once these retained earnings are exhausted, the firm will use new common stock as the form of common stock equity financing.

a. Calculate the specific cost of each source of financing. (Round to the nearest 0.1%.)

b. The firm uses the weights shown in the following table, which are based on target capital structure proportions, to calculate its weighted average cost of capital. (Round to the nearest 0.1%.)

Source of capital	Weight
Long-term debt	40%
Preferred stock	15
Common stock equity	45
Total	100%

(1) Calculate the single break point associated with the firm's financial situation. *(Hint:* This point results from the exhaustion of the firm's retained earnings.)

(2) Calculate the weighted average cost of capital associated with total new financing below the break point calculated in part (1).

(3) Calculate the weighted average cost of capital associated with total new financing above the break point calculated in part (1).

c. Using the results of part **b** along with the information shown in the following table on the available investment opportunities, draw the firm's weighted marginal cost of capital (WMCC) schedule and investment opportunities schedule (IOS) on the same set of axes (total new financing or investment on the *x* axis and weighted average cost of capital and IRR on the *y* axis).

Investment opportunity	Internal rate of return (IRR)	Initial investment
A	11.2%	$100,000
B	9.7	500,000
C	12.9	150,000
D	16.5	200,000
E	11.8	450,000
F	10.1	600,000
G	10.5	300,000

d. Which, if any, of the available investments do you recommend that the firm accept? Explain your answer. How much total new financing is required?

PROBLEMS

LG1 **10–1 Concept of cost of capital** Wren Manufacturing is in the process of analyzing its investment decision-making procedures. The two projects evaluated by the firm during the past month were projects 263 and 264. The basic variables surrounding each project analysis, using the IRR decision technique, and the resulting decision actions are summarized in the following table.

Basic variables	Project 263	Project 264
Cost	$64,000	$58,000
Life	15 years	15 years
IRR	8%	15%
Least-cost financing		
Source	Debt	Equity
Cost (after-tax)	7%	16%
Decision		
Action	Accept	Reject
Reason	8% IRR > 7% cost	15% IRR < 16% cost

a. Evaluate the firm's decision-making procedures, and explain why the acceptance of project 263 and rejection of project 264 may not be in the owners' best interest.
b. If the firm maintains a capital structure containing 40% debt and 60% equity, find its weighted average cost using the data in the table.
c. Had the firm used the weighted average cost calculated in part **b,** what actions would have been indicated relative to projects 263 and 264?
d. Compare and contrast the firm's actions with your findings in part **c.** Which decision method seems more appropriate? Explain why.

LG2 **10–2 Cost of debt using both methods** Currently, Warren Industries can sell 15-year, $1,000-par-value bonds paying *annual interest* at a 12% coupon rate. As a result of current interest rates, the bonds can be sold for $1,010 each; flotation costs of $30 per bond will be incurred in this process. The firm is in the 40% tax bracket.
a. Find the net proceeds from sale of the bond, N_d.
b. Show the cash flows from the firm's point of view over the maturity of the bond.
c. Use the *IRR approach* to calculate the before-tax and after-tax costs of debt.
d. Use the *approximation formula* to estimate the before-tax and after-tax costs of debt.
e. Compare and contrast the costs of debt calculated in parts **c** and **d.** Which approach do you prefer? Why?

LG2 **10–3 Cost of debt using the approximation formula** For each of the following $1,000-par-value bonds, assuming *annual interest* payment and a 40% tax rate, calculate the *after-tax* cost to maturity using the *approximation formula.*

Bond	Life	Underwriting fee	Discount (−) or premium (+)	Coupon interest rate
A	20 years	$25	−$20	9%
B	16	40	+ 10	10
C	15	30	− 15	12
D	25	15	Par	9
E	22	20	− 60	11

LG2 10–4 **Cost of preferred stock** Taylor Systems has just issued preferred stock. The stock has a 12% annual dividend and a $100 par value and was sold at $97.50 per share. In addition, flotation costs of $2.50 per share must be paid.

a. Calculate the cost of the preferred stock.

b. If the firm sells the preferred stock with a 10% annual dividend and nets $90.00 after flotation costs, what is its cost?

LG2 10–5 **Cost of preferred stock** Determine the cost for each of the following preferred stocks.

Preferred stock	Par value	Sale price	Flotation cost	Annual dividend
A	$100	$101	$9.00	11%
B	40	38	$3.50	8%
C	35	37	$4.00	$5.00
D	30	26	5% of par	$3.00
E	20	20	$2.50	9%

LG3 10–6 **Cost of common stock equity—CAPM** J&M Corporation common stock has a beta, b, of 1.2. The risk-free rate is 6%, and the market return is 11%.

a. Determine the risk premium on J&M common stock.

b. Determine the required return that J&M common stock should provide.

c. Determine J&M's cost of common stock equity using the CAPM.

LG3 10–7 **Cost of common stock equity** Ross Textiles wishes to measure its cost of common stock equity. The firm's stock is currently selling for $57.50. The firm expects to pay a $3.40 dividend at the end of the year (2004). The dividends for the past 5 years are shown in the following table.

Year	Dividend
2003	$3.10
2002	2.92
2001	2.60
2000	2.30
1999	2.12

After underpricing and flotation costs, the firm expects to net $52 per share on a new issue.

a. Determine the growth rate of dividends.

b. Determine the net proceeds, N_n, that the firm actually receives.

c. Using the constant-growth valuation model, determine the cost of retained earnings, k_r.

d. Using the constant-growth valuation model, determine the cost of new common stock, k_n.

LG3 **10–8 Retained earnings versus new common stock** Using the data for each firm shown in the following table, calculate the cost of retained earnings and the cost of new common stock using the constant-growth valuation model.

Firm	Current market price per share	Dividend growth rate	Projected dividend per share next year	Underpricing per share	Flotation cost per share
A	$50.00	8%	$2.25	$2.00	$1.00
B	20.00	4	1.00	0.50	1.50
C	42.50	6	2.00	1.00	2.00
D	19.00	2	2.10	1.30	1.70

LG4 **10–9 WACC—Book weights** Ridge Tool has on its books the amounts and specific (after-tax) costs shown in the following table for each source of capital.

Source of capital	Book value	Specific cost
Long-term debt	$700,000	5.3%
Preferred stock	50,000	12.0
Common stock equity	650,000	16.0

a. Calculate the firm's weighted average cost of capital using book value weights.
b. Explain how the firm can use this cost in the investment decision-making process.

LG4 **10–10 WACC—Book weights and market weights** Webster Company has compiled the information shown in the following table.

Source of capital	Book value	Market value	After-tax cost
Long-term debt	$4,000,000	$3,840,000	6.0%
Preferred stock	40,000	60,000	13.0
Common stock equity	1,060,000	3,000,000	17.0
Totals	$5,100,000	$6,900,000	

a. Calculate the weighted average cost of capital using book value weights.
b. Calculate the weighted average cost of capital using market value weights.
c. Compare the answers obtained in parts **a** and **b.** Explain the differences.

LG4 **10–11 WACC and target weights** After careful analysis, Dexter Brothers has determined that its optimal capital structure is composed of the sources and target market value weights shown in the following table.

Source of capital	Target market value weight
Long-term debt	30%
Preferred stock	15
Common stock equity	55
Total	100%

The cost of debt is estimated to be 7.2%; the cost of preferred stock is estimated to be 13.5%; the cost of retained earnings is estimated to be 16.0%; and the cost of new common stock is estimated to be 18.0%. All of these are after-tax rates. The company's debt represents 25%, the preferred stock represents 10%, and the common stock equity represents 65% of total capital on the basis of the market values of the three components. The company expects to have a significant amount of retained earnings available and does not expect to sell any new common stock.

a. Calculate the weighted average cost of capital on the basis of historical market value weights.

b. Calculate the weighted average cost of capital on the basis of target market value weights.

LG2 LG3 LG4 LG5

10–12 **Calculation of specific costs, WACC, and WMCC** Dillon Labs has asked its financial manager to measure the cost of each specific type of capital as well as the weighted average cost of capital. The weighted average cost is to be measured by using the following weights: 40% long-term debt, 10% preferred stock, and 50% common stock equity (retained earnings, new common stock, or both). The firm's tax rate is 40%.

Debt The firm can sell for $980 a 10-year, $1,000-par-value bond paying *annual interest* at a 10% coupon rate. A flotation cost of 3% of the par value is required in addition to the discount of $20 per bond.

Preferred stock Eight percent (annual dividend) preferred stock having a par value of $100 can be sold for $65. An additional fee of $2 per share must be paid to the underwriters.

Common stock The firm's common stock is currently selling for $50 per share. The dividend expected to be paid at the end of the coming year (2004) is $4. Its dividend payments, which have been approximately 60% of earnings per share in each of the past 5 years, were as shown in the following table.

Year	Dividend
2003	$3.75
2002	3.50
2001	3.30
2000	3.15
1999	2.85

It is expected that in order to sell, new common stock must be underpriced $5 per share, and the firm must also pay $3 per share in flotation costs. Dividend payments are expected to continue at 60% of earnings.

a. Calculate the specific cost of each source of financing. (Assume that $k_r = k_s$.)

b. If earnings available to common shareholders are expected to be $7 million, what is the break point associated with the exhaustion of retained earnings?

c. Determine the weighted average cost of capital between zero and the break point calculated in part **b.**

d. Determine the weighted average cost of capital just beyond the break point calculated in part **b.**

LG2 LG3 LG4 LG5

10–13 Calculation of specific costs, WACC, and WMCC Lang Enterprises is interested in measuring its overall cost of capital. Current investigation has gathered the following data. The firm is in the 40% tax bracket.

Debt The firm can raise an unlimited amount of debt by selling $1,000-par-value, 8% coupon interest rate, 20-year bonds on which *annual interest* payments will be made. To sell the issue, an average discount of $30 per bond would have to be given. The firm also must pay flotation costs of $30 per bond.

Preferred stock The firm can sell 8% preferred stock at its $95-per-share par value. The cost of issuing and selling the preferred stock is expected to be $5 per share. An unlimited amount of preferred stock can be sold under these terms.

Common stock The firm's common stock is currently selling for $90 per share. The firm expects to pay cash dividends of $7 per share next year. The firm's dividends have been growing at an annual rate of 6%, and this is expected to continue into the future. The stock must be underpriced by $7 per share, and flotation costs are expected to amount to $5 per share. The firm can sell an unlimited amount of new common stock under these terms.

Retained earnings When measuring this cost, the firm does not concern itself with the tax bracket or brokerage fees of owners. It expects to have available $100,000 of retained earnings in the coming year; once these retained earnings are exhausted, the firm will use new common stock as the form of common stock equity financing.

a. Calculate the specific cost of each source of financing. (Round answers to the nearest 0.1%.)

Source of capital	Weight
Long-term debt	30%
Preferred stock	20
Common stock equity	50
Total	100%

b. The firm's capital structure weights used in calculating its weighted average cost of capital are shown in the table at the bottom of page 416. (Round answer to the nearest 0.1%.)
(1) Calculate the single break point associated with the firm's financial situation. (*Hint:* This point results from exhaustion of the firm's retained earnings.)
(2) Calculate the weighted average cost of capital associated with total new financing below the break point calculated in part (1).
(3) Calculate the weighted average cost of capital associated with total new financing above the break point calculated in part (1).

LG4 LG5 LG6 **10–14 Integrative—WACC, WMCC, and IOS** Cartwell Products has compiled the data shown in the following table for the current costs of its three basic sources of capital—long-term debt, preferred stock, and common stock equity—for various ranges of new financing.

Source of capital	Range of new financing	After-tax cost
Long-term debt	$0 to $320,000	6%
	$320,000 and above	8
Preferred stock	$0 and above	17%
Common stock equity	$0 to $200,000	20%
	$200,000 and above	24

The company's capital structure weights used in calculating its weighted average cost of capital are shown in the following table.

Source of capital	Weight
Long-term debt	40%
Preferred stock	20
Common stock equity	40
Total	100%

a. Determine the break points and ranges of *total* new financing associated with each source of capital.
b. Using the data developed in part **a**, determine the break points (levels of *total* new financing) at which the firm's weighted average cost of capital will change.
c. Calculate the weighted average cost of capital for each range of total new financing found in part **b**. (*Hint:* There are three ranges.)
d. Using the results of part **c**, along with the following information on the available investment opportunities, draw the firm's weighted marginal cost of capital (WMCC) schedule and investment opportunities schedule (IOS) on the same set of axes (total new financing or investment on the x axis and weighted average cost of capital and IRR on the y axis).

Investment opportunity	Internal rate of return (IRR)	Initial investment
A	19%	$200,000
B	15	300,000
C	22	100,000
D	14	600,000
E	23	200,000
F	13	100,000
G	21	300,000
H	17	100,000
I	16	400,000

e. Which, if any, of the available investments do you recommend that the firm accept? Explain your answer.

CHAPTER 10 CASE Making Star Products' Financing/Investment Decision

Star Products Company is a growing manufacturer of automobile accessories whose stock is actively traded on the over-the-counter exchange. During 2003, the Dallas-based company experienced sharp increases in both sales and earnings. Because of this recent growth, Melissa Jen, the company's treasurer, wants to make sure that available funds are being used to their fullest. Management policy is to maintain the current capital structure proportions of 30% long-term debt, 10% preferred stock, and 60% common stock equity for at least the next 3 years. The firm is in the 40% tax bracket.

Star's division and product managers have presented several competing investment opportunities to Ms. Jen. However, because funds are limited, choices of which projects to accept must be made. The investment opportunities schedule (IOS) is shown in the following table.

Investment Opportunities Schedule (IOS) for Star Products Company

Investment opportunity	Internal rate of return (IRR)	Initial investment
A	15%	$400,000
B	22	200,000
C	25	700,000
D	23	400,000
E	17	500,000
F	19	600,000
G	14	500,000

To estimate the firm's weighted average cost of capital (WACC), Ms. Jen contacted a leading investment banking firm, which provided the financing cost data shown in the following table.

Financing Cost Data
Star Products Company

Long-term debt: The firm can raise \$450,000 of additional debt by selling 15-year, \$1,000-par-value, 9% coupon interest rate bonds that pay *annual interest.* It expects to net \$960 per bond after flotation costs. Any debt in excess of \$450,000 will have a before-tax cost, k_d, of 13%.

Preferred stock: Preferred stock, regardless of the amount sold, can be issued with a \$70 par value and a 14% annual dividend rate and will net \$65 per share after flotation costs.

Common stock equity: The firm expects dividends and earnings per share to be \$0.96 and \$3.20, respectively, in 2004 and to continue to grow at a constant rate of 11% per year. The firm's stock currently sells for \$12 per share. Star expects to have \$1,500,000 of retained earnings available in the coming year. Once the retained earnings have been exhausted, the firm can raise additional funds by selling new common stock, netting \$9 per share after underpricing and flotation costs.

Required

a. Calculate the cost of each source of financing, as specified:
   (1) Long-term debt, first \$450,000.
   (2) Long-term debt, greater than \$450,000.
   (3) Preferred stock, all amounts.
   (4) Common stock equity, first \$1,500,000.
   (5) Common stock equity, greater than \$1,500,000.

b. Find the break points associated with each source of capital, and use them to specify each of the ranges of total new financing over which the firm's weighted average cost of capital (WACC) remains constant.

c. Calculate the weighted average cost of capital (WACC) over each of the ranges of total new financing specified in part **b.**

d. Using your findings in part **c** along with the investment opportunities schedule (IOS), draw the firm's weighted marginal cost of capital (WMCC) and IOS on the same set of axes (total new financing or investment on the *x* axis and weighted average cost of capital and IRR on the *y* axis).

e. Which, if any, of the available investments would you recommend that the firm accept? Explain your answer.

WEB EXERCISE

Go to the St. Louis Federal Reserve Bank Web site *www.stls.frb.org*. Click on **Economic Research**; click on **Fred**; click on **Monthly Interest Rates**; and then click on **Bank Prime Loan Rate Changes—Historic Dates of Changes and Rates—1929.**

1. What was the prime interest rate in 1934?
2. What is the highest the prime interest rate has been? When was that?
3. What has been the highest prime interest rate since you were born?
4. What is the present prime interest rate?
5. Over the past 10 years, what was the lowest prime interest rate? What has been the highest prime interest rate over the past 10 years?

Now go to Barra's Web site *www.barra.com* and click on **Research + Indexes** and then on **S&P/Barra U.S. Equity Indexes.**

6. What was the average annual 10-year return on large-cap stocks, as measured by growth in the S&P 500 (annualized 10-year return)? How does this compare to your answers in question 5?

Remember to check the book's Web site at

www.aw.com/gitman

for additional resources, including additional Web exercises.

Across the Disciplines
Why This Chapter Matters To You

Accounting: You need to understand how to calculate and analyze operating and financial leverage and to be familiar with the tax effects of various capital structures.

Information systems: You need to understand the types of capital and what capital structure is, because you will provide much of the information needed in management's determination of the best capital structure for the firm.

Management: You need to understand leverage so that you can magnify returns for the firm's owners and to understand capital structure theory so that you can make decisions about the firm's optimal capital structure.

Marketing: You need to understand breakeven analysis, which you will use in pricing and product feasibility decisions.

Operations: You need to understand the impact of fixed and variable operating costs on the firm's breakeven point and its operating leverage, because these costs will have a major impact on the firm's risk and return.

Chapter 11
Leverage and Capital Structure

LEARNING GOALS

- LG1 Discuss the role of breakeven analysis, the operating breakeven point, and the effect of changing costs on it.
- LG2 Understand operating, financial, and total leverage and the relationships among them.
- LG3 Describe the types of capital, external assessment of capital structure, the capital structure of non-U.S. firms, and capital structure theory.
- LG4 Explain the optimal capital structure using a graphical view of the firm's cost-of-capital functions and a zero-growth valuation model.
- LG5 Discuss the EBIT–EPS approach to capital structure.
- LG6 Review the return and risk of alternative capital structures, their linkage to market value, and other important considerations related to capital structure.

Leverage involves the use of fixed costs to magnify returns. Its use in the capital structure of the firm has the potential to increase its return and risk. Leverage and capital structure are closely related concepts that are linked to capital budgeting decisions through the cost of capital. These concepts can be used to minimize the firm's cost of capital and maximize its owners' wealth. This chapter discusses leverage and capital-structure concepts and techniques and how the firm can use them to create the best capital structure.

LG1 LG2

Leverage

leverage
Results from the use of fixed-cost assets or funds to magnify returns to the firm's owners.

capital structure
The mix of long-term debt and equity maintained by the firm.

Leverage results from the use of fixed-cost assets or funds to magnify returns to the firm's owners. Generally, increases in leverage result in increased return and risk, whereas decreases in leverage result in decreased return and risk. The amount of leverage in the firm's **capital structure**—the mix of long-term debt and equity maintained by the firm—can significantly affect its value by affecting return and risk. Unlike some causes of risk, management has almost complete control over the risk introduced through the use of leverage. Because of its effect on value, the financial manager must understand how to measure and evaluate leverage, particularly when making capital structure decisions.

The three basic types of leverage can best be defined with reference to the firm's income statement, as shown in the general income statement format in Table 11.1.

- *Operating leverage* is concerned with the relationship between the firm's sales revenue and its earnings before interest and taxes, or EBIT. (EBIT is a descriptive label for *operating profits.*)
- *Financial leverage* is concerned with the relationship between the firm's EBIT and its common stock earnings per share (EPS).
- *Total leverage* is concerned with the relationship between the firm's sales revenue and EPS.

TABLE 11.1 General Income Statement Format and Types of Leverage

Operating leverage	Sales revenue	Total leverage
	Less: Cost of goods sold	
	Gross profits	
	Less: Operating expenses	
	Earnings before interest and taxes (EBIT)	
Financial leverage	Less: Interest	
	Net profits before taxes	
	Less: Taxes	
	Net profits after taxes	
	Less: Preferred stock dividends	
	Earnings available for common stockholders	
	Earnings per share (EPS)	

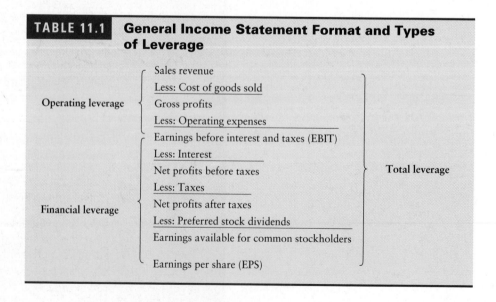

We will examine the three types of leverage concepts in detail in sections that follow. First, though, we will look at breakeven analysis, which lays the foundation for leverage concepts by demonstrating the effects of fixed costs on the firm's operations.

Breakeven Analysis

breakeven analysis
Indicates the level of operations necessary to cover all operating costs and the profitability associated with various levels of sales.

operating breakeven point
The level of sales necessary to cover all *operating costs;* the point at which EBIT = $0.

Breakeven analysis, sometimes called *cost-volume-profit analysis,* is used by the firm (1) to determine the level of operations necessary to cover all operating costs and (2) to evaluate the profitability associated with various levels of sales. The firm's **operating breakeven point** is the level of sales necessary to cover all *operating costs.* At that point, earnings before interest and taxes equals $0.[1]

The first step in finding the operating breakeven point is to divide the cost of goods sold and operating expenses into fixed and variable operating costs. *Fixed costs* are a function of time, not sales volume, and are typically contractual; rent, for example, is a fixed cost. *Variable costs* vary directly with sales and are a function of volume, not time; shipping costs, for example, are a variable cost.[2]

The Algebraic Approach

Using the following variables, we can recast the operating portion of the firm's income statement given in Table 11.1 into the algebraic representation shown in Table 11.2.

P = sale price per unit
Q = sales quantity in units
FC = fixed operating cost per period
VC = variable operating cost per unit

Rewriting the algebraic calculations in Table 11.2 as a formula for earnings before interest and taxes yields Equation 11.1:

$$\text{EBIT} = (P \times Q) - FC - (VC \times Q) \tag{11.1}$$

TABLE 11.2 Operating Leverage, Costs, and Breakeven Analysis

	Item	Algebraic representation
Operating leverage	Sales revenue	$(P \times Q)$
	Less: Fixed operating costs	$-\quad FC$
	Less: Variable operating costs	$-(VC \times Q)$
	Earnings before interest and taxes	EBIT

1. Quite often, the breakeven point is calculated so that it represents the point at which *all operating and financial costs* are covered. Our concern in this chapter is not with this overall breakeven point.

2. Some costs, commonly called *semifixed* or *semivariable,* are partly fixed and partly variable. An example is sales commissions that are fixed for a certain volume of sales and then increase to higher levels for higher volumes. For convenience and clarity, we assume that all costs can be classified as either fixed or variable.

Simplifying Equation 11.1 yields

$$\text{EBIT} = Q \times (P - VC) - FC \tag{11.2}$$

As noted above, the operating breakeven point is the level of sales at which all fixed and variable *operating costs* are covered—the level at which EBIT equals \$0. Setting EBIT equal to \$0 and solving Equation 11.2 for Q yield

$$Q = \frac{FC}{P - VC} \tag{11.3}$$

Q is the firm's operating breakeven point.

EXAMPLE Assume that Cheryl's Posters, a small poster retailer, has fixed operating costs of \$2,500, its sale price per unit (poster) is \$10, and its variable operating cost per unit is \$5. Applying Equation 11.3 to these data yields

$$Q = \frac{\$2{,}500}{\$10 - \$5} = \frac{\$2{,}500}{\$5} = 500 \text{ units}$$

At sales of 500 units, the firm's EBIT should just equal \$0. The firm will have positive EBIT for sales greater than 500 units and negative EBIT, or a loss, for sales less than 500 units. We can confirm this by substituting values above and below 500 units, along with the other values given, into Equation 11.1.

The Graphical Approach

Figure 11.1 presents in graphical form the breakeven analysis of the data in the preceding example. The firm's operating breakeven point is the point at which its *total operating cost*—the sum of its fixed and variable operating costs—equals sales revenue. At this point, EBIT equals \$0. The figure shows that for sales *below* 500 units, total operating cost exceeds sales revenue, and EBIT is less than \$0 (a loss). For sales *above* the breakeven point of 500 units, sales revenue exceeds total operating cost, and EBIT is greater than \$0.

Changing Costs and the Operating Breakeven Point

A firm's operating breakeven point is sensitive to a number of variables: fixed operating cost (FC), the sale price per unit (P), and the variable operating cost per unit (VC). The effects of increases or decreases in these variables can be readily seen by referring to Equation 11.3. The sensitivity of the breakeven sales volume (Q) to an *increase* in each of these variables is summarized in Table 11.3. As might be expected, an increase in cost (FC or VC) tends to increase the operating breakeven point, whereas an increase in the sale price per unit (P) decreases the operating breakeven point.

EXAMPLE Assume that Cheryl's Posters wishes to evaluate the impact of several options: (1) increasing fixed operating costs to \$3,000, (2) increasing the sale price per unit to

FIGURE 11.1

Breakeven Analysis
Graphical operating breakeven analysis

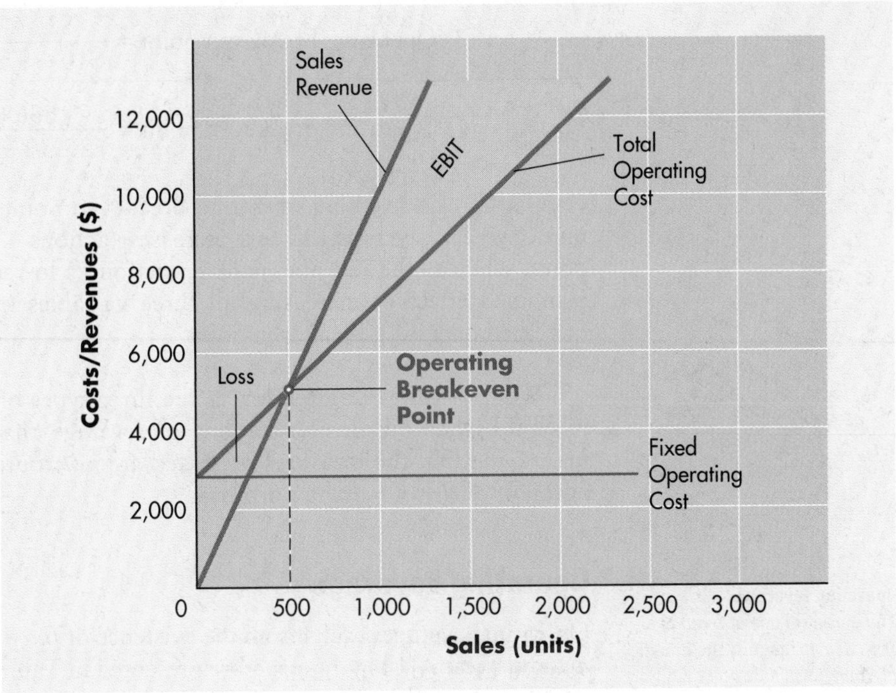

\$12.50, (3) increasing the variable operating cost per unit to \$7.50, and (4) simultaneously implementing all three of these changes. Substituting the appropriate data into Equation 11.3 yields the following results:

$$(1) \text{ Operating breakeven point} = \frac{\$3{,}000}{\$10 - \$5} = 600 \text{ units}$$

$$(2) \text{ Operating breakeven point} = \frac{\$2{,}500}{\$12.50 - \$5} = 333\tfrac{1}{3} \text{ units}$$

TABLE 11.3 Sensitivity of Operating Breakeven Point to Increases in Key Breakeven Variables

Increase in variable	Effect on operating breakeven point
Fixed operating cost *(FC)*	Increase
Sale price per unit *(P)*	Decrease
Variable operating cost per unit *(VC)*	Increase

Note: Decreases in each of the variables shown would have the opposite effect from their effect on operating breakeven point.

$$(3)\ \text{Operating breakeven point} = \frac{\$2{,}500}{\$10 - \$7.50} = 1{,}000 \text{ units}$$

$$(4)\ \text{Operating breakeven point} = \frac{\$3{,}000}{\$12.50 - \$7.50} = 600 \text{ units}$$

Comparing the resulting operating breakeven points to the initial value of 500 units, we can see that the cost increases (actions 1 and 3) raise the breakeven point, whereas the revenue increase (action 2) lowers the breakeven point. The combined effect of increasing all three variables (action 4) also results in an increased operating breakeven point. ▲

We now turn our attention to the three types of leverage. It is important to recognize that the demonstrations of leverage that follow are conceptual in nature and that the measures presented are *not* routinely used by financial managers for decision-making purposes.

Operating Leverage

operating leverage
The potential use of *fixed operating costs* to magnify the effects of changes in sales on the firm's earnings before interest and taxes.

Operating leverage results from the existence of *fixed operating costs* in the firm's income stream. Using the structure presented in Table 11.2, we can define **operating leverage** as the potential use of *fixed operating costs* to magnify the effects of changes in sales on the firm's earnings before interest and taxes.

EXAMPLE ▼ Using the data for Cheryl's Posters (sale price, $P = \$10$ per unit; variable operating cost, $VC = \$5$ per unit; fixed operating cost, $FC = \$2{,}500$), Figure 11.2 presents the operating breakeven graph originally shown in Figure 11.1. The additional notations on the graph indicate that as the firm's sales increase from 1,000 to 1,500 units (Q_1 to Q_2), its EBIT increases from \$2,500 to \$5,000 ($EBIT_1$ to $EBIT_2$). In other words, a 50% increase in sales (1,000 to 1,500 units) results in a 100% increase in EBIT (\$2,500 to \$5,000). Table 11.4 includes the data for

TABLE 11.4 The EBIT for Various Sales Levels

	Case 2		Case 1
	−50%		+50%
Sales (in units)	500	1,000	1,500
Sales revenue[a]	\$5,000	\$10,000	\$15,000
Less: Variable operating costs[b]	2,500	5,000	7,500
Less: Fixed operating costs	2,500	2,500	2,500
Earnings before interest and taxes (EBIT)	\$ 0	\$ 2,500	\$ 5,000
	−100%		+100%

[a]Sales revenue = \$10/unit × sales in units.
[b]Variable operating costs = \$5/unit × sales in units.

FIGURE 11.2

Operating Leverage
Breakeven analysis and operating leverage

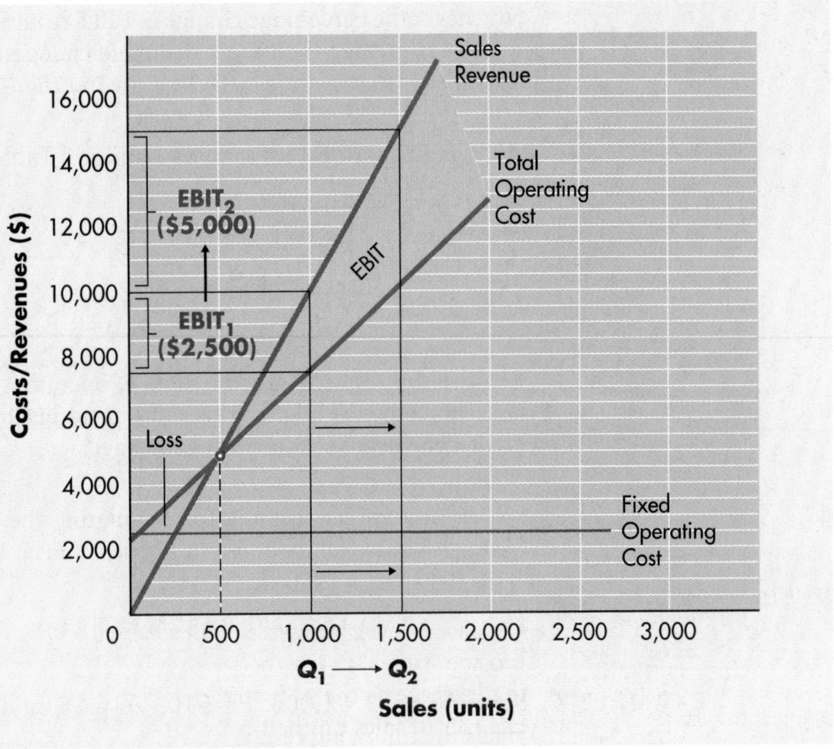

Figure 11.2 as well as relevant data for a 500-unit sales level. We can illustrate two cases using the 1,000-unit sales level as a reference point.

Case 1 A 50% *increase* in sales (from 1,000 to 1,500 units) results in a 100% *increase* in EBIT (from $2,500 to $5,000).

Case 2 A 50% *decrease* in sales (from 1,000 to 500 units) results in a 100% *decrease* in EBIT (from $2,500 to $0).

From the preceding example, we see that operating leverage works in *both directions*. When a firm has fixed operating costs, operating leverage is present. An increase in sales results in a more-than-proportional increase in EBIT; a decrease in sales results in a more-than-proportional decrease in EBIT.

Measuring the Degree of Operating Leverage (DOL)

degree of operating leverage (DOL)
The numerical measure of the firm's operating leverage.

The **degree of operating leverage (DOL)** is the numerical measure of the firm's operating leverage. It can be derived using the following equation:[3]

$$DOL = \frac{\text{Percentage change in EBIT}}{\text{Percentage change in sales}} \tag{11.4}$$

3. The degree of operating leverage also depends on the base level of sales used as a point of reference. The closer the base sales level used is to the operating breakeven point, the greater the operating leverage. *Comparison of the degree of operating leverage of two firms is valid only when the same base level of sales is used for both firms.*

Whenever the percentage change in EBIT resulting from a given percentage change in sales is greater than the percentage change in sales, operating leverage exists. This means that as long as DOL is greater than 1, there is operating leverage.

EXAMPLE ▼ Applying Equation 11.4 to cases 1 and 2 in Table 11.4 yields the following results:[4]

$$\text{Case 1:} \quad \frac{+100\%}{+50\%} = 2.0$$

$$\text{Case 2:} \quad \frac{-100\%}{-50\%} = 2.0$$

Because the result is greater than 1, operating leverage exists. For a given base level of sales, the higher the value resulting from applying Equation 11.4, the greater the degree of operating leverage. ▲

A more direct formula for calculating the degree of operating leverage at a base sales level, Q, is shown in Equation 11.5.

$$\text{DOL at base sales level } Q = \frac{Q \times (P - VC)}{Q \times (P - VC) - FC} \tag{11.5}$$

EXAMPLE ▼ Substituting $Q = 1{,}000$, $P = \$10$, $VC = \$5$, and $FC = \$2{,}500$ into Equation 11.5 yields the following result:

$$\text{DOL at 1,000 units} = \frac{1{,}000 \times (\$10 - \$5)}{1{,}000 \times (\$10 - \$5) - \$2{,}500} = \frac{\$5{,}000}{\$2{,}500} = 2.0$$

The use of the formula results in the same value for DOL (2.0) as that found by using Table 11.4 and Equation 11.4.[5] ▲

Fixed Costs and Operating Leverage

Changes in fixed operating costs affect operating leverage significantly. Firms sometimes can incur fixed operating costs rather than variable operating costs and at other times may be able to substitute one type of cost for the other. For example, a firm could make fixed-dollar lease payments rather than payments equal to a specified percentage of sales. Or it could compensate sales representatives with a fixed salary and bonus rather than on a pure percent-of-sales com-

4. Because the concept of leverage is *linear*, positive and negative changes of equal magnitude will always result in equal degrees of leverage when the same base sales level is used as a point of reference. This relationship holds for all types of leverage discussed in this chapter.

5. When total sales in dollars—instead of unit sales—are available, the following equation, in which TR = dollar level of base sales and TVC = total variable operating costs in dollars, can be used.

$$\text{DOL at base dollar sales } TR = \frac{TR - TVC}{TR - TVC - FC}$$

This formula is especially useful for finding the DOL for multiproduct firms. It should be clear that because in the case of a single-product firm, $TR = P \times Q$ and $TVC = VC \times Q$, substitution of these values into Equation 11.5 results in the equation given here.

TABLE 11.5 Operating Leverage and Increased Fixed Costs

	Case 2		Case 1
	−50%		+50%
Sales (in units)	500	1,000	1,500
Sales revenue[a]	$5,000	$10,000	$15,000
Less: Variable operating costs[b]	2,250	4,500	6,750
Less: Fixed operating costs	3,000	3,000	3,000
Earnings before interest and taxes (EBIT)	−$ 250	$ 2,500	$ 5,250
	−110%		+110%

[a]Sales revenue was calculated as indicated in Table 11.4.
[b]Variable operating costs = $4.50/unit × sales in units.

mission basis. The effects of changes in fixed operating costs on operating leverage can best be illustrated by continuing our example.

EXAMPLE

Assume that Cheryl's Posters exchanges a portion of its variable operating costs for fixed operating costs by eliminating sales commissions and increasing sales salaries. This exchange results in a reduction in the variable operating cost per unit from $5 to $4.50 and an increase in the fixed operating costs from $2,500 to $3,000. Table 11.5 presents an analysis like that in Table 11.4, but using the new costs. Although the EBIT of $2,500 at the 1,000-unit sales level is the same as before the shift in operating cost structure, Table 11.5 shows that the firm has increased its operating leverage by shifting to greater fixed operating costs.

With the substitution of the appropriate values into Equation 11.5, the degree of operating leverage at the 1,000-unit base level of sales becomes

$$\text{DOL at 1,000 units} = \frac{1{,}000 \times (\$10 - \$4.50)}{1{,}000 \times (\$10 - \$4.50) - \$3{,}000} = \frac{\$5{,}500}{\$2{,}500} = 2.2$$

Comparing this value to the DOL of 2.0 before the shift to more fixed costs makes it is clear that the higher the firm's fixed operating costs relative to variable operating costs, the greater the degree of operating leverage.

Financial Leverage

financial leverage
The potential use of *fixed financial costs* to magnify the effects of changes in earnings before interest and taxes on the firm's earnings per share.

Financial leverage results from the presence of *fixed financial costs* in the firm's income stream. Using the framework in Table 11.1, we can define **financial leverage** as the potential use of *fixed financial costs* to magnify the effects of changes in earnings before interest and taxes on the firm's earnings per share. The two fixed financial costs that may be found on the firm's income statement are (1) interest on debt and (2) preferred stock dividends. These charges must be paid regardless of the amount of EBIT available to pay them.[6]

EXAMPLE Chen Foods, a small Oriental food company, expects EBIT of $10,000 in the current year. It has a $20,000 bond with a 10% (annual) coupon rate of interest and an issue of 600 shares of $4 (annual dividend per share) preferred stock outstanding. It also has 1,000 shares of common stock outstanding. The annual interest on the bond issue is $2,000 (0.10 × $20,000). The annual dividends on the preferred stock are $2,400 ($4.00/share × 600 shares). Table 11.6 presents the EPS corresponding to levels of EBIT of $6,000, $10,000, and $14,000, assuming that the firm is in the 40% tax bracket. Two situations are shown:

Case 1 A 40% *increase* in EBIT (from $10,000 to $14,000) results in a 100% *increase* in earnings per share (from $2.40 to $4.80).

Case 2 A 40% *decrease* in EBIT (from $10,000 to $6,000) results in a 100% *decrease* in earnings per share (from $2.40 to $0).

The effect of financial leverage is such that an increase in the firm's EBIT results in a more-than-proportional increase in the firm's earnings per share, whereas a decrease in the firm's EBIT results in a more-than-proportional decrease in EPS.

TABLE 11.6 The EPS for Various EBIT Levels[a]

	Case 2 (−40%)		Case 1 (+40%)
EBIT	$6,000	$10,000	$14,000
Less: Interest (*I*)	2,000	2,000	2,000
Net profits before taxes	$4,000	$ 8,000	$12,000
Less: Taxes ($T = 0.40$)	1,600	3,200	4,800
Net profits after taxes	$2,400	$ 4,800	$ 7,200
Less: Preferred stock dividends (*PD*)	2,400	2,400	2,400
Earnings available for common (EAC)	$ 0	$ 2,400	$ 4,800
Earnings per share (EPS)	$\frac{\$0}{1{,}000} = \$0$	$\frac{\$2{,}400}{1{,}000} = \$2.40$	$\frac{\$4{,}800}{1{,}000} = \$4.80$
	−100%		+100%

[a]As noted in Chapter 1, for accounting and tax purposes, interest is a *tax-deductible expense,* whereas dividends must be paid from after-tax cash flows.

6. As noted in Chapter 7, although preferred stock dividends can be "passed" (not paid) at the option of the firm's directors, it is generally believed that payment of such dividends is necessary. *This text treats the preferred stock dividend as a contractual obligation, not only to be paid as a fixed amount, but also to be paid as scheduled.* Although failure to pay preferred dividends cannot force the firm into bankruptcy, it increases the common stockholders' risk because they cannot be paid dividends until the claims of preferred stockholders are satisfied.

Measuring the Degree of Financial Leverage (DFL)

degree of financial leverage (DFL)
The numerical measure of the firm's financial leverage.

The **degree of financial leverage (DFL)** is the numerical measure of the firm's financial leverage. Computing it is much like computing the degree of operating leverage. The following equation presents one approach for obtaining the DFL.[7]

$$\text{DFL} = \frac{\text{Percentage change in EPS}}{\text{Percentage change in EBIT}} \tag{11.6}$$

Whenever the percentage change in EPS resulting from a given percentage change in EBIT is greater than the percentage change in EBIT, financial leverage exists. This means that whenever DFL is greater than 1, there is financial leverage.

EXAMPLE ▼ Applying Equation 11.6 to cases 1 and 2 in Table 11.6 yields

$$\textbf{Case 1:} \quad \frac{+100\%}{+40\%} = 2.5$$

$$\textbf{Case 2:} \quad \frac{-100\%}{-40\%} = 2.5$$

In both cases, the quotient is greater than 1, so financial leverage exists. The higher this value, the greater the degree of financial leverage. ▲

A more direct formula for calculating the degree of financial leverage at a base level of EBIT is given by Equation 11.7, where the notation from Table 11.6 is used. Note that in the denominator, the term $1/(1-T)$ converts the after-tax preferred stock dividend to a before-tax amount for consistency with the other terms in the equation.

$$\text{DFL at base level EBIT} = \frac{\text{EBIT}}{\text{EBIT} - I - \left(PD \times \frac{1}{1-T}\right)} \tag{11.7}$$

EXAMPLE ▼ Substituting EBIT = \$10,000, I = \$2,000, PD = \$2,400, and the tax rate (T = 0.40) into Equation 11.7 yields the following result:

$$\text{DFL at \$10,000 EBIT} = \frac{\$10{,}000}{\$10{,}000 - \$2{,}000 - \left(\$2{,}400 \times \frac{1}{1-0.40}\right)}$$

$$= \frac{\$10{,}000}{\$4{,}000} = 2.5$$ ▲

Note that the formula given in Equation 11.7 provides a more direct method for calculating the degree of financial leverage than the approach illustrated using Table 11.6 and Equation 11.6.

7. This approach is valid only when the same base level of EBIT is used to calculate and compare these values. In other words, *the base level of EBIT must be held constant to compare the financial leverage associated with different levels of fixed financial costs.*

Total Leverage

total leverage
The potential use of *fixed costs, both operating and financial,* to magnify the effect of changes in sales on the firm's earnings per share.

We also can assess the combined effect of operating and financial leverage on the firm's risk by using a framework similar to that used to develop the individual concepts of leverage. This combined effect, or **total leverage,** can be defined as the potential use of *fixed costs, both operating and financial,* to magnify the effect of changes in sales on the firm's earnings per share. Total leverage can therefore be viewed as the *total impact of the fixed costs* in the firm's operating and financial structure.

EXAMPLE

Cables Inc., a computer cable manufacturer, expects sales of 20,000 units at $5 per unit in the coming year and must meet the following obligations: variable operating costs of $2 per unit, fixed operating costs of $10,000, interest of $20,000, and preferred stock dividends of $12,000. The firm is in the 40% tax bracket and has 5,000 shares of common stock outstanding. Table 11.7 presents the levels of earnings per share associated with the expected sales of 20,000 units and with sales of 30,000 units.

The table illustrates that as a result of a 50% increase in sales (from 20,000 to 30,000 units), the firm would experience a 300% increase in earnings per share (from $1.20 to $4.80). Although it is not shown in the table, a 50% decrease in sales would, conversely, result in a 300% decrease in earnings per share. The linear nature of the leverage relationship accounts for the fact that

TABLE 11.7 The Total Leverage Effect

		+50% →		
Sales (in units)	20,000	30,000		
Sales revenue[a]	$100,000	$150,000		
Less: Variable operating costs[b]	40,000	60,000	$\text{DOL} = \frac{+60\%}{+50\%} = 1.2$	
Less: Fixed operating costs	10,000	10,000		
Earnings before interest and taxes (EBIT)	$ 50,000	$ 80,000		
		+60% →		$\text{DTL} = \frac{+300\%}{+50\%} = 6.0$
Less: Interest	20,000	20,000		
Net profits before taxes	$ 30,000	$ 60,000		
Less: Taxes ($T = 0.40$)	12,000	24,000	$\text{DFL} = \frac{+300\%}{+60\%} = 5.0$	
Net profits after taxes	$ 18,000	$ 36,000		
Less: Preferred stock dividends	12,000	12,000		
Earnings available for common	$ 6,000	$ 24,000		
Earnings per share (EPS)	$\frac{\$6,000}{5,000} = \$1.20$	$\frac{\$24,000}{5,000} = \$4.80$		
		+300% →		

[a]Sales revenue = $5/unit × sales in units.
[b]Variable operating costs = $2/unit × sales in units.

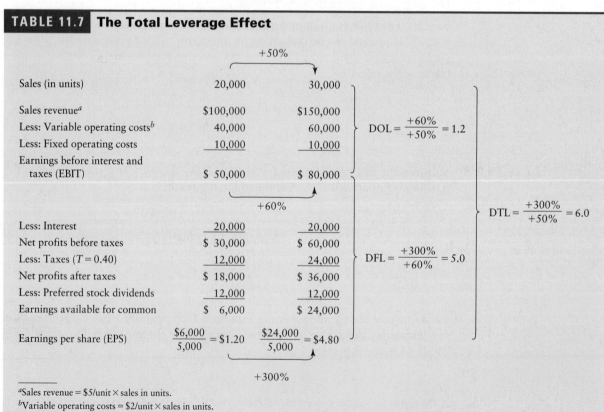

sales changes of equal magnitude in opposite directions result in EPS changes of equal magnitude in the corresponding direction. At this point, it should be clear that whenever a firm has fixed costs—operating or financial—in its structure, total leverage will exist.

Measuring the Degree of Total Leverage (DTL)

degree of total leverage (DTL) The numerical measure of the firm's total leverage.

The **degree of total leverage (DTL)** is the numerical measure of the firm's total leverage. It can be computed much as operating and financial leverage are computed. The following equation presents one approach for measuring DTL:[8]

$$\text{DTL} = \frac{\text{Percentage change in EPS}}{\text{Percentage change in sales}} \qquad (11.8)$$

Whenever the percentage change in EPS resulting from a given percentage change in sales is greater than the percentage change in sales, total leverage exists. This means that as long as the DTL is greater than 1, there is total leverage.

EXAMPLE Applying Equation 11.8 to the data in Table 11.7 yields

$$\text{DTL} = \frac{+300\%}{+50\%} = 6.0$$

Because this result is greater than 1, total leverage exists. The higher the value, the greater the degree of total leverage.

A more direct formula for calculating the degree of total leverage at a given base level of sales, Q, is given by Equation 11.9, which uses the same notation that was presented earlier:

$$\text{DTL at base sales level } Q = \frac{Q \times (P - VC)}{Q \times (P - VC) - FC - I - \left(PD \times \frac{1}{1 - T}\right)} \qquad (11.9)$$

EXAMPLE Substituting $Q = 20{,}000$, $P = \$5$, $VC = \$2$, $FC = \$10{,}000$, $I = \$20{,}000$, $PD = \$12{,}000$, and the tax rate ($T = 0.40$) into Equation 11.9 yields

DTL at 20,000 units

$$= \frac{20{,}000 \times (\$5 - \$2)}{20{,}000 \times (\$5 - \$2) - \$10{,}000 - \$20{,}000 - \left(\$12{,}000 \times \frac{1}{1 - 0.40}\right)}$$

$$= \frac{\$60{,}000}{\$10{,}000} = 6.0$$

Clearly, the formula used in Equation 11.9 provides a more direct method for calculating the degree of total leverage than the approach illustrated using Table 11.7 and Equation 11.8.

8. This approach is valid only when the same base level of sales is used to calculate and compare these values. In other words, *the base level of sales must be held constant if we are to compare the total leverage associated with different levels of fixed costs.*

The Relationship of Operating, Financial, and Total Leverage

Total leverage reflects the *combined impact* of operating and financial leverage on the firm. High operating leverage and high financial leverage will cause total leverage to be high. The opposite will also be true. The relationship between operating leverage and financial leverage is *multiplicative* rather than *additive*. The relationship between the degree of total leverage (DTL) and the degrees of operating leverage (DOL) and financial leverage (DFL) is given by Equation 11.10.

$$DTL = DOL \times DFL \tag{11.10}$$

EXAMPLE Substituting the values calculated for DOL and DFL, shown on the right-hand side of Table 11.7, into Equation 11.10 yields

$$DTL = 1.2 \times 5.0 = 6.0$$

The resulting degree of total leverage is the same value that we calculated directly in the preceding examples.

Review Questions

11–1 What is meant by the term *leverage?* How are operating leverage, financial leverage, and total leverage related to the income statement?

11–2 What is the *operating breakeven point?* How do changes in fixed operating costs, the sale price per unit, and the variable operating cost per unit affect it?

11–3 What is *operating leverage?* What causes it? How is the *degree of operating leverage (DOL)* measured?

11–4 What is *financial leverage?* What causes it? How is the *degree of financial leverage (DFL)* measured?

11–5 What is the general relationship among operating leverage, financial leverage, and the total leverage of the firm? Do these types of leverage complement each other? Why or why not?

LG3 LG4

The Firm's Capital Structure

Capital structure is one of the most complex areas of financial decision making because of its interrelationship with other financial decision variables.[9] Poor capital structure decisions can result in a high cost of capital, thereby lowering the NPVs of projects and making more of them unacceptable. Effective capital structure decisions can lower the cost of capital, resulting in higher NPVs and more acceptable projects—and thereby increasing the value of the firm. This section links together many of the concepts presented in Chapters 4, 5, 6, 7, and 10 and the discussion of leverage in this chapter.

9. Of course, although capital structure is financially important, it, like many business decisions, is generally not so important as the firm's products or services. In a practical sense, a firm can probably more readily increase its value by improving quality and reducing costs than by fine-tuning its capital structure.

Types of Capital

All of the items on the right-hand side of the firm's balance sheet, excluding current liabilities, are sources of capital. The following simplified balance sheet illustrates the basic breakdown of total capital into its two components, *debt capital* and *equity capital.*

Balance Sheet			
	Current liabilities		
	Long-term debt	Debt capital	Total capital
Assets	Stockholders' equity Preferred stock Common stock equity Common stock Retained earnings	Equity capital	

The various types and characteristics of *corporate bonds,* a major source of *debt capital,* were discussed in detail in Chapter 6. The cost of debt is lower than the cost of other forms of financing. Lenders demand relatively lower returns because they take the least risk of any long-term contributors of capital: (1) They have a higher priority of claim against any earnings or assets available for payment. (2) They can exert far greater legal pressure against the company to make payment than can holders of preferred or common stock. (3) The tax deductibility of interest payments lowers the debt cost to the firm substantially.

Unlike debt capital, which must be repaid at some future date, *equity capital* is expected to remain in the firm for an indefinite period of time. The two basic sources of equity capital are (1) preferred stock and (2) common stock equity, which includes common stock and retained earnings. Common stock is typically the most expensive form of equity, followed by retained earnings and then preferred stock. Our concern here is the relationship between debt and equity capital. Key differences between these two types of capital, relative to voice in management, claims on income and assets, maturity, and tax treatment, were summarized in Chapter 7, Table 7.1. Because of its secondary position relative to debt, suppliers of equity capital take greater risk than suppliers of debt capital and therefore must be compensated with higher expected returns.

External Assessment of Capital Structure

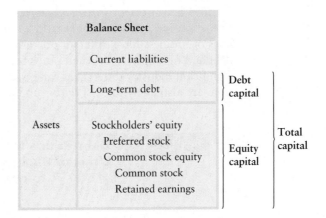

We saw earlier that *financial leverage* results from the use of fixed-cost financing, such as debt and preferred stock, to magnify return and risk. The amount of leverage in the firm's capital structure can affect its value by affecting return and risk. Those outside the firm can make a rough assessment of capital structure by using measures found in the firm's financial statements. Some of these important debt ratios were presented in Chapter 2. For example, a direct measure of the degree of indebtedness is the *debt ratio*. The higher this ratio, the greater the relative amount of debt (or financial leverage) in the firm's capital structure. Measures of the firm's ability to meet contractual payments associated with debt include the *times interest earned ratio* and the *fixed-payment coverage ratio*. These ratios provide indirect information on financial leverage. Generally, the smaller these ratios, the greater the firm's financial leverage and the less able it is to meet payments as they come due.

The level of debt (financial leverage) that is acceptable for one industry or line of business can be highly risky in another, because different industries and lines of business have different operating characteristics. Table 11.8 presents the debt and times interest earned ratios for selected industries and lines of business. Significant industry differences can be seen in these data. Differences in debt positions are also likely to exist *within* an industry or line of business.

TABLE 11.8 Debt Ratios for Selected Industries and Lines of Business (Fiscal Years Ended 4/1/00 Through 3/31/01)

Industry or line of business	Debt ratio	Times interest earned ratio
Manufacturing industries		
Books	65.2%	3.3
Dairy products	74.6	3.0
Electronic computers	55.4	3.4
Iron and steel forgings	62.7	2.3
Machine tools, metal cutting types	60.4	2.4
Wines & distilled alcoholic beverages	69.7	4.4
Women's, misses' & juniors' dresses	53.5	2.4
Wholesaling industries		
Furniture	69.4	3.0
General groceries	66.8	2.8
Men's and boys' clothing	60.8	2.6
Retailing industries		
Autos, new and used	76.1	1.4
Department stores	52.8	2.3
Restaurants	92.5	2.3
Service industries		
Accounting, auditing, bookkeeping	68.4	5.6
Advertising agencies	81.3	4.2
Auto repair—general	75.9	2.5
Insurance agents and brokers	94.1	4.1

Source: RMA Annual Statement Studies, 2001–2002 (fiscal years ended 4/1/00 through 3/31/01) (Philadelphia: Robert Morris Associates, 2001). Copyright © 2001 by Robert Morris Associates.

Note: Robert Morris Associates recommends that these ratios be regarded only as general guidelines and not as absolute industry norms. No claim is made as to the representativeness of these figures.

In Practice

FOCUS ON PRACTICE Enron Plays Hide and Seek with Debt

Enron Corp.'s December 31, 2000, balance sheet showed long-term debt of $10. 2 billion and $300 million in other financial obligations. These figures gave the company a 41 percent ratio of total obligations to total capitalization. That didn't seem out of line for a company in the capital-intensive energy industry.

Yet as the company's financial condition fell apart in the fall of 2001, investors and lenders discovered that Enron's true debt load was far beyond what its balance sheet indicated. By selling assets to perfectly legal special-purpose entities (SPEs), Enron had moved billions of dollars of debt off its balance sheet into subsidiaries, trusts, partnerships, and other creative financing arrangements. Former CFO Andrew Fastow claimed that these complex arrangements were disclosed in footnotes and that Enron was not liable for repayment of the debts of these SPEs.

Enron's required filing of Form 10-Q with the SEC, on November 19, 2001, told a different story: If its debt were to fall below investment grade, Enron would have to repay those off-balance-sheet partnership obligations. Ironically, its disclosure of about $4 billion in off-balance-sheet liabilities triggered the downgrade of its debt to "junk" status and accelerated debt repayment. Enron's secrecy about its off-balance-sheet ventures led to its loss of credibility in the investment community. Its stock and bond prices slid downward; its market value plunged $35 billion in about a month; and on December 2, 2001, Enron became the largest U.S. company ever to have filed for bankruptcy.

Enron is not alone in its use of off-balance-sheet debt. Most airlines have large aircraft leases structured through off-balance-sheet vehicles, although analysts and investors are aware that the true leverage is higher. **Pacific Gas & Electric**, **Southern California Edison**, and **Xerox** have also run into problems from off-balance-sheet debt obligations. Don't expect the Enron debacle to eliminate special-purpose entities, although the SEC has been calling for tighter consolidation rules. Companies like the flexibility that off-balance-sheet financing sources provide, not to mention that such financing makes debt ratios and returns look better.

Sources: Peter Behr, "Cause of Death: Mistrust," *Washington Post* (December 13, 2001), p. E1; Ronald Fink, "What Andrew Fastow Knew," *CFO* (January 1, 2002); and David Henry, "Who Else Is Hiding Debt?" *Business Week* (January 28, 2002).

Capital Structure of Non-U.S. Firms

In general, non-U.S. companies have much higher degrees of indebtedness than their U.S. counterparts. Most of the reasons for this are related to the fact that U.S. capital markets are much more developed than those elsewhere and have played a greater role in corporate financing than has been the case in other countries. In most European countries and especially in Japan and other Pacific Rim nations, large commercial banks are more actively involved in the financing of corporate activity than has been true in the United States. Furthermore, in many of these countries, banks are allowed to make large equity investments in nonfinancial corporations—a practice that is prohibited for U.S. banks. Finally, share ownership tends to be more tightly controlled among founding-family, institutional, and even public investors in Europe and Asia than it is for most large U.S. corporations. Tight ownership enables owners to understand the firm's financial condition better, resulting in their willingness to tolerate a higher degree of indebtedness.

On the other hand, similarities do exist between U.S. corporations and corporations in other countries. First, the same industry patterns of capital structure tend to be found all around the world. For example, in nearly all countries, pharmaceutical and other high-growth industrial firms tend to have lower debt ratios than do steel companies, airlines, and electric utility companies. Second, the capital structures of the largest U.S.-based multinational companies, which have access to many different capital markets around the world, typically resemble the capital structures of multinational companies from other countries more than they resemble those of smaller U.S. companies. Finally, the worldwide trend is away from reliance on banks for corporate financing and toward greater reliance on security issuance. Over time, the differences in the capital structures of U.S. and non-U.S. firms will probably lessen.

Capital Structure Theory

Scholarly research suggests that there is an optimal capital structure range. *It is not yet possible to provide financial managers with a specified methodology for use in determining a firm's optimal capital structure.* Nevertheless, financial theory does offer help in understanding how a firm's chosen financing mix affects the firm's value.

In 1958, Franco Modigliani and Merton H. Miller[10] (commonly known as "M and M") demonstrated algebraically that, assuming perfect markets,[11] the capital structure that a firm chooses does not affect its value. Many researchers, including M and M, have examined the effects of less restrictive assumptions on the relationship between capital structure and the firm's value. The result is a theoretical *optimal* capital structure based on balancing the benefits and costs of debt financing. The major benefit of debt financing is the tax shield, which allows interest payments to be deducted in calculating taxable income. The cost of debt financing results from (1) the increased probability of bankruptcy caused by debt obligations, (2) the *agency costs* of the lender's monitoring the firm's actions, and (3) the costs associated with managers having more information about the firm's prospects than do investors.

Tax Benefits

Allowing firms to deduct interest payments on debt when calculating taxable income reduces the amount of the firm's earnings paid in taxes, thereby making more earnings available for bondholders and stockholders. The deductibility of interest means the cost of debt, k_i, to the firm is subsidized by the government. Letting k_d equal the before-tax cost of debt and letting T equal the tax rate, from Chapter 10 (Equation 10.2), we have $k_i = k_d \times (1 - T)$.

Probability of Bankruptcy

The chance that a firm will become bankrupt because of an inability to meet its obligations as they come due depends largely on its level of both business risk and financial risk.

10. Franco Modigliani and Merton H. Miller, "The Cost of Capital, Corporation Finance, and the Theory of Investment," *American Economic Review* (June 1958), pp. 261–297.

11. Perfect-market assumptions include (1) no taxes, (2) no brokerage or flotation costs for securities, (3) symmetrical information—investors and managers have the same information about the firm's investment prospects, and (4) investor ability to borrow at the same rate as corporations.

Business Risk In Chapter 10, we defined *business risk* as the risk to the firm of being unable to cover its operating costs. In general, the greater the firm's *operating leverage*—the use of fixed operating costs—the higher its business risk. Although operating leverage is an important factor affecting business risk, two other factors—revenue stability and cost stability—also affect it. *Revenue stability* reflects the relative variability of the firm's sales revenues. Firms with reasonably stable levels of demand and with products that have stable prices have stable revenues. The result is low levels of business risk. Firms with highly volatile product demand and prices have unstable revenues that result in high levels of business risk. *Cost stability* reflects the relative predictability of input prices such as those for labor and materials. The more predictable and stable these input prices are, the lower the business risk; the less predictable and stable they are, the higher the business risk.

Business risk varies among firms, regardless of their lines of business, and is not affected by capital structure decisions. The level of business risk must be taken as a "given." The higher a firm's business risk, the more cautious the firm must be in establishing its capital structure. Firms with high business risk therefore tend toward less highly leveraged capital structures, and firms with low business risk tend toward more highly leveraged capital structures. We will hold business risk constant throughout the discussions that follow.

Financial Risk The firm's capital structure directly affects its *financial risk,* which is the risk to the firm of being unable to cover required financial obligations. The penalty for not meeting financial obligations is bankruptcy. The more fixed-cost financing—debt (including financial leases) and preferred stock—a firm has in its capital structure, the greater its financial leverage and risk. Financial risk depends on the capital structure decision made by the management, and that decision is affected by the business risk the firm faces. The *total risk* of a firm—business and financial risk combined—determines its probability of bankruptcy.

Agency Costs Imposed by Lenders

As noted in Chapter 1, the managers of firms typically act as *agents* of the owners (stockholders). The owners give the managers the authority to manage the firm for the owners' benefit. The *agency problem* created by this relationship extends not only to the relationship between owners and managers but also to the relationship between owners and lenders.

When a lender provides funds to a firm, the interest rate charged is based on the lender's assessment of the firm's risk. The lender–borrower relationship, therefore, depends on the lender's expectations for the firm's subsequent behavior. The borrowing rates are, in effect, locked in when the loans are negotiated. After obtaining a loan at a certain rate, the firm could increase its risk by investing in risky projects or by incurring additional debt. Such action could weaken the lender's position in terms of its claim on the cash flow of the firm. From another point of view, if these risky investment strategies paid off, the stockholders would benefit. Because payment obligations to the lender remain unchanged, the excess cash flows generated by a positive outcome from the riskier action would enhance the value of the firm to its owners. In other words, if the risky investments pay off, the owners receive all the benefits; but if the risky investments do not pay off, the lenders share in the costs.

Clearly, an incentive exists for the managers acting on behalf of the stockholders to "take advantage" of lenders. To avoid this situation, lenders impose certain monitoring techniques on borrowers, who as a result incur *agency costs*. The most obvious strategy is to deny subsequent loan requests or to increase the cost of future loans to the firm. Because this strategy is an after-the-fact approach, other controls must be included in the loan agreement. Lenders typically protect themselves by including provisions that limit the firm's ability to alter significantly its business and financial risk. These loan provisions tend to center on issues such as the minimum level of liquidity, asset acquisitions, executive salaries, and dividend payments.

By including appropriate provisions in the loan agreement, the lender can control the firm's risk and thus protect itself against the adverse consequences of this agency problem. Of course, in exchange for incurring agency costs by agreeing to the operating and financial constraints placed on it by the loan provisions, the firm should benefit by obtaining funds at a lower cost.

Asymmetric Information

Two surveys examined capital structure decisions.[12] Financial executives were asked which of two major criteria determined their financing decisions: (1) maintaining a *target capital structure* or (2) following a hierarchy of financing. This hierarchy, called a **pecking order,** begins with retained earnings, which is followed by debt financing and finally external equity financing. Respondents from 31 percent of Fortune 500 firms and from 11 percent of the (smaller) 500 largest over-the-counter firms answered target capital structure. Respondents from 69 percent of the Fortune 500 firms and 89 percent of the 500 largest OTC firms chose the pecking order.

pecking order
A hierarchy of financing that begins with retained earnings, which is followed by debt financing and finally external equity financing.

At first glance, on the basis of financial theory, this choice appears to be inconsistent with wealth maximization goals, but Stewart Myers has explained how "asymmetric information" could account for the pecking order financing preferences of financial managers.[13] **Asymmetric information** results when managers of a firm have more information about operations and future prospects than do investors. Assuming that managers make decisions with the goal of maximizing the wealth of existing stockholders, then asymmetric information can affect the capital structure decisions that managers make.

asymmetric information
The situation in which managers of a firm have more information about operations and future prospects than do investors.

Suppose, for example, that management has found a valuable investment that will require additional financing. Management believes that the prospects for the firm's future are very good and that the market, as indicated by the firm's current stock price, does not fully appreciate the firm's value. In this case, it would be advantageous to current stockholders if management raised the required funds using debt rather than issuing new stock. Using debt to raise funds is frequently

12. The results of the survey of Fortune 500 firms are reported in J. Michael Pinegar and Lisa Wilbricht, "What Managers Think of Capital Structure Theory: A Survey," *Financial Management* (Winter 1989), pp. 82–91, and the results of a similar survey of the 500 largest OTC firms are reported in Linda C. Hittle, Kamal Haddad, and Lawrence J. Gitman, "Over-the-Counter Firms, Asymmetric Information, and Financing Preferences," *Review of Financial Economics* (Fall 1992), pp. 81–92.

13. Stewart C. Myers, "The Capital Structure Puzzle," *Journal of Finance* (July 1984), pp. 575–592.

signal
A financing action by management that is believed to reflect its view of the firm's stock value; generally, debt financing is viewed as a *positive signal* that management believes the stock is "undervalued," and a stock issue is viewed as a *negative signal* that management believes the stock is "overvalued."

viewed as a **signal** that reflects management's view of the firm's stock value. Debt financing is a *positive signal* suggesting that management believes that the stock is "undervalued" and therefore a bargain. When the firm's positive future outlook becomes known to the market, the increased value will be fully captured by existing owners, rather than having to be shared with new stockholders.

If, however, the outlook for the firm is poor, management may believe that the firm's stock is "overvalued." In that case, it would be in the best interest of existing stockholders for the firm to issue new stock. Therefore, investors often interpret the announcement of a stock issue as a *negative signal*—bad news concerning the firm's prospects—and the stock price declines. This decrease in stock value, along with high underwriting costs for stock issues (compared to debt issues), make new stock financing very expensive. When the negative future outlook becomes known to the market, the decreased value is shared with new stockholders, rather than being fully captured by existing owners.

Because conditions of asymmetric information exist from time to time, firms should maintain some reserve borrowing capacity by keeping debt levels low. This reserve allows the firm to take advantage of good investment opportunities without having to sell stock at a low value and thus send signals that unduly influence the stock price.

The Optimal Capital Structure

What, then, *is* an optimal capital structure, even if it exists (so far) only in theory? To provide some insight into an answer, we will examine some basic financial relationships. It is generally believed that *the value of the firm is maximized when the cost of capital is minimized.* By using a modification of the simple zero-growth valuation model (see Equation 7.2 in Chapter 7), we can define the value of the firm, V, by Equation 11.11.

$$V = \frac{\text{EBIT} \times (1 - T)}{k_a} \tag{11.11}$$

where

EBIT = earnings before interest and taxes
T = tax rate
$\text{EBIT} \times (1 - T)$ = the after-tax operating earnings available to the debt and equity holders
k_a = weighted average cost of capital

Clearly, if we assume that EBIT is constant, the value of the firm, V, is maximized by minimizing the weighted average cost of capital, k_a.

Cost Functions

Figure 11.3(*a*) plots three cost functions—the cost of debt, the cost of equity, and the weighted average cost of capital (WACC)—as a function of financial leverage measured by the debt ratio (debt to total assets). The *cost of debt,* k_i, remains low because of the tax shield, but it slowly increases as leverage increases, to compensate lenders for increasing risk. The *cost of equity,* k_s, is above the cost of debt. It

FIGURE 11.3

Cost Functions and Value
Capital costs and the optimal capital structure

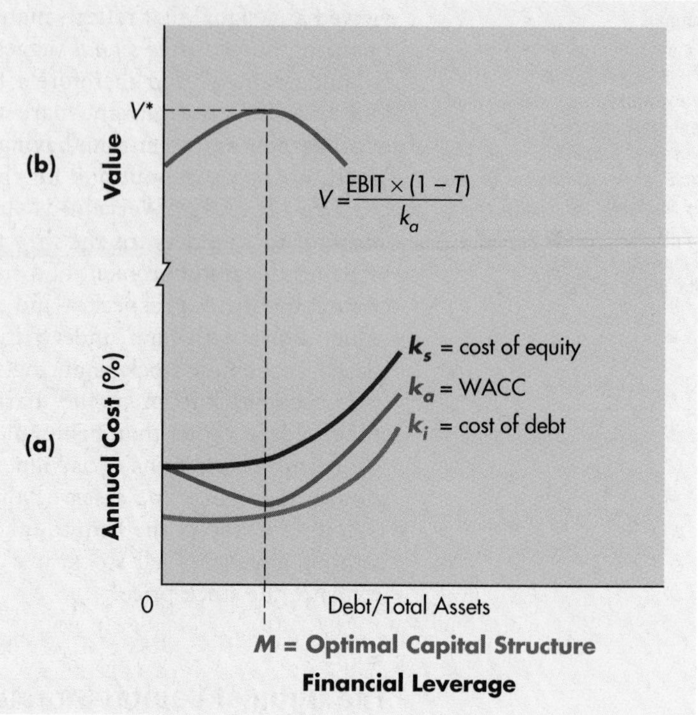

increases as financial leverage increases, but it generally increases more rapidly than the cost of debt. The cost of equity rises because the stockholders require a higher return as leverage increases, to compensate for the higher degree of financial risk.

The *weighted average cost of capital* (*WACC*) results from a weighted average of the firm's debt and equity capital costs. At a debt ratio of zero, the firm is 100 percent equity-financed. As debt is substituted for equity and as the debt ratio increases, the WACC declines because the debt cost is less than the equity cost ($k_i < k_s$). As the debt ratio continues to increase, the increased debt and equity costs eventually cause the WACC to rise (after point *M* in Figure 11.3(*a*)). This behavior results in a U-shaped, or saucer-shaped, weighted average cost-of-capital function, k_a.

A Graphical View of the Optimal Structure

optimal capital structure
The capital structure at which the weighted average cost of capital is minimized, thereby maximizing the firm's value.

Because the maximization of value, *V*, is achieved when the overall cost of capital, k_a, is at a minimum (see Equation 11.11), the **optimal capital structure** is that at which the weighted average cost of capital, k_a, is minimized. In Figure 11.3(*a*), point *M* represents the *minimum weighted average cost of capital*—the point of optimal financial leverage and hence of optimal capital structure for the firm. Figure 11.3(*b*) plots the value of the firm that results from substitution of k_a in Figure 11.3(*a*) for various levels of financial leverage into the zero-growth valuation model in Equation 11.11. As shown in Figure 11.3(*b*), at the optimal capital structure, point *M*, the value of the firm is maximized at V^*.

Generally, the lower the firm's weighted average cost of capital, the greater the difference between the return on a project and the WACC, and therefore the greater the owners' return. Simply stated, minimizing the weighted average cost of capital allows management to undertake a larger number of profitable projects, thereby further increasing the value of the firm.

As a practical matter, there is no way to calculate the optimal capital structure implied by Figure 11.3. Because it is impossible either to know or to remain at the precise optimal capital structure, firms generally try to operate in a *range* that places them near what they believe to be the optimal capital structure.

Review Questions

11–6 What is a firm's *capital structure?* What ratios assess the degree of financial leverage in a firm's capital structure?

11–7 In what ways are the capital structures of U.S. and non-U.S. firms different? How are they similar?

11–8 What is the major benefit of debt financing? How does it affect the firm's cost of debt?

11–9 What are *business risk* and *financial risk?* How does each of them influence the firm's capital structure decisions?

11–10 Briefly describe the *agency problem* that exists between owners and lenders. How do lenders cause firms to incur *agency costs* to resolve this problem?

11–11 How does *asymmetric information* affect the firm's capital structure decisions? How do the firm's financing actions give investors *signals* that reflect management's view of stock value?

11–12 How do the cost of debt, the cost of equity, and the weighted average cost of capital (WACC) behave as the firm's financial leverage increases from zero? Where is the *optimal capital structure?* What is its relationship to the firm's value at that point?

LG5

The EBIT–EPS Approach to Capital Structure

EBIT–EPS approach
An approach for selecting the capital structure that maximizes earnings per share (EPS) over the expected range of earnings before interest and taxes (EBIT).

One of the key variables affecting the market value of the firm's shares is its return to owners, as reflected by the firm's earnings. Therefore, earnings per share (EPS) can be conveniently used to analyze alternative capital structures. The **EBIT–EPS approach** to capital structure involves selecting the capital structure that maximizes EPS over the expected range of earnings before interest and taxes (EBIT).

Presenting a Financing Plan Graphically

To analyze the effects of a firm's capital structure on the owners' returns, we consider the relationship between earnings before interest and taxes (EBIT) and earnings per share (EPS). A constant level of EBIT—constant *business risk*—is assumed, to isolate the effect on returns of the financing costs associated with alternative capital structures. EPS is used to measure the owners' returns, which are expected to be closely related to share price.

The Data Required

To graph a financing plan, we need to know at least two EBIT–EPS coordinates. The approach for obtaining coordinates can be illustrated by an example.

EXAMPLE The current capital structure of JSG Company, a soft-drink manufacturer, is as shown in the following table. Note that JSG's capital structure currently contains only common stock equity; the firm has no debt or preferred stock. If for convenience we assume the firm has no current liabilities, its debt ratio (total liabilities ÷ total assets) is currently 0% ($0 ÷ $500,000); it therefore has *zero* financial leverage. Assume the firm is in the 40% tax bracket.

Current capital structure	
Long-term debt	$ 0
Common stock equity (25,000 shares @ $20)	500,000
Total capital (assets)	$500,000

EBIT–EPS coordinates for JSG's current capital structure can be found by assuming two EBIT values and calculating the EPS associated with them.[14] Because the EBIT–EPS graph is a straight line, any two EBIT values can be used to find coordinates. Here we arbitrarily use values of $100,000 and $200,000.

EBIT (assumed)	$100,000	$200,000
− Interest (rate × $0 debt)	0	0
Net profits before taxes	$100,000	$200,000
− Taxes ($T = 0.40$)	40,000	80,000
Net profits after taxes	$ 60,000	$120,000
EPS	$\frac{\$60,000}{25,000 \text{ sh.}} = \$2.40$	$\frac{\$120,000}{25,000 \text{ sh.}} = \$4.80$

14. A convenient method for finding one EBIT–EPS coordinate is to calculate the *financial breakeven point,* the level of EBIT for which the firm's EPS just equals $0. It is the level of EBIT needed just to cover all fixed financial costs—annual interest (I) and preferred stock dividends (PD). The equation for the financial breakeven point is

$$\text{Financial breakeven point} = I + \frac{PD}{1-T}$$

where T is the tax rate. It can be seen that when PD = $0, the financial breakeven point is equal to I, the annual interest payment.

FIGURE 11.4 **Graphic Presentation of a Financing Plan**
JSG Company's zero-leverage financing plan

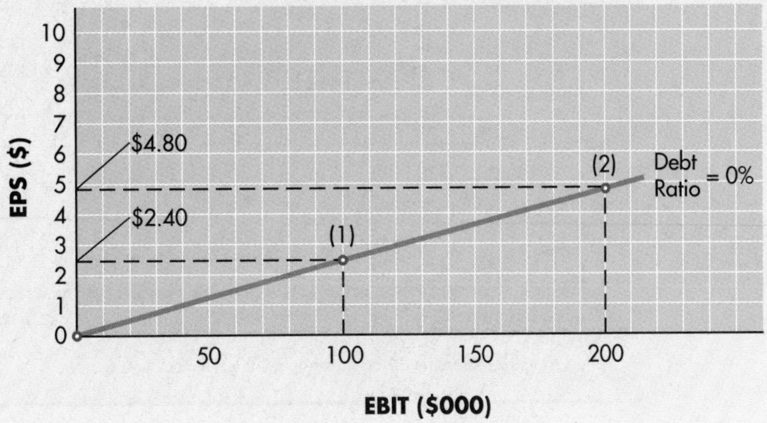

The two EBIT–EPS coordinates resulting from these calculations are (1) $100,000 EBIT and $2.40 EPS and (2) $200,000 EBIT and $4.80 EPS.

Plotting the Data

financial breakeven point
The level of EBIT necessary to just cover all *fixed financial costs;* the level of EBIT for which EPS = $0.

The two EBIT–EPS coordinates developed for JSG Company's current zero-leverage (debt ratio = 0 percent) situation can be plotted on a set of EBIT–EPS axes, as shown in Figure 11.4. The figure shows the level of EPS expected for each level of EBIT. For levels of EBIT below the x-axis intercept, a loss (negative EPS) results. Each of the x-axis intercepts is a **financial breakeven point,** the level of EBIT necessary to just cover all *fixed financial costs* (EPS = $0).

Comparing Alternative Capital Structures

We can compare alternative capital structures by graphing financing plans, as shown in Figure 11.4. The following example illustrates this procedure.

EXAMPLE

JSG Company, whose current zero-leverage capital structure was described in the preceding example, is contemplating shifting its capital structure to either of two leveraged positions. To maintain its $500,000 of total capital, JSG's capital structure will be shifted to greater leverage by issuing debt and using the proceeds to retire an equivalent amount of common stock. The two alternative capital structures result in debt ratios of 30% and 60%, respectively. The basic information on the current and two alternative capital structures is summarized in Table 11.9.

TABLE 11.9 Basic Information on JSG Company's Current and Alternative Capital Structures

Capital structure debt ratio (1)	Total assets[a] (2)	Debt [(1) × (2)] (3)	Equity [(2) − (3)] (4)	Interest rate on debt[b] (5)	Annual interest [(3) × (5)] (6)	Shares of common stock outstanding [(4) ÷ $20][c] (7)
0% (current)	$500,000	$ 0	$500,000	0 %	$ 0	25,000
30	500,000	150,000	350,000	10	15,000	17,500
60	500,000	300,000	200,000	16.5	49,500	10,000

[a]Because for convenience the firm is assumed to have no current liabilities, total assets equals total capital of $500,000.
[b]The interest rate on all debt increases with increases in the debt ratio due to the greater leverage and risk associated with higher debt ratios.
[c]The $20 value represents the book value of common stock equity.

Using the data in Table 11.9, we can calculate the coordinates needed to plot the 30% and 60% debt capital structures. For convenience, using the same $100,000 and $200,000 EBIT values used earlier to plot the current capital structure, we get the information in the following table.

	Capital structure			
	30% Debt ratio		60% Debt ratio	
EBIT (assumed)	$100,000	$200,000	$100,000	$200,000
− Interest (Table 11.9)	15,000	15,000	49,500	49,500
Net profits before taxes	$ 85,000	$185,000	$ 50,500	$150,500
− Taxes ($T = 0.40$)	34,000	74,000	20,200	60,200
Net profits after taxes	$ 51,000	$111,000	$ 30,300	$ 90,300
EPS	$\frac{\$51{,}000}{17{,}500\text{ sh.}} = \$2.91$	$\frac{\$111{,}000}{17{,}500\text{ sh.}} = \$6.34$	$\frac{\$30{,}300}{10{,}000\text{ sh.}} = \$3.03$	$\frac{\$90{,}300}{10{,}000\text{ sh.}} = \$9.03$

The two sets of EBIT–EPS coordinates developed in the preceding table, along with those developed for the current zero-leverage capital structure, are summarized and plotted on the EBIT–EPS axes in Figure 11.5. This figure shows that *each* capital structure is superior to the others in terms of maximizing EPS over certain ranges of EBIT: The zero-leverage capital structure (debt ratio = 0%) is superior to either of the other capital structures for levels of EBIT between $0 and $50,000. Between $50,000 and $95,500 of EBIT, the capital structure associated with a debt ratio of 30% is preferred. And at a level of EBIT above $95,500, the 60% debt ratio capital structure provides the highest earnings per share.[15]

15 An algebraic technique can be used to find the *indifference points* between the capital structure alternatives. Due to its relative complexity, this technique is not presented. Instead, emphasis is given here to the visual estimation of these points from the graph.

FIGURE 11.5 **EBIT–EPS Approach**
A comparison of selected capital structures for JSG Company

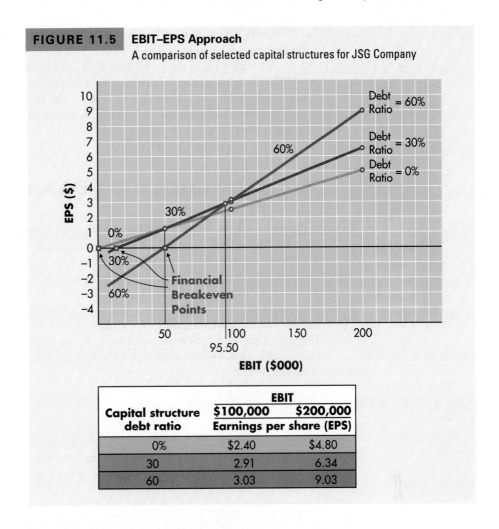

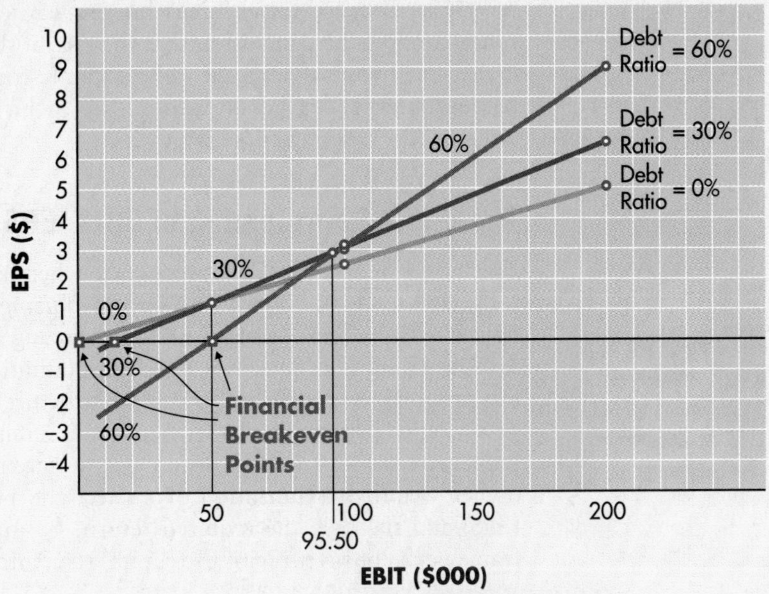

Capital structure debt ratio	EBIT $100,000	EBIT $200,000
	Earnings per share (EPS)	
0%	$2.40	$4.80
30	2.91	6.34
60	3.03	9.03

Considering Risk in EBIT–EPS Analysis

When interpreting EBIT–EPS analysis, it is important to consider the risk of each capital structure alternative. Graphically, the risk of each capital structure can be viewed in light of two measures: (1) the *financial breakeven point* (EBIT-axis intercept) and (2) the *degree of financial leverage* reflected in the slope of the capital structure line: *The higher the financial breakeven point and the steeper the slope of the capital structure line, the greater the financial risk.*

Further assessment of risk can be performed by using ratios. As financial leverage (measured by the debt ratio) increases, we expect a corresponding decline in the firm's ability to make scheduled interest payments (measured by the times interest earned ratio).

EXAMPLE Reviewing the three capital structures plotted for JSG Company in Figure 11.5, we can see that as the debt ratio increases, so does the financial risk of each alternative. Both the financial breakeven point and the slope of the capital structure lines increase with increasing debt ratios. If we use the $100,000 EBIT value, for example, the times interest earned ratio (EBIT ÷ interest) for the zero-leverage capital structure is infinity ($100,000 ÷ $0); for the 30% debt case, it is 6.67 ($100,000 ÷ $15,000); and for the 60% debt case, it is 2.02 ($100,000 ÷ $49,500). Because lower times interest earned ratios reflect higher risk, these ratios support the conclusion that the risk of the capital structures increases with increasing financial leverage. The capital structure for a debt ratio of 60% is riskier than that for a debt ratio of 30%, which in turn is riskier than the capital structure for a debt ratio of 0%.

The Basic Shortcoming of EBIT–EPS Analysis

The most important point to recognize when using EBIT–EPS analysis is that this technique tends to concentrate on *maximizing earnings* rather than maximizing owner wealth. The use of an EPS-maximizing approach generally ignores risk. If investors did not require risk premiums (additional returns) as the firm increased the proportion of debt in its capital structure, a strategy involving maximizing EPS would also maximize owner wealth. But because risk premiums increase with increases in financial leverage, the maximization of EPS *does not* ensure owner wealth maximization. To select the best capital structure, both return (EPS) and risk (via the required return, k_s) must be integrated into a valuation framework consistent with the capital structure theory presented earlier.

Review Question

11–13 Explain the *EBIT–EPS approach* to capital structure. Include in your explanation a graph indicating the *financial breakeven point;* label the axes. Is this approach consistent with maximization of the owners' wealth?

LG6

Choosing the Optimal Capital Structure

A wealth maximization framework for use in making capital structure decisions should include the two key factors of return and risk. This section describes the procedures for linking to market value the return and risk associated with alternative capital structures.

Linkage

To determine the firm's value under alternative capital structures, the firm must find the level of return that must be earned to compensate owners for the risk being incurred. Such a framework is consistent with the overall valuation framework developed in Chapters 6 and 7 and applied to capital budgeting decisions in Chapter 9.

The required return associated with a given level of financial risk can be estimated in a number of ways. Theoretically, the preferred approach would be first to estimate the beta associated with each alternative capital structure and then to use the CAPM framework presented in Equation 5.7 to calculate the required return, k_s. A more operational approach involves linking the financial risk associated with each capital structure alternative directly to the required return. Such an approach is similar to the CAPM-type approach demonstrated in Chapter 9 for linking project risk and required return (RADR). Here it involves estimating the required return associated with each level of financial risk, as measured by a statistic such as the coefficient of variation of EPS. Regardless of the approach used, one would expect the required return to increase as the financial risk increases.

EXAMPLE Expanding the JSG Company example presented earlier, we assume that the firm is attempting to choose the best of seven alternative capital structures—debt ratios of 0%, 10%, 20%, 30%, 40%, 50%, and 60%. For each of these structures the firm estimated the (1) EPS, (2) coefficient of variation of EPS, and (3) required return, k_s. These values are shown in columns 1 through 3 of Table 11.10. Note that EPS (in column 1) is maximized at a 50% debt ratio though the risk of EPS measured by its coefficient of variation (in column 2) is constantly increasing. As expected, the estimated required return of owners, k_s (in column 3), increases with increasing risk, as measured by the coefficient of variation of EPS (in column 2). Simply stated, for higher degrees of financial leverage—debt ratios—owners require higher rates of return.

Estimating Value

The value of the firm associated with alternative capital structures can be estimated by using one of the standard valuation models. If, for simplicity, we assume that all earnings are paid out as dividends, we can use a zero-growth valuation model such as that developed in Chapter 7. The model, originally stated in Equation 7.2, is restated here with EPS substituted for dividends (because in each year the dividends would equal EPS):

$$P_0 = \frac{\text{EPS}}{k_s} \qquad (11.12)$$

By substituting the expected level of EPS and the associated required return, k_s, into Equation 11.12, we can estimate the per-share value of the firm, P_0.

TABLE 11.10 Calculation of Share Value Estimates Associated with Alternative Capital Structures for JSG Company

Capital structure debt ratio	Expected EPS (1)	Estimated coefficient of variation of EPS (2)	Estimated required return, k_s (3)	Estimated share value [(1) ÷ (3)] (4)
0%	$2.40	0.71	.115	$20.87
10	2.55	0.74	.117	21.79
20	2.72	0.78	.121	22.48
30	2.91	0.83	.125	23.28
40	3.12	0.91	.140	22.29
50	3.18	1.07	.165	19.27
60	3.03	1.40	.190	15.95

EXAMPLE

We can now estimate the value of JSG Company's stock under each of the alternative capital structures. Substituting the expected EPS (column 1 of Table 11.10) and the required returns, k_s (column 3 of Table 11.10), into Equation 11.12 for each of the capital structures, we obtain the share values given in column 4 of Table 11.10. Plotting the resulting share values against the associated debt ratios, as shown in Figure 11.6, clearly illustrates that the maximum share value occurs at the capital structure associated with a debt ratio of 30%.

Maximizing Value versus Maximizing EPS

Throughout this text, the goal of the financial manager has been specified as maximizing owner wealth, not profit. Although there is some relationship between expected profit and value, there is no reason to believe that profit-maximizing strategies necessarily result in wealth maximization. It is therefore the wealth of the owners as reflected in the estimated share value that should serve as the criterion for selecting the best capital structure. A final look at JSG Company will highlight this point.

EXAMPLE

Further analysis of Figure 11.6 clearly shows that although the firm's profits (EPS) are maximized at a debt ratio of 50%, share value is maximized at a 30% debt ratio. Therefore, the preferred capital structure would be the 30% debt ratio. The two approaches provide different conclusions because EPS maximization does not consider risk.

FIGURE 11.6

Estimating Value
Estimated share value and EPS for alternative capital structures for JSG Company

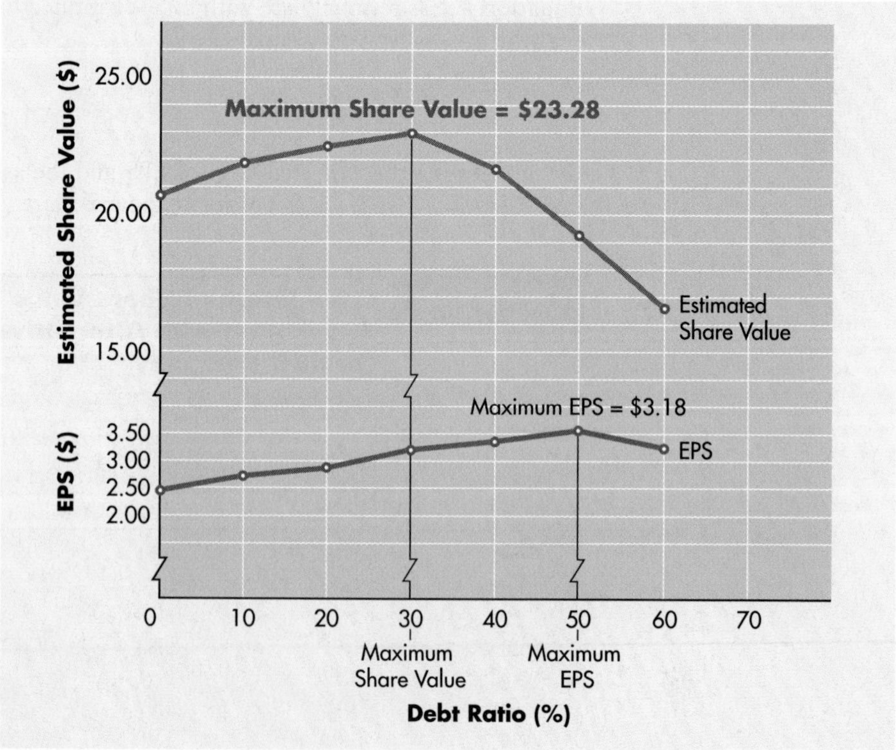

Some Other Important Considerations

Because there is really no practical way to calculate the optimal capital structure, any quantitative analysis of capital structure must be tempered with other important considerations. Some of the more important additional factors involved in capital structure decisions are summarized in Table 11.11.

TABLE 11.11 Important Factors to Consider in Making Capital Structure Decisions

Concern	Factor	Description
Business risk	Revenue stability	Firms that have stable and predictable revenues can more safely undertake highly leveraged capital structures than can firms with volatile patterns of sales revenue. Firms with growing sales tend to benefit from added debt because they can reap the positive benefits of financial leverage, which magnifies the effect of these increases.
	Cash flow	When considering a new capital structure, the firm must focus on its ability to generate the cash flows necessary to meet obligations. Cash forecasts reflecting an ability to service debts (and preferred stock) must support any shift in capital structure.
Agency costs	Contractual obligations	A firm may be contractually constrained with respect to the type of funds that it can raise. For example, a firm might be prohibited from selling additional debt except when the claims of holders of such debt are made subordinate to the existing debt. Contractual constraints on the sale of additional stock, as well as on the ability to distribute dividends on stock, might also exist.
	Management preferences	Occasionally, a firm will impose an internal constraint on the use of debt to limit its risk exposure to a level deemed acceptable to management. In other words, because of risk aversion, the firm's management constrains the firm's capital structure at a level that may or may not be the true optimum.
	Control	A management concerned about control may prefer to issue debt rather than (voting) common stock. Under favorable market conditions, a firm that wanted to sell equity could make a *preemptive offering* or issue *nonvoting shares* (see Chapter 7), allowing each shareholder to maintain proportionate ownership. Generally, only in closely held firms or firms threatened by takeover does control become a major concern in the capital structure decision.
Asymmetric information	External risk assessment	The firm's ability to raise funds quickly and at favorable rates depends on the external risk assessments of lenders and bond raters. The firm must therefore consider the impact of capital structure decisions both on share value and on published financial statements from which lenders and raters assess the firm's risk.
	Timing	At times when the general level of interest rates is low, debt financing might be more attractive; when interest rates are high, the sale of stock may be more appealing. Sometimes both debt and equity capital become unavailable at what would be viewed as reasonable terms. General economic conditions—especially those of the capital market—can thus significantly affect capital structure decisions.

Review Questions

11–14 Why do *maximizing EPS* and *maximizing value* not necessarily lead to the same conclusion about the optimal capital structure?

11–15 What important factors in addition to quantitative factors should a firm consider when it is making a capital structure decision?

SUMMARY

FOCUS ON VALUE

The amount of leverage (fixed-cost assets or funds) employed by a firm directly affects its risk, return, and share value. Generally, higher leverage raises, and lower leverage reduces, risk and return. Operating leverage is concerned with the level of fixed operating costs; financial leverage focuses on fixed financial costs, particularly interest on debt and any preferred stock dividends. The firm's financial leverage is determined by its capital structure—its mix of long-term debt and equity financing. Because of its fixed interest payments, the more debt a firm employs relative to its equity, the greater its financial leverage. The value of the firm is clearly affected by its degree of operating leverage and by the composition of its capital structure.

The financial manager must carefully consider the types of operating and financial costs the firm incurs, recognizing that with greater fixed costs comes higher risk. Major decisions with regard to both operating cost structure and capital structure must therefore focus on their impact on the firm's value. Only those leverage and capital structure decisions that are consistent with the firm's goal of **maximizing its stock price** should be implemented.

REVIEW OF LEARNING GOALS

LG1 **Discuss the role of breakeven analysis, the operating breakeven point, and the effect of changing costs on it.** Breakeven analysis measures the level of sales necessary to cover total operating costs. The operating breakeven point may be calculated algebraically, by dividing fixed operating costs by the difference between the sale price per unit and variable operating cost per unit, or it may be determined graphically. The operating breakeven point increases with increased fixed and variable operating costs and decreases with an increase in sale price, and vice versa.

LG2 **Understand operating, financial, and total leverage and the relationships among them.** Operating leverage is the use of fixed operating costs by the firm to magnify the effects of changes in sales on EBIT. The higher the fixed operating costs, the greater the operating leverage. Financial leverage is the use of fixed financial costs by the firm to magnify the effects of changes in EBIT on EPS. The higher the fixed financial costs—typically, interest on debt and preferred stock dividends—the greater the financial leverage. The total leverage of the firm is the use of fixed costs—both operating and financial—to magnify the effects of changes in sales on EPS. Total leverage reflects the combined effect of operating and financial leverage.

LG3 **Describe the types of capital, external assessment of capital structure, the capital structure of non-U.S. firms, and capital structure theory.** Two basic types of capital—debt capital and equity capital—make up a firm's capital structure. They differ with respect to voice in management, claims on income and assets, maturity, and tax treatment. Capital structure can be externally assessed by using financial ratios—debt ratio, times interest earned ratio, and fixed-payment coverage ratio. Non-U.S. companies tend to have much higher degrees of indebtedness than do their U.S. counterparts, primarily because U.S. capital markets are much more developed. Similarities between U.S. corporations and those of other countries include industry patterns of capital structure, large multinational company capital structures, and the trend toward greater reliance on securities issuance and less reliance on banks for financing.

Research suggests that there is an optimal capital structure that balances the firm's benefits and costs of debt financing. The major benefit of debt financing is the tax shield. The costs of debt financing include the probability of bankruptcy, caused by business and financial risk; agency costs imposed by lenders; and asymmetric information, which typically causes firms to raise funds in a pecking order of retained earnings, then debt, and finally external equity financing, in order to send positive signals to the market and thereby enhance the wealth of shareholders.

LG4 **Explain the optimal capital structure using a graphical view of the firm's cost-of-capital functions and a zero-growth valuation model.** The zero-growth valuation model can be used to define the firm's value as its after-tax EBIT divided by its weighted average cost of capital. Assuming that EBIT is constant, the value of the firm is maximized by minimizing its weighted average cost of capital (WACC). The optimal capital structure is the one that minimizes the WACC. Graphically, although both debt and equity costs rise with increasing financial leverage, the lower cost of debt causes the WACC to decline and then rise with increasing financial leverage. As a result, the firm's WACC exhibits a U-shape, whose minimum value defines the optimal capital structure that maximizes owner wealth.

LG5 **Discuss the EBIT–EPS approach to capital structure.** The EBIT–EPS approach evaluates capital structures in light of the returns they provide the firm's owners and their degree of financial risk. Under the EBIT–EPS approach, the preferred capital structure is the one that is expected to provide maximum EPS over the firm's expected range of EBIT. Graphically, this approach reflects risk in terms of the financial breakeven point and the slope of the capital structure line. The major shortcoming of EBIT–EPS analysis is that it concentrates on maximizing earnings rather than owners' wealth.

LG6 **Review the return and risk of alternative capital structures, their linkage to market value, and other important considerations related to capital structure.** The best capital structure can be selected by using a valuation model to link return and risk factors. The preferred capital structure is the one that results in the highest estimated share value, not the highest EPS. Other important nonquantitative factors, such as revenue stability, cash flow, contractual obligations, management preferences, control, external risk assessment, and timing, must also be considered when making capital structure decisions.

SELF-TEST PROBLEMS (Solutions in Appendix B)

LG1 LG2 ST 11–1 **Breakeven point and all forms of leverage** TOR most recently sold 100,000 units at \$7.50 each; its variable operating costs are \$3.00 per unit, and its fixed operating costs are \$250,000. Annual interest charges total \$80,000, and the firm has 8,000 shares of \$5 (annual dividend) preferred stock outstanding. It currently has 20,000 shares of common stock outstanding. Assume that the firm has a 40% tax rate.

a. At what level of sales (in units) would the firm break even on operations (that is, EBIT = \$0)?

b. Calculate the firm's earnings per share (EPS) in tabular form at (1) the current level of sales and (2) a 120,000-unit sales level.
c. Using the current *$750,000 level of sales as a base,* calculate the firm's degree of operating leverage (DOL).
d. Using the EBIT *associated with the $750,000 level of sales as a base,* calculate the firm's degree of financial leverage (DFL).
e. Use the degree of total leverage (DTL) concept to determine the effect (in percentage terms) of a 50% increase in TOR's sales *from the $750,000 base level* on its earnings per share.

LG5 **ST 11–2 EBIT–EPS analysis** Newlin Electronics is considering additional financing of $10,000. It currently has $50,000 of 12% (annual interest) bonds and 10,000 shares of common stock outstanding. The firm can obtain the financing through a 12% (annual interest) bond issue or through the sale of 1,000 shares of common stock. The firm has a 40% tax rate.
a. Calculate two EBIT–EPS coordinates for each plan by selecting any two EBIT values and finding their associated EPS values.
b. Plot the two financing plans on a set of EBIT–EPS axes.
c. On the basis of your graph in part **b,** at what level of EBIT does the bond plan become superior to the stock plan?

LG3 LG6 **ST 11–3 Optimal capital structure** Hawaiian Macadamia Nut Company has collected the following data with respect to its capital structure, expected earnings per share, and required return.

Capital structure debt ratio	Expected earnings per share	Required return, k_s
0%	$3.12	13%
10	3.90	15
20	4.80	16
30	5.44	17
40	5.51	19
50	5.00	20
60	4.40	22

a. Compute the estimated share value associated with each of the capital structures, using the simplified method described in this chapter (see Equation 11.12).
b. Determine the optimal capital structure on the basis of (1) maximization of expected earnings per share and (2) maximization of share value.
c. Which capital structure do you recommend? Why?

PROBLEMS

LG1 **11–1 Breakeven point—Algebraic** Kate Rowland wishes to estimate the number of flower arrangements she must sell at $24.95 to break even. She has estimated fixed operating costs of $12,350 per year and variable operating costs of $15.45 per arrangement. How many flower arrangements must Kate sell to break even on operating costs?

LG1 11–2 **Breakeven comparisons—Algebraic** Given the price and cost data shown in the accompanying table for each of the three firms, F, G, and H, answer the following questions.

Firm	F	G	H
Sale price per unit	$ 18.00	$ 21.00	$ 30.00
Variable operating cost per unit	6.75	13.50	12.00
Fixed operating cost	45,000	30,000	90,000

a. What is the operating breakeven point in units for each firm?
b. How would you rank these firms in terms of their risk?

LG1 11–3 **Breakeven point—Algebraic and graphical** Fine Leather Enterprises sells its single product for $129.00 per unit. The firm's fixed operating costs are $473,000 annually, and its variable operating costs are $86.00 per unit.
a. Find the firm's operating breakeven point in units.
b. Label the *x* axis "Sales (units)" and the *y* axis "Costs/Revenues ($)," and then graph the firm's sales revenue, total operating cost, and fixed operating cost functions on these axes. In addition, label the operating breakeven point and the areas of loss and profit (EBIT).

LG1 11–4 **Breakeven analysis** Barry Carter is considering opening a record store. He wants to estimate the number of CDs he must sell to break even. The CDs will be sold for $13.98 each, variable operating costs are $10.48 per CD, and annual fixed operating costs are $73,500.
a. Find the operating breakeven point in number of CDs.
b. Calculate the total operating costs at the breakeven volume found in part a.
c. If Barry estimates that at a minimum he can sell 2,000 CDs *per month*, should he go into the record business?
d. How much EBIT will Barry realize if he sells the minimum 2,000 CDs per month noted in part c?

LG1 11–5 **Breakeven point—Changing costs/revenues** JWG Company publishes *Creative Crosswords*. Last year the book of puzzles sold for $10 with variable operating cost per book of $8 and fixed operating costs of $40,000. How many books must JWG sell this year to achieve the breakeven point for the stated operating costs, given the following different circumstances?
a. All figures remain the same as last year.
b. Fixed operating costs increase to $44,000; all other figures remain the same.
c. The selling price increases to $10.50; all costs remain the same as last year.
d. Variable operating cost per book increases to $8.50; all other figures remain the same.

e. What conclusions about the operating breakeven point can be drawn from your answers?

LG2 **11–6 EBIT sensitivity** Stewart Industries sells its finished product for $9 per unit. Its fixed operating costs are $20,000, and the variable operating cost per unit is $5.

a. Calculate the firm's earnings before interest and taxes (EBIT) for sales of 10,000 units.
b. Calculate the firm's EBIT for sales of 8,000 and 12,000 units, respectively.
c. Calculate the percentage changes in sales (from the 10,000-unit base level) and associated percentage changes in EBIT for the shifts in sales indicated in part **b.**
d. On the basis of your findings in part **c,** comment on the sensitivity of changes in EBIT in response to changes in sales.

LG2 **11–7 Degree of operating leverage** Grey Products has fixed operating costs of $380,000, variable operating costs of $16 per unit, and a selling price of $63.50 per unit.

a. Calculate the operating breakeven point in units.
b. Calculate the firm's EBIT at 9,000, 10,000, and 11,000 units, respectively.
c. With 10,000 units as a base, what are the percentage changes in units sold and EBIT as sales move from the base to the other sales levels used in part **b?**
d. Use the percentages computed in part **c** to determine the degree of operating leverage (DOL).
e. Use the formula for degree of operating leverage to determine the DOL at 10,000 units.

LG2 **11–8 Degree of operating leverage—Graphical** Levin Corporation has fixed operating costs of $72,000, variable operating costs of $6.75 per unit, and a selling price of $9.75 per unit.

a. Calculate the operating breakeven point in units.
b. Compute the degree of operating leverage (DOL) for the following unit sales levels: 25,000, 30,000, 40,000. Use the formula given in the chapter.
c. Graph the DOL figures that you computed in part **b** (on the *y* axis) against sales levels (on the *x* axis).
d. Compute the degree of operating leverage at 24,000 units; add this point to your graph.
e. What principle do your graph and figures illustrate?

LG2 **11–9 EPS calculations** Southland Industries has $60,000 of 16% (annual interest) bonds outstanding, 1,500 shares of preferred stock paying an annual dividend of $5 per share, and 4,000 shares of common stock outstanding. Assuming that the firm has a 40% tax rate, compute earnings per share (EPS) for the following levels of EBIT:

a. $24,600
b. $30,600
c. $35,000

LG2 **11–10 Degree of financial leverage** Northwestern Savings and Loan has a current capital structure consisting of $250,000 of 16% (annual interest) debt and 2,000 shares of common stock. The firm pays taxes at the rate of 40%.

a. Using EBIT values of $80,000 and $120,000, determine the associated earnings per share (EPS).
b. Using $80,000 of EBIT as a base, calculate the degree of financial leverage (DFL).
c. Rework parts **a** and **b** assuming that the firm has $100,000 of 16% (annual interest) debt and 3,000 shares of common stock.

LG2 LG5 11–11 **DFL and graphical display of financing plans** Wells and Associates has EBIT of $67,500. Interest costs are $22,500, and the firm has 15,000 shares of common stock outstanding. Assume a 40% tax rate.
a. Use the degree of financial leverage (DFL) formula to calculate the DFL for the firm.
b. Using a set of EBIT–EPS axes, plot Wells and Associates' financing plan.
c. If the firm also has 1,000 shares of preferred stock paying a $6.00 annual dividend per share, what is the DFL?
d. Plot the financing plan, including the 1,000 shares of $6.00 preferred stock, on the axes used in part **b.**
e. Briefly discuss the graph of the two financing plans.

LG1 LG2 11–12 **Integrative—Multiple leverage measures** Play-More Toys produces inflatable beach balls, selling 400,000 balls a year. Each ball produced has a variable operating cost of $0.84 and sells for $1.00. Fixed operating costs are $28,000. The firm has annual interest charges of $6,000, preferred dividends of $2,000, and a 40% tax rate.
a. Calculate the operating breakeven point in units.
b. Use the degree of operating leverage (DOL) formula to calculate DOL.
c. Use the degree of financial leverage (DFL) formula to calculate DFL.
d. Use the degree of total leverage (DTL) formula to calculate DTL. Compare this to the product of DOL and DFL calculated in parts **b** and **c.**

LG2 11–13 **Integrative—Leverage and risk** Firm R has sales of 100,000 units at $2.00 per unit, variable operating costs of $1.70 per unit, and fixed operating costs of $6,000. Interest is $10,000 per year. Firm W has sales of 100,000 units at $2.50 per unit, variable operating costs of $1.00 per unit, and fixed operating costs of $62,500. Interest is $17,500 per year. Assume that both firms are in the 40% tax bracket.
a. Compute the degree of operating, financial, and total leverage for firm R.
b. Compute the degree of operating, financial, and total leverage for firm W.
c. Compare the relative risks of the two firms.
d. Discuss the principles of leverage that your answers illustrate.

LG1 LG2 11–14 **Various capital structures** Charter Enterprises currently has $1 million in total assets and is totally equity-financed. It is contemplating a change in capital structure. Compute the amount of debt and equity that would be outstanding if the firm were to shift to each of the following debt ratios: 10, 20, 30, 40, 50, 60, and 90%. (*Note:* The amount of total assets would not change.) Is there a limit to the debt ratio's value?

LG5 **11–15 EBIT–EPS and capital structure** Data-Check is considering two capital structures. The key information is shown in the following table. Assume a 40% tax rate.

Source of capital	Structure A	Structure B
Long-term debt	$100,000 at 16% coupon rate	$200,000 at 17% coupon rate
Common stock	4,000 shares	2,000 shares

a. Calculate two EBIT–EPS coordinates for each of the structures by selecting any two EBIT values and finding their associated EPS values.
b. Plot the two capital structures on a set of EBIT–EPS axes.
c. Indicate over what EBIT range, if any, each structure is preferred.
d. Discuss the leverage and risk aspects of each structure.
e. If the firm is fairly certain that its EBIT will exceed $75,000, which structure would you recommend? Why?

LG6 **11–16 EBIT–EPS and preferred stock** Litho-Print is considering two possible capital structures, A and B, shown in the following table. Assume a 40% tax rate.

Source of capital	Structure A	Structure B
Long-term debt	$75,000 at 16% coupon rate	$50,000 at 15% coupon rate
Preferred stock	$10,000 with an 18% annual dividend	$15,000 with an 18% annual dividend
Common stock	8,000 shares	10,000 shares

a. Calculate two EBIT–EPS coordinates for each of the structures by selecting any two EBIT values and finding their associated EPS values.
b. Graph the two capital structures on the same set of EBIT–EPS axes.
c. Discuss the leverage and risk associated with each of the structures.
d. Over what range of EBIT is each structure preferred?
e. Which structure do you recommend if the firm expects its EBIT to be $35,000? Explain.

LG6 **11–17 Optimal capital structure** Nelson Corporation has collected the following data associated with four possible capital structures.

Capital structure debt ratio	Expected EPS	Estimated coefficient of variation of EPS
0%	$1.92	.4743
20	2.25	.5060
40	2.72	.5581
60	3.54	.6432

The firm's research indicates that the marketplace assigns the following required returns to risky earnings per share.

Coefficient of variation of EPS	Estimated required return, ks
.43	15%
.47	16
.51	17
.56	18
.60	22
.64	24

a. Find the required return associated with each of the four capital structures.
b. Compute the estimated share value associated with each of the four capital structures using the simplified method described in this chapter (see Equation 11.12).
c. Determine the optimal capital structure based on (1) maximization of expected EPS and (2) maximization of share value.
d. Construct a graph (similar to Figure 11.6) showing the relationships in part **c.**
e. Which capital structure do you recommend? Why?

LG5 LG6 **11–18 Integrative—Optimal capital structure** Triple D Corporation wishes to analyze five possible capital structures—0%, 15%, 30%, 45%, and 60% debt ratios. The firm's total assets of $1 million are assumed to be constant. Its common stock has a book value of $25 per share, and the firm is in the 40% tax bracket. The following additional data have been gathered for use in analyzing the five capital structures under consideration.

Capital structure debt ratio	Interest rate on debt, k_d	Expected EPS	Required return, k_s
0%	0.0%	$3.60	10.0%
15	8.0	4.03	10.5
30	10.0	4.50	11.6
45	13.0	4.95	14.0
60	17.0	5.18	20.0

a. Calculate the amount of debt, the amount of equity, and the number of shares of common stock outstanding for each of the capital structures being considered.
b. Calculate the annual interest on the debt under each of the capital structures being considered. (*Note:* The interest rate given is applicable to *all* debt associated with the corresponding debt ratio.)
c. Calculate the EPS associated with $150,000 and $250,000 of EBIT for each of the five capital structures being considered.
d. Using the EBIT–EPS data developed in part **c**, plot the capital structures on the same set of EBIT–EPS axes, and discuss the ranges over which each is preferred. What is the major problem with the use of this approach?
e. Using the valuation model given in Equation 11.12 and the appropriate data, estimate the share value for each of the capital structures being considered.

f. Construct a graph similar to Figure 11.6 showing the relationships between the debt ratio (x axis) and expected EPS (y axis) and share value (y axis).
g. Referring to the graph in part **f**: Which structure is preferred if the goal is to maximize EPS? Which structure is preferred if the goal is to maximize share value? Which capital structure do you recommend? Explain.

CHAPTER 11 CASE Evaluating McGraw Industries' Capital Structure

McGraw Industries, an established producer of printing equipment, expects its sales to remain flat for the next 3 to 5 years because of both a weak economic outlook and an expectation of little new printing technology development over that period. On the basis of this scenario, the firm's management has been instructed by its board to institute programs that will allow it to operate more efficiently, earn higher profits, and, most important, maximize share value. In this regard, the firm's chief financial officer (CFO), Ron Lewis, has been charged with evaluating the firm's capital structure. Lewis believes that the current capital structure, which contains 10% debt and 90% equity, may lack adequate financial leverage. To evaluate the firm's capital structure, Lewis has gathered the data summarized in the following table on the current capital structure (10% debt ratio) and two alternative capital structures—A (30% debt ratio) and B (50% debt ratio)—that he would like to consider.

	Capital structure[a]		
Source of capital	Current (10% debt)	A (30% debt)	B (50% debt)
Long-term debt	\$1,000,000	\$3,000,000	\$5,000,000
Coupon interest rate[b]	9%	10%	12%
Common stock	100,000 shares	70,000 shares	40,000 shares
Required return on equity, k_s[c]	12%	13%	18%

[a]These structures are based on maintaining the firm's current level of \$10,000,000 of total financing.
[b]Interest rate applicable to *all* debt.
[c]Market-based return for the given level of risk.

Lewis expects the firm's earnings before interest and taxes (EBIT) to remain at its current level of \$1,200,000. The firm has a 40% tax rate.

Required

a. Use the current level of EBIT to calculate the times interest earned ratio for each capital structure. Evaluate the current and two alternative capital structures using the times interest earned and debt ratios.
b. Prepare a single EBIT–EPS graph showing the current and two alternative capital structures.
c. On the basis of the graph in part **b**, which capital structure will maximize McGraw's EPS at its expected level of EBIT of \$1,200,000? Why might this *not* be the best capital structure?

d. Using the zero-growth valuation model given in Equation 11.12, find the market value of McGraw's equity under each of the three capital structures at the $1,200,000 level of expected EBIT.

e. On the basis of your findings in parts **c** and **d,** which capital structure would you recommend? Why?

WEB EXERCISE

Go to the Web site *www.smartmoney.com*. In the column on the right under **Quotes & Research** enter the symbol **DIS**; click on **Stock Snapshot;** and then click on **Go.**

1. What is the name of the company? Click on **Financials.**
2. What are the 5-year high and the 5-year low for the company's debt/equity ratio (the ratio of long-term debt to stockholders' equity)?

At the bottom of this page under **Stock Search**, enter the next stock symbol from the list below and then click on **Submit**. Enter the name of the company in the matrix below and then click on **Financials**. Enter the 5-year high and low for the debt/equity ratio in the matrix for each of the stock symbols.

		Debt/equity ratio	
Symbol	Company name	5-yr. low	5-yr. high
DIS	________	______	______
AIT	________	______	______
MRK	________	______	______
LG	________	______	______
LUV	________	______	______
IBM	________	______	______
GE	________	______	______
BUD	________	______	______
PFE	________	______	______
INTC	________	______	______

3. Which of the companies have high debt/equity ratios?
4. Which of the companies have low debt/equity ratios?
5. Why do the companies that have a low debt/equity ratio use more equity even though it is more expensive than debt?

Remember to check the book's Web site at

www.aw.com/gitman

for additional resources, including additional Web exercises.

Chapter

12

Dividend Policy

LEARNING GOALS

- LG1 Understand cash dividend payment procedures and the role of dividend reinvestment plans.
- LG2 Describe the residual theory of dividends and the key arguments with regard to dividend irrelevance and relevance.
- LG3 Discuss the key factors involved in formulating a dividend policy.
- LG4 Review and evaluate the three basic types of dividend policies.
- LG5 Evaluate stock dividends from accounting, shareholder, and company points of view.
- LG6 Explain stock splits and stock repurchases and the firm's motivation for undertaking each of them.

Across the Disciplines

Why This Chapter Matters To You

Accounting: You need to understand the types of dividends and payment procedures for them because you will need to record and report the declaration and payment of dividends; you also will provide the financial data that management must have to make dividend decisions.

Information systems: You need to understand types of dividends, payment procedures, and the financial data that the firm must have to make and implement dividend decisions.

Management: In order to make appropriate dividend decisions for the firm, you need to understand types of dividends, the factors that affect dividend policy, types of dividend policies, and arguments about the relevance of dividends.

Marketing: You need to understand factors affecting dividend policy because you may want to argue that the firm would be better off keeping funds for the development of new products, rather than paying them out as dividends.

Operations: You need to understand factors affecting dividend policy because you may find that the firm's dividend policy imposes limitations on expansion.

Dividends represent a source of cash flow to stockholders and provide information about the firm's performance. Some stockholders expect to receive dividends. Others are content to see an increase in stock price and no dividends. The firm's dividend policy depends on various factors. This chapter considers whether dividends matter to stockholders and explains the key factors in dividend policy, basic types of dividend policies, and alternative forms of dividends.

LG1

Dividend Fundamentals

retained earnings
Earnings not distributed to owners as dividends; a form of *internal* financing.

Expected cash dividends are the key return variable from which owners and investors determine share value. They represent a source of cash flow to stockholders and provide information about the firm's current and future performance. Because **retained earnings**, earnings not distributed to owners as dividends, are a form of *internal* financing, the dividend decision can significantly affect the firm's *external* financing requirements. In other words, if the firm needs financing, the larger the cash dividend paid, the greater the amount of financing that must be raised externally through borrowing or through the sale of common or preferred stock. (Remember that although dividends are charged to retained earnings, they are actually paid out of cash.) The first thing to know about cash dividends is the procedures for paying them.

Cash Dividend Payment Procedures

Whether and in what amount to pay cash dividends to corporate stockholders is decided by the firm's board of directors at quarterly or semiannual meetings. The past period's financial performance and future outlook, as well as recent dividends paid, are key inputs to the dividend decision. The payment date of the cash dividend, if one is declared, must also be established.

Amount of Dividends

Whether dividends should be paid, and if so, in what amount, are important decisions that depend primarily on the firm's dividend policy. Most firms have a set policy with respect to the periodic dividend, but the firm's directors can change this amount, largely on the basis of significant increases or decreases in earnings.

Relevant Dates

If the directors of the firm declare a dividend, they also typically issue a statement indicating the dividend decision, the record date, and the payment date. This statement is generally quoted in the *Wall Street Journal* and other financial news media.

date of record (dividends)
Set by the firm's directors, the date on which all persons whose names are recorded as stockholders receive a declared dividend at a specified future time.

Record Date All persons whose names are recorded as stockholders on the **date of record** set by the directors receive a declared dividend at a specified future time. These stockholders are often referred to as *holders of record*.

ex dividend
Period, beginning 2 *business days* prior to the date of record, during which a stock is sold without the right to receive the current dividend.

Because of the time needed to make bookkeeping entries when a stock is traded, the stock begins selling **ex dividend** 2 *business days* prior to the date of record. Purchasers of a stock selling ex dividend do not receive the current dividend. A simple way to determine the first day on which the stock sells ex dividend is to subtract 2 days from the date of record; if a weekend intervenes, subtract 4 days. Ignoring general market fluctuations, the stock's price is expected to drop by the amount of the declared dividend on the ex dividend date.

payment date
Set by the firm's directors, the actual date on which the firm mails the dividend payment to the holders of record.

Payment Date The **payment date,** also set by the directors, is the actual date on which the firm mails the dividend payment to the holders of record. It is generally a few weeks after the record date. An example will clarify the various dates and the accounting effects.

EXAMPLE

At the quarterly dividend meeting of Rudolf Company, a distributor of office products, held on June 10, the directors declared an $0.80-per-share cash dividend for holders of record on Monday, July 1. The firm had 100,000 shares of common stock outstanding. The payment date for the dividend was August 1. Before the dividend was declared, the key accounts of the firm were as follows:

Cash	$200,000	Dividends payable	$ 0
		Retained earnings	1,000,000

When the dividend was announced by the directors, $80,000 of the retained earnings ($0.80 per share × 100,000 shares) was transferred to the dividends payable account. The key accounts thus became

Cash	$200,000	Dividends payable	$ 80,000
		Retained earnings	920,000

Rudolf Company's stock began selling ex dividend 2 *business days* prior to the date of record, which was June 27. This date was found by subtracting 4 days (a weekend intervened) from the July 1 date of record. Purchasers of Rudolf's stock on June 26 or earlier received the rights to the dividends; those who purchased the stock on or after June 27 did not. Assuming a stable market, Rudolf's stock price was expected to drop by approximately $0.80 per share when it began selling ex dividend on June 27. On August 1 the firm mailed dividend checks to the holders of record as of July 1. This produced the following balances in the key accounts of the firm:

Cash	$120,000	Dividends payable	$ 0
		Retained earnings	920,000

The net effect of declaring and paying the dividend was to reduce the firm's total assets (and stockholders' equity) by $80,000.

Dividend Reinvestment Plans

dividend reinvestment plans (DRIPs)
Plans that enable stockholders to use dividends received on the firm's stock to acquire additional shares—even fractional shares—at little or no transaction cost.

Today many firms offer **dividend reinvestment plans (DRIPs),** which enable stockholders to use dividends received on the firm's stock to acquire additional shares—even fractional shares—at little or no transaction cost. Some companies even allow investors to make their *initial purchases* of the firm's stock directly from the company without going through a broker. With DRIPs, plan participants typically can acquire shares at about 5 percent below the prevailing market price. From its point of view, the firm can issue new shares to participants more economically, avoiding the underpricing and flotation costs that would accompany the public sale of new shares. Clearly, the existence of a DRIP may enhance the market appeal of a firm's shares.

Review Questions

12–1 Who are *holders of record?* When does a stock sell *ex dividend?*

12–2 What benefit is available to participants in a *dividend reinvestment plan?* How might the firm benefit?

LG2

The Relevance of Dividend Policy

Numerous theories and empirical findings concerning dividend policy have been reported in the financial literature. Although this research provides some interesting insights about dividend policy, capital budgeting and capital structure decisions are generally considered far more important than dividend decisions. In other words, good investment and financing decisions should not be sacrificed for a dividend policy of questionable importance.

A number of key questions have yet to be resolved: Does dividend policy matter? What effect does dividend policy have on share price? Is there a model that can be used to evaluate alternative dividend policies in view of share value? Here we begin by describing the residual theory of dividends, which is used as a backdrop for discussion of the key arguments in support of dividend irrelevance and then those in support of dividend relevance.

The Residual Theory of Dividends

residual theory of dividends
A school of thought that suggests that the dividend paid by a firm should be viewed as a *residual*—the amount left over after all acceptable investment opportunities have been undertaken.

The **residual theory of dividends** is a school of thought that suggests that the dividend paid by a firm should be viewed as a *residual*—the amount left over after all acceptable investment opportunities have been undertaken. Using this approach, the firm would treat the dividend decision in three steps, as follows:

Step 1 Determine its optimal level of capital expenditures, which would be the level generated by the point of intersection of the investment opportunities schedule (IOS) and weighted marginal cost of capital (WMCC) schedule (see Chapter 10).

Step 2 Using the optimal capital structure proportions (see Chapter 11), estimate the total amount of equity financing needed to support the expenditures generated in Step 1.

Step 3 Because the cost of retained earnings, k_r, is less than the cost of new common stock, k_n, use retained earnings to meet the equity requirement determined in Step 2. If retained earnings are inadequate to meet this need, sell new common stock. If the available retained earnings are in excess of this need, distribute the surplus amount—the residual—as dividends.

According to this approach, as long as the firm's equity need exceeds the amount of retained earnings, no cash dividend is paid. The argument for this approach is that it is sound management to be certain that the company has the money it needs to compete effectively. This view of dividends suggests that the required return of investors, k_s, is *not* influenced by the firm's dividend policy—a premise that in turn implies that dividend policy is irrelevant.

EXAMPLE Overbrook Industries, a manufacturer of canoes and other small watercraft, has available from the current period's operations \$1.8 million that can be retained or paid out in dividends. The firm's optimal capital structure is at a debt ratio of 30%, which represents 30% debt and 70% equity. Figure 12.1 depicts the firm's weighted marginal cost of capital (WMCC) schedule along with three investment opportunities schedules. For each IOS, the level of total new financing or investment determined by the point of intersection of the IOS and the WMCC has been noted. For IOS_1, it is \$1.5 million, for IOS_2 \$2.4 million, and for IOS_3 \$3.2 million. Although only one IOS will exist in practice, it is useful to look at the possible dividend decisions generated by applying the residual theory in each of the three cases. Table 12.1 summarizes this analysis.

Table 12.1 shows that if IOS_1 exists, the firm will pay out \$750,000 in dividends, because only \$1,050,000 of the \$1,800,000 of available earnings is needed. A 41.7% payout ratio results. For IOS_2, dividends of \$120,000 (a payout ratio of 6.7%) result. Should IOS_3 exist, the firm would pay no dividends (a 0% payout ratio), because its retained earnings of \$1,800,000 would be less than the \$2,240,000 of equity needed. In this case, the firm would have to obtain additional new common stock financing to meet the new requirements generated by the intersection of the IOS_3 and WMCC. Depending on which IOS exists, the

FIGURE 12.1

WMCC and IOSs

WMCC and IOSs for Overbrook Industries

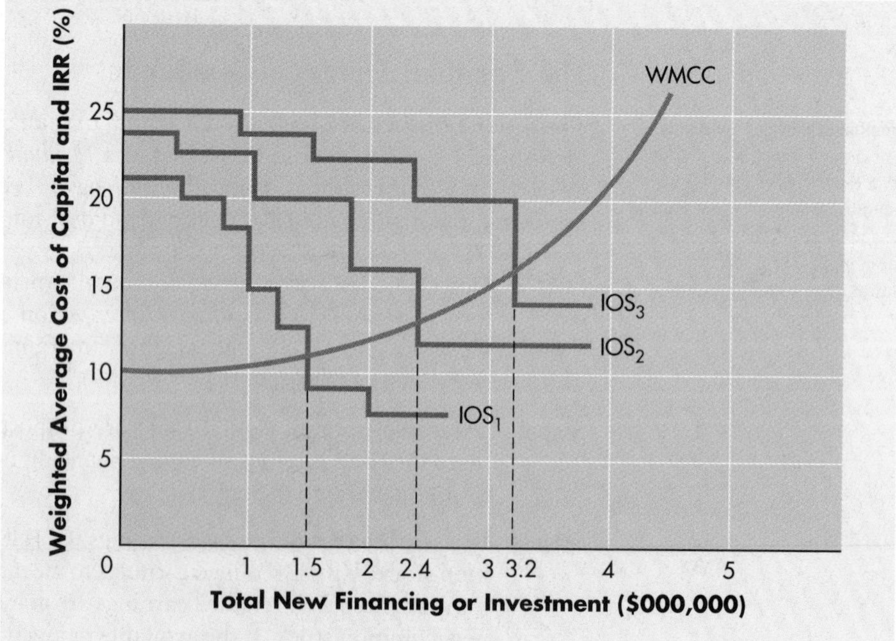

TABLE 12.1 Applying the Residual Theory of Dividends to Overbrook Industries for Each of Three IOSs (Shown in Figure 12.1)

Item	Investment opportunities schedules		
	IOS_1	IOS_2	IOS_3
(1) New financing or investment (Fig. 12.1)	$1,500,000	$2,400,000	$3,200,000
(2) Retained earnings available (given)	$1,800,000	$1,800,000	$1,800,000
(3) Equity needed [70% × (1)]	1,050,000	1,680,000	2,240,000
(4) Dividends [(2) − (3)]	$ 750,000	$ 120,000	$ 0[a]
(5) Dividend payout ratio [(4) ÷ (2)]	41.7%	6.7%	0%

[a]In this case, additional new common stock in the amount of $440,000 ($2,240,000 needed − $1,800,000 available) would have to be sold; no dividends would be paid.

firm's dividend would in effect be the residual, if any, remaining after all acceptable investments had been financed.

Arguments for Dividend Irrelevance

dividend irrelevance theory
Miller and Modigliani's theory that in a perfect world, the firm's value is determined solely by the earning power and risk of its assets (investments) and that the manner in which it splits its earnings stream between dividends and internally retained (and reinvested) funds does not affect this value.

informational content
The information provided by the dividends of a firm with respect to future earnings, which causes owners to bid up or down the price of the firm's stock.

The residual theory of dividends implies that if the firm cannot invest its earnings to earn a return (IRR) that is in excess of cost (WMCC), it should distribute the earnings by paying dividends to stockholders. This approach suggests that dividends represent an earnings residual rather than an active decision variable that affects the firm's value. Such a view is consistent with the **dividend irrelevance theory** put forth by Merton H. Miller and Franco Modigliani (M and M).[1] They argue that the firm's value is determined solely by the earning power and risk of its assets (investments) and that the manner in which it splits its earnings stream between dividends and internally retained (and reinvested) funds does not affect this value. M and M's theory suggests that in a perfect world (certainty, no taxes, no transactions costs, and no other market imperfections), the value of the firm is unaffected by the distribution of dividends.

However, studies have shown that large changes in dividends do affect share price. Increases in dividends result in increased share price, and decreases in dividends result in decreased share price. In response, M and M argue that these effects are attributable not to the dividend itself but rather to the **informational content** of dividends with respect to future earnings. In other words, say M and M, it is not the preference of shareholders for current dividends (rather than future capital gains) that is responsible for this behavior. Instead, investors view a change in dividends, up or down, as a *signal* that management expects future earnings to change in the same direction. An increase in dividends is viewed as a *positive signal,* and investors bid up the share price; a decrease in dividends is a *negative signal* that causes a decrease in share price as investors sell their shares.

1. Merton H. Miller and Franco Modigliani, "Dividend Policy, Growth and the Valuation of Shares," *Journal of Business* 34 (October 1961), pp. 411–433.

clientele effect
The argument that a firm attracts shareholders whose preferences for the payment and stability of dividends correspond to the payment pattern and stability of the firm itself.

M and M further argue that a **clientele effect** exists: A firm attracts shareholders whose preferences for the payment and stability of dividends correspond to the payment pattern and stability of the firm itself. Investors who desire stable dividends as a source of income hold the stock of firms that pay about the same dividend amount each period. Investors who prefer to earn capital gains are more attracted to growing firms that reinvest a large portion of their earnings, favoring growth over a stable pattern of dividends. Because the shareholders get what they expect, M and M argue, the value of their firm's stock is unaffected by dividend policy.

In summary, M and M and other proponents of dividend irrelevance argue that, all else being equal, an investor's required return—and therefore the value of the firm—is unaffected by dividend policy for three reasons:

1. The firm's value is determined solely by the earning power and risk of its assets.
2. If dividends do affect value, they do so solely because of their informational content, which signals management's earnings expectations.
3. A clientele effect exists that causes a firm's shareholders to receive the dividends they expect.

These views of M and M with respect to dividend irrelevance are consistent with the residual theory, which focuses on making the best investment decisions to maximize share value. The proponents of dividend irrelevance conclude that because dividends are irrelevant to a firm's value, the firm does not need to have a dividend policy. Although many research studies have been performed to validate or refute the dividend irrelevance theory, none has been successful in providing irrefutable evidence.

Arguments for Dividend Relevance

dividend relevance theory
The theory, advanced by Gordon and Lintner, that there is a direct relationship between a firm's dividend policy and its market value.

bird-in-the-hand argument
The belief, in support of *dividend relevance theory*, that investors see current dividends as less risky than future dividends or capital gains.

The key argument in support of **dividend relevance theory** is attributed to Myron J. Gordon and John Lintner,[2] who suggest that there is, in fact, a direct relationship between the firm's dividend policy and its market value. Fundamental to this proposition is their **bird-in-the-hand argument,** which suggests that investors see current dividends as less risky than future dividends or capital gains. "A bird in the hand is worth two in the bush." Gordon and Lintner argue that current dividend payments reduce investor uncertainty, causing investors to discount the firm's earnings at a lower rate and, all else being equal, to place a higher value on the firm's stock. Conversely, if dividends are reduced or are not paid, investor uncertainty will increase, raising the required return and lowering the stock's value.

Although many other arguments related to dividend relevance have been put forward, *empirical studies fail to provide conclusive evidence in support of the intuitively appealing dividend relevance argument.* In practice, however, the actions of both financial managers and stockholders tend to support the belief that

2. Myron J. Gordon, "Optimal Investment and Financing Policy," *Journal of Finance* 18 (May 1963), pp. 264–272, and John Lintner, "Dividends, Earnings, Leverage, Stock Prices, and the Supply of Capital to Corporations," *Review of Economics and Statistics* 44 (August 1962), pp. 243–269.

dividend policy does affect stock value.[3] Because we focus on the day-to-day behavior of firms, the remainder of this chapter is consistent with the belief that *dividends are relevant*—that each firm must develop a dividend policy that fulfills the goals of its owners and maximizes their wealth as reflected in the firm's share price.

Review Questions

12–3 Does following the *residual theory of dividends* lead to a stable dividend? Is this approach consistent with dividend relevance?

12–4 Contrast the basic arguments about dividend policy advanced by Miller and Modigliani (M and M) and by Gordon and Lintner.

LG3

Factors Affecting Dividend Policy

dividend policy
The firm's plan of action to be followed whenever a dividend decision is made.

The firm's **dividend policy** represents a plan of action to be followed whenever the dividend decision is made. Firms develop policies consistent with their goals. Before we review some of the popular types of dividend policies, we discuss the factors the are considered in establishing a dividend policy. These include legal constraints, contractual constraints, internal constraints, the firm's growth prospects, owner considerations, and market considerations.

Legal Constraints

Most states prohibit corporations from paying out as cash dividends any portion of the firm's "legal capital," which is typically measured by the par value of common stock. Other states define legal capital to include not only the par value of the common stock, but also any paid-in capital in excess of par. These *capital impairment restrictions* are generally established to provide a sufficient equity base to protect creditors' claims. An example will clarify the differing definitions of capital.

EXAMPLE The stockholders' equity account of Miller Flour Company, a large grain processor, is presented in the following table.

Miller Flour Company
Stockholders' Equity

Common stock at par	$100,000
Paid-in capital in excess of par	200,000
Retained earnings	140,000
Total stockholders' equity	$440,000

3. A common exception is small firms, because they frequently treat dividends as a residual remaining after all acceptable investments have been initiated. Small firms follow this course of action because they usually do not have ready access to capital markets. The use of retained earnings therefore is a key source of financing for growth, which is generally an important goal of a small firm.

In states where the firm's legal capital is defined as the par value of its common stock, the firm could pay out $340,000 ($200,000 + $140,000) in cash dividends without impairing its capital. In states where the firm's legal capital includes all paid-in capital, the firm could pay out only $140,000 in cash dividends.

An earnings requirement limiting the amount of dividends is sometimes imposed. With this restriction, the firm cannot pay more in cash dividends than the sum of its most recent and past retained earnings. However, *the firm is not prohibited from paying more in dividends than its current earnings.*[4]

EXAMPLE

Assume that Miller Flour Company, from the preceding example, in the year just ended has $30,000 in earnings available for common stock dividends. As the preceding table indicates, the firm has past retained earnings of $140,000. Thus it can legally pay dividends of up to $170,000.

excess earnings accumulation tax
The tax the IRS levies on retained earnings above $250,000 when it determines that the firm has accumulated an excess of earnings to allow owners to delay paying ordinary income taxes on dividends received.

If a firm has overdue liabilities or is legally insolvent or bankrupt, most states prohibit its payment of cash dividends. In addition, the Internal Revenue Service prohibits firms from accumulating earnings to reduce the owners' taxes. If the IRS can determine that a firm has accumulated an excess of earnings to allow owners to delay paying ordinary income taxes on dividends received, it may levy an **excess earnings accumulation tax** on any retained earnings above $250,000.

Contractual Constraints

Often the firm's ability to pay cash dividends is constrained by restrictive provisions in a loan agreement. Generally, these constraints prohibit the payment of cash dividends until a certain level of earnings has been achieved, or they may limit dividends to a certain dollar amount or percentage of earnings. Constraints on dividends help to protect creditors from losses due to the firm's insolvency.

Internal Constraints

The firm's ability to pay cash dividends is generally constrained by the amount of liquid assets (cash and marketable securities) available. Although it is possible for a firm to borrow funds to pay dividends, lenders are generally reluctant to make such loans because they produce no tangible or operating benefits that will help the firm repay the loan.

EXAMPLE

Miller Flour Company's stockholders' equity account presented earlier indicates that if the firm's legal capital is defined as all paid-in capital, the firm can pay $140,000 in dividends. If the firm has total liquid assets of $50,000 ($20,000 in cash plus marketable securities worth $30,000) and $35,000 of this is needed for operations, the maximum cash dividend the firm can pay is $15,000 ($50,000 − $35,000).

4. A firm that has an operating loss in the current period can still pay cash dividends as long as sufficient retained earnings against which to charge the dividend are available and, of course, as long as it has the cash with which to make the payments.

Growth Prospects

The firm's financial requirements are directly related to how much it expects to grow and what assets it will need to acquire. It must evaluate its profitability and risk to develop insight into its ability to raise capital externally. In addition, the firm must determine the cost and speed with which it can obtain financing. Generally, a large, mature firm has adequate access to new capital, whereas a rapidly growing firm may not have sufficient funds available to support its acceptable projects. A growth firm is likely to have to depend heavily on internal financing through retained earnings, and so it is likely to pay out only a very small percentage of its earnings as dividends. A more established firm is in a better position to pay out a large proportion of its earnings, particularly if it has ready sources of financing.

Owner Considerations

The firm must establish a policy that has a favorable effect on the wealth of the *majority* of owners. One consideration is the *tax status of a firm's owners.* If a firm has a large percentage of wealthy stockholders who are in a high tax bracket, it may decide to pay out a *lower* percentage of its earnings to allow the owners to delay the payment of taxes until they sell the stock. Of course, when the stock is sold, if the proceeds are in excess of the original purchase price, the capital gain will be taxed, possibly at a more favorable rate than the one applied to ordinary income. Lower-income shareholders, however, who need dividend income, will prefer a *higher* payout of earnings.

A second consideration is the *owners' investment opportunities.* A firm should not retain funds for investment in projects yielding lower returns than the owners could obtain from external investments of equal risk. If it appears that the owners have better opportunities externally, the firm should pay out a higher percentage of its earnings. If the firm's investment opportunities are at least as good as similar-risk external investments, a lower payout is justifiable.

A final consideration is the *potential dilution of ownership.* If a firm pays out a high percentage of earnings, new equity capital will have to be raised with common stock. The result of a new stock issue may be dilution of both control and earnings for the existing owners. By paying out a low percentage of its earnings, the firm can minimize the possibility of such dilution.

Market Considerations

An awareness of the market's probable response to certain types of policies is also helpful in formulating dividend policy. Stockholders are believed to value a *fixed or increasing level of dividends* as opposed to a fluctuating pattern of dividends. This belief is supported by the research of John Lintner[5], who found that corporate managers are averse to changing the dollar amount of dividends in response

5. John Lintner, "Distribution of Income of Corporations Among Dividends, Retained Earnings, and Taxes," *American Economic Review* 46 (May 1956), pp. 97–113.

In Practice

FOCUS ON ETHICS Were Ford Managers Hoarding Cash?

When managers don't pay dividends or pay only minimal dividends, they open themselves up to the charge that they are hoarding cash unnecessarily. Shareholders may believe this is unethical if they are convinced that managers are simply playing it too safe in order to protect their jobs and (by reducing the number of new stock or bond issues) to keep from having to answer to external funding sources. Some of these companies sell products in slow-growth markets and cannot point to future asset-funding requirements to justify their cash buildup. "Empire-building" behavior, whether investing in negative-NPV projects or hoarding cash, reminds us once again that shareholder wealth maximization has to be ethically constrained.

But this lesson can be taken too far. Automakers such as **Chrysler** and **Ford** have come under fire for investing too much in cash and short-term securities. Investor Kirk Kerkorian successfully forced Chrysler to make a one-time $1 billion payout to stockholders in 1996. Ford held the largest cash and security balances in corporate America: In 1999, when Jacques Nasser became CEO, its cash and securities totaled *$14 billion more than its entire debt.* Nasser invested chunks of that cash when acquiring **Volvo** and **Land Rover,** and he also initiated a combined $5.7 billion cash dividend and share repurchase. But maybe he went too far—or maybe his timing was bad. (Did you hear about the $3.5-billion tire replacement project?) In 2001, not only did Ford have to cut its normal quarterly dividend, but its debt was downgraded because investment bankers decided Ford was now in a "cash crisis." The *Wall Street Journal* stated that in hindsight, Ford management was wise to hoard cash against hard times, and investors were unwise to clamor for bigger payouts of cash to shareholders.

Caution and prudence are virtues—and these virtues provide ethical justification for managers accused of putting self-interest ahead of shareholder interests. "Virtue theory" focuses on the character of the decision maker, over and above merely doing one's duty. This area of ethics is now getting more attention, thanks to business guru Steven Covey and to ethicists such as Scott Rae, Kenman Wong, and Thomas Whetstone. In cases such as Ford's, it is probably wisest to give managers the benefit of the doubt.

to changes in earnings, particularly when earnings decline. In addition, stockholders are believed to value a policy of *continuous dividend payment.* Because regularly paying a fixed or increasing dividend eliminates uncertainty about the frequency and magnitude of dividends, the returns of the firm are likely to be discounted at a lower rate. This should result in an increase in the market value of the stock and therefore an increase in the owners' wealth.

A final market consideration is *informational content.* As noted earlier, shareholders often view a dividend payment as a *signal* of the firm's future success. A stable and continuous dividend is a *positive signal,* conveying the firm's good financial health. Shareholders are likely to interpret a passed dividend payment due to a loss or to very low earnings as a *negative signal.* The nonpayment of the dividend creates uncertainty about the future, which is likely to result in lower stock value. Owners and investors generally construe a dividend payment during a period of losses as an indication that the loss is merely temporary.

Review Question

12–5 What are the six factors that affect *dividend policy?* Briefly describe each of them.

LG4

Types of Dividend Policies

The firm's dividend policy must be formulated with two basic objectives in mind: providing for sufficient financing and maximizing the wealth of the firm's owners. Three of the more commonly used dividend policies are described in the following sections. A particular firm's cash dividend policy may incorporate elements of each.

Constant-Payout-Ratio Dividend Policy

dividend payout ratio
Indicates the percentage of each dollar earned that is distributed to the owners in the form of cash. It is calculated by dividing the firm's cash dividend per share by its earnings per share.

constant-payout-ratio dividend policy
A dividend policy based on the payment of a certain percentage of earnings to owners in each dividend period.

One type of dividend policy involves use of a constant payout ratio. The **dividend payout ratio** indicates the percentage of each dollar earned that is distributed to the owners in the form of cash. It is calculated by dividing the firm's cash dividend per share by its earnings per share. With a **constant-payout-ratio dividend policy,** the firm establishes that a certain percentage of earnings is paid to owners in each dividend period.

The problem with this policy is that if the firm's earnings drop or if a loss occurs in a given period, the dividends may be low or even nonexistent. Because dividends are often considered an indicator of the firm's future condition and status, the firm's stock price may thus be adversely affected.

EXAMPLE

Peachtree Industries, a miner of potassium, has a policy of paying out 40% of earnings in cash dividends. In periods when a loss occurs, the firm's policy is to pay no cash dividends. Data on Peachtree's earnings, dividends, and average stock prices for the past 6 years follow.

Year	Earnings/share	Dividends/share	Average price/share
2003	−$0.50	$0.00	$42.00
2002	3.00	1.20	52.00
2001	1.75	0.70	48.00
2000	− 1.50	0.00	38.00
1999	2.00	0.80	46.00
1998	4.50	1.80	50.00

Dividends increased in 2001 and in 2002 but decreased in the other years. In years of decreasing dividends, the firm's stock price dropped; when dividends increased, the price of the stock increased. Peachtree's sporadic dividend payments appear to make its owners uncertain about the returns they can expect.

Although some firms use a constant-payout-ratio dividend policy, it is *not* recommended.

Regular Dividend Policy

regular dividend policy
A dividend policy based on the payment of a fixed-dollar dividend in each period.

The **regular dividend policy** is based on the payment of a fixed-dollar dividend in each period. This policy provides the owners with generally positive information, thereby minimizing their uncertainty. Often, firms that use this policy increase the regular dividend once a *proven* increase in earnings has occurred. Under this policy, dividends are almost never decreased.

EXAMPLE The dividend policy of Woodward Laboratories, a producer of a popular artificial sweetener, is to pay annual dividends of $1.00 per share until per-share earnings have exceeded $4.00 for three consecutive years. At that point, the annual dividend is raised to $1.50 per share, and a new earnings plateau is established. The firm does not anticipate decreasing its dividend unless its liquidity is in jeopardy. Data for Woodward's earnings, dividends, and average stock prices for the past 12 years follow.

Year	Earnings/share	Dividends/share	Average price/share
2003	$4.50	$1.50	$47.50
2002	3.90	1.50	46.50
2001	4.60	1.50	45.00
2000	4.20	1.00	43.00
1999	5.00	1.00	42.00
1998	2.00	1.00	38.50
1997	6.00	1.00	38.00
1996	3.00	1.00	36.00
1995	0.75	1.00	33.00
1994	0.50	1.00	33.00
1993	2.70	1.00	33.50
1992	2.85	1.00	35.00

Whatever the level of earnings, Woodward Laboratories paid dividends of $1.00 per share through 2000. In 2001, the dividend increased to $1.50 per share because earnings in excess of $4.00 per share had been achieved for 3 years. In 2001, the firm also had to establish a new earnings plateau for further dividend increases. Woodward Laboratories' average price per share exhibited a stable, increasing behavior in spite of a somewhat volatile pattern of earnings.

target dividend-payout ratio
A dividend policy under which the firm attempts to pay out a certain *percentage* of earnings as a stated dollar dividend and adjusts that dividend toward a target payout as proven earnings increases occur.

low-regular-and-extra dividend policy
A dividend policy based on paying a low regular dividend, supplemented by an additional dividend when earnings are higher than normal in a given period.

extra dividend
An additional dividend optionally paid by the firm if earnings are higher than normal in a given period.

Often a regular dividend policy is built around a **target dividend-payout ratio.** Under this policy, the firm attempts to pay out a certain *percentage* of earnings, but rather than let dividends fluctuate, it pays a stated dollar dividend and adjusts that dividend toward the target payout as proven earnings increases occur. For instance, Woodward Laboratories appears to have a target payout ratio of around 35 percent. The payout was about 35 percent ($1.00 ÷ $2.85) when the dividend policy was set in 1992, and when the dividend was raised to $1.50 in 2001, the payout ratio was about 33 percent ($1.50 ÷ $4.60).

Low-Regular-and-Extra Dividend Policy

Some firms establish a **low-regular-and-extra dividend policy,** paying a low regular dividend, supplemented by an additional dividend when earnings are higher than normal in a given period. By calling the additional dividend an **extra dividend,** the firm avoids giving shareholders false hopes. This policy is especially common among companies that experience cyclical shifts in earnings.

By establishing a low regular dividend that is paid each period, the firm gives investors the stable income necessary to build confidence in the firm, and the extra dividend permits them to share in the earnings from an especially good period. Firms using this policy must raise the level of the regular dividend once proven increases in earnings have been achieved. The extra dividend should not be a regular event; otherwise, it becomes meaningless. The use of a target dividend-payout ratio in establishing the regular dividend level is advisable.

Review Question

12–6 Describe a constant-payout-ratio dividend policy, a regular dividend policy, and a low-regular-and-extra dividend policy. What are the effects of these policies?

LG5 LG6

Other Forms of Dividends

Dividends can be paid in forms other than cash. Here we discuss two other methods of paying dividends—stock dividends and stock repurchases—as well as a closely related topic, stock splits.

Stock Dividends

stock dividend
The payment, to existing owners, of a dividend in the form of stock.

A **stock dividend** is the payment, to existing owners, of a dividend in the form of stock. Often firms pay stock dividends as a replacement for or a supplement to cash dividends. Although stock dividends do not have a real value, stockholders may perceive them to represent something they did not have before.

Accounting Aspects

small (ordinary) stock dividend
A stock dividend representing less than 20 to 25 percent of the common stock outstanding when the dividend is declared.

In an accounting sense, the payment of a stock dividend is a shifting of funds between stockholders' equity accounts rather than a use of funds. When a firm declares a stock dividend, the procedures for announcement and distribution are the same as those described earlier for a cash dividend. The accounting entries associated with the payment of a stock dividend vary depending on its size. A **small (ordinary) stock dividend** is a stock dividend that represents less than 20 to 25 percent of the common stock outstanding when the dividend is declared. Small stock dividends are most common.

EXAMPLE

The current stockholders' equity on the balance sheet of Garrison Corporation, a distributor of prefabricated cabinets, is as shown in the following accounts.

Preferred stock	$ 300,000
Common stock (100,000 shares at $4 par)	400,000
Paid-in capital in excess of par	600,000
Retained earnings	700,000
Total stockholders' equity	$2,000,000

Garrison, which has 100,000 shares outstanding, declares a 10% stock dividend when the market price of its stock is $15 per share. Because 10,000 new shares (10% of 100,000) are issued at the prevailing market price of $15 per share, $150,000 ($15 per share × 10,000 shares) is shifted from retained earnings to the common stock and paid-in capital accounts. A total of $40,000 ($4 par × 10,000 shares) is added to common stock, and the remaining $110,000 [($15 − $4) × 10,000 shares] is added to the paid-in capital in excess of par. The resulting account balances are as follows:

Preferred stock	$ 300,000
Common stock (110,000 shares at $4 par)	440,000
Paid-in capital in excess of par	710,000
Retained earnings	550,000
Total stockholders' equity	$2,000,000

The firm's total stockholders' equity has not changed; funds have merely been *shifted* among stockholders' equity accounts.

The Shareholder's Viewpoint

The shareholder receiving a stock dividend typically receives nothing of value. After the dividend is paid, the per-share value of the shareholder's stock decreases in proportion to the dividend in such a way that the market value of his or her total holdings in the firm remains unchanged. The shareholder's proportion of ownership in the firm also remains the same, and *as long as the firm's earnings remain unchanged,* so does his or her share of total earnings. (However, if the firm's earnings and cash dividends increase when the stock dividend is issued, an increase in share value is likely to result.)

EXAMPLE Ms. X owned 10,000 shares of Garrison Corporation's stock. The company's most recent earnings were $220,000, and earnings are not expected to change in the near future. Before the stock dividend, Ms. X owned 10% (10,000 shares ÷ 100,000 shares) of the firm's stock, which was selling for $15 per share. Earnings per share were $2.20 ($220,000 ÷ 100,000 shares). Because Ms. X owned 10,000 shares, her earnings were $22,000 ($2.20 per share × 10,000 shares). After receiving the 10% stock dividend, Ms. X has 11,000 shares, which again is 10% of the ownership (11,000 shares ÷ 110,000 shares). The market price of the stock can be expected to drop to $13.64 per share [$15 × (1.00 ÷ 1.10)], which means that the market value of Ms. X's holdings is $150,000 (11,000 shares × $13.64 per share). This is the same as the initial value of her holdings (10,000 shares × $15 per share). The future earnings per share drops to $2 ($220,000 ÷ 110,000 shares) because the same $220,000 in earnings must now be divided among 110,000 shares. Because Ms. X still owns 10% of the stock, her share of total earnings is still $22,000 ($2 per share × 11,000 shares).

In summary, if the firm's earnings remain constant and total cash dividends do not increase, a stock dividend results in a lower per-share market value for the firm's stock.

The Company's Viewpoint

Stock dividends are more costly to issue than cash dividends, but certain advantages may outweigh these costs. Firms find the stock dividend a way to give owners something without having to use cash. Generally, when a firm needs to preserve cash to finance rapid growth, a stock dividend is used. When the stockholders recognize that the firm is reinvesting the cash flow so as to maximize future earnings, the market value of the firm should at least remain unchanged. However, if the stock dividend is paid so that cash can be retained to satisfy past-due bills, a decline in market value may result.

Stock Splits

stock split
A method commonly used to lower the market price of a firm's stock by increasing the number of shares belonging to each shareholder.

Although not a type of dividend, *stock splits* have an effect on a firm's share price similar to that of stock dividends. A **stock split** is a method commonly used to lower the market price of a firm's stock by increasing the number of shares belonging to each shareholder. In a 2-for-1 split, for example, two new shares are exchanged for each old share, with each new share worth half the value of each old share. A stock split has no effect on the firm's capital structure.

Quite often, a firm believes that its stock is priced too high and that lowering the market price will enhance trading activity. Stock splits are often made prior to issuing additional stock to enhance that stock's marketability and stimulate market activity. It is not unusual for a stock split to cause a slight increase in the market value of the stock, attributable to its informational content and to the fact that *total* dividends paid commonly increase slightly after a split.

EXAMPLE ▼ Delphi Company, a forest products concern, had 200,000 shares of \$2-par-value common stock and no preferred stock outstanding. Because the stock is selling at a high market price, the firm has declared a 2-for-1 stock split. The total before- and after-split stockholders' equity is shown in the following table.

Before split	
Common stock (200,000 shares at \$2 par)	\$ 400,000
Paid-in capital in excess of par	4,000,000
Retained earnings	2,000,000
Total stockholders' equity	\$6,400,000
After 2-for-1 split	
Common stock (400,000 shares at \$1 par)	\$ 400,000
Paid-in capital in excess of par	4,000,000
Retained earnings	2,000,000
Total stockholders' equity	\$6,400,000

The insignificant effect of the stock split on the firm's books is obvious. ▲

reverse stock split
A method used to raise the market price of a firm's stock by exchanging a certain number of outstanding shares for one new share.

Stock can be split in any way desired. Sometimes a **reverse stock split** is made: A certain number of outstanding shares are exchanged for one new share.

For example, in a 1-for-3 split, one new share is exchanged for three old shares. Reverse stock splits are initiated to raise the market price of a firm's stock when it is selling at too low a price to appear respectable.[6]

Stock Repurchases

stock repurchase
The repurchase by the firm of outstanding common stock in the marketplace; desired effects of stock repurchases are that they either enhance shareholder value or help to discourage an unfriendly takeover.

In recent years, firms have increased their repurchasing of outstanding common stock in the marketplace. The practical motives for **stock repurchases** include obtaining shares to be used in acquisitions, having shares available for employee stock option plans, and retiring shares. The recent increase in frequency and importance of stock repurchases is due to the fact that they either enhance shareholder value or help to discourage an unfriendly takeover. Stock repurchases enhance shareholder value by (1) reducing the number of shares outstanding and thereby raising earnings per share, (2) sending a *positive signal* to investors in the marketplace that management believes that the stock is undervalued, and (3) providing a temporary floor for the stock price, which may have been declining. The use of repurchases to discourage unfriendly takeovers is predicated on the belief that a corporate raider is less likely to gain control of the firm if there are fewer publicly traded shares available. Here we focus on retiring shares through repurchase, because this motive for repurchase is similar to the payment of cash dividends.

Stock Repurchases Viewed as a Cash Dividend

When common stock is repurchased for retirement, the underlying motive is to distribute excess cash to the owners. Generally, as long as earnings remain constant, the repurchase reduces the number of outstanding shares, raising the earnings per share and therefore the market price per share. In addition, certain owner tax benefits may result. The repurchase of common stock results in a type of *reverse dilution,* because the EPS and the market price of stock are increased by reducing the number of shares outstanding. The net effect of the repurchase is similar to the payment of a cash dividend.

EXAMPLE ▼

Benton Company, a national sportswear chain, has released the following financial data:

Earnings available for common stockholders	$1,000,000
Number of shares of common stock outstanding	400,000
Earnings per share ($1,000,000 ÷ 400,000)	$2.50
Market price per share	$50
Price/earnings (P/E) ratio ($50 ÷ $2.50)	20

The firm wants to use $800,000 of its earnings either to pay cash dividends or to repurchase shares. If the firm paid cash dividends, the amount of the dividend would be $2 per share ($800,000 ÷ 400,000 shares). If the firm paid $52 per

6. If a firm's stock is selling at a low price—possibly less than a few dollars—many investors are hesitant to purchase it because they believe it is "cheap." These somewhat unsophisticated investors correlate cheapness and quality, and they feel that a low-priced stock is a low-quality investment. A reverse stock split raises the stock price and increases per-share earnings.

share to repurchase stock, it could repurchase approximately 15,385 shares ($800,000 ÷ $52 per share). As a result of this repurchase, 384,615 shares (400,000 shares − 15,385 shares) of common stock would remain outstanding. Earnings per share (EPS) would rise to $2.60 ($1,000,000 ÷ 384,615). If the stock still sold at 20 times earnings (P/E = 20), its market price could be estimated by multiplying the new EPS by this P/E ratio (the *price/earnings multiple approach* presented in Chapter 7). The price would therefore rise to $52 per share ($2.60 × 20). In both cases, the stockholders would receive $2 per share: a $2 cash dividend in the dividend case or a $2 increase in share price ($50 per share to $52 per share) in the repurchase case.

Besides the advantage of an increase in per-share earnings, certain owner tax benefits also result. If the cash dividend were paid, the owners would have to pay ordinary income taxes on it, whereas the $2 increase in the market value of the stock that resulted from the repurchase would not be taxed until the owner sold the stock. Of course, when the stock is sold, the capital gain is taxed, but possibly at a more favorable rate than the one applied to ordinary income. The IRS is alleged to monitor firms that regularly repurchase stock and levies a penalty when it believes repurchases have been made to delay the payment of taxes by stockholders.

Accounting Entries

The accounting entries that result when common stock is repurchased are a reduction in cash and the establishment of a contra capital account called "treasury stock," which is shown as a deduction from stockholders' equity. The label *treasury stock* is used on the balance sheet to indicate the presence of repurchased shares.

The Repurchase Process

When a company intends to repurchase a block of outstanding shares, it should make shareholders aware of its intentions. Specifically, it should advise them of the purpose of the repurchase (acquisition, stock options, retirement) and the disposition (if any) planned for the repurchased shares (traded for shares of another firm, distribution to executives, or held in the treasury).

Three basic methods of repurchase are commonly used. One is to purchase shares on the *open market*. This places upward pressure on the price of shares if the number of shares being repurchased is reasonably large in comparison with the total number outstanding. The second method is through tender offers. A **tender offer** is a formal offer to purchase a given number of shares of a firm's stock at a specified price. The price at which a tender offer is made is set above the current market price to attract sellers. If the number of shares desired cannot be repurchased through the tender offer, open-market purchases can be used to obtain the additional shares. Tender offers are preferred when large numbers of shares are repurchased, because the company's intentions are clearly stated and each stockholder has an opportunity to sell shares at the tendered price. A third method that is sometimes used involves the purchase, on a *negotiated basis*, of a large block of shares from one or more major stockholders. Again, in this case, the firm has to state its intentions and make certain that the purchase price is

tender offer
A formal offer to purchase a given number of shares of a firm's stock at a specified price.

fair and equitable in view of the interests and opportunities of the remaining shareholders.

Review Questions

12–7 Why do firms issue *stock dividends?* Comment on the following statement: "I have a stock that promises to pay a 20 percent stock dividend every year, and therefore it guarantees that I will break even in 5 years."
12–8 Compare a *stock split* with a *stock dividend.*
12–9 What is the logic behind *repurchasing shares* of common stock to distribute excess cash to the firm's owners?

SUMMARY

FOCUS ON VALUE

Cash dividends are the cash flows that a firm distributes to its common stockholders. As noted in Chapter 7, a share of common stock gives its owner the right to receive all future dividends. The present value of all those future dividends expected over a firm's assumed infinite life determines the firm's stock value.

Dividends not only represent cash flows to shareholders but also contain useful information with regard to the firm's current and future performance. Such information affects the shareholders' perception of the firm's risk. A firm can also pay stock dividends, initiate stock splits, or repurchase stock. Each of these dividend-related actions can affect the firm's risk, return, and value as a result of their cash flows and informational content.

Although the theory with regard to the relevance of dividends is still evolving, the behavior of most firms and stockholders suggests that dividend policy affects share prices. It is therefore believed to be important for the financial manager to develop and implement a dividend policy that is consistent with the firm's goal of **maximizing stock price.**

REVIEW OF LEARNING GOALS

LG1 **Understand cash dividend payment procedures and the role of dividend reinvestment plans.** The cash dividend decision is normally made by the board of directors, which establishes the record and payment dates. Generally, the larger the dividend charged to retained earnings and paid in cash, the greater the amount of financing that must be raised externally. Some firms offer dividend reinvestment plans that allow stockholders to acquire shares in lieu of cash dividends.

LG2 **Describe the residual theory of dividends and the key arguments with regard to dividend irrelevance and relevance.** The residual theory suggests that dividends should be viewed as the earnings left after all acceptable investment opportunities have been undertaken. Miller and Modigliani argue in favor of dividend irrelevance, using a perfect world wherein information content and clientele effects exist. Gordon and Lintner advance the theory of dividend relevance, basing their argument on the uncertainty-reducing effect of dividends, supported by their bird-in-the-hand argument. Although the idea is intuitively appealing, empirical studies fail to provide clear support of dividend relevance. Even so, the actions of financial managers and stockholders tend to support the belief that dividend policy does affect stock value.

LG3 **Discuss the key factors involved in formulating a dividend policy.** A firm's dividend policy should provide for sufficient financing and maximize the wealth of the firm's owners. Dividend policy is affected by certain legal, contractual, and internal constraints, as well as by growth prospects, owner considerations, and market considerations. Legal constraints prohibit corporations from paying out as cash dividends any portion of the firm's "legal capital"; they also constrain firms with overdue liabilities and legally insolvent or bankrupt firms from paying cash dividends. Contractual constraints result from restrictive provisions in the firm's loan agreements. Internal constraints tend to result from a firm's limited availability of excess cash. Growth prospects affect the relative importance of retaining earnings rather than paying them out in dividends. The tax status of owners, the owners' investment opportunities, and the potential dilution of ownership are important owner considerations. Finally, market considerations are related to the stockholders' preference for the continuous payment of fixed or increasing streams of dividends and the perceived informational content of dividends.

LG4 **Review and evaluate the three basic types of dividend policies.** With a constant-payout-ratio dividend policy, the firm pays a fixed percentage of earnings to the owners each period; dividends move up and down with earnings, and no dividend is paid when a loss occurs. Under a regular dividend policy, the firm pays a fixed-dollar dividend each period; it increases the amount of dividends only after a proven increase in earnings has occurred. The low-regular-and-extra dividend policy is similar to the regular dividend policy, except that it pays an "extra dividend" in periods when the firm's earnings are higher than normal. The regular and the low-regular-and-extra dividend policies are generally preferred because their stable patterns of dividends reduce uncertainty.

LG5 **Evaluate stock dividends from accounting, shareholder, and company points of view.** Occasionally, firms pay stock dividends as a replacement for or supplement to cash dividends. The payment of stock dividends involves a shifting of funds between capital accounts rather than a use of funds. Shareholders receiving stock dividends receive nothing of value; the market value of their holdings, their proportion of ownership, and their share of total earnings remain unchanged. However, the firm may use stock dividends to satisfy owners and preserve its market value without having to use cash.

LG6 **Explain stock splits and stock repurchases and the firm's motivation for undertaking each of them.** Stock splits are used to enhance trading activity of a firm's shares by lowering or raising their market price. A stock split merely involves accounting adjustments; it has no effect on the firm's cash or on its capital structure. Stock repurchases can be made in lieu of cash dividend payments to retire outstanding shares. They reduce the number of outstanding shares and thereby increase earnings per share and the market price per share. They also delay the tax burden of shareholders.

SELF-TEST PROBLEM (Solution in Appendix B)

LG6 ST 12–1 **Stock repurchase** The Off-Shore Steel Company has earnings available for common stockholders of $2 million and has 500,000 shares of common stock outstanding at $60 per share. The firm is currently contemplating the payment of $2 per share in cash dividends.

a. Calculate the firm's current earnings per share (EPS) and price/earnings (P/E) ratio.

b. If the firm can repurchase stock at $62 per share, how many shares can be purchased in lieu of making the proposed cash dividend payment?
c. How much will the EPS be after the proposed repurchase? Why?
d. If the stock sells at the old P/E ratio, what will the market price be after repurchase?
e. Compare and contrast the earnings per share before and after the proposed repurchase.
f. Compare and contrast the stockholders' position under the dividend and repurchase alternatives.

PROBLEMS

LG1 **12–1 Dividend payment procedures** At the quarterly dividend meeting, Wood Shoes declared a cash dividend of $1.10 per share for holders of record on Monday, July 10. The firm has 300,000 shares of common stock outstanding and has set a payment date of July 31. Prior to the dividend declaration, the firm's key accounts were as follows:

Cash	$500,000	Dividends payable	$ 0
		Retained earnings	2,500,000

a. Show the entries after the meeting adjourned.
b. When is the *ex dividend* date?
c. What values would the key accounts have after the July 31 payment date?
d. What effect, if any, will the dividend have on the firm's total assets?
e. Ignoring general market fluctuations, what effect, if any, will the dividend have on the firm's stock price on the ex dividend date?

LG1 **12–2 Dividend payment** Kathy Snow wishes to purchase shares of Countdown Computing, Inc. The company's board of directors has declared a cash dividend of $0.80 to be paid to holders of record on Wednesday, May 12.
a. What is the last day that Kathy can purchase the stock (trade date) in order to receive the dividend?
b. What day does this stock begin trading "ex dividend"?
c. What change, if any, would you expect in the price per share when the stock begins trading on the ex dividend day?
d. If Kathy held the stock for less than one quarter and then sold it for $39 per share, would she achieve a higher investment return by (1) buying the stock *prior to* the ex dividend date at $35 per share and collecting the $0.80 dividend, or (2) buying it *on* the ex dividend date at $34.20 per share but not receiving the dividend?

LG2 **12–3 Residual dividend policy** As president of Young's of California, a large clothing chain, you have just received a letter from a major stockholder. The stockholder asks about the company's dividend policy. In fact, the stockholder has asked you to estimate the amount of the dividend that you are likely to pay next year. You have not yet collected all the information about the expected dividend payment, but you do know the following:

(1) The company follows a residual dividend policy.
(2) The total capital budget for next year is likely to be one of three amounts, depending on the results of capital budgeting studies that are currently under way. The capital expenditure amounts are $2 million, $3 million, and $4 million.
(3) The forecasted level of potential retained earnings next year is $2 million.
(4) The target or optimal capital structure is a debt ratio of 40%.

You have decided to respond by sending the stockholder the best information available to you.

a. Describe a *residual dividend policy.*
b. Compute the amount of the dividend (or the amount of new common stock needed) and the dividend payout ratio for each of the three capital expenditure amounts.
c. Compare, contrast, and discuss the amount of dividends (calculated in part **b**) associated with each of the three capital expenditure amounts.

LG3 12–4 **Dividend constraints** The Howe Company's stockholders' equity account is as follows:

Common stock (400,000 shares at $4 par)	$1,600,000
Paid-in capital in excess of par	1,000,000
Retained earnings	1,900,000
Total stockholders' equity	$4,500,000

The earnings available for common stockholders from this period's operations are $100,000, which have been included as part of the $1.9 million retained earnings.

a. What is the maximum dividend per share that the firm can pay? (Assume that legal capital includes *all* paid-in capital.)
b. If the firm has $160,000 in cash, what is the largest per-share dividend it can pay without borrowing?
c. Indicate the accounts and changes, if any, that will result if the firm pays the dividends indicated in parts **a** and **b**.
d. Indicate the effects of an $80,000 cash dividend on stockholders' equity.

LG3 12–5 **Dividend constraints** A firm has $800,000 in paid-in capital, retained earnings of $40,000 (including the current year's earnings), and 25,000 shares of common stock outstanding. In the current year, it has $29,000 of earnings available for the common stockholders.

a. What is the most the firm can pay in cash dividends to each common stockholder? (Assume that legal capital includes *all* paid-in capital.)
b. What effect would a cash dividend of $0.80 per share have on the firm's balance sheet entries?
c. If the firm cannot raise any new funds from external sources, what do you consider the key constraint with respect to the magnitude of the firm's dividend payments? Why?

LG4 **12–6 Alternative dividend policies** Over the last 10 years, a firm has had the earnings per share shown in the following table.

Year	Earnings per share
2003	$4.00
2002	3.80
2001	3.20
2000	2.80
1999	3.20
1998	2.40
1997	1.20
1996	1.80
1995	− 0.50
1994	0.25

a. If the firm's dividend policy were based on a constant payout ratio of 40% for all years with positive earnings and 0% otherwise, what would be the annual dividend for each year?

b. If the firm had a dividend payout of $1.00 per share, increasing by $0.10 per share whenever the dividend payout fell below 50% for two consecutive years, what annual dividend would the firm pay each year?

c. If the firm's policy were to pay $0.50 per share each period except when earnings per share exceed $3.00, when an extra dividend equal to 80% of earnings beyond $3.00 would be paid, what annual dividend would the firm pay each year?

d. Discuss the pros and cons of each dividend policy described in parts **a** through **c.**

LG4 **12–7 Alternative dividend policies** Given the earnings per share over the period 1996–2003 shown in the following table, determine the annual dividend per share under each of the policies set forth in parts **a** through **d.**

Year	Earnings per share
2003	$1.40
2002	1.56
2001	1.20
2000	− 0.85
1999	1.05
1998	0.60
1997	1.00
1996	0.44

a. Pay out 50% of earnings in all years with positive earnings.

b. Pay $0.50 per share and increase to $0.60 per share whenever earnings per share rise above $0.90 per share for two consecutive years.

c. Pay $0.50 per share except when earnings exceed $1.00 per share, in which case pay an extra dividend of 60% of earnings above $1.00 per share.

d. Combine policies in parts **b** and **c.** When the dividend is raised (in part **b**), raise the excess dividend base (in part **c**) from $1.00 to $1.10 per share.

e. Compare and contrast each of the dividend policies described in parts **a** through **d.**

LG5 12–8 **Stock dividend—Firm** Columbia Paper has the following stockholders' equity account. The firm's common stock has a current market price of $30 per share.

Preferred stock	$100,000
Common stock (10,000 shares at $2 par)	20,000
Paid-in capital in excess of par	280,000
Retained earnings	100,000
Total stockholders' equity	$500,000

a. Show the effects on Columbia of a 5% stock dividend.

b. Show the effects of (1) a 10% and (2) a 20% stock dividend.

c. In light of your answers to parts **a** and **b,** discuss the effects of stock dividends on stockholders' equity.

LG5 12–9 **Cash versus stock dividend** Milwaukee Tool has the following stockholders' equity account. The firm's common stock currently sells for $4 per share.

Preferred stock	$ 100,000
Common stock (400,000 shares at $1 par)	400,000
Paid-in capital in excess of par	200,000
Retained earnings	320,000
Total stockholders' equity	$1,020,000

a. Show the effects on the firm of a *cash* dividend of $0.01, $0.05, $0.10, and $0.20 per share.

b. Show the effects on the firm of a 1%, 5%, 10%, and 20% *stock* dividend.

c. Compare the effects in parts **a** and **b.** What are the significant differences between the two methods of paying dividends?

LG5 12–10 **Stock dividend—Investor** Sarah Warren currently holds 400 shares of Nutri-Foods. The firm has 40,000 shares outstanding. The firm most recently had earnings available for common stockholders of $80,000, and its stock has been selling for $22 per share. The firm intends to retain its earnings and pay a 10% stock dividend.

a. How much does the firm currently earn per share?

b. What proportion of the firm does Sarah Warren currently own?

c. What proportion of the firm will Ms. Warren own after the stock dividend? Explain your answer.
d. At what market price would you expect the stock to sell after the stock dividend?
e. Discuss what effect, if any, the payment of stock dividends will have on Ms. Warren's share of the ownership and earnings of Nutri-Foods.

LG5 **12–11 Stock dividend—Investor** Security Data Company has outstanding 50,000 shares of common stock currently selling at $40 per share. The firm most recently had earnings available for common stockholders of $120,000, but it has decided to retain these funds and is considering either a 5% or a 10% stock dividend in lieu of a cash dividend.

a. Determine the firm's current earnings per share.
b. If Sam Waller currently owns 500 shares of the firm's stock, determine his proportion of ownership currently and under each of the proposed stock dividend plans. Explain your findings.
c. Calculate and explain the market price per share under each of the stock dividend plans.
d. For each of the proposed stock dividends, calculate the earnings per share after payment of the stock dividend.
e. What is the value of Sam Waller's holdings under each of the plans? Explain.
f. Should Mr. Waller have any preference with respect to the proposed stock dividends? Why or why not?

LG6 **12–12 Stock split—Firm** Growth Industries' current stockholders' equity account is as follows:

Preferred stock	$ 400,000
Common stock (600,000 shares at $3 par)	1,800,000
Paid-in capital in excess of par	200,000
Retained earnings	800,000
Total stockholders' equity	$3,200,000

a. Indicate the change, if any, expected if the firm declares a 2-for-1 stock split.
b. Indicate the change, if any, expected if the firm declares a 1-for-1½ *reverse* stock split.
c. Indicate the change, if any, expected if the firm declares a 3-for-1 stock split.
d. Indicate the change, if any, expected if the firm declares a 6-for-1 stock split.
e. Indicate the change, if any, expected if the firm declares a 1-for-4 *reverse* stock split.

LG5 LG6 **12–13 Stock split versus stock dividend—Firm** Mammoth Corporation is considering a 3-for-2 stock split. It currently has the stockholders' equity position shown. The current stock price is $120 per share. The most recent period's earnings available for common stock is included in retained earnings.

Preferred stock	$ 1,000,000
Common stock (100,000 shares at $3 par)	300,000
Paid-in capital in excess of par	1,700,000
Retained earnings	10,000,000
Total stockholders' equity	$13,000,000

a. What effects on Mammoth would result from the stock split?
b. What change in stock price would you expect to result from the stock split?
c. What is the maximum cash dividend per share that the firm could pay on common stock before and after the stock split? (Assume that legal capital includes *all* paid-in capital.)
d. Contrast your answers to parts **a** through **c** with the circumstances surrounding a 50% stock dividend.
e. Explain the differences between stock splits and stock dividends.

LG6 **12–14 Stock repurchase** The following financial data on the Bond Recording Company are available:

Earnings available for common stockholders	$800,000
Number of shares of common stock outstanding	400,000
Earnings per share ($800,000 ÷ 400,000)	$2
Market price per share	$20
Price/earnings (P/E) ratio ($20 ÷ $2)	10

The firm is currently considering whether it should use $400,000 of its earnings to pay cash dividends of $1 per share or to repurchase stock at $21 per share.
a. Approximately how many shares of stock can the firm repurchase at the $21-per-share price, using the funds that would have gone to pay the cash dividend?
b. Calculate the EPS after the repurchase. Explain your calculations.
c. If the stock still sells at 10 times earnings, what will the market price be after the repurchase?
d. Compare the pre- and post-repurchase earnings per share.
e. Compare and contrast the stockholders' positions under the dividend and repurchase alternatives. What are the tax implications under each alternative?

CHAPTER 12 CASE Establishing General Access Company's Dividend Policy and Initial Dividend

General Access Company (GAC) is a fast-growing Internet access provider that initially went public in early 1997. Its revenue growth and profitability have steadily risen since the firm's inception in late 1995. GAC's growth has been financed through the initial common stock offering, the sale of bonds in 2000, and the retention of all earnings. Because of its rapid growth in revenue and profits, with only short-term earnings declines, GAC's common stockholders have been content to let the firm reinvest earnings to expand capacity to meet the growing demand for its services. This strategy has benefited most stockholders in terms of stock splits and capital gains. Since the company's initial public offering in 1997, GAC's stock twice has been split 2-for-1. In terms of total growth, the market price of GAC's stock, after adjustment for stock splits, has increased by 800 percent during the seven-year period 1997–2003.

Because GAC's rapid growth is beginning to slow, the firm's CEO, Marilyn McNeely, believes that its shares are becoming less attractive to investors. Ms. McNeely has had discussions with her CFO, Bobby Joe Rook, who believes that the firm must begin to pay cash dividends. He argues that many investors value regular dividends and that by beginning to pay them, GAC would increase the demand—and therefore the price—for its shares. Ms. McNeely decided that at the next board meeting she would propose that the firm begin to pay dividends on a regular basis.

Ms. McNeely realized that if the board approved her recommendation, it would have to (1) establish a dividend policy and (2) set the amount of the initial annual dividend. She had Mr. Rook prepare a summary of the firm's annual EPS. It is given in the following table.

Year	EPS
2003	$3.70
2002	4.10
2001	3.90
2000	3.30
1999	2.20
1998	0.83
1997	0.55

Mr. Rook indicated that he expects EPS to remain within 10% (plus or minus) of the most recent (2003) value during the next three years. His most likely estimate is an annual increase of about 5%.

After much discussion, Ms. McNeely and Mr. Rook agreed that she would recommend to the board one of the following types of dividend policies:

1. Constant-payout-ratio dividend policy
2. Regular dividend policy
3. Low-regular-and-extra dividend policy

Ms. McNeely realizes that her dividend proposal would significantly affect future financing opportunities and costs and the firm's share price. She also knows that she must be sure her proposal is complete and that it fully educates the board with regard to the long-term implications of each policy.

Required

a. Analyze each of the three dividend policies in light of GAC's financial position.
b. Which dividend policy would you recommend? Justify your recommendation.
c. What are the key factors to consider when setting the amount of a firm's initial annual dividend?

d. How should Ms. McNeely go about deciding what initial annual dividend she will recommend to the board?

e. In view of your dividend policy recommendation in part **b,** how large an initial dividend would you recommend? Justify your recommendation.

WEB EXERCISE

Go to the Web site *www.smartmoney.com*. In the column on the right under **Quotes & Research** enter the symbol **DIS**; click on **Stock Snapshot**; and then click on **Go**.

1. What is the name of the company?
2. What is its dividend amount? Its dividend frequency? Its dividend yield? Its return on equity (ROE)?

Enter those data into the matrix below. Then click on the **Key Ratios** tab and enter the current ROE. Enter the next stock symbol into the box on the bottom of the page under **Stock Search** and then click on **Submit**. Complete the following matrix in that manner.

Symbol	Company name	$ Amount	Dividend frequency	Yield %	ROE
DIS					
AIT					
MRK					
LG					
LUV					
IBM					
GE					
BUD					
PFE					
INTC					

3. Which of the companies have the lowest dividend yields?
4. Which of the companies have the highest dividend yields?
5. Looking at return on equity, can you draw any conclusions about the relationship between dividends and ROE?

Remember to check the book's Web site at

www.aw.com/gitman

for additional resources, including additional Web exercises.

Part 5

Short-Term Financial Decisions

Chapter

13

Working Capital and Current Assets Management

LEARNING GOALS

- **LG1** Understand short-term financial management, net working capital, and the related tradeoff between profitability and risk.
- **LG2** Describe the cash conversion cycle, its funding requirements, and the key strategies for managing it.
- **LG3** Discuss inventory management: differing views, common techniques, and international concerns.
- **LG4** Explain the credit selection process and the quantitative procedure for evaluating changes in credit standards.
- **LG5** Review the procedures for quantitatively considering cash discount changes, other aspects of credit terms, and credit monitoring.
- **LG6** Understand the management of receipts and disbursements, including float, speeding collections, slowing payments, cash concentration, zero-balance accounts, and investing in marketable securities.

Across the Disciplines

Why This Chapter Matters To You

Accounting: In order to record and report the firm's transactions, you need to understand the cash conversion cycle and the management of inventory, accounts receivable, and receipts and disbursements of cash.

Information systems: You need to understand the cash conversion cycle, inventory, accounts receivable, and receipts and disbursements of cash in order to design financial information systems that enhance effective short-term financial management.

Management: You need to understand management of working capital and current assets so that you can decide whether to finance the firm's funds requirements aggressively or conservatively.

Marketing: You need to understand credit selection and monitoring because sales will be affected by the availability of credit to purchasers; sales will also be affected by inventory management.

Operations: You need to understand the cash conversion cycle because you will be responsible for reducing the cycle through the efficient management of inventory levels and costs.

An important consideration for all firms is the ability to finance the transition from cash to inventories to receivables and back to cash. Various strategies exist for managing current assets in order to reduce the amount of financing needed to support this cycle. In addition to managing cash, firms also must manage the accounts that typically represent the firm's largest investment in current assets—inventories and accounts receivable. This chapter looks at the management of these various aspects of the firm's current assets.

LG1

Net Working Capital Fundamentals

The firm's balance sheet provides information about the structure of a firm's investments on the one hand and the structure of its financing sources on the other. The structures chosen should consistently lead to the maximization of the value of the owners' investment in the firm.

Important components of the firm's financial structure include the level of investment in current assets and the extent of current liability financing. In U.S. manufacturing firms, current assets account for about 40 percent of total assets; current liabilities represent about 26 percent of total financing. Therefore, it should not be surprising to learn that **short-term financial management**—managing current assets and current liabilities—is one of the financial manager's most important and time-consuming activities. A study of Fortune 1000 firms found that more than one-third of financial management time is spent managing current assets and about one-fourth of financial management time is spent managing current liabilities.

short-term financial management
Management of current assets and current liabilities.

The goal of short-term financial management is to manage each of the firm's current assets (inventory, accounts receivable, cash, and marketable securities) and current liabilities (accounts payable, accruals, and notes payable) to achieve a balance between profitability and risk that contributes positively to the firm's value. This chapter does not discuss the optimal level of current assets and current liabilities that a firm should have. That issue is unresolved in the financial literature. Here we first use net working capital to consider the basic relationship between current assets and current liabilities and then use the cash conversion cycle to consider the key aspects of current asset management. In the following chapter, we consider current liability management.

Net Working Capital

Current assets, commonly called **working capital,** represent the portion of investment that circulates from one form to another in the ordinary conduct of business. This idea embraces the recurring transition from cash to inventories to receivables and back to cash. As cash substitutes, *marketable securities* are considered part of working capital.

working capital
Current assets, which represent the portion of investment that circulates from one form to another in the ordinary conduct of business.

Current liabilities represent the firm's short-term financing, because they include all debts of the firm that come due (must be paid) in 1 year or less. These debts usually include amounts owed to suppliers (accounts payable), employees and governments (accruals), and banks (notes payable), among others.

net working capital
The difference between the firm's current assets and its current liabilities; can be *positive* or *negative.*

As noted in Chapter 8, **net working capital** is commonly defined as the difference between the firm's current assets and its current liabilities. When the current assets exceed the current liabilities, the firm has *positive net working capital.* When current assets are less than current liabilities, the firm has *negative net working capital.*

The conversion of current assets from inventory to receivables to cash provides the source of cash used to pay the current liabilities. The cash outlays for current liabilities are relatively predictable. When an obligation is incurred, the firm generally knows when the corresponding payment will be due. What is difficult to predict are the cash inflows—the conversion of the current assets to more liquid forms. The more predictable its cash inflows, the less net working capital a firm needs. Because most firms are unable to match cash inflows to outflows with certainty, current assets that more than cover outflows for current liabilities are usually necessary. In general, the greater the margin by which a firm's current assets cover its current liabilities, the better able it will be to pay its bills as they come due.

The Tradeoff Between Profitability and Risk

profitability
The relationship between revenues and costs generated by using the firm's assets—both current and fixed—in productive activities.

risk (of technical insolvency)
The probability that a firm will be unable to pay its bills as they come due.

technically insolvent
Describes a firm that is unable to pay its bills as they come due.

A tradeoff exists between a firm's profitability and its risk. **Profitability,** in this context, is the relationship between revenues and costs generated by using the firm's assets—both current and fixed—in productive activities. A firm's profits can be increased by (1) increasing revenues or (2) decreasing costs. **Risk,** in the context of short-term financial management, is the probability that a firm will be unable to pay its bills as they come due. A firm that cannot pay its bills as they come due is said to be **technically insolvent.** It is generally assumed that the greater the firm's net working capital, the lower its risk. In other words, the more net working capital, the more liquid the firm and therefore the lower its risk of becoming technically insolvent. Using these definitions of profitability and risk, we can demonstrate the tradeoff between them by considering changes in current assets and current liabilities separately.

Changes in Current Assets

How changing the level of the firm's current assets affects its profitability–risk tradeoff can be demonstrated using the ratio of current assets to total assets. This ratio indicates the *percentage of total assets* that is current. For purposes of illustration, we will assume that the level of total assets remains unchanged.[1] The effects on both profitability and risk of an increase or decrease in this ratio are summarized in the upper portion of Table 13.1. When the ratio increases—that is, when current assets increase—profitability decreases. Why? Because current assets are less profitable than fixed assets. Fixed assets are more profitable because they add more value to the product than that provided by current assets. Without fixed assets, the firm could not produce the product.

The risk effect, however, decreases as the ratio of current assets to total assets increases. The increase in current assets increases net working capital, thereby

1. In order to isolate the effect of changing asset and financing mixes on the firm's profitability and risk, we assume the level of total assets to be *constant* in this and the following discussion.

TABLE 13.1 Effects of Changing Ratios on Profits and Risk

Ratio	Change in ratio	Effect on profit	Effect on risk
$\frac{\text{Current assets}}{\text{Total assets}}$	Increase	Decrease	Decrease
	Decrease	Increase	Increase
$\frac{\text{Current liabilities}}{\text{Total assets}}$	Increase	Increase	Increase
	Decrease	Decrease	Decrease

reducing the risk of technical insolvency. In addition, as you go down the asset side of the balance sheet, the risk associated with the assets increases: Investment in cash and marketable securities is less risky than investment in accounts receivable, inventories, and fixed assets. Accounts receivable investment is less risky than investment in inventories and fixed assets. Investment in inventories is less risky than investment in fixed assets. The nearer an asset is to cash, the less risky it is. The opposite effects on profit and risk result from a decrease in the ratio of current assets to total assets.

Changes in Current Liabilities

How changing the level of the firm's current liabilities affects its profitability–risk tradeoff can be demonstrated by using the ratio of current liabilities to total assets. This ratio indicates the percentage of total assets that has been financed with current liabilities. Again, assuming that total assets remain unchanged, the effects on both profitability and risk of an increase or decrease in the ratio are summarized in the lower portion of Table 13.1. When the ratio increases, profitability increases. Why? Because the firm uses more of the less expensive current liabilities financing and less long-term financing. Current liabilities are less expensive because only notes payable, which represent about 20 percent of the typical manufacturer's current liabilities, have a cost. The other current liabilities are basically debts on which the firm pays no charge or interest. However, when the ratio of current liabilities to total assets increases, the risk of technical insolvency also increases, because the increase in current liabilities in turn decreases net working capital. The opposite effects on profit and risk result from a decrease in the ratio of current liabilities to total assets.

Review Questions

13–1 Why is *short-term financial management* one of the most important and time-consuming activities of the financial manager? What is *net working capital?*

13–2 What is the relationship between the predictability of a firm's cash inflows and its required level of net working capital? How are net working capital, liquidity, and *risk of technical insolvency* related?

13–3 Why does an increase in the ratio of current to total assets decrease both profits and risk as measured by net working capital? How do changes in the ratio of current liabilities to total assets affect profitability and risk?

LG2

The Cash Conversion Cycle

Central to short-term financial management is an understanding of the firm's cash conversion cycle.[2] This cycle frames discussion of the management of the firm's current assets in this chapter and that of the management of current liabilities in Chapter 14. Here, we begin by demonstrating the calculation and application of the cash conversion cycle.

Calculating the Cash Conversion Cycle

operating cycle (OC)
The time from the beginning of the production process to the collection of cash from the sale of the finished product.

A firm's **operating cycle** (OC) is the time from the beginning of the production process to collection of cash from the sale of the finished product. The operating cycle encompasses two major short-term asset categories: inventory and accounts receivable. It is measured in elapsed time by summing the *average age of inventory (AAI)* and the *average collection period (ACP)*.

$$OC = AAI + ACP \tag{13.1}$$

cash conversion cycle (CCC)
The amount of time a firm's resources are tied up; calculated by subtracting the average payment period from the *operating cycle*.

However, the process of producing and selling a product also includes the purchase of production inputs (raw materials) on account, which results in accounts payable. Accounts payable reduce the number of days a firm's resources are tied up in the operating cycle. The time it takes to pay the accounts payable, measured in days, is the *average payment period (APP)*. The operating cycle less the average payment period is referred to as the **cash conversion cycle** (CCC). It represents the amount of time the firm's resources are tied up. The formula for the cash conversion cycle is

$$CCC = OC - APP \tag{13.2}$$

Substituting the relationship in Equation 13.1 into Equation 13.2, we can see that the cash conversion cycle has three main components, as shown in Equation 13.3: (1) average age of the inventory, (2) average collection period, and (3) average payment period.

$$CCC = AAI + ACP - APP \tag{13.3}$$

Clearly, if a firm changes any of these time periods, it changes the amount of resources tied up in the day-to-day operation of the firm.

---

2. The conceptual model that is used in this section to demonstrate basic short-term financial management strategies was developed by Lawrence J. Gitman in "Estimating Corporate Liquidity Requirements: A Simplified Approach," *The Financial Review* (1974), pp. 79–88, and refined and operationalized by Lawrence J. Gitman and Kanwal S. Sachdeva in "A Framework for Estimating and Analyzing the Required Working Capital Investment," *Review of Business and Economic Research* (Spring 1982), pp 35–44.

FIGURE 13.1

Time Line for MAX Company's Cash Conversion Cycle

MAX Company's operating cycle is 100 days, and its cash conversion cycle is 65 days

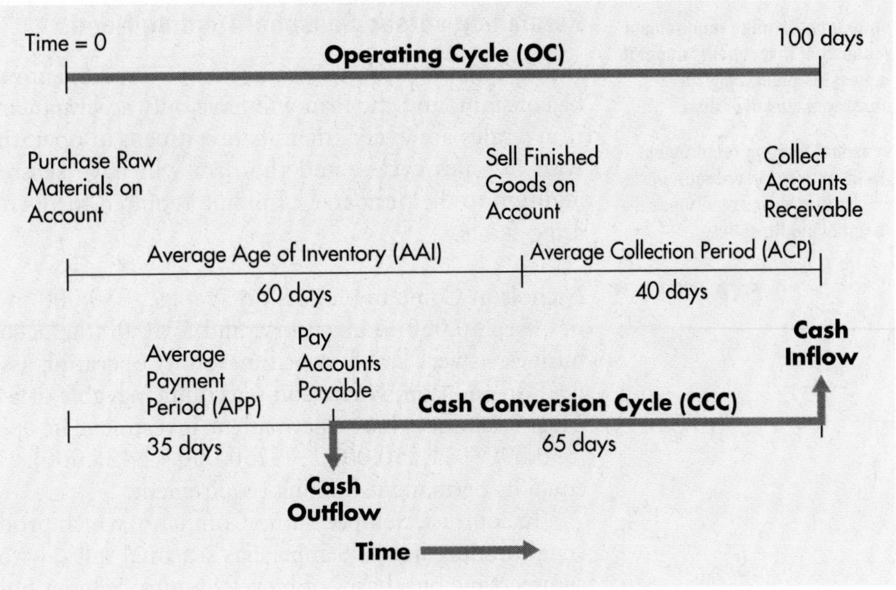

EXAMPLE

MAX Company, a producer of paper dinnerware, has annual sales of \$10 million, a cost of goods sold of 75% of sales, and purchases that are 65% of cost of goods sold. MAX has an average age of inventory (AAI) of 60 days, an average collection period (ACP) of 40 days, and an average payment period (APP) of 35 days. Thus the cash conversion cycle for MAX is 65 days (60 + 40 − 35). Figure 13.1 presents MAX Company's cash conversion cycle as a time line.

The resources MAX has invested in this cash conversion cycle (assuming a 360-day year) are

Inventory	= (\$10,000,000 × 0.75) × (60/360)	= \$1,250,000
+ Accounts receivable	= (10,000,000 × 40/360)	= 1,111,111
− Accounts payable	= (10,000,000 × 0.75 × 0.65) × (35/360)	= 473,958
	= Resources invested	= \$1,887,153

Changes in any of the time periods will change the resources tied up in operations. For example, if MAX could reduce the average collection period on its accounts receivable by 5 days, it would shorten the cash conversion time line and thus reduce the amount of resources MAX has invested in operations. For MAX, a 5-day reduction in the average collection period would reduce the resources invested in the cash conversion cycle by \$138,889 [\$10,000,000 × (5/360)].

Funding Requirements of the Cash Conversion Cycle

We can use the cash conversion cycle as a basis for discussing how the firm funds its required investment in operating assets. We first differentiate between permanent and seasonal funding needs and then describe aggressive and conservative seasonal funding strategies.

permanent funding requirement A constant investment in operating assets resulting from constant sales over time.

seasonal funding requirement An investment in operating assets that varies over time as a result of cyclic sales.

Permanent versus Seasonal Funding Needs

If the firm's sales are constant, then its investment in operating assets should also be constant, and the firm will have only a **permanent funding requirement.** If the firm's sales are cyclic, then its investment in operating assets will vary over time with its sales cycles, and the firm will have **seasonal funding requirements** in addition to the permanent funding required for its minimum investment in operating assets.

EXAMPLE

Nicholson Company holds, on average, $50,000 in cash and marketable securities, $1,250,000 in inventory, and $750,000 in accounts receivable. Nicholson's business is very stable over time, so its operating assets can be viewed as permanent. In addition, Nicholson's accounts payable of $425,000 are stable over time. Thus Nicholson has a permanent investment in operating assets of $1,625,000 ($50,000 + $1,250,0000 + $750,000 – $425,000). That amount would also equal its permanent funding requirement.

In contrast, Semper Pump Company, which produces bicycle pumps, has seasonal funding needs. Semper has seasonal sales, with its peak sales driven by the summertime purchases of bicycle pumps. Semper holds, at minimum, $25,000 in cash and marketable securities, $100,000 in inventory, and $60,000 in accounts receivable. At peak times, Semper's inventory increases to $750,000, and its accounts receivable increase to $400,000. To capture production efficiencies, Semper produces pumps at a constant rate throughout the year. Thus accounts payable remain at $50,000 throughout the year. Accordingly, Semper has a permanent funding requirement for its minimum level of operating assets of $135,000 ($25,000 + $100,000 + $60,000 – $50,000) and peak seasonal funding requirements (in excess of its permanent need) of $990,000 [($25,000 + $750,000 + $400,000 – $50,000) – $135,000]. Semper's total funding requirements for operating assets vary from a minimum of $135,000 (permanent) to a seasonal peak of $1,125,000 ($135,000 + $990,000). Figure 13.2 depicts these needs over time.

Aggressive versus Conservative Seasonal Funding Strategies

aggressive funding strategy A funding strategy under which the firm funds its seasonal requirements with short-term debt and its permanent requirements with long-term debt.

conservative funding strategy A funding strategy under which the firm funds both its seasonal and its permanent requirements with long-term debt.

Short-term funds are typically less expensive than long-term funds. (The yield curve is typically upward-sloping.) However, long-term funds allow the firm to lock in its cost of funds over a period of time and thus avoid the risk of increases in short-term interest rates. Also, long-term funding ensures that the required funds are available to the firm when needed. Short-term funding exposes the firm to the risk that it may not be able to obtain the funds needed to cover its seasonal peaks. Under an **aggressive funding strategy,** the firm funds its seasonal requirements with short-term debt and its permanent requirements with long-term debt. Under a **conservative funding strategy,** the firm funds both its seasonal and its permanent requirements with long-term debt.

EXAMPLE

Semper Pump Company has a permanent funding requirement of $135,000 in operating assets and seasonal funding requirements that vary between $0 and $990,000 and average $101,250. If Semper can borrow short-term funds at 6.25% and long-term funds at 8%, and if it can earn 5% on the investment of

FIGURE 13.2 **Semper Pump Company's Total Funding Requirements**
Semper Pump Company's peak funds need is $1,125,000, and its minimum need is $135,000

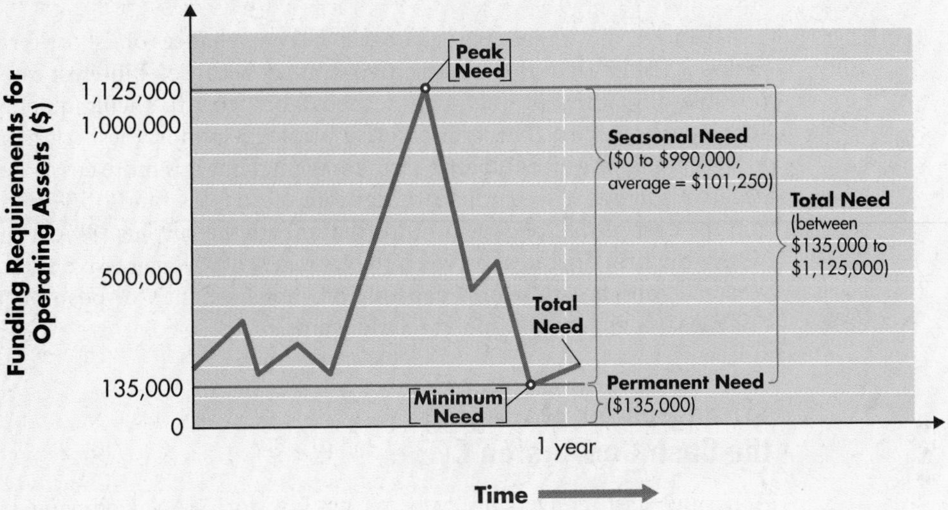

any surplus balances, then the annual cost of an aggressive strategy for seasonal funding will be

	Cost of short-term financing	$= 0.0625 \times \$101{,}250 =$	$ 6,328.13
+	Cost of long-term financing	$= 0.0800 \times 135{,}000 =$	10,800.00
−	Earnings on surplus balances[3]	$= 0.0500 \times 0 =$	0
	Total cost of aggressive strategy		$17,128.13

Alternatively, Semper can choose a conservative strategy, under which surplus cash balances are fully invested. (In Figure 13.2, this surplus will be the difference between the peak need of $1,125,000 and the total need, which varies between $135,000 and $1,125,000 during the year.) The cost of the conservative strategy will be

	Cost of short-term financing	$= 0.0625 \times \$ \quad 0 =$	$ 0
+	Cost of long-term financing	$= 0.0800 \times 1{,}125{,}000 =$	90,000.00
−	Earnings on surplus balances[4]	$= 0.0500 \times 888{,}750 =$	44,437.50
	Total cost of conservative strategy		$45,562.50

It is clear from these calculations that for Semper, the aggressive strategy is far less expensive than the conservative strategy. However, it is equally clear

3. Because under this strategy the amount of financing exactly equals the estimated funding need, no surplus balances exist.

4. The average surplus balance would be calculated by subtracting the sum of the permanent need ($135,000) and the average seasonal need ($101,250) from the seasonal peak need ($1,125,000) to get $888,750 ($1,125,000 − $135,000 − $101,250). This represents the surplus amount of financing that on average could be invested in short-term vehicles that earn a 5% annual return.

that Semper has substantial peak-season operating-asset needs and that it must have adequate funding available to meet the peak needs and ensure ongoing operations.

Clearly, the aggressive strategy's heavy reliance on short-term financing makes it riskier than the conservative strategy because of interest rate swings and possible difficulties in obtaining needed short-term financing quickly when seasonal peaks occur. The conservative strategy avoids these risks through the locked-in interest rate and long-term financing, but it is more costly because of the negative spread between the earnings rate on surplus funds (5% in the example) and the cost of the long-term funds that create the surplus (8% in the example). Where the firm operates, between the extremes of the aggressive and conservative seasonal funding strategies, depends on management's disposition toward risk and the strength of its banking relationships.

Strategies for Managing the Cash Conversion Cycle

A positive cash conversion cycle, as we saw for MAX Company in the earlier example, means the firm must use negotiated liabilities (such as bank loans) to support its operating assets. Negotiated liabilities carry an explicit cost, so the firm benefits by minimizing their use in supporting operating assets. Minimum negotiated liabilities can be realized through application of the following strategies:

1. *Turn over inventory as quickly as possible* without stockouts that result in lost sales.
2. *Collect accounts receivable as quickly as possible* without losing sales from high-pressure collection techniques.
3. *Manage mail, processing, and clearing time* to reduce them when collecting from customers and to increase them when paying suppliers.
4. *Pay accounts payable as slowly as possible* without damaging the firm's credit rating.

Techniques for implementing these four strategies are the focus of the remainder of this chapter and the following chapter.

Review Questions

13–4 What is the difference between the firm's *operating cycle* and its *cash conversion cycle?*

13–5 Why is it helpful to divide the funding needs of a seasonal business into its permanent and seasonal funding requirements when developing a funding strategy?

13–6 What are the benefits, costs, and risks of an *aggressive funding strategy* and of a *conservative funding strategy?* Under which strategy is the borrowing often in excess of the actual need?

13–7 Why is it important for a firm to minimize the length of its cash conversion cycle?

LG3

Inventory Management

The first component of the cash conversion cycle is the average age of inventory. The objective for managing inventory, as noted above, is to turn over inventory as quickly as possible without losing sales from stockouts. The financial manager tends to act as an advisor or "watchdog" in matters concerning inventory; he or she does not have direct control over inventory but does provide input to the inventory management process.

Differing Viewpoints About Inventory Level

Differing viewpoints about appropriate inventory levels commonly exist among a firm's finance, marketing, manufacturing, and purchasing managers. Each views inventory levels in light of his or her own objectives. The *financial manager's* general disposition toward inventory levels is to keep them low, to ensure that the firm's money is not being unwisely invested in excess resources. The *marketing manager,* on the other hand, would like to have large inventories of the firm's finished products. This would ensure that all orders could be filled quickly, eliminating the need for backorders due to stockouts.

The *manufacturing manager's* major responsibility is to implement the production plan so that it results in the desired amount of finished goods of acceptable quality at a low cost. In fulfilling this role, the manufacturing manager would keep raw materials inventories high to avoid production delays. He or she also would favor large production runs for the sake of lower unit production costs, which would result in high finished goods inventories.

The *purchasing manager* is concerned solely with the raw materials inventories. He or she must have on hand, in the correct quantities at the desired times and at a favorable price, whatever raw materials are required by production. Without proper control, in order to get quantity discounts or in anticipation of rising prices or a shortage of certain materials, the purchasing manager may purchase larger quantities of resources than are actually needed at the time.

Common Techniques for Managing Inventory

Numerous techniques are available for effectively managing the firm's inventory. Here we briefly consider four commonly used techniques.

The ABC System

ABC inventory system
Inventory management technique that divides inventory into three groups—A, B, and C, in descending order of importance and level of monitoring, on the basis of the dollar investment in each.

A firm using the **ABC inventory system** divides its inventory into three groups: A, B, and C. The A group includes those items with the largest dollar investment. Typically, this group consists of 20 percent of the firm's inventory items but 80 percent of its investment in inventory. The B group consists of items that account for the next largest investment in inventory. The C group consists of a large number of items that require a relatively small investment.

The inventory group of each item determines the item's level of monitoring. The A group items receive the most intense monitoring because of the high dollar investment. Typically, A group items are tracked on a perpetual inventory system that allows daily verification of each item's inventory level. B group items are frequently controlled through periodic, perhaps weekly, checking of their levels. C group items are monitored with unsophisticated techniques, such as the two-bin method. With the **two-bin method,** the item is stored in two bins. As an item is needed, inventory is removed from the first bin. When that bin is empty, an order is placed to refill the first bin while inventory is drawn from the second bin. The second bin is used until empty, and so on.

two-bin method
Unsophisticated inventory-monitoring technique that is typically applied to C group items and involves reordering inventory when one of two bins is empty.

The large dollar investment in A and B group items suggests the need for a better method of inventory management than the ABC system. The EOQ model, discussed next, is an appropriate model for the management of A and B group items.

The Economic Order Quantity (EOQ) Model

One of the most common techniques for determining the optimal order size for inventory items is the **economic order quantity (EOQ) model.** The EOQ model considers various costs of inventory and then determines what order size minimizes total inventory cost. EOQ assumes that the relevant costs of inventory can be divided into *order costs* and *carrying costs.* (The model excludes the actual cost of the inventory item.) Each of them has certain key components and characteristics.

economic order quantity (EOQ) model
Inventory management technique for determining an item's optimal order size, which is the size that minimizes the total of its *order costs* and *carrying costs.*

Order costs include the fixed clerical costs of placing and receiving orders: the cost of writing a purchase order, of processing the resulting paperwork, and of receiving an order and checking it against the invoice. Order costs are stated in dollars per order.

order costs
The fixed clerical costs of placing and receiving an inventory order.

Carrying costs are the variable costs per unit of holding an item of inventory for a specific period of time. Carrying costs include storage costs, insurance costs, the costs of deterioration and obsolescence, and the opportunity or financial cost of having funds invested in inventory. These costs are stated in dollars per unit per period.

carrying costs
The variable costs per unit of holding an item in inventory for a specific period of time.

Order costs decrease as the size of the order increases. Carrying costs, however, increase with increases in the order size. The EOQ model analyzes the tradeoff between order costs and carrying costs to determine the *order quantity that minimizes the total inventory cost.*

Mathematical Development of EOQ A formula can be developed for determining the firm's EOQ for a given inventory item, where

S = usage in units per period
O = order cost per order
C = carrying cost per unit per period
Q = order quantity in units

The first step is to derive the cost functions for order cost and carrying cost. The order cost can be expressed as the product of the cost per order and the number of orders. Because the number of orders equals the usage during the period divided by the order quantity (S/Q), the order cost can be expressed as follows:

$$\text{Order cost} = O \times S/Q \qquad (13.4)$$

The carrying cost is defined as the cost of carrying a unit of inventory per period multiplied by the firm's average inventory. The average inventory is the order quantity divided by 2 ($Q/2$), because inventory is assumed to be depleted at a constant rate. Thus carrying cost can be expressed as follows:

$$\text{Carrying cost} = C \times Q/2 \tag{13.5}$$

total cost of inventory
The sum of order costs and carrying costs of inventory.

The firm's **total cost of inventory** is found by summing the order cost and the carrying cost. Thus the total cost function is

$$\text{Total cost} = (O \times S/Q) + (C \times Q/2) \tag{13.6}$$

Because the EOQ is defined as the order quantity that minimizes the total cost function, we must solve the total cost function for the EOQ. The resulting equation is

$$\text{EOQ} = \sqrt{\frac{2 \times S \times O}{C}} \tag{13.7}$$

Although the EOQ model has weaknesses, it is certainly better than subjective decision making. Despite the fact that the use of the EOQ model is outside the control of the financial manager, the financial manager must be aware of its utility and must provide certain inputs, specifically with respect to inventory carrying costs.

reorder point
The point at which to reorder inventory, expressed as days of lead time × daily usage.

Reorder Point Once the firm has determined its economic order quantity, it must determine when to place an order. The **reorder point** reflects the firm's daily usage of the inventory item and the number of days needed to place and receive an order. Assuming that inventory is used at a constant rate, the formula for the reorder point is

$$\text{Reorder point} = \text{Days of lead time} \times \text{Daily usage} \tag{13.8}$$

safety stock
Extra inventory that is held to prevent stockouts of important items.

For example, if a firm knows it takes 3 days to place and receive an order, and if it uses 15 units per day of the inventory item, then the reorder point is 45 units of inventory (3 days × 15 units/day). Thus, as soon as the item's inventory level falls to the reorder point (45 units, in this case) an order will be placed at the item's EOQ. If the estimates of lead time and usage are correct, then the order will arrive exactly as the inventory level reaches zero. However, lead times and usage rates are not precise, so most firms hold **safety stock** (extra inventory) to prevent stockouts of important items.

EXAMPLE

MAX Company has an A group inventory item that is vital to the production process. This item costs \$1,500, and MAX uses 1,100 units of the item per year. MAX wants to determine its optimal order strategy for the item. To calculate the EOQ, we need the following inputs:

$$\text{Order cost per order} = \$150$$
$$\text{Carrying cost per unit per year} = \$200$$

Substituting into Equation 13.7, we get

$$\text{EOQ} = \sqrt{\frac{2 \times 1{,}100 \times \$150}{\$200}} \approx \underline{\underline{41}} \text{ units}$$

The reorder point for MAX depends on the number of days MAX operates per year. Assuming that MAX operates 250 days per year and uses 1,100 units of this item, its daily usage is 4.4 units $(1{,}100 \div 250)$. If its lead time is 2 days and MAX wants to maintain a safety stock of 4 units, the reorder point for this item is 12.8 units $[(2 \times 4.4) + 4]$. However, orders are made only in whole units, so the order is placed when the inventory falls to 13 units.

The firm's goal for inventory is to turn it over as quickly as possible without stockouts. Inventory turnover is best calculated by dividing cost of goods sold by average inventory. The EOQ model determines the optimal order size and, indirectly, through the assumption of constant usage, the average inventory. Thus the EOQ model determines the firm's optimal inventory turnover rate, given the firm's specific costs of inventory.

Just-in-Time (JIT) System

just-in-time (JIT) system
Inventory management technique that minimizes inventory investment by having materials arrive at exactly the time they are needed for production.

The **just-in-time (JIT) system** is used to minimize inventory investment. The philosophy is that materials should arrive at exactly the time they are needed for production. Ideally, the firm would have only work-in-process inventory. Because its objective is to minimize inventory investment, a JIT system uses no (or very little) safety stock. Extensive coordination among the firm's employees, its suppliers, and shipping companies must exist to ensure that material inputs arrive on time. Failure of materials to arrive on time results in a shutdown of the production line until the materials arrive. Likewise, a JIT system requires high-quality parts from suppliers. When quality problems arise, production must be stopped until the problems are resolved.

The goal of the JIT system is manufacturing efficiency. It uses inventory as a tool for attaining efficiency by emphasizing quality of the materials used and their timely delivery. When JIT is working properly, it forces process inefficiencies to surface.

Materials Requirement Planning (MRP) System

materials requirement planning (MRP) system
Inventory management technique that applies EOQ concepts and a computer to compare production needs to available inventory balances and determine when orders should be placed for various items on a product's *bill of materials.*

Many companies use a **materials requirement planning (MRP) system** to determine what materials to order and when to order them. MRP applies EOQ concepts to determine how much to order. By means of a computer, it simulates each product's bill of materials, inventory status, and manufacturing process. *The bill of materials* is simply a list of all the parts and materials that go into making the finished product. For a given production plan, the computer simulates materials requirements by comparing production needs to available inventory balances. On the basis of the time it takes for a product that is in process to move through the various production stages and the lead time required to get materials, the MRP system determines when orders should be placed for the various items on the bill of materials.

The advantage of the MRP system is that it forces the firm to consider its inventory needs more carefully. The objective is to lower the firm's inventory investment without impairing production. If the firm's opportunity cost of capital for investments of equal risk is 15 percent, every dollar of investment released from inventory increases before-tax profits by $0.15.

International Inventory Management

International inventory management is typically much more complicated for exporters in general, and for multinational companies in particular, than for purely domestic firms. The production and manufacturing economies of scale that might be expected from selling products globally may prove elusive if products must be tailored for individual local markets, as very frequently happens, or if actual production takes place in factories around the world. When raw materials, intermediate goods, or finished products must be transported long distances—particularly by ocean shipping—there will inevitably be more delays, confusion, damage, theft, and other difficulties than occur in a one-country operation. The international inventory manager therefore puts a premium on flexibility. He or she is usually less concerned about ordering the economically optimal quantity of inventory than about making sure that sufficient quantities of inventory are delivered where they are needed, when they are needed, and in a condition to be used as planned.

Review Questions

13–8 What are likely to be the viewpoints of each of the following managers about the levels of the various types of inventory: finance, marketing, manufacturing, and purchasing? Why is inventory an investment?

13–9 Briefly describe each of the following techniques for managing inventory: ABC system, economic order quantity (EOQ) model, just-in-time (JIT) system, and materials requirement planning (MRP) system.

13–10 What factors make managing inventory more difficult for exporters and multinational companies?

LG4

Accounts Receivable Management

The second component of the cash conversion cycle is the average collection period. This period is the average length of time from a sale on credit until the payment becomes usable funds for the firm. The average collection period has two parts. The first part is the time from the sale until the customer mails the payment. The second part is the time from when the payment is mailed until the firm has the collected funds in its bank account. The first part of the average collection period involves managing the credit available to the firm's customers, and the second part involves collecting and processing payments. This section of the chapter discusses the firm's accounts receivable credit management.

The objective for managing accounts receivable is to collect accounts receivable as quickly as possible without losing sales from high-pressure collection techniques. Accomplishing this goal encompasses three topics: (1) credit selection and standards, (2) credit terms, and (3) credit monitoring.

Credit Selection and Standards

credit standards
The firm's minimum requirements for extending credit to a customer.

Credit selection involves application of techniques for determining which customers should receive credit. This process involves evaluating the customer's creditworthiness and comparing it to the firm's **credit standards,** its minimum requirements for extending credit to a customer.

Five C's of Credit

five C's of credit
The five key dimensions—character, capacity, capital, collateral, and conditions—used by credit analysts to provide a framework for in-depth credit analysis.

One popular credit selection technique is the **five C's of credit,** which provides a framework for in-depth credit analysis. Because of the time and expense involved, this credit selection method is used for large-dollar credit requests. The five C's are

1. *Character:* The applicant's record of meeting past obligations.
2. *Capacity:* The applicant's ability to repay the requested credit, as judged in terms of financial statement analysis focused on cash flows available to repay debt obligations.
3. *Capital:* The applicant's debt relative to equity.
4. *Collateral:* The amount of assets the applicant has available for use in securing the credit. The larger the amount of available assets, the greater the chance that a firm will recover funds if the applicant defaults.
5. *Conditions:* Current general and industry-specific economic conditions, and any unique conditions surrounding a specific transaction.

Analysis via the five C's of credit does not yield a specific accept/reject decision, so its use requires an analyst experienced in reviewing and granting credit requests. Application of this framework tends to ensure that the firm's credit customers will pay, without being pressured, within the stated credit terms.

Credit Scoring

credit scoring
A credit selection method commonly used with high-volume/small-dollar credit requests; relies on a credit score determined by applying statistically derived weights to a credit applicant's scores on key financial and credit characteristics.

Credit scoring is a method of credit selection that is commonly used with high-volume/small-dollar credit requests. **Credit scoring** applies statistically derived weights for key financial and credit characteristics to predict whether a credit applicant will pay the requested credit in a timely fashion. Simply stated, the procedure results in a score that measures the applicant's overall credit strength, and the score is used to make the accept/reject decision for granting the applicant credit. Credit scoring is most commonly used by large credit card operations, such as those of banks, oil companies, and department stores. The purpose of credit scoring is to make a relatively informed credit decision quickly and inexpensively, recognizing that the cost of a single bad scoring decision is small. However, if bad debts from scoring decisions increase, then the scoring system must be re-evaluated. For a demonstration of credit scoring, including use of a spreadsheet for that purpose, see the book's Web site at *www.aw.com/gitman.*

Changing Credit Standards

The firm sometimes will contemplate changing its credit standards in order to improve its returns and create greater value for its owners. To demonstrate, consider the following changes and effects on profits expected to result from the *relaxation* of credit standards.

Effects of Relaxation of Credit Standards

Variable	Direction of change	Effect on profits
Sales volume	Increase	Positive
Investment in accounts receivable	Increase	Negative
Bad-debt expenses	Increase	Negative

If credit standards were tightened, the opposite effects would be expected.

EXAMPLE Dodd Tool, a manufacturer of lathe tools, is currently selling a product for \$10 per unit. Sales (all on credit) for last year were 60,000 units. The variable cost per unit is \$6. The firm's total fixed costs are \$120,000.

The firm is currently contemplating a *relaxation of credit standards* that is expected to result in the following: a 5% increase in unit sales to 63,000 units; an increase in the average collection period from 30 days (its current level) to 45 days; an increase in bad-debt expenses from 1% of sales (the current level) to 2%. The firm's required return on equal-risk investments, which is the opportunity cost of tying up funds in accounts receivable, is 15%.

To determine whether to relax its credit standards, Dodd Tool must calculate its effect on the firm's additional profit contribution from sales, the cost of the marginal investment in accounts receivable, and the cost of marginal bad debts.

Additional Profit Contribution from Sales Because fixed costs are "sunk" and therefore are unaffected by a change in the sales level, the only cost relevant to a change in sales is variable costs. Sales are expected to increase by 5%, or 3,000 units. The profit contribution per unit will equal the difference between the sale price per unit (\$10) and the variable cost per unit (\$6). The profit contribution per unit therefore will be \$4. The total additional profit contribution from sales will be \$12,000 (3,000 units × \$4 per unit).

Cost of the Marginal Investment in Accounts Receivable To determine the cost of the marginal investment in accounts receivable, Dodd must find the difference between the cost of carrying receivables under the two credit standards. Because its concern is only with the out-of-pocket costs, *the relevant cost is the variable cost.* The average investment in accounts receivable can be calculated by using the following formula:

$$\text{Average investment in accounts receivable} = \frac{\text{Total variable cost of annual sales}}{\text{Turnover of accounts receivable}} \qquad (13.9)$$

where

$$\text{Turnover of accounts receivable} = \frac{360}{\text{Average collection period}}$$

The total variable cost of annual sales under the present and proposed plans can be found as follows, using the variable cost per unit of $6.

Total variable cost of annual sales

Under present plan: ($6 × 60,000 units) = $360,000
Under proposed plan: ($6 × 63,000 units) = $378,000

The turnover of accounts receivable is the number of times each year that the firm's accounts receivable are actually turned into cash. It is found by dividing the average collection period into 360 (the number of days assumed in a year).

Turnover of accounts receivable

$$\text{Under present plan: } \frac{360}{30} = 12$$

$$\text{Under present plan: } \frac{360}{45} = 8$$

By substituting the cost and turnover data just calculated into Equation 13.9 for each case, we get the following average investments in accounts receivable:

Average investment in accounts receivable

$$\text{Under present plan: } \frac{\$360{,}000}{12} = \$30{,}000$$

$$\text{Under proposed plan: } \frac{\$378{,}000}{8} = \$47{,}250$$

The marginal investment in accounts receivable and its cost are calculated as follows:

Cost of marginal investment in accounts receivable

Average investment under proposed plan	$47,250
− Average investment under present plan	30,000
Marginal investment in accounts receivable	$17,250
× Required return on investment	0.15
Cost of marginal investment in A/R	$ 2,588

The resulting value of $2,588 is considered a cost because it represents the maximum amount that could have been earned on the $17,250 had it been placed in the best equal-risk investment alternative available at the firm's required return on investment of 15%.

Cost of Marginal Bad Debts The cost of marginal bad debts is found by taking the difference between the levels of bad debts before and after the proposed relaxation of credit standards.

Cost of marginal bad debts

Under proposed plan: $(0.02 \times \$10/\text{unit} \times 63{,}000 \text{ units})$ =	$12,600
Under present plan: $(0.01 \times \$10/\text{unit} \times 60{,}000 \text{ units})$ =	6,000
Cost of marginal bad debts	$ 6,600

Note that the bad-debt costs are calculated by using the sale price per unit ($10) to deduct not just the true loss of variable cost ($6) that results when a customer fails to pay its account, but also the profit contribution per unit (in this case $4) that is included in the "additional profit contribution from sales." Thus the resulting cost of marginal bad debts is $6,600.

Making the Credit Standard Decision To decide whether to relax its credit standards, the firm must compare the additional profit contribution from sales to the added costs of the marginal investment in accounts receivable and marginal bad debts. If the additional profit contribution is greater than marginal costs, credit standards should be relaxed.

EXAMPLE The results and key calculations related to Dodd Tool's decision whether to relax its credit standards are summarized in Table 13.2. The net addition to total profits resulting from such an action will be $2,812 per year. Therefore, the firm *should* relax its credits standards as proposed.

TABLE 13.2 The Effects on Dodd Tool of a Relaxation of Credit Standards

Additional profit contribution from sales		
[3,000 units × ($10 − $6)]		$12,000
Cost of marginal investment in A/R[a]		
Average investment under proposed plan:		
$\frac{\$6 \times 63{,}000}{8} = \frac{\$378{,}000}{8}$	$47,250	
Average investment under present plan:		
$\frac{\$6 \times 60{,}000}{12} = \frac{\$360{,}000}{12}$	30,000	
Marginal investment in A/R	$17,250	
Cost of marginal investment in A/R (0.15 × $17,250)		($ 2,588)
Cost of marginal bad debts		
Bad debts under proposed plan (0.02 × $10 × 63,000)	$12,600	
Bad debts under present plan (0.01 × $10 × 60,000)	6,000	
Cost of marginal bad debts		($ 6,600)
Net profit from implementation of proposed plan		$ 2,812

[a]The denominators 8 and 12 in the calculation of the average investment in accounts receivable under the proposed and present plans are the accounts receivable turnovers for each of these plans (360/45 = 8 and 360/30 = 12).

The procedure described here for evaluating a proposed change in credit standards is also commonly used to evaluate other changes in the management of accounts receivable. If Dodd Tool had been contemplating tightening its credit standards, for example, the cost would have been a reduction in the profit contribution from sales, and the return would have been from reductions in the cost of the investment in accounts receivable and in the cost of bad debts. Another application of this procedure is demonstrated later in the chapter.

Managing International Credit

Credit management is difficult enough for managers of purely domestic companies, and these tasks become much more complex for companies that operate internationally. This is partly because (as we have seen before) international operations typically expose a firm to *exchange rate risk*. It is also due to the dangers and delays involved in shipping goods long distances and in having to cross at least two international borders.

Exports of finished goods are usually priced in the currency of the importer's local market; most commodities, on the other hand, are priced in dollars. Therefore, a U.S. company that sells a product in Japan, for example, would have to price that product in Japanese yen and extend credit to a Japanese wholesaler in the local currency (yen). If the yen *depreciates* against the dollar before the U.S. exporter collects on its account receivable, the U.S. company experiences an exchange rate loss; the yen collected are worth fewer dollars than expected at the time the sale was made. Of course, the dollar could just as easily depreciate against the yen, yielding an exchange rate gain to the U.S. exporter. Most companies fear the loss more than they welcome the gain.

For a major currency such as the Japanese yen, the exporter can *hedge* against this risk by using the currency futures, forward, or options markets, but it is costly to do so, particularly for relatively small amounts. If the exporter is selling to a customer in a developing country—where 40 percent of U.S. exports are now sold—there will probably be no effective instrument available for protecting against exchange rate risk at any price. This risk may be further magnified because credit standards may be much lower (and acceptable collection techniques much different) in developing countries than in the United States. Although it may seem tempting just "not to bother" with exporting, U.S. companies no longer can concede foreign markets to international rivals. These export sales, if carefully monitored and (where possible) effectively hedged against exchange rate risk, often prove to be very profitable.

credit terms
The terms of sale for customers who have been extended credit by the firm.

cash discount
A percentage deduction from the purchase price; available to the credit customer who pays its account within a specified time.

Credit Terms

Credit terms are the terms of sale for customers who have been extended credit by the firm. Terms of *net 30* mean the customer has 30 days from the beginning of the credit period (typically *end of month* or *date of invoice)* to pay the full invoice amount. Some firms offer **cash discounts**, percentage deductions from the purchase price for paying within a specified time. For example, terms of *2/10 net*

30 mean the customer can take a 2 percent discount from the invoice amount if the payment is made within 10 days of the beginning of the credit period or can pay the full amount of the invoice within 30 days.

A firm's regular credit terms are strongly influenced by the firm's business. For example, a firm selling perishable items will have very short credit terms, because its items have little long-term collateral value; a firm in a seasonal business may tailor its terms to fit the industry cycles. A firm wants its regular credit terms to conform to its industry's standards. If its terms are more restrictive than its competitors', it will lose business; if its terms are less restrictive than its competitors', it will attract poor-quality customers that probably could not pay under the standard industry terms. The bottom line is that a firm should compete on the basis of quality and price of its product and service offerings, not its credit terms. Accordingly, the firm's regular credit terms should match the industry standards, but individual customer terms should reflect the riskiness of the customer.

Cash Discount

Including a cash discount in the credit terms is a popular way to achieve the goal of speeding up collections without putting pressure on customers. The cash discount provides an incentive for customers to pay sooner. By speeding collections, the discount decreases the firm's investment in accounts receivable (which is the objective), but it also decreases the per-unit profit. Additionally, initiating a cash discount should reduce bad debts because customers will pay sooner, and it should increase sales volume because customers who take the discount pay a lower price for the product. Accordingly, firms that consider offering a cash discount must perform a benefit–cost analysis to determine whether extending a cash discount is profitable.

EXAMPLE ▼ MAX Company has an average collection period of 40 days (turnover = 360/40 = 9). In accordance with the firm's credit terms of net 30, this period is divided into 32 days until the customers place their payments in the mail (not everyone pays within 30 days) and 8 days to receive, process, and collect payments once they are mailed. MAX is considering initiating a cash discount by changing its credit terms from net 30 to 2/10 net 30. The firm expects this change to reduce the amount of time until the payments are placed in the mail, resulting in an average collection period of 25 days (turnover = 360/25 = 14.4).

As noted earlier in the EOQ example (page 503), MAX has a raw material with current annual usage of 1,100 units. Each finished product produced requires 1 unit of this raw material at a variable cost of $1,500 per unit, incurs another $800 of variable cost in the production process, and sells for $3,000 on terms of net 30. MAX estimates that 80% of its customers will take the 2% discount and that offering the discount will increase sales of the finished product by 50 units (from 1,100 to 1,150 units) per year but will not alter its bad-debt percentage. MAX's opportunity cost of funds invested in accounts receivable is 14%. Should MAX offer the proposed cash discount? An analysis similar to that demonstrated earlier for the credit standard decision, presented in Table 13.3, shows a net loss

TABLE 13.3 Analysis of Initiating a Cash Discount for MAX Company

Additional profit contribution from sales		
[50 units × ($3,000 − $2,300)]		$35,000
Cost of marginal investment in A/R[a]		
Average investment presently (w/o discount):		
$\frac{\$2{,}300 \times 1{,}100 \text{ units}}{9} = \frac{\$2{,}530{,}000}{9}$	$281,111	
Average investment with proposed cash discount:[b]		
$\frac{\$2{,}300 \times 1{,}150 \text{ units}}{14.4} = \frac{\$2{,}645{,}000}{14.4}$	183,681	
Reduction in accounts receivable investment	$ 97,430	
Cost savings from reduced investments in accounts receivable (0.14 × $97,430)[c]		$13,640
Cost of cash discount (0.02 × 0.80 × 1,150 × $3,000)		($55,200)
Net profit from initiation of proposed cash discount		($ 6,560)

[a]In analyzing the investment in accounts receivable, we use the variable cost of the product sold ($1,500 raw materials cost + $800 production cost = $2,300 unit variable cost) instead of the sale price, because the variable cost is a better indicator of the firm's investment.

[b]The average investment in accounts receivable with the proposed cash discount is estimated to be tied up for an average of 25 days instead of the 40 days under the original terms.

[c]MAX's opportunity cost of funds is 14%.

from the cash discount of $6,560. Thus *MAX should not initiate the proposed cash discount.* However, other discounts may be advantageous.

Cash Discount Period

cash discount period
The number of days after the beginning of the credit period during which the cash discount is available.

The **cash discount period,** the number of days after the beginning of the credit period during which the cash discount is available, can be changed by the financial manager. The net effect of changes in this period is difficult to analyze because of the nature of the forces involved. For example, if a firm were to increase its cash discount period by 10 days (for example, changing its credit terms from 2/10 net 30 to 2/20 net 30), the following changes would be expected to occur: (1) Sales would increase, positively affecting profit. (2) Bad-debt expenses would decrease, positively affecting profit. (3) The profit per unit would decrease as a result of more people taking the discount, negatively affecting profit. The difficulty for the financial manager lies in assessing what impact an increase in the cash discount period would have on the firm's investment in accounts receivable. This investment will decrease because of non–discount takers now paying earlier. However, the investment in accounts receivable will increase for two reasons: (1) Discount takers will still get the discount but will pay later, and (2) new customers attracted by the new policy will result in new accounts receivable. If the firm were to decrease the cash discount period, the effects would be the opposite of those just described.

Credit Period

credit period
The number of days after the beginning of the credit period until full payment of the account is due.

Changes in the **credit period,** the number of days after the beginning of the credit period until full payment of the account is due, also affect a firm's profitability. For example, increasing a firm's credit period from net 30 days to net 45 days should increase sales, positively affecting profit. But both the investment in accounts receivable and bad-debt expenses would also increase, negatively affecting profit. The increased investment in accounts receivable would result from both more sales and generally slower pay, on average, as a result of the longer credit period. The increase in bad-debt expenses results from the fact that the longer the credit period, the more time available for a firm to fail, making it unable to pay its accounts payable. A decrease in the length of the credit period is likely to have the opposite effects. Note that the variables affected by an increase in the credit period behave in the same way they would have if the credit standards had been relaxed, as demonstrated earlier in Table 13.2.

Credit Monitoring

credit monitoring
The ongoing review of a firm's accounts receivable to determine whether customers are paying according to the stated credit terms.

The final issue a firm should consider in its accounts receivable management is credit monitoring. **Credit monitoring** is an ongoing review of the firm's accounts receivable to determine whether customers are paying according to the stated credit terms. If they are not paying in a timely manner, credit monitoring will alert the firm to the problem. Slow payments are costly to a firm because they lengthen the average collection period and thus increase the firm's investment in accounts receivable. Two frequently cited techniques for credit monitoring are average collection period and aging of accounts receivable. In addition, a number of popular collection techniques are used by firms.

Average Collection Period

The *average collection period* is the second component of the cash conversion cycle. As noted in Chapter 2, it is the average number of days that credit sales are outstanding. The average collection period has two components: (1) the time from sale until the customer places the payment in the mail and (2) the time to receive, process, and collect the payment once it has been mailed by the customer. The formula for finding the average collection period is

$$\text{Average collection period} = \frac{\text{Accounts receivable}}{\text{Average sales per day}} \qquad (13.10)$$

Assuming receipt, processing, and collection time is constant, the average collection period tells the firm, on average, when its customers pay their accounts.

Knowing its average collection period enables the firm to determine whether there is a general problem with accounts receivable. For example, a firm that has credit terms of net 30 would expect its average collection period (minus receipt, processing, and collection time) to equal about 30 days. If the actual collection period is significantly greater than 30 days, the firm has reason to review its credit operations. If the firm's average collection period is increasing over time, it has cause for concern about its accounts receivable management. A first step in analyzing an accounts receivable problem is to "age" the accounts receivable. By this process the firm can determine whether the problem exists in its accounts receivable in general or is attributable to a few specific accounts.

Aging of Accounts Receivable

aging of accounts receivable
A credit-monitoring technique that uses a schedule that indicates the percentages of the total accounts receivable balance that have been outstanding for specified periods of time.

The **aging of accounts receivable** requires the firm's accounts receivable to be broken down into groups on the basis of the time of origin. The breakdown is typically made on a month-by-month basis, going back 3 or 4 months. The result is a schedule that indicates the percentages of the total accounts receivable balance that have been outstanding for specified periods of time. Its purpose is to enable the firm to pinpoint problems.

If a firm with terms of net 30 has an average collection period (minus receipt, processing, and collection time) of 50 days, the firm will want to age its accounts receivable. If the majority of accounts are 2 months old, then the firm has a general problem and should review its accounts receivable operations. If the aging shows that most accounts are collected in about 35 days and a few accounts are way past due, then the firm should analyze and pursue collection of those specific past-due accounts.

Popular Collection Techniques

A number of collection techniques, ranging from letters to legal action, are employed. As an account becomes more and more overdue, the collection effort becomes more personal and more intense. In Table 13.4 the popular collection

TABLE 13.4 Popular Collection Techniques

Technique[a]	Brief description
Letters	After a certain number of days, the firm sends a polite letter reminding the customer of the overdue account. If the account is not paid within a certain period after this letter has been sent, a second, more demanding letter is sent.
Telephone calls	If letters prove unsuccessful, a telephone call may be made to the customer to request immediate payment. If the customer has a reasonable excuse, arrangements may be made to extend the payment period. A call from the seller's attorney may be used.
Personal visits	This technique is much more common at the consumer credit level, but it may also be effectively employed by industrial suppliers. Sending a local salesperson or a collection person to confront the customer can be very effective. Payment may be made on the spot.
Collection agencies	A firm can turn uncollectible accounts over to a collection agency or an attorney for collection. The fees for this service are typically quite high; the firm may receive less than 50 cents on the dollar from accounts collected in this way.
Legal action	Legal action is the most stringent step, an alternative to the use of a collection agency. Not only is direct legal action expensive, but it may force the debtor into bankruptcy without guaranteeing the ultimate receipt of the overdue amount.

[a]The techniques are listed in the order in which they are typically followed in the collection process.

techniques are listed, and briefly described, in the order typically followed in the collection process.

Review Questions

13–11 What is the role of the *five C's of credit* in the credit selection activity?

13–12 Explain why *credit scoring* is typically applied to consumer credit decisions rather than to mercantile credit decisions.

13–13 What are the basic tradeoffs in a *tightening* of credit standards?

13–14 Why are the risks involved in international credit management more complex than those associated with purely domestic credit sales?

13–15 Why do a firm's regular credit terms typically conform to those of its industry?

13–16 Why should a firm actively monitor the accounts receivable of its credit customers? How do the techniques of *average collection period* and *aging of accounts receivable* work?

LG6

Management of Receipts and Disbursements

As discussed in the previous section, the average collection period (the second component of the cash conversion cycle) has two parts: (1) the time from sale until the customer mails the payment and (2) the receipt, processing, and collection time. The third component of the cash conversion cycle, the average payment period, also has two parts: (1) the time from purchase of goods on account until the firm mails its payment and (2) the receipt, processing, and collection time required by the firm's suppliers. The receipt, processing, and collection time for the firm, both from its customers and to its suppliers, is the focus of receipts and disbursements management.

Float

float
Funds that have been sent by the payer but are not yet usable funds to the payee.

mail float
The time delay between when payment is placed in the mail and when it is received.

processing float
The time between receipt of a payment and its deposit into the firm's account.

clearing float
The time between deposit of a payment and when spendable funds become available to the firm.

Float refers to funds that have been sent by the payer but are not yet usable funds to the payee. Float is important in the cash conversion cycle because its presence lengthens both the firm's average collection period and its average payment period. However, the goal of the firm should be to shorten its average collection period and lengthen its average payment period. Both can be accomplished by managing float.

Float has three component parts:

1. **Mail float** is the time delay between when payment is placed in the mail and when it is received.
2. **Processing float** is the time between receipt of the payment and its deposit into the firm's account.
3. **Clearing float** is the time between deposit of the payment and when spendable funds become available to the firm. This component of float is attributable to the time required for a check to clear the banking system.

FIGURE 13.3

Float Time Line

Float resulting from a check issued and mailed by the payer company to the payee company

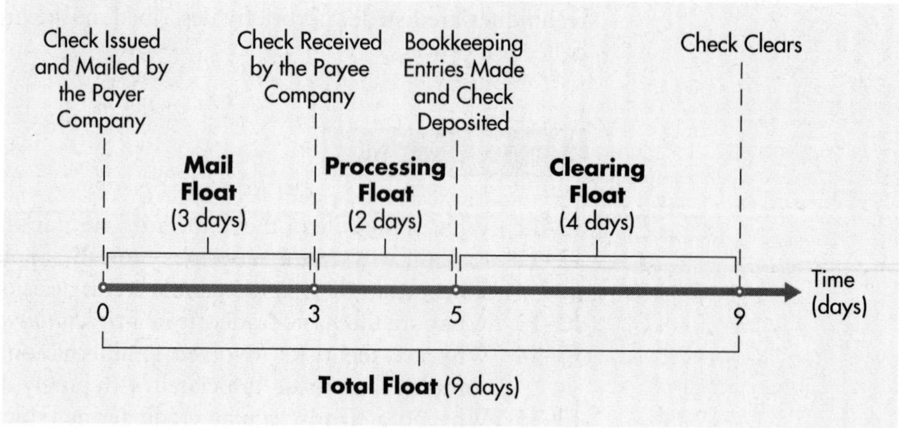

Figure 13.3 illustrates the key components of float resulting from the issuance and mailing of a check by the payer company to the payee company on day zero. The entire process required a total of 9 days: 3 days' mail float, 2 days' processing float, and 4 days' clearing float. To the payer company, the delay is disbursement float; to the payee company, the delay is collection float.

Some popular techniques for managing the component parts of float to speed up collections and slow down payments are described here.

Speeding Up Collections

Speeding up collections reduces customer *collection float* time and thus reduces the firm's average collection period, which reduces the investment the firm must make in its cash conversion cycle. In our earlier examples, MAX Company had annual sales of $10 million and 8 days of total collection float (receipt, processing, and collection time). If MAX can reduce its float time to 5 days, it will reduce its investment in the cash conversion cycle by $83,333 ([$10,000,000/360 days] × 3 days).

lockbox system
A collection procedure in which customers mail payments to a post office box that is emptied regularly by the firm's bank, who processes the payments and deposits them in the firm's account. This system speeds up collection time by reducing processing time as well as mail and clearing time.

A popular technique for speeding up collections is a lockbox system. A **lockbox system** works as follows: Instead of mailing payments to the company, customers mail payments to a post office box. The firm's bank empties the post office box regularly, processes each payment, and deposits the payments in the firm's account. Deposit slips, along with payment enclosures, are sent (or transmitted electronically) to the firm by the bank so that the firm can properly credit customers' accounts. Lockboxes are geographically dispersed to match the locations of the firm's customers. A lockbox system affects all three components of float. Lockboxes reduce mail time and often clearing time by being near the firm's customers. Lockboxes reduce processing time to nearly zero because the bank deposits payments before the firm processes them. Obviously a lockbox system reduces collection float time, but not without a cost; therefore, a firm must perform an economic analysis to determine whether to implement a lockbox system.

Lockbox systems are commonly used by large firms whose customers are geographically dispersed. However, a firm does not have to be large to benefit

In Practice

FOCUS ON ETHICS What Does It Do for You?

Lake Lillian, Minnesota, gained a mention in a Chicago-area media outlet, but not for being a hot fishing spot in this state of 10,000 lakes. An eagle-eyed Chicago consumer wondered why his 25-cent rebate check from **Illinois Bell** was drawn on a bank in Lake Lillian. He was told by a media investigator that many large corporations issued rebate checks drawn on a bank there in order to get more "float"—the time between when checks were issued and when the funds were deducted from their accounts. In reply, the particular bank justifiably insisted there was more to the story, noting its expertise in processing many small-dollar checks.

The cash management practice of "remote disbursing"—writing checks on banks located in geographically isolated locations to take advantage of the difficulty of presenting checks to them in a timely manner was common before the Federal Reserve issued a policy statement in 1979 to discourage the practice. Cash managers overlooked the fact that putting money in one's own pocket took it out of someone else's.

E.F. Hutton, at the time one of the most prominent stock brokers in the United States, took advantage of banks' inability to track deposits and transfers and gained interest-free use of multiple millions of dollars each day. Though many saw this as just "aggressive cash management," a 1985 U.S. Justice Department ruling saw it as fraud (because Hutton was using money that its banks had not yet collected from the check writer and without the bank's knowledge). Attorneys writing in *Bankers Magazine* urged cash managers not to use any type of remote disbursement in which the sole purpose is to increase check collection delays, thereby creating float. That float causes a "hold" to be placed on the funds so that the depositor cannot use them.

In response to E.F. Hutton's aggressive practices, the professional association to which many cash managers and treasurers belong implemented an ethical code. Anyone who is designated a "Certified Cash Manager" by the Association for Financial Professionals must agree to maintain the highest standards of conduct, including the standard to "refrain from intentional abuses of financial systems and markets."

Remote disbursing has largely disappeared. However, the fact that many cash managers still see nothing wrong with sending checks to the wrong address or changing disbursement banks to add a little more float shows that ethical codes do not guarantee ethical behavior. The odd locations of some "controlled disbursement accounts" today indicate that financial managers need one more reminder: The mere fact that something is legal does not necessarily make it moral or ethical. The Golden Rule—do to others as you would have them do to you—shows the inadvisability of remote disbursing.

from a lockbox. Smaller firms can also benefit from a lockbox system. The benefit to small firms often comes primarily from transferring the processing of payments to the bank.

Slowing Down Payments

Float is also a component of the firm's average payment period. In this case, the float is in the favor of the firm. The firm may benefit by increasing all three of the components of its *payment float.* One popular technique for increasing payment float is **controlled disbursing,** which involves the strategic use of mailing points and bank accounts to lengthen mail float and clearing float, respectively. This approach should be used carefully, though, because longer payment periods may strain supplier relations.

controlled disbursing
The strategic use of mailing points and bank accounts to lengthen mail float and clearing float, respectively.

In summary, a reasonable overall policy for float management is (1) to collect payments as quickly as possible, because once the payment is in the mail, the funds belong to the firm, and (2) to delay making payment to suppliers, because once the payment is mailed, the funds belong to the supplier.

Cash Concentration

cash concentration
The process used by the firm to bring lockbox and other deposits together into one bank, often called the *concentration bank.*

Cash concentration is the process used by the firm to bring lockbox and other deposits together into one bank, often called the *concentration bank*. Cash concentration has three main advantages. First, it creates a large pool of funds for use in making short-term cash investments. Because there is a fixed-cost component in the transaction cost associated with such investments, investing a single pool of funds reduces the firm's transaction costs. The larger investment pool also allows the firm to choose from a greater variety of short-term investment vehicles. Second, concentrating the firm's cash in one account improves the tracking and internal control of the firm's cash. Third, having one concentration bank enables the firm to implement payment strategies that reduce idle cash balances.

depository transfer check (DTC)
An unsigned check drawn on one of a firm's bank accounts and deposited in another.

There are a variety of mechanisms for transferring cash from the lockbox bank and other collecting banks to the concentration bank. One mechanism is a **depository transfer check (DTC),** which is an unsigned check drawn on one of the firm's bank accounts and deposited in another. For cash concentration, a DTC is drawn on each lockbox or other collecting bank account and deposited in the concentration bank account. Once the DTC has cleared the bank on which it is drawn (which may take several days), the transfer of funds is completed. Most firms currently provide deposit information by telephone to the concentration bank, which then prepares and deposits into its account the DTC drawn on the lockbox or other collecting bank account.

ACH (automated clearinghouse) transfer
Preauthorized electronic withdrawal from the payer's account and deposit into the payee's account via a settlement among banks by the *automated clearinghouse,* or *ACH.*

A second mechanism is an **ACH (automated clearinghouse) transfer,** which is a preauthorized electronic withdrawal from the payer's account. A computerized clearing facility (called the *automated clearinghouse,* or *ACH*) makes a paperless transfer of funds between the payer and payee banks. An ACH settles accounts among participating banks. Individual accounts are settled by respective bank balance adjustments. ACH transfers clear in one day. For cash concentration, an ACH transfer is made from each lockbox bank or other collecting bank to the concentration bank. An ACH transfer can be thought of as an electronic DTC, but because the ACH transfer clears in one day, it provides benefits over a DTC; however, both banks in the ACH transfer must be members of the clearinghouse.

wire transfer
An electronic communication that, via bookkeeping entries, removes funds from the payer's bank and deposits them in the payee's bank.

A third cash concentration mechanism is a **wire transfer.** A wire transfer is an electronic communication that, via bookkeeping entries, removes funds from the payer's bank and deposits them in the payee's bank. Wire transfers can eliminate mail and clearing float and may reduce processing float as well. For cash concentration, the firm moves funds using a wire transfer from each lockbox or other collecting account to its concentration account. Wire transfers are a substitute for DTC and ACH transfers, but they are more expensive.

It is clear that the firm must balance the costs and benefits of concentrating cash to determine the type and timing of transfers from its lockbox and other collecting accounts to its concentration account. The transfer mechanism selected should be the one that is most profitable. (The profit per period of any transfer mechanism equals earnings on the increased availability of funds minus the cost of the transfer system.)

Zero-Balance Accounts

zero-balance account (ZBA)
A disbursement account that always has an end-of-day balance of zero because the firm deposits money to cover checks drawn on the account only as they are presented for payment each day.

Zero-balance accounts (ZBAs) are disbursement accounts that always have an end-of-day balance of zero. The purpose is to eliminate nonearning cash balances in corporate checking accounts. A ZBA works well as a disbursement account under a cash concentration system.

ZBAs work as follows: Once all of a given day's checks are presented for payment from the firm's ZBA, the bank notifies the firm of the total amount of checks, and the firm transfers funds into the account to cover the amount of that day's checks. This leaves an end-of-day balance of $0 (zero dollars). The ZBA enables the firm to keep all of its operating cash in an interest-earning account, thereby eliminating idle cash balances. Thus a firm that used a ZBA in conjunction with a cash concentration system would need two accounts. The firm would concentrate its cash from the lockboxes and other collecting banks into an interest-earning account and would write checks against its ZBA. The firm would cover the exact dollar amount of checks presented against the ZBA with transfers from the interest-earning account, leaving the end-of-day balance in the ZBA at $0.

A ZBA is a disbursement management tool. As we discussed earlier, the firm would prefer to maximize its payment float. However, some cash managers feel that actively attempting to increase float time on payments is unethical. A ZBA enables the firm to maximize the use of float on each check without altering the float time of payments to its suppliers. Keeping all the firm's cash in an interest-earning account enables the firm to maximize earnings on its cash balances by capturing the full float time on each check it writes.

Investing in Marketable Securities

Marketable securities are short-term, interest-earning, money market instruments that can easily be converted into cash.[5] Marketable securities are classified as part of the firm's liquid assets. The firm uses them to earn a return on temporarily idle funds. To be truly marketable, a security must have (1) a ready market in order to minimize the amount of time required to convert it into cash, and (2) safety of principal, which means that it experiences little or no loss in value over time.

The securities that are most commonly held as part of the firm's marketable-securities portfolio are divided into two groups: (1) government issues, which have relatively low yields as a consequence of their low risk, and (2) nongovernment issues, which have slightly higher yields than government issues with similar maturities because of the slightly higher risk associated with them. Table 13.5 summarizes the key features and recent (May 1, 2002) yields for popular marketable securities.

Review Questions

13–17 What is *float* and what are its three components?

5. As explained in Chapter 1, the *money market* results from a financial relationship between the suppliers and demanders of short-term funds, that is, marketable securities.

TABLE 13.5 Features and Recent Yields on Popular Marketable Securities[a]

Security	Issuer	Description	Initial maturity	Risk and return	Yield on May 1, 2002[b]
Government Issues					
Treasury bills	U.S. Treasury	Issued weekly at auction; sold at a discount; strong secondary market	91 and 182 days	Lowest, virtually risk-free	1.73%
Treasury notes	U.S. Treasury	Stated interest rate; interest paid semiannually; strong secondary market	1 to 10 years	Low, but slightly higher than U.S. Treasury bills	1.79%
Federal agency issues	Agencies of federal government	Not an obligation of U.S. Treasury; strong secondary market	9 months to 30 years	Slightly higher than U.S. Treasury issues	1.80%[c]
Nongovernment Issues					
Negotiable certificates of deposit (CDs)	Commercial banks	Represent specific cash deposits in commercial banks; amounts and maturities tailored to investor needs; large denominations; good secondary market	1 month to 3 years	Higher than U.S. Treasury issues and comparable to commercial paper	1.83%
Commercial paper	Corporation with a high credit standing	Unsecured note of issuer; large denominations	3 to 270 days	Higher than U.S. Treasury issues and comparable to negotiable CDs	1.80%
Banker's acceptances	Banks	Results from a bank guarantee of a business transaction; sold at discount from maturity value	30 to 180 days	About the same as negotiable CDs and commercial paper but higher than U.S. Treasury issues	1.86%
Eurodollar deposits	Foreign banks	Deposits of currency not native to the country in which the bank is located; large denominations; active secondary market	1 day to 3 years	Highest, due to less regulation of depository banks and some foreign exchange risk	1.91%
Money market mutual funds	Professional portfolio management companies	Professionally managed portfolios of marketable securities; provide instant liquidity	None—depends on wishes of investor	Vary, but generally higher than U.S. Treasury issues and comparable to negotiable CDs and commercial paper	1.47%[d]
Repurchase agreements	Bank or security dealer	Bank or security dealer sells specific securities to firm and agrees to repurchase them at a specific price and time	Customized to purchaser's needs	Generally slightly below that associated with the outright purchase of the security	—

[a]The prime rate of interest at this time was 4.75%.

[b]Yields obtained for 3-month maturities of each security.

[c]Federal National Mortgage Association (Fannie Mae) constant maturity debt index is used here.

[d]The Dryfus Money Market Fund with an average maturity of 64 days is used here in the absence of any average-yield data. Comparatively low money market mutual fund yields occur when interest rates are historically low, as was the case in early 2002.

Source: Wall Street Journal, May 2, 2002, pp. C9, C10, and C14.

13–18 What are the firm's objectives with regard to collection float and to payment float?

13–19 What are the three main advantages of cash concentration?

13–20 What are three mechanisms of cash concentration? What is the objective of using a zero-balance account (ZBA) in a cash concentration system?

13–21 What two characteristics make a security marketable? Why are the yields on nongovernment marketable securities generally higher than the yields on government issues with similar maturities?

SUMMARY

FOCUS ON VALUE

It is important for a firm to maintain a reasonable level of net working capital. To do this, it must balance the high profit and high risk associated with low levels of current assets and high levels of current liabilities against the low profit and low risk that result from high levels of current assets and low levels of current liabilities. A strategy that achieves a reasonable balance between profits and liquidity should positively contribute to the firm's value.

Similarly, the firm should manage its cash conversion cycle by turning inventory quickly; collecting accounts receivable quickly; managing mail, processing, and clearing time; and paying accounts payable slowly. These strategies should enable the firm to manage its current accounts efficiently and to minimize the amount of required investment in operating assets.

The financial manager can use various techniques to manage inventory, accounts receivable, and cash receipts to reduce the amount of resources needed to support the business. Employing these strategies, and using various techniques to manage accounts payable and cash disbursements to shorten the cash conversion cycle, should minimize the firm's cash requirements, thereby positively contributing to its value. Clearly, active management of the firm's working capital and current assets should positively contribute to the firm's goal of **maximizing its stock price.**

REVIEW OF LEARNING GOALS

LG1 **Understand short-term financial management, net working capital, and the related tradeoff between profitability and risk.** Short-term financial management is focused on managing each of the firm's current assets (inventory, accounts receivable, cash, and marketable securities) and current liabilities (accounts payable, accruals, and notes payable) in a manner that positively contributes to the firm's value. Net working capital is the difference between current assets and current liabilities. Profitability is the relationship between revenues and costs. Risk, in the context of short-term financial decisions, is the probability that a firm will become technically insolvent—unable to pay its bills as they come due. Assuming a constant level of total assets, the higher a firm's ratio of current assets to total assets, the less profitable the firm, and the less risky it is. The converse is also true. With constant total assets, the higher a firm's ratio of current liabilities to total assets, the more profitable and the more risky the firm is. The converse of this statement is also true.

LG2 **Describe the cash conversion cycle, its funding requirements, and the key strategies for managing it.** The cash conversion cycle represents the amount of time a firm's resources are tied up. It has three components: (1) average age of inventory, (2) average collection period, and (3) average payment period. The length of the cash conversion cycle determines the amount of time resources are tied up in the firm's day-to-day operations. The firm's investment in short-term assets often consists of both permanent and seasonal funding requirements. The seasonal requirements can be financed using either a low-cost, high-risk, aggressive financing strategy or a high-cost, low-risk, conservative financing strategy. The firm's funding decision for its cash conversion cycle ultimately depends on management's disposition toward risk and the strength of the firm's banking relationships. To minimize its reliance on negotiated liabilities, the financial manager seeks to (1) turn over inventory as quickly as possible, (2) collect accounts receivable as quickly as possible, (3) manage mail, processing, and clearing time, and (4) pay accounts payable as slowly as possible. Use of these strategies should minimize the cash conversion cycle.

LG3 **Discuss inventory management: differing views, common techniques, and international concerns.** The viewpoints of marketing, manufacturing, and purchasing managers about the appropriate levels of inventory tend to cause higher inventories than those deemed appropriate by the financial manager. Four commonly used techniques for effectively managing inventory to keep its level low are (1) the ABC system, (2) the economic order quantity (EOQ) model, (3) the just-in-time (JIT) system, and (4) the materials requirement planning (MRP) system. International inventory managers place greater emphasis on making sure that sufficient quantities of inventory are delivered where they are needed, when they are needed, and in the right condition, than on ordering the economically optimal quantities.

LG4 **Explain the credit selection process and the quantitative procedure for evaluating changes in credit standards.** Credit selection and standards are concerned with applying techniques for determining which customers' creditworthiness is consistent with the firm's credit standards. Two popular credit selection techniques are the five C's of credit and credit scoring. Changes in credit standards can be evaluated mathematically by assessing the effects of a proposed change in profits on sales, the cost of accounts receivable investment, and bad-debt costs.

LG5 **Review the procedures for quantitatively considering cash discount changes, other aspects of credit terms, and credit monitoring.** Changes in credit terms (particularly the initiation of, or a change in, the cash discount) can be quantified in a way similar to that for changes in credit standards. Changes in the cash discount period can also be evaluated using similar methods. Credit monitoring, the ongoing review of customer payment of accounts receivable, frequently involves use of the average collection period and the aging of accounts receivable. A number of popular collection techniques are used by firms.

LG6 **Understand the management of receipts and disbursements, including float, speeding collections, slowing payments, cash concentration, zero-balance accounts, and investing in marketable securities.** Float refers to funds that have been sent by the payer but are not yet usable funds to the payee. The components of float are mail time, processing time, and clearing time. Float occurs in both the average collection period and the average payment period. One technique for speeding up collections to reduce collection float is a lockbox system. A popular technique for slowing payments to increase payment float is controlled disbursing, which involves strategic use of mailing points and bank accounts. The goal for managing operating cash is to balance the opportunity cost of nonearning balances against the transaction cost of temporary investments. Firms commonly use depository transfer checks (DTCs), ACH transfers, and wire transfers to transfer lockbox receipts to their concentration banks quickly. Zero-balance accounts (ZBAs) can be used to eliminate nonearning cash balances in corporate checking accounts. Marketable securities are short-term, interest-earning, money market instruments used by the firm to earn a return on temporarily idle funds. They may be government or nongovernment issues.

SELF-TEST PROBLEMS (Solutions in Appendix B)

LG2 **ST 13–1 Cash conversion cycle** Hurkin Manufacturing Company pays accounts payable on the tenth day after purchase. The average collection period is 30 days, and the average age of inventory is 40 days. The firm currently spends about $18 million on operating-cycle investments. The firm is considering a plan that would stretch its accounts payable by 20 days. If the firm pays 12% per year for its resource investment, what annual savings can it realize by this plan? Assume no discount for early payment of accounts payable and a 360-day year.

LG3 **ST 13–2 EOQ analysis** Thompson Paint Company uses 60,000 gallons of pigment per year. The cost of ordering pigment is $200 per order, and the cost of carrying the pigment in inventory is $1 per gallon per year. The firm uses pigment at a constant rate every day throughout the year.

a. Calculate the EOQ.

b. Assuming that it takes 20 days to receive an order once it has been placed, determine the reorder point in terms of gallons of pigment. (*Note:* Use a 360-day year.)

LG4 **ST 13–3 Relaxing credit standards** Regency Rug Repair Company is trying to decide whether it should relax its credit standards. The firm repairs 72,000 rugs per year at an average price of $32 each. Bad-debt expenses are 1% of sales, the average collection period is 40 days, and the variable cost per unit is $28. Regency expects that if it does relax its credit standards, the average collection period will increase to 48 days and that bad debts will increase to 1½% of sales. Sales will increase by 4,000 repairs per year. If the firm has a required rate of return on equal-risk investments of 14%, what recommendation would you give the firm? Use your analysis to justify your answer.

PROBLEMS

LG2 **13–1 Cash conversion cycle** American Products is concerned about managing cash efficiently. On the average, inventories have an age of 90 days, and accounts receivable are collected in 60 days. Accounts payable are paid approximately 30 days after they arise. The firm spends $30 million on operating-cycle investments each year, at a constant rate. Assume a 360-day year.

a. Calculate the firm's operating cycle.

b. Calculate the firm's cash conversion cycle.

c. Calculate the amount of resources needed to support the firm's cash conversion cycle.

d. Discuss how management might be able to reduce the cash conversion cycle.

LG2 **13–2 Changing cash conversion cycle** Camp Manufacturing turns over its inventory 8 times each year, has an average payment period of 35 days, and has an average collection period of 60 days. The firm's total annual outlays for operating-cycle investments are $3.5 million. Assume a 360-day year.

a. Calculate the firm's operating and cash conversion cycles.

b. Calculate the firm's daily cash operating expenditure. How much in resources must be invested to support its cash conversion cycle?

c. If the firm pays 14% for these resources, by how much would it increase its annual profits by *favorably* changing its current cash conversion cycle by 20 days?

LG2 13–3 **Multiple changes in cash conversion cycle** Garrett Industries turns over its inventory 6 times each year; it has an average collection period of 45 days and an average payment period of 30 days. The firm's annual operating-cycle investment is $3 million. Assume a 360-day year.

a. Calculate the firm's cash conversion cycle, its daily cash operating expenditure, and the amount of resources needed to support its cash conversion cycle.
b. Find the firm's cash conversion cycle and resource investment requirement if it makes the following changes simultaneously.
   (1) Shortens the average age of inventory by 5 days.
   (2) Speeds the collection of accounts receivable by an average of 10 days.
   (3) Extends the average payment period by 10 days.
c. If the firm pays 13% for its resource investment, by how much, if anything, could it increase its annual profit as a result of the changes in part **b**?
d. If the annual cost of achieving the profit in part **c** is $35,000, what action would you recommend to the firm? Why?

LG2 13–4 **Aggressive versus conservative seasonal funding strategy** Dynabase Tool has forecast its total funds requirements for the coming year as shown in the following table.

Month	Amount	Month	Amount
January	$2,000,000	July	$12,000,000
February	2,000,000	August	14,000,000
March	2,000,000	September	9,000,000
April	4,000,000	October	5,000,000
May	6,000,000	November	4,000,000
June	9,000,000	December	3,000,000

a. Divide the firm's monthly funds requirement into (1) a *permanent* component and (2) a *seasonal* component, and find the monthly average for each of these components.
b. Describe the amount of long-term and short-term financing used to meet the total funds requirement under (1) an *aggressive funding strategy* and (2) a *conservative funding strategy*. Assume that under the aggressive strategy, long-term funds finance permanent needs and short-term funds are used to finance seasonal needs.
c. Assuming that short-term funds cost 12% annually and that the cost of long-term funds is 17% annually, use the averages found in part **a** to calculate the total cost of each of the strategies described in part **b.**
d. Discuss the profitability–risk tradeoffs associated with the aggressive strategy and those associated with the conservative strategy.

LG3 13–5 **EOQ analysis** Tiger Corporation purchases 1,200,000 units per year of one component. The fixed cost per order is $25. The annual carrying cost of the item is 27% of its $2 cost.

a. Determine the EOQ under the following conditions: (1) no changes, (2) order cost of zero, and (3) carrying cost of zero.
b. What do your answers illustrate about the EOQ model? Explain.

LG3 13–6 **EOQ, reorder point, and safety stock** Alexis Company uses 800 units of a product per year on a continuous basis. The product has a fixed cost of $50 per order, and its carrying cost is $2 per unit per year. It takes 5 days to receive a shipment after an order is placed, and the firm wishes to hold 10 days' usage in inventory as a safety stock.
a. Calculate the EOQ.
b. Determine the average level of inventory. (*Note:* Use a 360-day year to calculate daily usage.)
c. Determine the reorder point.
d. Indicate which of the following variables change if the firm does not hold the safety stock: (1) order cost, (2) carrying cost, (3) total inventory cost, (4) reorder point, (5) economic order quantity. Explain.

LG4 13–7 **Accounts receivable changes without bad debts** Tara's Textiles currently has credit sales of $360 million per year and an average collection period of 60 days. Assume that the price of Tara's products is $60 per unit and that the variable costs are $55 per unit. The firm is considering an accounts receivable change that will result in a 20% increase in sales and a 20% increase in the average collection period. No change in bad debts is expected. The firm's equal-risk opportunity cost on its investment in accounts receivable is 14%.
a. Calculate the additional profit contribution from new sales that the firm will realize if it makes the proposed change.
b. What marginal investment in accounts receivable will result?
c. Calculate the cost of the marginal investment in accounts receivable.
d. Should the firm implement the proposed change? What other information would be helpful in your analysis?

LG4 13–8 **Accounts receivable changes with bad debts** A firm is evaluating an accounts receivable change that would increase bad debts from 2% to 4% of sales. Sales are currently 50,000 units, the selling price is $20 per unit, and the variable cost per unit is $15. As a result of the proposed change, sales are forecast to increase to 60,000 units.
a. What are bad debts in dollars currently and under the proposed change?
b. Calculate the cost of the marginal bad debts to the firm.
c. Ignoring the additional profit contribution from increased sales, if the proposed change saves $3,500 and causes no change in the average investment in accounts receivable, would you recommend it? Explain.
d. Considering *all* changes in costs and benefits, would you recommend the proposed change? Explain.
e. Compare and discuss your answers in parts c and d.

LG4 13–9 **Relaxation of credit standards** Lewis Enterprises is considering relaxing its credit standards to increase its currently sagging sales. As a result of the proposed relaxation, sales are expected to increase by 10% from 10,000 to 11,000 units during the coming year; the average collection period is expected to increase from 45 to 60 days; and bad debts are expected to increase from 1% to 3% of sales. The sale price per unit is $40, and the variable cost per unit is $31.

The firm's required return on equal-risk investments is 25%. Evaluate the proposed relaxation, and make a recommendation to the firm.

LG5 **13–10 Initiating a cash discount** Gardner Company currently makes all sales on credit and offers no cash discount. The firm is considering offering a 2% cash discount for payment within 15 days. The firm's current average collection period is 60 days, sales are 40,000 units, selling price is $45 per unit, and variable cost per unit is $36. The firm expects that the change in credit terms will result in an increase in sales to 42,000 units, that 70% of the sales will take the discount, and that the average collection period will fall to 30 days. If the firm's required rate of return on equal-risk investments is 25%, should the proposed discount be offered?

LG5 **13–11 Shortening the credit period** A firm is contemplating *shortening* its credit period from 40 to 30 days and believes that as a result of this change, its average collection period will decline from 45 to 36 days. Bad-debt expenses are expected to decrease from 1.5% to 1% of sales. The firm is currently selling 12,000 units but believes that as a result of the proposed change, sales will decline to 10,000 units. The sale price per unit is $56, and the variable cost per unit is $45. The firm has a required return on equal-risk investments of 25%. Evaluate this decision, and make a recommendation to the firm.

LG5 **13–12 Lengthening the credit period** Parker Tool is considering lengthening its credit period from 30 to 60 days. All customers will continue to pay on the net date. The firm currently bills $450,000 for sales and has $345,000 in variable costs. The change in credit terms is expected to increase sales to $510,000. Bad-debt expenses will increase from 1% to 1.5% of sales. The firm has a required rate of return on equal-risk investments of 20%.

a. What additional profit contribution from sales will be realized from the proposed change?
b. What is the cost of the marginal investment in accounts receivable?
c. What is the cost of the marginal bad debts?
d. Do you recommend this change in credit terms? Why or why not?

LG6 **13–13 Float** Simon Corporation has daily cash receipts of $65,000. A recent analysis of its collections indicated that customers' payments were in the mail an average of 2.5 days. Once received, the payments are processed in 1.5 days. After payments are deposited, it takes an average of 3 days for these receipts to clear the banking system.

a. How much collection float (in days) does the firm currently have?
b. If the firm's opportunity cost is 11%, would it be economically advisable for the firm to pay an annual fee of $16,500 to reduce collection float by 3 days? Explain why or why not.

LG6 **13–14 Lockbox system** Eagle Industries feels that a lockbox system can shorten its accounts receivable collection period by 3 days. Credit sales are $3,240,000 per year, billed on a continuous basis. The firm has other equally risky investments with a return of 15%. The cost of the lockbox system is $9,000 per year.

a. What amount of cash will be made available for other uses under the lockbox system?

b. What net benefit (cost) will the firm realize if it adopts the lockbox system? Should it adopt the proposed lockbox system?

LG6 **13–15 Zero-balance account** Union Company is considering establishment of a zero-balance account. The firm currently maintains an average balance of $420,000 in its disbursement account. As compensation to the bank for maintaining the zero-balance account, the firm will have to pay a monthly fee of $1,000 and maintain a $300,000 non-interest-earning deposit in the bank. The firm currently has no other deposits in the bank. Evaluate the proposed zero-balance account, and make a recommendation to the firm, assuming that it has a 12% opportunity cost.

CHAPTER 13 CASE Assessing Roche Publishing Company's Cash Management Efficiency

Lisa Pinto, vice president of finance at Roche Publishing Company, a rapidly growing publisher of college texts, is concerned about the firm's high level of short-term resource investment. She believes that the firm can improve the management of its cash and, as a result, reduce this investment. In this regard, she charged Arlene Bessenoff, the treasurer, with assessing the firm's cash management efficiency. Arlene decided to begin her investigation by studying the firm's operating and cash conversion cycles.

Arlene found that Roche's average payment period was 25 days. She consulted industry data, which showed that the average payment period for the industry was 40 days. Investigation of three similar publishing companies revealed that their average payment period was also 40 days. She estimated the annual cost of achieving a 40-day payment period to be $53,000.

Next, Arlene studied the production cycle and inventory policies. The average age of inventory was 120 days. She determined that the industry standard as reported in a survey done by *Publishing World*, the trade association journal, was 85 days. She estimated the annual cost of achieving an 85-day average age of inventory to be $150,000.

Further analysis showed Arlene that the firm's average collection period was 60 days. The industry average, derived from the trade association data and information on three similar publishing companies, was found to be 42 days—30% lower than Roche's. Arlene estimated that if Roche initiated a 2% cash discount for payment within 10 days of the beginning of the credit period, the firm's average collection period would drop from 60 days to the 42-day industry average. She also expected the following to occur as a result of the discount: Annual sales would increase from $13,750,000 to $15,000,000; bad debts would remain unchanged; and the 2% cash discount would be applied to 75% of the firm's sales. The firm's variable costs equal 80% of sales.

Roche Publishing Company is currently spending $12,000,000 per year on its operating-cycle investment, but it expects that initiating a cash discount will increase its operating-cycle investment to $13,100,000 per year. Arlene's concern was whether the firm's cash management was as efficient as it could be. Arlene knew that the company paid 12% annual interest for its resource investment and therefore viewed this value as the firm's required return. For this reason, she was concerned about the resource investment cost resulting from any inefficiencies in the management of Roche's cash conversion cycle.

Required

a. Assuming a constant rate for purchases, production, and sales throughout the year, what are Roche's existing operating cycle (OC), cash conversion cycle (CCC), and resource investment need?
b. If Roche can optimize operations according to industry standards, what would its operating cycle (OC), cash conversion cycle (CCC), and resource investment need be under these more efficient conditions?
c. In terms of resource investment requirements, what is the annual cost of Roche Publishing Company's operational inefficiency?
d. Evaluate whether Roche's strategy for speeding its collection of accounts receivable would be acceptable. What annual net profit or loss would result from implementation of the cash discount?
e. Use your finding in part **d**, along with the payables and inventory costs given, to determine the total annual cost the firm would incur to achieve the industry level of operational efficiency.
f. Judging on the basis of your findings in parts **c** and **e**, should the firm incur the annual cost to achieve the industry level of operational efficiency? Explain why or why not.

WEB EXERCISE

Go to the Web site *www.bankone.com*. Click on **Commercial** in the left column.

1. What are the general categories of business services that Bank One offers? (They are listed in the left column.)

Click on **Manage Cash.**

2. What cash management services does the bank offer? What are **Merchant Services** and **Stored-Value Cards**, and how do they help businesses manage cash?

Click on **Treasury Management Services** and then on **Products and Services** to get a list of seven different areas. Click on the appropriate area to answer the following questions.

3. Describe the services for the following areas and explain how they increase a firm's efficiency in managing its cash: (a) **Collections and Deposits,** (b) **Disbursements and Payments,** and (c) **E-Commerce.**

In one of the above areas, click on **ACH Services** and then on **What is ACH.**

4. Discuss the role of the ACH network, the process by which payments are made, and describe two types of electronic payment options.
5. Navigate the **International Banking** page and click on **Products and Services** and then on **Treasury.** What services does Bank One offer for **Collection, Disbursements,** and **Electronic Banking**? How do these offerings differ from its domestic services, and why?

Remember to check the book's Web site at

www.aw.com/gitman

for additional resources, including additional Web exercises.

Across the Disciplines
Why This Chapter Matters To You

Accounting: You need to understand how to analyze supplier credit terms in order to decide whether the firm should take or give up cash discounts; you also need to understand the various types of short-term loans, both unsecured and secured, that you will be required to record and report.

Information systems: You need to understand what data the firm will need in order to process accounts payable, track accruals, and meet bank loans and other short-term debt obligations in a timely manner.

Management: You need to know the sources of short-term loans so that if short-term financing is needed, you will understand its costs, both financial and ethical.

Marketing: You need to understand how accounts receivable and inventory can be used as loan collateral; the procedures used by the firm to secure short-term loans with such collateral could affect customer relationships.

Operations: You need to understand the use of accounts payable as a form of short-term financing and the effect on one's suppliers of stretching payables; you also need to understand the process by which a firm uses inventory as collateral.

Chapter

14 Current Liabilities Management

LEARNING GOALS

- LG1 Review the key components of a firm's credit terms and the procedures for analyzing them.
- LG2 Understand the effects of stretching accounts payable on their cost, and the use of accruals.
- LG3 Describe the interest rates and basic types of unsecured bank sources of short-term loans.
- LG4 Discuss the basic features of commercial paper and the key aspects of international short-term loans.
- LG5 Explain the characteristics of secured short-term loans and the use of accounts receivable as short-term-loan collateral.
- LG6 Describe the various ways in which inventory can be used as short-term-loan collateral.

529

Accounts payable and accruals represent forms of spontaneous financing for the firm. The longer the firm can hold the cash intended for those uses, the longer it can use those funds for its own purposes. Firms typically, though, must arrange for short-term loans to even out cash flows or to tide them over rough spots. This chapter looks at various aspects of current liabilities management—spontaneous liabilities and how best to manage them, and both unsecured and secured sources of short-term loans.

LG1 LG2

Spontaneous Liabilities

spontaneous liabilities
Financing that arises from the normal course of business; the two major short-term sources of such liabilities are accounts payable and accruals.

unsecured short-term financing
Short-term financing obtained without pledging specific assets as collateral.

Spontaneous liabilities arise from the normal course of business. The two major spontaneous sources of short-term financing are accounts payable and accruals. As the firm's sales increase, accounts payable increase in response to the increased purchases necessary to produce at higher levels. Also in response to increasing sales, the firm's accruals increase as wages and taxes rise because of greater labor requirements and the increased taxes on the firm's increased earnings. There is normally no explicit cost attached to either of these current liabilities, although they do have certain implicit costs. In addition, both are forms of **unsecured short-term financing**—short-term financing obtained without pledging specific assets as collateral. The firm should take advantage of these "interest-free" sources of unsecured short-term financing whenever possible.

Accounts Payable Management

Accounts payable are the major source of unsecured short-term financing for business firms. They result from transactions in which merchandise is purchased but no formal note is signed to show the purchaser's liability to the seller. The purchaser in effect agrees to pay the supplier the amount required in accordance with credit terms normally stated on the supplier's invoice. The discussion of accounts payable here is presented from the viewpoint of the purchaser.

Role in the Cash Conversion Cycle

accounts payable management
Management by the firm of the time that elapses between its purchase of raw materials and its mailing payment to the supplier.

The average payment period is the final component of the *cash conversion cycle* introduced in Chapter 13. The average payment period has two parts: (1) the time from the purchase of raw materials until the firm mails the payment and (2) payment float time (the time it takes after the firm mails its payment until the supplier has withdrawn spendable funds from the firm's account). In the preceding chapter, we discussed issues related to payment float time. Here we discuss the management by the firm of the time that elapses between its purchase of raw materials and its mailing payment to the supplier. This activity is **accounts payable management.**

The firm's goal is to pay as slowly as possible without damaging its credit rating. This means that accounts should be paid on the last day possible, given the supplier's stated credit terms. For example, if the terms are net 30, then the account should be paid 30 days from the *beginning of the credit period,* which is typically either the *date of invoice* or the *end of the month* (*EOM*) in which the purchase was made. This allows for the maximum use of an interest-free loan from the supplier and will not damage the firm's credit rating (because the account is paid within the stated credit terms).

EXAMPLE In the demonstration of the cash conversion cycle in Chapter 13 (see page 497), MAX Company had an average payment period of 35 days (consisting of 30 days until payment was mailed and 5 days of payment float), which resulted in average accounts payable of $473,958. Thus the daily accounts payable generated by MAX was $13,542 ($473,958/35). If MAX were to mail its payments in 35 days instead of 30, its accounts payable would increase by $67,710 ($13,542 × 5). As a result, MAX's cash conversion cycle would decrease by 5 days, and the firm would reduce its investment in operations by $67,710. Clearly, if this action did not damage MAX's credit rating, it would be in the company's best interest.

Analyzing Credit Terms

The credit terms that a firm is offered by its suppliers enable it to delay payments for its purchases. Because the supplier's cost of having its money tied up in merchandise after it is sold is probably reflected in the purchase price, the purchaser is already indirectly paying for this benefit. The purchaser should therefore carefully analyze credit terms to determine the best trade credit strategy. If a firm is extended credit terms that include a cash discount, it has two options—to take the cash discount or to give it up.

Taking the Cash Discount If a firm intends to take a cash discount, it should pay on the last day of the discount period. There is no cost associated with taking a cash discount.

EXAMPLE Lawrence Industries, operator of a small chain of video stores, purchased $1,000 worth of merchandise on February 27 from a supplier extending terms of 2/10 net 30 EOM. If the firm takes the cash discount, it must pay $980 [$1,000 − (0.02 × $1,000)] by March 10, thereby saving $20.

cost of giving up a cash discount
The implied rate of interest paid to delay payment of an account payable for an additional number of days.

Giving Up the Cash Discount If the firm chooses to give up the cash discount, it should pay on the final day of the credit period. There is an implicit cost associated with giving up a cash discount. The **cost of giving up a cash discount** is the implied rate of interest paid to delay payment of an account payable for an additional number of days. In other words, the amount is the interest being paid by the firm to keep its money for a number of days. This cost can be illustrated by a simple example. The example assumes that payment will be made on the last possible day (either the final day of the cash discount period or the final day of the credit period).

EXAMPLE In the preceding example, we saw that Lawrence Industries could take the cash discount on its February 27 purchase by paying $980 on March 10. If Lawrence gives up the cash discount, payment can be made on March 30. To keep its money for an extra 20 days, the firm must give up an opportunity to pay $980 for its $1,000 purchase. In other words, it will cost the firm $20 to

FIGURE 14.1

Payment Options
Payment options for Lawrence Industries

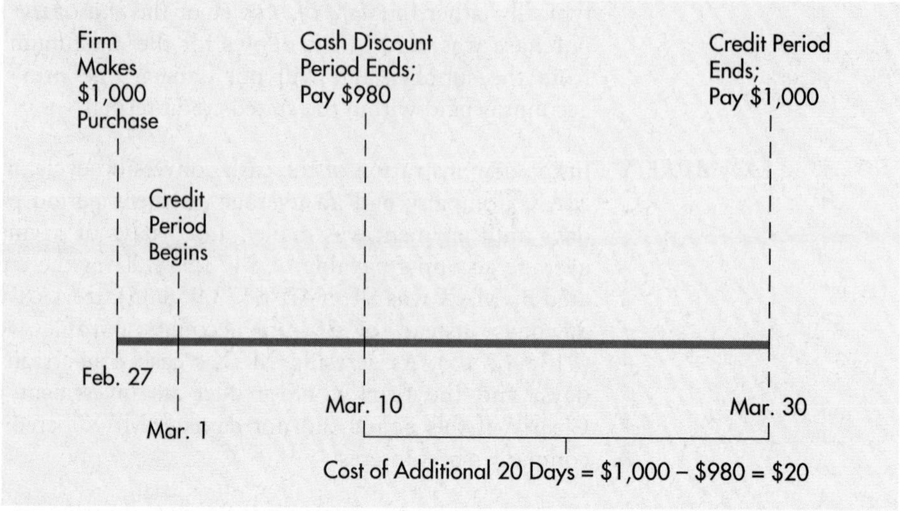

delay payment for 20 days. Figure 14.1 shows the payment options that are open to the company.

To calculate the cost of giving up the cash discount, the *true purchase price* must be viewed as the *discounted cost of the merchandise,* which is $980 for Lawrence Industries. The annual percentage cost of giving up the cash discount can be calculated using Equation 14.1:

$$\text{Cost of giving up cash discount} = \frac{CD}{100\% - CD} \times \frac{360}{N} \quad (14.1)$$

where

CD = stated cash discount in percentage terms
N = number of days that payment can be delayed by giving up the cash discount

Substituting the values for CD (2%) and N (20 days) into Equation 14.1 results in an annualized cost of giving up the cash discount of 36.73% [(2% ÷ 98%) × (360 ÷ 20)]. A 360-day year is assumed.

A simple way to *approximate* the cost of giving up a cash discount is to use the stated cash discount percentage, CD, in place of the first term of Equation 14.1:

$$\text{Approximate cost of giving up cash discount} = CD \times \frac{360}{N} \quad (14.2)$$

The smaller the cash discount, the closer the approximation to the actual cost of giving it up. Using this approximation, the cost of giving up the cash discount for Lawrence Industries is 36% [2% × (360 ÷ 20)].

Using the Cost of Giving Up a Cash Discount in Decision Making The financial manager must determine whether it is advisable to take a cash discount. Financial managers must remember that taking cash discounts may represent an important source of additional profitability.

TABLE 14.1 Cash Discounts and Associated Costs for Mason Products

Supplier	Credit terms	Approximate cost of giving up a cash discount
A	2/10 net 30 EOM	36.0%
B	1/10 net 55 EOM	8.0
C	3/20 net 70 EOM	21.6
D	4/10 net 60 EOM	28.8

EXAMPLE Mason Products, a large building-supply company, has four possible suppliers, each offering different credit terms. Otherwise, their products and services are identical. Table 14.1 presents the credit terms offered by suppliers A, B, C, and D and the cost of giving up the cash discounts in each transaction. The approximation method of calculating the cost of giving up a cash discount (Equation 14.2) has been used. The cost of giving up the cash discount from supplier A is 36%; from supplier B, 8%; from supplier C, 21.6%; and from supplier D, 28.8%.

If the firm needs short-term funds, which it can borrow from its bank at an interest rate of 13%, and if each of the suppliers is viewed *separately,* which (if any) of the suppliers' cash discounts will the firm give up? In dealing with supplier A, the firm takes the cash discount, because the cost of giving it up is 36%, and then borrows the funds it requires from its bank at 13% interest. With supplier B, the firm would do better to give up the cash discount, because the cost of this action is less than the cost of borrowing money from the bank (8% versus 13%). With either supplier C or supplier D, the firm should take the cash discount, because in both cases the cost of giving up the discount is greater than the 13% cost of borrowing from the bank.

The example shows that the cost of giving up a cash discount is relevant when one is evaluating a single supplier's credit terms in light of certain *bank borrowing costs.* However, other factors relative to payment strategies may also need to be considered. For example, some firms, particularly small firms and poorly managed firms, routinely give up *all* discounts because they either lack alternative sources of unsecured short-term financing or fail to recognize the implicit costs of their actions.

Effects of Stretching Accounts Payable

stretching accounts payable
Paying bills as late as possible without damaging the firm's credit rating.

A strategy that is often employed by a firm is **stretching accounts payable**—that is, paying bills as late as possible without damaging its credit rating. Such a strategy can reduce the cost of giving up a cash discount.

EXAMPLE Lawrence Industries was extended credit terms of 2/10 net 30 EOM. The cost of giving up the cash discount, assuming payment on the last day of the credit period, was found to be approximately 36% [2% × (360 ÷ 20)]. If the firm were

In Practice

FOCUS ON ETHICS Amazon Stays Ethical

Top managers in a tiny central Ohio company fret but say nothing publicly as a giant retailer routinely waits 120 days to pay its invoices marked "due in 30 days." The credit manager is quiet, partly because the company depends on this key account for survival and partly because "stretching payables" is the most widespread unethical practice in corporate America.

Unlike the retailer above, e-tailer **Amazon**, despite its size and marketing success, pays its suppliers on time amidst intense pressures on it to become profitable. Amazon has changed strategy, emphasizing profitability over growth. In fact, during 2001 it reported its first profit—1¢ per share. CFO Warren Jensen, describing the critical role management of working capital plays in the quest for profits, was quoted in *CFO* magazine as saying, "This isn't about trying to string our vendors out." Amazon has negative net working capital (that is, its current liabilities exceed current assets) but has chosen to employ just-in-time inventory delivery from book publishers—not delayed payments—to reduce the need for short-term bank loans. One advantage of Amazon's payables policy is that suppliers would be likely to work with Amazon should its cash position temporarily drop below that needed to cover payables.

In economic downturns, companies face even greater temptation to delay payments, and many do so. Stephen Payne, of REL Consultancy Group, warns that this unethical practice "can bite you in the rear end" as suppliers detect it and simply jack up prices to counter the effect. The buyer's average payment period represents its suppliers' average collection periods, after all.

Stretching payables is unethical for two reasons. First, the buyer is violating the terms of its trade credit agreement. Second, the buyer is in effect doing additional borrowing from its suppliers without their knowledge or authorization. "Everybody's doing it" is never a valid excuse for trying to add to shareholder wealth through such blatantly unethical behavior. Shareholder wealth maximization is once again seen to be subject to ethical constraints.

able to stretch its account payable to 70 days without damaging its credit rating, the cost of giving up the cash discount would be only 12% [$2\% \times (360 \div 60)$]. Stretching accounts payable reduces the implicit cost of giving up a cash discount.

Although stretching accounts payable may be financially attractive, it raises an important ethical issue: It may cause the firm to violate the agreement it entered into with its supplier when it purchased merchandise. Clearly, a supplier would not look kindly on a customer who regularly and purposely postponed paying for purchases.

Accruals

accruals
Liabilities for services received for which payment has yet to be made.

The second spontaneous source of short-term business financing is accruals. **Accruals** are liabilities for services received for which payment has yet to be made. The most common items accrued by a firm are wages and taxes. Because taxes are payments to the government, their accrual cannot be manipulated by the firm. However, the accrual of wages can be manipulated to some extent. This is accomplished by delaying payment of wages, thereby receiving an interest-free loan from employees who are paid sometime after they have performed the work. The pay period for employees who earn an hourly rate is often governed by union regulations or by state or federal law. However, in other cases, the frequency of payment is at the discretion of the company's management.

EXAMPLE Tenney Company, a large janitorial service company, currently pays its employees at the end of each work week. The weekly payroll totals $400,000. If the firm were to extend the pay period so as to pay its employees 1 week later throughout an entire year, the employees would in effect be lending the firm $400,000 for a year. If the firm could earn 10% annually on invested funds, such a strategy would be worth $40,000 per year ($0.10 \times \$400{,}000$).

Review Questions

14–1 What are the two major sources of spontaneous short-term financing for a firm? How do their balances behave relative to the firm's sales?

14–2 Is there a cost associated with *taking a cash discount?* Is there any cost associated with *giving up a cash discount?* How do short-term borrowing costs affect the cash discount decision?

14–3 What is "stretching accounts payable"? What effect does this action have on the cost of giving up a cash discount?

LG3 LG4

Unsecured Sources of Short-Term Loans

Businesses obtain unsecured short-term loans from two major sources, banks and commercial paper. Unlike the spontaneous sources of unsecured short-term financing, bank loans and commercial paper are negotiated and result from actions taken by the firm's financial manager. Bank loans are more popular, because they are available to firms of all sizes; commercial paper tends to be available only to large firms. In addition, international loans can be used to finance international transactions.

Bank Loans

short-term, self-liquidating loan
An unsecured short-term loan in which the use to which the borrowed money is put provides the mechanism through which the loan is repaid.

Banks are a major source of unsecured short-term loans to businesses. The major type of loan made by banks to businesses is the **short-term, self-liquidating loan.** These loans are intended merely to carry the firm through seasonal peaks in financing needs that are due primarily to buildups of inventory and accounts receivable. As inventories and receivables are converted into cash, the funds needed to retire these loans are generated. In other words, the use to which the borrowed money is put provides the mechanism through which the loan is repaid—hence the term *self-liquidating.* Banks lend unsecured, short-term funds in three basic ways: through single-payment notes, lines of credit, and revolving credit agreements. Before we look at these types of loans, we consider loan interest rates.

Loan Interest Rates

prime rate of interest (prime rate)
The lowest rate of interest charged by leading banks on business loans to their most important business borrowers.

The interest rate on a bank loan can be a fixed or a floating rate, typically based on the prime rate of interest. The **prime rate of interest (prime rate)** is the lowest rate of interest charged by leading banks on business loans to their most important business borrowers.[1] The prime rate fluctuates with changing supply-and-demand relationships for short-term funds.[2] Banks generally determine the rate to be charged to various borrowers by adding a premium to the prime rate to adjust it for the borrower's "riskiness." The premium may amount to 4 percent or more, although most unsecured short-term loans carry premiums of less than 2 percent.

fixed-rate loan
A loan with a rate of interest that is determined at a set increment above the prime rate and at which it remains fixed until maturity.

floating-rate loan
A loan with a rate of interest initially set at an increment above the prime rate and allowed to "float," or vary, above prime *as the prime rate varies* until maturity.

Fixed- and Floating-Rate Loans Loans can have either fixed or floating interest rates. On a **fixed-rate loan,** the rate of interest is determined at a set increment above the prime rate on the date of the loan and remains unvarying at that fixed rate until maturity. On a **floating-rate loan,** the increment above the prime rate is initially established, and the rate of interest is allowed to "float," or vary, above prime *as the prime rate varies* until maturity. Generally, the increment above the prime rate will be *lower* on a floating-rate loan than on a fixed-rate loan of equivalent risk, because the lender bears less risk with a floating-rate loan. As a result of the volatile nature of the prime rate during recent years, today *most short-term business loans are floating-rate loans.*

Method of Computing Interest Once the *nominal (or stated) annual rate* is established, the method of computing interest is determined. Interest can be paid either when a loan matures or in advance. If interest is paid *at maturity,* the *effective (or true) annual rate*—the actual rate of interest paid—for an assumed 1-year period[3] is equal to

$$\frac{\text{Interest}}{\text{Amount borrowed}} \tag{14.3}$$

Most bank loans to businesses require the interest payment at maturity.

discount loans
Loans on which interest is paid in advance by being deducted from the amount borrowed.

When interest is paid *in advance,* it is deducted from the loan so that the borrower actually receives less money than is requested. Loans on which interest is paid in advance are called **discount loans.** The *effective annual rate for a discount loan,* assuming a 1-year period, is calculated as

$$\frac{\text{Interest}}{\text{Amount borrowed} - \text{Interest}} \tag{14.4}$$

Paying interest in advance raises the effective annual rate above the stated annual rate.

EXAMPLE ▼ Wooster Company, a manufacturer of athletic apparel, wants to borrow \$10,000 at a stated annual rate of 10% interest for 1 year. If the interest on the loan is paid at maturity, the firm will pay \$1,000 (0.10 × \$10,000) for the use of the

1. A trend away from using the prime rate as a benchmark has begun in the United States in response to various borrower lawsuits against banks. Some banks now use the term *base rate* or *reference rate* rather than *prime rate* for pricing corporate and other loans. In fact, the use of the *London Interbank Offered Rate (LIBOR)* is gaining momentum as a base lending rate in the United States.

2. During the past 25 years, the prime rate has varied from a record high of 21.5% (December 1980) to a low of 4.75% (December 2001 through the middle of 2002). Since 1995, it has fluctuated in the range from a high of about 9.50% to a low of about 4.75%.

3. Effective annual rates (EARs) for loans with maturities of less than 1 year can be found by using the technique presented in Chapter 4 for finding EARs when interest is compounded more frequently than annually. See Equation 4.21.

$10,000 for the year. Substituting into Equation 14.3 reveals that the effective annual rate is therefore

$$\frac{\$1{,}000}{\$10{,}000} = 10.0\%$$

If the money is borrowed at the same *stated* annual rate for 1 year but interest is paid in advance, the firm still pays $1,000 in interest, but it receives only $9,000 ($10,000 − $1,000). The effective annual rate in this case is

$$\frac{\$1{,}000}{\$10{,}000 - \$1{,}000} = \frac{\$1{,}000}{\$9{,}000} = 11.1\%$$

Paying interest in advance thus makes the effective annual rate (11.1%) greater than the stated annual rate (10.0%).

Single-Payment Notes

single-payment note
A short-term, one-time loan made to a borrower who needs funds for a specific purpose for a short period.

A **single-payment note** can be obtained from a commercial bank by a creditworthy business borrower. This type of loan is usually a one-time loan made to a borrower who needs funds for a specific purpose for a short period. The resulting instrument is a *note,* signed by the borrower, that states the terms of the loan, including the length of the loan and the interest rate. This type of short-term note generally has a maturity of 30 days to 9 months or more. The interest charged is usually tied in some way to the prime rate of interest.

EXAMPLE

Gordon Manufacturing, a producer of rotary mower blades, recently borrowed $100,000 from each of two banks—bank A and bank B. The loans were incurred on the same day, when the prime rate of interest was 9%. Each loan involved a 90-day note with interest to be paid at the end of 90 days. The interest rate was set at $1\frac{1}{2}\%$ above the prime rate on bank A's *fixed-rate note.* Over the 90-day period, the rate of interest on this note will remain at $10\frac{1}{2}\%$ (9% prime rate + $1\frac{1}{2}\%$ increment) regardless of fluctuations in the prime rate. The total interest cost on this loan is $2,625 [$\$100{,}000 \times (10\frac{1}{2}\% \times 90/360)$]. The effective 90-day rate on this loan is 2.625% ($2,625/$100,000).

Assuming that the loan from bank A is rolled over each 90 days throughout the year under the same terms and circumstances, its effective *annual* interest rate is found by using Equation 4.23. Because the loan costs 2.625% for 90 days, it is necessary to compound $(1 + 0.02625)$ for four periods in the year (that is, 360/90) and then subtract 1:

$$\begin{aligned}\text{Effective annual rate} &= (1 + 0.02625)^4 - 1\\ &= 1.1092 - 1 = 0.1092 = \underline{\underline{10.92}}\%\end{aligned}$$

The effective annual rate of interest on the fixed-rate, 90-day note is 10.92%.

Bank B set the interest rate at 1% above the prime rate on its *floating-rate note.* The rate charged over the 90 days will vary directly with the prime rate. Initially, the rate will be 10% (9% + 1%), but when the prime rate changes, so will the rate of interest on the note. For instance, if after 30 days the prime rate rises to 9.5%, and after another 30 days it drops to 9.25%, the firm will be paying 0.833% for the first 30 days ($10\% \times 30/360$), 0.875% for the next 30 days ($10.5\% \times 30/360$), and 0.854% for the last 30 days ($10.25\% \times 30/360$). Its total interest cost will be \$2,562 [\$100,000 × (0.833% + 0.875% + 0.854%)], resulting in an effective 90-day rate of 2.562% (\$2,562/\$100,000).

Again, assuming the loan is rolled over each 90 days throughout the year under the same terms and circumstances, its effective *annual* rate is 10.65%:

$$\text{Effective annual rate} = (1 + 0.02562)^4 - 1$$
$$= 1.1065 - 1 = 0.1065 = \underline{\underline{10.65\%}}$$

Clearly, in this case the floating-rate loan would have been less expensive than the fixed-rate loan because of its generally lower effective annual rate.

Lines of Credit

line of credit
An agreement between a commercial bank and a business specifying the amount of unsecured short-term borrowing the bank will make available to the firm over a given period of time.

A **line of credit** is an agreement between a commercial bank and a business specifying the amount of unsecured short-term borrowing the bank will make available to the firm over a given period of time. It is similar to the agreement under which issuers of bank credit cards, such as MasterCard, Visa, and Discover, extend preapproved credit to cardholders. A line-of-credit agreement is typically made for a period of 1 year and often places certain constraints on the borrower. It is *not a guaranteed loan* but indicates that if the bank has sufficient funds available, it will allow the borrower to owe it *up to* a certain amount of money. The amount of a line of credit is the *maximum amount the firm can owe the bank* at any point in time.

When applying for a line of credit, the borrower may be required to submit such documents as its cash budget, its pro forma income statement, its pro forma balance sheet, and its recent financial statements. If the bank finds the customer acceptable, the line of credit will be extended. The major attraction of a line of credit from the bank's point of view is that it eliminates the need to examine the creditworthiness of a customer each time it borrows money.

Interest Rates The interest rate on a line of credit is normally stated as a floating rate—the *prime rate plus a premium.* If the prime rate changes, the interest rate charged on new *as well as outstanding* borrowing automatically changes. The amount a borrower is charged in excess of the prime rate depends on its creditworthiness. The more creditworthy the borrower, the lower the premium (interest increment) above prime, and vice versa.

operating-change restrictions
Contractual restrictions that a bank may impose on a firm's financial condition or operations as part of a line-of-credit agreement.

Operating-Change Restrictions In a line-of-credit agreement, a bank may impose **operating-change restrictions,** which give it the right to revoke the line if any major changes occur in the firm's financial condition or operations. The firm is usually required to submit up-to-date, and preferably audited, financial statements for periodic review. In addition, the bank typically needs to be informed of shifts in key managerial personnel or in the firm's operations before changes take place. Such changes may affect the future success and debt-paying ability of the firm and thus could alter its credit status. If the bank does not agree with the proposed changes and the firm makes them anyway, the bank has the right to revoke the line of credit.

Compensating Balances To ensure that the borrower will be a good customer, many short-term unsecured bank loans—single-payment notes and lines

compensating balance
A required checking account balance equal to a certain percentage of the amount borrowed from a bank under a line-of-credit or revolving credit agreement.

of credit—require the borrower to maintain, in a checking account, a **compensating balance** equal to a certain percentage of the amount borrowed. Compensating balances of 10 to 20 percent are frequently required. A compensating balance not only forces the borrower to be a good customer of the bank but may also raise the interest cost to the borrower.

EXAMPLE

Estrada Graphics, a graphic design firm, has borrowed $1 million under a line-of-credit agreement. It must pay a stated interest rate of 10% and maintain, in its checking account, a compensating balance equal to 20% of the amount borrowed, or $200,000. Thus it actually receives the use of only $800,000. To use that amount for a year, the firm pays interest of $100,000 (0.10 × $1,000,000). The effective annual rate on the funds is therefore 12.5% ($100,000 ÷ $800,000), 2.5% more than the stated rate of 10%.

If the firm normally maintains a balance of $200,000 or more in its checking account, the effective annual rate equals the stated annual rate of 10% because none of the $1 million borrowed is needed to satisfy the compensating-balance requirement. If the firm normally maintains a $100,000 balance in its checking account, only an additional $100,000 will have to be tied up, leaving it with $900,000 of usable funds. The effective annual rate in this case would be 11.1% ($100,000 ÷ $900,000). Thus a compensating balance raises the cost of borrowing *only if* it is larger than the firm's normal cash balance.

annual cleanup
The requirement that for a certain number of days during the year borrowers under a line of credit carry a zero loan balance (that is, owe the bank nothing).

Annual Cleanups To ensure that money lent under a line-of-credit agreement is actually being used to finance seasonal needs, many banks require an **annual cleanup.** This means that the borrower must have a loan balance of zero—that is, owe the bank nothing—for a certain number of days during the year. Insisting that the borrower carry a zero loan balance for a certain period ensures that short-term loans do not turn into long-term loans.

All the characteristics of a line-of-credit agreement are negotiable to some extent. Today, banks bid competitively to attract large, well-known firms. A prospective borrower should attempt to negotiate a line of credit with the most favorable interest rate, for an optimal amount of funds, and with a minimum of restrictions. Borrowers today frequently pay fees to lenders instead of maintaining deposit balances as compensation for loans and other services. The lender attempts to get a good return with maximum safety. Negotiations should produce a line of credit that is suitable to both borrower and lender.

Revolving Credit Agreements

revolving credit agreement
A line of credit *guaranteed* to a borrower by a commercial bank regardless of the scarcity of money.

commitment fee
The fee that is normally charged on a *revolving credit agreement;* it often applies to the average unused balance of the borrower's credit line.

A **revolving credit agreement** is nothing more than a *guaranteed line of credit.* It is guaranteed in the sense that the commercial bank assures the borrower that a specified amount of funds will be made available regardless of the scarcity of money. The interest rate and other requirements are similar to those for a line of credit. It is not uncommon for a revolving credit agreement to be for a period greater than 1 year. Because the bank guarantees the availability of funds, a **commitment fee** is normally charged on a revolving credit agreement. This fee often applies to the average unused balance of the borrower's credit line. It is normally about 0.5 percent of the *average unused portion* of the line.

EXAMPLE REH Company, a major real estate developer, has a \$2 million revolving credit agreement with its bank. Its average borrowing under the agreement for the past year was \$1.5 million. The bank charges a commitment fee of 0.5%. Because the average unused portion of the committed funds was \$500,000 (\$2 million − \$1.5 million), the commitment fee for the year was \$2,500 (0.005 × \$500,000). Of course, REH also had to pay interest on the actual \$1.5 million borrowed under the agreement. Assuming that \$160,000 interest was paid on the \$1.5 million borrowed, the effective cost of the agreement was 10.83% [(\$160,000 + \$2,500)/\$1,500,000]. Although more expensive than a line of credit, a revolving credit agreement can be less risky from the borrower's viewpoint, because the availability of funds is guaranteed.

Commercial Paper

commercial paper
A form of financing consisting of short-term, unsecured promissory notes issued by firms with a high credit standing.

Commercial paper is a form of financing that consists of short-term, unsecured promissory notes issued by firms with a high credit standing. Generally, only quite large firms of unquestionable financial soundness are able to issue commercial paper. Most commercial paper has maturities ranging from 3 to 270 days. Although there is no set denomination, it is generally issued in multiples of \$100,000 or more. A large portion of the commercial paper today is issued by finance companies; manufacturing firms account for a smaller portion of this type of financing. Businesses often purchase commercial paper, which they hold as marketable securities, to provide an interest-earning reserve of liquidity.

Interest on Commercial Paper

Commercial paper is sold at a discount from its *par,* or *face, value.* The interest paid by the issuer of commercial paper is determined by the size of the discount and the length of time to maturity. The actual interest earned by the purchaser is determined by certain calculations, illustrated by the following example.

EXAMPLE Bertram Corporation, a large shipbuilder, has just issued \$1 million worth of commercial paper that has a 90-day maturity and sells for \$980,000. At the end of 90 days, the purchaser of this paper will receive \$1 million for its \$980,000 investment. The interest paid on the financing is therefore \$20,000 on a principal of \$980,000. The effective 90-day rate on the paper is 2.04% (\$20,000/\$980,000). Assuming that the paper is rolled over each 90 days throughout the year, the effective annual rate for Bertram's commercial paper, found by using Equation 4.23, is 8.41% $[(1 + 0.0204)^4 - 1]$.

An interesting characteristic of commercial paper is that its interest cost is *normally* 2 to 4 percent below the prime rate. In other words, firms are able to raise funds more cheaply by selling commercial paper than by borrowing from a commercial bank. The reason is that many suppliers of short-term funds do not have the option, as banks do, of making low-risk business loans at the prime rate. They can invest safely only in marketable securities such as Treasury bills and commercial paper. The yields on these marketable securities on May 1, 2002, when the prime rate of interest was 4.75 percent, were about 1.73 percent for 3-month Treasury bills and about 1.80 percent for 3-month commercial paper.

Although the stated interest cost of borrowing through the sale of commercial paper is normally lower than the prime rate, the *overall cost* of commercial paper may not be less than that of a bank loan. Additional costs include the fees paid by most issuers to obtain the bank line of credit used to back the paper, fees paid to obtain third-party ratings used to make the paper more salable, and flotation costs. In addition, even if it is slightly more expensive to borrow from a commercial bank, it may at times be advisable to do so to establish a good working relationship with a bank. This strategy ensures that when money is tight, funds can be obtained promptly and at a reasonable interest rate.

International Loans

In some ways, arranging short-term financing for international trade is no different from financing purely domestic operations. In both cases, producers must finance production and inventory and then continue to finance accounts receivable before collecting any cash payments from sales. In other ways, however, the short-term financing of international sales and purchases is fundamentally different from that of strictly domestic trade.

International Transactions

The important difference between international and domestic transactions is that payments are often made or received in a foreign currency. Not only must a U.S. company pay the costs of doing business in the foreign exchange market, but it also is exposed to *exchange rate risk*. A U.S.-based company that exports goods and has accounts receivable denominated in a foreign currency faces the risk that the U.S. dollar will appreciate in value relative to the foreign currency. The risk to a U.S. importer with foreign-currency-denominated accounts payable is that the dollar will depreciate. Although *exchange rate risk* can often be *hedged* by using currency forward, futures, or options markets, doing so is costly and is not possible for all foreign currencies.

Typical international transactions are large in size and have long maturity dates. Therefore, companies that are involved in international trade generally have to finance larger dollar amounts for longer time periods than companies that operate domestically. Furthermore, because foreign companies are rarely well known in the United States, some financial institutions are reluctant to lend to U.S. exporters or importers, particularly smaller firms.

Financing International Trade

letter of credit
A letter written by a company's bank to the company's foreign supplier, stating that the bank guarantees payment of an invoiced amount if all the underlying agreements are met.

Several specialized techniques have evolved for financing international trade. Perhaps the most important financing vehicle is the **letter of credit,** a letter written by a company's bank to the company's foreign supplier, stating that the bank guarantees payment of an invoiced amount if all the underlying agreements are met. The letter of credit essentially substitutes the bank's reputation and creditworthiness for that of its commercial customer. A U.S. exporter is more willing to sell goods to a foreign buyer if the transaction is covered by a letter of credit issued by a well-known bank in the buyer's home country.

Firms that do business in foreign countries on an ongoing basis often finance their operations, at least in part, in the local market. A company that has an assembly plant in Mexico, for example, might choose to finance its purchases of Mexican goods and services with peso funds borrowed from a Mexican bank. This not only minimizes exchange rate risk but also improves the company's business ties to the host community. Multinational companies, however, sometimes finance their international transactions through dollar-denominated loans from international banks. The *Eurocurrency loan markets* allow creditworthy borrowers to obtain financing on very attractive terms.

Transactions Between Subsidiaries

Much international trade involves transactions between corporate subsidiaries. A U.S. company might, for example, manufacture one part in an Asian plant and another part in the United States, assemble the product in Brazil, and sell it in Europe. The shipment of goods back and forth between subsidiaries creates accounts receivable and accounts payable, but the parent company has considerable discretion about how and when payments are made. In particular, the parent can minimize foreign exchange fees and other transaction costs by "netting" what affiliates owe each other and paying only the net amount due, rather than having both subsidiaries pay each other the gross amounts due.

Review Questions

14–4 How is the *prime rate of interest* relevant to the cost of short-term bank borrowing? What is a *floating-rate loan?*

14–5 How does the *effective annual rate* differ between a loan requiring interest payments *at maturity* and another, similar loan requiring interest *in advance?*

14–6 What are the basic terms and characteristics of a *single-payment note?* How is the *effective annual rate* on such a note found?

14–7 What is a *line of credit?* Describe each of the following features that are often included in these agreements: (**a**) operating-change restrictions; (**b**) compensating balance; and (**c**) annual cleanup.

14–8 What is a *revolving credit agreement?* How does this arrangement differ from the line-of-credit agreement? What is a *commitment fee?*

14–9 How is *commercial paper* used to raise short-term funds? Who can issue commercial paper? Who buys commercial paper?

14–10 What is the important difference between international and domestic transactions? How is a *letter of credit* used in financing international trade transactions? How is "netting" used in transactions between subsidiaries?

LG5 LG6

Secured Sources of Short-Term Loans

secured short-term financing
Short-term financing (loan) that has specific assets pledged as collateral.

When a firm has exhausted its sources of unsecured short-term financing, it may be able to obtain additional short-term loans on a secured basis. **Secured short-term financing** has specific assets pledged as collateral. The *collateral* commonly takes the form of an asset, such as accounts receivable or inventory. The lender

security agreement
The agreement between the borrower and the lender that specifies the collateral held against a secured loan.

obtains a security interest in the collateral through the execution of a **security agreement** with the borrower that specifies the collateral held against the loan. In addition, the terms of the loan against which the security is held form part of the security agreement. They specify the conditions required for the security interest to be removed, along with the interest rate on the loan, repayment dates, and other loan provisions. A copy of the security agreement is filed in a public office within the state—typically, a county or state court. Filing provides subsequent lenders with information about which assets of a prospective borrower are unavailable for use as collateral. The filing requirement protects the lender by legally establishing the lender's security interest.

Characteristics of Secured Short-Term Loans

Although many people believe that holding collateral as security reduces the risk of a loan, lenders do not usually view loans in this way. Lenders recognize that holding collateral can reduce losses if the borrower defaults, but *the presence of collateral has no impact on the risk of default.* A lender requires collateral to ensure recovery of some portion of the loan in the event of default. What the lender wants above all, however, is to be repaid as scheduled. In general, lenders prefer to make less risky loans at lower rates of interest than to be in a position in which they must liquidate collateral.

Collateral and Terms

Lenders of secured short-term funds prefer collateral that has a duration closely matched to the term of the loan. Current assets—accounts receivable and inventory—are the most desirable short-term-loan collateral, because they can normally be converted into cash much sooner than fixed assets. Thus the short-term lender of secured funds generally accepts only liquid current assets as collateral.

percentage advance
The percent of the book value of the collateral that constitutes the principal of a secured loan.

Typically, the lender determines the desirable **percentage advance** to make against the collateral. This percentage advance constitutes the principal of the secured loan and is normally between 30 and 100 percent of the book value of the collateral. It varies according to the type and liquidity of collateral.

The interest rate that is charged on secured short-term loans is typically *higher* than the rate on unsecured short-term loans. Lenders do not normally consider secured loans less risky than unsecured loans. In addition, negotiating and administering secured loans is more troublesome for the lender than negotiating and administering unsecured loans. The lender therefore normally requires added compensation in the form of a service charge, a higher interest rate, or both.

Institutions Extending Secured Short-Term Loans

commercial finance companies
Lending institutions that make *only* secured loans—both short-term and long-term—to businesses.

The primary sources of secured short-term loans to businesses are commercial banks and finance companies. Both institutions deal in short-term loans secured primarily by accounts receivable and inventory. The operations of commercial banks have already been described. **Commercial finance companies** are lending institutions that make *only* secured loans—both short-term and long-term—to businesses. Unlike banks, finance companies are not permitted to hold deposits.

Only when its unsecured and secured short-term borrowing power from the commercial bank is exhausted will a borrower turn to the commercial finance company for additional secured borrowing. Because the finance company generally ends up with higher-risk borrowers, its interest charges on secured short-term loans are usually higher than those of commercial banks. The leading U.S. commercial finance companies include the CIT Group and GE Capital.

The Use of Accounts Receivable as Collateral

Two commonly used means of obtaining short-term financing with accounts receivable are *pledging accounts receivable* and *factoring accounts receivable.* Actually, only a pledge of accounts receivable creates a secured short-term loan; factoring really entails the *sale* of accounts receivable at a discount. Although factoring is not actually a form of secured short-term borrowing, it does involve the use of accounts receivable to obtain needed short-term funds.

Pledging Accounts Receivable

pledge of accounts receivable
The use of a firm's accounts receivable as security, or collateral, to obtain a short-term loan.

A **pledge of accounts receivable** is often used to secure a short-term loan. Because accounts receivable are normally quite liquid, they are an attractive form of short-term-loan collateral.

The Pledging Process When a firm requests a loan against accounts receivable, the lender first evaluates the firm's accounts receivable to determine their desirability as collateral. The lender makes a list of the acceptable accounts, along with the billing dates and amounts. If the borrowing firm requests a loan for a fixed amount, the lender needs to select only enough accounts to secure the funds requested. If the borrower wants the maximum loan available, the lender evaluates all the accounts to select the maximum amount of acceptable collateral.

After selecting the acceptable accounts, the lender normally adjusts the dollar value of these accounts for expected returns on sales and other allowances. If a customer whose account has been pledged returns merchandise or receives some type of allowance, such as a cash discount for early payment, the amount of the collateral is automatically reduced. For protection from such occurrences, the lender normally reduces the value of the acceptable collateral by a fixed percentage.

lien
A publicly disclosed legal claim on collateral.

Next, the percentage to be advanced against the collateral must be determined. The lender evaluates the quality of the acceptable receivables and the expected cost of their liquidation. This percentage represents the principal of the loan and typically ranges between 50 and 90 percent of the face value of acceptable accounts receivable. To protect its interest in the collateral, the lender files a **lien,** which is a publicly disclosed legal claim on the collateral. For an example of the complete pledging process, see the book's Web site at *www.aw.com/gitman.*

nonnotification basis
The basis on which a borrower, having pledged an account receivable, continues to collect the account payments without notifying the account customer.

notification basis
The basis on which an account customer whose account has been pledged (or factored) is notified to remit payment directly to the lender (or factor).

Notification Pledges of accounts receivable are normally made on a **nonnotification basis,** meaning that a customer whose account has been pledged as collateral is not notified. Under the nonnotification arrangement, the borrower still collects the pledged account receivable, and the lender trusts the borrower to remit these payments as they are received. If a pledge of accounts receivable is made on a **notification basis,** the customer is notified to remit payment directly to the lender.

Pledging Cost The stated cost of a pledge of accounts receivable is normally 2 to 5 percent above the prime rate. In addition to the stated interest rate, a service charge of up to 3 percent may be levied by the lender to cover its administrative costs. Clearly, pledges of accounts receivable are a high-cost source of short-term financing.

Factoring Accounts Receivable

factoring accounts receivable
The outright sale of accounts receivable at a discount to a *factor* or other financial institution.

factor
A financial institution that specializes in purchasing accounts receivable from businesses.

Factoring accounts receivable involves selling them outright, at a discount, to a financial institution. A **factor** is a financial institution that specializes in purchasing accounts receivable from businesses. Some commercial banks and commercial finance companies also factor accounts receivable. Although it is not the same as obtaining a short-term loan, factoring accounts receivable is similar to borrowing with accounts receivable as collateral.

Factoring Agreement A factoring agreement normally states the exact conditions and procedures for the purchase of an account. The factor, like a lender against a pledge of accounts receivable, chooses accounts for purchase, selecting only those that appear to be acceptable credit risks. Where factoring is to be on a continuing basis, the factor will actually make the firm's credit decisions, because this will guarantee the acceptability of accounts.[4] Factoring is normally done on a *notification basis,* and the factor receives payment of the account directly from the customer. In addition, most sales of accounts receivable to a factor are made on a **nonrecourse basis.** This means that the factor agrees to accept all credit risks. Thus, if a purchased account turns out to be uncollectible, the factor must absorb the loss.

nonrecourse basis
The basis on which accounts receivable are sold to a factor with the understanding that the factor accepts all credit risks on the purchased accounts.

Typically, the factor is not required to pay the firm until the account is collected or until the last day of the credit period, whichever occurs first. The factor sets up an account similar to a bank deposit account for each customer. As payment is received or as due dates arrive, the factor deposits money into the seller's account, from which the seller is free to make withdrawals as needed.

In many cases, if the firm leaves the money in the account, a *surplus* will exist on which the factor will pay interest. In other instances, the factor may make *advances* to the firm against uncollected accounts that are not yet due. These advances represent a negative balance in the firm's account, on which interest is charged.

Factoring Cost Factoring costs include commissions, interest levied on advances, and interest earned on surpluses. The factor deposits in the firm's account the book value of the collected or due accounts purchased by the factor, less the commissions. The commissions are typically stated as a 1 to 3 percent discount from the book value of factored accounts receivable. The *interest levied on advances* is generally 2 to 4 percent above the prime rate. It is levied on the actual

4. The use of credit cards such as MasterCard, Visa, and Discover by consumers has some similarity to factoring, because the vendor that accepts the card is reimbursed at a discount for purchases made with the card. The difference between factoring and credit cards is that cards are nothing more than a line of credit extended by the issuer, which charges the vendors a fee for accepting the cards. In factoring, the factor does not analyze credit until after the sale has been made; in many cases (except when factoring is done on a continuing basis), the initial credit decision is the responsibility of the vendor, not the factor that purchases the account.

amount advanced. The *interest paid on surpluses* is generally between 0.2 and 0.5 percent per month. An example of the factoring process is included on the book's Web site at *www.aw.com/gitman.*

Although its costs may seem high, factoring has certain advantages that make it attractive to many firms. One is the ability it gives the firm to *turn accounts receivable immediately into cash* without having to worry about repayment. Another advantage of factoring is that it ensures a *known pattern of cash flows.* In addition, if factoring is undertaken on a continuing basis, the firm *can eliminate its credit and collection departments.*

The Use of Inventory as Collateral

Inventory is generally second to accounts receivable in desirability as short-term loan collateral. Inventory normally has a market value that is greater than its book value, which is used to establish its value as collateral. A lender whose loan is secured with inventory will probably be able to sell that inventory for at least book value if the borrower defaults on its obligations.

The most important characteristic of inventory being evaluated as loan collateral is *marketability,* which must be considered in light of its physical properties. A warehouse of *perishable* items, such as fresh peaches, may be quite marketable, but if the cost of storing and selling the peaches is high, they may not be desirable collateral. *Specialized items,* such as moon-roving vehicles, are not desirable collateral either, because finding a buyer for them could be difficult. When evaluating inventory as possible loan collateral, the lender looks for items with very stable market prices that have ready markets and that lack undesirable physical properties.

Floating Inventory Liens

floating inventory lien
A secured short-term loan against inventory under which the lender's claim is on the borrower's inventory in general.

A lender may be willing to secure a loan under a **floating inventory lien,** which is a claim on inventory in general. This arrangement is most attractive when the firm has a stable level of inventory that consists of a diversified group of relatively inexpensive merchandise. Inventories of items such as auto tires, screws and bolts, and shoes are candidates for floating-lien loans. Because it is difficult for a lender to verify the presence of the inventory, the lender generally advances less than 50 percent of the book value of the average inventory. The interest charge on a floating lien is 3 to 5 percent above the prime rate. Commercial banks often require floating liens as extra security on what would otherwise be an unsecured loan. Floating-lien inventory loans may also be available from commercial finance companies. An example of a floating lien is included on the book's Web site at *www.aw.com/gitman.*

Trust Receipt Inventory Loans

trust receipt inventory loan
A secured short-term loan against inventory under which the lender advances 80 to 100 percent of the cost of the borrower's relatively expensive inventory items in exchange for the borrower's promise to repay the lender, with accrued interest, immediately after the sale of each item of collateral.

A **trust receipt inventory loan** often can be made against relatively expensive automotive, consumer durable, and industrial goods that can be identified by serial number. Under this agreement, the borrower keeps the inventory, and the lender may advance 80 to 100 percent of its cost. The lender files a *lien* on all the items financed. The borrower is free to sell the merchandise but is trusted to remit the amount lent, along with accrued interest, to the lender immediately after the sale. The lender then releases the lien on the item. The lender makes periodic checks of the borrower's inventory to make sure that the required amount of collateral remains in the hands of the borrower. The interest charge to the borrower is normally 2 percent or more above the prime rate.

Trust receipt loans are often made by manufacturers' wholly owned financing subsidiaries, known as *captive finance companies,* to their customers. Captive finance companies are especially popular in industries that manufacture consumer durable goods, because they provide the manufacturer with a useful sales tool. For example, General Motors Acceptance Corporation (GMAC), the financing subsidiary of General Motors, grants these types of loans to its dealers. Trust receipt loans are also available through commercial banks and commercial finance companies.

Warehouse Receipt Loans

warehouse receipt loan
A secured short-term loan against inventory under which the lender receives control of the pledged inventory collateral, which is stored by a designated warehousing company on the lender's behalf.

A **warehouse receipt loan** is an arrangement whereby the lender, who may be a commercial bank or commercial finance company, receives control of the pledged inventory collateral, which is stored by a designated agent on the lender's behalf. After selecting acceptable collateral, the lender hires a warehousing company to act as its agent and take possession of the inventory.

Two types of warehousing arrangements are possible. A *terminal warehouse* is a central warehouse that is used to store the merchandise of various customers. The lender normally uses such a warehouse when the inventory is easily transported and can be delivered to the warehouse relatively inexpensively. Under a *field warehouse* arrangement, the lender hires a field warehousing company to set up a warehouse on the borrower's premises or to lease part of the borrower's warehouse to store the pledged collateral. Regardless of which type of warehouse is used, the warehousing company places a guard over the inventory. Only on written approval of the lender can any portion of the secured inventory be released by the warehousing company.

The actual lending agreement specifically states the requirements for the release of inventory. As in the case of other secured loans, the lender accepts only collateral that is believed to be readily marketable and advances only a portion—generally 75 to 90 percent—of the collateral's value. The specific costs of warehouse receipt loans are generally higher than those of any other secured lending arrangements because of the need to hire and pay a warehousing company to guard and supervise the collateral. The basic interest charged on warehouse receipt loans is higher than that charged on unsecured loans, generally ranging from 3 to 5 percent above the prime rate. In addition to the interest charge, the borrower must absorb the costs of warehousing by paying the warehouse fee, which is generally between 1 and 3 percent of the amount of the loan. The borrower is normally also required to pay the insurance costs on the warehoused merchandise. An example of the procedures and costs of a warehouse receipt loan is included on the book's web site at *www.aw.com/gitman.*

Review Questions

14–11 Are secured short-term loans viewed as more risky or less risky than unsecured short-term loans? Why?

14–12 In general, what interest rates and fees are levied on secured short-term loans? Why are these rates generally *higher* than the rates on unsecured short-term loans?

14–13 Describe and compare the basic features of the following methods of using *accounts receivable* to obtain short-term financing: (**a**) pledging accounts receivable, and (**b**) factoring accounts receivable. Be sure to mention the institutions that offer each of them.

14–14 For the following methods of using *inventory* as short-term loan collateral, describe the basic features of each, and compare their use: (**a**) floating lien; (**b**) trust receipt loan; and (**c**) warehouse receipt loan.

SUMMARY

FOCUS ON VALUE

Current liabilities represent an important and generally inexpensive source of financing for a firm. The level of short-term (current liabilities) financing employed by a firm affects its profitability and risk. Accounts payable are an inexpensive spontaneous source of short-term financing. They should be paid as late as possible without damaging the firm's credit rating. This strategy will reduce the firm's required investment in operating assets. If vendors offer cash discounts, the firm must consider the economics of giving up versus taking the discount. Accruals, another spontaneous liability, should be maximized because they represent free financing. Notes payable, which represent negotiated short-term financing, can be obtained from banks on an unsecured basis. They should be obtained at the lowest cost under the best possible terms. Large, well-known firms can obtain unsecured short-term financing through the sale of commercial paper. On a secured basis, the firm can obtain loans from banks or commercial finance companies, using either accounts receivable or inventory as collateral.

The financial manager must obtain the right quantity and form of current liabilities financing in order to provide the lowest-cost funds with the least risk. Such a strategy should positively contribute to the firm's goal of **maximizing the stock price.**

REVIEW OF LEARNING GOALS

LG1 **Review the key components of a firm's credit terms and the procedures for analyzing them.** The major spontaneous source of short-term financing is accounts payable, which are the primary source of short-term funds. Accounts payable result from credit purchases of merchandise. The key features of this form of financing are summarized in part I of Table 14.2. Credit terms may differ with respect to the credit period, cash discount, cash discount period, and beginning of the credit period. The cost of giving up cash discounts is a factor in deciding whether to take or give up a cash discount. Cash discounts should be given up only when a firm in need of short-term funds must pay an interest rate on borrowing that is greater than the cost of giving up the cash discount.

LG2 **Understand the effects of stretching accounts payable on their cost, and the use of accruals.** Stretching accounts payable can lower the cost of giving up a cash discount. This is because the firm can keep its money longer if it gives up the discount.

TABLE 14.2 Summary of Key Features of Common Sources of Short-Term Financing

Type of short-term financing	Source	Cost or conditions	Characteristics
I. Spontaneous liabilities			
Accounts payable	Suppliers of merchandise	No stated cost except when a cash discount is offered for early payment.	Credit extended on open account for 0 to 120 days. The largest source of short-term financing.
Accruals	Employees and government	Free.	Result because wages (employees) and taxes (government) are paid at discrete points in time after the service has been rendered. Hard to manipulate this source of financing.
II. Unsecured sources of short-term loans			
Bank sources			
(1) Single-payment notes	Commercial banks	Prime plus 0% to 4% risk premium—fixed or floating rate.	A single-payment loan used to meet a funds shortage expected to last only a short period of time.
(2) Lines of credit	Commercial banks	Prime plus 0% to 4% risk premium—fixed or floating rate. Often must maintain 10% to 20% compensating balance and clean up the line annually.	A prearranged borrowing limit under which funds, if available, will be lent to allow the borrower to meet seasonal needs.
(3) Revolving credit agreements	Commercial banks	Prime plus 0% to 4% risk premium—fixed or floating rate. Often must maintain 10% to 20% compensating balance and pay a commitment fee of approximately 0.5% of the average unused balance.	A line-of-credit agreement under which the availability of funds is guaranteed. Often for a period greater than 1 year.
Commercial paper	Business firms—both nonfinancial and financial	Generally 2% to 4% below the prime rate of interest.	An unsecured short-term promissory note issued by the most financially sound firms.

(continued)

TABLE 14.2 Summary of Key Features of Common Sources of Short-Term Financing (continued)

Type of short-term financing	Source	Cost or conditions	Characteristics
III. Secured sources of short-term loans			
Accounts receivable collateral			
(1) Pledging	Commercial banks and commercial finance companies	2% to 5% above prime plus up to 3% in fees. Advance 50% to 90% of collateral value.	Selected accounts receivable are used as collateral. The borrower is trusted to remit to the lender on collection of pledged accounts. Done on a non-notification basis.
(2) Factoring	Factors, commercial banks, and commercial finance companies	1% to 3% discount from face value of factored accounts. Interest of 2% to 4% above prime levied on advances. Interest between 0.2% and 0.5% per month earned on surplus balances left with factor.	Selected accounts are sold—generally without recourse—at a discount. All credit risks go with the accounts. Factor will lend (make advances) against uncollected accounts that are not yet due. Factor will also pay interest on surplus balances. Typically done on a notification basis.
Inventory collateral			
(1) Floating liens	Commercial banks and commercial finance companies	3% to 5% above prime. Advance less than 50% of collateral value.	A loan against inventory in general. Made when firm has stable inventory of a variety of inexpensive items.
(2) Trust receipts	Manufacturers' captive financing subsidiaries, commercial banks, and commercial finance companies	2% or more above prime. Advance 80% to 100% of cost of collateral.	Loan against relatively expensive automotive, consumer durable, and industrial goods that can be identified by serial number. Collateral remains in possession of borrower, who is trusted to remit proceeds to lender upon its sale.
(3) Warehouse receipts	Commercial banks and commercial finance companies	3% to 5% above prime plus a 1% to 3% warehouse fee. Advance 75% to 90% of collateral value.	Inventory used as collateral is placed under control of the lender either through a terminal warehouse or through a field warehouse. A third party—a warehousing company—guards the inventory for the lender. Inventory is released only on written approval of the lender.

Accruals, which result primarily from wage and tax obligations, are virtually free. The key features of this spontaneous liability are summarized in part I of Table 14.2.

LG3 **Describe the interest rates and basic types of unsecured bank sources of short-term loans.** Banks are the major source of unsecured short-term loans to businesses. The interest rate on these loans is tied to the prime rate of interest by a risk premium and may be fixed or floating. It should be evaluated by using the effective annual rate. This rate is calculated differently, depending on whether interest is paid when the loan matures or in advance. Bank loans may take the form of a single-payment note, a line of credit, or a revolving credit agreement. The key features of the various types of bank loans are summarized in part II of Table 14.2.

LG4 **Discuss the basic features of commercial paper and the key aspects of international short-term loans.** Commercial paper is an unsecured IOU issued by firms with a high credit standing. The key features of commercial paper are summarized in part II of Table 14.2. International sales and purchases expose firms to exchange rate risk. They are larger and of longer maturity than typical transactions, and they can be financed by using a letter of credit, by borrowing in the local market, or through dollar-denominated loans from international banks. On transactions between subsidiaries, "netting" can be used to minimize foreign exchange fees and other transaction costs.

LG5 **Explain the characteristics of secured short-term loans and the use of accounts receivable as short-term-loan collateral.** Secured short-term loans are those for which the lender requires collateral—typically, current assets such as accounts receivable or inventory. Only a percentage of the book value of acceptable collateral is advanced by the lender. These loans are more expensive than unsecured loans; collateral does not lower the risk of default, and increased administrative costs result. Both commercial banks and commercial finance companies make secured short-term loans. Both pledging, which is the use of accounts receivable as loan collateral, and factoring, which is the outright sale of accounts receivable at a discount, involve the use of accounts receivable to obtain needed short-term funds. The key features of loans using accounts receivable as collateral are summarized in part III of Table 14.2.

LG6 **Describe the various ways in which inventory can be used as short-term-loan collateral.** Inventory can be used as short-term-loan collateral under a floating lien, a trust receipt arrangement, or a warehouse receipt loan. The key features of loans using inventory as collateral are summarized in part III of Table 14.2.

SELF-TEST PROBLEM (Solution in Appendix B)

LG1 LG2 **ST 14–1 Cash discount decisions** The credit terms for each of three suppliers are shown in the following table.

Supplier	Credit terms
X	1/10 net 55 EOM
Y	2/10 net 30 EOM
Z	2/20 net 60 EOM

a. Determine the *approximate* cost of giving up the cash discount from each supplier.

b. Assuming that the firm needs short-term financing, indicate whether it would be better to give up the cash discount or take the discount and borrow from a bank at 15% annual interest. Evaluate each supplier *separately* using your findings in part **a.**

c. What impact, if any, would the fact that the firm could stretch its accounts payable (net period only) by 20 days from supplier Z have on your answer in part **b** relative to this supplier?

PROBLEMS

LG1 **14–1 Payment dates** Determine when a firm must pay for purchases made and invoices dated on November 25 under each of the following credit terms.

a. net 30 date of invoice
b. net 30 EOM
c. net 45 date of invoice
d. net 60 EOM

LG1 **14–2 Cost of giving up cash discounts** Determine the cost of giving up cash discounts under each of the following terms of sale.

a. 2/10 net 30
b. 1/10 net 30
c. 2/10 net 45
d. 3/10 net 45
e. 1/10 net 60
f. 3/10 net 30
g. 4/10 net 180

LG1 **14–3 Credit terms** Purchases made on credit are due in full by the end of the billing period. Many firms extend a discount for payment made in the first part of the billing period. The original invoice contains a type of "short-hand" notation that explains the credit terms that apply.

a. Write the short-hand expression of credit terms for each of the following.

Cash discount	Cash discount period	Credit period	Beginning of credit period
1%	15 days	45 days	date of invoice
2	10	30	end of month
2	7	28	date of invoice
1	10	60	end of month

b. For each of the sets of credit terms in part **a**, calculate the number of days until full payment is due for invoices dated March 12.
c. For each of the sets of credit terms, calculate the cost of giving up the cash discount.
d. If the firm's cost of short-term financing is 8%, what would you recommend in regard to taking the discount or giving it up in each case?

LG1 **14–4 Cash discount versus loan** Erica Stone works in an accounts payable department. She has attempted to convince her boss to take the discount on the 3/10 net 45 credit terms most suppliers offer, but her boss argues that giving up the 3% discount is less costly than a short-term loan at 14%. Prove to whoever is wrong that the other is correct.

LG1 LG2 **14–5 Cash discount decisions** Prairie Manufacturing has four possible suppliers, all of whom offer different credit terms. Except for the differences in credit terms, their products and services are virtually identical. The credit terms offered by these suppliers are shown in the following table.

Supplier	Credit terms
J	1/10 net 30 EOM
K	2/20 net 80 EOM
L	1/20 net 60 EOM
M	3/10 net 55 EOM

a. Calculate the *approximate* cost of giving up the cash discount from each supplier.

b. If the firm needs short-term funds, which are currently available from its commercial bank at 16%, and if each of the suppliers is viewed *separately*, which, if any, of the suppliers' cash discounts should the firm give up? Explain why.

c. What impact, if any, would the fact that the firm could stretch its accounts payable (net period only) by 30 days from supplier M have on your answer in part **b** relative to this supplier?

LG2 14–6 **Changing payment cycle** Upon accepting the position of chief executive officer and chairman of Reeves Machinery, Frank Cheney changed the firm's weekly payday from Monday afternoon to the following Friday afternoon. The firm's weekly payroll was $10 million, and the cost of short-term funds was 13%. If the effect of this change was to delay check clearing by 1 week, what *annual* savings, if any, were realized?

LG2 14–7 **Spontaneous sources of funds, accruals** When Tallman Haberdashery, Inc., merged with Meyers Men's Suits, Inc., Tallman's employees were switched from a weekly to a bi-weekly pay period. Tallman's weekly payroll amounted to $750,000. The cost of funds for the combined firms is 11%. What annual savings, if any, are realized by this change of pay period?

LG3 14–8 **Cost of bank loan** Data Back-Up Systems has obtained a $10,000, 90-day bank loan at an annual interest rate of 15%, payable at maturity. (*Note:* Assume a 360-day year.)

a. How much interest (in dollars) will the firm pay on the 90-day loan?

b. Find the effective 90-day rate on the loan.

c. Annualize your result in part **b** to find the effective annual rate for this loan, assuming that it is rolled over every 90 days throughout the year under the same terms and circumstances.

LG3 14–9 **Effective annual rate** A financial institution made a $10,000, 1-year discount loan at 10% interest, requiring a compensating balance equal to 20% of the face value of the loan. Determine the effective annual rate associated with this loan.

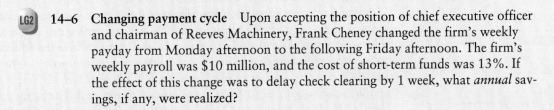

LG3 14–10 **Compensating balances and effective annual rates** Lincoln Industries has a line of credit at Bank Two that requires it to pay 11% interest on its borrowing and to maintain a compensating balance equal to 15% of the amount borrowed. The firm has borrowed $800,000 during the year under the agreement. Calculate the effective annual rate on the firm's borrowing in each of the following circumstances:

a. The firm normally maintains no deposit balances at Bank Two.
b. The firm normally maintains $70,000 in deposit balances at Bank Two.
c. The firm normally maintains $150,000 in deposit balances at Bank Two.
d. Compare, contrast, and discuss your findings in parts **a, b,** and **c.**

LG3 14–11 **Compensating balance vs. discount loan** Weathers Catering Supply, Inc., needs to borrow $150,000 for 6 months. State Bank has offered to lend the funds at a 9% annual rate subject to a 10% compensating balance. Frost Finance Co. has offered to lend the funds at a 9% annual rate with discount-loan terms. The principal of both loans would be payable at maturity as a single sum.

a. Calculate the effective annual rate of interest on each loan.
b. What could Weathers do that would reduce the effective annual rate on the State Bank loan?

LG3 14–12 **Integrative—Comparison of loan terms** Cumberland Furniture wishes to establish a prearranged borrowing agreement with its local commercial bank. The bank's terms for a line of credit are 3.30% over the prime rate, and each year the borrowing must be reduced to zero for a 30-day period. For an equivalent revolving credit agreement, the rate is 2.80% over prime with a commitment fee of 0.50% on the average unused balance. With both loans, the required compensating balance is equal to 20% of the amount borrowed. The prime rate is currently 8%. Both agreements have $4 million borrowing limits. The firm expects on average to borrow $2 million during the year no matter which loan agreement it decides to use.

a. What is the effective annual rate under the line of credit?
b. What is the effective annual rate under the revolving credit agreement? (*Hint:* Compute the ratio of the dollars that the firm will pay in interest and commitment fees to the dollars that the firm will effectively have use of.)
c. If the firm does expect to borrow an average of half the amount available, which arrangement would you recommend for the borrower? Explain why.

LG4 14–13 **Cost of commercial paper** Commercial paper is usually sold at a discount. Fan Corporation has just sold an issue of 90-day commercial paper with a face value of $1 million. The firm has received initial proceeds of $978,000.

a. What effective annual rate will the firm pay for financing with commercial paper, assuming that it is rolled over every 90 days throughout the year?
b. If a brokerage fee of $9,612 was paid from the initial proceeds to an investment banker for selling the issue, what effective annual rate will the firm pay, assuming that the paper is rolled over every 90 days throughout the year?

LG5 14–14 **Accounts receivable as collateral** Kansas City Castings (KCC) is attempting to obtain the maximum loan possible using accounts receivable as collateral. The firm extends net-30-day credit. The amounts that are owed KCC by its 12 credit customers, the average age of each account, and customer's average payment period are as shown in the following table.

Customer	Account receivable	Average age of account	Average payment period of customer
A	$37,000	40 days	30 days
B	42,000	25	50
C	15,000	40	60
D	8,000	30	35
E	50,000	31	40
F	12,000	28	30
G	24,000	30	70
H	46,000	29	40
I	3,000	30	65
J	22,000	25	35
K	62,000	35	40
L	80,000	60	70

a. If the bank will accept all accounts that can be collected in 45 days or less as long as the customer has a history of paying within 45 days, which accounts will be acceptable? What is the total dollar amount of accounts receivable collateral? (*Note:* Accounts receivable that have an average age greater than the customer's average payment period are also excluded.)

b. In addition to the conditions in part a, the bank recognizes that 5% of credit sales will be lost to returns and allowances. Also, the bank will lend only 80% of the acceptable collateral (after adjusting for returns and allowances). What level of funds would be made available through this lending source?

LG5 **14–15 Accounts receivable as collateral** Springer Products wishes to borrow $80,000 from a local bank using its accounts receivable to secure the loan. The bank's policy is to accept as collateral any accounts that are normally paid within 30 days of the end of the credit period, as long as the average age of the account is not greater than the customer's average payment period. Springer's accounts receivable, their average ages, and the average payment period for each customer are shown in the following table. The company extends terms of net 30 days.

Customer	Account receivable	Average age of account	Average payment period of customer
A	$20,000	10 days	40 days
B	6,000	40	35
C	22,000	62	50
D	11,000	68	65
E	2,000	14	30
F	12,000	38	50
G	27,000	55	60
H	19,000	20	35

a. Calculate the dollar amount of acceptable accounts receivable collateral held by Springer Products.

b. The bank reduces collateral by 10% for returns and allowances. What is the level of acceptable collateral under this condition?
c. The bank will advance 75% against the firm's acceptable collateral (after adjusting for returns and allowances). What amount can Springer borrow against these accounts?

LG3 LG5 **14–16 Accounts receivable as collateral, cost of borrowing** Maximum Bank has analyzed the accounts receivable of Scientific Software, Inc. The bank has chosen eight accounts totaling $134,000 that it will accept as collateral. The bank's terms include a lending rate set at prime + 3% and a 2% commission charge. The prime rate currently is 8.5%.
a. The bank will adjust the accounts by 10% for returns and allowances. It then will lend up to 85% of the adjusted acceptable collateral. What is the maximum amount that the bank will lend to Scientific Software?
b. What is Scientific Software's effective annual rate of interest if it borrows $100,000 for 12 months? For 6 months? For 3 months? (Assume that the prime rate remains at 8.5% during the life of the loan.)

LG5 **14–17 Factoring** Blair Finance factors the accounts of the Holder Company. All eight factored accounts are shown in the following table, with the amount factored, the date due, and the status on May 30. Indicate the amounts that Blair should have remitted to Holder as of May 30 and the dates of those remittances. Assume that the factor's commission of 2% is deducted as part of determining the amount of the remittance.

Account	Amount	Date due	Status on May 30
A	$200,000	May 30	Collected May 15
B	90,000	May 30	Uncollected
C	110,000	May 30	Uncollected
D	85,000	June 15	Collected May 30
E	120,000	May 30	Collected May 27
F	180,000	June 15	Collected May 30
G	90,000	May 15	Uncollected
H	30,000	June 30	Collected May 30

LG1 LG6 **14–18 Inventory financing** Raymond Manufacturing faces a liquidity crisis—it needs a loan of $100,000 for 30 days. Having no source of additional unsecured borrowing, the firm must find a secured short-term lender. The firm's accounts receivable are quite low, but its inventory is considered liquid and reasonably good collateral. The book value of the inventory is $300,000, of which $120,000 is finished goods.
(1) City-Wide Bank will make a $100,000 *trust receipt* loan against the finished goods inventory. The annual interest rate on the loan is 12% on the outstanding loan balance plus a 0.25% administration fee levied against the $100,000 initial loan amount. Because it will be liquidated as inventory is sold, the average amount owed over the month is expected to be $75,000.

(2) Sun State Bank will lend \$100,000 against a *floating lien* on the book value of inventory for the 30-day period at an annual interest rate of 13%.
(3) Citizens' Bank and Trust will lend \$100,000 against a *warehouse receipt* on the finished goods inventory and charge 15% annual interest on the outstanding loan balance. A 0.5% warehousing fee will be levied against the average amount borrowed. Because the loan will be liquidated as inventory is sold, the average loan balance is expected to be \$60,000.

a. Calculate the dollar cost of each of the proposed plans for obtaining an initial loan amount of \$100,000.
b. Which plan do you recommend? Why?
c. If the firm had made a purchase of \$100,000 for which it had been given terms of 2/10 net 30, would it increase the firm's profitability to give up the discount and not borrow as recommended in part **b?** Why or why not?

CHAPTER 14 CASE Selecting Kanton Company's Financing Strategy and Unsecured Short-Term Borrowing Arrangement

Morton Mercado, the CFO of Kanton Company, carefully developed the estimates of the firm's total funds requirements for the coming year. These are shown in the following table.

Month	Total funds	Month	Total funds
January	\$1,000,000	July	\$6,000,000
February	1,000,000	August	5,000,000
March	2,000,000	September	5,000,000
April	3,000,000	October	4,000,000
May	5,000,000	November	2,000,000
June	7,000,000	December	1,000,000

In addition, Morton expects short-term financing costs of about 10% and long-term financing costs of about 14% during that period. He developed the three possible financing strategies that follow:

Strategy 1—Aggressive: Finance seasonal needs with short-term funds and permanent needs with long-term funds.

Strategy 2—Conservative: Finance an amount equal to the peak need with long-term funds and use short-term funds only in an emergency.

Strategy 3—Tradeoff: Finance \$3,000,000 with long-term funds and finance the remaining funds requirements with short-term funds.

Using the data on the firm's total funds requirements, Morton estimated the average annual short-term and long-term financing requirements for each strategy in the coming year, as shown in the following table.

	Average annual financing		
Type of financing	Strategy 1 (aggressive)	Strategy 2 (conservative)	Strategy 3 (tradeoff)
Short-term	$2,500,000	$ 0	$1,666,667
Long-term	1,000,000	7,000,000	3,000,000

To ensure that, along with spontaneous financing from accounts payable and accruals, adequate short-term financing will be available, Morton plans to establish an unsecured short-term borrowing arrangement with its local bank, Third National. The bank has offered either a line-of-credit agreement or a revolving credit agreement. Third National's terms for a line of credit are an interest rate of 2.50% above the prime rate, and the borrowing must be reduced to zero for a 30-day period during the year. On an equivalent revolving credit agreement, the interest rate would be 3.00% above prime with a commitment fee of 0.50% on the average unused balance. Under both loans, a compensating balance equal to 20% of the amount borrowed would be required. The prime rate is currently 7%. Both the line-of-credit agreement and the revolving credit agreement would have borrowing limits of $1,000,000. For purposes of his analysis, Morton estimates that Kanton will borrow $600,000 on the average during the year, regardless which financing strategy and loan arrangement it chooses.

Required

a. Determine the total annual cost of each of the three possible financing strategies.

b. Assuming that the firm expects its current assets to total $4 million throughout the year, determine the average amount of net working capital under each financing strategy. (*Hint:* Current liabilities equal average short-term financing.)

c. Using the net working capital found in part **b** as a measure of risk, discuss the profitability–risk tradeoff associated with each financing strategy. Which strategy would you recommend to Morton Mercado for Kanton Company? Why?

d. Find the effective annual rate under:

(1) The line-of-credit agreement.

(2) The revolving credit agreement. (*Hint:* Find the ratio of the dollars that the firm will pay in interest and commitment fees to the dollars that the firm will effectively have use of.)

e. If the firm does expect to borrow an average of $600,000, which borrowing arrangement would you recommend to Kanton? Explain why.

WEB EXERCISE

Go to the Web site *www.21stfinancialsolutions.com*.

1. Click on **What Is Factoring**? What are factoring's advantages?
2. In the left-hand navigation bar, click on **Is factoring for You**? What are the additional benefits, and what types of companies can use factoring to their advantage?

3. Using the information in **How factoring works**, summarize the factoring process.

Next, go to the Web site *www.wellsfargo.com*.

4. On the top navigation bar, click on **commercial services**. Under **Business Lending and Leasing**, click on **commercial loans**.
   a. What types of loans does the bank offer businesses?
   b. Click on each of the four categories and summarize the type of loan and its uses.
5. At the top of the page, click on the link for **factoring services**.
   a. Describe the two types of factoring services.
   b. Click on **Wells Fargo Business Credit**. What features does Wells Fargo offer its factoring customers?

Remember to check the book's Web site at

www.aw.com/gitman

for additional resources, including additional Web exercises.

Appendix A

Financial Tables

TABLE A–1 Future Value Interest Factors for One Dollar Compounded at i Percent for n Periods:

$$FVIF_{i,n} = (1+i)^n$$

TABLE A–2 Present Value Interest Factors for One Dollar Discounted at i Percent for n Periods:

$$PVIF_{i,n} = \frac{1}{(1+i)^n}$$

TABLE A–3 Future Value Interest Factors for a One-Dollar Ordinary Annuity Compounded at i Percent for n Periods:

$$FVIFA_{i,n} = \sum_{t=1}^{n} (1+i)^{t-1}$$

TABLE A–4 Present Value Interest Factors for a One-Dollar Annuity Discounted at i Percent for n Periods:

$$PVIFA_{i,n} = \sum_{t=1}^{n} \frac{1}{(1+i)^t}$$

TABLE A–1 **Future Value Interest Factors for One Dollar Compounded at *i* Percent for *n* Periods: $FVIF_{i,n} = (1+i)^n$**

Period	1%	2%	3%	4%	5%	6%	7%	8%	9%	10%	11%	12%	13%	14%	15%	16%	17%	18%	19%	20%
1	1.010	1.020	1.030	1.040	1.050	1.060	1.070	1.080	1.090	1.100	1.110	1.120	1.130	1.140	1.150	1.160	1.170	1.180	1.190	1.200
2	1.020	1.040	1.061	1.082	1.102	1.124	1.145	1.166	1.188	1.210	1.232	1.254	1.277	1.300	1.322	1.346	1.369	1.392	1.416	1.440
3	1.030	1.061	1.093	1.125	1.158	1.191	1.225	1.260	1.295	1.331	1.368	1.405	1.443	1.482	1.521	1.561	1.602	1.643	1.685	1.728
4	1.041	1.082	1.126	1.170	1.216	1.262	1.311	1.360	1.412	1.464	1.518	1.574	1.630	1.689	1.749	1.811	1.874	1.939	2.005	2.074
5	1.051	1.104	1.159	1.217	1.276	1.338	1.403	1.469	1.539	1.611	1.685	1.762	1.842	1.925	2.011	2.100	2.192	2.288	2.386	2.488
6	1.062	1.126	1.194	1.265	1.340	1.419	1.501	1.587	1.677	1.772	1.870	1.974	2.082	2.195	2.313	2.436	2.565	2.700	2.840	2.986
7	1.072	1.149	1.230	1.316	1.407	1.504	1.606	1.714	1.828	1.949	2.076	2.211	2.353	2.502	2.660	2.826	3.001	3.185	3.379	3.583
8	1.083	1.172	1.267	1.369	1.477	1.594	1.718	1.851	1.993	2.144	2.305	2.476	2.658	2.853	3.059	3.278	3.511	3.759	4.021	4.300
9	1.094	1.195	1.305	1.423	1.551	1.689	1.838	1.999	2.172	2.358	2.558	2.773	3.004	3.252	3.518	3.803	4.108	4.435	4.785	5.160
10	1.105	1.219	1.344	1.480	1.629	1.791	1.967	2.159	2.367	2.594	2.839	3.106	3.395	3.707	4.046	4.411	4.807	5.234	5.695	6.192
11	1.116	1.243	1.384	1.539	1.710	1.898	2.105	2.332	2.580	2.853	3.152	3.479	3.836	4.226	4.652	5.117	5.624	6.176	6.777	7.430
12	1.127	1.268	1.426	1.601	1.796	2.012	2.252	2.518	2.813	3.138	3.498	3.896	4.334	4.818	5.350	5.936	6.580	7.288	8.064	8.916
13	1.138	1.294	1.469	1.665	1.886	2.133	2.410	2.720	3.066	3.452	3.883	4.363	4.898	5.492	6.153	6.886	7.699	8.599	9.596	10.699
14	1.149	1.319	1.513	1.732	1.980	2.261	2.579	2.937	3.342	3.797	4.310	4.887	5.535	6.261	7.076	7.987	9.007	10.147	11.420	12.839
15	1.161	1.346	1.558	1.801	2.079	2.397	2.759	3.172	3.642	4.177	4.785	5.474	6.254	7.138	8.137	9.265	10.539	11.974	13.589	15.407
16	1.173	1.373	1.605	1.873	2.183	2.540	2.952	3.426	3.970	4.595	5.311	6.130	7.067	8.137	9.358	10.748	12.330	14.129	16.171	18.488
17	1.184	1.400	1.653	1.948	2.292	2.693	3.159	3.700	4.328	5.054	5.895	6.866	7.986	9.276	10.761	12.468	14.426	16.672	19.244	22.186
18	1.196	1.428	1.702	2.026	2.407	2.854	3.380	3.996	4.717	5.560	6.543	7.690	9.024	10.575	12.375	14.462	16.879	19.673	22.900	26.623
19	1.208	1.457	1.753	2.107	2.527	3.026	3.616	4.316	5.142	6.116	7.263	8.613	10.197	12.055	14.232	16.776	19.748	23.214	27.251	31.948
20	1.220	1.486	1.806	2.191	2.653	3.207	3.870	4.661	5.604	6.727	8.062	9.646	11.523	13.743	16.366	19.461	23.105	27.393	32.429	38.337
21	1.232	1.516	1.860	2.279	2.786	3.399	4.140	5.034	6.109	7.400	8.949	10.804	13.021	15.667	18.821	22.574	27.033	32.323	38.591	46.005
22	1.245	1.546	1.916	2.370	2.925	3.603	4.430	5.436	6.658	8.140	9.933	12.100	14.713	17.861	21.644	26.186	31.629	38.141	45.923	55.205
23	1.257	1.577	1.974	2.465	3.071	3.820	4.740	5.871	7.258	8.954	11.026	13.552	16.626	20.361	24.891	30.376	37.005	45.007	54.648	66.247
24	1.270	1.608	2.033	2.563	3.225	4.049	5.072	6.341	7.911	9.850	12.239	15.178	18.788	23.212	28.625	35.236	43.296	53.108	65.031	79.496
25	1.282	1.641	2.094	2.666	3.386	4.292	5.427	6.848	8.623	10.834	13.585	17.000	21.230	26.461	32.918	40.874	50.656	62.667	77.387	95.395
30	1.348	1.811	2.427	3.243	4.322	5.743	7.612	10.062	13.267	17.449	22.892	29.960	39.115	50.949	66.210	85.849	111.061	143.367	184.672	237.373
35	1.417	2.000	2.814	3.946	5.516	7.686	10.676	14.785	20.413	28.102	38.574	52.799	72.066	98.097	133.172	180.311	243.495	327.988	440.691	590.657
40	1.489	2.208	3.262	4.801	7.040	10.285	14.974	21.724	31.408	45.258	64.999	93.049	132.776	188.876	267.856	378.715	533.846	750.353	1051.642	1469.740
45	1.565	2.438	3.781	5.841	8.985	13.764	21.002	31.920	48.325	72.888	109.527	163.985	244.629	363.662	538.752	795.429	1170.425	1716.619	2509.583	3657.176
50	1.645	2.691	4.384	7.106	11.467	18.419	29.456	46.900	74.354	117.386	184.559	288.996	450.711	700.197	1083.619	1670.669	2566.080	3927.189	5988.730	9100.191

Using the Calculator to Compute the Future Value of a Single Amount

Before you begin, make sure to clear the memory, ensure that you are in the *end mode* and that your calculator is set for *one payment per year*, and set the number of decimal places that you want (usually two for dollar-related accuracy).

SAMPLE PROBLEM

You place $800 in a savings account at 6% compounded annually. What is your account balance at the end of 5 years?

Hewlett-Packard HP 12C, 17 BII, and 19 BII[a]

Input	Function
800	PV
5	N
6	I%YR
	FV

Solution[b]
1070.58

[a]For the 12C, you would use the n key instead of the N key and use the i key instead of the I%YR key.
[b]The minus sign that precedes the solution should be ignored.

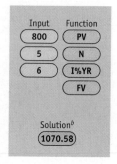

TABLE A–1 (Continued)

Period	21%	22%	23%	24%	25%	26%	27%	28%	29%	30%	31%	32%	33%	34%	35%	40%	45%	50%
1	1.210	1.220	1.230	1.240	1.250	1.260	1.270	1.280	1.290	1.300	1.310	1.320	1.330	1.340	1.350	1.400	1.450	1.500
2	1.464	1.488	1.513	1.538	1.562	1.588	1.613	1.638	1.664	1.690	1.716	1.742	1.769	1.796	1.822	1.960	2.102	2.250
3	1.772	1.816	1.861	1.907	1.953	2.000	2.048	2.097	2.147	2.197	2.248	2.300	2.353	2.406	2.460	2.744	3.049	3.375
4	2.144	2.215	2.289	2.364	2.441	2.520	2.601	2.684	2.769	2.856	2.945	3.036	3.129	3.224	3.321	3.842	4.421	5.063
5	2.594	2.703	2.815	2.932	3.052	3.176	3.304	3.436	3.572	3.713	3.858	4.007	4.162	4.320	4.484	5.378	6.410	7.594
6	3.138	3.297	3.463	3.635	3.815	4.001	4.196	4.398	4.608	4.827	5.054	5.290	5.535	5.789	6.053	7.530	9.294	11.391
7	3.797	4.023	4.259	4.508	4.768	5.042	5.329	5.629	5.945	6.275	6.621	6.983	7.361	7.758	8.172	10.541	13.476	17.086
8	4.595	4.908	5.239	5.589	5.960	6.353	6.767	7.206	7.669	8.157	8.673	9.217	9.791	10.395	11.032	14.758	19.541	25.629
9	5.560	5.987	6.444	6.931	7.451	8.004	8.595	9.223	9.893	10.604	11.362	12.166	13.022	13.930	14.894	20.661	28.334	38.443
10	6.727	7.305	7.926	8.594	9.313	10.086	10.915	11.806	12.761	13.786	14.884	16.060	17.319	18.666	20.106	28.925	41.085	57.665
11	8.140	8.912	9.749	10.657	11.642	12.708	13.862	15.112	16.462	17.921	19.498	21.199	23.034	25.012	27.144	40.495	59.573	86.498
12	9.850	10.872	11.991	13.215	14.552	16.012	17.605	19.343	21.236	23.298	25.542	27.982	30.635	33.516	36.644	56.694	86.380	129.746
13	11.918	13.264	14.749	16.386	18.190	20.175	22.359	24.759	27.395	30.287	33.460	36.937	40.745	44.912	49.469	79.371	125.251	194.620
14	14.421	16.182	18.141	20.319	22.737	25.420	28.395	31.691	35.339	39.373	43.832	48.756	54.190	60.181	66.784	111.119	181.614	291.929
15	17.449	19.742	22.314	25.195	28.422	32.030	36.062	40.565	45.587	51.185	57.420	64.358	72.073	80.643	90.158	155.567	263.341	437.894
16	21.113	24.085	27.446	31.242	35.527	40.357	45.799	51.923	58.808	66.541	75.220	84.953	95.857	108.061	121.713	217.793	381.844	656.841
17	25.547	29.384	33.758	38.740	44.409	50.850	58.165	66.461	75.862	86.503	98.539	112.138	127.490	144.802	164.312	304.911	553.674	985.261
18	30.912	35.848	41.523	48.038	55.511	64.071	73.869	85.070	97.862	112.454	129.086	148.022	169.561	194.035	221.822	426.875	802.826	1477.892
19	37.404	43.735	51.073	59.567	69.389	80.730	93.813	108.890	126.242	146.190	169.102	195.389	225.517	260.006	299.459	597.625	1164.098	2216.838
20	45.258	53.357	62.820	73.863	86.736	101.720	119.143	139.379	162.852	190.047	221.523	257.913	299.937	348.408	404.270	836.674	1687.942	3325.257
21	54.762	65.095	77.268	91.591	108.420	128.167	151.312	178.405	210.079	247.061	290.196	340.446	398.916	466.867	545.764	1171.343	2447.515	4987.883
22	66.262	79.416	95.040	113.572	135.525	161.490	192.165	228.358	271.002	321.178	380.156	449.388	530.558	625.601	736.781	1639.878	3548.896	7481.824
23	80.178	96.887	116.899	140.829	169.407	203.477	244.050	292.298	349.592	417.531	498.004	593.192	705.642	838.305	994.653	2295.829	5145.898	11222.738
24	97.015	118.203	143.786	174.628	211.758	256.381	309.943	374.141	450.974	542.791	652.385	783.013	938.504	1123.328	1342.781	3214.158	7461.547	16834.109
25	117.388	144.207	176.857	216.539	264.698	323.040	393.628	478.901	581.756	705.627	854.623	1033.577	1248.210	1505.258	1812.754	4499.816	10819.242	25251.164
30	304.471	389.748	497.904	634.810	807.793	1025.904	1300.477	1645.488	2078.208	2619.936	3297.081	4142.008	5194.516	6503.285	8128.426	24201.043	69348.375	191751.000
35	789.716	1053.370	1401.749	1861.020	2465.189	3258.053	4296.547	5653.840	7423.988	9727.598	12719.918	16598.906	21617.363	28096.695	36448.051	130158.687	*	*
40	2048.309	2846.941	3946.340	5455.797	7523.156	10346.879	14195.051	19426.418	26520.723	36117.754	49072.621	66519.313	89962.188	121388.437	163433.875	700022.688	*	*
45	5312.758	7694.418	11110.121	15994.316	22958.844	32859.457	46897.973	66748.500	94739.937	134102.187	*	*	*	*	*	*	*	*
50	13779.844	20795.680	31278.301	46889.207	70064.812	104354.562	154942.687	229345.875	338440.000	497910.125	*	*	*	*	*	*	*	*

*Not shown because of space limitations.

Texas Instruments, BA-35, BAII, and BAII Plus[c]

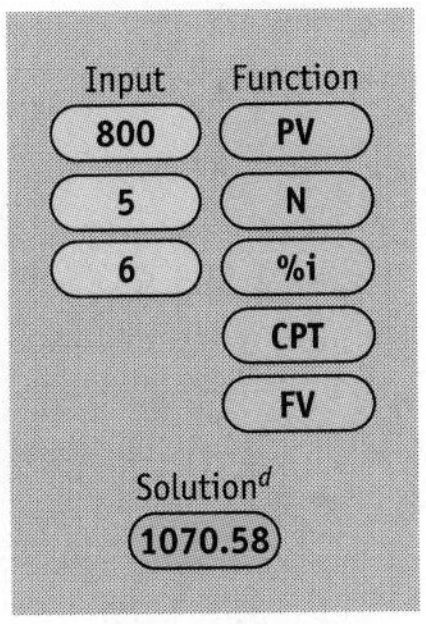

[c]For the Texas Instruments BAII, you would use the 2nd key instead of the CPT key; for the Texas Instruments BAII Plus, you would use the I/Y key instead of the %i key.

[d]If a minus sign precedes the solution, it should be ignored.

TABLE A–2 Present Value Interest Factors for One Dollar Discounted at *i* Percent for *n* Periods: $PVIF_{i,n} = \frac{1}{(1+i)^n}$

Period	1%	2%	3%	4%	5%	6%	7%	8%	9%	10%	11%	12%	13%	14%	15%	16%	17%	18%	19%	20%
1	.990	.980	.971	.962	.952	.943	.935	.926	.917	.909	.901	.893	.885	.877	.870	.862	.855	.847	.840	.833
2	.980	.961	.943	.925	.907	.890	.873	.857	.842	.826	.812	.797	.783	.769	.756	.743	.731	.718	.706	.694
3	.971	.942	.915	.889	.864	.840	.816	.794	.772	.751	.731	.712	.693	.675	.658	.641	.624	.609	.593	.579
4	.961	.924	.888	.855	.823	.792	.763	.735	.708	.683	.659	.636	.613	.592	.572	.552	.534	.516	.499	.482
5	.951	.906	.863	.822	.784	.747	.713	.681	.650	.621	.593	.567	.543	.519	.497	.476	.456	.437	.419	.402
6	.942	.888	.837	.790	.746	.705	.666	.630	.596	.564	.535	.507	.480	.456	.432	.410	.390	.370	.352	.335
7	.933	.871	.813	.760	.711	.665	.623	.583	.547	.513	.482	.452	.425	.400	.376	.354	.333	.314	.296	.279
8	.923	.853	.789	.731	.677	.627	.582	.540	.502	.467	.434	.404	.376	.351	.327	.305	.285	.266	.249	.233
9	.914	.837	.766	.703	.645	.592	.544	.500	.460	.424	.391	.361	.333	.308	.284	.263	.243	.225	.209	.194
10	.905	.820	.744	.676	.614	.558	.508	.463	.422	.386	.352	.322	.295	.270	.247	.227	.208	.191	.176	.162
11	.896	.804	.722	.650	.585	.527	.475	.429	.388	.350	.317	.287	.261	.237	.215	.195	.178	.162	.148	.135
12	.887	.789	.701	.625	.557	.497	.444	.397	.356	.319	.286	.257	.231	.208	.187	.168	.152	.137	.124	.112
13	.879	.773	.681	.601	.530	.469	.415	.368	.326	.290	.258	.229	.204	.182	.163	.145	.130	.116	.104	.093
14	.870	.758	.661	.577	.505	.442	.388	.340	.299	.263	.232	.205	.181	.160	.141	.125	.111	.099	.088	.078
15	.861	.743	.642	.555	.481	.417	.362	.315	.275	.239	.209	.183	.160	.140	.123	.108	.095	.084	.074	.065
16	.853	.728	.623	.534	.458	.394	.339	.292	.252	.218	.188	.163	.141	.123	.107	.093	.081	.071	.062	.054
17	.844	.714	.605	.513	.436	.371	.317	.270	.231	.198	.170	.146	.125	.108	.093	.080	.069	.060	.052	.045
18	.836	.700	.587	.494	.416	.350	.296	.250	.212	.180	.153	.130	.111	.095	.081	.069	.059	.051	.044	.038
19	.828	.686	.570	.475	.396	.331	.277	.232	.194	.164	.138	.116	.098	.083	.070	.060	.051	.043	.037	.031
20	.820	.673	.554	.456	.377	.312	.258	.215	.178	.149	.124	.104	.087	.073	.061	.051	.043	.037	.031	.026
21	.811	.660	.538	.439	.359	.294	.242	.199	.164	.135	.112	.093	.077	.064	.053	.044	.037	.031	.026	.022
22	.803	.647	.522	.422	.342	.278	.226	.184	.150	.123	.101	.083	.068	.056	.046	.038	.032	.026	.022	.018
23	.795	.634	.507	.406	.326	.262	.211	.170	.138	.112	.091	.074	.060	.049	.040	.033	.027	.022	.018	.015
24	.788	.622	.492	.390	.310	.247	.197	.158	.126	.102	.082	.066	.053	.043	.035	.028	.023	.019	.015	.013
25	.780	.610	.478	.375	.295	.233	.184	.146	.116	.092	.074	.059	.047	.038	.030	.024	.020	.016	.013	.010
30	.742	.552	.412	.308	.231	.174	.131	.099	.075	.057	.044	.033	.026	.020	.015	.012	.009	.007	.005	.004
35	.706	.500	.355	.253	.181	.130	.094	.068	.049	.036	.026	.019	.014	.010	.008	.006	.004	.003	.002	.002
40	.672	.453	.307	.208	.142	.097	.067	.046	.032	.022	.015	.011	.008	.005	.004	.003	.002	.001	.001	.001
45	.639	.410	.264	.171	.111	.073	.048	.031	.021	.014	.009	.006	.004	.003	.002	.001	.001	.001	*	*
50	.608	.372	.228	.141	.087	.054	.034	.021	.013	.009	.005	.003	.002	.001	.001	.001	*	*	*	*

*PVIF is zero to three decimal places.

Using the Calculator to Compute the Present Value of a Single Amount

Before you begin, make sure to clear the memory, ensure that you are in the *end mode* and that your calculator is set for *one payment per year,* and set the number of decimal places that you want (usually two for dollar-related accuracy).

Sample Problem

You want to know the present value of $1,700 to be received at the end of 8 years, assuming an 8% discount rate.

Hewlett-Packard HP 12C, 17 BII, and 19 BII[a]

Input	Function
1700	FV
8	N
8	I%YR
	PV

Solution[b]

918.46

[a]For the 12C, you would use the n key instead of the N key and use the i key instead of the I%YR key.
[b]The minus sign that precedes the solution should be ignored.

TABLE A–2 (Continued)

Period	21%	22%	23%	24%	25%	26%	27%	28%	29%	30%	31%	32%	33%	34%	35%	40%	45%	50%
1	.826	.820	.813	.806	.800	.794	.787	.781	.775	.769	.763	.758	.752	.746	.741	.714	.690	.667
2	.683	.672	.661	.650	.640	.630	.620	.610	.601	.592	.583	.574	.565	.557	.549	.510	.476	.444
3	.564	.551	.537	.524	.512	.500	.488	.477	.466	.455	.445	.435	.425	.416	.406	.364	.328	.296
4	.467	.451	.437	.423	.410	.397	.384	.373	.361	.350	.340	.329	.320	.310	.301	.260	.226	.198
5	.386	.370	.355	.341	.328	.315	.303	.291	.280	.269	.259	.250	.240	.231	.223	.186	.156	.132
6	.319	.303	.289	.275	.262	.250	.238	.227	.217	.207	.198	.189	.181	.173	.165	.133	.108	.088
7	.263	.249	.235	.222	.210	.198	.188	.178	.168	.159	.151	.143	.136	.129	.122	.095	.074	.059
8	.218	.204	.191	.179	.168	.157	.148	.139	.130	.123	.115	.108	.102	.096	.091	.068	.051	.039
9	.180	.167	.155	.144	.134	.125	.116	.108	.101	.094	.088	.082	.077	.072	.067	.048	.035	.026
10	.149	.137	.126	.116	.107	.099	.092	.085	.078	.073	.067	.062	.058	.054	.050	.035	.024	.017
11	.123	.112	.103	.094	.086	.079	.072	.066	.061	.056	.051	.047	.043	.040	.037	.025	.017	.012
12	.102	.092	.083	.076	.069	.062	.057	.052	.047	.043	.039	.036	.033	.030	.027	.018	.012	.008
13	.084	.075	.068	.061	.055	.050	.045	.040	.037	.033	.030	.027	.025	.022	.020	.013	.008	.005
14	.069	.062	.055	.049	.044	.039	.035	.032	.028	.025	.023	.021	.018	.017	.015	.009	.006	.003
15	.057	.051	.045	.040	.035	.031	.028	.025	.022	.020	.017	.016	.014	.012	.011	.006	.004	.002
16	.047	.042	.036	.032	.028	.025	.022	.019	.017	.015	.013	.012	.010	.009	.008	.005	.003	.002
17	.039	.034	.030	.026	.023	.020	.017	.015	.013	.012	.010	.009	.008	.007	.006	.003	.002	.001
18	.032	.028	.024	.021	.018	.016	.014	.012	.010	.009	.008	.007	.006	.005	.005	.002	.001	.001
19	.027	.023	.020	.017	.014	.012	.011	.009	.008	.007	.006	.005	.004	.004	.003	.002	.001	*
20	.022	.019	.016	.014	.012	.010	.008	.007	.006	.005	.005	.004	.003	.003	.002	.001	.001	*
21	.018	.015	.013	.011	.009	.008	.007	.006	.005	.004	.003	.003	.003	.002	.002	.001	*	*
22	.015	.013	.011	.009	.007	.006	.005	.004	.004	.003	.003	.002	.002	.002	.001	.001	*	*
23	.012	.010	.009	.007	.006	.005	.004	.003	.003	.002	.002	.002	.001	.001	.001	*	*	*
24	.010	.008	.007	.006	.005	.004	.003	.003	.002	.002	.002	.001	.001	.001	.001	*	*	*
25	.009	.007	.006	.005	.004	.003	.003	.002	.002	.001	.001	.001	.001	.001	.001	*	*	*
30	.003	.003	.002	.002	.001	.001	.001	.001	*	*	*	*	*	*	*	*	*	*
35	.001	.001	.001	.001	*	*	*	*	*	*	*	*	*	*	*	*	*	*
40	*	*	*	*	*	*	*	*	*	*	*	*	*	*	*	*	*	*
45	*	*	*	*	*	*	*	*	*	*	*	*	*	*	*	*	*	*
50	*	*	*	*	*	*	*	*	*	*	*	*	*	*	*	*	*	*

**PVIF* is zero to three decimal places.

Texas Instruments, BA-35, BAII, and BAII Plus[c]

Input	Function
1700	FV
8	N
8	%i
	CPT
	FV

Solution[d]

918.46

[c]For the Texas Instruments BAII, you would use the 2nd key instead of the CPT key; for the Texas Instruments BAII Plus, you would use the I/Y key instead of the %i key.

[d]If a minus sign precedes the solution, it should be ignored.

TABLE A–3 Future Value Interest Factors for a One-Dollar Ordinary Annuity Compounded at *i* Percent for *n* Periods: $FVIFA_{i,n} = \sum_{t=1}^{n} (1+i)^{t-1}$

Period	1%	2%	3%	4%	5%	6%	7%	8%	9%	10%	11%	12%	13%	14%	15%	16%	17%	18%	19%	20%
1	1.000	1.000	1.000	1.000	1.000	1.000	1.000	1.000	1.000	1.000	1.000	1.000	1.000	1.000	1.000	1.000	1.000	1.000	1.000	1.000
2	2.010	2.020	2.030	2.040	2.050	2.060	2.070	2.080	2.090	2.100	2.110	2.120	2.130	2.140	2.150	2.160	2.170	2.180	2.190	2.200
3	3.030	3.060	3.091	3.122	3.152	3.184	3.215	3.246	3.278	3.310	3.342	3.374	3.407	3.440	3.472	3.506	3.539	3.572	3.606	3.640
4	4.060	4.122	4.184	4.246	4.310	4.375	4.440	4.506	4.573	4.641	4.710	4.779	4.850	4.921	4.993	5.066	5.141	5.215	5.291	5.368
5	5.101	5.204	5.309	5.416	5.526	5.637	5.751	5.867	5.985	6.105	6.228	6.353	6.480	6.610	6.742	6.877	7.014	7.154	7.297	7.442
6	6.152	6.308	6.468	6.633	6.802	6.975	7.153	7.336	7.523	7.716	7.913	8.115	8.323	8.535	8.754	8.977	9.207	9.442	9.683	9.930
7	7.214	7.434	7.662	7.898	8.142	8.394	8.654	8.923	9.200	9.487	9.783	10.089	10.405	10.730	11.067	11.414	11.772	12.141	12.523	12.916
8	8.286	8.583	8.892	9.214	9.549	9.897	10.260	10.637	11.028	11.436	11.859	12.300	12.757	13.233	13.727	14.240	14.773	15.327	15.902	16.499
9	9.368	9.755	10.159	10.583	11.027	11.491	11.978	12.488	13.021	13.579	14.164	14.776	15.416	16.085	16.786	17.518	18.285	19.086	19.923	20.799
10	10.462	10.950	11.464	12.006	12.578	13.181	13.816	14.487	15.193	15.937	16.722	17.549	18.420	19.337	20.304	21.321	22.393	23.521	24.709	25.959
11	11.567	12.169	12.808	13.486	14.207	14.972	15.784	16.645	17.560	18.531	19.561	20.655	21.814	23.044	24.349	25.733	27.200	28.755	30.403	32.150
12	12.682	13.412	14.192	15.026	15.917	16.870	17.888	18.977	20.141	21.384	22.713	24.133	25.650	27.271	29.001	30.850	32.824	34.931	37.180	39.580
13	13.809	14.680	15.618	16.627	17.713	18.882	20.141	21.495	22.953	24.523	26.211	28.029	29.984	32.088	34.352	36.786	39.404	42.218	45.244	48.496
14	14.947	15.974	17.086	18.292	19.598	21.015	22.550	24.215	26.019	27.975	30.095	32.392	34.882	37.581	40.504	43.672	47.102	50.818	54.841	59.196
15	16.097	17.293	18.599	20.023	21.578	23.276	25.129	27.152	29.361	31.772	34.405	37.280	40.417	43.842	47.580	51.659	56.109	60.965	66.260	72.035
16	17.258	18.639	20.157	21.824	23.657	25.672	27.888	30.324	33.003	35.949	39.190	42.753	46.671	50.980	55.717	60.925	66.648	72.938	79.850	87.442
17	18.430	20.012	21.761	23.697	25.840	28.213	30.840	33.750	36.973	40.544	44.500	48.883	53.738	59.117	65.075	71.673	78.978	87.067	96.021	105.930
18	19.614	21.412	23.414	25.645	28.132	30.905	33.999	37.450	41.301	45.599	50.396	55.749	61.724	68.393	75.836	84.140	93.404	103.739	115.265	128.116
19	20.811	22.840	25.117	27.671	30.539	33.760	37.379	41.446	46.018	51.158	56.939	63.439	70.748	78.968	88.211	98.603	110.283	123.412	138.165	154.739
20	22.019	24.297	26.870	29.778	33.066	36.785	40.995	45.762	51.159	57.274	64.202	72.052	80.946	91.024	102.443	115.379	130.031	146.626	165.417	186.687
21	23.239	25.783	28.676	31.969	35.719	39.992	44.865	50.422	56.764	64.002	72.264	81.698	92.468	104.767	118.809	134.840	153.136	174.019	197.846	225.024
22	24.471	27.299	30.536	34.248	38.505	43.392	49.005	55.456	62.872	71.402	81.213	92.502	105.489	120.434	137.630	157.414	180.169	206.342	236.436	271.028
23	25.716	28.845	32.452	36.618	41.430	46.995	53.435	60.893	69.531	79.542	91.147	104.602	120.203	138.295	159.274	183.600	211.798	244.483	282.359	326.234
24	26.973	30.421	34.426	39.082	44.501	50.815	58.176	66.764	76.789	88.496	102.173	118.154	136.829	158.656	184.166	213.976	248.803	289.490	337.007	392.480
25	28.243	32.030	36.459	41.645	47.726	54.864	63.248	73.105	84.699	98.346	114.412	133.333	155.616	181.867	212.790	249.212	292.099	342.598	402.038	471.976
30	34.784	40.567	47.575	56.084	66.438	79.057	94.459	113.282	136.305	164.491	199.018	241.330	293.192	356.778	434.738	530.306	647.423	790.932	966.698	1181.865
35	41.659	49.994	60.461	73.651	90.318	111.432	138.234	172.314	215.705	271.018	341.583	431.658	546.663	693.552	881.152	1120.699	1426.448	1816.607	2314.173	2948.294
40	48.885	60.401	75.400	95.024	120.797	154.758	199.630	259.052	337.872	442.580	581.812	767.080	1013.667	1341.979	1779.048	2360.724	3134.412	4163.094	5529.711	7343.715
45	56.479	71.891	92.718	121.027	159.695	212.737	285.741	386.497	525.840	718.881	986.613	1358.208	1874.086	2590.464	3585.031	4965.191	6879.008	9531.258	13203.105	18280.914
50	64.461	84.577	112.794	152.664	209.341	290.325	406.516	573.756	815.051	1163.865	1668.723	2399.975	3459.344	4994.301	7217.488	10435.449	15088.805	21812.273	31514.492	45496.094

Using the Calculator to Compute the Future Value of an Ordinary Annuity

Before you begin, make sure to clear the memory, ensure that you are in the *end mode* and that your calculator is set for *one payment per year,* and set the number of decimal places that you want (usually two for dollar-related accuracy).

Sample Problem

You want to know what the future value will be at the end of 5 years if you place five end-of-year deposits of $1,000 in an account paying 7% annually. What is your account balance at the end of 5 years?

Hewlett-Packard HP 12C, 17 BII, and 19 BII[a]

Input	Function
1000	PMT
5	N
7	I%YR
	FV

Solution[b]
5750.74

[a]For the 12C, you would use the n key instead of the N key and use the i key instead of the I%YR key.

[b]The minus sign that precedes the solution should be ignored.

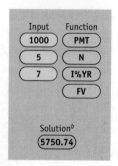

TABLE A-3 (Continued)

Period	21%	22%	23%	24%	25%	26%	27%	28%	29%	30%	31%	32%	33%	34%	35%	40%	45%	50%
1	1.000	1.000	1.000	1.000	1.000	1.000	1.000	1.000	1.000	1.000	1.000	1.000	1.000	1.000	1.000	1.000	1.000	1.000
2	2.210	2.220	2.230	2.240	2.250	2.260	2.270	2.280	2.290	2.300	2.310	2.320	2.330	2.340	2.350	2.400	2.450	2.500
3	3.674	3.708	3.743	3.778	3.813	3.848	3.883	3.918	3.954	3.990	4.026	4.062	4.099	4.136	4.172	4.360	4.552	4.750
4	5.446	5.524	5.604	5.684	5.766	5.848	5.931	6.016	6.101	6.187	6.274	6.362	6.452	6.542	6.633	7.104	7.601	8.125
5	7.589	7.740	7.893	8.048	8.207	8.368	8.533	8.700	8.870	9.043	9.219	9.398	9.581	9.766	9.954	10.946	12.022	13.188
6	10.183	10.442	10.708	10.980	11.259	11.544	11.837	12.136	12.442	12.756	13.077	13.406	13.742	14.086	14.438	16.324	18.431	20.781
7	13.321	13.740	14.171	14.615	15.073	15.546	16.032	16.534	17.051	17.583	18.131	18.696	19.277	19.876	20.492	23.853	27.725	32.172
8	17.119	17.762	18.430	19.123	19.842	20.588	21.361	22.163	22.995	23.858	24.752	25.678	26.638	27.633	28.664	34.395	41.202	49.258
9	21.714	22.670	23.669	24.712	25.802	26.940	28.129	29.369	30.664	32.015	33.425	34.895	36.429	38.028	39.696	49.152	60.743	74.887
10	27.274	28.657	30.113	31.643	33.253	34.945	36.723	38.592	40.556	42.619	44.786	47.062	49.451	51.958	54.590	69.813	89.077	113.330
11	34.001	35.962	38.039	40.238	42.566	45.030	47.639	50.398	53.318	56.405	59.670	63.121	66.769	70.624	74.696	98.739	130.161	170.995
12	42.141	44.873	47.787	50.895	54.208	57.738	61.501	65.510	69.780	74.326	79.167	84.320	89.803	95.636	101.840	139.234	189.734	257.493
13	51.991	55.745	59.778	64.109	68.760	73.750	79.106	84.853	91.016	97.624	104.709	112.302	120.438	129.152	138.484	195.928	276.114	387.239
14	63.909	69.009	74.528	80.496	86.949	93.925	101.465	109.611	118.411	127.912	138.169	149.239	161.183	174.063	187.953	275.299	401.365	581.858
15	78.330	85.191	92.669	100.815	109.687	119.346	129.860	141.302	153.750	167.285	182.001	197.996	215.373	234.245	254.737	386.418	582.980	873.788
16	95.779	104.933	114.983	126.010	138.109	151.375	165.922	181.867	199.337	218.470	239.421	262.354	287.446	314.888	344.895	541.985	846.321	1311.681
17	116.892	129.019	142.428	157.252	173.636	191.733	211.721	233.790	258.145	285.011	314.642	347.307	383.303	422.949	466.608	759.778	1228.165	1968.522
18	142.439	158.403	176.187	195.993	218.045	242.583	269.885	300.250	334.006	371.514	413.180	459.445	510.792	567.751	630.920	1064.689	1781.838	2953.783
19	173.351	194.251	217.710	244.031	273.556	306.654	343.754	385.321	431.868	483.968	542.266	607.467	680.354	761.786	852.741	1491.563	2584.665	4431.672
20	210.755	237.986	268.783	303.598	342.945	387.384	437.568	494.210	558.110	630.157	711.368	802.856	905.870	1021.792	1152.200	2089.188	3748.763	6648.508
21	256.013	291.343	331.603	377.461	429.681	489.104	556.710	633.589	720.962	820.204	932.891	1060.769	1205.807	1370.201	1556.470	2925.862	5436.703	9973.762
22	310.775	356.438	408.871	469.052	538.101	617.270	708.022	811.993	931.040	1067.265	1223.087	1401.215	1604.724	1837.068	2102.234	4097.203	7884.215	14961.645
23	377.038	435.854	503.911	582.624	673.626	778.760	900.187	1040.351	1202.042	1388.443	1603.243	1850.603	2135.282	2462.669	2839.014	5737.078	11433.109	22443.469
24	457.215	532.741	620.810	723.453	843.032	982.237	1144.237	1332.649	1551.634	1805.975	2101.247	2443.795	2840.924	3300.974	3833.667	8032.906	16579.008	33666.207
25	554.230	650.944	764.596	898.082	1054.791	1238.617	1454.180	1706.790	2002.608	2348.765	2753.631	3226.808	3779.428	4424.301	5176.445	11247.062	24040.555	50500.316
30	1445.111	1767.044	2160.459	2640.881	3227.172	3941.953	4812.891	5873.172	7162.785	8729.805	10632.543	12940.672	15737.945	19124.434	23221.258	60500.207	154105.313	383500.000
35	3755.814	4783.520	6090.227	7750.094	9856.746	12527.160	15909.480	20188.742	25596.512	32422.090	41028.887	51868.563	65504.199	82634.625	104134.500	325394.688	*	*
40	9749.141	12936.141	17153.691	22728.367	30088.621	39791.957	52570.707	69376.562	91447.375	120389.375	*	*	*	*	*	*	*	*
45	25294.223	34970.230	48300.660	66638.937	91831.312	126378.937	173692.875	238384.312	326686.375	447005.062	*	*	*	*	*	*	*	*

*Not shown because of space limitations.

Texas Instruments, BA-35, BAII, and BAII Plus[c]

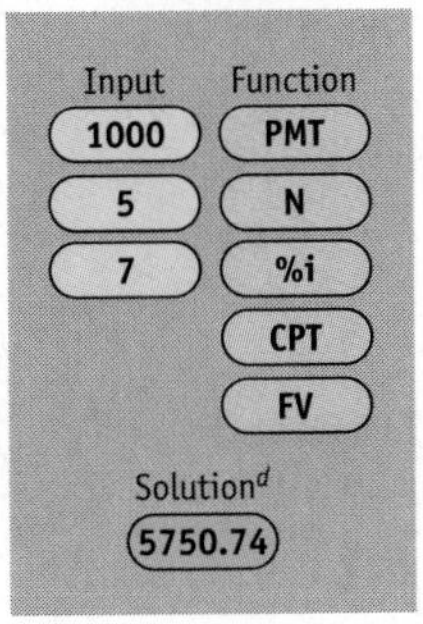

[c]For the Texas Instruments BAII, you would use the 2nd key instead of the CPT key; for the Texas Instruments BAII Plus, you would use the I/Y key instead of the %i key.

[d]If a minus sign precedes the solution, it should be ignored.

TABLE A–4 **Present Value Interest Factors for a One-Dollar Annuity Discounted at *i* Percent for *n* Periods:** $PVIFA_{i,n} = \sum_{t=1}^{n} \frac{1}{(1+i)^t}$

Period	1%	2%	3%	4%	5%	6%	7%	8%	9%	10%	11%	12%	13%	14%	15%	16%	17%	18%	19%	20%
1	.990	.980	.971	.962	.952	.943	.935	.926	.917	.909	.901	.893	.885	.877	.870	.862	.855	.847	.840	.833
2	1.970	1.942	1.913	1.886	1.859	1.833	1.808	1.783	1.759	1.736	1.713	1.690	1.668	1.647	1.626	1.605	1.585	1.566	1.547	1.528
3	2.941	2.884	2.829	2.775	2.723	2.673	2.624	2.577	2.531	2.487	2.444	2.402	2.361	2.322	2.283	2.246	2.210	2.174	2.140	2.106
4	3.902	3.808	3.717	3.630	3.546	3.465	3.387	3.312	3.240	3.170	3.102	3.037	2.974	2.914	2.855	2.798	2.743	2.690	2.639	2.589
5	4.853	4.713	4.580	4.452	4.329	4.212	4.100	3.993	3.890	3.791	3.696	3.605	3.517	3.433	3.352	3.274	3.199	3.127	3.058	2.991
6	5.795	5.601	5.417	5.242	5.076	4.917	4.767	4.623	4.486	4.355	4.231	4.111	3.998	3.889	3.784	3.685	3.589	3.498	3.410	3.326
7	6.728	6.472	6.230	6.002	5.786	5.582	5.389	5.206	5.033	4.868	4.712	4.564	4.423	4.288	4.160	4.039	3.922	3.812	3.706	3.605
8	7.652	7.326	7.020	6.733	6.463	6.210	5.971	5.747	5.535	5.335	5.146	4.968	4.799	4.639	4.487	4.344	4.207	4.078	3.954	3.837
9	8.566	8.162	7.786	7.435	7.108	6.802	6.515	6.247	5.995	5.759	5.537	5.328	5.132	4.946	4.772	4.607	4.451	4.303	4.163	4.031
10	9.471	8.983	8.530	8.111	7.722	7.360	7.024	6.710	6.418	6.145	5.889	5.650	5.426	5.216	5.019	4.833	4.659	4.494	4.339	4.192
11	10.368	9.787	9.253	8.760	8.306	7.887	7.499	7.139	6.805	6.495	6.207	5.938	5.687	5.453	5.234	5.029	4.836	4.656	4.486	4.327
12	11.255	10.575	9.954	9.385	8.863	8.384	7.943	7.536	7.161	6.814	6.492	6.194	5.918	5.660	5.421	5.197	4.988	4.793	4.611	4.439
13	12.134	11.348	10.635	9.986	9.394	8.853	8.358	7.904	7.487	7.013	6.750	6.424	6.122	5.842	5.583	5.342	5.118	4.910	4.715	4.533
14	13.004	12.106	11.296	10.563	9.899	9.295	8.745	8.244	7.786	7.367	6.982	6.628	6.302	6.002	5.724	5.468	5.229	5.008	4.802	4.611
15	13.865	12.849	11.938	11.118	10.380	9.712	9.108	8.560	8.061	7.606	7.191	6.811	6.462	6.142	5.847	5.575	5.324	5.092	4.876	4.675
16	14.718	13.578	12.561	11.652	10.838	10.106	9.447	8.851	8.313	7.824	7.379	6.974	6.604	6.265	5.954	5.668	5.405	5.162	4.938	4.730
17	15.562	14.292	13.166	12.166	11.274	10.477	9.763	9.122	8.544	8.022	7.549	7.120	6.729	6.373	6.047	5.749	5.475	5.222	4.990	4.775
18	16.398	14.992	13.754	12.659	11.690	10.828	10.059	9.372	8.756	8.201	7.702	7.250	6.840	6.467	6.128	5.818	5.534	5.273	5.033	4.812
19	17.226	15.679	14.324	13.134	12.085	11.158	10.336	9.604	8.950	8.365	7.839	7.366	6.938	6.550	6.198	5.877	5.584	5.316	5.070	4.843
20	18.046	16.352	14.878	13.590	12.462	11.470	10.594	9.818	9.129	8.514	7.963	7.469	7.025	6.623	6.259	5.929	5.628	5.353	5.101	4.870
21	18.857	17.011	15.415	14.029	12.821	11.764	10.836	10.017	9.292	8.649	8.075	7.562	7.102	6.687	6.312	5.973	5.665	5.384	5.127	4.891
22	19.661	17.658	15.937	14.451	13.163	12.042	11.061	10.201	9.442	8.772	8.176	7.645	7.170	6.743	6.359	6.011	5.696	5.410	5.149	4.909
23	20.456	18.292	16.444	14.857	13.489	12.303	11.272	10.371	9.580	8.883	8.266	7.718	7.230	6.792	6.399	6.044	5.723	5.432	5.167	4.925
24	21.244	18.914	16.936	15.247	13.799	12.550	11.469	10.529	9.707	8.985	8.348	7.784	7.283	6.835	6.434	6.073	5.746	5.451	5.182	4.937
25	22.023	19.524	17.413	15.622	14.094	12.783	11.654	10.675	9.823	9.077	8.422	7.843	7.330	6.873	6.464	6.097	5.766	5.467	5.195	4.948
30	25.808	22.396	19.601	17.292	15.373	13.765	12.409	11.258	10.274	9.427	8.694	8.055	7.496	7.003	6.566	6.177	5.829	5.517	5.235	4.979
35	29.409	24.999	21.487	18.665	16.374	14.498	12.948	11.655	10.567	9.644	8.855	8.176	7.586	7.070	6.617	6.215	5.858	5.539	5.251	4.992
40	32.835	27.356	23.115	19.793	17.159	15.046	13.332	11.925	10.757	9.779	8.951	8.244	7.634	7.105	6.642	6.233	5.871	5.548	5.258	4.997
45	36.095	29.490	24.519	20.720	17.774	15.456	13.606	12.108	10.881	9.863	9.008	8.283	7.661	7.123	6.654	6.242	5.877	5.552	5.261	4.999
50	39.196	31.424	25.730	21.482	18.256	15.762	13.801	12.233	10.962	9.915	9.042	8.304	7.675	7.133	6.661	6.246	5.880	5.554	5.262	4.999

Using the Calculator to Compute the Present Value of an Annuity

Before you begin, make sure to clear the memory, ensure that you are in the *end mode* and that your calculator is set for *one payment per year,* and set the number of decimal places that you want (usually two for dollar-related accuracy).

SAMPLE PROBLEM

You want to know what the present value of an annuity of $700 received at the end of each year for 5 years, given a discount rate of 8%.

Hewlett-Packard HP 12C, 17 BII, and 19 BII[a]

Input	Function
700	PMT
5	N
8	I%YR
	PV

Solution[b]

2794.90

[a]For the 12C, you would use the n key instead of the N key and use the i key instead of the I%YR key.

[b]The minus sign that precedes the solution should be ignored.

TABLE A–4 (Continued)

Period	21%	22%	23%	24%	25%	26%	27%	28%	29%	30%	31%	32%	33%	34%	35%	40%	45%	50%
1	.826	.820	.813	.806	.800	.794	.787	.781	.775	.769	.763	.758	.752	.746	.741	.714	.690	.667
2	1.509	1.492	1.474	1.457	1.440	1.424	1.407	1.392	1.376	1.361	1.346	1.331	1.317	1.303	1.289	1.224	1.165	1.111
3	2.074	2.042	2.011	1.981	1.952	1.923	1.896	1.868	1.842	1.816	1.791	1.766	1.742	1.719	1.696	1.589	1.493	1.407
4	2.540	2.494	2.448	2.404	2.362	2.320	2.280	2.241	2.203	2.166	2.130	2.096	2.062	2.029	1.997	1.849	1.720	1.605
5	2.926	2.864	2.803	2.745	2.689	2.635	2.583	2.532	2.483	2.436	2.390	2.345	2.302	2.260	2.220	2.035	1.876	1.737
6	3.245	3.167	3.092	3.020	2.951	2.885	2.821	2.759	2.700	2.643	2.588	2.534	2.483	2.433	2.385	2.168	1.983	1.824
7	3.508	3.416	3.327	3.242	3.161	3.083	3.009	2.937	2.868	2.802	2.739	2.677	2.619	2.562	2.508	2.263	2.057	1.883
8	3.726	3.619	3.518	3.421	3.329	3.241	3.156	3.076	2.999	2.925	2.854	2.786	2.721	2.658	2.598	2.331	2.109	1.922
9	3.905	3.786	3.673	3.566	3.463	3.366	3.273	3.184	3.100	3.019	2.942	2.868	2.798	2.730	2.665	2.379	2.144	1.948
10	4.054	3.923	3.799	3.682	3.570	3.465	3.364	3.269	3.178	3.092	3.009	2.930	2.855	2.784	2.715	2.414	2.168	1.965
11	4.177	4.035	3.902	3.776	3.656	3.544	3.437	3.335	3.239	3.147	3.060	2.978	2.899	2.824	2.752	2.438	2.185	1.977
12	4.278	4.127	3.985	3.851	3.725	3.606	3.493	3.387	3.286	3.190	3.100	3.013	2.931	2.853	2.779	2.456	2.196	1.985
13	4.362	4.203	4.053	3.912	3.780	3.656	3.538	3.427	3.322	3.223	3.129	3.040	2.956	2.876	2.799	2.469	2.204	1.990
14	4.432	4.265	4.108	3.962	3.824	3.695	3.573	3.459	3.351	3.249	3.152	3.061	2.974	2.892	2.814	2.478	2.210	1.993
15	4.489	4.315	4.153	4.001	3.859	3.726	3.601	3.483	3.373	3.268	3.170	3.076	2.988	2.905	2.825	2.484	2.214	1.995
16	4.536	4.357	4.189	4.033	3.887	3.751	3.623	3.503	3.390	3.283	3.183	3.088	2.999	2.914	2.834	2.489	2.216	1.997
17	4.576	4.391	4.219	4.059	3.910	3.771	3.640	3.518	3.403	3.295	3.193	3.097	3.007	2.921	2.840	2.492	2.218	1.998
18	4.608	4.419	4.243	4.080	3.928	3.786	3.654	3.529	3.413	3.304	3.201	3.104	3.012	2.926	2.844	2.494	2.219	1.999
19	4.635	4.442	4.263	4.097	3.942	3.799	3.664	3.539	3.421	3.311	3.207	3.109	3.017	2.930	2.848	2.496	2.220	1.999
20	4.657	4.460	4.279	4.110	3.954	3.808	3.673	3.546	3.427	3.316	3.211	3.113	3.020	2.933	2.850	2.497	2.221	1.999
21	4.675	4.476	4.292	4.121	3.963	3.816	3.679	3.551	3.432	3.320	3.215	3.116	3.023	2.935	2.852	2.498	2.221	2.000
22	4.690	4.488	4.302	4.130	3.970	3.822	3.684	3.556	3.436	3.323	3.217	3.118	3.025	2.936	2.853	2.498	2.222	2.000
23	4.703	4.499	4.311	4.137	3.976	3.827	3.689	3.559	3.438	3.325	3.219	3.120	3.026	2.938	2.854	2.499	2.222	2.000
24	4.713	4.507	4.318	4.143	3.981	3.831	3.692	3.562	3.441	3.327	3.221	3.121	3.027	2.939	2.855	2.499	2.222	2.000
25	4.721	4.514	4.323	4.147	3.985	3.834	3.694	3.564	3.442	3.329	3.222	3.122	3.028	2.939	2.856	2.499	2.222	2.000
30	4.746	4.534	4.339	4.160	3.995	3.842	3.701	3.569	3.447	3.332	3.225	3.124	3.030	2.941	2.857	2.500	2.222	2.000
35	4.756	4.541	4.345	4.164	3.998	3.845	3.703	3.571	3.448	3.333	3.226	3.125	3.030	2.941	2.857	2.500	2.222	2.000
40	4.760	4.544	4.347	4.166	3.999	3.846	3.703	3.571	3.448	3.333	3.226	3.125	3.030	2.941	2.857	2.500	2.222	2.000
45	4.761	4.545	4.347	4.166	4.000	3.846	3.704	3.571	3.448	3.333	3.226	3.125	3.030	2.941	2.857	2.500	2.222	2.000
50	4.762	4.545	4.348	4.167	4.000	3.846	3.704	3.571	3.448	3.333	3.226	3.125	3.030	2.941	2.857	2.500	2.222	2.000

Texas Instruments, BA-35, BAII, and BAII Plus[c]

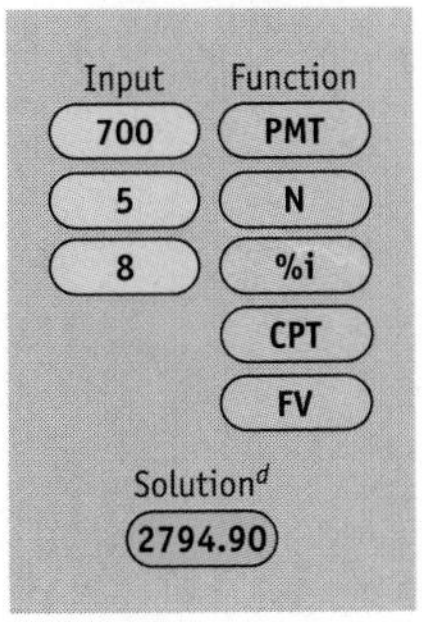

[c]For the Texas Instruments BAII, you would use the 2nd key instead of the CPT key; for the Texas Instruments BAII Plus, you would use the I/Y key instead of the %i key.

[d]If a minus sign precedes the solution, it should be ignored.

Appendix B

Solutions to Self-Test Problems

Chapter 1

ST 1–1 **a.** Capital gains = \$180,000 sale price − \$150,000 original purchase price = \$30,000

b. Total taxable income = \$280,000 operating earnings + \$30,000 capital gain = \$310,000

c. Firm's tax liability:

Using Table 1.5:

$$\begin{aligned}\text{Total taxes due} &= \$22{,}250 + [0.39 \times (\$310{,}000 - \$100{,}000)]\\ &= \$22{,}250 + (0.39 \times \$210{,}000) = \$22{,}250 + \$81{,}900\\ &= \underline{\underline{\$104{,}150}}\end{aligned}$$

d. $\text{Average tax rate} = \dfrac{\$104{,}150}{\$310{,}000} = \underline{\underline{33.6\%}}$

Marginal tax rate = 39%

Chapter 2

ST 2–1

Ratio	Too high	Too low
Current ratio = current assets/current liabilities	May indicate that the firm is holding excessive cash, accounts receivable, or inventory.	May indicate poor ability to satisfy short-term obligations.
Inventory turnover = CGS/inventory	May indicate lower level of inventory, which may cause stockouts and lost sales.	May indicate poor inventory management, excessive inventory, or obsolete inventory.
Times interest earned = earnings before interest and taxes/interest	X	May indicate poor ability to pay contractual interest payments.
Gross profit margin = gross profits/sales	Indicates the low cost of merchandise sold relative to the sales price; may indicate noncompetitive pricing and potential lost sales.	Indicates the high cost of the merchandise sold relative to the sales price; may indicate either a low sales price or a high cost of goods sold.
Return on total assets = net profits after taxes/total assets	X	Indicates ineffective management in generating profits with the available assets.

ST 2–2

O'Keefe Industries
Balance Sheet
December 31, 2003

Assets		Liabilities and Stockholders' Equity	
Cash	$ 30,000	Accounts payable	$ 120,000
Marketable securities	25,000	Notes payable	160,000[e]
Accounts receivable	200,000[a]	Accruals	20,000
Inventories	225,000[b]	Total current liabilities	$ 300,000[d]
Total current assets	$ 480,000	Long-term debt	$ 600,000[f]
Net fixed assets	$1,020,000[c]	Stockholders' equity	$ 600,000
Total assets	$1,500,000	Total liabilities and stockholders' equity	$1,500,000

[a]Average collection period (ACP) = 40 days
ACP = Accounts receivable/Average sales per day
40 = Accounts receivable/($1,800,000/360)
40 = Accounts receivable/$5,000
$200,000 = Accounts receivable

[b]Inventory turnover = 6.0
Inventory turnover = Cost of goods sold/Inventory
6.0 = [Sales × (1 = Gross profit margin)]/Inventory
6.0 = [$1,800,000 × (1 = 0.25)]/Inventory
$225,000 = Inventory

[c]Total asset turnover = 1.20
Total asset turnover = Sales/Total assets
1.20 = $1,800,000/Total assets
$1,500,000 = Total assets
Total assets = Current assets + Net fixed assets
$1,500,000 = $480,000 + Net fixed assets
$1,020,000 = Net fixed assets

[d]Current ratio = 1.60
Current ratio = Current assets/Current liabilities
1.60 = $480,000/Current liabilities
$300,000 = Current liabilities

[e]Notes payable = Total current liabilities − Accounts payable − Accruals
= $300,000 − $120,000 − $20,000
= $160,000

[f]Debt ratio = 0.60
Debt ratio = Total liabilities/Total assets
0.60 = Total liabilities/$1,500,000
$900,000 = Total liabilities
Total liabilities = Current liabilities + Long-term debt
$900,000 = $300,000 + Long-term debt
$600,000 = Long-term debt

Chapter 3

ST 3–1 a. Depreciation Schedule

Year	Cost[a] (1)	Percentages (from Table 3.2) (2)	Depreciation [(1) × (2)] (3)
1	$150,000	20%	$ 30,000
2	150,000	32	48,000
3	150,000	19	28,500
4	150,000	12	18,000
5	150,000	12	18,000
6	150,000	5	7,500
	Totals	100%	$150,000

[a]$140,000 asset cost + $10,000 installation cost.

b. Accounting definition:

Year	EBIT (1)	Interest (2)	Net profits before taxes [(1) – (2)] (3)	Taxes [0.40 × (3)] (4)	Net profits after taxes [(3) – (4)] (5)	Depreciation (from part a, col. 3) (6)	Cash Flows from operations [(5) + (6)] (7)
1	$160,000	$15,000	$145,000	$58,000	$87,000	$30,000	$117,000
2	160,000	15,000	145,000	58,000	87,000	48,000	135,000
3	160,000	15,000	145,500	58,000	87,000	28,500	115,500
4	160,000	15,000	145,000	58,000	87,000	18,000	105,000
5	160,000	15,000	145,000	58,000	87,000	18,000	105,000
6	160,000	15,000	145,500	58,000	87,000	7,500	94,500

Financial definition:

Year	EBIT (1)	Taxes (from part b, col. 4) (2)	Depreciation (from part a, col. 3) (6)	Operating cash flows [(1) – (2) + (3)] (4)
1	$160,000	$58,000	$30,000	$132,000
2	160,000	58,000	48,000	150,000
3	160,000	58,000	28,500	130,500
4	160,000	58,000	18,000	120,000
5	160,000	58,000	18,000	120,000
6	160,000	58,000	7,500	109,500

c. Change in net fixed assets in year 6 = $0 – $7,500 = –$7,500
NFAI in year 6 = –$7,500 + $7,500 = $0
Change in current assets in year 6 = $110,000 – $90,000 = $20,000
Change in (Accounts payable + Accruals) in year 6 = ($45,000 + $7,000) – ($40,000 + $8,000) = $52,000 – $48,000 = $4,000
NCAI in year 6 = $20,000 – $4,000 = $16,000

For year 6

FCF = OCF – NFAI – NCAI

= $109,500* – $0 – $16,000 = $93,500

*From part **b** financial definition, column 4 value for year 6.

d. In part **b** we can see that in each of the six years, the operating cash flow is greater when viewed from a financial perspective than when viewed from a strict accounting point of view. This difference results from the fact that the accounting definition includes interest as an operating flow, whereas the financial definition excludes it. This causes (in this case) each year's accounting flow to be $15,000 below the financial flow; $15,000 is equal to the amount of interest in each year as stated in the problem. The free cash flow (FCF) calculated in part **c** for year 6 represents the cash flow available to investors—providers of debt and equity—after covering all operating needs and paying for net fixed asset investment (NFAI) and net current asset investment (NCAI) that occurred during the year.

Caroll Company Cash Budget April–June						Accounts receivable at end of June	
	February	March	April	May	June	July	August
Forecast sales	$500	$600	$400	$200	$200		
Cash sales (0.30)	$150	$180	$120	$ 60	$ 60		
Collections of A/R							
Lagged 1 month [(0.7 × 0.7) = 0.49]		245	294	196	98	$ 98	
Lagged 2 months [(0.3 × 0.7) = 0.21]			105	126	84	42	$42
						$140 + $42 = $182	
Total cash receipts			$519	$382	$242		
Less: Total cash disbursements			600	500	200		
Net cash flow			($ 81)	($118)	$ 42		
Add: Beginning cash			115	34	(84)		
Ending cash			$ 34	($ 84)	($ 42)		
Less: Minimum cash balance			25	25	25		
Required total financing (notes payable)			—	$ 109	$ 67		
Excess cash balance (marketable securities)			$ 9	—	—		

ST 3–2 a.

b. Caroll Company would need a maximum of $109 in financing over the 3-month period.

c.

Account	Amount	Source of amount
Cash	$ 25	Minimum cash balance—June
Notes payable	67	Required total financing—June
Marketable securities	0	Excess cash balance—June
Accounts receivable	182	Calculation at right of cash budget statement

ST 3–3 a.

Euro Designs, Inc.,
Pro Forma Income Statement
for the Year Ended December 31, 2004

Sales revenue (given)	$3,900,000
Less: Cost of goods sold (0.55)[a]	2,145,000
Gross profits	$1,755,000
Less: Operating expenses (0.12)[b]	468,000
Operating profits	$1,287,000
Less: Interest expense (given)	325,000
Net profits before taxes	$ 962,000
Less: Taxes (0.40 × $962,000)	384,800
Net profits after taxes	$ 577,200
Less: Cash dividends (given)	320,000
To retained earnings	$ 257,200

[a]From 2003: CGS/Sales = $1,925,000/$3,500,000 = 0.55.
[b]From 2003: Oper. Exp./Sales = $420,000/$3,500,000 = 0.12.

b. The percent-of-sales method may underestimate actual 2004 pro forma income by assuming that all costs are variable. If the firm has fixed costs, which by definition would not increase with increasing sales, the 2004 pro forma income would probably be underestimated.

Chapter 4

ST 4–1 a. *Bank A:*

$FV_3 = \$10{,}000 \times FVIF_{4\%/3yrs} = \$10{,}000 \times 1.125 = \underline{\underline{\$11{,}250}}$

(Calculator solution = $11,248.64)

Bank B:

$FV_3 = \$10{,}000 \times FVIF_{4\%/2,2 \times 3yrs} = \$10{,}000 \times FVIF_{2\%,6yrs}$

$= \$10{,}000 \times 1.126 = \underline{\underline{\$11{,}260}}$

(Calculator solution = $11,261.62)

Bank C:

$FV_3 = \$10{,}000 \times FVIF_{4\%/4,4 \times 3\text{yrs}} = \$10{,}000 \times FVIF_{1\%,12\text{yrs}}$
$= \$10{,}000 \times 1.127 = \underline{\underline{\$11{,}270}}$

(Calculator solution = \$11,268.25)

b. *Bank A:*

EAR $= (1 + 4\%/1)^1 - 1 = (1 + 0.04)^1 - 1 = 1.04 - 1 = 0.04 = \underline{\underline{4}}\%$

Bank B:

EAR $= (1 + 4\%/2)^2 - 1 = (1 + 0.02)^2 - 1 = 1.0404 - 1 = 0.0404 = \underline{\underline{4.04}}\%$

Bank C:

EAR $= (1 + 4\%/4)^4 - 1 = (1 + 0.01)^4 - 1 = 1.0406 - 1 = 0.0406 = \underline{\underline{4.06}}\%$

c. Ms. Martin should deal with Bank C: The quarterly compounding of interest at the given 4% rate results in the highest future value as a result of the corresponding highest effective annual rate.

d. *Bank D:*

$FV_3 = \$10{,}000 \times FVIF_{4\%,3\text{yrs}}$ (continuous compounding)
$= \$10{,}000 \times e^{0.04 \times 3} = \$10{,}000 \times e^{0.12}$
$= \$10{,}000 \times 1.127497$
$= \underline{\underline{\$11{,}274.97}}$

This alternative is better than Bank C; it results in a higher future value because of the use of continuous compounding, which with otherwise identical cash flows always results in the highest future value of any compounding period.

ST 4–2 **a.** On a purely subjective basis, annuity Y looks more attractive than annuity X because it provides \$1,000 more each year than does annuity X. Of course, the fact that X is an annuity due means that the \$9,000 would be received at the beginning of the first year, unlike the \$10,000 at the end of the year, and this makes annuity X awfully tempting.

b. *Annuity X:*

$FVA_6 = \$9{,}000 \times FVIFA_{15\%,6\text{yrs}} \times (1 + 0.15)$
$= \$9{,}000 \times 8.754 \times 1.15 = \underline{\underline{\$90{,}603.90}}$

(Calculator solution = \$90,601.19)

Annuity Y:

$FVA_6 = \$10{,}000 \times FVIFA_{15\%,6\text{yrs}}$
$= \$10{,}000 \times 8.754 = \underline{\underline{\$87{,}540.00}}$

(Calculator solution = \$87,537.38)

c. Annuity X is more attractive, because its future value at the end of year 6, FVA_6, of \$90,603.90 is greater than annuity Y's end-of-year-6 future value, FVA_6, of \$87,540.00. The subjective assessment in part **a** was incorrect. The benefit of receiving annuity X's cash inflows at the beginning of each year appears to have outweighed the fact that annuity Y's annual cash inflow, which occurs at the end of each year, is \$1,000 larger (\$10,000 vs. \$9,000) than annuity X's.

ST 4–3 *Alternative A:*

Cash flow stream:

$PVA_5 = \$700 \times PVIFA_{9\%,5yrs}$

$= \$700 \times 3.890 = \underline{\underline{\$2,723}}$

(Calculator solution = \$2,722.76)

Single amount: $\underline{\underline{\$2,825}}$

Alternative B:

Cash flow stream:

Year (n)	Cash flow (1)	$FVIF_{9\%,n}$ (2)	Present value [(1) × (2)] (3)
1	\$1,100	0.917	\$1,088.70
2	900	0.842	757.80
3	700	0.772	540.40
4	500	0.708	354.00
5	300	0.650	195.00
		Present value	\$2,855.90

(Calculator solution = \$2,856.41)

Single amount: $\underline{\underline{\$2,800}}$

Conclusion: Alternative B in the form of a cash flow stream is preferred because its present value of \$2,855,90 is greater than the other three values.

ST 4–4 $FVA_5 = \$8,000$; $FVIFA_{7\%,5yrs} = 5.751$; $PMT = ?$

$FVA_n = PMT \times (FVIFA_{k,n})$ [Equation 4.14 or 4.22]

$\$8,000 = PMT \times 5.751$

$PMT = \$8,000/5.751 = \underline{\underline{\$1,391.06}}$

(Calculator solution = \$1,391.13)

Judi should deposit \$1,391.06 at the end of each of the 5 years to meet her goal of accumulating \$8,000 at the end of the fifth year.

Chapter 5

ST 5–1 a. Expected return, $\bar{k} = \frac{\Sigma \text{Returns}}{3}$ *(Equation 5.2a in footnote 1)*

$$\bar{k}_A = \frac{12\% + 14\% + 16\%}{3} = \frac{42\%}{3} = \underline{\underline{14\%}}$$

$$\bar{k}_B = \frac{16\% + 14\% + 12\%}{3} = \frac{42\%}{3} = \underline{\underline{14\%}}$$

$$\bar{k}_C = \frac{12\% + 14\% + 16\%}{3} = \frac{42\%}{3} = \underline{\underline{14}}\%$$

b. Standard deviation, $\sigma_k = \sqrt{\frac{\sum_{i=1}^{n}(k_i - \bar{k})^2}{n-1}}$ (*Equation 5.3a in footnote 2*)

$$\sigma_{k_A} = \sqrt{\frac{(12\% - 14\%)^2 + (14\% - 14\%)^2 + (16\% - 14\%)^2}{3-1}}$$

$$= \sqrt{\frac{4\% + 0\% + 4\%}{2}} = \sqrt{\frac{8\%}{2}} = \underline{\underline{2}}\%$$

$$\sigma_{k_B} = \sqrt{\frac{(16\% - 14\%)^2 + (14\% - 14\%)^2 + (12\% - 14\%)^2}{3-1}}$$

$$= \sqrt{\frac{4\% + 0\% + 4\%}{2}} = \sqrt{\frac{8\%}{2}} = \underline{\underline{2}}\%$$

$$\sigma_{k_C} = \sqrt{\frac{(12\% - 14\%)^2 + (14\% - 14\%)^2 + (16\% - 14\%)^2}{3-1}}$$

$$= \sqrt{\frac{4\% + 0\% + 4\%}{2}} = \sqrt{\frac{8\%}{2}} = \underline{\underline{2}}\%$$

c.

	Annual expected returns	
Year	Portfolio AB	Portfolio AC
2004	(0.50 × 12%) + (0.50 × 16%) = 14%	(0.50 × 12%) + (0.50 × 12%) = 12%
2005	(0.50 × 14%) + (0.50 × 14%) = 14%	(0.50 × 14%) + (0.50 × 14%) = 14%
2006	(0.50 × 16%) + (0.50 × 12%) = 14%	(0.50 × 16%) + (0.50 × 16%) = 16%

Over the 3-year period:

$$\bar{k}_{AB} = \frac{14\% + 14\% + 14\%}{3} = \frac{42\%}{3} = \underline{\underline{14}}\%$$

$$\bar{k}_{AC} = \frac{12\% + 14\% + 16\%}{3} = \frac{42\%}{3} = \underline{\underline{14}}\%$$

d. AB is perfectly negatively correlated.
AC is perfectly positively correlated.

e. Standard deviation of the portfolios

$$\sigma_{k_{AB}} = \sqrt{\frac{(14\% - 14\%)^2 + (14\% - 14\%)^2 + (14\% - 14\%)^2}{3-1}}$$

$$= \sqrt{\frac{0\% + 0\% + 0\%}{2}} = \sqrt{\frac{0\%}{2}} = \underline{\underline{0\%}}$$

$$\sigma_{k_{AC}} = \sqrt{\frac{(12\% - 14\%)^2 + (14\% - 14\%)^2 + (16\% - 14\%)^2}{3-1}}$$

$$= \sqrt{\frac{4\% + 0\% + 4\%}{2}} = \sqrt{\frac{8\%}{2}} = \underline{\underline{2\%}}$$

f. Portfolio AB is preferred, because it provides the same return (14%) as AC but with less risk $[(\sigma_{k_{AB}} = 0\%) < (\sigma_{k_{AC}} = 2\%)]$.

ST 5–2 a. When the market return increases by 10%, the project's required return would be expected to increase by 15% ($1.50 \times 10\%$). When the market return decreases by 10%, the project's required return would be expected to decrease by 15% $[1.50 \times (-10\%)]$.

b. $k_j = R_F + [b_j \times (k_m - R_F)]$
$= 7\% + [1.50 \times (10\% - 7\%)]$
$= 7\% + 4.5\% = \underline{\underline{11.5\%}}$

c. No, the project should be rejected, because its *expected* return of 11% is less than the 11.5% return *required* from the project.

d. $k_j = 7\% + [1.50 \times (9\% - 7\%)]$
$= 7\% + 3\% = \underline{\underline{10\%}}$

The project would now be acceptable, because its *expected* return of 11% is now in excess of the *required* return, which has declined to 10% as a result of investors in the marketplace becoming less risk-averse.

Chapter 6

ST 6–1 a. $B_0 = I \times (PVIFA_{k_d,n}) + M \times (PVIF_{k_d,n})$
$I = 0.08 \times \$1{,}000 = \$80$
$M = \$1{,}000$
$n = 12$ yrs

(1) $k_d = 7\%$
$B_0 = \$80 \times (PVIFA_{7\%,12\text{yrs}}) + \$1{,}000 \times (PVIF_{7\%,12\text{yrs}})$
$= (\$80 \times 7.943) + (\$1{,}000 \times 0.444)$
$= \$635.44 + \$444.00 = \underline{\underline{\$1{,}079.44}}$

(Calculator solution = $1,079.43)

(2) $k_d = 8\%$
$B_0 = \$80 \times (PVIFA_{8\%,12\text{yrs}}) + \$1{,}000 \times (PVIF_{8\%,12\text{yrs}})$
$= (\$80 \times 7.536) + (\$1{,}000 \times 0.397)$
$= \$602.88 + \$397.00 = \underline{\underline{\$999.88}}$

(Calculator solution = $1,000)

(3) $k_d = 10\%$

$$B_0 = \$80 \times (PVIFA_{10\%,12\text{yrs}}) + \$1{,}000 \times (PVIF_{10\%,12\text{yrs}})$$
$$= (\$80 \times 6.814) + (\$1{,}000 \times 0.319)$$
$$= \$545.12 + \$319.00 = \underline{\underline{\$864.12}}$$

(Calculator solution = $863.73)

b. (1) $k_d = 7\%$, $B_0 = \$1{,}079.44$; sells at a *premium*

(2) $k_d = 8\%$, $B_0 = \$999.88 \approx \$1{,}000.00$; sells at its *par value*

(3) $k_d = 10\%$, $B_0 = \$864.12$; sells at a *discount*

c. $$B_0 = \frac{I}{2} \times (PVIFA_{k_d/2,2n}) + M \times (PVIF_{k_d/2,2n})$$
$$= \frac{\$80}{2} \times (PVIFA_{10\%/2,2\times 12\text{periods}}) + \$1{,}000 \times (PVIF_{10\%/2,2\times 12\text{periods}})$$
$$= \$40 \times (PVIFA_{5\%,24\text{periods}}) + \$1{,}000 \times (PVIF_{5\%,24\text{periods}})$$
$$= (\$40 \times 13.799) + (\$1{,}000 \times 0.310)$$
$$= \$551.96 + \$310.00 = \underline{\underline{\$861.96}}$$

(Calculator solution = $862.01)

ST 6–2 **a.** $B_0 = \$1{,}150$

$I = 0.11 \times \$1{,}000 = \$110$

$M = \$1{,}000$

$n = 18$ yrs

$\$1{,}150 = \$110 \times (PVIFA_{k_d,18\text{yrs}}) + \$1{,}000 \times (PVIF_{k_d,18\text{yrs}})$

Because if $k_d = 11\%$, $B_0 = \$1{,}000 = M$, try $k_d = 10\%$.

$$B_0 = \$110 \times (PVIFA_{10\%,18\text{yrs}}) + \$1{,}000 \times (PVIF_{10\%,18\text{yrs}})$$
$$= (\$110 \times 8.201) + (\$1{,}000 \times 0.180)$$
$$= \$902.11 + \$180.00 = \$1{,}082.11$$

Because $\$1{,}082.11 < \$1{,}150$, try $k_d = 9\%$.

$$B_0 = \$110 \times (PVIFA_{9\%,18\text{yrs}}) + \$1{,}000 \times (PVIF_{9\%,18\text{yrs}})$$
$$= (\$110 \times 8.756) + (\$1{,}000 \times 0.212)$$
$$= \$963.16 + \$212.00 = \$1{,}175.16$$

Because the $1,175.16 value at 9% is higher than $1,150, and the $1,082.11 value at 10% rate is lower than $1,150, the bond's yield to maturity must be between 9% and 10%. Because the $1,175.16 value is closer to $1,150, rounding to the nearest whole percent, the YTM is 9%. (By using interpolation, the more precise YTM value is 9.27%.)

(Calculator solution = 9.26%)

b. The calculated YTM of 9+% is below the bond's 11% coupon interest rate, because the bond's market value of $1,150 is above its $1,000 par value. Whenever a bond's market value is above its par value (it sells at a *premium*), its YTM will be below its coupon interest rate; when a bond sells at *par,* the YTM will equal its coupon interest rate; and when the bond sells for less than par (at a *discount*), its YTM will be greater than its coupon interest rate.

Chapter 7

ST 7–1 $D_0 = \$1.80/\text{share}$
$k_s = 12\%$

a. *Zero growth:*

$$P_0 = \frac{D_1}{k_s} = \frac{D_1 = D_0 = \$1.80}{0.12} = \underline{\underline{\$15}}/\text{share}$$

b. *Constant growth, g = 5%:*
$D_1 = D_0 \times (1 + g) = \$1.80 = (1 + 0.05) = \$189/\text{share}$

$$P_0 = \frac{D_1}{k_s} + g = \frac{\$1.89}{0.12 - 0.05} = \frac{\$1.89}{0.07} = \underline{\underline{\$27}}/\text{share}$$

ST 7–2 a. **Step 1:** Present value of free cash flow from end of 2008 to infinity measured at the end of 2007.
$FCF_{2008} = \$1{,}500{,}000 \times (1 + 0.04) = \$1{,}560{,}000$

$$\text{Value of } FCF_{2008 \to \infty} = \frac{\$1{,}560{,}000}{0.10 - 0.04} = \frac{\$1{,}560{,}000}{0.06} = \underline{\underline{\$26{,}000{,}000}}$$

Step 2: Add the value found in Step 1 to the 2007 FCF.
Total $FCF_{2007} = \$1{,}500{,}000 + \$26{,}000{,}000 = \underline{\underline{\$27{,}500{,}000}}$

Step 3: Find the sum of the present values of the *FCFs* for 2004 through 2007 to determine company value, V_C.

Year (t)	FCF_t (1)	$PVIF_{10\%,t}$ (2)	Present Value of FCF_t [(1) × (2)] (3)
2004	$ 800,000	0.909	$ 727,200
2005	1,200,000	0.826	991,200
2006	1,400,000	0.751	1,051,400
2007	27,500,000	0.683	18,782,500
		Value of entire company, V_C =	$21,552,300

(Calculator solution = $21,553,719)

b. Common Stock value, $V_S = V_C - V_D - V_P$
$V_C = \$21{,}552{,}300$ (calculated in part **a**)
$V_D = \$12{,}500{,}000$ (given)
$V_P = \$0$ (given)
$V_S = \$21{,}552{,}300 - \$12{,}500{,}000 - \$0 = \underline{\underline{\$9{,}052{,}300}}$
(Calculator solution = $9,053,719)

c. $\text{Price per share} = \dfrac{\$9{,}052{,}300}{500{,}000} = \underline{\underline{\$18.10}}/\text{share}$

(Calculator solution = $18.11/share)

Chapter 8

ST 8–1 a. Book value = Installed cost − Accumulated depreciation

Installed cost = $50,000

Accumulated depreciation = $50,000 × (0.20 + 0.32 + 0.19 + 0.12)
= $50,000 × 0.83 = $41,500

Book value = $50,000 − $41,500 = $8,500

b. Taxes on sale of old equipment:

Capital gain = Sale price − Initial purchase price
= $55,000 − $50,000 = $5,000

Recaptured depreciation = Initial purchase price − Book value
= $50,000 − $8,500 = $41,500

Taxes = (0.40 × $5,000) + (0.40 × $41,500)
= $2,000 + $16,600 = $18,600

(Calculator solution = $18.11/share)

c. Initial investment:

Installed cost of new equipment		
Cost of new equipment	$75,000	
+ Installation costs	5,000	
Total installed cost—new		$80,000
− After-tax proceeds from sale of old equipment		
Proceeds from sale of old equipment	$55,000	
− Taxes on sale of old equipment	18,600	
Total after-tax proceeds—old		36,400
+ Change in net working capital		15,000
Initial investment		$58,600

ST 8–2 a. Initial investment:

Installed cost of new machine		
Cost of new Cost of new machine	$140,000	
+ Installation costs	10,000	
Total installed cost—new (depreciable value)		$150,000
− After-tax proceeds from sale of old machine		
Proceeds from sale of old machine	$ 42,000	
− Taxes on sale of old machine[1]	9,120	
Total after-tax proceeds—old		32,880
+ Change in net working capital[2]		20,000
Initial investment		$137,120

[1]Book value of old machine = $40,000 − [(0.20 + 0.32) × $40,000]
= $40,000 − (0.52 × $40,000)
= $40,000 − $20,800 = $19,200

Capital gain = $42,000 − $40,000 = $2,000

Recaptured depreciation = $40,000 − $19,200 = $20,800

Taxes = (0.40 × $2,000) + (.40 × $20,800) = $800 + $8,320 = $9,120

[2]Change in net working capital = +$10,000 + $25,000 − $15,000
= $35,000 − $15,000 = $20,000

b. Incremental operating cash inflows:

Calculation of Depreciation Expense

Year	Cost (1)	Applicable MACRS depreciation percentages (from Table 3.2) (2)	Depreciation [(1) × (2)] (3)
With new machine			
1	$150,000	33%	$ 49,500
2	150,000	45	67,500
3	150,000	15	22,500
4	150,000	7	10,500
		Totals 100%	$150,000
With old machine			
2	$ 40,000	19% (year-3 depreciation)	$ 7,600
2	40,000	12 (year-4 depreciation)	4,800
3	40,000	12 (year-5 depreciation)	4,800
4	40,000	5 (year-6 depreciation)	2,000
		Total	$19,200[a]

[a]The total of $19,200 represents the book value of the old machine at the end of the second year, which was calculated in part **a.**

Calculation of Operating Cash Inflows

	Year 1	2	3	4
With new machine				
Profits before depr. and taxes[a]	$120,000	$130,000	$130,000	$ 0
− Depreciation[b]	49,500	67,500	22,500	10,500
Net profits before taxes	$ 70,500	$ 62,500	$107,500	−$10,500
− Taxes (rate = 40%)	28,200	25,000	43,000	− 4,200
Net profits after taxes	$ 42,300	$ 37,500	$ 64,500	−$ 6,300
+ Depreciation[b]	49,500	67,500	22,500	10,500
Operating cash inflows	$ 91,800	$105,000	$ 87,000	$ 4,200
With old machine				
Profits before depr. and taxes[a]	$ 70,000	$ 70,000	$ 70,000	$ 0
− Depreciation[c]	7,600	4,800	4,800	2,000
Net profits before taxes	$ 62,400	$ 65,200	$ 65,200	−$ 2,000
− Taxes (rate = 40%)	24,960	26,080	26,080	− 800
Net profits after taxes	$ 37,440	$ 39,120	$ 39,120	−$ 1,200
+ Depreciation	7,600	4,800	4,800	2,000
Operating cash inflows	$ 45,040	$ 43,920	$ 43,920	$ 800

[a]Given in the problem.
[b]From column 3 of the preceding table, top.
[c]From column 3 of the preceding table, bottom.

Calculation of Incremental Operating Cash Inflows

	Operating cash inflows		
Year	New machine[a] (1)	Old machine[a] (2)	Incremental (relevant) [(1) − (2)] (3)
1	$ 91,800	$45,040	$46,760
2	105,000	43,920	61,080
3	87,000	43,920	43,080
4	4,200	800	3,400

[a]From the final row for the respective machine in the preceding table.

c. Terminal cash flow (end of year 3):

After-tax proceeds from sale of new machine		
Proceeds from sale of new machine	$35,000	
Total after-tax proceeds—new[1]	9,800	
Total after-tax proceeds—new		$25,200
− After-tax proceeds from sale of old machine		
Proceeds from sale of old machine	$ 0	
− Tax on sale of old machine[2]	− 800	
Total after-tax proceeds—old		800
+ Change in net working capital		20,000
Terminal cash flow		$44,400

[1]Book value of new machine at end of year 3
$= \$150,000 - [(0.33 + 0.45 + 0.15) \times \$150,000] = \$150,000 - (0.93 \times \$150,000)$
$= \$15,000 - \$139,500 = \$10,500)$
Tax on sale $= 0.40 \times (\$35,000 \text{ sale price} - \$10,500 \text{ book value})$
$= 0.40 \times \$24,500 = \underline{\$9,800}$
[2]Book value of old machine at end of year 3
$= \$40,000 - [(0.20 + 0.32 + 0.19 + 0.12 + 0.12) \times \$40,000] = \$40,000 - (0.95 \times \$40,000)$
$= \$40,000 - \$38,000 = \$2,000$
Tax on sale $= 0.40 \times (\$0 \text{ sale price} - \$2,000 \text{ book value})$
$= 0.40 \times (-\$2,500 = -\underline{\underline{\$800}}$ (i.e., \$800 tax saving)

d.

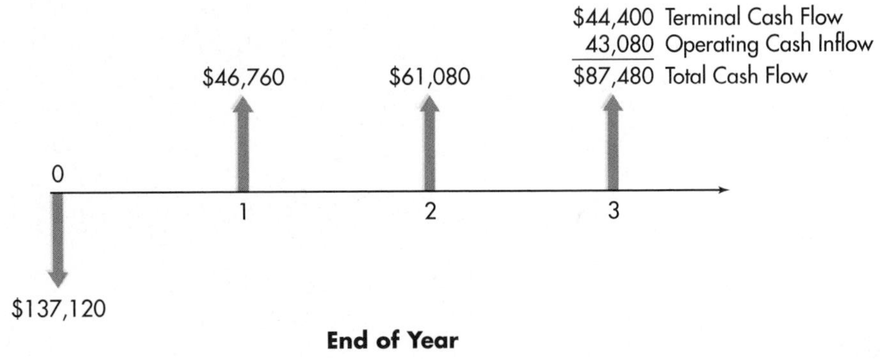

Note: The year-4 incremental operating cash inflow of \$3,400 is not directly included; it is instead reflected in the book values used to calculate the taxes on sale of the machines at the end of year 3 and is therefore part of the terminal cash flow.

Chapter 9

ST 9–1 **a.** Payback period:

Project M: $\frac{\$28{,}500}{\$10{,}000} = \underline{\underline{2.85}}$ years

Project N:

Year (t)	Cash inflows (CF_t)	Cumulative cash inflows
1	\$11,000	\$11,000
2	10,000	21,000 ←
3	9,000	30,000
4	8,000	38,000

$$2 + \frac{\$27{,}000 - \$21{,}000}{\$9{,}000} \text{ years}$$

$$2 + \frac{\$6{,}000}{\$9{,}000} \text{ years} = \underline{\underline{2.67}} \text{ years}$$

b. Net present value (NPV):

$$\begin{aligned}\text{Project M: NPV} &= (\$10{,}000 \times PVIFA_{14\%,4\text{yrs}}) - \$28{,}500\\ &= (\$10{,}000 \times 2.914) - \$28{,}500\\ &= \$29{,}140 - \$28{,}500 = \underline{\underline{\$640}}\end{aligned}$$

(Calculator solution = \$637.12)

Project N:

Year (t)	Cash inflows (CF_t) (1)	$PVIF_{14\%,t}$ (2)	Present value at 14% [(1) × (2)] (3)
1	\$11,000	0.877	\$ 9,647
2	10,000	0.769	7,690
3	9,000	0.675	6,075
4	8,000	0.592	4,736
	Present value of cash inflows		\$28,148
	− Initial investment		27,000
	Net present value (NPV)		\$ 1,148

(Calculator solution = \$1,155.18)

c. Internal rate of return (IRR):

Project M: $\dfrac{\$28{,}500}{\$10{,}000} = 2.850$

$PVIFA_{IRR,4yrs} = 2.850$

From Table A–4:

$PVIFA_{15\%,4yrs} = 2.855$

$PVIFA_{16\%,4yrs} = 2.798$

IRR = $\underline{\underline{15}}$% (2.850 is closest to 2.855)

(Calculator solution = 15.09%)

Project N:

$$\text{Average annual cash inflow} = \frac{\$11{,}000 + \$10{,}000 + \$9{,}000 + \$8{,}000}{4}$$

$$= \frac{\$38{,}000}{4} = \$9{,}500$$

$$PVIFA_{k,4yrs} = \frac{\$27{,}000}{\$9{,}500} = 2.842$$

$k \approx 15\%$

Try 16%, because there are more cash inflows in early years.

Year (t)	CF_t (1)	$PVIF_{16\%,t}$ (2)	Present value at 16% [(1) × (2)] (3)	$PVIF_{17\%,t}$ (4)	Present value at 17% [(1) × (4)] (5)
1	$11,000	0.862	$ 9,482	0.855	$ 9,405
2	10,000	0.743	7,430	0.731	7,310
3	9,000	0.641	5,769	0.624	5,616
4	8,000	0.552	4,416	0.534	4,272
	Present value of cash inflows		$27,097		$26,603
	− Initial investment		27,000		27,000
	NPV		$ 97		−$ 397

IRR = $\underline{\underline{16}}$% (rounding to nearest whole percent)

(Calculator solution = 16.19%)

d.

	Project M	Project N
Payback period	2.85 years	2.67 years[a]
NPV	$640	$1,148[a]
IRR	15%	16%[a]

[a]Preferred project.

Project N is recommended, because it has the shorter payback period and the higher NPV, which is greater than zero, and the larger IRR, which is greater than the 14% cost of capital.

e. Net present value profiles:

Data

Discount rate	NPV Project M	NPV Project N
0%	$11,500[a]	$11,000[b]
14	640	1,148
15	0	—
16	—	0

[a]($10,000 + $10,000 + $10,000 + $10,000) − $28,500
= $40,000 − $28,500
= $11,500

[b]($11,000 + $10,000 + $9,000 + $8,000) − $27,000
= $38,000 − $27,000
= $11,000

From the NPV profile that follows, it can be seen that if the firm has a cost of capital below approximately 6% (exact value is 5.75%), conflicting rankings of the projects would exist using the NPV and IRR decision techniques. Because the firm's cost of capital is 14%, it can be seen in part **d** that no conflict exists.

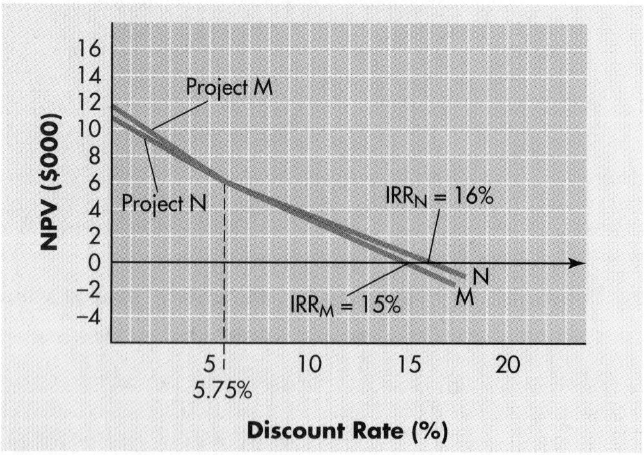

ST 9–2 a. $NPV_A = (\$7,000 \times PVIFA_{10\%,3yrs}) - \$15,000$

$= (\$7,000 \times 2.487) - \$15,000$

$= \$17,409 - \$15,000 = \underline{\underline{\$2,409}}$

(Calculator solution = $2,407.96)

$NPV_B = (\$10{,}000 \times PVIFA_{10\%,3yrs}) - \$20{,}000$
$= (\$10{,}000 - 2.487) - \$20{,}000$
$= \$24{,}870 - \$20{,}000 = \underline{\underline{\$4{,}870}}*$

(Calculator solution = \$4,868.52)

*Preferred project, because higher NPV.

b. From the CAPM-type relationship, the risk-adjusted discount rate (*RADR*) for project A, which has a risk index of 0.4, is 9%; for project B, with a risk index of 1.8, the *RADR* is 16%.

$NPV_A = (\$7{,}000 \times PVIFA_{9\%,3yrs}) - \$15{,}000$
$= (\$7{,}000 \times 2.531) - \$15{,}000$
$= \$17{,}717 - \$15{,}000 = \underline{\underline{\$2{,}717}}*$

(Calculator solution = \$2,719.06)

$NPV_B = (\$10{,}000 \times PVIFA_{16\%,3yrs}) - \$20{,}000$
$= (\$10{,}000 \times 2.246) - \$20{,}000$
$= \$22{,}460 - \$20{,}000 = \underline{\underline{\$2{,}460}}$

(Calculator solution = \$2,458.90)

*Preferred project, because higher NPV.

c. When the differences in risk were ignored in part **a,** project B was preferred over project A; but when the higher risk of project B is incorporated into the analysis using risk-adjusted discount rates in part **b,** *project A is preferred over project B.* Clearly, project A should be implemented.

Chapter 10

ST 10–1 **a.** Cost of debt, k_i (using approximation formula)

$$k_d = \frac{I + \dfrac{\$1{,}000 - N_d}{n}}{\dfrac{N_d + \$1{,}000}{2}}$$

$I = 0.10 \times \$1{,}000 = \$100$

$N_d = \$1{,}000 - \$30 \text{ discount} - \$20 \text{ flotation cost} = \$950$

$n = 10$ years

$$k_d = \frac{\$100 + \dfrac{\$1{,}000 - \$950}{10}}{\dfrac{\$950 + \$1{,}000}{2}} = \frac{\$100 + \$5}{\$975} = 10.8\%$$

(Calculator solution = 10.8%)

$k_i = k_d \times (1 - T)$

$T = 0.40$

$k_i = 10.8\% \times (1 - 0.40) = \underline{\underline{6.5}}\%$

Cost of preferred stock, k_p

$$k_p = \frac{D_p}{N_p}$$

$D_p = 0.11 \times \$100 = \$11$
$N_p = \$100 - \$4 \text{ flotation cost} = \$96$

$$k_p = \frac{\$11}{\$96} = \underline{\underline{11.5}}\%$$

Cost of retained earnings, k_r

$$k_r = k_s = \frac{D_1}{P_0} + g$$

$$= \frac{\$6}{\$80} + 6.0\% = 7.5\% + 6.0\% = \underline{\underline{13.5}}\%$$

Cost of new common stock, k_n

$$k_n = \frac{D_1}{N_n} + g$$

$D_1 = \$6$
$N_n = \$80 - \$4 \text{ underpricing} - \$4 \text{ flotation cost} = \$72$
$g = 6.0\%$

$$k_n = \frac{\$6}{\$72} + 6.0\% = 8.3\% + 6.0\% = \underline{\underline{14.3}}\%$$

b. (1) Break point, *BP*

$$BP_{\text{common equity}} = \frac{AF_{\text{common equity}}}{w_{\text{common equity}}}$$

$AF_{\text{common equity}} = \$225{,}000$
$w_{\text{common equity}} = 45\%$

$$BP_{\text{common equity}} = \frac{\$225{,}000}{0.45} = \$500{,}000$$

(2) WACC for total new financing $< \$500{,}000$

Source of capital	Weight (1)	Cost (2)	Weighted cost [(1) × (2)] (3)
Long-term debt	.40	6.5%	2.6%
Preferred stock	.15	11.5	1.7
Common stock equity	.45	13.5	6.1
Totals	1.00		10.4%

Weighted average cost of capital = 10.4%

(3) WACC for total new financing > \$500,000

Source of capital	Weight (1)	Cost (2)	Weighted cost [(1) × (2)] (3)
Long-term debt	.40	6.5%	2.6%
Preferred stock	.15	11.5	1.7
Common stock equity	.45	14.3	6.4
Totals	1.00		10.7%

Weighted average cost of capital = 10.7%

c. IOS data for graph

Investment opportunity	Internal rate of return (IRR)	Initial investment	Cumulative investment
D	16.5%	$200,000	$ 200,000
C	12.9	150,000	350,000
E	11.8	450,000	800,000
A	11.2	100,000	900,000
G	10.5	300,000	1,200,000
F	10.1	600,000	1,800,000
B	9.7	500,000	2,300,000

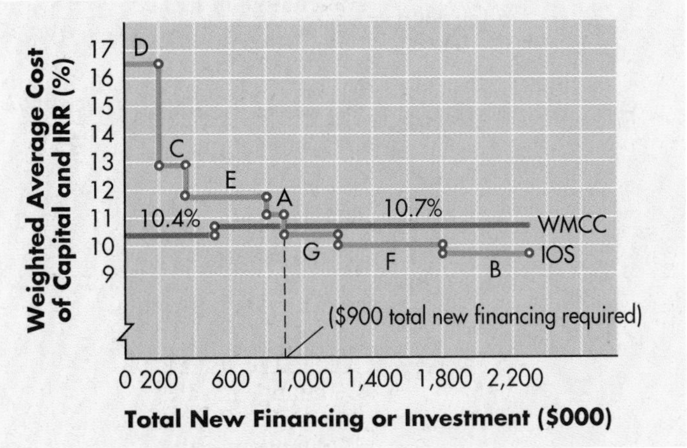

d. Projects D, C, E, and A should be accepted because their respective IRRs exceed the WMCC. They will require $900,000 of total new financing.

Chapter 11

ST 11–1 a. $Q = \dfrac{FC}{P - VC}$

$$= \frac{\$250{,}000}{\$7.50 - \$3.00} = \frac{\$250{,}000}{\$4.50} = \underline{\underline{55{,}556}} \text{ units}$$

b.

		+20%	
Sales (in units)	100,000		120,000
Sales revenue (units × \$7.50/unit)	\$750,000		\$900,000
Less: Variable operating costs (units × \$3.00/unit)	300,000		360,000
Less: Fixed operating costs	250,000		250,000
Earnings before interest and taxes (EBIT)	\$200,000		\$290,000
		+45%	
Less: Interest	80,000		80,000
Net profits before taxes	\$120,000		\$210,000
Less: Taxes ($T = 0.40$)	48,000		84,000
Net profits after taxes	\$ 72,000		\$126,000
Less: Preferred dividends (8,000 shares × \$5.00/share)	40,000		40,000
Earnings available for common	\$ 32,000		\$ 86,000
Earnings per share (EPS)	\$32,000/20,000 = \$1.60/share		\$86,000/20,000 = \$4.30/share
		+169%	

c. $$\text{DOL} = \frac{\%\text{ change in EBIT}}{\%\text{ change in sales}} = \frac{+45\%}{+20\%} = \underline{\underline{2.25}}$$

d. $$\text{DFL} = \frac{\%\text{ change in EPS}}{\%\text{ change in EBIT}} = \frac{+169\%}{+45\%} = \underline{\underline{3.76}}$$

e. $$\text{DTL} = \text{DOL} \times \text{DFL}$$
$$= 2.25 \times 3.76 = \underline{\underline{8.46}}$$

Using the other DTL formula:

$$\text{DTL} = \frac{\%\text{ change in EPS}}{\%\text{ change in sales}}$$

$$8.46 = \frac{\%\text{ change in EPS}}{+50\%}$$

$$\%\text{ change in EPS} = 8.46 \times 0.50 = 4.23 = \underline{\underline{+423\%}}$$

ST 11–2

Data summary for alternative plans

Source of capital	Plan A (bond)	Plan B (stock)
Long-term debt	\$60,000 at 12% annual interest	\$50,000 at 12% annual interest
Annual interest =	0.12 = \$60,000 = \$7,200	0.12 × \$50,000 = \$6,000
Common stock	10,000 shares	11,000 shares

a.

	Plan A (bond)		Plan B (stock)	
EBIT[a]	$30,000	$40,000	$30,000	$40,000
Less: Interest	7,200	7,200	6,000	6,000
Net profits before taxes	$22,800	$32,800	$24,000	$34,000
Less: Taxes ($T = 0.40$)	9,120	13,120	9,600	13,600
Net profits after taxes	$13,680	$19,680	$14,400	$20,400
EPS (10,000 shares)	$1.37	$1.97		
(11,000 shares)			$1.31	$1.85

[a]Values were arbitrarily selected; other values could have been used.

Coordinates

	EBIT	
	$30,000	$40,000
Financing plan	Earnings per share (EPS)	
A (Bond)	$1.37	$1.97
B (Stock)	1.31	1.85

b.

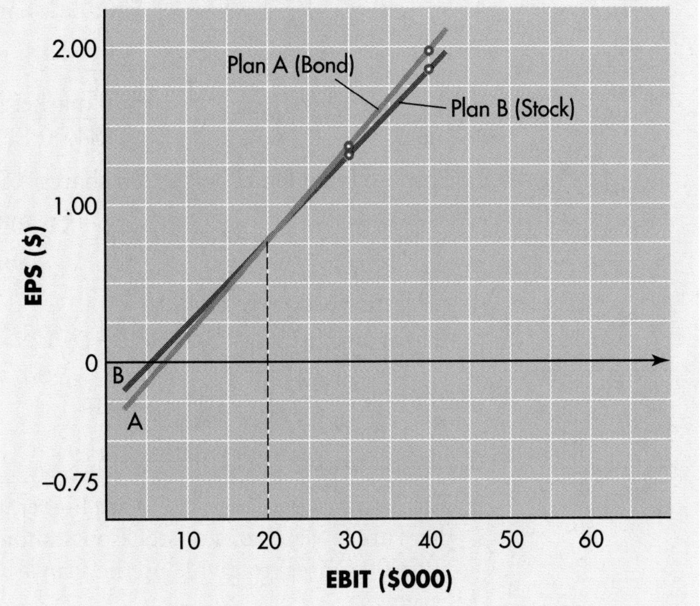

c. The bond plan (Plan A) becomes superior to the stock plan (Plan B) at *around $20,000* of EBIT, as represented by the dashed vertical line in the figure in part **b.** (*Note:* The actual point is $19,200, which was determined algebraically by using a technique described in more advanced texts.)

ST 11–3 a.

Capital structure debt ratio	Expected EPS (1)	Required return, k_s (2)	Estimated share value [(1) ÷ (2)] (3)
0%	$3.12	.13	$24.00
10	3.90	.15	26.00
20	4.80	.16	30.00
30	5.44	.17	32.00
40	5.51	.19	29.00
50	5.00	.20	25.00
60	4.40	.22	20.00

b. Using the table in part **a:**

(1) Maximization of EPS: *40% debt ratio,* EPS = $5.51/share (see column 1).

(2) Maximization of share value: *30% debt ratio,* share value = $32.00 (see column 3).

c. Recommend *30% debt ratio,* because it results in the maximum share value and is therefore consistent with the firm's goal of owner wealth maximization.

Chapter 12

ST 12–1 a. Earnings per share (EPS) = $\dfrac{\$2{,}000{,}000 \text{ earnings available}}{500{,}000 \text{ shares of common outstanding}}$

$= \underline{\underline{\$4.00}}/\text{share}$

Price/earnings (P/E) ratio = $\dfrac{\$60 \text{ market price}}{\$4.00 \text{ EPS}} = \underline{\underline{15}}$

b. Proposed dividends = 500,000 shares × $2 per share = $1,000,000

Shares that can be repurchased = $\dfrac{\$1{,}000{,}000}{\$62} = \underline{\underline{16{,}129}}$ shares

c. *After proposed repurchase:*

Shares outstanding = 500,000 − 16,129 = 483,871

$\text{EPS} = \dfrac{\$2{,}000{,}000}{483{,}871} = \underline{\underline{\$4.13}}/\text{share}$

d. Market price = $4.13/share × 15 = $\underline{\underline{\$61.95}}$/share

e. The earnings per share (EPS) are higher after the repurchase, because there are fewer shares of stock outstanding (483,871 shares versus 500,000 shares) to divide up the firm's $2,000,000 of available earnings.

f. In both cases, the stockholders would receive $2 per share—a $2 cash dividend in the dividend case or an approximately $2 increase in share price ($60.00 per share to $61.95 per share) in the repurchase case. [*Note:*

The difference of \$0.05 per share (\$2.00 − \$1.95) difference is due to rounding.]

Chapter 13

ST 13–1

Basic data		
Time component	Current	Proposed
Average payment period (APP)	10 days	30 days
Average collection period (ACP)	30 days	30 days
Average age of inventory (AAI)	40 days	40 days

Cash conversion cycle (CCC) = AAI + ACP − APP

$$CCC_{current} = 40 \text{ days} + 30 \text{ days} - 10 \text{ days} = 60 \text{ days}$$
$$CCC_{proposed} = 40 \text{ days} + 30 \text{ days} - 30 \text{ days} = \underline{40} \text{ days}$$
$$\text{Reduction in CCC} \quad \underline{\underline{20}} \text{ days}$$

Annual operating cycle investment = \$18,000,000
Daily expenditure = \$18,000,000 ÷ 360 = \$50,000
Reduction in resource investment = \$50,000 × 20 days = \$1,000,000
Annual profit increase = 0.12 × \$1,000,000 = $\underline{\underline{\$120{,}000}}$

ST 13–2 a. *Data:*

$S = 60{,}000$ gallons
$O = \$200$ per order
$C = \$1$ per gallon per year

Calculation:

$$EOQ = \sqrt{\frac{2 \times S \times O}{C}}$$
$$= \sqrt{\frac{2 \times 60{,}000 \times \$200}{\$1}}$$
$$= \sqrt{24{,}000{,}000}$$
$$= \underline{\underline{4{,}899}} \text{ gallons}$$

b. *Data:*

Lead time = 20 days
Daily usage = 60,000 gallons/360 days
= 166.67 gallons/day

Calculation:

Reorder point = lead time in days × daily usage
= 20 days × 166.67 gallons/day
= $\underline{\underline{3{,}333.4}}$ gallons

ST 13–3 Tabular Calculation of the Effects of Relaxing Credit Standards on Regency Rug Repair Company:

Additional profit contribution from sales		
[4,000 rugs × ($32 avg. sale price − $28 var. cost)]		$16,000
Cost of marginal investment in accounts receivable		
Average investment under proposed plan:		
$\frac{(\$28 \times 76{,}000 \text{ rugs})}{360/48} = \frac{\$2{,}128{,}000}{7.5}$	$283,733	
Average investment under present plan:		
$\frac{(\$28 \times 72{,}000 \text{ rugs})}{360/40} = \frac{\$2{,}016{,}000}{9}$	224,000	
Marginal investment in A/R	$ 59,733	
Cost of marginal investment in A/R (0.14 × $59,733)		($ 8,363)
Cost of marginal bad debts		
Bad debts under proposed plan (0.015 × $32 × 76,000 rugs)	$ 36,480	
Bad debts under present plan (0.010 × $32 × 72,000 rugs)	23,040	
Cost of marginal bad debts		($13,440)
Net loss from implementation of proposed plan		($ 5,803)

Recommendation: Because a net loss of $5,803 is expected to result from relaxing credit standards, *the proposed plan should not be implemented.*

Chapter 14

ST 14–1 a.

Supplier	Approximate cost of giving up cash discount
X	1% × [360/(55 − 10)] = 1% × 360/45 = 1% × 8 = 8%
Y	2% × [360/(30 − 10)] = 2% × 360/20 = 2% × 18 = 36%
Z	2% × [360/(60 − 20)] = 2% × 360/40 = 2% × 9 = 18%

b.

Supplier	Recommendation
X	8% cost of giving up discount < 15% interest cost from bank; therefore, *give up discount.*
Y	36% cost of giving up discount > 15% interest cost from bank; therefore, *take discount and borrow from bank.*
Z	18% cost of giving up discount > 15% interest cost from bank; therefore, *take discount and borrow from bank.*

c. Stretching accounts payable for supplier Z would change the cost of giving up the cash discount to

$$2\% \times [360/[(60 + 20) - 20]) = 2\% \times 360/60 = 2\% \times 6 = 12\%$$

In this case, in light of the 15% interest cost from the bank, the recommended strategy in part **b** would be to *give up the discount,* because the 12% cost of giving up the discount would be less than the 15% interest cost from the bank.

Appendix C

Answers to Selected End-of-Chapter Problems

The following list of answers to selected problems and portions of problems is included to provide "check figures" for use in preparing detailed solutions to end-of-chapter problems requiring calculations. For problems that are relatively straightforward, the key answer is given; for more complex problems, answers to a number of parts of the problem are included. Detailed calculations are not shown—only the final and, in some cases, intermediate answers, which should help to confirm whether the correct solution is being developed. Answers to problems involving present and future value were solved by using the appropriate tables; calculator solutions are not given. For problems containing a variety of cases for which similar calculations are required, the answers for only one or two cases have been included. The only verbal answers included are simple yes-or-no or "choice of best alternative" responses; answers to problems requiring detailed explanations or discussions are not given.

The problems and portions of problems for which answers have been included were selected randomly; therefore, there is no discernible pattern to the choice of problem answers given. The answers given are based on what are believed to be the most obvious and reasonable assumptions related to the given problem; in some cases, other reasonable assumptions could result in equally correct answers.

1–1 a. Ms. Harper has unlimited liability: $60,000
c. Ms. Harper has limited liability

1–4 a. $19,700
b. $72,800
c. 21.3%

1–7 e. Total tax liability: $206,400

1–8 a. Earnings after tax: $18,000

1–9 b. Asset X: $100
Asset Y: $2,000

2–3 a. Net profit after tax: $19,250

2–4 a. Earnings per share: $1.162

2–6 Initial sales price: $9.50

2–7 b. Earnings per share: $2.36
c. Cash dividend per share: $1.50

2–9 a.

Current ratio	2000: 1.88	2002: 1.79
Quick ratio	2000: 1.22	2002: 1.24
Net working capital		2002: $9,900

2–11 a. 45 days

2–12

	Creek	*Industry*
Debt ratio	0.73	0.51
Times interest earned	3.00	7.30

2–13 a.

	Pelican	*Timberland*
(1) Debt ratio	10%	50%
(2) Times interest earned	62.5	12.5

b.

	Pelican	*Timberland*
(1) Operating margin	25%	25%
(2) Net profit margin	14.8%	13.8%
(3) ROA	36.9%	34.5%
(4) ROE	41.0%	69.0%

2–16 a.

	Actual 2003
Current Ratio:	1.04
Average collection period:	56 days
Debt ratio:	61.3%
Net profit margin:	4.1%
Return on equity:	11.3%

2–14 a. 2003 Johnson ROE = 21.21%
Industry ROE = 14.46%

3–5 b. $13.367
c. $10,537

3–11 a. To retained earnings: $146,600
b. To retained earnings: $157,400

3–12 a. Total assets: $1,383,000
Total current liabilities: $510,000
External funds required: $53,000

3–14 a. To retained earnings: $32,500
c. $11,250

4–3 C: 3 years $< n <$ 4 years

4–4 A: $530.60
D: $78.450

4–6 a. (1) $15,456

4–10 B: $6,020
D $80,250

4–17 a. (1) A: $36,217.50
(2) A: $39,114.90

4–18 a. (1) C: $2,821.70
(2) C: $3,386.04

4–21 b. $30,950.64

4–23 b. B: $1,000,000
D: $1,200,000

4–25 a. A: $3,862.50

4–27 b. B: $26,039

4–30 a. $22,215

4–32 a. (1) Annual: $8,810
Semiannual: $8,955
Quarterly: $9,030

4–35 b. B: 12.6%
D: 17.0%

4–38 B: $2,439.32

4–41 a. $60,000
b. $3,764.82

4–42 A: $4,656.58
B: $10,619.47
C: $7,955.87

4–46 a. A: $12\% < i < 13\%$
Calculator solution 12.47%
C: $2\% < i < 3\%$
Calculator solution 2.50%

4–48 a. B: $8\% < i < 9\%$
Calculator solution 8.02%
D: $10\% < i < 11\%$
Calculator solution 10.03%

4–53 A: $17 < n < 18$
Calculator solution 17.79
D: $18 < n < 19$
Calculator solution 18.68

5–1 a. X: 12.50%
Y: 12.36%

5–2 A: 25%

5–4 a. A: 8%
B: 20%

5–5 a. R: 10%
S: 20%
b. R: 25%
S: 25.5%

5–8 a. (4) Project 257 CV: .368
Project 432 CV: .354

5–9 a. F: 4%
b. F: 13.38%
c. F: 3.345

5–10 b. Portfolio return: 15.5%
c. Standard deviation: 1.511%

5–15 a. 18% increase
b. 9.6% decrease
c. No change

5–19 A: 8.9%
D: 15%
5–21 b. 10%
6–2 a. A: 9%
B: 12%
6–5 b. $175,000
c. $113,750
6–7 b. $8,791.40
6–8 C: $16,660.00
D: $9,717.00
6–10 a. $1,156.88
6–14 a.
(1) $1,120.23
(2) $1,000.00
(3) $896.01
6–17 a. A: approximate: 12.36%
Calculator solution: 12.71%
C: approximate: 10.38%
Calculator solution: 10.22%
E: approximate: 8.77%
Calculator solution: 8.95%
6–19 A: $1,152.35
C: $464.72
E: $76.11
7–1 b. 800,000 shares
7–3 A: $15.00
C: $11.00
D: $25.50
7–6 a. $20
b. $12
7–8 a. $68.82
b. $60.95
7–9 A: $24.00
B: $40.00
E: $18.75
7–10 a. $37.75
b. $60.40
7–13 a. (1) $5,021,250
(2) $5,411,250
(3) $4,049,331
b. $2,191,331
c. $10.96
7–15 a. Book value: $36.00
b. Liquidation value: $30.20
7–16 A: $18.60
B: $45.00
E: $76.50
8–1 a. Operating expenditure
d. Operating expenditure
f. Capital expenditure
8–4

Year	*Relevant cash flow*
1	$4,000
2	$6,000
4	$10,000

8–6 A: $275,500
B: $26,800
8–7 a. $23,200
b. @ $100,000: $30,720
@ $56,000: $13,120
8–8 a. Total tax: $49,600
d. Total tax: ($6,400)
8–11 Initial investment $22,680
8–12 a. Initial investment: $18,240
c. Initial investment: $23,100
8–14 c. Cash inflow, Year 3: $584,000
8–16 b. Incremental cash flow, Year 3: $1,960
8–18 Terminal cash flow: $76,640
9–2 a. Machine 1: 4 years, 8 months
Machine 2: 5 years, 3 months
9–4 a. $3,246 Accept
b. −$5,131 Reject
9–5 a. $2,675 Accept
b. −$805 Reject
9–8 a. Project A: 3.08 years
Project C: 2.38 years
b. Project C: NPV $5,451
9–9 a. Project A: 17%
Project D: 21%
9–12 a. NPV = $1,222
b. IRR = 12%
c. Accept
9–17 a. Initial Investment: $1,480,000
b.

Year	*Cash Flow*
1	$656,000
2	761,600
3	647,200
4	585,600
5	585,600
6	44,000

c. 2.1 years
d. NPV = $959,289
IRR = 35%
9–22 a. Range A: $1,600
9–23 b. Project A:
Pessimistic: $73
Most likely: $1,609
Optimistic: $3,145
9–26 a. Project E: $2,130;
Project F: $1,678
c. Project E: $834;
Project F: $1,678
10–2 a. $980
d. 7.36% after tax
10–6 a. 6%
b. 12%
10–7 d. 16.54%
10–9 a. 13.55%
b. 12.985%

10–12 e. Breakpoint common stock: $5,880,000
f. 7.02%
g. 7.07%
11–1 1,300
11–4 a. 21,000 CDs
b. $293,580
d. $10,500
11–7 a. 8,000 units
b. @10,000 units: $95,000
11–10 b. 2
c. 1.25
11–16 a. Structure A:
EBIT $30,000: EPS $1.125
Structure B:
EBIT $50,000: EPS 2.28
12–4 a. $4.75 per share
b. $0.40 per share
12–6 a.

Year	*$ Dividend*
1994	0.10
1998	0.96
2001	1.28
2003	1.60

c.

Year	*$ Dividend*
1994	0.50
1998	0.50
2001	0.66
2003	1.30

12–8 a. Common stock: $21,000
Paid in capital: $294,000
Retained earnings: $85,000
12–10 a. $2.00
d. $20.00 per share
12–12 a. 1,200,000 shares @ $1.50 par
d. 3,600,000 shares @ $0.50 par
12–14 a. 19,047 shares
b. $2.10
13–1 a. OC = 150 days
b. CCC = 120 days
c. $10,000,000
13–2 b. CCC = 70 days
c. $27,222
13–4 a. Average season requirement: $4,000,000
13–6 a. 200 units
b. 122.2 units
c. 33.33 units
13–9 Loss from implementation: $4,721
13–11 Loss from implementation: $11,895
13–13 a. 7 days
b. $21,450
14–2 a. 36.73%
b. 18.18%
e. 7.27%
14–6 $1,300,000
14–7 $82,500
14–9 14.29%
14–10 a. Effective rate: 12.94%
b. Effective rate: 11.73%
14–13 a. Effective rate: 2.25%
b. Effective annual rate: 13.69%
14–17

	Amount remitted
A:	$196,000
C:	$107,800
F:	$176,400
G:	$ 88,200

Appendix D

Instructions for Using the *PMF Brief* CD-ROM Software

The *PMF Brief* CD-ROM contains three applications: the *PMF Tutor,* the *PMF Problem-Solver,* and the *PMF Excel Spreadsheet Templates.* These solutions are designed to run on any computer running Windows 98, ME, NT 4.0, 2000, or XP and Microsoft Excel version 97, 2000, or XP or higher. Be sure to visit the book's Web site at *http://www.aw.com/gitman* to see if any updates have been made to this software since the book was published.

For your convenience, chapter and section references are shown on the screen for each associated computation in the *Problem-Solver* and the *Tutor.* As noted in the text preface as well as in Chapter 1, applicability of the software throughout the text and the study guide is keyed to related text discussions, end-of-chapter problems, and end-of-chapter and end-of-part cases by icons for all of the computational routines. Thus you can integrate the procedures on the disk with the corresponding text discussions.

What Is the *PMF Tutor?*

The *PMF Tutor* is an Excel workbook containing a collection of managerial finance problem types with the problems varied by random-number generation. Its purpose is to give you an essentially unlimited number of problems to work through so that you can practice until you are satisfied that you understand a concept. In using the *Tutor,* the following sequence should produce the best results:

1. **Work the problem first yourself.** It is tempting to save time by letting the computer solve the problem for you and then studying the computer's answer. You won't learn much that way. Even if you make mistakes when you try the problem on your own, you will learn from those mistakes.

2. **Enter your answer.** The computer will check your answer against the correct answer.
3. **Check the solution.** If you do not get the same answer as the computer, check your work step by step against the correct solution displayed on the computer screen. Doing so will help you to pinpoint your mistakes. Practice each type of problem until you have genuinely mastered it. When you take the course exams, you won't be able to fake your knowledge level. So don't stop until you're sure that you have mastered the concepts.

The *Tutor* uses random-number generation to choose the specific numbers, so it is unlikely that you will ever see a combination of numbers twice. This gives you an effectively unlimited number of practice problems. The only limit is your willingness to practice.

What Is the *PMF Problem-Solver?*

The *PMF Problem-Solver* is an Excel workbook containing a collection of financial computation worksheets. The purpose of the *PMF Problem-Solver* is to aid the student's learning and understanding of managerial finance by providing a fast and easy method for performing the often time-consuming mathematical computations required. It is not the intent of the *PMF Problem-Solver* to eliminate the need for learning the various concepts but, rather, to assist in solving the problems once the appropriate formulas have been studied. The *PMF Problem-Solver* differs from the *Tutor* in that it solves for the answer, given the input data supplied by the user, whereas the *Tutor* supplies the input data and looks to the student to perform the calculations. Use the *Tutor* to practice application of basic concepts. Then use the *PMF Problem-Solver* to save computational time once you understand the concepts.

What Are the *PMF Excel Spreadsheet Templates?*

The *PMF Excel Spreadsheet Templates* are preprogrammed Excel worksheets, with one file for each problem. The worksheets enable students to enter data and solve problems using Microsoft Excel—the most commonly used spreadsheet software. The worksheet files correspond to selected end-of-chapter problems, and the worksheet file names are based on the chapter number and the problem number.

Hardware and Software Requirements

To use the *PMF Brief* CD-ROM, you must have the following:

- an IBM-compatible PC
- Microsoft Windows 98, ME, NT 4.0, 2000, or XP
- Microsoft Excel Version 97, 2000, or XP

Installing the Software

1. Insert the *PMF Brief* CD-ROM into your CD-ROM drive.
2. An autorun will automatically lead you through the installation process. If your CD is configured to bypass this autorun, select Start | Run | D:setup.exe, where D:\ is the drive letter of your CD-ROM.
3. Follow the instructions on the screen to install the files to your hard drive.

You can also access the spreadsheets directly on the CD-ROM. All of the individual files are available in the PMF folder.

Be sure to store the CD-ROM in a safe place in case you need to install the software again at a later time. Or you can download a fresh copy from the book's Web site.

The *PMF Tutor*

Running the *PMF Tutor*

To run the *PMF Tutor,* either double-click on its desktop shortcut or select Start | Programs | PMF Brief CD-ROM Software | Start PMF Tutor.

When the *PMF Tutor* is loaded, you will see the following introductory screen:

FIGURE D-1

Excel *PMF Tutor* Start-up Screen Showing the Main Menu

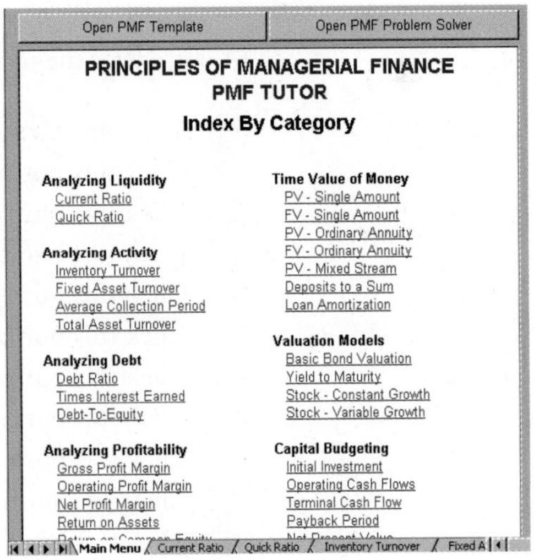

Using the *PMF Tutor*

From the *PMF Tutor* main menu, click on the name of a specific problem type. Each tutorial will open with a new problem ready for you to solve. The following is an example *Tutor* problem:

FIGURE D-2

Excel *PMF Tutor* Sample Problem

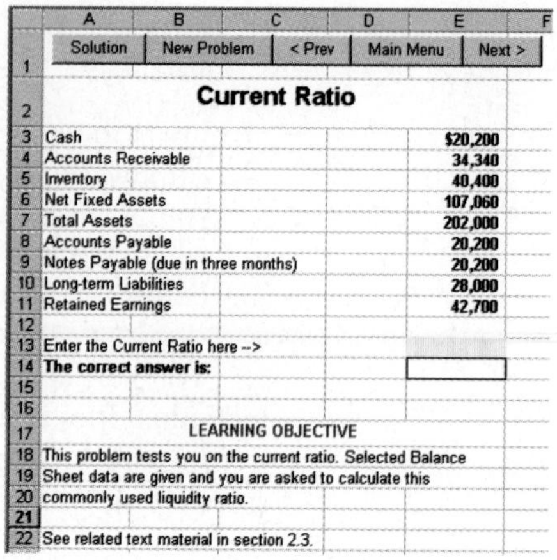

Solution / New Problem / < Prev / Main Menu / Next >	
Current Ratio	
Cash	$20,200
Accounts Receivable	34,340
Inventory	40,400
Net Fixed Assets	107,060
Total Assets	202,000
Accounts Payable	20,200
Notes Payable (due in three months)	20,200
Long-term Liabilities	28,000
Retained Earnings	42,700
Enter the Current Ratio here -->	
The correct answer is:	
LEARNING OBJECTIVE	
This problem tests you on the current ratio. Selected Balance Sheet data are given and you are asked to calculate this commonly used liquidity ratio.	
See related text material in section 2.3.	

There are five buttons at the top of the window for each tutorial:

- Solution—Click this to see the problem solution.
- New Problem—Click this to see new problem data.
- Prev—Click this to move to the previous tutorial problem.
- Main—Click this to return to the *PMF Tutor* main menu.
- Next—Click this to move to the next tutorial problem.

Using the *PMF Tutor* Toolbar

The *PMF Tutor* has a toolbar that also facilitates navigation and tasks. The 14 buttons of the toolbar are explained in the following list.

Click this button to open the *PMF Templates.*
Click this button to open the *Problem-Solver.*
Click this button to go to the main menu.
Click this button to go to the previous tutorial.
Click this button to go to the next tutorial.
Click this button to go to the last sheet.
Click this button to set the zoom factor for the tutorial.
Click this button to make a new problem in the current tutorial.
Click this button to check the solution to the current problem.
Click this button to open the Windows calculator to facilitate your solution.
Click this button to print the current tutorial sheets.
Click this button to preview the printing of the current tutorial sheets.
Click this button to learn more about the developer, KMT Software.
Click this button to view Help for *PMF Tutor.*

When you are ready to solve a particular tutorial problem, you may want to follow these steps:

1. Review the learning objective. Each tutorial has a learning objective situated just below the problem. Learning objectives provide a brief description of what each problem is testing you on and note the associated section in the textbook where the material is covered.
2. Review the problem data and calculate your answer.
3. Enter your answer in the yellow cell. *Note:* If the problem calls for a percentage, be sure to enter the percentage in decimal form (for example, enter 20% as .2) or to enter the number followed by the percent sign (that is, type 20% and then press Enter).
4. Check your solution.
5. If you need more practice, click the New Problem button and begin with Step 1.

The *PMF Problem-Solver*

Running the *PMF Problem-Solver*

To run the *PMF Problem-Solver,* either double-click on its desktop shortcut or select Start | Programs | PMF Brief CD-ROM Software | Start PMF Problem Solver.

Using the *PMF Problem-Solver*

From the *PMF Problem-Solver* main menu, click on the name of a specific calculation. Here is the *PMF Problem-Solver* main menu:

FIGURE D-3

Excel *PMF Problem-Solver* Start-up Screen Showing the Main Menu

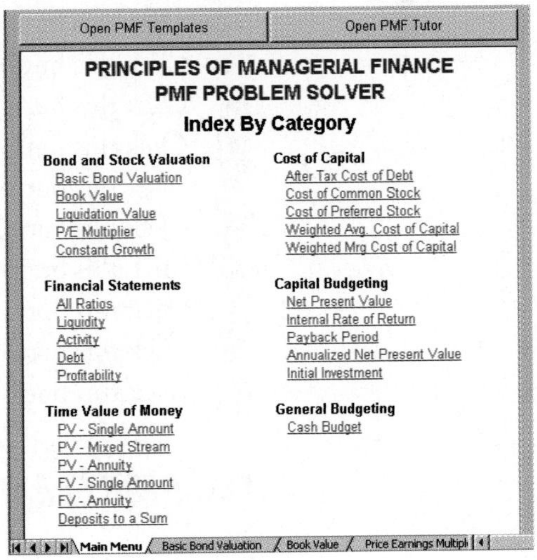

Using a *PMF Problem-Solver* worksheet is simple. You enter your inputs in the yellow cells. You can move between these cells by using your mouse or by

FIGURE D–4

Excel *PMF Problem-Solver* Sample Problem

	A	B	C	D	E	F
1						
2			**Basic Bond Valuation**			
3	Par Value of the Bond				$1,000	
4	Years to Maturity				10	
5	Required Rate of Return				12.000%	
6	Coupon Rate of Bond				10.000%	
7	Payment of interest:					
8	Annual ◉ Semi-annual ○					
9						
10	**Value of the bond is:**				$887.00	
11						
12						
13			DESCRIPTION			
14	Use this worksheet to determine the value of a bond. If the					
15	bond pays interest on an semi-annual basis (twice per year),					
16	be sure to selection the semi-annual option button.					
17						
18	This material is covered in section 6.4.					
19						

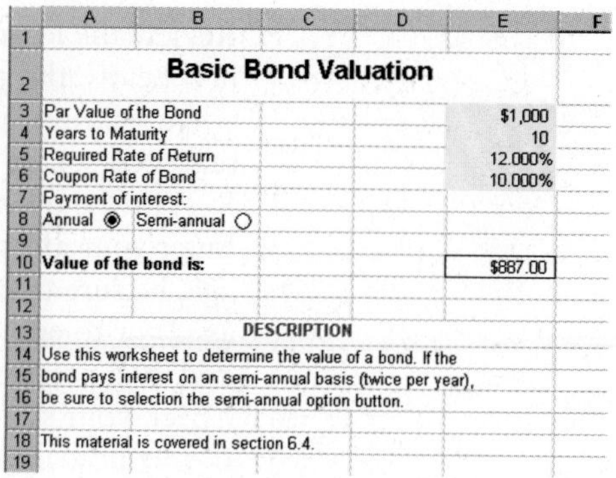

pressing the Tab on your keyboard. If any of your inputs involve percentages (such as an interest rate of 10.5%), either enter the percentage in decimal form (that is, enter .105 for 10.5%) or enter the percentage following the format number followed by the percent sign (that is, type 10.5% and then press Enter).

Figure D–4 shows a sample *Problem-Solver* problem.

The *PMF Problem-Solver* has a toolbar that also facilitates navigation and tasks. The 12 buttons of the toolbar are explained below.

Using the *Problem-Solver* Toolbar

The *Problem-Solver* has a toolbar that performs a variety of functions depending on which button you select. The toolbar includes the following buttons and functions:

Click this button to open the *PMF Templates*.

Click this button to open the *Tutor*.

Click this button to go to the main menu.

Click this button to go to the previous sheet.

Click this button to go to the next sheet.

Click this button to go to the last sheet.

Click this button to set the zoom factor for the *Solver*.

Click this button to open the Windows calculator to facilitate your solution.

Click this button to print the *Solver* sheets.

Click this button to preview the printing of the current *Solver* sheets.

Click this button to learn more about the developer, KMT Software.

Click this button to view Help for *PMF Problem-Solver*.

The *PMF Excel Spreadsheet Templates*

Running the *PMF Excel Spreadsheet Templates*

To run one of the *PMF Excel Spreadsheet Templates*, either double-click on its desktop shortcut or select Start | Programs | PMF Brief CD-ROM Software | Start PMF Templates.

Using the *PMF Excel Spreadsheet Templates*

The *PMF Excel Spreadsheet Templates* describe the problem from the chapter material. You then enter the inputs in the yellow highlighted cells. If any of your inputs involve percentages (such as an interest rate of 10.5%), either enter the percentage in decimal form (that is, enter .105 for 10.5%) or enter the percentage following the format number followed by the percent sign (that is, type 10.5% and then press Enter).

Each of the *PMF Excel Spreadsheet Templates* has a description of the problem at the top of the worksheet, and the answer is listed below. The screen shot in Figure D–5 shows a typical problem description. The answer is made available as shown in Figure D–6 below the problem description.

FIGURE D–5

Example *PMF Excel Spreadsheet Templates* Sample Problem Description

	A	B	C	D	E	F	G	H
1								
2			**PRINCIPLES OF MANAGERIAL FINANCE**					
3								
4	**1-8 Interest versus Dividend Income**							
5	During the year just ended, Shering Distributors, Inc., had pretax earnings from operations of $490,000. In							
6	addition, during the year it received $20,000 in income from interest on bonds it held in Zig Manuafcturing and							
7	received $20,000 in income from dividends on its 5% common stock holding in Tank Industries. Shering is in							
8	the 40% tax bracket and is eligible for a 70% dividend exclusion on its Tank Industries stock.							
9								
10	a.	Calculate the firm's tax on its operating earnings only.						
11								
12	b.	Find the tax and after-tax amount attributable to the interest income from						
13		the Zig Manufacturing bonds.						
14								
15	c.	Find the tax and after-tax amount attributable to the dividend income from						
16		the Tank Industries, Inc., common stock.						
17								
18	d.	Compare, contrast, and discuss the after-tax amounts resulting from the						
19		interest income and dividend income calculated in b. and c.						
20								
21	e.	What is the firm's total tax liability for the year?						
22								

FIGURE D–6

Example *PMF Excel Spreadsheet Templates* Sample Answer

	A	B	C	D	E	F	G	H
24								
25	**Answer:**							
26								
27	a.	Tax on operating earnings =					$0	
28								
29	b. & c.				b. Interest Income		c. Dividend Income	
30		Before-tax amount						
31		Less: Applicable exclusion						
32		Taxable Amount			$0		$0	
33		Tax (40%)						
34		After-tax amount			$0		$0	
35								
36	d.	The after-tax amount of dividends received, $17,600, exceeds the after-tax amount of interest, $12,000,						
37		due to the 70% corporate dividend exclusion. This increases the attractiveness of stock investments by						
38		one corporation in another relative to bond investments.						
39								
40	e.	Total tax liability :						
41			Taxes from operating earnings			$0		
42			+ Taxes on interest income			0		
43			+ Taxes on dividend income			0		
44			Total Tax Liability			$0		
45								

The data entry cells are clearly highlighted in yellow. When you enter your data, the worksheet automatically calculates the new answer.

Using the *PMF Spreadsheet* Toolbar

Each *PMF Spreadsheet* has a toolbar that performs a variety of functions depending on which button you select. The toolbar includes the following buttons and functions:

Click this button to open the *PMF Templates.*
Click this button to open the *Tutor.*
Click this button to go to the main menu.
Click this button to go to the previous sheet.
Click this button to go to the next sheet.
Click this button to go to the last sheet.
Click this button to set the zoom factor for the *Solver.*
Click this button to open the Windows calculator to facilitate your solution.
Click this button to print the *Solver* sheets.
Click this button to preview the printing of the current *Solver* sheets.
Click this button to learn more about the developer, KMT Software.
Click this button to view Help for *PMF Problem-Solver.*

Glossary

ABC inventory system Inventory management technique that divides inventory into three groups—A, B, and C, in descending order of importance and level of monitoring, on the basis of the dollar investment in each. (Chapter 13)

ability to service debts The ability of a firm to make the payments required on a scheduled basis over the life of a debt. (Chapter 2)

accept–reject approach The evaluation of capital expenditure proposals to determine whether they meet the firm's minimum acceptance criterion. (Chapter 8)

accounts payable management Management by the firm of the time that elapses between its purchase of raw materials and its mailing payment to the supplier. (Chapter 14)

accrual basis In preparation of financial statements, recognizes revenue at the time of sale and recognizes expenses when they are incurred. (Chapter 1)

accruals Liabilities for services received for which payment has yet to be made. (Chapter 14)

ACH (automated clearinghouse) transfer Preauthorized electronic withdrawal from the payer's account and deposit into the payee's account via a settlement among banks by the *automated clearinghouse,* or *ACH.* (Chapter 13)

activity ratios Measure the speed with which various accounts are converted into sales or cash—inflows or outflows. (Chapter 2)

after-tax proceeds from sale of old asset The difference between the old asset's sale proceeds and any applicable taxes or tax refunds related to its sale. (Chapter 8)

agency costs The costs borne by stockholders to minimize agency problems. (Chapter 1)

agency problem The likelihood that managers may place personal goals ahead of corporate goals. (Chapter 1)

aggressive funding strategy A funding strategy under which the firm funds its seasonal requirements with short-term debt and its permanent requirements with long-term debt. (Chapter 13)

aging of accounts receivable A credit-monitoring technique that uses a schedule that indicates the percentages of the total accounts receivable balance that have been outstanding for specified periods of time. (Chapter 13)

American depositary receipts (ADRs) Claims issued by U.S. banks representing ownership of shares of a foreign company's stock held on deposit by the U.S. bank in the foreign market and issued in dollars to U.S. investors. (Chapter 7)

angel capitalists (angels) Wealthy individual investors who do not operate as a business but invest in promising early-stage companies in exchange for a portion of the firm's equity. (Chapter 7)

annual cleanup The requirement that for a certain number of days during the year borrowers under a line of credit carry a zero loan balance (that is, owe the bank nothing). (Chapter 14)

annual percentage rate (APR) The *nominal annual rate* of interest, found by multiplying the periodic rate by the number of periods in 1 year, that must be disclosed to consumers on credit cards and loans as a result of "truth-in-lending laws." (Chapter 4)

annual percentage yield (APY) The *effective annual rate* of interest that must be disclosed to consumers by banks on their savings products as a result of "truth-in-savings laws." (Chapter 4)

annuity A stream of equal periodic cash flows, over a specified time period. These cash flows can be *inflows* of returns earned on investments or *outflows* of funds invested to earn future returns. (Chapter 4)

annuity due An annuity for which the cash flow occurs at the *beginning* of each period. (Chapter 4)

articles of partnership The written contract used to formally establish a business partnership. (Chapter 1)

asymmetric information The situation in which managers of a firm have more information about operations and future prospects than do investors. (Chapter 11)

authorized shares The number of shares of common stock that a firm's corporate charter allows it to issue. (Chapter 7)

average age of inventory Average number of days' sales in inventory. (Chapter 2)

average collection period The average amount of time needed to collect accounts receivable. (Chapter 2)

average payment period The average amount of time needed to pay accounts payable. (Chapter 2)

average tax rate A firm's taxes divided by its taxable income. (Chapter 1)

balance sheet Summary statement of the firm's financial position at a given point in time. (Chapter 2)

bar chart The simplest type of probability distribution; shows only a limited number of outcomes and associated probabilities for a given event. (Chapter 5)

benchmarking A type of *cross-sectional analysis* in which the firm's ratio values are compared to those of a key competitor or group of competitors that it wishes to emulate. (Chapter 2)

beta coefficient (*b*) A relative measure of nondiversifiable risk. An *index* of the degree of movement of an asset's return in response to a change in the *market return.* (Chapter 5)

bird-in-the-hand argument The belief, in support of *dividend relevance theory,* that investors see current dividends as less risky than future dividends or capital gains. (Chapter 12)

board of directors Group elected by the firm's stockholders and having ultimate authority to guide corporate affairs and make general policy. (Chapter 1)

bond Long-term debt instrument used by business and government to raise large sums of money, generally from a diverse group of lenders. (Chapter 1)

bond indenture A legal document that specifies both the rights of the bondholders and the duties of the issuing corporation. (Chapter 6)

book value The strict accounting value of an asset, calculated by subtracting its accumulated depreciation from its installed cost. (Chapter 8)

book value per share The amount per share of common stock that would be received if all of the firm's assets were *sold for their exact book (accounting) value* and the proceeds remaining after paying all liabilities (including preferred stock) were divided among the common stockholders. (Chapter 7)

book value weights Weights that use accounting values to measure the proportion of each type of capital in the firm's financial structure. (Chapter 10)

break point The level of *total* new financing at which the cost of one of the financing components rises, thereby causing an upward shift in the *weighted marginal cost of capital (WMCC).* (Chapter 10)

breakeven analysis Indicates the level of operations necessary to cover all operating costs and the profitability associated with various levels of sales. (Chapter 11)

business risk The risk to the firm of being unable to cover operating costs. (Chapter 10)

call feature A feature included in nearly all corporate bond issues that gives the issuer the opportunity to repurchase bonds at a stated *call price* prior to maturity. (Chapter 6)

call premium The amount by which a bond's *call price* exceeds its par value. (Chapter 6)

call price The stated price at which a bond may be repurchased, by use of a *call feature,* prior to maturity. (Chapter 6)

capital The long-term funds of a firm; all items on the right-hand side of the firm's balance sheet, *excluding current liabilities.* (Chapter 7)

capital asset pricing model (CAPM) Describes the relationship between the required return, k_s, and the nondiversifiable risk of the firm as measured by the beta coefficient, *b*. (Chapters 5 and 10)

capital budgeting The process of evaluating and selecting long-term investments that are consistent with the firm's goal of maximizing owner wealth. (Chapter 8)

capital budgeting process Five distinct but interrelated steps: *proposal generation, review and analysis, decision making, implementation,* and *follow-up*. (Chapter 8)

capital expenditure An outlay of funds by the firm that is expected to produce benefits over a period of time *greater than* 1 year. (Chapter 8)

capital gain The amount by which the sale price of an asset exceeds the asset's initial purchase price. (Chapter 1)

capital market A market that enables suppliers and demanders of *long-term funds* to make transactions. (Chapter 1)

capital rationing The financial situation in which a firm has only a fixed number of dollars available for capital expenditures, and numerous projects compete for these dollars. (Chapter 8)

capital structure The mix of long-term debt and equity maintained by the firm. (Chapter 11)

carrying costs The variable costs per unit of holding an item in inventory for a specific period of time. (Chapter 13)

cash basis Recognizes revenues and expenses only with respect to actual inflows and outflows of cash. (Chapter 1)

cash bonuses Cash paid to management for achieving certain performance goals. (Chapter 1)

cash budget (cash forecast) A statement of the firm's planned inflows and outflows of cash that is used to estimate its short-term cash requirements. (Chapter 3)

cash concentration The process used by the firm to bring lockbox and other deposits together into one bank, often called the *concentration bank.* (Chapter 13)

cash conversion cycle (CCC) The amount of time a firm's resources are tied up; calculated by subtracting the average payment period from the *operating cycle.* (Chapter 13)

cash disbursements All outlays of cash by the firm during a given financial period. (Chapter 3)

cash discount A percentage deduction from the purchase price; available to the credit customer who pays its account within a specified time. (Chapter 13)

cash discount period The number of days after the beginning of the credit period during which the cash discount is available. (Chapter 13)

cash receipts All of a firm's inflows of cash in a given financial period. (Chapter 3)

change in net working capital The difference between a change in current assets and a change in current liabilities. (Chapter 8)

clearing float The time between deposit of a payment and when spendable funds become available to the firm. (Chapter 13)

clientele effect The argument that a firm attracts shareholders whose preferences for the payment and stability of dividends correspond to the payment pattern and stability of the firm itself. (Chapter 12)

closely owned (stock) All common stock of a firm owned by a small group of investors (such as a family). (Chapter 7)

coefficient of variation (CV) A measure of relative dispersion that is useful in comparing the risks of assets with differing expected returns. (Chapter 5)

collateral trust bonds See Table 6.3 (Chapter 6)

commercial finance companies Lending institutions that make *only* secured loans—both short-term and long-term—to businesses. (Chapter 14)

commercial paper A form of financing consisting of short-term, unsecured promissory notes issued by firms with a high credit standing. (Chapter 14)

commitment fee The fee that is normally charged on a *revolving credit agreement;* it often applies to the average unused balance of the borrower's credit line. (Chapter 14)

common stock The purest and most basic form of corporate ownership. (Chapter 1)

common-size income statement An income statement in which each item is expressed as a percentage of sales. (Chapter 2)

compensating balance A required checking account balance equal to a certain percentage of the amount borrowed from a bank under a line-of-credit or revolving credit agreement. (Chapter 14)

compound interest Interest that is earned on a given deposit and has become part of the principal at the end of a specified period. (Chapter 4)

conflicting rankings Conflicts in the ranking given a project by NPV and IRR, resulting from *differences in the magnitude and timing of cash flows.* (Chapter 9)

conservative funding strategy A funding strategy under which the firm funds both its seasonal and its permanent requirements with long-term debt. (Chapter 13)

constant-growth model A widely cited dividend valuation approach that assumes that dividends will grow at a constant rate, but a rate that is less than the required return. (Chapter 7)

constant-growth valuation (Gordon) model Assumes that the value of a share of stock equals the present value of all future dividends (assumed to grow at a constant rate) that it is expected to provide over an infinite time horizon. (Chapter 10)

constant-payout-ratio dividend policy A dividend policy based on the payment of a certain percentage of earnings to owners in each dividend period. (Chapter 12)

continuous compounding Compounding of interest an infinite number of times per year at intervals of microseconds. (Chapter 4)

continuous probability distribution A probability distribution showing all the possible outcomes and associated probabilities for a given event. (Chapter 5)

controlled disbursing The strategic use of mailing points and bank accounts to lengthen mail float and clearing float, respectively. (Chapter 13)

controller The firm's chief accountant, who is responsible for the firm's accounting activities, such as corporate accounting, tax management, financial accounting, and cost accounting. (Chapter 1)

conventional cash flow pattern An initial outflow followed only by a series of inflows. (Chapter 8)

conversion feature (preferred stock) A feature of *convertible preferred stock* that allows holders to change each share into a stated number of shares of common stock. (Chapter 7)

conversion feature (bonds) A feature of *convertible bonds* that allows bondholders to change each bond into a stated number of shares of common stock. (Chapter 6)

corporate bond A debt instrument indicating that a corporation has borrowed a certain amount of money and promises to repay it in the future under clearly defined terms. (Chapter 6)

corporation An artificial being created by law (often called a "legal entity"). (Chapter 1)

correlation coefficient A measure of the degree of correlation between two series. (Chapter 5)

correlation A statistical measure of the relationship between any two series of numbers representing data of any kind. (Chapter 5)

cost of a new issue of common stock, k_n The cost of common stock, net of underpricing and associated flotation costs. (Chapter 10)

cost of capital The rate of return that a firm must earn on the projects in which it invests to maintain its market value and attract funds. (Chapter 10)

cost of common stock equity, k_s The rate at which investors discount the expected dividends of the firm to determine its share value. (Chapter 10)

cost of giving up a cash discount The implied rate of interest paid to delay payment of an account payable for an additional number of days. (Chapter 14)

cost of long-term debt, k_i The after-tax cost today of raising long-term funds through borrowing. (Chapter 10)

cost of new asset The net outflow necessary to acquire a new asset. (Chapter 8)

cost of preferred stock, k_p The ratio of the preferred stock dividend to the firm's net proceeds from the sale of preferred stock; calculated by dividing the annual dividend, D_p, by the net proceeds from the sale of the preferred stock, N_p. (Chapter 10)

cost of retained earnings, k_r The same as the cost of an *equivalent fully subscribed issue of additional common stock,* which is equal to the cost of common stock equity, k_s. (Chapter 10)

coupon interest rate The percentage of a bond's par value that will be paid annually, typically in two equal semiannual payments, as interest. (Chapter 6)

coverage ratios Ratios that measure the firm's ability to pay certain fixed charges. (Chapter 2)

credit monitoring The ongoing review of a firm's accounts receivable to determine whether customers are paying according to the stated credit terms. (Chapter 13)

credit period The number of days after the beginning of the credit period until full payment of the account is due. (Chapter 13)

credit scoring A credit selection method commonly used with high-volume/small-dollar credit requests; relies on a credit score determined by applying statistically derived weights to a credit applicant's scores on key financial and credit characteristics. (Chapter 13)

credit standards The firm's minimum requirements for extending credit to a customer. (Chapter 13)

credit terms The terms of sale for customers who have been extended credit by the firm. (Chapter 13)

cross-sectional analysis Comparison of different firms' financial ratios at the same point in time; involves comparing the firm's ratios to those of other firms in its industry or to industry averages. (Chapter 2)

cumulative preferred stock Preferred stock for which all passed (unpaid) dividends in arrears, along with the current dividend, must be paid before dividends can be paid to common stockholders. (Chapter 7)

current assets Short-term assets, expected to be converted into cash within 1 year or less. (Chapter 2)

current liabilities Short-term liabilities, expected to be paid within 1 year or less. (Chapter 2)

current ratio A measure of liquidity calculated by dividing the firm's current assets by its current liabilities. (Chapter 2)

date of record (dividends) Set by the firm's directors, the date on which all persons whose names are recorded as stockholders receive a declared dividend at a specified future time. (Chapter 12)

debentures See Table 6.3 (Chapter 6)

debt capital All long-term borrowing incurred by a firm, including bonds. (Chapter 7)

debt ratio Measures the proportion of total assets financed by the firm's creditors. (Chapter 2)

decision trees A behavioral approach that uses diagrams to map the various investment decision alternatives and payoffs, along with their probabilities of occurrence. (Chapter 9)

degree of financial leverage (DFL) The numerical measure of the firm's financial leverage. (Chapter 11)

degree of indebtedness Measures the amount of debt relative to other significant balance sheet amounts. (Chapter 2)

degree of operating leverage (DOL) The numerical measure of the firm's operating leverage. (Chapter 11)

degree of total leverage (DTL) The numerical measure of the firm's total leverage. (Chapter 11)

depository transfer check (DTC) An unsigned check drawn on one of a firm's bank accounts and deposited in another. (Chapter 13)

depreciable life Time period over which an asset is depreciated. (Chapter 3)

depreciation The systematic charging of a portion of the costs of fixed assets against annual revenues over time. (Chapter 3)

dilution of ownership Occurs when a new stock issue results in each present shareholder having a claim on a *smaller* part of the firm's earnings than previously. (Chapter 7)

discount The amount by which a bond sells at a value that is less than its par value. (Chapter 6)

discount loans Loans on which interest is paid in advance by being deducted from the amount borrowed. (Chapter 14)

discounting cash flows The process of finding present values; the inverse of compounding interest. (Chapter 4)

diversifiable risk The portion of an asset's risk that is attributable to firm-specific, random causes; can be eliminated through diversification. Also called *unsystematic risk*. (Chapter 5)

dividend irrelevance theory Miller and Modigliani's theory that in a perfect world, the firm's value is determined solely by the earning power and risk of its assets (investments) and that the manner in which it splits its earnings stream between dividends and internally retained (and reinvested) funds does not affect this value. (Chapter 12)

dividend payout ratio Indicates the percentage of each dollar earned that is distributed to the owners in the form of cash. It is calculated by dividing the firm's cash dividend per share by its earnings per share. (Chapter 12)

dividend per share (DPS) The dollar amount of cash distributed during the period on behalf of each outstanding share of common stock. (Chapter 2)

dividend policy The firm's plan of action to be followed whenever a dividend decision is made. (Chapter 12)

dividend reinvestment plans (DRIPs) Plans that enable stockholders to use dividends received on the firm's stock to acquire additional shares—even fractional shares—at little or no transaction cost. (Chapter 12)

dividend relevance theory The theory, advanced by Gordon and Lintner, that there is a direct relationship between a firm's dividend policy and its market value. (Chapter 12)

dividends Periodic distributions of earnings to the stockholders of a firm. (Chapter 1)

double taxation Occurs when the already once-taxed earnings of a corporation are distributed as cash dividends to stockholders, who must pay taxes on them. (Chapter 1)

DuPont formula Multiplies the firm's *net profit margin* by its *total asset turnover* to calculate the firm's *return on total assets (ROA)*. (Chapter 2)

DuPont system of analysis System used to dissect the firm's financial statements and to assess its financial condition. (Chapter 2)

earnings per share (EPS) The amount earned during the period on behalf of each outstanding share of common stock, calculated by dividing the period's total earnings available for the firm's common stockholders by the number of shares of common stock outstanding. (Chapter 1)

EBIT–EPS approach An approach for selecting the capital structure that maximizes earnings per share (EPS) over the expected range of earnings before interest and taxes (EBIT). (Chapter 11)

economic order quantity (EOQ) model Inventory management technique for determining an item's optimal order size, which is the size that minimizes the total of its *order costs* and *carrying costs*. (Chapter 13)

economic value added A popular measure used by many firms to determine whether an investment contributes positively to the owners' wealth; calculated by subtracting the cost of funds used to finance an investment from its after-tax operating profits. (Chapter 1)

effective (true) annual rate (EAR) The annual rate of interest actually paid or earned. (Chapter 4)

efficient market (Chapter 1)

efficient market A market that allocates funds to their most productive uses as a result of competition among wealth-maximizing investors that determines and publicizes prices that are believed to be close to their true value; a market with the following characteristics: many small investors, all having the same information and expectations with respect to securities; no restrictions on investment, no taxes, and no transaction costs; and rational investors, who view securities similarly and are risk-averse, preferring higher returns and lower risk. (Chapters 1 and 5)

efficient-market hypothesis Theory describing the behavior of an assumed "perfect" market in which (1) securities are typically in equilibrium, (2) security prices fully reflect all public information available and react swiftly to new information, and, (3) because stocks are fairly priced, investors need not waste time looking for mispriced securities. (Chapter 7)

efficient portfolio A portfolio that maximizes return for a given level of risk or minimizes risk for a given level of return. (Chapter 5)

ending cash The sum of the firm's beginning cash and its net cash flow for the period. (Chapter 3)

equipment trust certificates See Table 6.3 (Chapter 6)

equity capital The long-term funds provided by the firm's owners, the stockholders. (Chapter 7)

ethics Standards of conduct or moral judgment. (Chapter 1)

Eurobond market The market in which corporations and governments typically issue bonds denominated in dollars and sell them to investors located outside the United States. (Chapter 1)

Eurobond A bond issued by an international borrower and sold to investors in countries with currencies other than the currency in which the bond is denominated. (Chapter 6)

Eurocurrency market International equivalent of the domestic money market. (Chapter 1)

ex dividend Period, beginning 2 *business days* prior to the date of record, during which a stock is sold without the right to receive the current dividend. (Chapter 12)

excess cash balance The (excess) amount available for investment by the firm if the period's ending cash is greater than the desired minimum cash balance; assumed to be invested in marketable securities. (Chapter 3)

excess earnings accumulation tax The tax the IRS levies on retained earnings above $250,000 when it determines that the firm has accumulated an excess of earnings to allow owners to delay paying ordinary income taxes on dividends received. (Chapter 12)

exchange rate risk The danger that an unexpected change in the exchange rate between the dollar and the currency in which a project's cash flows are denominated will reduce the market value of that project's cash flow. (Chapter 9)

expectations theory The theory that the yield curve reflects investor expectations about future interest rates; an increasing inflation expectation results in an upward-sloping yield curve, and a decreasing inflation expectation results in a downward-sloping yield curve (Chapter 6)

expected value of a return ($\bar{k}$) The most likely return on a given asset. (Chapter 5)

extendible notes See Table 6.4 (Chapter 6)

external financing required ("plug" figure) Under the judgmental approach for developing a pro forma balance sheet, the amount of external financing needed to bring the statement into balance. (Chapter 3)

external forecast A sales forecast based on the relationships observed between the firm's sales and certain key external economic indicators. (Chapter 3)

extra dividend An additional dividend optionally paid by the firm if earnings are higher than normal in a given period. (Chapter 12)

factor A financial institution that specializes in purchasing accounts receivable from businesses. (Chapter 14)

factoring accounts receivable The outright sale of accounts receivable at a discount to a *factor* or other financial institution. (Chapter 14)

federal funds Loan transactions between commercial banks in which the Federal Reserve banks become involved. (Chapter 1)

finance The art and science of managing money. (Chapter 1)

Financial Accounting Standards Board (FASB) Standard No. 52 Mandates that U.S.-based companies translate their foreign-currency-denominated assets and liabilities into dollars, for consolidation with the parent company's financial statements. This is done by using the *current rate (translation) method.* (Chapter 2)

Financial Accounting Standards Board (FASB) The accounting profession's rule-setting body, which authorizes *generally accepted accounting principles (GAAP).* (Chapter 2)

financial breakeven point The level of EBIT necessary to just cover all *fixed financial costs;* the level of EBIT for which EPS = $0. (Chapter 11)

financial institution An intermediary that channels the savings of individuals, businesses, and governments into loans or investments. (Chapter 1)

financial leverage multiplier (FLM) The ratio of the firm's total assets to its common stock equity. (Chapter 2)

financial leverage The magnification of risk and return introduced through the use of fixed-cost financing, such as debt and preferred stock. (Chapter 2)

financial leverage The potential use of *fixed financial costs* to magnify the effects of changes in earnings before interest and taxes on the firm's earnings per share. (Chapter 11)

financial manager Actively manages the financial affairs of any type of business, whether financial or nonfinancial, private or public, large or small, profit-seeking or not-for-profit. (Chapter 1)

financial markets Forums in which suppliers of funds and demanders of funds can transact business directly. (Chapter 1)

financial planning process Planning that begins with long-term, or *strategic,* financial plans that in turn guide the formulation of short-term, or *operating,* plans and budgets. (Chapter 3)

financial risk The risk to the firm of being unable to cover required financial obligations (interest, lease payments, preferred stock dividends). (Chapter 10)

financial services The part of finance concerned with the design and delivery of advice and financial products to individuals, business, and government. (Chapter 1)

financing flows Cash flows that result from debt and equity financing transactions; includes incurrence and repayment of debt, cash inflow from the sale of stock, and cash outflows to pay cash dividends or repurchase stock. (Chapter 3)

five C's of credit The five key dimensions—character, capacity, capital, collateral, and conditions—used by credit analysts to provide a framework for in-depth credit analysis. (Chapter 13)

fixed-payment coverage ratio Measures the firm's ability to meet all fixed-payment obligations. (Chapter 2)

fixed-rate loan A loan with a rate of interest that is determined at a set increment above the prime rate and at which it remains fixed until maturity. (Chapter 14)

flat yield curve A yield curve that reflects relatively similar borrowing costs for both short- and longer-term loans. (Chapter 6)

float Funds that have been sent by the payer but are not yet usable funds to the payee. (Chapter 13)

floating inventory lien A secured short-term loan against inventory under which the lender's claim is on the borrower's inventory in general. (Chapter 14)

floating-rate bonds See Table 6.4 (Chapter 6)

floating-rate loan A loan with a rate of interest initially set at an increment above the prime rate and allowed to "float," or vary, above prime *as the prime rate varies* until maturity. (Chapter 14)

flotation costs The total costs of issuing and selling a security. (Chapter 10)

foreign bond Bond that is issued by a foreign corporation or government and is denominated in the investor's home currency and sold in the investor's home market. (Chapters 1 and 6)

foreign direct investment The transfer of capital, managerial, and technical assets to a foreign country. (Chapter 8)

foreign exchange manager The manager responsible for monitoring and managing the firm's exposure to loss from currency fluctuations. (Chapter 1)

free cash flow (FCF) The amount of cash flow available to investors (creditors and owners) after the firm has met all operating needs and paid for investments in net fixed assets and net current assets. (Chapter 3)

free cash flow valuation model A model that determines the value of an entire company as the present value of its expected free cash flows discounted at the firm's *weighted average cost of capital,* which is its expected average future cost of funds over the long run. (Chapter 7)

future value The value of a present amount at a future date, found by applying *compound interest* over a specified period of time. (Chapter 4)

future value interest factor The multiplier used to calculate, at a specified interest rate, the future value of a present amount as of a given time. (Chapter 4)

future value interest factor for an ordinary annuity The multiplier used to calculate the future value of an *ordinary annuity* at a specified interest rate over a given period of time. (Chapter 4)

generally accepted accounting principles (GAAP) The practice and procedure guidelines used to prepare and maintain financial records and reports; authorized by the *Financial Accounting Standards Board (FASB).* (Chapter 2)

Gordon model A common name for the *constant-growth model* that is widely cited in dividend valuation. (Chapter 7)

gross profit margin Measures the percentage of each sales dollar remaining after the firm has paid for its goods. (Chapter 2)

historical weights Either book or market value weights based on *actual* capital structure proportions. (Chapter 10)

incentive plans Management compensation plans that tend to tie management compensation to share price; most popular incentive plan involves the grant of *stock options.* (Chapter 1)

income bonds See Table 6.3 (Chapter 6)

income statement Provides a financial summary of the firm's operating results during a specified period. (Chapter 2)

incremental cash flows The *additional* cash flows—outflows or inflows—expected to result from a proposed capital expenditure. (Chapter 8)

independent projects Projects whose cash flows are unrelated or independent of one another; the acceptance of one *does not eliminate* the others from further consideration. (Chapter 8)

informational content The information provided by the dividends of a firm with respect to future earnings, which causes owners to bid up or down the price of the firm's stock. (Chapter 12)

initial investment The relevant cash outflow for a proposed project at time zero. (Chapter 8)

initial public offering (IPO) The first public sale of a firm's stock. (Chapter 7)

installation costs Any added costs that are necessary to place an asset into operation. (Chapter 8)

installed cost of new asset The cost of the asset plus its installation costs; equals the asset's depreciable value. (Chapter 8)

intercorporate dividends Dividends received by one corporation on common and preferred stock held in other corporations. (Chapter 1)

interest rate risk The chance that interest rates will change and thereby change the required return and bond value. Rising rates, which result in decreasing bond values, are of greatest concern. (Chapter 6)

interest rate The compensation paid by the borrower of funds to the lender; from the borrower's point of view, the cost of borrowing funds. (Chapter 6)

intermediate cash inflows Cash inflows received prior to the termination of a project. (Chapter 9)

internal forecast A sales forecast based on a buildup, or consensus, of sales forecasts through the firm's own sales channels. (Chapter 3)

internal rate of return (IRR) A sophisticated capital budgeting technique; the discount rate that equates the NPV of an investment opportunity with $0 (because the present value of cash inflows equals the initial investment); it is the compound annual rate of return that the firm will earn if it invests in the project and receives the given cash inflows. (Chapter 9)

internal rate of return approach An approach to capital rationing that involves graphing project IRRs in descending order against the total dollar investment, to determine the group of acceptable projects. (Chapter 9)

international equity market A market that allows corporations to sell blocks of shares to investors in a number of different countries simultaneously. (Chapter 1)

inventory turnover Measures the activity, or liquidity, of a firm's inventory. (Chapter 2)

inverted yield curve A *downward-sloping* yield curve that indicates generally cheaper long-term borrowing costs than short-term borrowing costs. (Chapter 6)

investment banker Financial intermediary that specializes in selling new security issues and advising firms with regard to major financial transactions. (Chapter 7)

investment flows Cash flows associated with purchase and sale of both fixed assets and business interests. (Chapter 3)

investment opportunities schedule (IOS) A ranking of investment possibilities from best (highest return) to worst (lowest return); the graph that plots project IRRs in descending order against total dollar investment. (Chapters 9 and 10)

issued shares The number of shares of common stock that have been put into circulation; the sum of outstanding shares and treasury stock. (Chapter 7)

judgmental approach A simplified approach for preparing the pro forma balance sheet under which the values of certain balance sheet accounts are estimated and the firm's external financing is used as a balancing, or "plug," figure. (Chapter 3)

junk bonds See Table 6.4 (Chapter 6)

just-in-time (JIT) system Inventory management technique that minimizes inventory investment by having materials arrive at exactly the time they are needed for production. (Chapter 13)

letter of credit A letter written by a company's bank to the company's foreign supplier, stating that the bank guarantees payment of an invoiced amount if all the underlying agreements are met. (Chapter 14)

letter to stockholders Typically, the first element of the annual stockholders' report and the primary communication from management. (Chapter 2)

leverage Results from the use of fixed-cost assets or funds to magnify returns to the firm's owners. (Chapter 11)

lien A publicly disclosed legal claim on collateral. (Chapter 14)

line of credit An agreement between a commercial bank and a business specifying the amount of unsecured short-term borrowing the bank will make available to the firm over a given period of time. (Chapter 14)

liquidation value per share The *actual amount* per share of common stock that would be received if all of the firm's assets were *sold for their market value,* liabilities (including preferred stock) were paid, and any remaining money were divided among the common stockholders. (Chapter 7)

liquidity A firm's ability to satisfy its short-term obligations *as they come due.* (Chapter 2)

liquidity preferences General preferences of investors for shorter-term securities. (Chapter 6)

liquidity preference theory Theory suggesting that for any given issuer, long-term interest rates tend to be higher than short-term rates because (1) lower liquidity and higher responsiveness to general interest rate movements of longer-term securities exists and (2) borrower willingness to pay a higher rate for long-term financing; causes the yield curve to be upward-sloping. (Chapter 6)

loan amortization The determination of the equal periodic loan payments necessary to provide a lender with a specified interest return and to repay the loan principal over a specified period. (Chapter 4)

loan amortization schedule A schedule of equal payments to repay a loan. It shows the allocation of each loan payment to interest and principal. (Chapter 4)

lockbox system A collection procedure in which customers mail payments to a post office box that is emptied regularly by the firm's bank, who processes the payments and deposits them in the firm's account. This system speeds up collection time by reducing processing time as well as mail and clearing time. (Chapter 13)

London Interbank Offered Rate (LIBOR) The base rate that is used to price all Eurocurrency loans. (Chapter 1)

long-term debt Debts for which payment is not due in the current year. (Chapter 2)

long-term (strategic) financial plans Lay out a company's planned financial actions and the anticipated impact of those actions over periods ranging from 2 to 10 years. (Chapter 3)

low-regular-and-extra dividend policy A dividend policy based on paying a low regular dividend, supplemented by an additional dividend when earnings are higher than normal in a given period. (Chapter 12)

mail float The time delay between when payment is placed in the mail and when it is received. (Chapter 13)

managerial finance Concerns the duties of the financial manager in the business firm. (Chapter 1)

marginal analysis Economic principle that states that financial decisions should be made and actions taken only when the added benefits exceed the added costs. (Chapter 1)

marginal tax rate The rate at which *additional income* is taxed. (Chapter 1)

market/book (M/B) ratio Provides an assessment of how investors view the firm's performance. Firms expected to earn high returns relative to their risk typically sell at higher M/B multiples. (Chapter 2)

market ratios Relate a firm's market value, as measured by its current share price, to certain accounting values. (Chapter 2)

market return The return on the market portfolio of all traded securities. (Chapter 5)

market segmentation theory Theory suggesting that the market for loans is segmented on the basis of maturity and that the supply of and demand for loans within each segment determine its prevailing interest rate; the slope of the yield curve is determined by the general relationship between the prevailing rates in each segment. (Chapter 6)

market value weights Weights that use market values to measure the proportion of each type of capital in the firm's financial structure. (Chapter 10)

marketable securities Short-term debt instruments, such as U.S. Treasury bills, commercial paper, and negotiable certificates of deposit issued by government, business, and financial institutions, respectively. (Chapter 1)

materials requirement planning (MRP) system Inventory management technique that applies EOQ concepts and a computer to compare production needs to available inventory balances and determine when orders should be placed for various items on a product's *bill of materials.* (Chapter 13)

mixed stream A stream of unequal periodic cash flows that reflect no particular pattern. (Chapter 4)

modified accelerated cost recovery system (MACRS) System used to determine the depreciation of assets for tax purposes. (Chapter 3)

modified DuPont formula Relates the firm's *return on total assets (ROA)* to its *return on common equity (ROE)* using the *financial leverage multiplier (FLM).* (Chapter 2)

money market A financial relationship created between suppliers and demanders of *short-term funds.* (Chapter 1)

mortgage bonds See Table 6.3 (Chapter 6)

mutually exclusive projects Projects that compete with one another, so that the acceptance of one *eliminates* from further consideration all other projects that serve a similar function. (Chapter 8)

negatively correlated Describes two series that move in opposite directions. (Chapter 5)

net cash flow The mathematical difference between the firm's cash receipts and its cash disbursements in each period. (Chapter 3)

net present value (NPV) A sophisticated capital budgeting technique; found by subtracting a project's initial investment from the present value of its cash inflows discounted at a rate equal to the firm's cost of capital. (Chapter 9)

net present value approach An approach to capital rationing that is based on the use of present values to determine the group of projects that will maximize owners' wealth. (Chapter 9)

net present value profile Graph that depicts a project's NPVs for various discount rates. (Chapter 9)

net proceeds Funds actually received from the sale of a security. (Chapter 10)

net profit margin Measures the percentage of each sales dollar remaining after all costs and expenses, *including* interest, taxes, and preferred stock dividends, have been deducted. (Chapter 2)

net working capital The difference between the firm's current assets and its current liabilities; can be *positive* or *negative.* (Chapters 8 and 13)

nominal (stated) annual rate Contractual annual rate of interest charged by a lender or promised by a borrower. (Chapter 4)

noncash charge An expense deducted on the income statement but does not involve the actual outlay of cash during the period; includes depreciation, amortization, and depletion. (Chapter 3)

nonconventional cash flow pattern An initial outflow followed by a series of inflows *and* outflows. (Chapter 8)

noncumulative preferred stock Preferred stock for which passed (unpaid) dividends do not accumulate. (Chapter 7)

nondiversifiable risk The relevant portion of an asset's risk attributable to market factors that affect all firms; cannot be eliminated through diversification. Also called *systematic risk.* (Chapter 5)

nonnotification basis The basis on which a borrower, having pledged an account receivable, continues to collect the account payments without notifying the account customer. (Chapter 14)

nonrecourse basis The basis on which accounts receivable are sold to a factor with the understanding that the factor accepts all credit risks on the purchased accounts. (Chapter 14)

nonvoting common stock Common stock that carries no voting rights; issued when the firm wishes to raise capital through the sale of common stock but does not want to give up its voting control. (Chapter 7)

no-par preferred stock Preferred stock with no stated face value but with a stated annual dollar dividend. (Chapter 7)

normal yield curve An *upward-sloping* yield curve that indicates generally cheaper short-term borrowing costs than long-term borrowing costs. (Chapter 6)

notes to the financial statements Footnotes detailing information on the accounting policies, procedures, calculations, and transactions underlying entries in the financial statements. (Chapter 2)

notification basis The basis on which an account customer whose account has been pledged (or factored) is notified to remit payment directly to the lender (or factor). (Chapter 14)

operating breakeven point The level of sales necessary to cover all *operating costs;* the point at which EBIT = $0. (Chapter 11)

operating cash flow (OCF) The cash flow a firm generates from its normal operations; calculated as EBIT − taxes + depreciation. (Chapter 3)

operating cash inflows The incremental after-tax cash inflows resulting from implementation of a project during its life. (Chapter 8)

operating cycle (OC) The time from the beginning of the production process to the collection of cash from the sale of the finished product. (Chapter 13)

operating expenditure An outlay of funds by the firm resulting in benefits received *within* 1 year. (Chapter 8)

operating flows Cash flows directly related to sale and production of the firm's products and services. (Chapter 3)

operating leverage The potential use of *fixed operating costs* to magnify the effects of changes in sales on the firm's earnings before interest and taxes. (Chapter 11)

operating profit margin Measures the percentage of each sales dollar remaining after all costs and expenses *other than* interest, taxes, and preferred stock dividends are deducted; the "pure profits" earned on each sales dollar. (Chapter 2)

operating-change restrictions Contractual restrictions that a bank may impose on a firm's financial condition or operations as part of a line-of-credit agreement. (Chapter 14)

opportunity costs Cash flows that could be realized from the best alternative use of an owned asset. (Chapter 8)

optimal capital structure The capital structure at which the weighted average cost of capital is minimized, thereby maximizing the firm's value. (Chapter 11)

order costs The fixed clerical costs of placing and receiving an inventory order. (Chapter 13)

ordinary annuity An annuity for which the cash flow occurs at the *end* of each period. (Chapter 4)

ordinary income Income earned through the sale of a firm's goods or services. (Chapter 1)

organized securities exchanges Tangible organizations that act as *secondary markets* where outstanding securities are resold. (Chapter 1)

outstanding shares The number of shares of common stock held by the public. (Chapter 7)

over-the-counter (OTC) exchange An intangible market for the purchase and sale of securities not listed by the organized exchanges. (Chapter 1)

paid-in capital in excess of par The amount of proceeds in excess of the par value received from the original sale of common stock. (Chapter 2)

par value (stock) A relatively useless value for a stock established for legal purposes in the firm's corporate charter. (Chapter 7)

partnership A business owned by two or more people and operated for profit. (Chapter 1)

par-value preferred stock Preferred stock with a stated face value that is used with the specified dividend percentage to determine the annual dollar dividend. (Chapter 7)

payback period The amount of time required for a firm to recover its initial investment in a project, as calculated from *cash inflows*. (Chapter 9)

payment date Set by the firm's directors, the actual date on which the firm mails the dividend payment to the holders of record. (Chapter 12)

pecking order A hierarchy of financing that begins with retained earnings, which is followed by debt financing and finally external equity financing. (Chapter 11)

percentage advance The percent of the book value of the collateral that constitutes the principal of a secured loan. (Chapter 14)

percent-of-sales method A simple method for developing the pro forma income statement; it forecasts sales and then expresses the various income statement items as percentages of projected sales. (Chapter 3)

perfectly negatively correlated Describes two *negatively correlated* series that have a *correlation coefficient* of −1. (Chapter 5)

perfectly positively correlated Describes two *positively correlated* series that have a *correlation coefficient* of +1. (Chapter 5)

performance plans Plans that tie management compensation to measures such as EPS, growth in EPS, and other ratios of return. *Performance shares* and/or *cash bonuses* are used as compensation under these plans. (Chapter 1)

performance shares Shares of stock given to management for meeting stated performance goals. (Chapter 1)

permanent funding requirement A constant investment in operating assets resulting from constant sales over time. (Chapter 13)

perpetuity An annuity with an infinite life, providing continual annual cash flow. (Chapter 4)

pledge of accounts receivable The use of a firm's accounts receivable as security, or collateral, to obtain a short-term loan. (Chapter 14)

political risk Risk that arises from the possibility that a host government will take actions harmful to foreign investors or that political turmoil in a country will endanger investments there. (Chapter 5)

portfolio A collection, or group, of assets. (Chapter 5)

positively correlated Describes two series that move in the same direction. (Chapter 5)

preemptive right Allows common stockholders to maintain their *proportionate* ownership in the corporation when new shares are issued. (Chapter 7)

preferred stock A special form of ownership having a fixed periodic dividend that must be paid prior to payment of any common stock dividends. (Chapter 1)

premium The amount by which a bond sells at a value that is greater than its par value. (Chapter 6)

present value The current dollar value of a future amount—the amount of money that would have to be invested today at a given interest rate over a specified period to equal the future amount. (Chapter 4)

present value interest factor The multiplier used to calculate, at a specified discount rate, the present value of an amount to be received in a future period. (Chapter 4)

present value interest factor for an ordinary annuity The multiplier used to calculate the present value of an *ordinary annuity* at a specified discount rate over a given period of time. (Chapter 4)

president or chief executive officer (CEO) Corporate official responsible for managing the firm's day-to-day operations and carrying out the policies established by the board of directors. (Chapter 1)

price/earnings multiple approach A popular technique used to estimate the firm's share value; calculated by multiplying the firm's expected earnings per share (EPS) by the average price/earnings (P/E) ratio for the industry. (Chapter 7)

price/earnings (P/E) ratio Measures the amount that investors are willing to pay for each dollar of a firm's earnings; the higher the P/E ratio, the greater is investor confidence. (Chapter 2)

primary market Financial market in which securities are initially issued; the only market in which the issuer is directly involved in the transaction. (Chapter 1)

prime rate of interest (prime rate) The lowest rate of interest charged by leading banks on business loans to their most important business borrowers. (Chapter 14)

principal The amount of money on which interest is paid. (Chapter 4)

private placement The sale of a new security issue, typically bonds or preferred stock, directly to an investor or group of investors. (Chapter 1)

privately owned (stock) All common stock of a firm owned by a single individual. (Chapter 7)

pro forma statements Projected, or forecast, income statements and balance sheets. (Chapter 3)

probability The *chance* that a given outcome will occur. (Chapter 5)

probability distribution A model that relates prob-abilities to the associated outcomes. (Chapter 5)

proceeds from sale of old asset The cash inflows, net of any *removal* or *cleanup costs,* resulting from the sale of an existing asset. (Chapter 8)

processing float The time between receipt of a payment and its deposit into the firm's account. (Chapter 13)

profitability The relationship between revenues and costs generated by using the firm's assets—both current and fixed—in productive activities. (Chapter 13)

prospectus A portion of a security registration statement that describes the key aspects of the issue, the issuer, and its management and financial position. (Chapter 7)

proxy battle The attempt by a nonmanagement group to gain control of the management of a firm by soliciting a sufficient number of proxy votes. (Chapter 7)

proxy statement A statement giving the votes of a stockholder to another party. (Chapter 7)

public offering The nonexclusive sale of either bonds or stocks to the general public. (Chapter 1)

publicly owned (stock) Common stock of a firm owned by a broad group of unrelated individual or institutional investors. (Chapter 7)

putable bonds See Table 6.4 (Chapter 6)

quarterly compounding Compounding of interest over four periods within the year. (Chapter 4)

quick (acid-test) ratio A measure of liquidity calculated by dividing the firm's current assets minus inventory by its current liabilities. (Chapter 2)

quotations Information on bonds, stocks, and other securities, including current price data and statistics on recent price behavior. (Chapter 6)

range A measure of an asset's risk, which is found by subtracting the pessimistic (worst) outcome from the optimistic (best) outcome. (Chapter 5)

ranking approach The ranking of capital expenditure projects on the basis of some predetermined measure, such as the rate of return. (Chapter 8)

ratio analysis Involves methods of calculating and interpreting financial ratios to analyze and monitor the firm's performance. (Chapter 2)

real options Opportunities that are embedded in capital projects that enable managers to alter their cash flows and risk in a way that affects project acceptability (NPV). Also called *strategic options.* (Chapter 9)

real rate of interest The rate that creates an equilibrium between the supply of savings and the demand for investment funds in a perfect world, without inflation, where funds suppliers and demanders are indifferent to the term of loans or investments and have no liquidity preference, and where all outcomes are certain. (Chapter 6)

recaptured depreciation The portion of an asset's sale price that is above its book value and below its initial purchase price. (Chapter 8)

recovery period The appropriate depreciable life of a particular asset as determined by MACRS. (Chapter 3)

red herring A preliminary prospectus made available to prospective investors during the waiting period between the registration statement's filing with the SEC and its approval. (Chapter 7)

regular dividend policy A dividend policy based on the payment of a fixed-dollar dividend in each period. (Chapter 12)

relevant cash flows The *incremental cash outflow (investment) and resulting subsequent inflows* associated with a proposed capital expenditure. (Chapter 8)

reorder point The point at which to reorder inventory, expressed as days of lead time × daily usage. (Chapter 13)

required return The cost of funds obtained by selling an ownership interest; it reflects the funds supplier's level of expected return. (Chapter 6)

required total financing Amount of funds needed by the firm if the ending cash for the period is less than the desired minimum cash balance; typically represented by notes payable. (Chapter 3)

residual theory of dividends A school of thought that suggests that the dividend paid by a firm should be viewed as a *residual*—the amount left over after all acceptable investment opportunities have been undertaken. (Chapter 12)

restrictive covenants Provisions in a *bond indenture* that place operating and financial constraints on the borrower. (Chapter 6)

retained earnings The cumulative total of all earnings, net of dividends, that have been retained and reinvested in the firm since its inception; earnings not distributed to owners as dividends; a form of *internal* financing. (Chapters 2 and 12)

return on common equity (ROE) Measures the return earned on the common stockholders' investment in the firm. (Chapter 2)

return on total assets (ROA) Measures the overall effectiveness of management in generating profits with its available assets; also called the *return on investment (ROI)*. (Chapter 2)

return The total gain or loss experienced on an investment over a given period of time; calculated by dividing the asset's cash distributions during the period, plus change in value, by its beginning-of-period investment value. (Chapter 5)

reverse stock split A method used to raise the market price of a firm's stock by exchanging a certain number of outstanding shares for one new share. (Chapter 12)

revolving credit agreement A line of credit *guaranteed* to a borrower by a commercial bank regardless of the scarcity of money. (Chapter 14)

rights Financial instruments that permit stockholders to purchase additional shares at a price below the market price, in direct proportion to their number of owned shares. (Chapter 7)

risk The chance of financial loss or, more formally, the *variability of returns associated with a given asset.* (Chapters 1 and 5)

risk (in capital budgeting) The chance that a project will prove unacceptable or, more formally, the degree of variability of cash flows. (Chapter 9)

risk (of technical insolvency) The probability that a firm will be unable to pay its bills as they come due. (Chapter 13)

risk premium The amount by which the interest rate or required return on a security exceeds the risk-free rate of interest, R_F; it varies with specific issuer and issue characteristics. (Chapter 6)

risk-adjusted discount rate (RADR) The rate of return that must be earned on a given project to compensate the firm's owners adequately—that is, to maintain or improve the firm's share price. (Chapter 9)

risk-averse The attitude toward risk in which an increased return is required for an increase in risk. (Chapters 1 and 5)

risk-free rate of interest, R_F The required return on a risk-free asset, typically a 3-month *U.S. Treasury bill.* (Chapters 5 and 6)

safety stock Extra inventory that is held to prevent stockouts of important items. (Chapter 13)

sales forecast The prediction of the firm's sales over a given period, based on external and/or internal data; used as the key input to the short-term financial planning process. (Chapter 3)

scenario analysis A behavioral approach that evaluates the impact on the firm's return of simultaneous changes in *a number of variables.* (Chapter 9)

seasonal funding requirement An investment in operating assets that varies over time as a result of cyclic sales. (Chapter 13)

secondary market Financial market in which preowned securities (those that are not new issues) are traded. (Chapter 1)

secured short-term financing Short-term financing (loan) that has specific assets pledged as collateral. (Chapter 14)

Securities and Exchange Commission (SEC) The federal regulatory body that governs the sale and listing of securities. (Chapter 2)

securities exchanges Organizations that provide the marketplace in which firms can raise funds through the sale of new securities and purchasers can resell securities. (Chapter 1)

security agreement The agreement between the borrower and the lender that specifies the collateral held against a secured loan. (Chapter 14)

security market line (SML) The depiction of the *capital asset pricing model* (*CAPM*) as a graph that reflects the required return in the marketplace for each level of nondiversifiable risk (beta). (Chapter 5)

selling group A large number of brokerage firms that join the originating investment banker(s); each accepts responsibility for selling a certain portion of a new security issue. (Chapter 7)

semiannual compounding Compounding of interest over two periods within the year. (Chapter 4)

sensitivity analysis An approach for assessing risk that uses several possible-return estimates to obtain a sense of the variability among outcomes. (Chapters 5 and 9)

short-term (operating) financial plans Specify short-term financial actions and the anticipated impact of those actions. (Chapter 3)

short-term financial management Management of current assets and current liabilities. (Chapter 13)

short-term, self-liquidating loan An unsecured short-term loan in which the use to which the borrowed money is put provides the mechanism through which the loan is repaid. (Chapter 14)

signal A financing action by management that is believed to reflect its view of the firm's stock value; generally, debt financing is viewed as a *positive signal* that management believes the stock is "undervalued," and a stock issue is viewed as a *negative signal* that management believes the stock is "overvalued." (Chapter 11)

simulation A statistics-based behavioral approach that applies predetermined probability distributions and random numbers to estimate risky outcomes. (Chapter 9)

single-payment note A short-term, one-time loan made to a borrower who needs funds for a specific purpose for a short period. (Chapter 14)

sinking-fund requirement A restrictive provision often included in a bond indenture, providing for the systematic retirement of bonds prior to their maturity. (Chapter 6)

small (ordinary) stock dividend A stock dividend representing less than 20 to 25 percent of the common stock outstanding when the dividend is declared. (Chapter 12)

sole proprietorship A business owned by one person and operated for his or her own profit. (Chapter 1)

spontaneous liabilities Financing that arises from the normal course of business; the two major short-term sources of such liabilities are accounts payable and accruals. (Chapter 14)

stakeholders Groups such as employees, customers, suppliers, creditors, owners, and others who have a direct economic link to the firm. (Chapter 1)

standard debt provisions Provisions in a *bond indenture* specifying certain record-keeping and general business practices that the bond issuer must follow; normally, they do not place a burden on a financially sound business. (Chapter 6)

standard deviation (σ_k) The most common statistical indicator of an asset's risk; it measures the dispersion around the *expected value.* (Chapter 5)

statement of cash flows Provides a summary of the firm's operating, investment, and financing cash flows and reconciles them with changes in its cash and marketable securities during the period. (Chapter 2)

statement of retained earnings Reconciles the net income earned during a given year, and any cash dividends paid, with the change in retained earnings between the start and the end of that year. (Chapter 2)

stock dividend The payment, to existing owners, of a dividend in the form of stock. (Chapter 12)

stock options An incentive allowing managers to purchase stock at the market price set at the time of the grant. (Chapter 1)

stock purchase warrants Instruments that give their holders the right to purchase a certain number of shares of the issuer's common stock at a specified price over a certain period of time. (Chapter 6)

stock repurchase The repurchase by the firm of outstanding common stock in the marketplace; desired effects of stock repurchases are that they either enhance shareholder value or help to discourage an unfriendly takeover. (Chapter 12)

stock split A method commonly used to lower the market price of a firm's stock by increasing the number of shares belonging to each shareholder. (Chapter 12)

stockholders The owners of a corporation, whose ownership, or *equity,* is evidenced by either common stock or preferred stock. (Chapter 1)

stockholders' report Annual report that publicly owned corporations must provide to stockholders; it summarizes and documents the firm's financial activities during the past year. (Chapter 2)

stretching accounts payable Paying bills as late as possible without damaging the firm's credit rating. (Chapter 14)

subordinated debentures See Table 6.3 (Chapter 6)

subordination In a bond indenture, the stipulation that subsequent creditors agree to wait until all claims of the *senior debt* are satisfied. (Chapter 6)

sunk costs Cash outlays that have already been made (past outlays) and therefore have no effect on the cash flows relevant to a current decision. (Chapter 8)

supervoting shares Stock that carries with it multiple votes per share rather than the single vote per share typically given on regular shares of common stock. (Chapter 7)

target capital structure The desired optimal mix of debt and equity financing that most firms attempt to maintain. (Chapter 10)

target dividend-payout ratio A dividend policy under which the firm attempts to pay out a certain *percentage* of earnings as a stated dollar dividend and adjusts that dividend toward a target payout as proven earnings increases occur. (Chapter 12)

target weights Either book or market value weights based on *desired* capital structure proportions. (Chapter 10)

tax on sale of old asset Tax that depends on the relationship among the old asset's sale price, initial purchase price, and *book value,* and on existing government tax rules. (Chapter 8)

technically insolvent Describes a firm that is unable to pay its bills as they come due. (Chapter 13)

tender offer A formal offer to purchase a given number of shares of a firm's stock at a specified price. (Chapter 12)

term structure of interest rates The relationship between the interest rate or rate of return and the time to maturity. (Chapter 6)

terminal cash flow The after-tax nonoperating cash flow occurring in the final year of a project. It is usually attributable to liquidation of the project. (Chapter 8)

time line A horizontal line on which time zero appears at the leftmost end and future periods are marked from left to right; can be used to depict investment cash flows. (Chapter 4)

times interest earned ratio Measures the firm's ability to make contractual interest payments; sometimes called the *interest coverage ratio.* (Chapter 2)

time-series analysis Evaluation of the firm's financial performance over time using financial ratio analysis. (Chapter 2)

total asset turnover Indicates the efficiency with which the firm uses its assets to generate sales. (Chapter 2)

total cost of inventory The sum of order costs and carrying costs of inventory. (Chapter 13)

total leverage The potential use of *fixed costs, both operating and financial,* to magnify the effect of changes in sales on the firm's earnings per share. (Chapter 11)

total risk The combination of a security's nondiversifiable and diversifiable risk. (Chapter 5)

transfer prices Prices that subsidiaries charge each other for the goods and services traded between them. (Chapter 9)

treasurer The firm's chief financial manager, who is responsible for the firm's financial activities, such as financial planning and fund raising, making capital expenditure decisions, and managing cash, credit, the pension fund, and foreign exchange. (Chapter 1)

treasury stock The number of shares of outstanding stock that have been repurchased by the firm. (Chapter 7)

trust receipt inventory loan A secured short-term loan against inventory under which the lender advances 80 to 100 percent of the cost of the borrower's relatively expensive inventory items in exchange for the borrower's promise to repay the lender, with accrued interest, immediately after the sale of each item of collateral. (Chapter 14)

trustee A paid individual, corporation, or commercial bank trust department that acts as the third party to a bond indenture and can take specified actions on behalf of the bondholders if the terms of the indenture are violated. (Chapter 6)

two-bin method Unsophisticated inventory-monitoring technique that is typically applied to C group items and involves reordering inventory when one of two bins is empty. (Chapter 13)

U.S. Treasury bills (T-bills) Short-term IOUs issued by the U.S. Treasury; considered the *risk-free asset.* (Chapter 5)

uncorrelated Describes two series that lack any interaction and therefore have a *correlation coefficient* close to zero. (Chapter 5)

underpriced Stock sold at a price below its current market price, P_0. (Chapter 10)

underwriting The role of the *investment banker* in bearing the risk of reselling, at a profit, the securities purchased from an issuing corporation at an agreed-on price. (Chapter 7)

underwriting syndicate A group formed by an investment banker to share the financial risk associated with *underwriting* new securities. (Chapter 7)

unlimited funds The financial situation in which a firm is able to accept all independent projects that provide an acceptable return. (Chapter 8)

unlimited liability The condition of a sole proprietorship (or general partnership) allowing the owner's total wealth to be taken to satisfy creditors. (Chapter 1)

unsecured short-term financing Short-term financing obtained without pledging specific assets as collateral. (Chapter 14)

valuation The process that links risk and return to determine the worth of an asset. (Chapter 6)

venture capital Privately raised external equity capital used to fund early-stage firms with attractive growth prospects. (Chapter 7)

venture capitalists (VCs) Providers of venture capital; typically, formal businesses that maintain strong oversight over the firms they invest in and that have clearly defined exit strategies. (Chapter 7)

warehouse receipt loan A secured short-term loan against inventory under which the lender receives control of the pledged inventory collateral, which is stored by a designated warehousing company on the lender's behalf. (Chapter 14)

weighted average cost of capital (WACC), k_a Reflects the expected average future cost of funds over the long run; found by weighting the cost of each specific type of capital by its proportion in the firm's capital structure. (Chapter 10)

weighted marginal cost of capital (WMCC) schedule Graph that relates the firm's weighted average cost of capital to the level of total new financing. (Chapter 10)

weighted marginal cost of capital (WMCC) The firm's weighted average cost of capital (WACC) associated with its *next dollar* of total new financing. (Chapter 10)

wire transfer An electronic communication that, via bookkeeping entries, removes funds from the payer's bank and deposits them in the payee's bank. (Chapter 13)

working capital Current assets, which represent the portion of investment that circulates from one form to another in the ordinary conduct of business. (Chapter 13)

yield curve A graph of the relationship between the debt's remaining time to maturity (x axis) and its yield to maturity (y axis); it shows the pattern of annual returns on debts of equal quality and different maturities. Graphically depicts the *term structure of interest rates.* (Chapter 6)

yield to maturity (YTM) The rate of return that investors earn if they buy a bond at a specific price and hold it until maturity. (Assumes that the issuer makes all scheduled interest and principal payments as promised. (Chapter 6)

zero- (or low-) coupon bonds See Table 6.4 (Chapter 6)

zero-balance account (ZBA) A disbursement account that always has an end-of-day balance of zero because the firm deposits money to cover checks drawn on the account only as they are presented for payment each day. (Chapter 13)

zero-growth model An approach to dividend valuation that assumes a constant, nongrowing dividend stream. (Chapter 7)

Sources

Bold page numbers indicate location of feature.

15: "Business Ethics: A Perspective," by Robert A. Cooke in Arthur Andersen *Cases on Business Ethics* (Chicago: Arthur Andersen, September 1991), pp. 2 and 5. Copyright © 1991 Arthur Andersen. All rights reserved. Reprinted by Permission. **46:** Table of Industry Average Ratios (2001) for Selected Lines of Business from "Industry Norms and Key Business Ratios," Copyright © 2001 Dun & Bradstreet, Inc. Reprinted with permission. **192:** Table of Historic Returns for Selected Security Investments (1926–2000), Source: *Stocks, Bonds, Bills and Inflation 2001 Yearbook®*, © 2001 Ibbotson Associates, Inc. Based on copyrighted works by Ibbotson and Sinquefield. All rights reserved. Used with permission. **199:** Table of Historical Returns and Standard Deviations for Selected Security Investments (1926–2000), Source: *Stocks, Bonds, Bills and Inflation, 2001 Yearbook®*, © 2001 Ibbotson Associates, Inc. Based on copyrighted works by Ibbotson and Sinquefield. All rights reserved. Used with permission. **209:** Table of Beta Coefficients for Selected Stocks, *Value Line Investment Survey* (New York: Value Line Publishing, March 8, 2002). Reprinted with permission. **239:** Selected bond quotations, *Wall Street Journal*, April 23, 2002, p. C14. Reprinted with permission. **275:** Announcement of public offering of common stock dated 3/21/02 by Ribopharm, Inc. Reprinted with permission. **278:** Stock Quotations, *Wall Street Journal*, Monday, March 18, 2002, p. C4. Reprinted with permission. **436:** Table of Debt Ratios for Selected Industries and Lines of Business (Fiscal Years Ended 4/1/00 Through 3/31/01), © 2001 by RMA-The Risk Management Association. All rights reserved. No part of this table may be reproduced or utilized in any form or by any means, electronic or mechanical, including photocopying, recording or by an information storage and retrieval system without permission in writing from RMA-The Risk Management Association. **520:** Features and Recent Yields on Popular Marketable Securities, *Wall Street Journal*, May 2, 2002, pp. C9, C10, and C14. Reprinted with permission.

Index